ANABAPTIST HISTORY
AND THEOLOGY:
AN INTRODUCTION

C. Arnold Snyder

Pandora Press
51 Pandora Avenue N.
Kitchener, Ontario

ANABAPTIST HISTORY AND THEOLOGY:
AN INTRODUCTION

Copyright © 1995 by C. Arnold Snyder
       Pandora Press
       33 Kent Avenue
       Kitchener, Ontario, N2G 3R2

Co-published with Herald Press,
       Scottdale, Pennsylvania/Waterloo, Ontario
International Standard Book Number: 0-9698762-0-3
Printed in Canada on acid-free paper

First Printing, July 1995
Second Printing, December 1995
Third Printing, May 2002

Cover illustration:
    From an engraving by Jan Luiken (1649-1712) depicting the Anabaptist martyr Pieter Pieters Beckjen teaching a "little flock." Anabaptist congregations were forced to meet in secret. Since Pieter was a boatman, meeting for worship and instruction on his boat afforded some natural protection. The engraving appears in the English edition of the *Martyrs Mirror* on page 739. A brief description of Pieter, and the judgment pronounced against him, is found on pages 738-740. He was burned at the stake at Amsterdam February 26, 1569.

Table of Contents

Preface

Some books have a longer gestation periods than others. This one has been many years in the making. I was introduced to what became my perennial questions when, as an undergraduate at the University of Waterloo in the mid-1970s I enrolled in "The Radical Reformation," a course taught at Conrad Grebel College by Professor Walter Klaassen. The question was posed: How can the "Anabaptist movement" be defined and described? The question I was left with then, still preoccupies me: How best might the "Anabaptist story" be told?

I will confess, I did only moderately well in Dr. Klaassen's course. But one thing led to another, as it sometimes does: Walter Klaassen became my trusted advisor in graduate studies, and a member of my dissertation committee at McMaster University. In truth, he was my *Doktorvater*. Walter and Ruth became close friends and mentors for Linda and me during those years of study and growing families. In 1985, when I joined the faculty of Conrad Grebel College, Walter and I became colleagues. Since his retirement a few years ago, I have come full circle and found myself teaching "Walter's course," The Radical Reformation. Perhaps this book ought to be seen as my attempt to write a more credible take home exam, seventeen years later. Certainly the basic questions remain the same: How can the Anabaptist movement be described? What is the clearest and best way to tell this interesting and complex historical tale?

The text Walter had us read in 1974 was the incomparable *The Radical Reformation* by George H. Williams (Philadelphia: Westminster Press, 1962). It was an altogether impressive, encyclopedic treatment of the subject, and more than a little daunting for an undergraduate. It has since been replaced by an even more impressive third edition, of the same title, that runs to more than 1500 pages (Kirksville, Mo.: Sixteenth Century Journal Publishers, 1992). As a teacher of that subject, I quickly discovered that although there were excellent monographs on specialized aspects of the radical reformation, no comprehensive, synthetic texts, beyond the work of Williams, were available. This remained true even when the focus was narrowed to sixteenth century "Anabaptist Studies," a subset of radical reformation studies. Perhaps Williams' tour de force simply discouraged other scholars in the field from attempting synthetic overviews, even along more modest lines.

This book is the end result of the search for a text that would, first of all, provide a fairly concise narrative describing the birth and evolution of the sixteenth century Anabaptist movement. From the start I intended this book to be accessible to university students. I also hoped that this telling of the Anabaptist story would have something to say to people in the churches, and especially to those interested in the Anabaptist roots (historical and theological) of the Believers' Church tradition. All the same, the effort was made to incorporate scholarly advances in Anabaptist studies into the narrative itself, which of course complicated the narrative.

The attempt to walk this tightrope, clinging to narrative clarity on the one hand and academic respectability on the other, has not always succeeded. At times complex matters have been deceptively oversimplified in the telling; at other times, pedantic instincts have complicated unecessarily what should have been said more simply. I apologize both to those who may be confused by the intrusion of academic nit picking, and to my colleagues in the field who will find far too many nits unpicked. Nevertheless, every attempt has been made to take seriously the very rich tradition of academic research into sixteenth century Anabaptism, and to incorporate the best of that research into an accessible story.

In a further effort to make this material more accessible, two versions of the text have been prepared. This present volume is the "full edition" text which contains more complete descriptions and discussions (particularly in section C), the usual scholarly documentation, a bibliography, and an appendix on Anabaptist historiography. A considerably condensed version, following the same format and order (the "Abridged Student Edition" under the same title), has been prepared for use in the classroom and in other settings where a more concise narrative would be more helpful than scholarly apparatus. It is the author's hope that readers of either volume will be left with a better understanding of the complex Reformation movement we have come to call Anabaptism.

A very useful collection of Anabaptist sources in translation is Walter Klaassen's *Anabaptism in Outline* (Scottdale, Pa.: Herald Press, 1981). Cross references to this collection will be made at appropriate places in this text, in order to help readers who wish to augment the narrative with a parallel exploration of Anabaptist writings. Readers who wish to explore primary texts in more depth will want to refer to the eight volumes of the *Classics of the Radical Reformation* series (Herald Press), of which *Anabaptism in Outline* is volume three. In this series will be found the translated writings of Michael Sattler, Pilgram Marpeck, Conrad Grebel, Balthasar Hubmaier, Dirk Philips, David Joris, and most recently, Andreas Karlstadt. As always, those who read the original languages (German and Dutch) will have access to a much wider spectrum of source materials. The bibliography contains a representative, though not exhaustive, listing of published Anabaptists sources in both English and the original languages.

Various photocopied "incarnations" of this text have been used in past years in courses taught at Conrad Grebel College and other Mennonite and Baptist institutions, in locations as far afield as Ontario, Indiana, Central America (Nicaragua, Honduras, Costa Rica, Guatemala), Colombia, the Netherlands, and Switzerland. Critical feedback from those many students of history and theology has been invaluable in shaping the present book; I am indebted to them all. I also owe a large debt of thanks to colleagues and friends who took the time to comment and correct many errors at various stages in the process. Deserving of special thanks are Walter Klaassen, whose observations were invaluable as always, and my Conrad Grebel College colleague, historical researcher *par excellence*, Werner Packull, who took time away from work on his own latest monograph in order to offer help with mine. Thanks as well to C.J. Dyck, Ray Gingerich, Brad Gregory, Leonard Gross, Linda Huebert Hecht, Ted Koontz, Alan Kreider, Jerry Moon, Wayne Pipkin, John Rempel, John Roth, Shirley Showalter, James Stayer, Peter Stucky, Hildi Froese Tiessen, and Sjouke Voolstra for their invaluable encouragement to me, and their engagement with me. Also to Joe Springer, of the Mennonite Historical Library, Goshen, Indiana; to Frau Dr. B. Stadler, of the Staatsarchiv, Zürich; and to Dr. Piet Visser, Universiteitsbibliotheek, Amsterdam, for their support and assistance throughout.

Special thanks is due to the Mennonite Historical Library for graciously allowing me to reproduce illustrations from their holdings. The engravings and woodcuts in this book appear courtesy of the Mennonite Historical Library.

A sabbatical leave from Conrad Grebel College (1992/93) and a research grant from the Social Sciences and Humanities Research Council of Canada provided the necessary time and resources for the completion of this project. Gilbert Fast kindly contributed his editing skills in the final stages, and August Kroger solved a myriad of digital problems in the late going.

To my most "significant others," Linda, Carrie, Christian, Clifford, Karl, and Edna, thanks for the good-natured patience as the obsession with "the book" stretched into years. And finally, special thanks are due to my son, Clifford, who worked with me in producing this book for Pandora Press. His interest in geography and computers has taken printed form in the maps he prepared for this volume and in the general layout and production of the printed book.

C. Arnold Snyder
Conrad Grebel College
August, 1995

Abbreviations

ARG = *Archiv für Reformationsgeschichte*

Ausbund = *Ausbund, das ist Etliche schöne Christliche Lieder, wie sie in dem Gefängnis zu Passau in dem Schloss von den Schweizer-Brüdern und von andern rechtglaubigen Christen hin und her gedichtet worden.* First edition 1564; second expanded edition 1583. Subsequent editions to the present essentially reproduce the 1583 edition, with some minor additions. I have used an edition published at Elkhart, Indiana: Mennonitischen Verlagshandlung, 1880.

CGR = *The Conrad Grebel Review.*

CWMS = *The Complete Writings of Menno Simons*, trans. by Leonard Verduin (Scottdale, Pa.: Herald Press, 1956).

ME = *The Mennonite Encyclopedia* (Scottdale, Pa.: Herald Press, 1955).

MQR = *The Mennonite Quarterly Review.*

QGTS, 1 = L. von Muralt and W. Schmid, eds., *Quellen zur Geschichte der Täufer in der Schweiz*, 1. Band, Zürich (Zürich: Theologischer Verlag, 1952).

QGTS, 2 = Heinold Fast, ed., *Quellen zur Geschichte der Täufer in der Schweiz*, 2. Band, Ostschweiz (Zürich: Theologischer Verlag, 1973).

QGTS, 3 = [Unpublished. Ms. used with permission of Dr. Martin Haas.] Martin Haas, ed., *Quellen zur Geschichte der Täufer in der Schweiz*, 3. Band. (Aarau, Bern, Solothurn).

QGTS, 4 = Martin Haas, ed., *Quellen zur Geschichte der Täufer in der Schweiz*, 4. Band, Drei Täufergespräche in Bern und im Aargau (Zürich: Theologischer Verlag, 1974).

STAZ = Staatsarchiv Zürich.

TA, *Baden und Pfalz* = Manfred Krebs, ed., *Quellen zur Geschichte der Täufer: Baden und Pfalz* (Gütersloh: Bertelsmann Verlag, 1951).

TA, *Hesse* = Günther Franz, ed., *Urkundliche Quellen zur hessischen Reformationsgeschichte* (Marburg: N. G. Elwert'sche Velagsbuchhandlung, 1951).

TA, *Elsass, 1* = Manfred Krebs and Hans Georg Rott, eds., *Quellen zur Geschichte der Täufer, VII. Band, Elsaß, I. Teil: Stadt Straßburg 1522-1532* (Gütersloh: Gerd Mohn, 1959).

TA, *Elsass, 2* = Manfred Krebs and Hans Georg Rott, eds., *Quellen zur Geschichte der Täufer, VIII. Band, Elsaß, II. Teil: Stadt Straßburg 1533-1535* (Gütersloh: Gerd Mohn, 1960).

Maps and Illustrations

Maps

Illustrations (courtesy of the Mennonite Historical Library, Goshen, Indiana)

Introduction

Anabaptism was a church reform movement born at the time and in the context of the Protestant Reformation, an unwanted and unloved "stepchild" of the mainline reformers, all of whom disavowed responsibility for their unruly offspring. Anabaptism became a "church" movement when adherents insisted that the properly biblical way of forming the church was through the freely chosen baptism of adult believers. The true church, they maintained, was made up only of persons who had, in full conscience and choice, publicly committed themselves to the Body of Christ on earth. They thus baptized each other following personal confessions of faith, in spite of the fact that they had all been baptized as infants. The continued existence of the "baptizing" reform movement marked a crucial step in the development of present day "Believers' Churches." The direct descendants of the Anabaptists are the present day Mennonites, Amish, Hutterites, and some groups of "Brethren"; the indirect descendants of the Anabaptists are above all the Baptists, the largest Believers' Church denomination today.

The descriptive term Anabaptist was applied to this reforming movement very soon after the first adult baptisms took place in 1525, and has remained in use to this day. *Anabaptista* was a Latin rendering of Greek words which, when combined, meant "rebaptizer." This negative descriptive term was an ancient one, known in the church from fourth century on. In Justinian's legal code, rebaptism was one of two heresies that merited the death penalty; the other capital heresy was anti-trinitarianism.[1] The exact sixteenth century German equivalent term describing an adherent of the "baptizing" movement was *Wiedertaufer*, and the German term soon took on all the negative legal and heretical connotations of the Latin original, including the implication that "rebaptism" was a capital offense against the state.

From a strictly religious perspective, raising the question of the proper form of baptism in the sixteenth century context was an instance of an appeal to the authority of Scripture alone; it was a call to test traditional baptismal practices by the light of the Scriptures. But in social terms, granting religious freedom of choice to just anyone, woman or man, common or noble, clergy or lay, challenged traditional social hierarchies. In political terms, making baptism a matter of free adult choice threatened the uniformity of religious confession and practice in political territories. Sixteenth century political wisdom demanded the monopoly and control of religion by the rulers of any given state. The Reformation did not modify this understanding, but only served to intensify the problem: Christendom no longer was united under the religious authority of Rome; who then, if not the civil authority, was to decide questions of church doctrine and polity?

In response to the break up of Christendom following the Reformation, a ruling political/religious principle was declared at the Peace of Ausgburg in 1555, namely "cuius regio, eius religio" (the religion of the rulers must be the religion of their subjects), a principle that applied only to the Catholic and Lutheran denominations in the Holy Roman Empire, and not to Calvinism or Anabaptism. Nevertheless the Peace of Augsburg demonstrated the political conviction of the age: religion was considered the essential political "glue" that bound subjects to the rulers of territories. The religious freedom required by voluntarily-chosen adult baptism was deemed seditious and dangerous to political stability by virtually all political authorities.

Given this political reality, espousing Anabaptism in the sixteenth century was no "purely religious" option, but rather was a faith decision that directly confronted and challenged the social, religious, and political status quo. Anabaptists were sought out, persecuted, jailed, dispossessed, exiled and put to death by Lutheran, Reformed, and Catholic cities and rulers well into the seventeenth century, although persecution was most ferocious in the Catholic regions. Denied political legitimacy virtually everywhere, the Anabaptist movement was driven underground, where it survived in more or less clandestine fashion (depending upon the level of official or unofficial toleration in a given locale) in much the same way as had the outlawed Cathars and Waldensians in the Middle Ages. As had been the case with the medieval "heretical" groups, Anabaptist members came to be drawn primarily from the labouring classes and joined secret conventicles led by lay pastors. In both cases a clandestine doctrinal literature circulated within the network of conventicles, carried by ministers and evangelists, and memorized by the faithful. This material, most often in handwritten form, was usually conveyed orally to converts. Often there were pre-arranged greetings and signals in order to gain entry to secret worship meetings. The arrest of a travelling pastor or leader was a cataclysmic event for this small network of conventicles, because leaders often carried incriminating letters and lists of addresses, and those arrested were routinely subjected to torture in order to extract more details about the movement.

Writing an introductory history of this clandestine, grass roots reforming movement has proved to be a complex undertaking. The bulk of historical sources documenting the Anabaptist movement are court records (many of them now published) covering an area from Austria to the Netherlands, written in a variety of German and Dutch dialects. The "baptizing" movement held important teachings in common, as will be noted in more detail below, but being a grass roots movement, there also emerged a bewildering variety of unique local teachings and practices. Recent studies have highlighted local particularities, adding to the complexity of the descriptive task.

The Anabaptist movement has been interpreted and described in widely differing ways, from the sixteenth century to the present, often along ideological lines.[2]

For Martin Luther and Heinrich Bullinger the Anabaptists were fanatics and heretics, and until this century Protestant historians simply followed Luther's lead in describing the movement. For the spiritualist Sebastian Franck, who knew many Anabaptists personally, they were sincere and pious people (although tending toward legalism, he said) who were unjustly persecuted by so-called Christians. Already in the sixteenth century Mennonite and Hutterite writers appreciated Franck's dissenting historical view, and borrowed freely from his writings. For Friedrich Engels (Karl Marx's associate) the Anabaptists were proto-socialist shock troops, an underground network of Müntzerite revolutionaries. For the twentieth century Mennonite historian Harold S. Bender, the "evangelical Anabaptists" originated in Switzerland and excluded all spiritualist and revolutionary "crazies." The "Anabaptists" so defined were the heroic "purely religious," nonresistant parents-in-the-faith of modern day Mennonites. This reading has been challenged in the past two decades by the "polygenesis" historians, who have demonstrated that the "baptizing" movement originated in more places than just Switzerland, and must be described objectively as including *all* sixteenth century "adult baptizers," not just those who might qualify as exemplary twentieth century Mennonites.[3]

The description of Anabaptism which follows has been shaped by published and archival Anabaptist primary sources and the author's own studies in the field. This telling of the Anabaptist story also is indebted to a wide range of historical scholarship: the Mennonite "recovery" of Anabaptism put into motion by Harold Bender beginning in the late 1920s; the "Radical Reformation" scholarship of George H. Williams and Roland Bainton; the "polygenesis" revisionist scholarship which contested Bender's theory of Anabaptist origins; and the social history approach which, thanks to dialogue with Marxist scholars, has highlighted political, social, and economic factors involved in the emergence of Anabaptism, rather than looking simply to the development of religious ideas. All of these interpretations have added important elements to the telling of this story.

The dependence of this "Introduction" upon these earlier studies will be plain to the observant reader. Nevertheless, this text is an attempt at a new synthesis and organization of the historical and theological material, and an attempt to integrate insights from different (and sometimes antagonistic) historical methodologies. Large-scale historical events (such as "the Reformation" or "the Anabaptist movement") can be thought of as thick and complex fabrics, woven from many different threads of "causality." The historian attempts first to untangle and understand the weave, and then attempts to reconstruct something of the colour, texture, shape, and "feel" of the cloth in a "narrative," a word tapestry in story form. In some ways, poetry would be a more powerful medium for this task than is narrative. Descriptive narrative shows its limitations when it attempts to "recreate" complex objects or events, such as paintings or musical performances, with words. The precious old quilt is brought out from the trunk and admired. It is "objectively" there as a fact. But it is not a matter of "objective science" when someone describing the quilt thinks that the combination of red and blue made it particularly striking, or when someone else is convinced that the tracing effect of a particular green thread is the element that held it all together. In the end, if the narrators have some skill in observation and description, and if readers read with equal skill, a fair *impression* of the quilt will have been passed on. But "Ode to a Quilt" may have done as well, and in the end, neither story nor ode (however skillfully done) is the quilt itself.

Two things can be mentioned about this particular "word tapestry" of the Anabaptist movement. First, the traditional quarrel between "secular" historians and theologians has been quite deliberately ignored, since insights from both sides are needed. There is no worthy telling of the Anabaptist story that excludes the social, economic, and political forces that helped shape the movement in its origins and development. At the same time, the Anabaptist story can only make sense if the religious *ideas* that the protagonists said were important to them, are taken seriously as "reasons for action."

In the second place, an effort has been made to begin including Anabaptist women in the narrative. As readers of the Anabaptist court records well know, women played a central role in the spread and the survival of the movement, but their colours and threads have been largely absent from earlier accounts. The author recognizes that much more could and should have been done to integrate the story of Anabaptist women more fully into the narrative as a whole. The absence of women's voices is most evident in the story of "origins" and in the discussions of theological developments which (in time-honoured fashion) have relied primarily on records left behind by prominent Anabaptist men. Perhaps these limitations can be more adequately addressed in a future edition. In this text the role of Anabaptist women emerges primarily in anecdotal material, when we touch upon the communication of Anabaptist ideas (chapter 7), the theory and practice of equality (chapter 18, which deals directly with the role of Anabaptist women in the movement), and marriage (chapter 19). Chapters 18 and 19 are somewhat longer than the norm in order to be able to include individual stories that deserve to be better known. Readers interested in knowing more about the subject may wish to consult the forthcoming collection, *Profiles of Anabaptist Women*.[4]

The chronological scope of this introduction to the Anabaptist movement is limited to the sixteenth century, apart from an occasional necessary foray into the seventeenth. We wish to tell the story of the emergence and development of the baptizing movement up to the point at which it stabilized into the ongoing Mennonite, Swiss Brethren, and Hutterite denominational "traditions." In order to tell the Anabaptist story in this longer-range fashion the material has been organized into four chronological and topical sections. The organizational scheme is oriented around the points of the emergence, initial consolidation, development, and re-consolidation of the Anabaptist church reform movement. This process involved not only dialogue with changing social, economic and political realities, but also dialogue, change, and development of religious ideas that were important to the Anabaptists themselves.

Since the Anabaptists increasingly were marginalized from civil society as the sixteenth century progressed, much of the essential "development" of the movement took place through "intramural" dialogue and disagreement. Our study moves increasingly "inside" the Anabaptist movement (in section C) in order to clarify how differences in biblical interpretation shaped the later surviving Anabaptist traditions. This approach admittedly leaves to one side the ecumenical dimensions of dialogue with other Christian groups (the "disputations" and other discussions), and the particularities of later social and political arrangements in specific territories—two important historical "threads" that could not be included in this "weave."

The Anabaptist movement began with sixteenth century aspirations for broad and sweeping social and religious change, but ended with the consolidation of sectarian church boundaries. The major sections of the study are thus devoted to a) the central reforming "precursors" to the Anabaptist movement; b) the emergence of the "baptizing" movement as such; c) change and development within the movement itself, in theory and practice (by far the longest and most complex section); and d) a concluding view of the "consolidated" movement as it appeared towards the end of the sixteenth century.

A. The Context: Reformation and Radical Reformation

The first section of the study builds upon the work of social historians of the Reformation and the work of "Radical Reformation" scholars. A few years ago Robert Scribner summarized what now is becoming a truism for social historians of the Reformation: "The Reformation" no longer can be defined in terms of its most famous representatives; rather the Reformation must be seen as a complex of social, political, economic and religious processes that necessarily include the ideas, aspirations, and actions of the masses of people.[5] This observation has important consequences for our understanding of the Radical Reformation generally, and of Anabaptism more particularly.

The predominantly theological definition of the Reformation tended to centre around Martin Luther, defining other contemporary movements by means of comparison with his critiques and categories. While such an approach certainly told a good part of the story, especially for those like Andreas Karlstadt who began their careers as followers of Luther, nevertheless it also distorted crucial historical realities. The "Radical Reformation," for example, was defined as "radical" with reference to the "mainline" or "magisterial" reform of the Protestant theologians, obscuring its own links to the radical reforming movement and socio/economic movements of various kinds.[6]

This first section of the study will outline the emergence of the sixteenth century "evangelical" reforming stream, placing it first in the late medieval context, going on to describe the emergence of the "radical" evangelical reforming stream. Historians today recognize that the Anabaptist movement cannot be understood simply as "the Reformation taken to its proper ends" (Harold Bender's phrase), but rather that there were intervening "radical" reformers and movements that functioned as important precursors to the Anabaptist movement. The historical and theological context for Anabaptism thus emerges when we outline the views of Andreas Karlstadt, Thomas Müntzer, and Caspar Schwenckfeld, and describe some of the objectives pursued in the Peasants' War.

B. The Setting of Initial Boundaries: 1525-1540

The second major section of this study presents an overview of the most heavily researched area of Anabaptist studies, namely its "origins." The most widely accepted historical description of sixteenth century Anabaptism now speaks of "polygenesis," that is, of several geographical and ideological points of origins of Anabaptism. The origins of three primary Anabaptist "streams" will be identified and described in some detail: Swiss Anabaptism, South German/Austrian Anabaptism, and North German/Dutch Anabaptism. We will look first to the origin, theological core, and spread of Swiss and South German/Austrian Anabaptism. These two Anabaptist streams emerged almost simultaneously, and interacted for five years (1525-1530) before North German/Dutch Anabaptism began.

When the Anabaptist story has been told from the perspective of its origins, the movement as such has tended to disappear and sometimes has been described as at least three or more "Anabaptisms." A central thesis of this book (it was a lesson learned from the "polygenesis" historians) is that the "Anabaptist movement" included *all* the "adult baptizers" of the sixteenth century. However, our further thesis is that the "baptizing movement" centred around, and grew out of, a core of fundamental, shared teachings.[7] It was a commitment to this core of theological and reforming principles that first identified Anabaptism as a religious reform movement distinct from the mainline "evangelical" and late medieval Catholic traditions. Furthermore, this essential theological core was present in all three geographical expressions of Anabaptism and provided the internal dialogical agenda for further definition and development within the movement. We may say that where the prevailing description of Anabaptism in recent decades has been concerned above all with distinct origins and differences between Anabaptists, we are also interested in tracing the story of the points of identity that stand at the Anabaptist "origins."[8]

The story of the geographical spread of Anabaptism is complex. In this book we will devote several chapters to this theme, in order to provide glimpses into the process. Included in the story of the setting of initial boundaries is a chapter describing some of the communication dynamics that underlay the spread of Anabaptism among the "common people" of the sixteenth century; a chapter providing an overview of the geographical spread and development of "early" (Swiss and South German) Anabaptism up to ca. 1530; and a chapter examining the origin and spread of North German/Dutch Anabaptism. This section concludes with an overview of three interpretive approaches to Scripture that lay at the root of subsequent Anabaptist disagreements.

C. The Development of Anabaptism: 1525-ca.1600

The points of identity seen in the "core" Anabaptist teachings answered some crucial questions posed by the early evangelical reforming movement, and set the baptizing movement apart from other streams of reform. But as a church reform movement, Anabaptism posed a host of new questions that were debated subsequently among Anabaptists of different persuasions. The Anabaptist story cannot be told without describing the many points of tension and difference, change and development, and eventual solutions found by those who made up the "baptizing movement" itself. Early Anabaptism was in many respects a diffuse and varied phenomenon that developed *only over time* into rigidly defined "separatist" (or "sectarian") forms. In our telling of the Anabaptist story, we wish to explore in particular the tensional, dialogical process (the "conversations" about faith essentials) that led to the establishment of later traditions. We have organized our description of these further "conversations" around three descriptive categories which correspond to three major points of historical transition in sixteenth century society at large: the political, the socio-economic, and the religious. Of course, in the sixteenth century context, *all* of these questions were considered "religious."

1. Anabaptism and Political Reality

There was no early agreement among Anabaptists on how individual believers, or the church generally, should relate to the world of politics, or to "the world" in general. In this section of our survey we will look briefly at the political context into which Anabaptism was born, and examine the variety of scriptural arguments presented by different Anabaptists in defence of their respective points of view. We will pay particular attention to the development of Anabaptist positions concerning "the sword" (government authority) and "the oath."

2. Anabaptism and Socio-economic Reality

The Anabaptist movement had significant roots in radically egalitarian readings of Scripture and movements of social reform. Although the possibility of reforming society at large according to egalitarian principles became an impossible dream after the failure of the Peasants' War in 1525, and then with the collapse of the apocalyptic dream of Münster after 1535, egalitarian principles survived in the Anabaptist movement as expressions of how God intended disciples to live together. In this section of our study we will examine how Anabaptist positions developed concerning economic principles of conduct, the role of women in the movement and in questions of marriage.

3. Anabaptism and Religious Reform

The Anabaptists understood all of the above questions to be matters of "religious" reform, applying both to individuals (repentance and rebirth) and the community of believers, the church (the Body of Christ). This section of our study will survey questions that related most directly to church polity, doctrine, and practice. In particular the Anabaptist emphasis on regeneration of believers and the living of a "new life," when combined with the Anabaptist emphasis on the ban (church discipline), led to the establishment of increasingly rigid community boundaries over time. We will trace this process, looking also to Anabaptist debates and developments concerning the use of the central Anabaptist "external ceremonies" of water baptism, the ban, and the Lord's Supper.

D. Conclusion

When we look back at the development of the Anabaptist movement from the vantage point of the surviving groups we are able to identify internal patterns of tension and change that led from plural beginnings (albeit around a core consensus) to clearly defined ecclesial traditions by the end of the sixteenth century. The Anabaptist story told in this way provides elements for continuing the dialogue begun in the sixteenth century, especially for those who stand in Believers' Church traditions. There was nothing theologically, politically, or socially inevitable about the sixteenth century patterns of development; had other choices been made, the history would read differently. But certain choices were made, and certain political and social realities had to be faced. What survived, then, was not necessarily "right" simply because it survived. It is the author's conviction that it is important, especially for those within Believers' Churches, to understand and reflect upon the issues and the processes that by the end of the sixteenth century had led to the definition of the Anabaptist theological and ecclesial traditions. In an effort to encapsulate those issues and processes, the first of two concluding chapters will compare and contrast the later Swiss, Hutterite, and Mennonite traditions with the core teachings of the early Anabaptist movement.

In spite of the fact that it is currently out of fashion for historians to address openly the question of the possible meaning or relevance of their subjects of study, the final chapter will leave the field of historical research and narrative proper, and will pose questions about the possible "contemporary relevance" of Anabaptist history for present day Believers' Churches. The discussion initiated there grows out of the author's own location within the Mennonite faith tradition, and is an attempt to carry the historical conversations further. Thus the material presented in the Epilogue may well not be relevant to those readers interested simply in an historical account of the Anabaptist movement. Readers not sharing an interest in issues facing contemporary Believers' Churches may wish to omit reading the Epilogue altogether. Those who do pass over the concluding chapter will not lose any of the essential story of sixteenth century Anabaptism, but they will miss a dandy sermon.

End Notes

[1] Harold Bender and Robert Friedmann, "Anabaptist," ME, I, p. 113.

[2] For a review of the historiography, see the Appendix, below.

[3] James Stayer, Werner Packull, and Klaus Deppermann, "From Monogenesis to Polygenesis: The Historical Discussion of Anabaptist Origins," MQR 49(1975), pp. 83-122.

[4] Arnold Snyder and Linda Huebert Hecht, eds., *Profiles of Anabaptist Women* (Wilfrid Laurier University Press, forthcoming).

[5] Scribner defines "the Reformation" as "a complex, extended historical process, going well beyond the endeavours of one man or one tendency, and involving social, political and wider religious issues." Robert Scribner, *The German Reformation* (Atlantic Highlands, N.J.: Humanities Press, 1986), p. 5.

[6] As Robert Scribner notes, the Radicals or Anabaptists "are still seen as somehow marginal to the development of the 'mainstream' Reformation. This is a measure of how far the confessional historiography produced by erastian churches has influenced views of the Reformation, obscuring the fact that there were many strands in the original evangelical movements." *Ibid.*, p. 45.

[7] The general outlines of the Anabaptist theological core, as distinguished from Protestant and Roman Catholic theology, have been drawn in a little book which has yet to be superseded: Walter Klaassen's *Anabaptism: Neither Catholic nor Protestant* (Waterloo, Ont.: Conrad Press, 1973).

[8] Argued in more detail in Arnold Snyder, "Beyond Polygenesis: Recovering the Unity and Diversity of Anabaptist Theology," in H. Wayne Pipkin, ed., *Essays in Anabaptist Theology* (Elkhart, Ind.: Institute of Mennonite Studies, 1994), pp. 1-33, and in response to J. Denny Weaver, CGR 13(Spring, 1995), pp. 210-15.

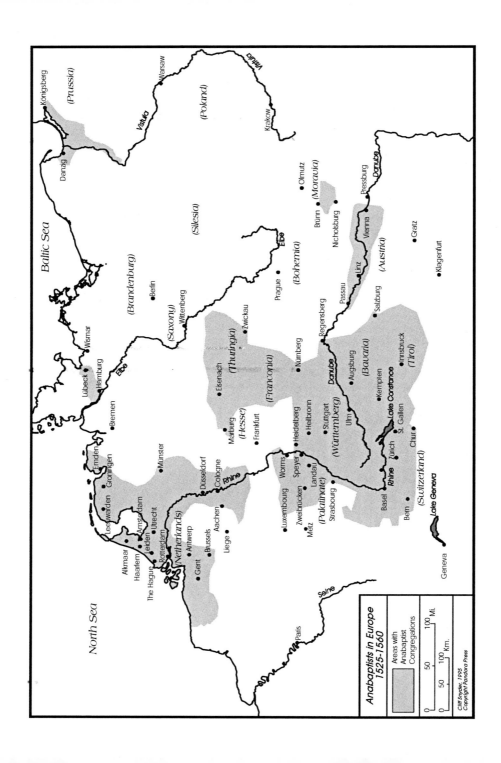

Anabaptists in Europe
1525–1560

Areas with
Anabaptist
Congregations

0   50   100 Mi.

0   50   100 Km.

Cliff Snyder, 1995
Copyright Pandora Press

North Sea

Baltic Sea

Paris

Seine

(Netherlands)

Alkmaar
Haarlem
The Hague
Leiden
Rotterdam
Amsterdam
Utrecht
Leeuwarden
Groningen
Emden

Gent
Antwerp
Brussels
Aachen
Liege

Münster
Düsseldorf
Cologne
Rhine

(Palatinate)

Luxembourg
Metz
Zweibrücken
Speyer
Landau
Strasbourg

Worms
Heidelberg
Heilbronn
Stuttgart

(Württemberg)

(Hesse)
Marburg
Frankfurt

(Franconia)
Eisenach
(Thuringia)
Zwickau
Nürnberg

Bremen
Hamburg
Lübeck
Wismar

(Brandenburg)
Berlin

(Saxony)
Wittenberg

Elbe

(Silesia)

(Poland)
Warsaw
Krakow

Vistula

(Prussia)
Königsberg
Danzig

(Bohemia)
Prague

Regensberg
Passau
Danube

(Moravia)
Olmütz
Brünn
Nicholsburg

Pressburg
Danube

(Austria)
Vienna
Linz
Gratz
Klagenfurt
Salzburg

(Bavaria)
Augsburg
Kempten
Ulm

Lake Constance
Innsbruck
(Tirol)

St. Gallen
Chur
Zürich
Basel
Bern
Rhine

(Switzerland)

Lake Geneva
Geneva

Chapter 1

The Late Medieval Tradition
and the Early Reformation Challenge

The Crises in Late Medieval Society

Modern historians distinguish between social, economic, political and religious elements in society. Such distinctions were still foreign in the sixteenth century, which assumed the medieval ideal of the *corpus christianum*: the interpenetration and interdependence of all of these elements were thought to make up a unified social/religious "Christian body," a social, political and religious whole. Nevertheless by the sixteenth century the medieval ideal had been in the process of disintegration for some time. The religious breakup which has come to be called the Reformation was only one more step in the collapse of the old, unworkable ideal of "Christendom."

Political transitions

The late medieval period witnessed the beginning of the end for the theocratic ideals that had characterized the high medieval period. The monumental struggle between the reformed popes and the Holy Roman Emperors led ultimately to the destruction of both pretenders for ultimate theocratic power. By the end of the thirteenth century, the emergent political powers in Europe were the national monarchies and by the sixteenth century these included especially France, Spain, and England. The Holy Roman Emperor also remained a serious contender for political power, contingent on his ability to centralize power and authority in Germany, Austria, and other territories of the "Holy Roman Empire." That possibility, however, seemed remote, given the incoherent collection of principalities and free imperial cities that formed the heart of the Empire in Germany.

Politically, then, sixteenth century Europe was dominated by national monarchies, with a possibility always lurking of a re-emergent Holy Roman Empire. The papacy, as a political power, controlled a second-rate Italian state, competing with other Italian states for advantages in peninsular politics. It had been humbled by the King of France during the "Babylonian Captivity" in Avignon (1309-1377), torn by internal dissension during the Great Schism (1378-1417), and narrowly missed being reduced to a parliamentary monarchy following the Council of Constance (1414-1417). The Renaissance popes of the fifteenth and early sixteenth centuries, capitalizing on the finances of their international religious empire, managed a fair show of power in the Italian peninsula, but they were ill prepared to play a unifying role in European politics as a whole. In fact, their role was just the opposite—a cause for dissension.

Luther's prince, Frederick of Saxony, was an imperial elector—obviously a key political player in the eyes of both the pope and the secular rulers. Early in 1519, the pope was backing Frederick for election as Holy Roman Emperor. In the eyes of the Holy See, he was a more acceptable candidate (being weaker politically) than the front runners Charles of the house of Habsburg or Francis I of France. Thus when Frederick protected his star professor, Martin Luther, the pope went along. But it was Charles who was elected the fifth Holy Roman Emperor in June, 1519; he called a meeting of the Estates (the Diet of Worms) for April 1521, to which Luther was summoned and at which he refused to recant. The famous scene, with Luther declaring to the Emperor "Here I stand. I can do no other" took place at that time. Luther had the subsequent good fortune of being defended and protected by a prince strong enough to provide him a space for his religious reform, but such protection and cooperation could not be assumed everywhere. In effect, Frederick of Saxony stood between Luther and a "radical" fate such as had awaited John Hus, who was burned at the stake a century earlier for defying the papacy.

All kings, princes, and town councils considering an "evangelical" ecclesiastical reform had to weigh the political consequences of allowing reform to take place. Often a choice for "the Reformation" came to rest on questions of political alignments and possibilities rather than on justification by grace through faith or theological issues as such. The consequences of failing to win over any political authorities to one's point of view were devastating. Without such support any reforming movement would be left in a political no-man's-land, in a position of absolute vulnerability. This unenviable result was especially visible in the eventual fate of the Anabaptist movement. The fact that in the end, the Anabaptists came to accept political illegitimacy, rather than compromising their religious principles, was in the eyes of contemporaries a sign of their "radicality."

The Anabaptist movement needed to define its own position in matters of church and state, in the context of the political crises and realities of the sixteenth century and in light of the call to biblical reform. Although a fairly uniform Anabaptist tradition of teaching concerning church and state had emerged by the end of the sixteenth century, it did not arrive full-blown with the first adult baptisms. The road on the way to agreement was full of pitfalls and complex detours. It involved not only a variety of external political factors in different territories and regions, but also a variety of internal "biblical" answers to the question of how the church should relate to political power. We will devote a section of our study below to "Anabaptism and Political Reality," paying particular attention to the development of Anabaptist positions on the sword and the oath.

Socio-economic transition

By the sixteenth century the fundamental transition had begun from an agriculturally based feudal system (favouring the landholding aristocracy, who collected rents in kind from their properties) to a capitalist system (favouring the urban bourgeoisie who controlled capital, and stimulated trade, commerce and industry). The socio-economic transition was carried out by an alliance of the bourgeoisie with the emerging monarchs. Cities and towns would make alliances with monarchs (that is, they bought their freedom, negotiated trading and commercial rights, rights to charge duties, etc.); they would pay taxes for their privileges, which generated revenue for the king. Thus the burghers moved away from dependence on the landed aristocracy and agriculture, into independent commercial and capitalistic ventures.

At the same time kings strengthened their hands against the aristocracy by generating revenue not dependent on the landholding class. This had significant repercussions in terms of military power. In an earlier time, only the landholding aristocracy had the means to provide cavalry, i.e., mounted and armoured knights. By the sixteenth century, the invention of gunpowder had rendered the knight in armour, as well as the castle, an anachronism (thanks to bullets and cannonballs, respectively). A king now needed only money with which to buy sufficient infantry (mercenaries) and field guns; this money came from the towns and the revenues generated by trade and commerce.

As members of the nobility began losing ground in the economic battle, they began pressing their tenants for more revenue. The deck was stacked against the landowner, since rents traditionally were paid in kind and were traditionally non-negotiable, being set by customary law. The aristocracy, however, was starved for cash, needed to buy the goods imported by the merchants. From the thirteenth century on, landowners struggled to convert payments in kind into cash payments. There were corresponding struggles of resistance among the peasantry. However, the landowners slowly managed to extract more cash from their serfs and tenant farmers. By the sixteenth century, however, inflation had begun to set in, and the fixed rents (cash or otherwise) no longer provided sufficient wealth for the landowning class. The great Peasants' War of 1525, which coincided with the Reformation and gained ideological legitimacy from it, can be seen as one more battle in this on-going struggle between the landowners and the peasants. Although the aristocracy won the battle decisively in 1525, ultimately they lost the war for economic supremacy to the rising bourgeosie.

The church did not escape this socio-economic conflict for the simple reason that the medieval and late medieval church formed an integral part of the agrarian feudal system. In pre-Reformation Germany, for example, the church controlled approximately one third of the land, and exercised lordship over the peasants on that land. The upper clergy of the church, who were with few exceptions drawn from the nobility, formed an integral part of the aristocracy of Europe and were dependent, as was the aristocracy, on the revenues produced by their serfs and tenant farmers. The monasteries were particularly efficient exploiters of land and rural labour. Added to these revenues, of course, were the obligatory tithes and church taxes extracted from serfs and tenants to which the ecclesiastical lords were entitled. All of this only increased peasant resentment against the clergy.

The response of the "common people" to the financial exactions of the church was a strong and, at times, violent anticlericalism. This manifested itself in the medieval and late-medieval "heretical" movements as well as in movements of lay piety and movements of outright social rebellion, often directed against ecclesiastical lords with special zeal. This strong anticlerical sentiment was something that could be exploited by territorial rulers, especially in German lands, where anti-curial feeling ran high. There was much to be gained.

Given the substantial economic power of the late medieval church, there were significant political and economic dimensions to "reform" for the privileged classes of society. A ruler could widen his economic base and strengthen his political power by appropriating church lands to himself—lands traditionally controlled by the noble families or the church itself. Likewise in the cities, the struggle between the patrician classes and the guilds (described as "the rabble" by the patricians) often centred on the question of who was to control the "reform." The social and economic dimensions of reform thus played a crucial role in the acceptance of religious ideas. Some religious ideas lent themselves more readily to the support of the elites; some lent themselves more in support of "popular" interests.

Among the peasantry and some poorer urban classes "reform" meant primarily a social change and a change in church polity and church economics: very often the common people expressed a desire to control the morals of their priests and pastors by controlling appointments, and they likewise wished to use tithe revenues in their own parishes, rather than having those tithes go to support some cathedral canon or distant scholar. And they dreamed of a more egalitarian society where they too would have a political and religious voice. The study of the "Radical Reformation" takes on further dimensions when these grass roots movements for social and economic reform are understood as also forming a crucial part of the Reformation as such.

The question would remain: were perceived church abuses to be resolved in a way that conformed to the agitation of the commoners, or would old church privileges and revenues simply accrue to new masters? Luther opted for a conservative solution against which other positions came to be seen as "radical," but these positions were not yet evident in the early 1520s.[1]

There is ample evidence that after 1520 many common people came to base their requests on the Bible, and saw themselves as part of what Luther was writing about. From their perspective, "reform" was a call for a more just and equal society. In 1525, during the Peasants' War, Luther clarified in no uncertain terms that he had meant no such thing. The Peasants' War of 1525 and the subsequent Anabaptist movement, while they appealed to the Bible and Reformation writings, exhibited strong communitarian, egalitarian, and anticlerical sentiments whose roots lay clearly in the long history of socio-economic abuses of the preceding centuries.

It is important for our story to note the process by which the political powers in various localities came to define the limits of social and economic reform. In particular some recent studies on the Peasants' War have argued that peasant proposals were not necessarily "utopian," and may well have functioned, had they been implemented.[2] Furthermore, the historical and ideological links that connect Anabaptism and the Peasants' War have suggested that many of the aspirations of the peasants survived and were carried forward in the Anabaptist religious communities. In the context of an emerging capitalism, for example, the early Anabaptists unequivocally declared themselves to be against the charging of interest and the accumulation of surplus capital. In their egalitarianism and communitarianism the Anabaptists hearkened back to earlier communal traditions, rather than looking forward to the coming "individualism" of the capitalist revolution. Much in the manner of medieval "heretics" like Peter Waldo, the Anabaptists were to be classified as "radical" thanks to their stubborn and thoroughgoing conservative interpretation of Scripture. We will devote a separate section of our study below to the development of Anabaptist positions on social and economic questions.

Religious transition

We state only the obvious when we say that by the sixteenth century there was a growing and painful discrepancy between the medieval church's universal claims to religious authority and the not-so-subtle scramble for church revenue and the moral decadence of lower and higher clergy. Any call for reform—and the calls were loud and insistent in the century before the Reformation—would have to deal with the problem of simony (buying and selling of church offices), absentee clerics, low moral standards, and ill-prepared clergy. From the perspective of the common people, any "reformation" of the church would have to correct these failings, but it also would have to speak to their spiritual hunger. The yearning for reform arose not only from dissatisfaction, but also from a substratum of fervent lay piety, spirituality, and practice.

There was also an intellectual debate and critique beginning to take shape in the century before the Reformation, largely limited to the halls of academia (with the glaring exception of fifteenth century Bohemia), conducted in Latin by a privileged, educated few. The great sixteenth century Reformation issues and slogans escaped the narrow confines of university debate, and learned to speak German, Dutch, French and English. The freedom of a Christian, justification by grace through faith, Scripture alone, the priesthood of all believers, and "at once justified and a sinner" were ideas that could be found in any town square or tavern, published in cheap pamphlets on the newly-invented printing press. In ways not completely understood, they reached the common people and found a startling resonance there.

The Dogmatic and Ecclesial Reality

The high claims made by the church in the High Middle Ages were summed up nicely at the Fourth Lateran Council (1215) which decreed, among other things, that outside the church and its seven sacraments there was no salvation. This central dogmatic formulation still stood in the late medieval church: the church was the sole mediator between a sinful humanity and damnation, on the one hand, and God and salvation, on the other. It was a church made up not only of the living, but also of the dead. The mystical communion of saints included those awaiting further grace in purgatory, as well as the Saviour, the Blessed Virgin, and the saints who had proceeded directly to heaven. The superfluous or "left over" merits of Christ, Mary, and the saints could be utilized to reduce the penalty for sin for those still living, as well as for those already dead but undergoing cleansing in purgatory. The papacy claimed the power to draw upon this "Treasury of Merit," at its discretion. The infamous "indulgences" that called forth Luther's 95 theses in 1517 were papal documents that promised just such remission of sin's penalty. Indulgences were only one small part of the general sacrament of penance, but as it happened, Luther's questioning of the salvific value of indulgences soon brought the entire sacramental edifice into question.

The seven sacraments of the medieval church were baptism, the Eucharist, ordination, confirmation, penance, marriage, and extreme unction. A sacrament was understood to be a "visible sign of invisible grace." The waters of baptism, for example, were the visible sign that conveyed the invisible grace that removed the stain of original sin from the soul of the one baptized. Outside of exceptional circumstances, these visible signs could only convey invisible grace when administered by someone who had been duly and properly ordained. Ordination, in turn, was only valid if administered by a properly ordained bishop standing in the line of apostolic succession represented by the pope, the bishop of Rome. Thus the dispensation of saving grace was entirely in the hands of the clergy of the church, under the authority of the pope. Or, said more elegantly, there was no salvation outside the church.

The supernatural powers conveyed by ordination created a "clerical" class as distinct from the "laity." There were two kinds of clergy, with distinct functions: "regular" clergy were those who had taken monastic vows and so were subject to a rule of life (a *regula*); the "secular" clergy were ordained priests, under no monastic rule of life. The spiritual powers of the secular clergy were displayed in the administration of all the sacraments, but they were visible particularly in the celebration of the Eucharist. At the words of institution, "This is my Body," the elements of the host (the bread) and the wine were said to be transubstantiated into the body and the blood of Christ. The word itself was adapted from Aristotelian physics to explain a religious mystery. All physical things, Aristotle had said, could be reduced to substance and accidents. The substance of any thing was the essence that it shared with other things of the same kind: the substance of a tree was its "treeness" or the properties it shared with all other trees, such as having a root system, a trunk, and branches. The accidental properties of any particular tree were its own distinctive size, colour, shape, number of branches, etc.

When this physics of substance and accidents was applied to the mystery of the Eucharist, it was held that when the priest said the words of institution, the substance of the bread and the wine changed invisibly into the substance of the body and blood of Christ (hence *transubstantiation*), while the accidents remained the same. That is, the particular bread and wine still looked and tasted (accidental qualities) like bread and wine, but an invisible change of substance had occurred through the priestly

mediation. The belief that Christ was physically (substantially) present in the consecrated host led to the common practice of adoration of the host as a form of devotion,
meditation, and prayer.

This description of late medieval sacramentalism can lead to the mistaken
impression that the spirituality of the era was dominated "from above" by the secular clergy and the sacraments, and that the laity were mere passive recipients of the
grace the clergy dispensed. The situation was much more complex.[3] The evidence
suggests that there was a marked increase in traditional religious practices initiated
and funded by the laity in the late medieval period, right up to the time of the Reformation. On this there is agreement, but there is little agreement on how to interpret
this increase in religious activity.[4] Some historians suggest that the rise in traditional
observance actually reflects the rising anxiety of the laity concerning salvation.[5] Other
historians have warned against extrapolating too much from Luther's particular experience of anxiety.[6] All agree, however, that the phenomenon of increasing lay piety
on the eve of the Reformation presents a complex picture.

Lay Piety

The empirical evidence for an increase in lay piety is a marked upswing in the
foundation of new chapels and churches, and the continuing popularity of endowed
Masses for the dead, pilgrimages, and the commissioning of the production of images
of the saints. Added to this are the increased activities of religious confraternities
which hired their own priests to celebrate Masses for the dead and occasionally endowed their own preachers. These confraternities initiated popular feasts,
processsions, plays, and pageants. The image of a silent and subservient laity dominated by an overpowering clergy simply does not fit the facts of lay piety in the late
middle ages: these same clergy were often hired by the laity themselves to perform
sacramental functions the laity desired.[7] Nevertheless, the confusing fact remains
that within a very few years, great numbers of these same lay people would repudiate much of what they had so recently held sacred. As Collinson notes, the Reformation iconoclasts were not attacking something "medieval," but rather destroying "what
was new and freshly painted."[8]

Some lay movements verged into the heretical (Cathars, Waldensians) or
marginally orthodox (Beghards, Beguines). The Sacramentarian movement in the
Netherlands was of the former variety in that it challenged the medieval church's
view on the sacrament of the altar. Sacramentarianism was of particular significance
for the development of Reformation views on the Supper, and for the eventual reception of Anabaptism in the Low Countries. The Sacramentarians in the Netherlands
emerged in the late medieval period and openly opposed any notion of transubstantiation.[9] George H. Williams notes that this opposition was due not so much to skepticism
as it was to a "devout spiritualization of the sacrament" which could not conceive of the
association of materiality with the true Body of Christ. Williams notes further:

> The fact that Sacramentism deprived one sacrament of its
> sacrificatory character *ex opere operato* and that Anabaptism in con-

trast would give enhanced prominence to another does not obscure the spiritualizing trait common to both processes.[10]

Clerical and lay interest in mysticism and "things of the Spirit" expressed itself sometimes in orthodox ways, but at other times and places the "spiritualizing" impulse could threaten directly the sacramental edifice. When Anabaptism arrived in the Netherlands in 1530, it found that sacramentarian piety had prepared the way. Many Anabaptists in the Netherlands, notably Menno Simons and David Joris, had been introduced to doubts about the efficacy of the sacraments by the Sacramentarians.

Just as the laity in 1450 showed initiative in their religious expressions, so also the common people after 1517 showed little inclication to walk in lockstep with the major reformers. The Anabaptist movement in particular illustrates the survival of a lay piety that in some ways repudiated late medieval religious forms and practices, but that in other ways continued earlier forms of piety that the mainline reformers wished to repudiate.

In this connection it is important to note that a significant portion of late medieval lay piety was modelled upon the ideals of monastic piety. Only ordained priests had the power to transubstantiate bread and wine, but the ascetic ideals of the monks and nuns could be mirrored by any truly zealous lay person. It should not be surprising that the most religiously committed laity of the late medieval period found ways of paralleling the religiosity of the monks and nuns. The lay religious communities of Beghards and Beguines that sprang up without benefit of clerical leadership or sanction are the most striking examples of lay initiative and piety in a monastic mode; the ideals remained poverty, chastity, and separation from the world. The "Modern Devotion" movement also shared these same ideals. Steven Ozment notes the proliferation of these "devotional options" among the laity of the late middle ages, and comments further that "almost all were restorational in nature, that is, basically attempts to return to the example of the Apostles." Writing from the mainstream Protestant perspective, Ozment argues that this late medieval emphasis on a "purer asceticism" was not of the same "spirit" as later Reformation piety.[11] While this may be true of the reforms of Luther and Zwingli, the same cannot be said for the Anabaptist reform, which continued to resonate to the late medieval monastic ideal of "ascetic" and "restorationist" piety.[12]

There was no typical form of late medieval piety. Within the dogmatic framework of sacramental teaching and practice there flourished side by side exalted mystical forms of unitive prayer, ascetic programmes of renewal, participation in bawdy street plays, pilgrimages to shrines, and the purchase of indulgences as acts of penance. Calls for reform would necessarily evoke different responses depending upon the hearer's commitments. Nevertheless, in light of what was to come, it is fair to say that late medieval piety was shaped by very fundamental presuppositions that would come under serious question with the advent of Luther's critiques. Three of these central presuppositions were:

1. The conviction that the church was a mystical body that included the *active* participation of the dead as well as the living. This conviction, on which rested much of what characterized lay piety in the late middle ages, was shared not only by those who made pilgrimages or commissioned Masses for the dead, but by virtually everyone. Salvation within this mystical body depended in large measure upon the activity of the living, in conjunction with the benefits that could be conferred by the sainted dead. Acts of penance, deeds of virtue and self-denial, and sacramental acts all played active roles in the saving process of justification before God the judge.

2. The conviction that sacramental powers resided with the clergy of the church, who were duly ordained within a hierarchy headed by the pope. Outside this sacramental structure, which existed as the only mediator of God's saving grace, there was no salvation. Furthermore, final doctrinal and interpretive authority within the church was held to reside with the papacy.

3. The conviction that "laity who desired a full spiritual life should live as nearly like clergy as possible."[13] It was generally accepted that full time, observant, "regular" clergy had an advantage in the economy of salvation, particularly in matters of penance. This conviction often led to parallel efforts among the laity.

The Challenge of Luther's Ideas

Martin Luther's 95 theses were not calculated to overthrow the existing church. Sparked by the sale of indulgences, they were a critique of an abused practice, not of the structure that sponsored the practice. But one thing led to another. In his university lectures on Romans (1513-1517) Luther already had come to his radical understanding of saving faith, and it soon became evident that he was questioning the foundations of medieval church doctrine and practice. In 1520 Luther published three remarkable writings that provided many of the basic concepts and slogans for the early "evangelical" reforming movement.[14] Luther had thrown down the gauntlet in public, in print, and in German, and the papacy responded with a bull entitled *Exsurge Domine*, which condemned 41 proposition extracted from Luther's publications. By January 1521 an unrepentant Luther had been excommunicated by the pope.

The revolutionary power of Luther's reforming ideas lay in its challenge to prevailing assumptions about the nature of authority, the church, and salvation. Four of these principles in particular soon were circulating at the popular level.

1. *Scripture Alone.* In his writings of 1520 Luther emphasized repeatedly that the authority of Scripture is above that of the papacy: it is Scripture that judges humankind, including the papacy, and not vice versa. This appeal to the ultimate authority of Scripture, prepared as it had been by Wycliff, Hus, and others, challenged the interpretive powers of the church hierarchy, and appeared to place all church practices before the bar of Scripture alone. We say "appeared to place" because Luther's appeal to Scripture failed to resolve the crucial question of who (if not the church hierarchy) was to be the authoritative interpreter of Scripture. Luther's assumption (incorrect, but shared by most evangelical reformers before 1525) was that Scripture was "clear" and would need no further interpretation.

2. *Priesthood of all Believers.* Luther argued that all believers are equally "priests" by virtue of baptism. Ordination, said Luther, does not leave an indelible mark on the soul; furthermore, the authority to ordain pastors lies with the congregation. Luther's challenge was plain: the supposed "powers" conferred through ordination upon the clergy did not exist. Therefore the entire sacramental edifice resting upon that supposed clerical power was a house built upon sand. It appeared, furthermore, that Luther was conferring great powers upon the laity by erasing the clergy/laity distinction altogether. The laity, said Luther, had the right to interpret Scripture for themselves; it appeared that he also was arguing that the laity had an equal right to function as "priests" within the church, and that congregations had authority over their pastors.

3. *Salvation by Grace through Faith.* Whereas the medieval church held that the clergy and the sacraments were central in mediating grace, Luther argued that salvation was by "faith alone," and not by any "works." By "works" Luther meant the numerous works of penance as well as other "good works" that were supposed to confer merit and contribute to justification in the sacramental understanding. Luther's understanding of salvation emphatically removed the sacramental church from its previous mediatorial function, and appeared to place all individual believers directly before God.

4. *At the same time Justified and yet a Sinner.* Luther's understanding of salvation by faith *alone* challenged the ascetic rationale underlying much of medieval spirituality: it had been assumed that with proper disposition, effort, and exercise, human beings were capable of growing in virtue, and that growth in virtue would contribute to salvation. The highest exemplars of this potential growth in virtue were the saints, most of whom had devoted themselves to the "religious" life under a monastic rule. To the contrary, said Luther, human beings are justified not by any actual virtue they can attain (for they can attain no virtue in God's sight), but only because God considers them "just" *for Christ's sake.* Righteousness is *imputed* to human beings because of their faith in Christ, but no human being actually becomes righteous. Luther's understanding of salvation "by faith alone" was a repudiation of the ascetic rationale underlying centuries of spiritual practice.

Luther's initial reforming ideas were fruitful beyond his own expectations. But as presented in his great reform writings of 1520 they were not yet a programme of reform. His ideas circulated as popular slogans that gave rise to a variety of reforming programmes that, as it happened, were not always what Luther himself came to endorse. Luther's critique meant, for example, that it no longer made sense to pray before images of saints, to light candles there, or to make pilgrimages to holy relics. Following Luther's lead, the basic spiritual question appeared to be directed within, to one's personal faith in Christ. This posed some difficult practical questions. What was to be done with holy pictures, relics, statues, and the like? Was a "biblical" church one that had been "cleansed" of these "human inventions," and should such "cleansing" proceed as soon as possible? What form of public and private piety should now take the place of those older forms?

Along with the "desacralizing" of holy images and objects Luther also appeared to "desacralize" the sacraments. Meditation and prayer that had focused on the "presence of Christ" in the consecrated host, and the popular celebrations and feasts associated with *Corpus Christi*, were now said to be much ado about nothing. How then were sacramental practices in the church to be understood? Does baptism have any value *apart from faith*, given that the water remains only water, even after a priest has blessed it? And if faith must accompany the waters of baptism, what then is the theological rationale supporting the baptism of infants, who clearly have no personal faith? How is the Supper to be understood, if Christ is not present in the elements through transubstantiation?

Luther also appeared to have removed the fundamental distinction between clergy and laity, and to have empowered the laity in spiritual matters. But Luther's understanding of salvation also had removed "ascetic" assumptions that underlay the highest spiritual aspirations of medieval people. If human beings are saved by being *considered* righteous, and not by *becoming* righteous, how should Christian piety manifest itself? What was to become of the pursuit of virtue, of ascetic self-denial, of the avoidance of sin, of growth in humility?

Luther's eventual answer to these practical questions gave concrete shape to the "Lutheran" branch of reform. Luther argued for a slow pace of reform, and that keeping many older forms was harmless. His position was "if it is not forbidden in Scripture, it is allowed in practice." In ecclesial practice the Lutheran reform looked and felt more conservative than radical. Concerning baptism of infants, Luther said that the faith of the parents and godparents effectively substituted for the absent faith of the infant; concerning the Supper, Luther rejected transubstantiation while maintaining that Christ was physically present "with" the elements, and that the real body and blood of Christ was physically eaten with the elements, even by those who lacked faith.

These eventual Lutheran answers were not obvious in 1520, or for some years to come. In the euphoria and unclarity of those early years Luther's reforming principles and slogans were developed in a more "radical" manner by persons who also considered themselves to be part of the evangelical reform. Out of this "Radical Reformation" eventually emerged the Anabaptist stream of reform.

Conclusion

The threads that went into making up the Reformation were many, varied, and complex. They were "political" both within and without the church itself. The political struggle within the church was the conciliar struggle: an effort to reform the church "in head and members" had been attempted at the Council of Constance, was foiled by the Renaissance popes, but did achieve some measure of success at Trent. The wider political struggle witnessed the curtailing of papal power and the breakup of Christendom, as the various European political powers did battle with each other and against the Ottoman Turks in a dizzying whirl of shifting alliances that often looked to religious questions only secondarily. In the wider political context the survival of a "magisterial Reformation" must be seen as the result of fortuitous political circumstances.

The call for reform also took place at the higher intellectual levels of the universities. There the struggle was theological, involving theories of authority, (conciliar and scriptural), salvation, grace, free will, works, etc. But the reforming struggle among the intellectual elite could also concentrate on moral reform, with a strong demand for lives that fit the words. The humanists (the best known of whom was Erasmus) carried this particular torch. It was this latter stream that found its strongest echo among the common people, not so much because of direct humanist influence, but more likely because the humanists and the commoners shared a common late medieval concern for the reformation of morals within the church.

Finally, the call for reform surged up from the bottom of the socio-economic heap, that is, from the common people. It was the great mass of commoners, both city and country dwellers, who responded to the Protestant reformers' strong critiques of medieval (Roman) sacramental religion, as well as to the calls for a new authority in Scripture and a more responsive and moral clergy. On this initial note, humanists, "Catholic" reformers, Lutherans, and commoners were in agreement. There was a honeymoon, but it would not last long. As the papacy began to draw the line of authority with Luther outside it, the Reformation movement began to fragment. The humanists were the first to abandon the united front, Erasmus choosing to stay with the "mother" church. For the common people, the line would be drawn definitively in 1525, with the Peasants' War. This struggle would leave many outside not only the sphere of the papal church, but also outside the Protestant ones. The Radical Reformation is, above all, the reformation of these latter people—those who were left (or who chose to stand) outside the "legitimate" limits soon defined by Roman Catholicism and mainline Protestantism.

End Notes

[1] "There came a point when Luther's theology had to be embodied in institutions. Moreover, the Peasants' War of 1525, the visitations of 1527 and 1530, the formation of the League of Schmalkalden in 1531—these and similar events in the late 1520s and early 1530s were both cause and effect of a transition from a revolutionary movement made up primarily of ideologically committed individuals to a more conservative movement led by rulers of territories and city states. Political considerations, though never absent in the development of Luther's Reformation, came to exert an increasingly important role." Mark U. Edwards, Jr., "Martin Luther," in Steven Ozment, ed., *Reformation Europe: A Guide to Research* (St. Louis: Center for Reformation Research, 1982), pp. 68-69.

[2] For this and following points see especially James M. Stayer, *The German Peasants' War and Anabaptist Community of Goods* (Montreal and Kingston: McGill-Queen's University Press, 1991).

[3] "It was a serious mistake to think of late medieval religion as a commodity provided by the clergy for lay people, which as customers they either understood or misunderstood, accepted or rejected." Patrick Collinson, "The late Medieval Church and its Reformation, 1400-1600," in John McManners, ed., *The Oxford Illustrated History of Christianity* (Oxford: Oxford University Press, 1992), p. 252. For a survey of the scholarship, see Francis Oakley, "Religious and Ecclesiastical Life on the Eve of the Reformation," in Steven Ozment, ed., *Reformation Europe: A Guide to Research* (St. Louis: Center for Reformation Research, 1982), pp. 5-32.

[4] See Steven Ozment, *The Age of Reform: 1250-1550* (New Haven: Yale University Press, 1980), pp. 205ff.

[5] Ozment follows a common Protestant interpretation, suggesting that "The failure of the late medieval church to provide a theology and spirituality that could satisfy and discipline religious hearts and minds was the most important religious precondition of the Reformation." *Ibid.*, p. 208.

[6] "There is no reason to suppose that the majority lived in that perpetual mood of morbid *angst* with which Jan Huizinga characterized ... late medieval culture." So Collinson, "Late Medieval Church," p. 256.

[7] *Ibid.*, p. 252.

[8] *Ibid.*, p. 254.

[9] See Williams, *Radical* (1992), chapter 2.4.

[10] *Ibid.*, p. 99.

[11] Ozment, *Age of Reform*, pp. 220-21.

[12] See Kenneth Davis, *Anabaptism and Asceticism* (Scottdale, Pa.: Herald Press, 1974). Although Davis makes too much of tenuous historical connections between Anabaptism and the "Erasmian" piety of the *Devotio Moderna*, his book nonetheless illustrates convincingly the "ascetic" cast of Anabaptist spirituality. See also Arnold Snyder, *The Life and Thought of Michael Sattler* (Scottdale, Pa.: Herald Press, 1984).

[13] Ozment, *Age of Reform*, p. 219.

[14] They were: *An Appeal to the Christian Nobility, On the Babylonian Captivity of the Church*, and *A Treatise on Christian Liberty*.

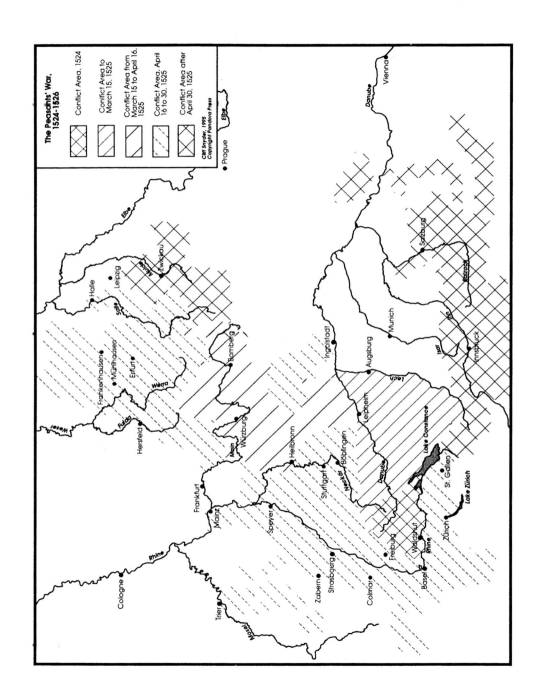

Cliff Snyder, 1995
Copyright Pandora Press

**The Peasants' War,
1524–1526**

Conflict Area, 1524

Conflict Area to
March 15, 1525

Conflict Area from
March 15 to April 16,
1525

Conflict Area, April
16 to 30, 1525

Conflict Area after
April 30, 1525

Prague

Vienna

Elbe

Zwickau

Leipzig

Halle

Saale

Mulde

Elbe

Salzburg

Salzach

Munich

Ingolstadt

Augsburg

Inn

Innsbruck

Frankenhausen

Mühlhausen

Erfurt

Werra

Bamberg

Leipheim

Lech

Isar

Hersfeld

Fulda

Weser

Würzburg

Main

Lake Constance

Frankfurt

Heilbronn

Stuttgart

Böblingen

Neckar

Danube

St. Gallen

Mainz

Speyer

Strasbourg

Zabern

Colmar

Freiburg

Waldshut

Basel

Rhine

Zürich

Lake Zürich

Cologne

Rhine

Trier

Mosel

Chapter 2

The Emergence of Radical Reform

The Anabaptist understanding of reform owed a fundamental debt to the earliest "evangelical" critiques of the medieval church, but Anabaptism also grew out of, and carried forward, the critiques directed by "radical" evangelical reformers against Wittenberg and Zürich. For this reason the Anabaptist story cannot be told apart from the important mediating influences of Andreas Karlstadt, Thomas Müntzer, Caspar Schwenckfeld, and others. Tracing some of these influences, as we will do below, does not tell the entire story, for many other names and movements could be added to the list.[1] Nevertheless, it does go a long way toward introducing the Radical Reformation context and critique out of which Anabaptism emerged and of which it formed a part.

Andreas Karlstadt

Among the reformers who have come to be labelled "radical" reformers, none was closer to Martin Luther than was Andreas Karlstadt.[2] Although it was Andreas Karlstadt who promoted Martin Luther to the doctorate at the University of Wittenberg in 1512, it was Luther who would take the lead in the reforming movement, eventually pushing the elder Karlstadt to the margins. The differences between them were, initially, not theological differences but had more to do with the pace of reform. Karlstadt had taken over reform in Wittenberg after Luther's exile to the Wartburg in 1521, but there had been public disputations, iconoclastic riots, and the celebration of the first evangelical Mass on Christmas day, 1522. On the 6th of March, 1522, Martin Luther returned to Wittenberg, preached eight powerful sermons, and "restored old custom": "Only after the word had convinced the weak [and the princes] should old customs and practices be changed."[3] Karlstadt's leading role in Wittenberg was at an end. In the summer of 1523, Karlstadt took up the post of pastor at Orlamünde, a parish he held as a sinecure. It was here that he instituted, however briefly, church reforms as he saw fit, and it was here that his distinctive theological perspectives, *vis-a-vis* Luther, became evident.

Karlstadt's Orlamünde Theology
Scripture Alone

Already by 1521, Karlstadt had a different conception of Scripture as the measure of reform than did Luther. Karlstadt was willing to allow *no* human tradition to remain, and called rather for a reform of the church only according to what had been commanded in Scripture.[4] While Luther was willing to accept the basic structure of the Mass, for instance, and a very sacramental view of the Supper, Karlstadt purged the sanctuary of images and radically undid the sacramental view. A second crucial difference between Karlstadt and Luther concerned the role of the Spirit as it related to the letter of Scripture. Both Luther and Karlstadt insisted that a literal reading of Scripture was primary, and that Scripture must be read Christocentrically.[5] Both insisted that the external word was the means of grace by which faith was born.[6] Nevertheless, Karlstadt insisted further that the external word (whether read or heard) could be *interpreted* properly only through the power of the Holy Spirit. Already in 1521 Karlstadt insisted that "even 'extensive reading is not sufficient unless you have the Spirit of God.' Many who can discuss the Scriptures and excite others are cold and do not rejoice personally in the truth."[7] Karlstadt's emphasis on the active role of the Spirit in the interpretation of Scripture would be taken up in the Anabaptist movement, and would remain a feature of the "radical" appropriation of Scripture alone.

Salvation by Grace through Faith

At the heart of Luther's theology was the teaching of justification of sinners before God by grace through faith in Christ's sacrificial death. Karlstadt agreed, but believed that God's saving grace would remake and regenerate sinners, leading them to a subsequent life of discipleship and obedience.[8] In Karlstadt's view, grace is efficacious, and faith results in an overcoming of sin. The differences between Luther and Karlstadt concerning the nature of divine grace were mirrored also in their respective anthropologies. There was no free will possible for Luther, but rather the human will was bound to sin in this life, dependent upon God's predestination. Karlstadt, to the contrary, argued that grace freed the human will to choose or not to choose salvation.[9] Karlstadt understood sin as being essentially volitional, namely as willing other than what God wills.[10] Since sin is of this nature, the conquering of sin must take place by means of *Gelassenheit*, or "yieldedness" of one's will and desires to do God's will. Thus Karlstadt, as would the Anabaptists after him, spoke of the "obedience of faith," and demanded a life of visible conformity to Christ. This emphasis hearkened back to late medieval ascetic spiritual ideals; it was not what Luther had in mind.

Priesthood of all Believers

Whether or not Luther intended it to sound that way, the "priesthood of all believers" was a slogan that implied an egalitarian church: all believers had the right (so it appeared) to interpret Scripture and to judge clergy on the basis of it, all in virtue of their Christian baptism. But Luther soon made clear that he had not meant to establish a "free church." His non-egalitarian position became crystal clear in 1525, during the Peasants' War, when he backed the princes against the peasants. Karlstadt, on the other hand, gave a heightened role to the laity.

The question of "priesthood" was central to sacramental questions. Do physical elements *convey* divine grace and, if so, what role is played by the "priesthood" in bringing this about? Karlstadt radically severed the reception of grace from any physical elements; the "priests" would mediate grace by proclaiming the Word, something the laity could do as well as any ordained clergy. While Luther came to insist on an essential continuity with the Roman Catholic sacramental and mediatory understanding for baptism and the Supper, Karlstadt returned the elements of baptismal water and eucharistic bread and wine back to the "natural world." What really counted was the inner spiritual reality of faith, regeneration by the Holy Spirit, and the new life which resulted. Karlstadt was able to carry through a consistent priesthood of believers in large part because of the removal of the liturgical and ritualistic function of "priests."[11] This view would appear also in the Anabaptist movement, which in its early years emphasized the right of the laity (when informed by the Spirit) to preach, interpret Scripture, and preside over the Lord's Supper, without benefit of "ordination" outside of the Spirit's presence.

Ecclesiology

Because of Karlstadt's understanding of the necessity of regeneration following faith in Christ, his view of the church was that it would be a community of those who have been regenerated.[12] He had little patience with Luther's admonition that reform should proceed slowly to "spare the weak." Furthermore, it was within the context of the regenerate congregation that the ordinances of baptism and the Supper were to be placed. Both are external signs of an internal yieldedness and rebirth.[13] Although Karlstadt did not institute the rebaptism of adults following confession of faith, he did argue against infant baptism and in favour of adult baptism. This followed directly from his regenerationist soteriology: "Since regeneration is the prerequisite for baptism, infant baptism is not permissible."[14] Likewise the Supper is not a "means of grace," but is a memorial to be utilized by those who have been regenerated by grace through faith.[15] In this important way Karlstadt, although never an "Anabaptist" in a formal sense, nevertheless laid the necessary groundwork for the emergence of Anabaptism.

Finally, Karlstadt upheld a radically egalitarian vision of the church. The priesthood of all believers remained primary for him; he also supported the election of pastors by the congregation, the correction of those pastors by the congregation, and the power of the congregation to "bind and loose."[16] The similarity of Karlstadt's ecclesiology to that of the later Anabaptist movement is striking.

Conclusion

When Karlstadt's Orlamünde theology is considered from the point of view of spirituality, it is clear that he stood in closer continuity with late medieval piety than did Luther. Karlstadt's emphasis on an efficacious grace that regenerates and sanctifies sinners, leading to a visibly new life, hearkened back to the theme of "sanctification" in the late medieval framework. So did Karlstadt's understanding of the potentialities of the human person: he believed, as Luther did not, that human beings were capable of being regenerated by the Spirit of God in this life, that they were capable of becoming righteous. Likewise Karlstadt's understanding of sin as essentially volitional, opened the door to an ascetic approach to the Christian life: walking in obedience was possible for Karlstadt, if one learned to "yield oneself" to the Spirit and grace of God. This understanding left a place for the spiritual exercise of "preparing for grace," with the expectation of real growth in the Christian life as a result. Finally, the church for Karlstadt was a community of the reborn, a kind of ascetic lay order committed to living new lives in community.

At the same time, Karlstadt also went further than did Luther in rejecting other aspects of traditional piety. He was far more anticlerical than was Luther, and rejected any mediatory role for the clergy, save the "preaching of the Word." He enhanced the role of the laity far more than would Luther, arguing for the right of the laity to interpret Scripture and to elect and discipline their own pastors. Karlstadt was willing to subordinate sacraments to faith in a way Luther was not. And Karlstadt's approach to Scripture was at once more biblicistic (only what is commanded is allowed) and pneumatic (only those with the Spirit can interpret correctly) than was Luther's view.

Karlstadt's differences with Luther played an important role in delineating an alternative stream of reform in the "evangelical" movement. His influence as a mediator of this alternative stream of reform is undeniable; Calvin Pater has called him the "father" of the Baptist movement.[17] Although some clear differences are evident between Karlstadt and the Anabaptists—such as the role Karlstadt maintained for Christian rulers—and although crucial historical links are no longer extant—such as Karlstadt's writing on baptism—his influence on at least the Swiss Anabaptist stream no longer is in doubt.[18] Karlstadt blazed an alternative evangelical reforming trail upon which many an Anabaptist would tread subsequently.

Thomas Müntzer

There was in all likelihood no person more vilified by learned contemporaries than the infamous Thomas Müntzer, the "destroyer of unbelievers" or, alternatively, "the Satan from Allstedt."[19] Müntzer was concerned from the start of his career with the reform of the existing church; he was branded as a "Lutheran" already in 1519, and thanks to Luther's intervention he was called in May 1520 to fill a vacant post in the church in Zwickau. Müntzer already differed from Luther at this early stage by opposing infant baptism and by promoting what Williams calls a "Spiritualist hermeneutics."[20] Müntzer held to the Lutheran view of *sola scriptura*, but he held that both Testaments needed to be interpreted by the Holy Spirit working in believers. Müntzer's mystical doctrine of spiritual suffering also was in evidence, modifying Luther's understanding of "faith

THOMAS MUNCER PREDIGER TOT ALSTAT,

TOMAS MVNCER PREDIGER ZV ALSTET IN DVRINGEN.

alone." It was on this inner birth of the Spirit through suffering that Müntzer pinned his reforming hopes: When the original internal order is restored to human hearts, then the kingdom of this world will be given over to the elect.

As a consequence of Müntzer's understanding, he saw humanity divided between sheep and goats, the righteous and the unrighteous. The righteous "sheep" are those who have *experienced* faith, which has come to them through deep suffering; the unrighteous "goats" are those who have "stolen" their faith. Primary among the "godless" goats, said Müntzer, were the clergy themselves, and Luther himself soon became the primary example.[21] By 1521 Müntzer had become convinced that the End Times had arrived and that "a new apostolic church must gather the elect and separate them from worldly people."[22]

By 1525 Müntzer came to see "in the peasant revolt the end of the fifth monarchy prophecied in Daniel..."[23] Convinced that he was participating in the End Times scenario, Müntzer urged the peasants assembled at Frankenhausen to battle against the professional army of the Landgrave, Philip of Hesse. The result was an unholy slaughter in which an estimated 6,000 peasants lost their lives; there were a total of six casualties in Philip's army.[24] After the slaughter, Müntzer was discovered hiding in an attic of the town. He eventually was brought to recantation; toward the end of May, 1525, he was beheaded in Mühlhausen.

Müntzer's Theology
Scripture Alone

Thomas Müntzer became an "evangelical" reformer because he embraced the authority of Scripture over against the authority of the Roman Catholic hierarchy. But he emphasized the hermeneutical role of the living Spirit even more emphatically than did Karlstadt. In this his approach was more mystical and spiritualistic than strictly exegetical. Müntzer considered any reading of Scripture inauthentic which was not grounded on a "living experience" of faith. Everyone in his day, he said, liked to "dress up in Scripture," and talk about the faith of the apostles, but the only price they wished to pay was to "stagger around mad-drunk."[25]

Müntzer's strong emphasis on the "inner word," on the direct teaching by the Spirit of God as the true word, solidly separated Müntzer's understanding of "the Word" from Luther's. Although Karlstadt also emphasized the work of the Spirit in the proper interpretation of Scripture, Müntzer's was yet a stronger spiritualism that did not follow Karlstadt's tendency to find "laws of behaviour" in Scripture; Müntzer's approach, furthermore, opened up the possibilty of direct, non-scriptural revelations. There are, then, both strong similarities in the "spiritualism" of Karlstadt and Müntzer's respective approaches to Scripture, as well as differences in emphases. Both Karlstadt's and Müntzer's respective approaches to the question of the relationship of spirit to letter would find representatives within the subsequent Anabaptist tradition of reform.

Salvation by grace through faith

Thomas Müntzer assumed that only some would be chosen for salvation, but those who are so chosen will know it because the process of salvation will include a painful spiritual purging, an uprooting of self, and a re-making of the inner person. This is a view that stands conceptually close to Karlstadt's view of spiritual regeneration, while not identical with it because of Müntzer's stronger emphasis on the painful process of coming to faith. For Müntzer, one's heart must be "ploughed" before faith can be born. This understanding owed much to the mystical tradition, and much less to Luther. His critique of Luther's "faith alone" was that it was a preaching of "sweetness alone." True faith, as opposed to the counterfeit variety, will not be learned in books, said Müntzer, but rather in "poverty of spirit," something akin to what the mystics called the "dark night of the soul." In a strikingly similar way (and thoroughly in tune with late medieval ascetic expectations) Karlstadt and Müntzer critiqued Luther's understanding of salvation for not demanding more in the way of regeneration of believers. Karlstadt was more disposed to expect particular ethical results from this rebirth; Müntzer concentrated more on the process leading up to the birth of faith. These differences in emphasis would be echoed in the later expressions of Anabaptism.

Priesthood of all Believers and Ecclesiology

Because his reforming career was abruptly cut short, it is difficult to say how Thomas Müntzer would have structured his church in subsequent years. In Allstedt he seemed quite comfortable with a traditional "priestly" role as a preacher of the word and presider over the sacraments of the church. His liturgical work retained the traditional form of the Mass, and although he criticized infant baptism, nevertheless he continued to perform the ceremony. All of this drew the criticism of Conrad Grebel who, in his 1524 letter to Müntzer said: "We understand that you have put the Mass into German and introduced new German songs and we have seen them. This cannot be right..."[26] Grebel was influenced by Karlstadt's more radically biblicist ecclesiology. Whether Thomas Müntzer eventually would have moved into a more explicit "believers' church" ecclesiology remains a moot point, given his early demise—although his understanding of the "elect" who are reborn spiritually certainly contained the possible seeds for such a development.

On the other hand, because of the strong spiritualism at the heart of his thought, there did seem to be an openness on Müntzer's part to accepting "pneumatic authority" no matter on whom it fell. It must be noted here, as we have noted above concerning Karlstadt, that the emphasis on the work of the Spirit in the interpretation of Scripture meant that such interpretation was now open to all who had in turn opened themselves to the Spirit. This radical interpretive egalitarianism, common to both Karlstadt and Müntzer, would continue in the Anabaptist tradition, particularly during the earlier more "pneumatic" phases of the movement.

Apocalypticism

Müntzer's growing conviction that he was living in the Last Days certainly pushed him in a socially radical direction, although it appears that he was headed there from the start. Granted that even Martin Luther believed that he was living in the Last Days, still Müntzer drew far more radical implications from this than did Luther or Karlstadt. Müntzer threw caution to the wind, and spoke with anticipation of the purging which was about to be visited upon the ungodly. Just as God must root out the weeds in the believer's heart, so also will He weed out the ungodly from the world before the End. In contrast to Müntzer's "revolutionary" apocalypticism, Andreas Karlstadt showed little enthusiasm for End Times speculation, nor was he overly fond of the prophetic books of the Bible (e.g., Daniel, Esdras, Revelation). This lack of apocalyptic enthusiasm was shared also by the Swiss Anabaptists, in the same way that Müntzer's apocalypticism came to be reflected in early South German Anabaptism. Certainly Karlstadt shared none of Müntzer's enthusiasm for the "uprooting of the godless." The differences between them were brought out explicitly at the beginning of the upheaval of the Peasants' War, when Karlstadt wrote personally to Müntzer rejecting the latter's invitation to join his "league."[27] Karlstadt and Müntzer took rather different paths leading away from Wittenberg which led them to contrasting ecclesiological and social-political conclusions. These differing tendencies would become evident also in the Anabaptist descendants they inspired.

Conclusion

Thomas Müntzer's continuation of late medieval themes is evident. In contrast to Luther, Müntzer's understanding of the "Word of God" owed more to the mystical tradition: the "Word" was living, spiritual power, recognized in the souls of believers, not the "literal word" of the scholars and exegetes. Here Müntzer went beyond Karlstadt as well, for although Karlstadt also emphasized the role of the Spirit in the interpretation of Scripture, he did not suggest that extra-biblical revelation was possible or reliable. Thomas Müntzer, to the contrary, did open this possibility. On the basis of his reliance on the Holy Spirit, he was more willing to sever the link with the written word. What counted most were the inner experiences of the living God. The tension between spirit and letter, evident here, would remain a contentious issue among the Anabaptists as well, the resolution of which gave a definite "shape" to the Anabaptist traditions passed on into the seventeenth century and beyond.

In the matter of salvation, Müntzer and Karlstadt critiqued Luther in essentially the same manner, and on the basis of the same late medieval presuppositions. Karlstadt and Müntzer shared the language and conception of late medieval mysticism in their use of the concepts of human free will, *Gelassenheit*, the volitional nature of sin, the possibility and necessity of regeneration and a new life. Thomas Müntzer, however, concentrated much more on the preliminary process by which individuals would come to "true faith"; Karlstadt focused more attention on the biblical shape of the ecclesial community that would result from the association of regenerate individuals.

Finally, Thomas Müntzer's strongly apocalyptic convictions influenced all other aspects of his thought. His emphasis on the living Spirit was a reflection of his conviction that in these "End Times" the Spirit would be poured out in new and powerful ways; his reading of Scripture was coloured by the conviction that the events of the Last Days had been predicted in the prophetic books of the Bible; the parallel he drew between the "inner ploughing of the soul" and the historical "winnowing of the godless" was ruled by his apocalyptic conviction as well. In all these ways Müntzer went well beyond Luther and Karlstadt and outlined a reform path that was followed by a significant number of influential early Anabaptists.

The Peasants' War

Church historians (in particular, Reformation historians) have been accustomed to denying that the Peasants' War had anything essential to do with the Reformation. This attitude can be traced back directly to Martin Luther, who vehemently repudiated any such connection with his own reform efforts.[28] Scholars now have come to a very different conclusion: the Peasants' War clearly did have socio-economic roots (grievances concerning serfdom, forced service to lords, etc.), but it would have been unthinkable without the religious justification provided by Martin Luther and the other mainline reformers. The broader social and economic dimensions of "reform" become clear when one looks at the specific articles and grievances of the peasants.[29]

The Peasants' War was no unified movement, but rather a combined series of regional uprisings.[30] But in number and scope it was a tremendous event, drawing in as many as 300,000 persons, with an estimated 100,000 casualties.[31] It is common to divide the Peasants' War into five phases and regions, the earliest in the Black Forest already in 1524, the last continuing in the Tirol into 1526. (See map on p. 24). But the most concentrated period of conflict took place from January to July, 1525, with May 1525 representing the height of the conflict. In that month the affected regions were: the Upper Rhine, Upper Swabia (the places of origin of the conflict), Alsace, Württemberg, Franconia, Thuringia, and the Tirol.[32] The uprising thus was an extremely complex series of local uprisings all of which manifested the particularities of region and place. The peasants and commoners lacked a coherent leadership that could exploit numerical, military and political advantage, and they were therefore vulnerable to the nobles' strategy of military confrontation, one band and army at a time. Nevertheless, the revolt was a social and political convulsion of great magnitude, that came close to achieving a revolutionary political re-alignment in German speaking lands. For the purposes of our own concern with the Radical Reformation, the following observations are in order.

First, it is clear that the revolt was not primarily a religious event. It was a search for social, economic and political redress which found ideological legitimation in Reformation concepts. But for that latter reason the uprising everywhere tended to coalesce around biblical and Reformation language, which provided a broader rallying cry than did local grievances with particular landlords. Some Anabaptists and future Anabaptists participated in, and were committed to the goals of the Peasants' War. We may think here especially of Balthasar Hubmaier in Waldshut, and Hans Hut's and Melchior Rinck's commitments to Thomas Müntzer's aims; the revolt in the Tirol probably also prepared the way for the Anabaptist movement which followed, particularly in some areas. The connections between Anabaptism and the Peasants' War—so long denied by Mennonite scholars and others—appears now to be undeniable. James Stayer's recent study summarizes recent conclusions so well that we will cite it at length here.

> The Peasants' War ... was significantly connected with the begin-
> nings of Anabaptism. In the Waldshut-Schaffhausen-St Gallen area,
> particularly in the rural villages, it caused a temporary breakdown
> of magisterial authority for most of 1525, thereby enabling Swiss
> Anabaptism to spread behind its smoke-screen. Much more impor-
> tant, in eastern Hesse, Thuringia and Franconia, veterans of the
> Peasants' War provided the major leadership and probably most of
> the rank and file of the early Anabaptist movement. . . . Perhaps
> most important of all, but still an hypothesis awaiting documenta-
> tion, the Tyrolean Peasants' War may have alienated the mass of the
> population so completely from the Hapsburg government and the
> Roman Church that it shaped the indispensable preconditions for
> the creation of Jakob Hutter's 'New Tyrol' in Moravia.[33]

Anabaptism cannot be separated from the social and political aims of the group of
"common people" which formed its base of membership.

The Anabaptist stream of Reformation lived on in part because the mainline
reformers disassociated reform of social and economic abuses from the theological
and ecclesiological reform of the church. Anabaptist communities, on the other hand,
continued to address moral, social, and economic questions as part of their *religious*
reform. Peasant concerns were echoed especially in the continuing Anabaptist critique of clerical immorality and inferior cure of souls. This was an issue of who was to
control the appointment, sustenance, and discipline of pastors. The peasants' demand that local communities elect their own pastors, that those pastors be supported
economically by the communities they served, and that they be morally accountable
to those communities (and subject to the discipline of those communities) were all
demands that were carried forward in Anabaptism, but not within mainline Protestantism. Likewise the peasants' call for more just economic relationships among Christians, and their opposition to "usury," also was continued within Anabaptism, as will
be seen in a later chapter. Finally, the egalitarian social ideal articulated by the peasants was achieved, in part, in the Anabaptist communities where it was often repeated that "God is no respecter of persons." Particularly in matters of conscience
and religious conviction, maintained the Anabaptists, all human beings stood equally
before God and would have to answer to God. While this may seem like a "religious"
point, and not a socially revolutionary one, the social and political radicality of such an
attitude was plainly evident to the political authorities. In the sixteenth century, religious dissent was also civil dissent.

Conclusion

Luther's intemperate conduct during the peasants' uprising—he called on the
princes to slay as many of the "mad dog" peasants as possible—effectively ended
the wide grassroots nature of his Reformation programme.[34] Anabaptism recruited
not only peasants and craftsmen disaffected with social and economic conditions, but
also (and more importantly) won over religiously motivated common people to a more

egalitarian and radical current of reform, in which they were called upon to appropriate the message of Scripture for themselves, and to reform their lives according to the guidelines of Scripture.[35] The Anabaptist insistence that questions of usury, economic sharing, moral accountability and community discipline were also *spiritual* matters echoed concerns voiced in the peasants' movement that were not found in either Wittenberg or Zürich. Although persecuted and virtually extinguished in some regions, Anabaptism survived in attenuated form to become an alternative Reformation movement of the common people in the years following 1525.

Caspar Schwenckfeld

Caspar Schwenckfeld von Ossig (1489-1561) was an aristocrat from Silesia who, like Karlstadt and Müntzer, became an early convert to the Lutheran reform.[36] Like them, he also found his reasons to disagree with Luther and also exerted some influence on parts of the Anabaptist movement. By 1522 this enthusiastic Silesian "evangelical" had become advisor in church affairs to Duke Frederick II at Liegnitz. By 1529, however, Schwenckfeld had left Silesia in a self-imposed exile. Three events conspired to bring this about: increasing political pressure from Ferdinand of Hapsburg, who had come to rule the duchy of Silesia in 1526; Schwenckfeld's own estrangement from Luther because of Schwenckfeld's doubts about Luther's conception of saving faith; and Schwenckfeld's steady movement in a spiritualist direction. In April of 1529, Schwenckfeld made a "discreet withdrawal" from the territory and remained a wanderer and itinerant lay theologian for the rest of his life.[37] In Strasbourg, where he found refuge from 1529 to 1534, Schwenckfeld came into frequent contact with a wide variety of Anabaptists (Swiss Brethren, Pilgram Marpeck, Melchior Hoffman). During his stay in the city Schwenckfeld influenced Melchior Hoffman's christological speculations and (a decade later) argued his spiritualist reforming position con-

SCHWENKFELD.

cerning Christology and the Supper against Pilgram Marpeck. Following his stay in Strasbourg, Schwenckfeld found temporary refuge in Ulm and Esslingen. He ended his life in hiding, protected by old friends and benefactors. He died in Ulm in 1561, after a prolonged illness.[38]

Schwenckfeld's Early Theology

Caspar Schwenckfeld had been converted to "evangelical" reform by reading Martin Luther, and from the start he identified himself with the Lutheran reform movement. But the Holy Spirit and the interior life of the spirit of believers played a much larger role for Schwenckfeld than it did for Luther. Central for Schwenckfeld from the start of his evangelical career was the doctrine of justification by faith, but his view—it became increasingly clear—was not consonant with Luther's. Likewise Schwenckfeld's understanding of the Eucharist stood a long distance from Luther's, and led Luther himself to repudiate Schwenckfeld in 1526.

Scripture Alone

Caspar Schwenckfeld has been described as a "spiritualist" because of his continuing and consistent emphasis on the interior action of the Spirit in the hearts of believers. It was the inner Word which brought salvation, not the outer, literal word.[39] Nevertheless, this emphasis on the inner Word did not mean that the outer Word was of no value to Schwenckfeld: he continued to study and exegete Scripture, he encouraged the preaching of the Word in public services, and invariably, he argued his spiritualist points of view scripturally. Still, he maintained that a true exposition of the Word could be done only by those who had been taught by the Spirit.[40] Schwenckfeld's emphasis on the role of the Holy Spirit in the interpretation of Scripture recalls the critiques of Luther by Andreas Karlstadt and Thomas Müntzer, even though Schwenckfeld expressed his views in more moderate and cultured tones.

Salvation by Faith

Martin Luther's critique of the Roman Catholic sacramental and penitential understanding of salvation, which he characterized as "works righteousness," was replaced by Luther's conviction that human beings are saved from sin solely by faith in Christ's sacrifice. This doctrine Caspar Schwenckfeld embraced wholeheartedly. Nevertheless, Schwenckfeld believed that once faith had come to the human heart through the grace of God and the action of the Holy Spirit, this spiritual reality transformed the natures of the children of Adam.[41] Schwenckfeld's understanding of salvation thus mirrored in its general outlines (but with no visible lines of dependence) the dissenting evangelical views of Karlstadt and Müntzer: human beings are justified by *becoming* righteous, by the power of God (not by human effort as such), freed and empowered to begin a process of sanctification. He opposed Luther's "bondage of the will" and doctrine of predestination; his was a more optimistic anthropology and pneumatology.[42] Although the "old Adam" cannot keep God's commandments (loving God and neighbour), "it is not impossible for the new regenerate man, that is, for all Christians who believe in Christ, to keep them."[43]

Schwenckfeld, like Karlstadt and Müntzer, was concerned with the moral and ethical side of reform; the moral reform of the church, he believed, would be brought to fruition only as a result of the activity of the Holy Spirit in the hearts of believers. A true faith born of the Spirit would, of necessity, result in a new life manifesting that faith; salvation would be a process of progressive sanctification. There could be no *simul iustus et peccator* (justified and a sinner at the same time) for Schwenckfeld, as there could not be either for Karlstadt or Müntzer. Faith meant for Schwenckfeld a spiritual bond "between the righteous celestial Christ and the formerly sinful, but now regenerated believer."[44]

The Supper and Baptism

Building on the view that faith is a spiritual bond between the believer and the risen Christ, Schwenckfeld redefined the Lord's Supper. Already by July 1525 Schwenckfeld was convinced, on his reading of John 6, that Christ was not physically present in the elements of the Supper, and he sent a writing to Luther and others which argued this point of view.[45] By October of that same year Schwenckfeld's friend, Valentine Crautwald, had helped him to a further understanding. Concerning the words of institution, "This is my body," Crautwald and Schwenckfeld concluded that the body of Christ indicated in the words of institution was "a mystical flesh upon which only those who perceived Christ spiritually might feed."[46] Schwenckfeld wrote:

> Eating means . . . partaking of the nature of Christ through true faith. The bodily food is transferred into our nature, but the spiritual food changes us into itself, that is, the divine nature, so that we become partakers of it.[47]

In this way Schwenckfeld moved away from the traditional sacramental position in which there was a physical and real presence of Christ's body in or with the elements. At the same time by his formulation Schwenckfeld could retain a "real" (though spiritual) presence of Christ: believers partook in the mystical body of Christ, because of their inward faith. But on the crucial question of whether the inner feeding was in any way intrinsically related to the outer eating of earthly elements, Schwenckfeld said emphatically that they were *not* intrinsically related—even though the two might coincide on occasion.[48]

At about the same time, Schwenckfeld also addressed the question of baptism. As might be expected, Schwenckfeld emphasized the inner, spiritual baptism. Schwenckfeld, like Karlstadt and Müntzer, opposed the baptism of infants because the rite was dependent upon the "outward" element of water, and not upon "inward" faith.[49] Water baptism, said Schwenckfeld in 1526, must follow catechetical instruction and an inner baptism of the Spirit. Nevertheless, although he opposed infant baptism as a misuse, Schenckfeld did not commend or practise rebaptism. Since the essential baptism was a spiritual, interior baptism, Schwenckfeld "simply looked for a baptism by the Holy Spirit at some point in the unfolding of each Christian life, either conjointly with, prior to, or after water baptism."[50]

The question of how the inner life was related to the outer life of church ordinances was answered in a decisively spiritual mode by Schwenckfeld.[51] Although Schwenckfeld saw a decisive separation between spirit and flesh, inner and outer,[52] and although the salvific accent fell on the activity of the living Word, the inner life, and spiritual regeneration, nevertheless Schwenckfeld still maintained a place for the external life of the church as a testimony to, and a manifestation of the inner rebirth.[53] Outer ceremonies were not bound to the inner life of the Spirit in any essential or mediating way, but they could, when properly used, "point toward" grace and salvation.[54] Schwenckfeld's spiritualist answer would pose a problematic alternative for Anabaptists who shared with him an emphasis on the necessary interior work of the Holy Spirit.

Christology

Because of Schwenckfeld's fundamental conviction that the spiritual and material realms (divine/creature; spiritual/physical) were distinct and separate from each other, the christological question became primary. The fact that God had taken on human flesh in the person of Jesus appeared to contradict the dualistic principle that Schwenckfeld accepted as axiomatic.[55] If, as Schwenckfeld believed, the "creaturely" was in fact the "antithesis to the divine," how were the two natures of Christ to be explained and reconciled? How could salvation be mediated to humankind by a "creaturely" Jesus?

In explaining the incarnation Schwenckfeld maintained that God was "the true, *natural* father not only of the eternal Word, but of Jesus's humanity as well."[56] Jesus was not simply born of God in His divinity, and of Mary in His humanity, but rather owed *both* directly to God. Christ participated "in the essence and nature of divinity," said Schwenckfeld, "because he himself, also according to his flesh, body, and soul was divinely adorned and made glorious and rich by birth from God his father."[57] Thus the origin of Christ's human flesh was God the Father, and not a combination of God and the Virgin Mary. This answer helped Schwenckfeld avoid the conclusion that Jesus was a "creature," and helped explain the unique "divine humanness" of Jesus, but it looked suspiciously like an heretical docetic teaching.[58] As a result, Schwenckfeld was forced to clarify his understanding of the Virgin Mary's role in the incarnation. Schwenckfeld argued that

> the Virgin Mary was the true and natural mother of Christ. The Word assumed genuine human flesh directly from her and from no other source or substance. Despite the special nature of Christ's conception, the maternal functions remained natural and the child developed and was born in normal fashion, but with no harm to Mary.[59]

In this way Schwenckfeld tried to explain that a real "conception" (with God as father) had taken place in the Virgin Mary and that Jesus was "truly human." But in order to protect his notion of the divine, non-creaturely flesh of Christ, Schwenckfeld soon found himself defending the doctrine of the sinless flesh of Mary, and eventually the doctrine of Mary's own immaculate conception. In this way did Schwenckfeld work to show how "the flesh of Jesus was and was not ours," and to guarantee that both the truly divine and truly human (but not "creaturely") natures of Christ be recognized.[60]

This brief sketch does not begin to do justice to the complexity of Schwenckfeld's theological argument and position, but at least this much of his view must be described in order to place a good part of the Anabaptist movement in perspective.[61] Andreas Karlstadt influenced the early Swiss Brethren views on baptism and the Supper; Thomas Müntzer passed on some of his mysticism and apocalypticism to South German Anabaptism through Hans Hut; Caspar Schwenckfeld's christological views lived on, in modified form, in North German/Dutch Anabaptism, mediated by Melchior Hoffman to all Melchiorites, including Menno Simons. We will revisit christological questions again in chapter 25 below.

Conclusion

It is evident that Caspar Schwenckfeld's dissatisfaction with Luther's understanding of salvation by faith alone paralleled in some important respects the objections of Andreas Karlstadt and Thomas Müntzer. On the other hand, Schwenckfeld's spiritualist emphasis, which was expressed dogmatically in his docetic Christology, was premised upon a strong dichotomy between the "spirit" and the "flesh" in a way not seen in Karlstadt or Müntzer. Schwenckfeld emphasized the "spirit" side of the spirit/flesh polarity in a way that brought all "creaturely" or "created" things into question. This "spiritualization" was simultaneously a radical "desacralization" of all things physical. The question for Schwenckfeld, and for other like minded persons (of whom there would be some in Anabaptist circles) was what connection there could be, if any, between "outward things" like church ordinances or ceremonies (such as baptism and the Supper) and the spiritual realities to which they pointed. Taken to its logical extreme the spiritualist position denied any "spiritual" relevance to outward observances, seeing in "ceremonies" only human deformations of spiritual realities.

The "spiritualist" way of conceiving the relationship between inner and outer realities (spirit/flesh) led to a distinctive piety or spirituality, especially when it was combined with a regenerationist pneumatology and optimistic anthropology. The Anabaptist movement would struggle long with the spiritualist option. The reason for the attraction of the spiritualist point of view was not that Schwenckfeld himself persuaded so many Anabaptists, but rather because most Anabaptists shared with Schwenckfeld the basic premise that spiritual realities, not physical tokens, were of the essence.

Summary

From the surveys above it should be evident that although Luther's early critique of the medieval church was instrumental in setting into motion an "evangelical" reform movement, the interpretation of how such a reform was to be carried out varied widely. Rather than seeing these "radical" interpretations as "deformations," it is truer to the nature and development of the reforming phenomenon of the sixteenth century to say simply that the Reformation included within its scope, all of these tendencies and interpretations, and more.

The three radical reformers and the movement of the peasants surveyed above do not exhaust the early "Radical Reformation" story, but outlining the views of Karlstadt, Müntzer, Schwenckfeld, and the peasants is a necessary, if minimal, beginning to telling the Anabpatist story. Anabaptism did not emerge *ex nihilo* (out of nothing) as a result of *simply* a pure and earnest Bible reading, but rather it mirrored and echoed radical critiques of those who had gone before. Early Anabaptism would take those critiques some steps further, abandoning some emphases and developing others.

End Notes

[1] For an encyclopedic treatment of the wide variety of Radical Reformation influences on Anabaptism, see the unsurpassed work of George Williams, *Radical Reformation* (1992 edition).

[2] Ronald J. Sider, *Andreas Bodenstein von Karlstadt: The Development of His Thought, 1517-1525* (Leiden: Brill, 1974), and also the summary account in Ronald J. Sider, "Andreas Bodenstein von Karlstadt: Between Liberal and Radical," in Hans-Jürgen Goertz, ed., *Profiles of Radical Reformers* (Scottdale, Pa.: Herald Press, 1982), pp. 45-53.

[3] *Ibid.*, pp. 172-73.

[4] Calvin Pater, *Karlstadt as the Father of the Baptist Movements: The Emergence of Lay Protestantism* (Toronto: Univ. of Toronto Press, 1984), pp. 23-24.

[5] Sider, *Karlstadt*, pp. 91-92.

[6] *Ibid.*, pp. 118-19.

[7] *Ibid.*, pp. 120-21.

[8] Pater notes that salvation for Karlstadt has three stages: 1. flesh, Adam; 2. spirit (annihilation, union, God); 3. incorporation (body, new creation, Christ). Pater, *Karlstadt*, p. 50. Cf. Sider, *Karlstadt*, p. 212.

[9] Pater, *Karlstadt*, p. 46.

[10] Sider, *Karlstadt*, p. 213. Karlstadt also saw sin as "having excessive delight and concern for the self or creatures." *Ibid.*, p. 216.

[11] See Pater, *Karlstadt*, p. 56.

[12] Sider, *Karlstadt*, p. 283.

[13] *Ibid.*, p. 291.

[14] *Ibid.*, pp. 292-93.

[15] *Ibid.*, p. 297.

[16] Pater, *Karlstadt*, pp. 66-78. Pater argues that Karlstadt's emphasis on binding and loosing could be the source for the subsequent emphasis on the ban among the Swiss Anabaptists, *ibid.*, pp. 60-62.

[17] See Pater, *Karlstadt*, pp. 107-08. I would agree with Liechty's critique that Pater has claimed too extensive an influence for Karlstadt. See Daniel Liechty, *Andreas Fischer and the Sabbatarian Anabaptists* (Scottdale, Pa.: Herald Press, 1988), p. 127, n. 2.

[18] See Pater, *Karlstadt*, pp. 80-91. For a study of Karlstadt's effect on the reformation at Strasbourg, see Hans-Werner Müsing, "Karlstadt und die Entstehung der Strassburger Täufergemeinde," in Marc Lienhard, ed., *The Origins and Characteristics of Anabaptism*, (The Hague, 1977), pp. 169-195.

[19] A good popular biography is Hans-Jürgen Goertz, "Thomas Müntzer: Revolutionary in a Mystical Spirit," in Hans-Jürgen Goertz, *Profiles of Radical Reformers* (Scottdale, Pa.: Herald Press, 1982), pp. 29-44. The year 1989 marked the quincentenary of his birth, which was celebrated by numerous major publications. See James Stayer, "Thomas Müntzer in 1989: A Review Article," *Sixteenth Century Journal* 21(1990), pp. 655-70.

Also useful and accessible is Williams, *Radical Reformation*, (1992), pp. 120-136; 162-165. A translation of Müntzer's works is now available in English. See Peter Matheson, *The Collected Works of Thomas Müntzer* (Edinburgh: T & T Clark, 1988).

[20] Williams, *Radical*, p. 125.

[21] Goertz, "Müntzer," pp. 33-35. Cf. Williams, *Radical*, pp. 126-27.

[22] Williams, *Radical*, p. 127.

[23] Williams, *Radical*, p. 164.

[24] Goertz, "Müntzer," p. 40; Williams, *Radical*, p. 165.

[25] Matheson, *Works*, pp. 197-98.

[26] Matheson, *Works*, p. 123.

[27] Letter of Karlstadt to Müntzer, July 19, 1524, in Matheson, *Works*, pp. 91-92. See also the letter from the "people of Orlamünde to those of Allstedt on the Christian way to fight," in *ibid.*, pp. 93-94.

[28] "Luther quite sincerely regarded the commoners' upheaval of 1525 as a carnal perversion of 'his' Gospel." James Stayer, *The German Peasants' War and Anabaptist Community of Goods* (Montreal and Kingston: McGill-Queen's University Press, 1991), p. 35.

[29] See the excellent collection of documents from the Peasants' War, edited and translated by Tom Scott and Bob Scribner, *The German Peasants' War: A History in Documents* (London: Humanities Press, 1991). Also, note the detailed argumentation in Stayer, *German Peasants' War*, pp. 50-54.

[30] Stayer, *Peasants' War*, pp. 20ff.

[31] Numbers cited in Stayer, *German Peasants' War*, p. 20.

[32] *Ibid.*, p. 22.

[33] *Ibid.*, p. 92.

[34] Hermann Mühlfort, Mayor of Zwickau and a Lutheran, wrote in June of 1525: "Doctor Martin has fallen into great disfavor with the common people, also with both the learned and unlearned: his writing is regarded as having been too fickle. (Mühlfort then surveys the publication of Luther's three tracts on the Peasant's War). In the third tract (*Against the Robbing and Murdering Hordes of Peasants*) ... he called for the private and public murder of the peasants... Is the devil, and those who do this, to be our Lord God? Here I do not agree. . . . There was enough murdering of peasants, burghers, women, and children taking place... Martin has not done well in Zwickau and in the countryside and towns; he has written the truth in condemning rebellion, but the poor have been greatly forgotten." Scott and Scribner, *German Peasants' War*, document #157.

[35] Best demonstrated in Stayer, *German Peasants' War*. His central thesis is that "Anabaptist community of goods was the logical continuation of the social Gospel of the Reformation ..., a very radical, albeit non-violent, expression of the commoners' Reformation during and after the suppression of the Peasants' War." p. 7.

[36] For a brief biography, see Horst Weigelt, "Caspar von Schwenckfeld: Proclaimer of the Middle Way," in Hans-Jürgen Goertz, ed., *Profiles of Radical Reformers* (Scottdale, Pa.: Herald Press, 1982), pp. 214-225. Also Selina G. Schultz, *Caspar Schwenckfeld von Ossig (1489-1561)...* (Norristown, Pa.: The Board of Publication of the Schwenckfelder Church, 1946); R. Emmet McLaughlin, *Caspar Schwenckfeld, Reluctant Radical: His Life to 1540* (New Haven: Yale University Press, 1986); Peter C. Erb, *Schwenckfeld and Early Schwenckfelders* (Pennsburg, Pa.: Schwenckfelder Library, 1986); Paul L. Maier, *Caspar Schwenckfeld on the Person and Work of Christ* (Assen: VanGorcum, 1959); and Williams, *Radical, passim*.

[37] Williams, *Radical*, pp. 210-11.

[38] *Ibid.*, p. 1237.

[39] See Maier, *Schwenckfeld*, p. 26, and Gottfried Seebass, "Caspar Schwenckfeld's Understanding of the Old Testament," in Peter C. Erb, ed., *Schwenckfeld and Early Schwenkfeldianism: Papers Presented at the Colloquium on Schwenckfeld and the Schwenkfelders* (Pennsburg, Pa.: Schwenkfelder Library, 1986), p. 96.

[40] "Faith is necessary before one can understand the outer word of the Scripture." *Ibid.*, p. 96. So also Maier, *Schwenckfeld*, p. 28: "The Holy Scriptures constitute the norm of theology, but only a spiritual understanding of the Bible is its normative interpretation."

[41] Weigelt, "Schwenckfeld," pp. 215-16.

[42] See Maier, *Schwenckfeld*, ch. 7, "Anthropological Presuppositions," pp. 41-44.

[43] Cited in Williams, *Radical*, p. 204.

[44] *Ibid.*, p. 204.

[45] On Schwenckfeld's view of the Supper, see Maier, *Schwenckfeld*, pp. 18-23; Williams, *Radical*, p. 204.

[46] *Ibid.*, p. 205.

[47] Cited in Maier, *Schwenckfeld*, p. 22; also in Williams, *Radical*, p. 207.

[48] Maier, *Schwenckfeld*, pp. 20-21. "The outer communion ... remained only a theoretical possibility with Schwenckfeld, while the inner observance received the predominating emphasis in his theology." *Ibid.*, p. 21.

[49] "The inner baptism of the Holy Spirit comforts, strengthens, and assures the believing soul of inner man. The outer baptism of the man or minister, however, comforts, strengthens and assures the believing flesh or outer man, so that the whole man is comforted, assured, and blessed. The external assurance, however, requires the priority of the internal." Cited in Maier, *Schwenckfeld*, p. 24.

[50] Williams, *Radical*, p. 208.

[51] Arguing against those who, like Zwingli, appealed to circumcision as prefiguring infant baptism, Schwenckfeld maintained that "Only those, such as the Jews, who cling to the external can parallel baptism and circumcision. Schwenckfeld ironically notes that infant baptism and circumcision are rather similar: before God neither have *any* importance." So Seebaß, in Erb, ed., *Schwenckfeld*, p. 90.

[52] Maier speaks of the "axiomatic cosmological, ontological, philosophical, and psychological dualism" of his theology. Maier, *Schwenckfeld*, p. 14.

[53] "Christians are a free, good-willed people thanks to the work of the Holy Spirit, God, and Christ who are at complete liberty to work in them. Schwenckfeld, however, does not wish to do away with the formalities of sermons, sacraments, church orders, and ministry. They are necessary for the admonishment and encouragement of men to learn and praise God and to thank him for what he has worked inwardly in them." *Ibid.*, p. 92.

[54] *Ibid.*, p. 17.

[55] See *ibid.*, pp. 34ff.

[56] *Ibid.*, pp. 54-55.

[57] Cited in *ibid.*, p. 55.

[58] Docetism was the teaching (held especially by the Gnostics) that Jesus' humanity was apparent, not real.

[59] Maier, *Schwenckfeld*, p. 56. Maier notes "a certain ambivalence in Schwenckfeld's doctrine of the incarnation," given the fact that he was attempting to safeguard the divine origin of Jesus' flesh, but also did not wish to sever Jesus' bond with humankind.

[60] *Ibid.*, pp. 57-58, esp. p. 58, n. 1.

[61] For fuller details, see especially Maier, *Schwenckfeld*.

Chapter 3

The Radical Reformation Revisited

The Theological "Shape" of Radical Reform

As is evident in the foregoing sketches, the historian of the Radical Reformation is faced with the classic problem of the "forest and the trees" in attempting to tell the story of this branch of reform. There is no easy equating of Karlstadt, Müntzer, Schwenckfeld, and the peasants, for the particular differences between them all are numerous and in many cases, substantial. But on the other hand, when we step back from individual cases and look to broader issues—to the "shape" of these radical critiques—it also is true that there was a remarkable similarity in the "radical" rejection of Luther and his views. Our survey has emphasized these similarities. Looked at from this longer range, the radical reformers belong in another theological "forest" than did Luther; moreover, the radical reformers share a kinship that places them together in the *same* theological forest, apart from Luther. Without negating the value of careful distinction between radical reforming individuals we may also say that there is something important to be learned in noting the broad commonalities between their views.

Scripture Alone

The divergent approaches to the authority of Scripture taken by Luther, Karlstadt, Müntzer, and the peasants, pointed very early on to the achilles heel of the evangelical movement: appeal to the authority of Scripture encouraged a multiplicity of views, not uniformity. On the other hand, the radical reformers who most strongly influenced the Anabaptist movement all critiqued Luther's scriptural approach in a very similar way, appealing to the necessity of reading the letter of Scripture in the power of the Holy Spirit. This spiritualistic critique had important social and ecclesiological consequences because of the egalitarian nature of the claim: if biblical truth is known by letter and spirit together, anyone graced with the Holy Spirit will be able to interpret Scripture correctly. Conversely, anyone who lacks the Holy Spirit simply is not fitted to be able to interpret Scripture correctly.

The insistence by the radical reformers that "spirit *and* letter" belonged together (their interpretation of Luther's "sola scriptura") had radical consequences that drove the thin edge of the wedge between "radical" and "mainline" evangelical reformers. Anticlerical critique—which had helped form a united evangelical front in the early years—would now be directed not only against Roman Catholic clergy who "denied Scripture" by appealing to traditional church interpretive authority, but also against "evangelical learned scribes" who appealed to the letter of Scripture but "lacked the Spirit." The egalitarian nature of an appeal to "Scripture and Spirit" meant that scriptural questions were not to be decided automatically by the scholar-theologian-preacher in the employ of a prince or city council who would make definitive reference to the Hebrew and Greek texts. If the Holy Spirit was the ultimate authority by which scriptural questions were to be decided, the result was an interpretive anarchy which, the sixteenth century authorities were convinced (and not without reason), was politically dangerous. The radical insistence on "Scripture *and* Spirit" contained the seeds of Believers' Church thinking, and threatened the "state church" monopoly of scriptural interpretation.

Salvation by Grace through Faith

At the very heart of the joint critiques of Karlstadt, Müntzer and Schwenckfeld was their rejection of Luther's soteriology. This was no insignificant objection. After all, this was Luther's central theological point: human beings are saved by faith in Christ's sacrifice, through God's grace and election, and not by any human effort or merit. The radical reformers embraced the soteriological emphasis on grace and faith, but disagreed with Luther's conclusion that saving faith changed one's "legal" status before God (forensic justification) but *did not* change one's essential human condition as a sinner (at once justified and a sinner). They argued, rather, that saving faith works in believers to *transform* them in the here and now, and that believers thus transformed would participate in some way in the salvation process. This fundamental point of difference indicated two areas more in which Karlstadt, Müntzer and Schwenckfeld agreed with each other and jointly disagreed with Luther, namely in their general anthropological and pneumatological presuppositions.

The Nature of the Human Person

The radical reformers we have surveyed agreed that human beings are radically sinful beings, in need of redemption. But together they disagreed with Luther on whether sinful human beings are capable of moving beyond sin in this life. None of these radical reformers were "Pelagian"; that is, none of them maintained that human beings could move salvifically beyond sin by dint of human effort. But they held that human beings could, by the power and grace of God and the Holy Spirit, be remade in their human natures so that they would at least be on the path to sanctification in this life. Furthermore, they held that God's grace opened up the possibility of choice for the sinner: God's grace enabled sinners to choose freely either the path of salvation, or the path to perdition. Here the radical reformers decisively parted company with Luther, who denied the possibility of free will, and upheld the doctrine of predestination. Furthermore, Luther denied that any salvifically relevant human regeneration could take place: believers will live better lives out of gratitude, of course (and Luther's sermons give ample evidence of his concern for such "good works" subsequent to faith), but for Luther no "works" of any kind can have a bearing on *salvation*, which depends alone on God's gracious election and Christ's sacrifice.

The Holy Spirit

We have already noted the importance of the Holy Spirit to the radical reformers' understanding of the evangelical scriptural principle. In the context of soteriology, the Holy Spirit was seen as the power of God which conveyed faith to believers. The radical reformers agreed with Luther that the grace of God which grants saving faith is a "prevenient" grace (it "comes before" faith, and cannot be "earned" by good works). Nevertheless, they insisted that saving grace is also an "efficacious" grace which has the power to remake human nature. Thus the radical reformers could speak of "rebirth," "regeneration by the Spirit," and the "new life" which emerged as the result of the action of the Holy Spirit. By the power of God, sinners come to repentance and believe the Gospel; by that same power of God they are reborn and regenerated by the Holy Spirit, and become new persons. These new persons then live lives that give witness to the sanctification that God's grace is working in their lives. In a significant way, one's inner state of grace will be visible externally. Karlstadt, Müntzer, and Schwenckfeld thus expected a "reform" of the church not simply through a "preaching of the Word," but because those convicted by the *living* Word would be regenerated and so live new lives.

Karlstadt, Müntzer and Schwenckfeld alike critiqued the lack of moral and ethical reform in churches which preached a forensic justification. This perceived deficiency in the mainline reform they attributed to, in Müntzer's words, the preaching of a "sweet Christ" who required for salvation only that one have faith. For these three reformers, on the contrary, accepting the good news of salvation through Christ meant also "yielding" inwardly before God and being remade into a new person. This fundamental agreement between Karlstadt, Müntzer and Schwenckfeld points to their common rootage in late medieval piety, which allowed for the linkage of grace and regeneration in a continuous process of sanctification *leading to* justification before God. Each of these radical reformers may have had different points of access to this late medieval tradition, but in terms of soteriology the results were essentially the same. And, because of their agreement that God's grace could and would regenerate believers, these reformers also expected the "preaching of the Gospel" to result in a visibly reformed (i.e. moral) church. While these reformers did not agree in the working out of their respective ecclesiologies, the soteriological principles they held in common provided the essential underpinning for the emergence of a believers' church ecclesiology in the Anabaptist movement.

Baptism and the Supper

Karlstadt and Müntzer were agreed that God's grace opens the possibility of response for the sinner (freedom of the will), and that faith means believing and accepting God's gracious offer of pardon through Christ. All of this meant, however, that infant baptism was a rite that no longer made sense theologically, for infants do not make personal faith decisions, nor are they regenerated after choosing to live new lives. If the water was just water, and no longer a visible sign that conferred invisible grace, then water baptism could be no more than an outer witness to a more essential and inward baptism. That is, the outer baptism was a sign that an individual had in fact consciously "yielded" inwardly to the working of God—something no infant could possibly do. And yet further, the New Testament evidence concerning baptism seemed weighted heavily in favour of adult baptism. Although neither Karlstadt, Müntzer or Schwenckfeld took the step of rebaptizing adults on confession of faith, nevertheless they provided the essential logic for the practice of adult baptism by their critique of the practice of infant baptism.

In the matter of the Lord's Supper these radical reformers were in close agreement in rejecting a "real presence" in the elements—although this seems to have been less of an issue with Müntzer. But again, their rejection of Roman Catholic sacramentalism, and their emphasis on an inner working of the Holy Spirit leading to rebirth, regeneration and sanctification led them to think of the Supper in a more spiritualist fashion than would Luther.

Priesthood of all Believers

Karlstadt, Müntzer and Schwenckfeld were in agreement with the apparent meaning of Luther's phrase "a priesthood of all believers." That is, they agreed that the Roman Catholic clergy were not especially privileged with regard to the sacraments, and that any Christian could perform "priestly" functions by virtue of Christian baptism. Luther, however, soon backed away from the egalitarian implications suggested by the provocative phrase; the radical reformers did not. "Priests" are not "made" by virtue of an "indelible mark on the soul" (ordination), conferred by a clerical hierarchy based on "apostolic succession." Rather, pastors are those chosen by the Spirit of God to proclaim the Gospel; there cannot be a centrally controlled "priesthood." At best there can perhaps be an "election" or commissioning by a local congregation—something to which Luther appealed early on, in his struggle against the medieval church.

The call for congregational election and congregational disciplining of pastors was widespread in the Peasants' War. So also was the call for fiscal reform, and the demand that local tithes be controlled and spent in the parishes which furnished the tithes. This certainly was one way of interpreting a "priesthood of all believers," but it was not the way Luther intended. The spiritual calling of pastors, along with the congregational validation of that call, was to survive only in the early Anabaptist movement.

It must be said that the radical reformers who were to have the strongest influence on the Anabaptist movement shared significant theological commonalities that place them in close proximity to one another (in the same theological "forest" if one will), and at the same time at some distance from Martin Luther—even though he was their shared point of "evangelical" theological origin. This is not to downplay significant differences between Karlstadt, Müntzer, and Schwenckfeld, but rather to suggest that the theological presuppositions and principles they shared were of fundamental significance. These theological commonalitites made them partners in the sixteenth century reforming conversation. They shared and spoke a spiritual, soteriological, anthropological, and sociological language which Luther did not speak.

The fact that the Anabaptist movement also came to speak that same "radical" theological language, and encountered problems with the mainline Reformation leaders at exactly the same points as had the earlier radical reformers, can suggest two things. It can of course suggest direct lines of influence from the radical reformers to Anabaptists. In some individual cases these lines of mediation and influence are clear, as has been noted above and will be noted again. But how are we to explain the appearance of these radical teachings among the masses of people who made up the rank and file of the Anabaptist movement? What explains the acceptance of an optimistic anthropology and pneumatology of regeneration in an illiterate peasant of a remote rural village of Switzerland? Here historians, dependent upon written records, encounter mostly silence, for the influence of a Karlstadt or a Müntzer cannot be "demonstrated" in the absence of documentary evidence. It does not seem likely that there was any such direct influence on such a wide scale.

Perhaps a good part of the answer to this more difficult question of the origin and spread of the radical reforming ideas that eventually found a voice in the Anabaptist movement lies in the way that historians have conceived of the "origination" and "spread" of ideas. The cases of the radical reformers we have surveyed above suggest that reforming ideas were never imprinted upon "blank slates," but found differing echoes in different recipients. In the cases of literate and learned radical reformers, we have access to writings which allow us to trace a part of the process of theological appropriation. It is not so for the great majority of common people who also came to accept radical reforming premises, for they were predominantly illiterate, but the absence of written treatises does not mean that the masses of people therefore were simply "recipients" of ideas, or that they had no means of communicating their own ideas.

It is evident that radical reforming ideas were circulated widely among the common people, usually by lesser-known figures who mediated by oral means, slogans, basic premises and interpretations of Scripture and reform. Furthermore, these basic premises, we must conclude, were not mediated to "blank slates" but rather either found, or did not find, a corresponding echo in the unlettered hearers of those ideas. Thus looking to literate and published interpreters of reform will tell a partial, though important part of the story: there were influential figures such as Karlstadt, Müntzer and Schwenckfeld who enunciated basic terms of reference for radical reform. The other side of the story, however, requires a thesis less easily demonstrated. What led many thousands of common people to accept these premises as true and even self-evident? The answer to this question, suggested by the surprising uniformity in crucial theological presuppositions in all branches of Anabaptism, is that the radical reformers were giving voice to *widely shared* ideas about the meaning of reform, salvation, regeneration, and sanctification.

The origins of Anabaptism undoubtedly lie in large measure in the radical reformers who first articulated an alternative view of "evangelical" reform; but they also lie in the regenerationist and ascetic tradition of late medieval piety which conceived of salvation in terms of sanctification. Perhaps it is for this reason that, in spite of differing points of Radical Reformation origin of Anabaptism, the resulting movement bears a distinctive theological "shape" and shares fundamental terms of reference that defined it as a movement over against other reforming movements.

Conclusion

We return in conclusion to the question of piety and spiritual practice. There were options that were opened and closed by the reforming currents emerging from Luther's early critique of late medieval doctrine and practice. We may summarize with the following points.

1. All "evangelical" reformers accepted the appeal to the authority of Scripture, but in what way would the "Word of God" be expected to inform one's spirituality? A blanket appeal to "Scripture" opened up a host of new, unanswered, but crucial questions.

—Was the "Word" essentially an inner word, or an outer, written word? If it was the former, then "hearing the Word of God" would indicate a process of inward discernment; if the latter, a process of understanding the written text of Scripture.

—If the "living Word of God" was seen as an inner, spiritual word, were extrabiblical revelations (dreams, visions, prophecies) to be sought and valued on par with written Scripture?

—If the "Word of God" was understood to be the written biblical word, should the written Scripture be combed for a concrete "rule of life" for believers which should be followed literally?

—If the "Word of God" was seen to be the written Scripture, should one seek to discover the esoteric secrets of the Last Days within its prophetic books?

—If the "Word" was the written text which came to life when it was preached, did it have to be exegeted by linguistic and theological experts who had access to the most reliable versions in the original languages?

All of these possibilities, and more, were opened by the apparently simple expedient of appealing to the authority of "Scripture alone." The emergence of alternative "evangelical" views, we can see in retrospect, should have been a foregone conclusion. The historical process of development demonstrates that it was possible to be in the "evangelical" reforming camp by one's acceptance of the authority of Scripture, and yet differ widely concerning its interpretation and meaning for one's spiritual life.

2. The most obvious late medieval spiritual practices that evangelicals repudiated related to the sacrament of penance and the mediation of the saints. A huge field of popular piety was removed at one stroke. But how was "faith alone" to be understood in practice? There was more than just one interpretation. On this score the "radical" reformers turned out to be more conservative than Luther, and re-

tained the ascetic, late medieval piety that saw humankind as capable of regeneration and a new life in the here and now; that saw grace as efficacious; that expected "true" faith to lead to moral reform; and that assumed that external behaviour was a good sign of the presence or absence of faith. The consequences for spirituality were enormous. In spite of the removal of the "works" of penance, the spirituality of the radical reformers continued to appeal to the ascetic ideals of late medieval piety.

3. Crucial questions were raised about the nature and function of the sacraments.

—If all Christians are priests, may all Christians then "make" sacraments?

—If, on the contrary, no one has the power to "make" a grace-conveying sacrament out of a physical object, then what principles explain what happens in the actions of corporate worship?

—If physical objects always remain just that, does the faith of the recipient "make" a sacrament more than just a physical celebration?

—Is Christ made physically present *at all* in this world? How?

—Should baptism and the Supper simply be celebrated as "inward" events in which spiritual realities are experienced individually?

More questions of this kind could be listed. Given the centrality of corporate worship to Christian spirituality, the answers to these questions were extremely important. The sacramental edifice had been challenged, but what was to be put in its place, on what theological basis, and with what results for Christian spiritual practice and piety?

It was in the midst of this kind of upheaval that the reforming movement emerged that came to be labelled "Anabaptism." It answered some of the questions posed above, drew some specific conclusions, and thus chose a particular theological and reforming path that set it apart from other reforming streams.

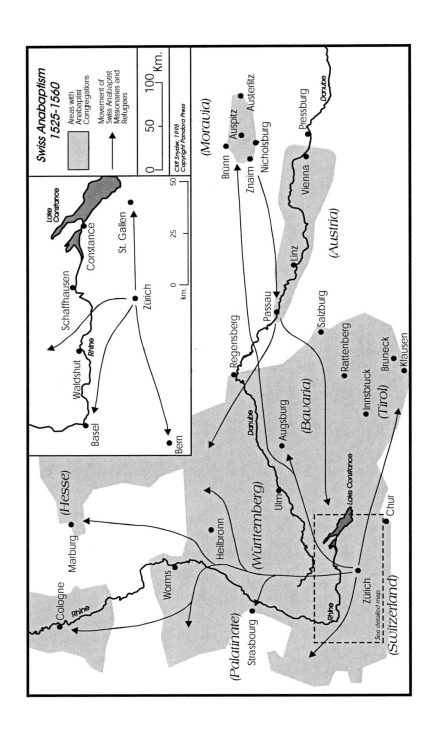

Swiss Anabaptism 1525-1560

Areas with Anabaptist Congregations

Movement of Swiss Anabaptist Missionaries and Refugees

0   50   100 Km.

Cliff Snyder, 1995
Copyright Pandora Press

(Moravia)

Austerlitz
Auspitz
Brünn
Znaim
Nicholsburg

Pressburg

Vienna

(Austria)

Linz

Salzburg

Passau

Regensberg

Rattenberg

Innsbruck
Bruneck
Klausen

(Tirol)

(Bavaria)

Danube

Augsburg

Ulm

Lake Constance

Chur

(Hesse)

Marburg

Cologne

Rhine

Worms

Heilbronn

(Württemberg)

(Palatinate)

Strasbourg

Zürich

Rhine

See detailed map

(Switzerland)

Lake Constance

Constance

Schaffhausen

Rhine

Waldshut

St. Gallen

Zürich

Basel

Bern

0   25   50
km.

Chapter 4

The Origins of Swiss Anabaptism

The story of the beginnings of Swiss Anabaptism has often been told beginning with Zwingli's reformation of Zürich, passing to the eventual disaffection of Conrad Grebel and Felix Mantz, and leading inexorably to the separated pacifism of the Schleitheim Articles. But the Swiss Anabaptist story also must include, among others, the Anabaptist pastor and theologian Balthasar Hubmaier. Hubmaier was wooed by Conrad Grebel himself, and baptized by Wilhelm Reublin, a member of Grebel's circle. Thus part of the story of Swiss Anabaptism includes, of necessity, Hubmaier's reform of the city of Waldshut, and the military alliance struck between Anabaptist Waldshut and the Black Forest Peasant troops in 1525. Also part of the Swiss Anabaptist story are ambiguous figures such as Wilhelm Reublin and Hans Krüsi, Anabaptist pastors preaching in rebellious rural communities during the Peasants' War, who accepted armed protection by peasants-in-arms.

There can be no doubt that after the failure of the Peasants' Revolt in late 1525, and with the spread of the Schleitheim Articles of 1527, the Swiss Brethren assumed a strongly separatist and pacifist stand. What polygenesis historians have illuminated for us is the movement along the way to the well-known outcome, the various positions assumed on the path to Schleitheim, and the discernible influences along that way.

Zürich and Zwingli

The first rebaptism of adults in the Reformation period occurred in Zürich in January, 1525. They were carried out by former followers of Ulrich Zwingli, the reformer of that city. The story of Swiss Anabaptism, then, is closely tied with the reform of Zürich under Zwingli, although the influence of Karlstadt is discernible, and the Zürich radical group also read Thomas Müntzer's tracts.

Ulrich Zwingli had been a Roman Catholic priest in the Swiss town of Glarus from 1506 to 1516, accepting a post as preacher in the pilgrimage town of Einsiedeln, which he occupied from 1516 to 1518. He was a scholar, part of the humanist current of reform, and dedicated himself to the study of Greek and Hebrew. Erasmus' views had some influence on his thought. In 1518 Zwingli accepted a post as people's preacher at the Grossminster in Zürich. It is clear that he owed some debt to Martin Luther, in a general sense, but his path to reform was distinct from Luther's, owing much more to humanism, sacramentist influences from the Netherlands, and the influence of Andreas Karlstadt.[1]

By 1522, Zwingli was speaking the new language of the Reformation, and had begun to preach sermons that were, essentially, expositions of Gospel texts. Some of his ideas resulted in the breaking of the Lenten fast of 1522 by a group of Zwingli's followers—they gathered together and ate sausages. Zwingli also preached against images (idolatry) and clerical celibacy (as a Catholic priest he had been living with a concubine). By the end of 1522, Zwingli had resigned his post as priest, and had accepted the post of preacher under the direct control of the city council. He was well on his way to winning over the city council in favour of his reform ideas, but his position required some political skill.

Zwingli's reform proceeded, then, by means of civic conciliar action. There is some evidence that Zwingli's sermons were calculated to incite unrest from the grass roots, pressuring the council for change, following which a conciliar disputation would be held, under Zwingli's direction, and the council would prudently decide what would be made law in Zürich. In this context, Zwingli skillfully played the man in the middle. But something was bound to break—and eventually it did, when Zwingli's more radical followers disagreed with him over the slow pace of reform. This break recalls, not without reason, the similar rupture between Karlstadt and Luther in 1522 at the base of which was the question of the speed and extent of reform, and the "sparing of the weak."

The Zürich Radicals to 1524

The followers of Zwingli that came to be labelled "radicals" took Zwingli at his word, in particular concerning the study of Scripture. Many of the radicals who later became Anabaptists had been meeting together to study the Bible since 1522. The first focus of the radical movement, following the sausages, was the question of images, the Mass, and in general, anticlericalism as represented by the issue of the tithe. Among the Zürich followers of Zwingli were Conrad Grebel and Felix Mantz, both educated urbanites; Wilhelm Reublin came to the area after a turbulent time of reform preaching in Basel, and took up a pastorate in the neighboring Swiss town of Witikon late in 1522; he was aided by Simon Stumpf of Höngg. There was a large cast of lesser players, both within the city and in the countryside.

Serious radical agitation for fundamental church reform began outside of the city itself, in the countryside governed by Zürich. The focus was the tithe, an issue taken up later by the peasants in 1525. Early in 1523, both Reublin and Stumpf began preaching in their country churches that the local congregations should stop paying the tithe, because the income was going to support "good for nothing monks, who have stolen their living from the people long enough."[2] The Zürich council ruled that the tithe should continue to be paid, and that the reform of the countriside would be decided, not by the communities themselves, but by Zürich. The city council would not allow the basic economic structure to be tampered with, and it had no intention of letting church incomes slip out of its grasp.

The radicals in the countryside did not give up, however. The next issue was the question of images. Simon Stumpf preached openly concerning the "idolatry" of images in his country church (a theme also preached by Zwingli) and his congregation took matters into their own hands, "purifying" their sanctuary in unruly fashion by smashing images. Similar incidents began to occur in and around Zürich. The Zürich council decided to hold a public disputation in October 1523, concerning images and the Mass, following this radical challenge in the churches of Stumpf and Reublin.

At this same time, Balthasar Hubmaier was intiating a reform in the Austrian city of Waldshut very much like the one unfolding in Zürich; he took part in the October disputation in Zürich, defending a Zwinglian position on the Mass, saying that it was no sacrifice. Hubmaier called for an understanding of the Supper as a memorial, called for the Mass to be said in the vernacular, and called for it to be celebrated "in both kinds," i.e., that the recipients should receive both the bread and the wine. Hubmaier would later break with Zwingli on the question of infant baptism, but on the question of the Supper, he like the other Zürich radicals and virtually all Anabaptists subsequently, would follow a "sacramentarian" understanding of the Lord's Supper.[3]

Following the Zürich disputation on the Mass of October 1523, Zwingli prudently decided to implement reforms according to the rather conservative wishes of the city council: the council had decreed that the time for radical changes in church reform had not yet arrived. Zwingli's reluctance caused some of his radical followers to begin an even more serious critique of the pace of Zürich reform. It was here that the critiques of Karlstadt and Müntzer concerning Luther's "sparing of the weak" found a decided echo among Conrad Grebel and his compatriots.

We can note that the radical movement in and around Zürich owed its beginnings to a wholesale effort at scriptural church reform. It was a critique directed against existing Roman practices, sharing in the general Reformation anticlerical sentiment: unworthy local pastors, tithes, images in the churches, and the continued celebration of the Mass in absence of, or in opposition to, scriptural commands ordering such practices.[4] The next point of attack of the radicals was a logical one, prepared as it had been by the critiques of Karlstadt and Müntzer, namely the question of baptism.[5]

Baptism

There is some evidence that as late as 1523, Zwingli himself had been doubtful as to the validity of infant baptism.[6] The issue of baptism had not yet been resolved as a Reformation issue: if salvation is by faith through grace, and grace is not conferred by means of sacraments, of what use is infant baptism?[7] In particular it was not clear why Zwingli, with his spiritualized view of the sacraments, would insist on infant baptism: the water itself, he said, was only a sign of an inner change, just as the elements of the Supper were only memorials of a past sacrifice and a testimony to an inner faith in Christ's sacrifice. Thus the logic of the case would seem to have been pushing Zwingli away from infant baptism, towards adult baptism. In any case, the radicals again forced Zürich's hand. Early in 1524, the inhabitants of Witikon and Zollikon refused to allow their newborn infants to be baptized, following the preaching of Wilhelm Reublin and Johannes Brötli. Within Zürich itself, the issue of baptism was taken up by Grebel and Mantz.

A series of private talks were held between the radicals and their former teacher Zwingli, who published a book he hoped would end the matter. His main argument there was that the New Testament neither commanded nor forbade infant baptism; therefore, the testimony of the Old Testament had to be considered decisive. Zwingli argued that baptism had to be seen as the equivalent of Old Testament circumcision: infants who were to be educated into the faith were baptized as the symbol of their incorporation into the faith community.[8] The disruptions of the radicals continued: some sermons were interrupted, and some infants—notably Grebel's daughter—remained unbaptized. Zürich's response was to call a public disputation on baptism for January, 1525. This was held, and the result was predictable: the council decreed that Grebel and Mantz were to desist from any more agitation in the city, that all infants were to be baptized; the foreigners were expelled from the territory; they had eight days in which to leave. Among the latter were Reublin and Brötli.

Very shortly following the council mandate (dated January 21, 1525) a group of the Zürich radicals gathered at Felix Mantz's house. According to a contemporary account, Grebel, Mantz, George Blaurock and others were present. They discussed the events of the day, and then the account says: "After fear lay greatly upon them, they called upon God in heaven, that he should show mercy to them. Then George arose and asked Conrad for God's sake to baptize him; and this he did. After that he baptized the others also."[9] In this way the first "rebaptisms" took place. Of course, they were not understood as rebaptisms at all, but rather as the only true baptism. A definitive break with the Zwinglian reform had taken place.

Although further nuances in baptismal theology would become evident, the essential argument for adult baptism was presented at the first disputation on baptism in Zürich. According to Heinrich Bullinger's report, Felix Mantz, Conrad Grebel and Wilhelm Reublin argued that

> infants could not believe or understand what baptism is. Baptism should be given to believers to whom the gospel had previously been preached, who have understood it, and who thereupon requested baptism for themselves, and killing the old Adam, desired to live a new life. Because infants knew nothing of this, baptism did not apply to them. For this they drew on Scripture from the Gospels and the Acts of the Apostles and pointed out that the apostles had not baptized infants but only adult discerning people.[10]

Bullinger did not give the biblical citations used in the public disputation, but from Grebel's published concordance (1525) on the subjects of faith and baptism and later Swiss Brethren argumentation, it is safe to assume that central passages presented were Matthew 28:18-20, Mark 16:15-16, Acts 2:38, Acts 9:17-19, Acts 16:17-34, and Acts 19:1-5.[11]

The passages from Matthew and Mark outline a particular order in Christ's great commission: go forth and teach, then baptize those who believe, following which, have them obey my commandments. This sequence of events, argued the earliest

Anabaptists, outlined the "proper biblical order" concerning baptism. It was this line of argumentation that would reappear in virtually all branches of the Anabaptist movement. Less often noted is the emphasis in Grebel's concordance on the necessary work of the Spirit of God in bringing about faith—the fact that faith "comes from heaven" is a central theme of the first part. The passages from Acts provide examples of the apostolic practice of baptism, including the notable case of rebaptism in Acts 19:5. These passages emphasized not only the necessary conjunction of profession of faith and baptism, but also the role of the Holy Spirit in the process.[12] Implicit in the earliest Swiss statements on baptism, then, is the "inner baptism" of the Spirit which brings faith, and results in the outer baptism of water. Hubmaier's detailed biblical defence of adult baptism and his description of a three-fold baptism of spirit, water, and blood, soon to appear in print, repeats and builds upon many of these earliest passages and interpretations.

The Spread of Anabaptism from Zürich

The baptism movement spread rather quickly to neighbouring towns and cities. In part this seems to have been a deliberate attempt on the part of the Zürich radicals to win adherents to an alternative vision of reform: they were hoping their vision of reform would supplant Zwingli's. In part the spread of Anabaptism also was a result of the deportation orders handed down to all Anabaptist "foreigners" by the Zürich council. The first town to be evangelized by the Anabaptists was neighbouring Zollikon, where the movement flourished for several months, in spite of mass arrests by the Zürich authorities. The baptizing movement also spread west towards Basel and Bern, and east to St. Gall and Appenzell. More significant in the context of 1525 was the spread of the movement to the north of Zürich, to Schaffhausen, Hallau and Waldshut, where the Anabaptists encountered the growing movement of peasant unrest.

Balthasar Hubmaier

In spite of the early leadership of Conrad Grebel, Felix Mantz, and George Blaurock, none of these persons wrote or published significant works in defence of adult baptism. This task fell to Balthasar Hubmaier, an early Swiss Anabaptist leader of surpassing importance.[13]

Balthasar Hubmaier had been born around 1480 in Friedberg, near Augsburg.[14] He received a good early education, took orders, and attended the University of Freiburg in the Breisgau, where he studied theology with Johannes Eck—later Luther's opponent at the Leipzig disputation. When Eck moved to the University of Ingolstadt in 1510, Hubmaier first succeeded him as rector of the university of Freiburg, and then followed Eck to Ingolstadt two years later, where he earned his doctorate in theology. By 1515 he was elected prorector of the University of Ingolstadt, but in 1516 he left suddenly (for unknown reasons) to take on the post of cathedral preacher in Regensburg. He spent the next four years in Regensburg, a time marked by a nasty preaching campaign against the Jewish population of that city. Eventually their synagogue was destroyed and all Jews were forced to leave the city in February 1519. On the ruins of the synagogue a chapel was erected dedicated to Mary which, with Hubmaier preaching to excited crowds, became a major pilgrimage centre virtually overnight.

In 1520, at the height of these events, Hubmaier again left for unexplainable reasons, and took a preaching position in the town of Waldshut, which was under the lordship of the Austrian Hapsburgs. Here he began to turn in the evangelical direction; he was now reading Erasmus, Melanchthon and Luther as well as studying the Pauline epistles. By 1523 he was solidly "evangelical," and by Spring of the following year he had prepared a reformation programme for Waldshut. Hapsburg political pressure required him to flee to neighbouring Schaffhausen for a time, but he was able to return to Waldshut in October of 1524 and instituted evangelical church reforms: images and relics were removed from the church, and the Mass was celebrated in German. The Hapsburgs, traditional enemies of the Swiss cantons, continued to threaten action but in response a troop of volunteer soldiers from Zürich marched to reinforce Waldshut. Among these volunteers were members of the emerging "radical" evangelical circle in Zürich.

It was in the midst of this tense situation that the Peasants' War broke out in earnest, and almost simultaneously the first "rebaptisms" took place in Zürich. As the reformer of Waldshut, Hubmaier got involved in both movements. In March of 1525 Reublin and Grebel made several trips to Waldshut, to visit Hubmaier. At this same time Waldshut already was in a political alliance with the rebellious Black Forest peasants. On Easter Sunday, 1525, Reublin baptized Hubmaier, who in turn baptized around three hundred Waldshut citizens during the Easter season alone. In time the majority of Waldshut citizens accepted rebaptism, including most of the city council. Hubmaier immediately took up his pen and composed some of the basic works defending the baptism of adults.[15] Waldshut became an "Anabaptist city," but at the same time it also actively supported the rebellious peasants with supplies and troops; they, in turn, provided military defence for the city against its Austrian lords.

In the meantime, in the nearby town of Hallau, Reublin and Brötli came to be accepted as the town pastors. They preached and baptized in the local church, and were defended by armed men when threatened with arrest. The city of Schaffhausen also came very close to accepting adult baptism as its official position. This early Anabaptism was no sectarian movement of separation from the world, but rather was closely involved with the movement of social reform represented by the peasants.

It is at this point that Harold Bender's depiction of Swiss Anabaptist origins has been substantially revised. As Martin Haas, James Stayer and others have argued, the Swiss Anabaptist movement began as a grass roots, alternative movement of popular reform, not as a separatist and thoroughly pacifist movement. Central to this revision of the earlier depiction of Swiss Anabaptism as a separatist, pacifist movement has been a close examination of the question of "the sword of government" in the first two years of the Swiss movement. A description of the historical phenomenon will be included here. Chapter 13 below will look in more detail at the development of Swiss Anabaptist teachings on the sword and the oath.

Swiss Anabaptism and the Sword

Conrad Grebel and Felix Mantz were thoroughly committed to a nonresistant position; on this the documentation leaves no room for doubt. But central questions remain: What were the intellectual origins of their nonresistance, and more importantly, may one assume that because Grebel and Mantz were nonresistant, therefore Swiss Anabaptism was also uniformly nonresistant?

In trying to trace the origins of the Grebel and Mantz positions on the sword, we cannot consider Zwingli to have been a direct influence. One possible source might have been humanism. The humanism of Erasmus influenced Zwingli greatly, and although Zwingli did not adopt Erasmus' pacifism, it is possible that Grebel and Mantz, as aspiring humanist scholars, might have been influenced by the general humanist interest in pacifism. But the direct evidence of such influence is limited. We have one fleeting reference in Conrad Grebel's early correspondence. In a letter to Vadian in August of 1520, Grebel notes that "With nothing else to do, I have read the *Philirenus*, Myconius' dialogue 'on not going to war,' which by reason of its truth deserves to become a classic." Grebel seems to be enthusiastic, but after telling Vadian that he cannot send the manuscript to him to read, Grebel notes that Vadian "can do without" it—a surprisingly lukewarm endorsement of a book arguing what would later become a central Swiss Brethren teaching.[16]

It may be that humanism helped form the pacifism of the Zürich Anabaptists, but if this was the case the lines of influence are no longer discernible. The next reference to pacifism in the Grebel writings appears in the September, 1524 letter to Thomas Müntzer. What led Grebel to the pacifism he espouses in that letter remains hidden from view. It may well be that, as Harold Bender suggested, a direct reading of Scripture was primarily responsible for Grebel and Mantz's rejection of warfare for the Christian. At any rate, Grebel now argued clearly that Christians "must reach the fatherland of eternal rest not by slaying the physical but the spiritual. They use neither worldly sword nor war, since killing has ceased with them entirely."[17]

Grebel's fundamental argument concerning the sword is based on an uncompromising commitment to New Testament guidelines as establishing church practice. This becomes apparent in a postscript, where Grebel writes to Müntzer: "Hujuff's brother writes that you have preached against the princes, that they should be combatted with the fist. If that is true, or if you intend to defend war, the tablets, chanting, or other things for which you do not find a clear word [i.e. of Scripture] ... I admonish you ... to desist."[18] Although this is not yet Scheitheim pacifism of the uncompromisingly separatist variety, nor an argument for an "imitation of Christ" ethic, it is biblical pacifism nonetheless, and moving in the general direction of Schleitheim.

Felix Mantz's writings give witness to an equally committed pacifism, rooted in obedience to the commandments of Scripture, but giving evidence of a deeper Christocentrism.[19] At his hearing before the Zürich Council (late 1526 or early 1527) Mantz argued that no magistrate may kill a person, since no Scripture can be cited to justify it. While Mantz also argued that Christians must follow Christ's example, he denied holding to separatism, but rather said that all those who did not believe as he did "should be allowed to remain in their faith."[20] Shortly thereafter the Zürich authorites sentenced Mantz to death by drowning. In his farewell song, Mantz is decidedly more separatist in his conclusions: those who wield the sword do not show the love or mercy of Christ, nor follow his example, although they wish to be called shepherds and teachers. The true servants of Christ do not hate or murder. Those who take the sword demonstrate that they are Satan's children, and they will receive their just reward, if they do not repent.[21]

> The true love of Christ shall not destroy the enemy; he that would be an heir with Christ is taught that he must be merciful, as the Father in heaven is merciful. . . . Christ also never hated any one; neither did his true servants, but they continued to follow Christ in the true way, as He went before them.[22]

In contrast to Grebel's writings, Mantz's farewell song gives evidence of a significant Christocentric spirituality that foreshadows Schleitheim's later formulation on the sword, although lacking Schleitheim's separatist finality. There is no doubt that a strong rejection of the sword was present in Anabaptist beginnings in Zürich.

Not all the Swiss Anabaptists, however, were moving in lock-step with Grebel and Mantz on this question, nor does nonresistance seem to have been a requirement for membership in the Swiss movement prior to Schleitheim, as the case of Hubmaier demonstrates.[23] In spite of his having been wooed personally by Conrad Grebel and baptized by Wilhelm Reublin, a member of the Zürich Anabaptist group, Balthasar Hubmaier and other Swiss Anabaptists were not won over by pacifistic Anabaptism. Hubmaier supported Waldshut's participation in the Peasants' War, and in his later writing "On the Sword," expressed his disagreement with pacifistic Anabaptism—as we will see in more detail in a later chapter. Although Hubmaier was an Anabaptist through and through, and insisted on baptism following an adult confession of faith, submission to community discipline, and a memorial Supper closed to all but those baptized as adults, he did not understand these elements to be "separatist" or "sectarian" in the common understanding of these terms. Hubmaier expected the voluntary and disciplined church to be a governmentally sanctioned church of the majority, with members of the Anabaptist church participating fully in all social and governmental functions, including civil police actions and war. "Separation," if it were to come, would come either if someone did not wish to join the majority church, or if a baptized member of the church failed to repent from sin and had to be banned from the church. In either case the onus fell on the individual who did not conform, rather than on the nonconformity of the "separated community."[24]

Two Swiss Anabaptist pastors who directly benefitted from peasant protection were Wilhelm Reublin and Johannes Brötli, both co-workers with Grebel and Mantz. As noted above, it was Wilhelm Reublin who, after making several trips to Waldshut with Conrad Grebel, finally baptized Balthasar Hubmaier on Easter Sunday (April 15), 1525. Reublin and Brötli centred their activity in the town of Hallau, located between Zürich and Waldshut. At Hallau the peasants' revolt and Anabaptism merged: most of the citizenry accepted rebaptism (performed in the local church), and troops from Hallau joined the Black Forest peasants as well as participating in a variety of local armed conflicts—including the armed defence of their Anabaptist pastors.[25] The conclusion is inescapable that along with preaching baptism following confession of faith, Reublin and Brötli also were allowing that the sword could be used in a "just cause."

In the area of St. Gall, Hans Krüsi led a similar movement which merged Anabaptism with peasant aspirations.[26] Krüsi also had worked closely with Conrad Grebel, in the St. Gall district, and had in his possession the concordance put together by Conrad Grebel listing Bible passages on faith and baptism—later printed in Augsburg under Krüsi's name. Nevertheless, Krüsi was not a consistent pacifist. The peasants in the Anabaptist villages where he preached organized themselves for defence, and pledged themselves to defend their preacher with arms—a pledge which they failed to carry out when Krüsi was apprehended in the middle of the night— much to Krüsi's vocal disappointment. As he was being taken away by the authorities, Krüsi is said to have shouted at the top of his lungs, "Where are you now, you who promised to help me?!"[27] Hans Krüsi was burned at the stake in the Catholic Canton of Lucerne on July 27, 1525.

The Grüningen area, south-west of Zürich, also saw the blending of peasant unrest with Anabaptist concerns. It was in the Grüningen district that Conrad Grebel, Felix Mantz and George Blaurock carried out an extensive missionizing activity following the first rebaptisms. Nevertheless, Grüningen Anabaptism was a continuation of, and not a radical break from, the social, political, and economic concerns of the peasantry.[28] In April of 1525 the Grüningen peasantry sacked three religious establishments, including the monastery at Rüti. A recent detailed historical study has demonstrated that the ringleaders of that movement became central leaders in the stubborn Grüningen Anabaptist movement. Many of the grievances articulated by the peasants survived in Anabaptist form in Grüningen.[29] Swiss Anabaptism in 1525, then, was not uniformly pacifist, apolitical, or separatist, even among the "Grebel circle."

By the end of 1525, Waldshut had fallen to the Swabian League, as had all the territory north of Zürich. The peasants' revolt had failed, and Anabaptism had no political centre of support anywhere at all in the Swiss territories. In this hostile environment, many abandoned the movement; for those who stayed, a growing emphasis on separation from the world became more and more prevalent. The reality of the matter was that the local authorities in Zürich, St. Gall, Bern and Basel had begun taking ever stronger civil measures against the baptizing dissenters. Zürich promulgated a mandate which decreed death by drowning for those who rebaptized others, and imprisonment and fines for those who accepted baptism. By January, 1527, Protestant Zürich had executed its first heretic: Felix Mantz, former student and friend of Zwingli, learned in Greek and Hebrew, had rebaptized contrary to the Council's mandate. He was arrested, tried, and drowned in the Limmat river on January 5, 1527. If Anabaptism was to survive, it would do so not as a widespread reform, but as a persecuted, underground movement.

Michael Sattler and the Schleitheim Articles

It was within this tense setting that Michael Sattler emerged as a leader of the Swiss Brethren in the Summer of 1526.[30] His pilgrimage had begun in the Benedictine monastery of St. Peter's of the Black Forest, near the city of Freiburg. He had reached the rank of prior, second in command of the monastery. The monastery had begun a process of strict observant reform by 1519 or 1520, and it is likely—although by no means certain—that Sattler, as prior, was in favour of that reform. In 1525, the Black Forest troop of peasants—containing, as we have noted, volunteer fighters from Anabaptist Waldshut and Hallau—took the monastery of St. Peter's of the Black Forest, on their way to a successful siege of the city of Freiburg.[31]

Unfortunately, we can only conjecture about Sattler's whereabouts at that time, or his movements subsequent to the taking of St. Peter's, but the next time we find Sattler in the historical record, he appears in Zürich court documents with two men from the Waldshut area. He swore an oath that he would have nothing to do with Anabaptism in the future, and was released. Did Sattler leave the monastery in the midst of the peasant unrest, and was he first introduced to Anabaptism by brethren in the Black Forest troop? We will probably never know for certain, even though the circumstantial evidence suggests that it was so.

Whether it was Michael Sattler or Michael Wüst who came to reside in the Swiss village of Klingnau, in the house of Hans Kuenzi, learning how to weave, remains a disputed question.[32] But it is certain that by the summer of 1526 Michael Sattler had committed himself fully to the Anabaptist cause, and began preaching, teaching and baptizing in the same Swiss villages where the peasants had earlier taken up arms. His work took him then into the Strasbourg area, where he preached and baptized in the neighboring city of Lahr, and into Strasbourg itself, where he pleaded for the release of imprisoned Anabaptists (among them, Jakob Groß) and held talks with Martin Bucer and Wolfgang Capito, reformers of that city. In a letter to them, Michael Sattler expressed what would become a central theme in the

Schleitheim Articles: there are two kingdoms, one under the lordship of Christ and the other under the domination of Satan. There can be no commerce between them. Christians, therefore, separate from all that is outside the Kingdom of Christ.[33] It was this radical separatism, in which all manner of armed resistance or governmental involvement ("the sword") was rejected as "outside the perfection of Christ," that soon came to define the Swiss Brethren position.

On February 24, 1527, these ideas and others appeared in a document we have come to call the Schleitheim Articles.[34] These articles are the first systematic detailing of Swiss Anabaptist views, and as such they mark a "crystallization point" for the Swiss movement. There are seven articles detailed in the document:

1. Baptism
2. Ban
3. Supper
4. Separation from the world and all evil.
5. Election of shepherds by the congregation.
6. Sword
7. Oath.

Of these articles, the first three were held in common with the Anabaptists who had gone before, from Hubmaier, to Grebel, to Reublin; these three articles would be held in common with Anabaptists in other regions as well. They called for the baptism of adults following confession of faith; those who accepted such a baptism signified by that baptism that they placed themselves under the discipline of the community (the ban) to be corrected if they erred; and those who accepted baptism and community discipline (and only those so committed) then celebrated the Supper of remembrance, unity and fellowship together.

New elements were introduced, however, with articles four through seven. The strong stress on separation from the world was a clear contribution from the ex-monk Sattler.[35] It was a common emphasis in his known writings. He called there for a church that knowingly and purposefully distanced itself from society, rejecting society's values. It expected judgement to fall soon on the sinful world, and would not partake of either the sin or the punishment. The article on the election of the shepherd picked up a demand of the peasants: that pastors be elected and disciplined by local congregations. Article six put forward an uncompromising pacifism. The final article on the oath forbade oath taking of any kind: one's speech should be yea or nay, and no more. This meant that followers of Schleitheim would not be able to swear the common feudal and civil oaths of allegiance that were standard fare for sixteenth century citizens.

The upshot of articles four through seven was that those who accepted rebaptism in the Schleitheim mold also were separating themselves totally from involvement in society at large. They were establishing an alternative society, in the world, but not of it. Unlike the peasants and militant Swiss Anabaptists of 1525, the Schleitheim group did not hope to reform the world according to a utopian pattern; they had given up on the world and were withdrawing from it, awaiting the divine judgement of the Last Days which they believed was imminent. But articles four through seven were not universally accepted in the Anabaptism that emerged elsewhere, as will be seen in the chapters which follow.

Significant also is the "Congregational Order" that appears to have circulated with the earliest versions of the Schleitheim Articles.[36] The "Order" also contained seven points "which all brothers and sisters of the entire congregation should agree to hold to." Briefly summarized, the articles were:

1. Members are to meet together "at least three or four times a week" for teaching and mutual exhortation.

2. Brothers and sisters are to read and exegete the Bible together, and read the Psalter daily at home.

3. None shall be frivolous, in the meeting or outside.

4. All are pledged to correct one another.

5. There is to be a "common fund" from which help will be given to those who have need: "none shall have anything of his own."

6. There shall be no gluttony at the meetings.

7. The Supper should be celebrated as often as there is a fellowship gathering.[37]

Notable in this list is the emphasis on a rudimentary "community of goods" that in fact was one of the common Anabaptist emphases in all branches of the movement.

It was the separatist, "apolitical," pacifist and non-swearing Anabaptism of Schleitheim that would come to predominate in Swiss Anabaptism after 1527. As such it would survive in isolated pockets of resistance in some Swiss mountains and valleys, and in some regions of Alsace and Bern. Many Swiss emigrated eastwards to Moravia, and we will trace some of the influences of this sectarian and pacifist Anabaptism below. Others fled to the Palatinate, down the Rhine and eventually even into Hesse and the Netherlands. The later Swiss Brethren, then, were not geographically "Swiss," but rather were described as "Swiss Brethren" in a doctrinal sense.

As for Michael Sattler, he was arrested in Austrian territory shortly following the Schleitheim meeting, was tried in the town of Rottenburg on the Neckar river, in Württemberg, and was sentenced to a horrible death: he had part of his tongue cut off, was then forged to a cart, had his flesh ripped from him eight times with red hot tongs, following which he was to be burned at the stake. This was carried out on May 20, 1527. His wife Margareta, who was arrested with him, was drowned two days later after refusing to recant.[38]

Conclusion

The origins of Swiss Anabaptism were unique within Anabaptism as a whole. The theological influences of Zwingli and Karlstadt are visible among the early Zürich radicals; some distant influence from Thomas Müntzer also is evident. But local political and religious pressures meant that Swiss Anabaptism moved quickly from being a movement aspiring to territorial reform, to a movement defining itself as separatist—all within the space of two short years. With the Schleitheim Articles the boundaries of Swiss Anabaptism began to be set in a sectarian and pacifist mould. But the questions of separation from the world, the extent and limits of involvement in the world and society, the extent and limits of sword bearing (or participation in government) would remain debated issues in the *larger* Anabaptist movement for several decades more. When we include, as we must, Balthasar Hubmaier among the Swiss Anabaptists, we may say that the debate concerning the role of government and the sword was not finally settled, even among the Swiss, at least until Nicholsburg, in 1528.

Swiss Anabaptism was unique, then, in that it moved to a sectarian position in a very short time. All surviving Anabaptist groups eventually arrived at similar affirmations, but the path leading there was filled with inter-Anabaptist discussion, testing, and dissension as the concrete implications of the Anabaptist beliefs were defined.

End Notes

[1] Williams, *Radical Reformation* (1962), pp. 86-9.

[2] Snyder, *Life and Thought*, pp. 67-8.

[3] Williams, *Radical Reformation* (1962), pp. 90-1. For a more nuanced treatment of Hubmaier's relationship to Zwingli concerning the Supper, see John Rempel, *The Lord's Supper in Anabaptism* (Scottdale, Pa.: Herald Press, 1993), chapter 2.

[4] Snyder, *Life and Thought*, pp. 68-69.

[5] See Calvin Pater, *Karlstadt as the Father of the Baptist Movements: The Emergence of Lay Protestantism* (Toronto: Univ. of Toronto Press, 1984).

[6] So reported Hubmaier. See Wayne Pipkin and John H. Yoder, eds., *Balthasar Hubmaier* (Scottdale, Pa.: Herald Press, 1989), pp. 257-58.

[7] George Williams notes, "the magisterial reformers themselves, in their initial emphasis on salvation by faith alone, had to grope for a while before coming down firmly in defense of the traditional practice of infant baptism, either by stressing the entirety of the Christian life from birth to death as metaphorically a baptismal dying and rising with Christ (Luther), or by insisting on birthright baptism as the New Covenantal equivalent of circumcision (Zwingli and Bullinger), or by interpreting it as a civil-ecclesiastical pledge to nurture progeny in an urban or national Christocracy (Bucer)." *Radical* (1992), p. 432.

[8] Snyder, *Life and Thought*, pp. 69-70.

[9] Cited in Snyder, *Life and Thought*, p. 70.

[10] Translation from Harder, *Sources*, p. 335; original in Bullinger, *Reformationsgeschichte*, I, pp. 238-39 (incorrectly cited as pp. 258-59 in Harder).

[11] Only the scriptural references of Grebel's concordance are given in Harder, *Sources*, pp. 427-28. For the full impact of the argument the original must be consulted, in QGTS, 2, pp. 265-73.

[12] Also notable is the citing of John 3:5: unless you are born of water and the spirit you cannot enter the Kingdom of Heaven. QGTS, 2, p. 272.

[13] Hubmaier has been unfairly marginalized in Mennonite histories primarily because he was not a

pacifist. Oddly enough, polygenesis historians, focusing as they do on the "sword" as a central issue, also tend to marginalize Hubmaier as an "atypical" Anabaptist. In fact, Hubmaier probably did more to define an early theological core of Anabaptist teaching than did any one else. His writings on baptism continued to be cited verbatim by Swiss Brethren into the seventeenth century.

[14] For a brief biography of Hubmaier, see Christof Windhorst, "Balthasar Hubmaier: Professor, Preacher, Politician," in Hans-Jürgen Goertz, ed., *Profiles of Radical Reformers* (Scottdale, Pa.: Herald Press, 1982), pp. 144-157. For a more detailed treatment, see Torsten Bergsten, *Balthasar Hubmaier: Anabaptist Theologian and Martyr*, trans. by W.R. Estep, Jr. (Valley Forge, Pa.: Judson Press, 1978).

[15] See especially "On the Christian Baptism of Believers," in Pipkin and Yoder, *Hubmaier*, pp. 95-149.

[16] Leland Harder, ed., *The Sources of Swiss Anabaptism* (Scottdale, Pa.: Herald Press, 1985), 118-119. Note the discussion of Erasmian pacifism on p. 608, n. 11.

[17] *Ibid.*, p. 290.

[18] *Ibid.*, p. 293.

[19] For the biblical arguments concerning baptism, see Mantz's "Protestation" in QGTS, 1, pp. 23-28; translation by Ernst Correll and Harold Bender, "Conrad Grebel's (sic) Petition of Protest and Defense to the Zurich Council in 1523," in *Goshen College Record Review and Supplement* (Jan., 1926), pp. 23-26.

[20] QGTS, 1, p. 216.

[21] QGTS, 1, pp. 218-221. Gottfried Locher has argued that Mantz's song is the earliest version, with the prose rendering a later work by an anonymous editor. Gottfried Locher, "Felix Manz' Abschiedsworte an seine Mitbrüder vor der Hinrichtung 1527: Spiritualität und Theologie. Die Echtheit des Liedes 'Bey Christo will ich bleiben'," *Zwingliana* XVII (1986), pp. 11-24.

[22] Felix Mantz' Farewell Letter, *Martyrs' Mirror*, p. 415.

[23] The evidence from Zollikon, where the Anabaptist movement was initiated directly by Grebel, Mantz and Blaurock, indicates that nonresistance was not yet a defining feature of the movement. See Arnold Snyder, "Zollikon Anabaptism and the Sword," MQR 69(April, 1995), pp. 205-225.

[24] In later years reformed clergy, among them Bucer and Ambrosius Blaurer, would adopt positions close to Hubmaier's, especially in relation to church discipline. Bucer and Blaurer had some success in persuading Anabaptists to recant by providing for a more stringent discipline within their churches. See Werner Packull, "The Melchiorites and the Ziegenhain Order of Discipline, 1538-39," in Walter Klaassen, ed., *Anabaptism Revisited* (Scottdale, Pa.: Herald Press, 1992), pp. 11-28.

[25] Snyder, *Life and Thought*, pp. 71-73; James Stayer, "Reublin and Brötli: The Revolutionary Beginnings of Swiss Anabaptism," in Marc Lienhard, ed., *The Origins and Characteristics of Anabaptism* (The Hague: Nijhoff, 1977), pp. 83-102.

[26] Heinold Fast, "Hans Krüsis Büchlein über Glauben und Taufe," in Cornelius J. Dyck, ed., *A Legacy of Faith*, (Newton, Kan.: Faith and Life Press, 1962), pp. 197-231. Stayer, *Sword*, pp. 110-111.

[27] Fast, "Büchlein," pp. 221-222.

[28] See Matthias Hui, "Von Bauernaufstand zur Täuferbewegung," *Mennonitische Geschichtsblätter*, 46 (1989), pp. 113-144.

[29] Above all, a strong anticlericalism carried over into Grüningen Anabaptism, expressed positively in the Anabaptist insistence on the congregational election of pastors. Agitation against tithe payment also continued. Hui, "Von Bauernaufstand," pp. 136-37.

[30] Snyder, *Life and Thought*.

[31] Snyder, *Life and Thought*, p. 87.

[32] See Heinold Fast, "Michael Sattler's Baptism: Some Comments," MQR 60(July, 1986), pp. 364-373, and Arnold Snyder, "Michael Sattler's Baptism: Some Comments in Reply to Heinold Fast," MQR 62(October, 1988), pp. 496-506.

[33] The letter to Bucer and Capito is found in Yoder, *Legacy*, pp. 21-24.

[34] Text in *ibid.*, pp. 34-43.

[35] Some controversy has been generated concerning the question of the "monastic" influence on Sattler. Compare Dennis Martin, "Monks, Mendicants, and Anabaptists: Michael Sattler and the Benedictines Reconsidered," MQR 60(April, 1986), pp. 139-164, and Arnold Snyder, "Michael Sattler, Benedictine: Dennis Martin's Objections Reconsidered," MQR 61(July, 1987), pp. 262-279.

[36] Text in *ibid.*, pp. 44-45.

[37] Yoder, *Legacy*, pp. 44-5.

[38] Snyder, *Life and Thought*, pp. 100-104.

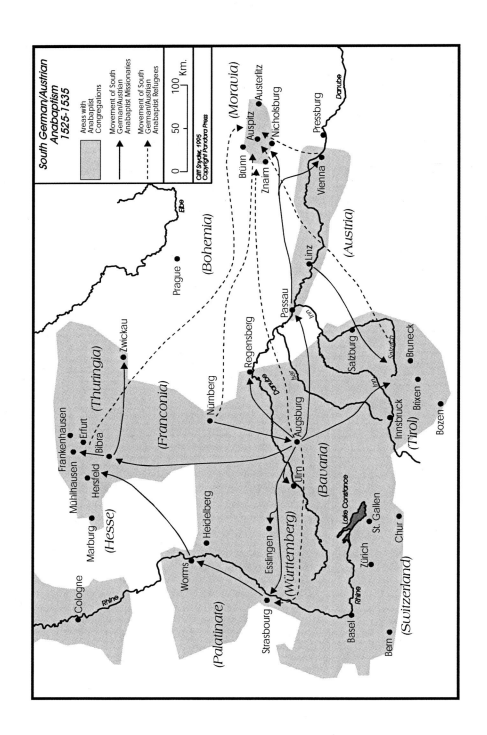

South German/Austrian Anabaptism 1525-1535

Areas with Anabaptist Congregations

Movement of South German/Austrian Anabaptist Missionaries

Movement of South German/Austrian Anabaptist Refugees

0   50   100 Km.

Cliff Snyder, 1995
Copyright Pandora Press

(Moravia)

Austerlitz

Auspitz

Nicholsburg

Znaim

Brünn

Pressburg

Danube

Vienna

(Austria)

Linz

(Bohemia)

Prague

Passau

Regensberg

Inn

Salzburg

Salzach

Bruneck

(Thuringia)

Zwickau

(Franconia)

Nürnberg

Danube

Isar

Augsburg

(Bavaria)

Innsbruck

(Tirol)

Brixen

Bozen

Frankenhausen

Mühlhausen

Erfurt

Bibra

Hersfeld

(Hesse)

Marburg

Heidelberg

Ulm

Lake Constance

St. Gallen

Chur

Esslingen

(Württemberg)

Zürich

Cologne

Rhine

Worms

(Palatinate)

Strasbourg

Basel

Rhine

Bern

(Switzerland)

Elbe

Chapter 5

The Origins of South German/Austrian Anabaptism

Polygenesis historians have modified our understanding of the nature of early Swiss Anabaptism, but even more significantly, they have pointed to different intellectual and historical origins of other Anabaptist movements. This is particularly evident in recent studies of the South German/Austrian Anabaptist movement.[1] The roots of South German/Austrian Anabaptism are not to be found in the Zürich reformation or in the theology of Ulrich Zwingli, but rather in ashes of the Peasant's War of 1525 and the theologies of Thomas Müntzer, Hans Denck, and Hans Hut.

Just as the story of Swiss Anabaptism must begin with Ulrich Zwingli, so must the story of South German Anabaptism begin with Thomas Müntzer, even though Müntzer was not an Anabaptist, never having practiced adult baptism.[2] As noted above, Müntzer's convictions finally led him to the forefront of the peasants' revolt in Thuringia. Also present at the disastrous battle of Frankenhausen were two followers of Thomas Müntzer who would soon play leading roles in Central and South German Anabaptism: Melchior Rinck, who participated as a combatant, and Hans Hut, who was arrested at Frankenhausen while allegedly plying his trade as a bookseller.

Hans Denck

Before tracing the career of Hans Hut, we must introduce Hans Denck, another important early Anabaptist leader in the South German movement.[3] Hans Denck was born sometime around 1500 in Bavaria and attended the University of Ingolstadt from 1517 to 1520. A humanist scholar, well versed in Latin, Greek and Hebrew, he came to Basel in 1522, worked as a proofreader in various print shops, and identified with the evangelical reform movement led by Johannes Oecolampadius, upon whose recommendation Denck received a teaching appointment in 1523 at the St. Sebald school in Nuremberg. Once in Nuremberg, Denck began to associate with the circle of mystical humanists and to identify with the radical currents of reform that had found a strong resonance in those circles.[4]

Nuremberg's move in a reforming direction was carried out under the leadership of a strong Lutheran party, but from 1523 to 1525 the ideas and writings of Karlstadt and Müntzer began circulating in Nuremberg and found an immediate response in the mystical humanist party. Denck had been strongly influenced by the Rhenish mysticism of Tauler and Suso, thus sharing some of the same theological roots as Müntzer and Karlstadt. There were also personal contacts, the exact details of which are no longer clear. Nevertheless, Hans Denck probably came to know both Thomas Müntzer and Heinrich Pfeiffer in Nuremberg on the occasion of their visits to that city in 1524. Hans Hut, at this time an active member of Müntzer's circle, came to Nuremberg on at least two occassions to have some of Müntzer's writings printed, and testified later that he had stayed with Denck at least once in 1524.[5] By January of 1525, Hans Denck had been called before the Nuremberg city council to be examined for his orthodoxy by the Lutheran pastors, led by Andreas Osiander. His answers failed to satisfy the council and he was expelled from the city. Hans Denck was now clearly on the radical side of the growing radical/mainline rift developing within the evangelical reform movement.[6]

Following his banishment from Nuremberg, Denck appeared next in the Swiss city of Schwyz, where he was imprisoned briefly for preaching against infant baptism. Coming next to St. Gall, he consorted with the Anabaptists gathered around Johannes Krüsi, the "not-so-pacifist" Anabaptist preacher; Denck, however, had probably not yet accepted adult baptism. It was reported that Denck was teaching universalism, namely that in the end, all persons (perhaps even Satan) would be saved.[7] By September of 1525, Denck was in the South German city of Augsburg, where he would remain for a year and a month. At some point—whether in Augsburg or at some point prior to his arrival there—he accepted baptism, and became an active Anabaptist leader. It was during his sojourn in Augsburg that Denck would write three important works: *Whether God is the Cause of Evil*, *Of the Law of God*, and *He Who Truly Loves the Truth*.[8] In Augsburg Denck also met Balthasar Hubmaier, who was passing though the city on his way to Nicholsburg, Moravia, following his imprisonment and expulsion from Zürich. And, in the spring of 1526 (May 3), in a watershed event for the history of South German Anabaptism, Hans Denck baptized Hans Hut into the movement.

By late summer of 1526 Denck came to the attention of Urbanus Rhegius, reformer of Augsburg. They had private discussions, and a public disputation was arranged. Hans Denck, however, left town before the disputation could take place and by November of 1526 was in Strasbourg. His one-month stay in that city was punctuated with possible disagreements with Michael Sattler—about which we know little—and overt disagreements with Martin Bucer—about which we know more. Bucer and Denck carried out a public debate before several hundred citizens on December 22 and 23, 1526 with the result that the council, at Bucer's urging, expelled Denck from the city. He fled to the imperial city of Worms, stopping on the way at Landau, where he had a public disputation concerning baptism with the local pastor, Johann Bader.[9]

The six months Hans Denck would spend in Worms would be very fruitful ones. Besides collaborating with Ludwig Hätzer on a translation of the Old Testament prophets, he also joined forces with Melchior Rinck in promoting Anabaptist reform in the city; they succeeded in converting Jacob Kautz and Hilarius, both young Lutheran preachers, to the Anabaptist cause. It was also in Worms that Denck composed his most Anabaptist writing, *Concerning True Love*. But this all came to an end when, in early June of 1527, Jacob Kautz posted seven Anabaptist theses on the door of the Dominican church in Worms and provoked a swift civic response. By July 1, Kautz and Hilarius had been banned, as had also Melchior Rinck; Denck and Hätzer then left the city.[10]

In August of 1527, Hans Denck took part in some meetings of the "Martyrs' Synod" in and around Augsburg, as will be detailed further below, following which he withdrew to Basel. By this time he had become disillusioned by Anabaptist divisions and, at the urging of his old friend Oecolampadius, he composed an apology which came to be called (posthumously and misleadingly) his *Recantation*.[11] He died in Basel in mid-November of 1527, a victim of the plague.

Central to Hans Denck's understanding of reform was the importance of the inner Word over that of the outer word, although like Müntzer and Schwenckfeld, he quoted Scripture constantly. This emphasis on the inner word, and a questioning of infant baptism, had gotten him expelled from Nuremberg in 1525; the inner, mystical emphasis in his thought would remain a constant for Denck throughout all his peregrinations and changes. In contrast to Müntzer, however, Denck was a mystic without a hammer. Of all early Anabaptist leaders, Hans Denck was the least dogmatic. He called for religious toleration, since he considered outward ceremonies to be largely secondary. What truly counted was the inner life. As Werner Packull has noted, this interior emphasis was egalitarian and anticlerical: the Spirit could and did speak to all, not just to the literate doctors of theology. Although there are no demonstrated connections between Denck and the Peasants' War, he agreed with Müntzer and Karlstadt in the appeal to mystical roots, the call for spiritual self-surrender, the egalitarian stress on the Spirit, as well as in his anticlericalism.

It was Hans Denck's acceptance of water baptism as the outer sign of inner repentance and commitment that defined him as an Anabaptist, although he did move away from a firm commitment to the "ceremonies" of water baptism and the Lord's Supper just before his death. During his Anabaptist phase, however, Denck maintained that for those who inwardly accepted God's gracious offer of a new life in Christ, the next step was water baptism, "the sign of the Covenant, [which] is to be given and not to be denied to any of those who by the power of God have been invited to it through the knowledge of genuine Love and who desire such Love and agree to be followers."[12] The covenant of baptism, said Denck, "means that whoever is baptized into the death of Christ is baptized in order that he might die to the old Adam as (Christ) has died and that he may walk in a new life with Christ as He (Christ) was raised."[13] Thus the outer sign of baptism indicated publicly that one had made an

inner commitment thenceforth to live a new life in Christ.[14] Here the ethical emphasis emerged as strongly in Denck's thought as in that of other Anabaptists: salvation
is not dependent on "imputed righteousness" on the basis of faith in Christ alone, but
rather salvation involves living a sanctified life, in the power of Christ's Spirit.[15] Hans
Denck joined other Anabaptists in opposing the Protestant understanding of justification by faith alone, imputed righteousness, and "at once justified and a sinner."[16]

Hans Hut

Hans Hut was born around 1490
in Haina, in Central Germany. Hut was a
bookbinder and a bookpeddler who also
fulfilled the office of sexton in the town
of Bibra for four years. He was described
in a warrant for his arrest as "a very
learned, clever fellow, a fair length of a
man [i.e., tall], a rustic person with
cropped brown hair, a pale yellow mous-
tache, dressed in gray woolen pants, a
broad gray hat, and at times a black riding
coat."[17] From 1521 on his bookselling
activity took him to Würzburg, Bamberg,
Nuremberg, Passau and into Austria, as
well as to Wittenberg, where he showed
a preference for Karlstadt's and
Müntzer's views.[18] When Thomas
Müntzer had to flee Mühlhausen in September of 1524 he spent a night and a

day at Hut's house, and entrusted Hut with the task of having his *Vindication and
Refutation* printed in Nuremberg, where Hut had contact with Hans Denck. By the
end of 1524, Hut refused to have his child baptized in Bibra and, given the choice of
having his child baptized or being exiled, he chose exile.

The Peasants' War was now well underway in Central Germany, and by Hut's
presence at the fateful battle of Frankenhausen, it is evident that he was a close
follower of Müntzer; in fact, he was a signed member of Thomas Müntzer's "Eternal
Covenant." After the defeat of the peasant forces at Frankenhausen, we find Hut
preaching at Bibra, castigating the clergy for celebrating the Mass only for pay. He
promised his hearers that God would punish them, but even more it was claimed that
he said "The subjects should murder all the authorities, for the opportune time has
arrived; the power is in their hands."[19] Of course Hut had to leave Bibra again, and
apparently resumed his bookselling peregrinations, finally accepting baptism in

Augsburg, in May, 1526 from Hans Denck.

Following his baptism, Hans Hut developed an amazing itinerant ministry. Even a partial list of the places where he founded Anabaptist congregations is impressive. Among them are: Haina, Coburg, Königsberg (Franconia), Ostheim, Bamberg, Erlangen, Nuremberg, Uttenreuth, Augsburg, Passau, Nikolsburg, Vienna, Melk, Steyr, Freistadt, Linz, Laufen, and Salzburg; there were in addition very many smaller villages and rural locations where Hut baptized. All of this Hut accomplished in less than a year and a half of Anabaptist activity, for he was arrested in Augsburg in September, 1527, shortly after the "Martyrs' Synod." After suffering horrible tortures (he was racked severely and repeatedly) he died in prison under mysterious circumstances, asphyxiating as the result of a fire in his cell. In the absence of a living Hans Hut, the court publicly condemned his lifeless body to death and burned it at the stake.

Hut retained much of Thomas Müntzer's teachings, and much less of Denck's. Like Müntzer, Hut emphasised God's grace as a purging of the soul, the necessity of suffering while this purging was taking place, the reception of a living Spirit in all believers, and a preaching about the imminent End Times. So close are the parallels that Hans Hut's major writing on baptism was for some time thought to be a writing by Thomas Müntzer.[20] There is some justice to Gottfried Seebass' judgement that Hut's theology represents "a cruder version of Müntzer's basic assumptions."[21] In particular, Müntzer's emphasis on the necessity of suffering was taken up by Hut's "Gospel of all Creatures." According to Hut, God had revealed in all creation the fundamental "gospel" that lower orders of creation must "suffer" the will of the higher orders of creation: just as animals must suffer at the hands of human beings, so also human beings must be subject to, and suffer, at the hands of God.[22] This call to *Gelassenheit*, or giving place to God's will, and the call to accept the suffering that such yielding would entail, was thoroughly Müntzerian.

Hut's understanding of baptism illustrates his unique blending of Anabaptist emphases seen elsewhere, with Müntzer's views. Hut's defence of water baptism restates the Anabaptist themes that the Gospel is to be preached, after which, when faith results, baptism is to be given. Baptism is a covenant sign that incorporates believers into the fellowship of the Christian Church; the outer baptism "follows preaching and faith," and is a sign or covenant of the "true reality."[23] As Rollin Armour notes, this formulation recalls Hubmaier's three steps, seen already in the earliest Swiss Anabaptism: preaching, faith, and water baptism.[24] Like Hubmaier, Hut also spoke of a three-fold baptism of spirit, water and blood, thus echoing previously articulated Anabaptist understandings of baptism.[25] Nevertheless, Hut also introduced new emphases that recall his previous allegiance to Thomas Müntzer.

Although the spiritualist emphasis was present in Swiss understandings of baptism, Hut developed the concept of the "inner baptism" further. For Hut the "es-

**The angel from the east seals the 144,000 elect,
Revelation 7:3**

sential" or true baptism begins with knowledge of God, deepens in a process of suffering and doubt, and is fulfilled through the work of the Spirit. Hut's understanding, drawn from Müntzer and perhaps also from Denck, points to roots in German mysticism and concentrates on the spiritual process of coming to "true faith."[26] A second original theme that emerged in Hut's baptismal practice was his linking of water baptism with the sealing of the 144,000 elect of the Last Days (Revelation 7:3): Hut typically baptized followers on the forehead with this mark of the elect of the Last Days. With this practice, Hut's blending of Müntzer's apocalyptic convictions with Anabaptism is most evident. Thus in baptismal teaching and practice, Hans Hut gave the practice of Anabaptist baptism, mystical and apocalyptic emphases not seen previously, which point to his own theological origins as a follower of Thomas Müntzer.

Melchior Rinck

In tracing the story of Melchior Rinck we look to Central Germany—to Hesse, Saxony, and Thuringia—and to a person who was in close contact with both Thomas Müntzer and Hans Denck.[27] Melchior Rinck was born in 1492 or 1493, apparently of peasant parents from Hesse. He received a good education at the Universities of Leipzig and Erfurt, where he excelled in classical languages: his nickname was "the Greek," an allusion to his linguistic skill. Rinck was an early convert to evangelical reform: already in 1523, as chaplain in Hersfeld, Rinck had begun to preach in a reformed mode, following the lead of the Hersfeld pastor Heinrich

Fuchs, who had been in the evangelical camp since 1521.[28] Their preaching eventually brought about a confrontation with the abbot and the city council, a small revolt in the city, and an order by Philip of Hesse that the two pastors be arrested and expelled from Hessian territory. Their supporters in Hersfeld saw that they were released from prison, given money, and escorted safely across the Hessian border. Early in 1524, through the intervention of Jakob Strauss, Melchior Rinck did find a post as a Lutheran preacher first in Oberhausen, and then in Eckhardshausen, near Eisenach.

Late in 1524 or early in 1525 Rinck married Anna, daughter of the Lutheran supporter Hans Eckhart. Given Rinck's later accusation that Anna had married him not out of love or free choice, but in order to find a "quiet life," it seems a safe assumption that at the time of his marriage Rinck was not yet a follower of Müntzer, for Müntzer's life was anything but "quiet" already by 1524. Thomas Müntzer returned to Mühlhausen in late February 1525, and Rinck was on the battlefield in Frankenhausen by May 1525. As Erich Geldbach notes, Rinck "must have fallen very suddenly under Müntzer's influence."[29]

Unfortunately, details are lacking concerning Rinck's involvement with Müntzer and the Peasants' War. Rinck later did not deny that he had been involved in the Peasants' War, although he did deny any leadership role; his opponents claimed that he had been a leader more zealous than either Müntzer or Pfeiffer.[30] In fact, although later opponents may have exaggerated his importance for polemical purposes, Rinck's involvement in the Peasants' War was not innocent or incidental: he was a leading combatant (a captain) at Frankenhausen.[31] Unfortunately, Rinck (perhaps understandably) never clarified his own relationship to Thomas Müntzer during the years 1523 to 1525. From the few surviving writings from Rinck's hand—all from a later date—no more than what may be a general influence of Müntzer is still discernible.[32] Certainly Müntzer left a far stronger theological imprint on Hans Hut than he did on Melchior Rinck.

Rinck's whereabouts and activities after the defeat of the peasants are unknown until January 1527, when he appeared in Landau in conversation with the Reformed pastor Johannes Bader. Bader appears to have been leaning in an Anabaptist direction, but then changed his mind and supported infant baptism. Hans Denck passed through Landau sometime between January 9 and 20, on his way from Strasbourg to Worms. Denck and Bader held a disputation on January 20, the proceedings of which Bader published; in reply, Melchior Rinck wrote a "Refutation."[33] What evidence there is suggests that Hans Denck baptized Melchior Rinck, probably sometime in January 1527.[34] In any case, Denck and Rinck now made their way to Worms and worked there together for the Anabaptist cause. Hans Denck, as noted above, set to work with Ludwig Hätzer translating the prophets; there is evidence to suggest that Rinck played a major role in converting Jacob Kautz and Hilarius to

Anabaptism.[35] In the spring of 1527, Melchior Rinck, along with Ludwig Hätzer and Hans Denck, was implicated in the "Seven Articles" Kautz posted prominently on a church door.[36] Rinck's involvement with the South German Anabaptist branch is thus unmistakeable.

After his expulsion from Worms Melchior Rinck again disappeared for a time from the historical record. He surfaced again evangelizing for Anabaptism in and around Hersfeld in the summer of 1528, where he had formerly worked as chaplain, in the territory bordering Hesse and ducal Saxony. When he presented a written petition to be allowed to preach publicly in the parish church in Hersfeld, word reached the Margrave Philip of Hesse, who summoned Rinck to his hunting lodge and interviewed him personally. Given the option of expulsion or an examination by Philip's theologians at the University of Marburg, Rinck chose the latter. The articles discussed at that August, 1528 debate are still extant, and provide us with a little insight into Rinck's Anabaptist teachings.[37]

Erich Geldbach has shown convincingly that the general argument and structure of Rinck's articles closely parallels that seen in Hans Denck's booklet "Concerning True Love," published in the previous year at Worms. Nevertheless, although Rinck's writing emphasizes love much as Denck's, it displays none of Denck's emphasis on the "inner word," nor for that matter is there any trace of Müntzer's "revolutionary eschatology" in Rinck's 1528 thinking, as there had been in Hut's.[38] Melchior Rinck may have been "influenced" by Müntzer in 1525, he was probably baptized and clearly "influenced" by Denck in 1527, but he remained very much his own person theologically.[39]

As a result of the debate, Rinck was expelled from Hessian territory in the summer of 1528. He is known to have baptized someone in November of that year in Franconia, and to have passed through the territory in Fulda early in 1529, returning soon to preach again near Hersfeld. He was arrested yet again in Hessian territory in April of 1529 and, with characteristic leniency, Philip of Hesse had him held in the monastery of Haina until May, 1531, when he was released without any penalty except the condition that he remain out of Hessian and Saxon territories.[40] This condition Rinck violated immediately, returning to the same general area near Hersfeld again: he was arrested for the last time in the town of Vacha while preaching on a favourite Anabaptist baptismal text, Mark 16:16.[41]

Although John Frederick, Duke of Saxony, now pressured for a death sentence, Philip of Hesse resisted and pronounced instead a sentence of life imprisonment for Rinck. For the next twenty years Melchior Rinck heroically resisted all attempts to dissuade him from his Anabaptist belief—he was visited by Peter Tasch after the latter's recantation of Anabaptism, as well as by Martin Bucer, but all to no avail. He was still living in prison in 1553 at sixty years of age. There is no further notice of him in the historical record; it is assumed that he died in prison, probably before 1560.[42]

The "origins" of Melchior Rinck's Anabaptism are to be found firmly in the Müntzer/Denck tradition. Nevertheless, one could hardly arrive at such a conclusion by a mere analysis of his writings or the testimonies of those whom he instructed in Anabaptism. We find in Rinck a strong anticlericalism, but nothing beyond what was commonly seen among Anabaptists. Like all Anabaptists, Rinck rejected Luther's understanding of salvation by faith, and upheld the standard Anabaptist view that emphasized the necessity of good works.[43] The historical records indicate that Rinck was concerned above all with baptism, and that his teaching resembled most of all that of the Swiss Brethren in its biblically literal foundation—although no "dependence" is suggested by this.[44] Although he taught that baptism in water had to follow one's "having been taught of God," he showed no tendency to depreciate water baptism in favour of an inner, spiritual baptism. There is no evidence that Rinck shared Denck's mystical and spiritualist bent.[45] Likewise, Rinck did not emphasize baptism as an apocalyptic sign of the 144,000 elect, as did Hut, although he appears to have baptized by making a sign of the cross on the forehead.[46] While there is some sporatic evidence that he may have preached that the End Times were near, this was no pronounced emphasis in his teaching as it had been with Müntzer and with Hut. The testimonies of those whom he taught identify the core of his teaching as: coming to faith from hearing the Word (that is, being taught by God), repenting, being baptized, and living a new life.

South German Anabaptism after Hut and Denck

In spite of the true generalization that at its origins it was a more "mystical," "spiritualistic," and "apocalyptic" Anabaptism, the South German movement showed little uniformity in its development after 1527. This "problem" of divergent Anabaptist expressions within South German Anabaptism was explained by Werner Packull as being the result of "mutations from Hut-Denck Anabaptism,"[47] although it appears that "mutation" was more the rule than the exception. Part of the reason for these "mutations" was a loss of leadership. Just as Swiss Anabaptism lost its original leadership very quickly (Grebel in 1526, Mantz and Sattler in 1527, Hubmaier in 1528, Blaurock in 1529), so also the founding South German Anabaptist leaders disappeared quickly from the scene (Denck and Hut both perished in 1527).

Werner Packull has spoken of the "devolution" of Hut's movement, especially following the failure of his End Times prophecies and his own death, and the "evolution" of a more sectarian, congregational Anabaptism. In fact this process seems to have been underway from the very start. Four primary groupings have been identified that "mutated" from the Hut-Denck beginnings: those who developed Hut's militant apocalypticism a few steps further (e.g., Augustine Bader); direct heirs of Hans Denck's mystical and spiritualist tendencies (Bünderlin, Entfelder, and eventually, Kautz); transitional figures who synthesized mysticism, apocalypticism, and separated congregationalism (Schiemer, Schlaffer) who went on to influence the Anabaptism of Pilgram Marpeck, on the one hand, and the communitarian Hutterite movement, on the other; finally, we may mention the "Central German" stream that evolved after its own fashion along separatist lines, in spite of its Denck-Hut lineage (Melchior Rinck). In what follows we will give a brief overview of these various groupings and developments.

Augustine Bader

A direct continuation of Hut's militant apocalypticism is associated above all with the name of Augustine Bader. The bizarre story of Bader's attempt to keep Hut's apocalyptic hopes alive is part of the South German Anabaptist story that stands closest to Hut's own emphases; Bader's hopes for the millenium and the rule of his own son as the Messiah were ended by his arrest and execution in March of 1530.[48] There was an openness by Hut and some of his followers to direct visions, revelations and prophecies such as inspired Augustine Bader. In spite of the demise of Bader, and the relatively small number of persons involved in his movement, individual "prophets" in the Hut tradition remained active. Some migrated to Strasbourg, where they would play important roles in Melchiorite Anabaptism after 1530. However, the prophetic, apocalyptic strand of Anabaptism very quickly moved to the margins of the South German movement; after 1530 it played an insignificant role. Nevertheless, prophetic apocalypticism did continue to play an important role in North German/Dutch Anabaptism, reaching a climax at Münster. With the fall of the city in 1535, apocalyptic expectation progressively decreased in importance in the north as well.

Hans Bünderlin and Christian Entfelder

Hans Bünderlin and Christian Entfelder, both representatives of the mystical spiritualist Anabaptist stream, have been described as "homeless minds."[49] As with Hans Denck himself, these individuals passed through an Anabaptist phase, but eventually came to embrace a spiritualized Christianity that had little use for the "external ceremonies" of baptism and the Lord's Supper, or for an emphasis on the written Word. The tension between the spirit and the letter and the inner and outer realms was brought into particular focus by these Anabaptists. The theological issues raised by the spiritualists were among some of the most important to be faced by the Anabaptist movement. We will return to Bünderlin and Entfelder when we look at Anabaptism in Strasbourg.

Leonhard Schiemer and Hans Schlaffer

Leonhard Schiemer fit well into the South German Anabaptist context, for his writings give evidence of his having received much from late medieval mystical thought.[50] He had been a Franciscan monk for six years, left the monastery and became a tailor, witnessed the debate between Hut and Hubmaier in Nicholsburg, was baptized by Hut in Vienna, participated in the Martyrs' Synod in Augsburg, and soon was captured in the Tirol and martyred in January, 1528. He had been an Anabaptist all of six months. His writings emphasize suffering purgation and a soteriology that began with the presence of the divine Spirit in human beings. He also assimilated Hut's Gospel of all Creatures and Hut's concern for the things of the End Times. Nevertheless, Schiemer did not focus on a coming time of vengeance, when the righteous would finally get the chance to use their swords, nor on the suffering of inner purgation. Rather, Schiemer's response to the events of the End Times, which he was sure he was witnessing, was to call for separated communities of believers who would be willing to suffer the ultimate consequences, just as their Head had suffered. In Packull's words, "Schiemer in his own person epitomized the transition from a purely internalized cross mysticism to an Anabaptist theology of martyrdom."[51] Schiemer also emphasized strong community discipline (an element not emphasized to the same degree by Hut himself) and in general called for stringent ethical standards. In these matters, and in the matter of the sword, he stood closer to Denck and the Swiss than to Hut; there is some limited evidence of Swiss contact in Schiemer's case.[52]

Like Hut and Schiemer, Hans Schlaffer also emphasized suffering and the Gospel of All Creatures, and he expected the imminent return of Christ.[53] Hans Schlaffer had been a parish priest who had moved in an evangelical direction already by 1526; it is not known when he was baptized, but like Schiemer, he would have been an Anabaptist for only a short time prior to his martyrdom. He was martyred shortly after Leonhard Schiemer, in January of 1528. Schlaffer like Schiemer had moved beyond Hut and closer to the Swiss understanding, particularly in his conception of a separated, suffering fellowship. In his doctrine of the sword Hans Schlaffer gave no evidence of Hut's expectation of participation in divine vengeance.

Schiemer and Schlaffer represent transitional figures in South German and Austrian Anabaptism. They were baptized by Hut, but moved in the direction of "a more confessional sectarian movement."[54] The "internalized cross mysticism" of Müntzer and Hut became externalized in a martyr theology, appropriated later by virtually all the surviving Anabaptist groups, but especially by the Hutterites and the followers of Pilgram Marpeck who remembered Schiemer and Schlaffer as martyrs. Just as importantly, Schiemer and Schlaffer demonstrate how quickly Hut's Anabaptism could and did move into a separated congregational mode. The Anabaptism of Schiemer and Schlaffer was transitional in the fact that their apocalypticism and mysticism (already toned down from Hut's accustomed levels) would be toned down even further in the communities of Pilgram Marpeck and the Hutterites; likewise, the germinating separatist ecclesiology of Schiemer and Schlaffer would emerge with even more strength in the majority of South German groups.

Pilgram Marpeck[55]

Pilgram Marpeck was born around 1495 into a family of wealth and influence in the Tirol; his father Heinrich had been a city and mining magistrate in Rattenberg, Tirol. Pilgram himself became a member of Rattenberg's city council, served as Mayor in 1522, and occupied the powerful position of mining magistrate from 1525 until his resignation from that post in 1528.[56] Even after his conversion to Anabaptism and his departure from the Tirol, Marpeck remained willing to participate in civil service posts, as long as his conscience was not compromised.

It appears that Marpeck was won over to evangelical views through contact with Jakob Strauss and Stephan Castenbaur (Agricola); from 1520 on Marpeck had many opportunities to hear the new views defended. However Marpeck became an Anabaptist in the end; he reported later that he was unhappy with the "fleshly freedom" of the evangelicals, and was won over by the "obedience of faith" of the Anabaptists.[57] While details are missing, it appears that Leonard Schiemer and Hans Schlaffer helped shape Marpeck's Anabaptist views; Leonhard Schiemer's arrest, torture, trial and death by fire in Rattenberg finally led to Marpeck's resignation from his governmental post in Rattenburg in January 1528.[58]

On leaving the Tirol, Pilgram and his wife Anna travelled first to the Bohemian mining town of Krumau, where there was a substantial Anabaptist congregation, and appear also to have spent some time in Austerlitz, Moravia. According to one report, an Anabaptist congregation there commissioned Marpeck an elder, and sent him to Strasbourg. By late summer of 1528, Pilgram and Anna had moved to Strasbourg where Pilgram worked as an engineer in the employ of the city, and functioned also as an Anabaptist leader (1528-1532). He was forced into exile following a dispute with the city's preachers. After a period of wandering that took him from Switzerland to Moravia (1533-1544), Marpeck found employment in Augsburg where he ended his days, quietly leading a small Anabaptist group in that city (1544-1556).

Marpeck's thought was more indebted to German mysticism and Hans Denck than to the Swiss or Schleitheim. Nevertheless, his path led between the spiritualist descendants of Hans Denck, such as Bünderlin, Kautz and Entfelder, on the one hand, and the Swiss and the Hutterites on the other. He was in direct conversation with virtually all Anabaptist parties (except for the Dutch, where little evidence exists of direct contact). Against the spiritualists Marpeck stressed the incarnate Christ and the necessity of visible church ordinances, while against the more literal-minded Swiss and Hutterites, he stressed the freedom of the Spirit and the centrality of love. Thus although Marpeck argued for a visible and separated church against the spiritualists, he opposed a "legalistic" use of the ban and the insistence on external ordinances of separation such as the Swiss followers of Schleitheim were elaborating.[59]

Because of Marpeck's mediating position between spiritualist Anabaptists on the one hand, and the more literalistic and separatist Swiss and Hutterites on the other, his writings provide a particularly clear window into inter-Anabaptist dialogues. Although the groups led by Marpeck did not, as far as we know, survive much past the sixteenth century, in his person Marpeck represented a pivotal dialogue partner in the Swiss/South German Anabaptist context up to the middle of the sixteenth century.

Conclusion

We may note in conclusion two emphases unique to South German Anabaptism, in comparison to Swiss Anabaptism. First of all, much of South German Anabaptism had strong mystical roots, seen in Thomas Müntzer, Hans Denck and Hans Hut, which stressed the inner work of the Holy Spirit in believers. Werner Packull noted that these Anabaptists "took their theological starting point not from the Reformers but from a popularized medieval mystical tradition."[60] The second emphasis that set South German Anabaptism apart from the Swiss Anabaptism that preceded it was a very live apocalyptic expectation, which is most evident in Hans Hut, but by contrast is far less conspicuous in Denck and Rinck. The apocalyptic strand in fact would have a rather limited reach and life span in South German Anabaptism, given Hut's demise in 1527 and the failure of his prediction that Christ would return by 1528. The mystical strand of South German Anabaptist thought, combined with an emphasis on suffering, would prove longer-lived and, in many ways, the more influential of these teachings.

The tradition of German mysticism as appropriated by Müntzer, Hut, and Denck gave to much of South German/Austrian Anabaptism a spiritualist cast which distinguished it, up to a point, from the more biblicistic Swiss. As we have seen, however, this was far less the case with Melchior Rinck, who (oddly enough) also stands in the Müntzer/Denck line. In the second place, there was a marked stress on suffering as a way of conforming to the way of Christ, initially in the painful coming to faith, but also in the later Christian walk. Third, there was a strong willingness towards community of goods in Hut's Anabaptism and among his followers—although such a tendency was not unique to the South German movement. Fourth, there was a stronger identification with the social upheaval of the Peasants' War in this Anabaptist movement, which was reflected in Hut's doctrine of the sword (to be reviewed in a later chapter) and perhaps in a stronger anticlericalism than seen elsewhere. And finally, the failure of Hut's End Times predictions, and the continuing contact between a variety of Anabaptist "tendencies" (including the more separatist Swiss tradition), moved the surviving South German Anabaptist movement into accepting positions very close to Schleitheim's separatism.

End Notes

[1] See here especially the work of Werner Packull, *Mysticism and the Early South German-Austrian Anabaptist Movement, 1525-1531* (Scottdale, Pa.: Herald Press, 1977); Gottfried Seebaß, "Müntzers Erbe: Werk, Leben un Theologie des Hans Hut (1527)," Habilitationsschrift der Theologischen Fakultät der Friedrich-Alexander Universität zu Erlangen-Nürnberg (1972); and James Stayer, *Anabaptists and the Sword*, (Lawrence, Kan.: Coronado Press, 1972).

[2] On Thomas Müntzer, see Gordon Rupp, *Patterns of Reformation* (London: Epworth Press, 1969); Hans-Jürgen Goertz, "Thomas Müntzer," in Hans-Jürgen Goertz, ed., *Profiles of Radical Reformers*, (Scottdale, Pa.: Herald Press, 1982), pp. 29-44.

[3] See Werner Packull, "Hans Denck: Fugitive from Dogmatism," in Hans-Jürgen Goertz, ed., *Profiles of Radical Reformers*, (Scottdale, Pa.: Herald Press, 1982), pp. 62-71; and *idem.*, *Mysticism and the Early South German-Austrian Anabaptist Movement, 1525-1531* (Scottdale, Pa.: Herald Press, 1977), chapter 2. Also "Das Leben Dencks" in Walter Fellmann, ed., *Hans Denck Schriften*, 2. Teil (Gütersloh: Bertelsmann Verlag, 1956), pp. 8-19.

[4] Packull, "Denck," pp. 62-3.

[5] Packull, *Mysticism*, pp. 37-9.

[6] "In Nuremberg [Denck] was undeniably in contact with and part of that faction which, employing ideas of Müntzer and Carlstadt, drew upon mystical sources to combat and criticize the Lutheran Reformation." So Packull, *Mysticism*, p. 39. See Denck's "Confession" to the Nuremberg council in Fellmann, *Hans Denck Schriften*, 2. Teil, pp. 20-26.

[7] See the discussion in Packull, *Mysticism*, pp. 40-44.

[8] Critical texts of these writings in Walter Fellmann, ed., *Hans Denck Schriften*, 2. Teil (Gütersloh: Bertelsmann Verlag, 1956), pp. 27-74.

[9] Williams, *Radical* (1992), pp. 260-61; Packull, "Denck," p. 64.

[10] *Ibid.*, p. 261-63.

[11] Critical texts of *True Love* and the *Recantation* in Fellmann, *Hans Denck Schriften*, 2. Teil, pp. 75-86; 104-110 respectively.

[12] Hans Denck, "Concerning Genuine Love," (1527), in Edward J. Furcha, ed. and trans., *Selected Writings of Hans Denck* (Pittsburgh: Pickwick Press, 1975), p. 109.

[13] Hans Denck, "Confession to the City Council of Nürnberg, 1525," in Edward J. Furcha, ed. and trans., *Selected Writings of Hans Denck* (Pittsburgh: Pickwick Press, 1975), p. 19.

[14] "Holiness means to have separated oneself once and for all from the evil world and from all filth of the flesh to serve God the Lord only. This is indicated and witnessed to by water baptism because in it one declares the old life to be wicked and desires henceforth to walk in the new life." Hans Denck, "Concerning Genuine Love," (1527), in Edward J. Furcha, ed. and trans., *Selected Writings of Hans Denck* (Pittsburgh: Pickwick Press, 1975), pp. 110-111.

[15] "Through His suffering Christ has made satisfaction for the sin of all men. Otherwise no man could be saved... He who depends on the merits of Christ, but continues, nonetheless in a carnal, animal-like existence, holds Christ in utter disregard... As long as we are in the old life, we do not yet truly believe, nor do we want to be good and innocent." Hans Denck, "Recantation," (1528), in Edward J. Furcha, ed. and trans., *Selected Writings of Hans Denck* (Pittsburgh: Pickwick Press, 1975), pp. 124-25.

[16] "Indeed, he has made satisfaction and has levelled the path which no man could otherwise find that one may walk therein and reach life. Whoever does not walk it, does not reach life; for him the path is useless. He has fulfilled the Law, not to place us above it, but to give us an example to follow Him." Hans Denck, "The Law of God" (1526), in Edward J. Furcha, ed. and trans., *Selected Writings of Hans Denck* (Pittsburgh: Pickwick Press, 1975), p. 49. "They (the Protestants) say thoughtlessly and without making any distinctions ... 'Peace, peace;

simply believe and you are accepted and everything is in order.' O you miserable little people; how readily you entrust your soul to dangerous foxes; but you do not trust even for the smallest bit of bread, the shepherd and guardian who can protect you." Hans Denck, "Divine Order," in *ibid.*, p. 97.

[17] Gottfried Seebass, "Hans Hut: The Suffering Avenger," in Hans-Jürgen Goertz, ed., *Profiles of Radical Reformers* (Scottdale, Pa.: Herald Press, 1982), p. 54; see pp. 54-61 for a biographical sketch; Hans-Dieter Schmid, "Das Hutsche Täufertum. Ein Beitrag zur Charakterisierung einer täuferischen Richtung aus der Frühzeit der Täuferbewegung," *Historische Jahrbuch*, XCI (1971), pp. 327-44.

[18] Hans Guderian, *Die Täufer in Augsburg* (Pfaffenhofen: Ludwig Verlag, 1984), p. 63.

[19] Cited in Williams, *Radical*, pp. 167-68; cf. Guderian, *Täufer in Augsburg*, p. 63.

[20] See the discussion in Armour, *Baptism*, pp. 64-75.

[21] Gottfried Seebass, "Hans Hut: The Suffering Avenger" in Hans-Jürgen Goertz, ed., *Profiles of Radical Reformers* (Scottdale, Pa.: Herald Press, 1982), p. 57.

[22] "In the 'gospel of all creatures' is nothing else signified and preached than simply Christ crucified, but not Christ alone as Head, but the whole Christ with all members, this is the Christ which all creatures preach and teach. The whole Christ has to suffer in all members... . . . The eternal power and divinity will be perceived when a man truly recognizes it in the creatures or works from the creation of the world." Hut, "Mystery of Baptism," in Klaassen, *Outline*, p. 49.

[23] Klaassen, *Outline*, p. 170.

[24] See Armour, *Baptism*, p. 77, for the citation from Hut and this observation.

[25] See Armour, *Baptism*, pp. 92-93, for a comparison.

[26] See Armour, *Baptism*, pp. 79-86, for a detailed discussion.

[27] On Rinck in general, John S. Oyer, *Lutheran Reformers Against Anabaptists* (The Hague: Nijhoff, 1964), chapters II and III. See also Erich Geldbach, "Toward a more ample biography of the Hessian Anabaptist leader Melchior Rinck," MQR 48(July, 1974), pp. 371-72. Also, see ME, IV, "Rink," pp. 336-38 (in some cases, superseded); Williams, *Radical*, p. 168; 663-65; Ruth Weiß, "Die Herkunft der osthessischen Täufer," ARG 50(1959), pp. 3-9.

[28] Geldbach, "Melchior Rinck," p. 372. Fuchs subsequently also became a follower of Müntzer, and was killed in the battle of Frankenhausen. Oyer, *Lutheran*, p. 53.

[29] Geldbach, "Melchior Rinck," p. 373.

[30] The evidence in collated in Weiß, "Herkunft," pp. 4-5.

[31] So Stayer, *Sword*, p. 193; Williams, *Radical*, p. 168.

[32] See the discussion in Oyer, *Lutheran*, p. 106-110.

[33] Bader's writing was titled "Brüderliche warnung für dem newen Abgöttischen orden der Widertäuffer" (1527). On Rinck's "Widerlegung," see Gerhard Neumann, "A Newly Discovered Manuscript of Melchior Rinck," MQR 25(July, 1961), pp. 197-217.

[34] Geldbach, "Melchior Rinck," pp. 374-75. Oyer notes that "the association with Denk must have been decisive in enabling [Rinck] to restructure his theological outlook after the catastrophe in Central Germany." Oyer, *Lutheran*, p. 54.

[35] Geldbach, "Melchior Rinck," p. 375 follows Weiß, "Herkunft," p. 7 in concluding that a local chronicler's reference to a "learned Melchior Hoffman's" role in converting Kautz must refer to Melchior Rinck.

[36] According to a contemporary chronicler, the original copy began "Jacob Kautz, minister at Worms, with his brothers Hätzer, Denck and Rinck..." Cited in Packull, *Mysticism*, p. 57, and n. 168. The articles themselves are found in TA, *Baden und Pfalz*, pp. 113-114.

[37] See TA, *Hesse*, pp. 3-16; on these events, Oyer, *Lutheran*, pp. 56-7; Williams, *Radical*, pp. 663ff.

[38] Geldbach, "Melchior Rinck," p. 378, concludes from the lack of eschatological material that "not a trace of Müntzer's revolutionary eschatology had remained in Rinck's theology by the summer of 1528, if he had ever held this view." There is, however, a sharp anticlerical bite in the charges brought by Balthasar Raidt of Hersfeld against Rinck that recalls Müntzer more than Denck. Raidt charged that Rinck had insulted the "gospel of Jesus

Christ" and had said that "it is a false, hypocritical, dissembling gospel and all who follow Martin Luther and teach in that way, are leading the people to the devil. For although truly Luther at first had God's Spirit, he had certainly now become a devil and the very antichrist." TA, *Hesse*, p. 4. Rinck objected to this wording, and restated his meaning at his hearing.

[39] Stayer's efforts to uncover Rinck's views on the sword and government by means of an analysis of all the relevant data failed to discover any evident continuation of either Müntzer's or Hut's views. See *Sword*, pp. 193-96.

[40] Geldbach, "Melchior Rinck," pp. 379-80; Weiß, "Herkunft," p. 8.

[41] The report of the arrest notes that Rinck was arrested at a meeting along with twelve others, that he had preached there "and especially on the gospel of Mark, the last chapter, where according to the manner of their sect, [he] preached that Jesus Christ our saviour instituted baptism." TA, *Hesse*, p. 42.

[42] Accounts of Rinck's last years in other biographical sketches should be checked against Geldbach, "Melchior Rinck," pp. 382-83.

[43] Oyer, *Lutheran*, pp. 75-8.

[44] Oyer notes that baptism was even more central to Rinck than it was to the Swiss. See Oyer's comments in *Lutheran*, pp. 80-83.

[45] Rinck tied Spirit to Letter in a way that Denck did not; in fact, Rinck very often (as for instance in baptismal or marriage questions) was downright literalistic. See *ibid.*, pp. 86-87.

[46] *Ibid.*, p. 83.

[47] *Ibid.*, p. 110.

[48] On some of the variant expressions of Hut's Anabaptism, and especially good details on Bader, see Packull, *Mysticism*, pp. 118-138.

[49] See Packull, *Mysticism*, pp. 155-175, for a thorough review of Bünderlin and Entfelder.

[50] See the treatment in Packull, *Mysticism*, pp. 106-113.

[51] Packull, *Mysticism*, p. 112.

[52] *Ibid.*

[53] On Schlaffer, see *ibid.*, pp. 113-117.

[54] *Ibid.*, p. 117.

[55] See Stephen B. Boyd, *Pilgram Marpeck: His Life and Social Theology*, (Durham, N.C.: Duke University Press, 1992).

[56] *Ibid.*, pp. 5-12.

[57] *Ibid.*, p. 13.

[58] See Boyd, *Marpeck*, pp. 22-25; also Stayer, *Sword*, pp. 177-187 for the Marpeck circle's view of the sword.

[59] William Klassen, "Pilgram Marpeck: Liberty without Coercion," in Hans-Jürgen Goertz, ed., *Profiles of Radical Reformers* (Scottdale, Pa.: Herald Press, 1982), pp. 169-170. Klassen notes that Marpeck's time in Grisons (1532-44) was marked by success in engineering, but failure in communication with Swiss. "They, following the lines of Schleitheim, showed no reluctance in using the ban, and appeared to be concerned with spelling out ascetic rules of how the Christian was to live. For Marpeck, standing in the ethical tradition of Denck, the importance of love was increasingly stressed." *Ibid.*, pp. 171-72.

[60] Stayer, Packull, and Deppermann, "Polygenesis," MQR 49(April, 1975), p. 110.

Chapter 6

The Theological and Ecclesiological Core of Anabaptism

The Anabaptist "theological forest" had a unique and distinctive "shape" and character that marked it as *Anabaptist,* in spite of individual differences in origin and emphasis. It is a central thesis of this book that there are good reasons for maintaining the term "Anabaptist" for all of the sixteenth century "baptizing" groups, regardless of their differing origins. This chapter will identify the theological and ecclesiological core that was shared by all Swiss and South German/Austrian Anabaptists; we will see later that Melchior Hoffman's Anabaptism, born in Strasbourg in 1530 and transplanted into the Lowlands that same year, also embraced this same "core."

Hubmaier's Catechism of 1526[1]

Hubmaier's catechism is particularly valuable as a beginning reference point for identifying Anabaptist distinctives because it is a very early, and also an unusually comprehensive, Anabaptist expression of theological and ecclesiological fundamentals. Reference to the catechism here is not meant to indicate that Hubmaier was the "definitive" early Anabaptist theologian, or that this writing itself was "normative" for the movement, for there is no evidence that the catechism was used outside Nicholsburg. Hubmaier's catechism is useful for our purposes because the Anabaptist essentials he enumerated systematically were echoed (less systematically) by Anabaptists elsewhere. In the early Anabaptist context, the systematic nature of Hubmaier's catechism was unusual, but its content was unexceptional.

Hubmaier composed his catechism in 1526 with a view to educating new church members. The catechism is written in dialogue form between "Leonhart" and "Hans," and is structured in two main sections, the first dealing primarily with dogmatic questions, the second elaborating distinctive features of Anabaptist practice and belief, often drawn in contrast to prevailing belief and practice. The outline of the order of topics taken up in the catechism is as follows.

Part I
God; Christ; Sin
Ten Commandments; Repentance; Prayer
Promise and Gospel; Faith (The Apostles' Creed)
Baptism (Spirit, Water, and Blood)
Church (Universal and Particular)
Ban (Fraternal Admonition)
Part II
Lord's Supper (a memorial); Confession of Sin
Fasting; Restraint of Tongue; Sabbath Observance

Against the Veneration of Saints, Miracles, Images
Hearing God's Word in Church
Love
Sin, Redemption, Works and Grace
Outward and Inward Call of God
Genuine Good Works
Judgement Day; Eternal Life
Persecution; Hell

As this outline demonstrates, Hubmaier's catechism was comprehensive indeed. In what follows we will isolate elements of this catechism that will appear again in all branches of the Anabaptist movement, as we will have occasion to note throughout the following chapters.

Anabaptist views shared with Christian confessions

The Creed

Hubmaier included in his catechism instruction on the universal or ecumenical fundamentals of the faith, in particular the teaching of the Ten Commandments (Pipkin/Yoder, 346), the teaching of the Lord's Prayer (347) and the teaching of the Apostles' Creed (348-9) In addressing the reality of "second generation" believers to be raised within the church, Hubmaier recognized the need for the youth of the church to learn these basics of the Christian faith.

Hubmaier was not alone in his appeal to the Creed as the grounding of Christian faith. Acceptance of the historical Christian *doxa* or teachings, as summarized in the ecumenical Creeds and symbols, was common to all Anabaptist movements. The Anabaptists were orthodox in their understanding of the central elements of the faith with one major and one minor exception, as we will see. Although the Apostles' Creed did not form a central part of Anabaptist worship, as far as we know, it was commonly taught and appealed to in all branches of the movement.[2] Nevertheless, there was one glaring exception to the general doctrinal orthodoxy of Anabaptism, and this was Melchiorite Christology which has been described as "monophysite" or even "docetic." That is, Melchior Hoffman taught that Jesus had one, divine nature and only took on an appearance of humanity or "creatureliness." We will examine Melchiorite Christology further in later chapters. The "minor" heterodox exception that could be named in addition would be a tendency towards anti-trinitarianism in Silesia and by some individuals in the Netherlands.[3] These caveats aside, it can be said that the accusations of "Anabaptist heresy" by contemporaries were usually not allegations that Anabaptists had abandoned common Christian affirmations of faith, but rather were directed against Anabaptist church practices such as believers' baptism, the ban, an exclusive and memorial Lord's Supper, etc.

While Anabaptists generally affirmed the Apostles' Creed (commonly called the "twelve articles of the faith") nevertheless they followed common Christian practice by investing creedal affirmations with their own particular (Anabaptist) meanings. As one example of this process of "reinterpretation" we may consider the Anabaptist understanding of the affirmation "I believe in the holy universal church."

Establishing the true Christian church was central to Anabaptism, but that church was not understood in the medieval sense. Thus Hubmaier's exposition of the Creed says "I also believe and confess one holy universal Christian church, that is, *a communion of saints*..." (238)[4] The further definition of a "holy universal church" as a "communion of saints," although it goes beyond creedal affirmations in defining an essential component of Anabaptist ecclesiology, nevertheless it is not "heterodox," any more than the medieval ecclesiological arrangement had been heterodox. Still, these further definitions were crucial in delineating the confessional boundaries of various denominational groups. Toward the end of the sixteenth century the Anabaptists followed the lead of the Protestant denominations and began elaborating "confessions of faith" which outlined distinctive Anabaptist beliefs in more detail.[5]

Views shared with Evangelical/Protestant groups
Anti-Sacramentalism

Hubmaier's catechism articulates a thorough rejection of Roman Catholic sacramentalism. Hubmaier composed the following catechetical exchange concerning the Lord's Supper: "*Leonhart*: Is the bread not the body of Christ and the wine his crimson blood, as the Maoz-priests have been telling us? *Hans*: By no means; the bread and wine are nothing but memorial symbols of Christ's suffering and death for the forgiveness of our sins." (354-55) Even more strongly, in answer to the question "what is the Mass," Hubmaier has "Hans" reply: "It is the very idol and abomination, spoken of by the Prophet Daniel..." (355) Likewise concerning baptism, Hubmaier wrote the following: "*Leonhart*: What is your opinion of the infant baptism which the water-priests use? *Hans*: Nothing other than that the adult child gives a bath to the young child, thereby depriving it of the real water baptism of Christ." (350)

Anabaptists everywhere were agreed that neither priests nor sacraments were capable of conveying God's grace or of initiating the Christian life of the spirit, thus following the Protestant critique. This rejection of sacramental efficacy was the first step towards Anabaptist baptism, for if the water could not convey grace or confer salvation *ex opere operato* (by the performance of the act), on what basis was infant baptism to be defended? Said in terms of Protestant soteriology, the question was "If we are saved by grace through faith, and not by sacramental mediation, how then can infant baptism be continued, since infants do not have faith?" Although different answers to this question came from Lutherans to Reformed to Anabaptists, the posing of the question was common to all "evangelical" groups that questioned the medieval sacramental understanding. A crucial step in the direction of the eventual Anabaptist answer was provided by the radical reformers who first questioned the validity of infant baptism, as we have seen above.

On the eucharistic question that later would split apart the Protestant Reformation, the Anabaptists were united in holding that the Lord's Supper was a memorial, pointing to their theological kinship to the Reformed branch of Protestantism on this particular issue. There were no Anabaptists who took up the Lutheran view of the Supper, although Pilgram Marpeck—apparently influenced by Luther—came the closest to retaining a "sacramental" view.[6]

The anti-sacramentalism of the Anabaptists identifies their point of departure within the general evangelical protest of the sixteenth century. Virtually all of the first generation Anabaptist leaders were inspired, in the first instance, by this evangelical critique, even though they came to part company with the mainline reformers in their understanding of what would take the place of the sacramental view. They were aided in this process by the radical reformers, who defined crucial terms of further evangelical reform in a mode distinct from the mainline Protestant answers.

Anticlericalism

Hubmaier and virtually all Anabaptists shared in the anticlericalism of the early Protestant reformers. Their language could be just as intemperate (although probably not as inventive) as that of the more famous reformers. In his preface to the Catechism Hubmaier noted:

> Indeed, it is in many cases manifest what incompetent shepherds and pastors have been forced upon us by popes, bishops, provosts, abbots, and also by secular emperors, kings, princes, and nobles, by their bulls and mandates, such as courtisans, donkey curriers, fornicators, adulterers, procurers, gamblers, drunkards, and foolish rouges, whom we would in truth not have trusted to herd our pigs and goats, but still we had to accept them as our souls' shepherds. They have become nothing but thieves and murderers... (342)

Such anticlericalism was common within the Anabaptist movement generally, although the focus of Anabaptist anticlericalism very soon widened to include the Protestant clerics as well as the Catholic.[7] It can be said that the closest practical institution of a priesthood of all believers would be seen within early Anabaptism, although that phenomenon also was not destined to last.

The Authority of Scripture

The positive side of the Protestant critique of the teaching authority of the Roman Catholic church hierarchy was the insistence on the final authority of Scripture. The Anabaptists followed the Protestant reformers on this point. In his preface to "A Christian Catechism," Hubmaier gave thanks that God's "saving, living, and eternal Word admonished and instructed us and so clearly taught us that we henceforth know thoroughly how to navigate only by the glow and star of his holy Word." (340) What is called for is a testing and trying of all teachings "by the plumb line of the Bible." (343) The Scriptures remained the final authority in all matters of faith.

It would become evident soon enough that this "scriptural principle" was not a facile answer to all questions of faith and practice, but in taking this point of departure the Anabaptists recognized themselves to be a part of the "evangelical" movement in the sixteenth century. Again, their path away from the mainline Protestant position was first marked out by radical reformers who were the first "evangelicals" to diverge from Luther's understanding of the scriptural principle.

Salvation by Grace through Faith

In soteriology too the Anabaptists took their point of departure from the Protestant, rather than the medieval church: salvation depended in the first instance on God's grace and the human response of faith, and not on any sacramental or penitential mediation. Hubmaier's catechism expresses this "evangelical" insight in the following way: "*Leonhart*: Show me ... a message of the gospel. *Hans*: Christ died for the sake of our sins, and arose for the sake of our justification, Rom. 4:25. *Leonhart*: What follows from this message? *Hans*: Faith. *Leonhart*: What is faith? *Hans*: Faith is the realization of the unspeakable mercy of God, his gracious favor and goodwill, which he bears to us through his most beloved Son Jesus Christ, whom he did not spare and delivered him to death for our sakes that sin might be paid for, and we might be reconciled to him and with the assurance of our hearts cry to him: Abba, Father, our Father who are (sic) in heaven." (348)

In accepting the principle of salvation by grace through faith, the Anabaptists again gave evidence of their "evangelical" point of departure. Nevertheless, as we have seen above and as we will see below, this point of departure could be developed in different directions; Anabaptist soteriology was in fact distinct from mainline "evangelical" soteriology, as well as from the soteriology of the medieval church. The closest similarity in soteriology is to be found among the radical reformers who differed with Luther.

Anabaptist Doctrinal Emphases

It should be clear from the above that Anabaptists shared important fundamental positions with the evangelical (Protestant) stream. Nevertheless they came to form part of the Radical Reformation stream by accepting some critiques of the radical reformers who had preceded them in criticizing Luther and Zwingli. The Anabaptists became an identifiable movement when they developed radical reforming emphases in new doctrinal and ecclesial directions.

Pneumatology: the activity of the Holy Spirit.

Anabaptism of all kinds was based on a lively pneumatology, on the expectation that God's Spirit needed to work in the hearts of human beings in order to initiate and sustain the life of faith.[8] This is visible even in Hubmaier, who was one of the least "pneumatic" of Anabaptist leaders. For Hubmaier the necessary working of the Spirit was expressed as the first of three "baptisms" which he called the baptisms of the Spirit, of water, and of blood. The baptism of the Spirit is "an inner illumination of our hearts that takes place by the Holy Spirit, through the living Word of God." (362) Hubmaier linked the work of the Holy Spirit to the hearing of the Word in a way not usually seen among other early Anabaptists, but nevertheless sounds a thoroughly Anabaptist note in his insistence on an inward spiritual rebirth and regeneration and the first step in the process of salvation.

Spirit and Letter

The Anabaptist emphasis on the active working of the Spirit of God meant that Anabaptist "biblicism" always was mediated by the expectation that the Spirit would illuminate and provide the proper understanding of Scripture. Thus although the Anabaptists accepted the "scriptural principle" as a point of departure, it would be more accurate to say that in their view, divine authority needed to be based on *"Scripture and Spirit together,"* rather than the "Scripture alone" of Luther.

Hubmaier expressed this understanding in the following way: *"Leonhart*: How does God draw or call a person? *Hans*: In two forms, outwardly and inwardly. The outward drawing occurs through the public proclamation of his holy gospel... The inward drawing is this, that God also illuminates the person's soul inwardly, so that it understands the incontrovertible truth, convinced by the Spirit and the preached Word in such a way that one must in one's own conscience confess that this is the case and it cannot be otherwise." (362) It is here, in the Anabaptist connection between the Bible and the Spirit as the highest authorities, that we can speak of a necessary "spirit/letter" linkage as constitutive of shared Anabaptist belief. As we have seen above, this linkage was first articulated in the "evangelical" camp by radical reformers.

Soteriology

Although Anabaptists always maintained that believers are saved by grace through faith, the similarity to mainline Protestantism teaching was in this first step alone. For Hubmaier as for other Anabaptists, the faith that would lead to salvation was a faith that bore visible fruit in repentance, conversion, regeneration, obedience, and a new life dedicated to the love of God and the neighbour, by the power of the Holy Spirit (i.e., discipleship). Righteousness was not simply imputed to the sinner for Christ's sake, as Luther had maintained; but rather being saved meant *becoming righteous* by the power of the risen Christ.[9]

This understanding stood closer to the late medieval tradition by its denial of the radical depravity of all humankind and by its insistence on the essential and necessary unity of the inner life of the spirit with the outer life of obedience and discipleship. We must note here the essential Anabaptist linkage between the life of faith and the life of obedience, that is, between the inner and the outer lives of believers. And again, this soteriological emphasis on regeneration and obedience was not original to the Anabaptists, but was first articulated in an "evangelical" context by the radical reformers.

Faith and Works: Discipleship

The active working of the Spirit of God was the crucial first step without which there could be no "life of discipleship." The pneumatological strain in all of early Anabaptism points not only to the importance of the "spirit/letter" linkage for Anabaptists, but also to the necessary connection they made between the inner life of the spirit (faith, rebirth, regeneration) and the outer life of discipleship (obedience). This is seen clearly in Hubmaier's discussion of faith. Directly following his assertions concerning faith (cited above), "Leonhard" initiates the following dialogue: "How many kinds of faith are there? *Hans*: Two kinds, namely a dead one and a living one. *Leonhart*: What is a dead faith? *Hans*: One that is unfruitful and without the works of love, James 2:17. *Leonhart*: What is a living faith? *Hans*: One that produces the fruits of the Spirit and works through love, Gal. 5." (348) This "inner/outer" connection, basing discipleship on a "living faith," was also constitutive of the Anabaptist theological approach. It too was prefigured by the radical reformers.

Anthropology (The following two anthropological points can be seen as corollaries of the above Anabaptist emphases).

Gelassenheit.

Although the word "Gelassenheit" is not found in all Anabaptist testimonies, the reality indicated by that term is visible in the Anabaptist movement as a whole. The concept itself was central to Anabaptist theology and spirituality. Believers were called to yield inwardly to the Spirit of God, outwardly to the community and to outward discipline, and finally, in the face of a hostile world, believers could be called upon to give way before God's greater purposes by accepting a martyr's death. The necessary unity between the "inner life" of believers—believing, yielded to, and regenerated by the Spirit of God—and their "outer lives" of discipleship and community life (visible baptism, celebration of the Supper, community discipline, martyrdom), is seen here again.[10] The principle of "yieldedness" has roots in late medieval mysticism and piety, and was central to the radical reformers who diverged from Luther.

Doctrines of Sin and Free Will.

In order for human beings to be able to respond and yield to God's call in Christ to repentance and a new life, they must be free to respond. All Anabaptists held that human beings were made free (by God's grace) to accept, or not accept, the call of God in Christ. In this respect also, Anabaptist theology stands closer to late medieval teaching than it does to mainstream Protestantism, as reference to the debate between Luther and Erasmus on the freedom of the human will makes clear.

Hubmaier broached the subject of the free versus the bound will in his catechism, arguing that the human will was bound in sin following Adam's fall, but the fallen will was restored again through Christ "although captive in the sinful and poisoned body." (360) Hubmaier's point was that "the image or inbreathing of God is still in us all, although captive and as a live spark covered with cold ashes is still alive and will steam if heavenly water is poured on it." (360) Thus there is something of good in human beings, but which yet needs a further step in order to be truly good: "If we are now again to become free in the spirit and healthy in the soul ... then this must take place through a rebirth..." This rebirth takes place "by the word of his power in which we are really made whole and free again." (361) Thus the heavenly rebirth is a double gift of grace, first through Christ's sacrifice which restores the Adamic Fall, and then through the offer of rebirth to the sinner who is still captive. The sinner, however, is "free" to refuse this second grace, to condemnation, or accept it to salvation. Hubmaier elaborated his doctrine of the free will further in two later writings.[11]

While most Anabaptists did not discuss the fine points of the Fall, nor did any elaborate a theological anthropology as did Hubmaier, still all Anabaptists held to a doctrine of free will, while at the same time insisting that salvation was a gift of grace, not a payment for meritorious works. The basic logic of Hubmaier's position was repeated throughout the movement; the same basic logic had been argued by the radical reformers, over against Luther.

The Last Days

Most Anabaptists, like virtually all Christians in the sixteenth century, were convinced that they were living in the Last Days, and that Christ's return was imminent—although Hubmaier provides few examples of this.[12] A popular way of understanding what this might mean (with roots in the medieval Joachite tradition) was to conceive of the Last Days as that time in which Christ's Spirit would be poured out on humankind, resulting in dreams, visions and direct revelations just as it had been in the time of the Old Testament prophets. Likewise, a strong conviction that these were the Last Days led many Anabaptists to scrutinize the prophetic books of Scripture in order to discover there the "signs of the times."

As is well known, there were differences among the Anabaptists on the question of the genuineness of direct "revelations" such as dreams and visions, and a scriptural approach that attempted to discover the secrets of God's timetable in the biblical prophetic books. Nevertheless, it is important to note that because of the strong pneumatology that underlay Anabaptism as such, virtually *all* Anabaptists were open to some measure of the revelatory power of the Holy Spirit; and, because of the strong stress on the authority of Scripture, all Anabaptists took the biblical words of prophecy seriously as well. The differences that arose later in the movement can best be understood as differences of degree, not differences in kind, along a spirit/letter *continuum.* Anabaptist apocalyptic expectation, at one level at least, can be seen as a natural working out of the necessary conjunction of spirit and letter. But even more, Anabaptists saw themselves occupying a period in history that was radically new, that stood close to the end of all time.

Anabaptist Ecclesiology

The majority of the doctinal emphases noted above could be found outside the Anabaptist movement as well as within it, as for instance with Karlstadt and Müntzer. It is because of its ecclesiology that Anabaptism came to define a separate stream of reform, in distinction from the radical reformers, none of whom established separate churches on the basis of sacramental signs. It was adult baptism, above all, that set the Anabaptist movement apart as a visible and separate stream of radical reform. In Hubmaier's catechism, immediately following the discussion of faith comes the question "After faith what do you desire?" Hubmaier has Hans answer: "Water baptism." (349) For the Anabaptists, an individual response to God's call led immediately into community through water baptism.

The ecclesiological dimension was central to Anabaptist theology, particularly in the insistence that the church was to be the visible Body of Christ. For Hubmaier and other Anabaptists the biblical model of "Christian community" was the community of yielded, regenerated, faithful, baptized, committed and obedient believers—a "community of saints." The anchor of Anabaptist theology and spirituality was this community, formed first by the spiritual, and then the water baptism of believers, maintained by fraternal admonition, and nurtured by the Supper of the Lord (celebrated as a memorial and a pledge by those who had committed themselves to the church in baptism), by communal worship and visible expressions of love among the members of the body.

At least four marks of this "visible community of saints" can be identified as universally Anabaptist: baptism, the ban, the Supper, and mutual aid. The first three of these also were elaborated in a programatic way in the first three of the Schleitheim Articles of 1527.

Water Baptism

The inner call of God's Spirit, or the "baptism of the Spirit" as Hubmaier called it, demanded an outward and visible response from those who had been inwardly called and who had freely accepted the call. It was by public water baptism that one confessed one's sins before the congregation of God's people, testified to one's faith in the forgiveness of sins through Christ, and was incorporated into the fellowship of the church, accepting the fraternal responsibilities that went along with membership in the church. (349) Water baptism signified that the inner yieldedness to Christ had already taken place (the water was the "covenant of a good conscience"); it signified that the believer was now yielding to the Body of Christ on earth (the church); and it signified a willingness to suffer all for Christ and the brother and sister. Baptism meant moving from "the world" to "the Body of Christ," the church.[13]

Although it is true that the term "Anabaptist" was used to denigrate the movement by its opponents, and also that the Anabaptists themselves preferred to be called by the term "Brethren," nevertheless contemporary critics of the movement were close to the mark when they emphasized baptism on confession of faith as a central teaching by which to identify the Brethren. If the Brethren had been content to emphasize the baptism of the Spirit, and had abandoned the outer baptism of water there would have been no "Anabaptist movement." The "spiritualizing" solution of suspending the outer sign remained a temptation for Anabaptists in the sixteenth century, as we will see below. Nevertheless, it was the stubborn maintenance of the outward pledge of baptism in water to God and the church that formed a significant visible ecclesiological boundary for all so called Anabaptists.

Why, if the water contained no saving power as water, did the Brethren continue to insist on water baptism? The answer is not simply that they were being true to the biblical command to believe and be baptised, in that order—although this was the most common answer given by Anabaptists questioned in prison. Just as fundamentally, water baptism was a pledge, promise, or vow to the believing community, the true church of believers, on which pledge the subsequent Christian life was based. Water baptism was the outer mark of an inner change; the baptized church was then the visible gathering of the inwardly regenerated. The "obedience of faith" required not simply inward assent to the Spirit, but also an outward witness and commitment to a regenerated life *in community* with others who also had made the same pledge. In this way the visible church, the true church, the Body of Christ on earth, was built on the basis of outward signs of an inner change. The Anabaptist movement became a "movement" because of a conviction that the inner and the outer realities could not be separated or severed from one another.

The Ban

For Hubmaier and the Anabaptists generally, the reform of the church would never be complete until members of the church committed themselves to that church freely and consciously, and by their public baptism also committed themselves to the discipline of the community. In his catechism Hubmaier stated that through baptism one

> publicly and orally vows to God and agrees in the strength of God the Father, Son, and Holy Spirit that he will henceforth believe and live according to his divine Word. And if he should trespass herein he will accept brotherly admonition, according to Christ's order, Matt. 18:15ff. (349)

The church not only had the power to discipline, admonish, and correct; Christ had given it the power to bind and to loose, on earth and in heaven. The extreme of discipline—excommunication—was to be performed only for "refusal to be reconciled to the brother or to desist from sin." (353) Ideally, of course, the aim was not to exclude, but to win back the sinner and be able to accept such a person back "with joy, as the father did his prodigal son..." (354)

In order for such community discipline to function, there had to be a prior theological understanding that one's outer life closely reflects the state of one's inner life. Furthermore, the "reform" of the outer life had to be seen as essential to a "healthy" inner life. If on the other hand saving faith is, in essence, known only to God and therefore invisible, the ban is not only unnecessary, it is the height of presumption. But if, as the Anabaptists believed, the inner and the outer lives are two sides of the same coin, so to speak (and the church is conceived as the Body of Christ on earth, with the power to bind and to loose, Matt. 18), then the ban becomes fundamental to the soteriological *and* the church reform processes. In many ways the ban in Anabaptism took the place of the Roman Catholic rite of confession and absolution, providing a context for the "loosing" of the penalty for sin by the church. Seen from another perspective, the Anabaptist ban was an answer to how the church might be reformed "in head and members."

The Supper

As noted above, for Hubmaier and all Anabaptists the Lord's Supper was understood as a memorial of Christ's death and sacrifice. But more concretely, Hubmaier says that the Lord's Supper is

> a public sign and testimonial of the love in which one brother obligates himself to another before the congregation that just as they now break and eat the bread with each other and share and drink the cup, likewise they wish now to sacrifice and shed their body and blood for one another..." (354)

The Supper, then, is "a sign of the obligation to brotherly love," which is pledged not on the strength of human will but "in the strength of our Lord Jesus Christ, whose suffering they are now commemorating in the Supper." (354-5) Just as water baptism testifies that one is serious about the demand to love God above all—that one has died to self and risen in Christ—so the Supper testifies to one's seriousness in loving the neighbour as oneself. This "horizontal" understanding of the Supper as a *response* and a *pledge* is typically Anabaptist.

Mutual Aid

From the start, membership in the Body of Christ meant ultimate allegiance to that body in economic, social and political matters. Within this Body of Christ a new life had begun, governed by the Spirit of Christ and modeled on the example of His life and that of the apostles. This meant that economic relationships within the church were no longer to proceed as they did "in the world." Likewise hierarchical relationships based on social class were challenged; submission to the "community of saints" had a "levelling" effect. We will see in section C.2 below how these initial Anabaptist convictions came into concrete expression in different groups, over time.

The emphasis on a *visible* church, which was understood to be a part of God's kingdom incarnate, underlined the importance of the "outward" elements of belief; baptism, the ban, the Supper, and renewed social and economic relationships served as signs and seals of that commitment to the visible "members of Christ's body." Thus the church and the world remained in a tension that was not present in quite the same way in the Protestant and Catholic churches. It was within the tension of this church/world polarity that the concrete working out of Anabaptist eschatology also would take shape.

Consequences of Faith: Suffering and Martyrdom

Anabaptists were not the only Christians to suffer persecution and martyrdom in the sixteenth century. Nevertheless, because of the near-universal condemnation of Anabaptism in western Europe, the movement soon faced more systematic persecution, with its accompanying physical suffering and martyrdom, than was the case for other Christian groups. Hubmaier reflected on that reality in this way: Following inward regeneration and the outward witness in water, the "baptism of blood" could be expected to take place. The phrase "baptism of blood" rightly evokes images of martyrdom; Hubmaier meant to evoke such images, for he insisted that suffering and persecution would necessarily be the lot of true believers. But it is important to note that when Hubmaier speaks of the baptism of blood he is not referring in the first instance to a martyr's death. He is speaking of the continuing path of yielding one's desires daily to the will of God. The "baptism of blood" is a daily practice in the discipline of obedience. Hubmaier clarified this point further in an earlier writing: "The flesh must daily be killed since it wants only to live and reign according to its own lusts. Here the Spirit of Christ prevails and gains the victory. Then the person brings forth good fruits which give testimony of a good tree. Day and night he practices all those things which concern the praise of God and brotherly love. By this the old Adam is martyred, killed, and carried to the grave. This is a summary and right order of a whole Christian life which begins in the Word of God."[14]

At the same time, the "baptism of blood" could be much more than simply a "mortification of the flesh," or an ascetic exercise—it could be a call to accept the

Torture of Geleyn the Shoemaker

fact that one's own blood would be shed. If a believer were called to witness to the truth by accepting death—as was Hubmaier himself—the way to the greatest test of faith and obedience would have been prepared by daily practice in the "third baptism," the "daily mortification of the flesh until death." (350) The existence of a deep and common theological rationale for the ultimate "outer testimony of the flesh" in suffering and martyrdom can easily be discerned in the records documenting the martyrdom of thousands of Anabaptists in all parts of Europe.

The "Shape" of Anabaptist Theology

Readers who recall the discussion in chapter 3 above may well be struck by the fundamental coincidences between the Radical Reformation positions of Karlstadt, Müntzer and Schwenckfeld, and the Anabaptist "doctrinal" positions described above. In fact, the basic "doctrinal shape" of Anabaptist theology was delineated by those radical reformers and mediated directly to significant leaders of the Anabaptist movement. The radical reformers provided an alternative interpretation of "evangelical reform" that clearly set key terms of reference also for the Anabaptist movement.

The emphasis of the radical reformers on the interpretive and regenerating activity of the Holy Spirit (efficacious grace) marked out a significant theological path also followed by the Anabaptists. It was this active pneumatology that called for a "life of discipleship"—an emphasis not original to the Anabaptists, but one that they did embrace heartily. Because of this efficacious grace, the radical reformers and the Anabaptists alike expected visible and external signs of the inner working of grace. They shared a vision of church reform based on regenerationist principles. The most significant point of coincidence between Karlstadt and Müntzer, on the one hand, and the Anabaptists on the other can be summarized as a common soteriological vision which took its point of departure from Luther's critique of Roman Catholic soteriology (Luther's salvation by grace through faith), but which rejected Luther's understanding of forensic justification and called instead for an inner/outer transformation and a process of sanctification of believers.

The anthropological insistence on freedom of the will also reappeared in Anabaptism, with a corresponding difference in how Anabaptists and mainline reformers would conceive of human participation in the matter of salvation. For the radical reformers and Anabaptists alike, God's grace frees human beings to choose either salvation or damnation. This principle was important from a church reforming perspective: believers were *responsible* for the lives they came to lead. Following Christ was a conscious choice, not a matter of predestination; believers willingly subjected themselves to discipline; the church thus was a visible community of saints.

In sum, Anabaptism was not so much "Protestantism taken to its proper ends" as it was *Radical* Protestantism taken some ecclesiological steps further. Seen from the Anabaptist perspective, the critique and alternative theological outline of the radical reformers provided a crucial transitional framework of theological reforming principles. What the Anabaptists elaborated further, on the basis of the radical evangelical critique, was an *ecclesiology* that set Anabaptism apart from reformers and radical reformers alike.

The radical reformers also had prepared the way for Anabaptist ecclesiological distinctives with their critique of infant baptism, their calls for church discipline, and their sacramentarian view of the Lord's Supper. But it was Anabaptism as such that came to insist that the only proper, biblical understanding of church reform was the establishment of freely chosen adult baptism on confession of faith, by which believers pledged themselves to community discipline and solidarity with the other members of the Body of Christ on earth.

Conclusion

The general doctrinal and ecclesiological principles enumerated in this chapter were universally held by "adult baptizers" in the sixteenth century, and so may be said to constitute the "theological and ecclesiological core" of the Anabaptist movement that can be seen taking shape from Switzerland to Moravia to Friesland. On this basis alone there is reason to retain the descriptive term "Anabaptist" for all of the "baptizing" groups, in spite of differing origins and regional and individual differences. It was this shared theological core that provided guidelines for Anabaptist communities as they attempted to put into practice and actualize their theological principles in their various historical situations. The Anabaptists themselves recognized that they were neither Roman Catholics *nor* "Evangelicals" (later called "Protestants"), but rather were "brethren" of yet another movement. The disagreements that took place subsequently between the Anabaptists themselves, while they were strongly held and often led to schism, nevertheless took place between people who agreed on the above essentials, even while they disagreed on the *implications* of these essentials for the life of faith.[15]

It must be said further that it is only when we look *within* the boundaries of this body of belief, *within* the limits of this field of agreement, that we can understand the development of Anabaptism over the course of the sixteenth century and into the seventeenth. The disagreements Anabaptists came to have with one another were hammered out on this common anvil of shared belief. The working out of those differences led eventually to "denominational" expressions of Anabaptism.

We may, in conclusion, note a few features of the "theological and ecclesiological core" of early Anabaptism, outlined above, that have not received sufficient emphasis in previous delineations. The most important of these is Anabaptist pneumatology. There was, after all, some justice in Karl Holl's contention (against Ernst Troeltsch) that "Above all the Anabaptists placed the weight on the 'Spirit,' in contrast with mere learning and a literal understanding."[16] Although Holl wished to connect all "Anabaptists" with Thomas Müntzer (and in this was mistaken), nevertheless he made a valid point: Without its strong pneumatic base, Anabaptism would have been a far different movement—or most probably, no "movement" at all. The work of the Spirit provided the essential underpinning for biblical interpretation, for conversion and rebirth leading to baptism, and for discipleship (as the enabling power which made discipleship possible). Anabaptist ethics and ecclesiology rested on the living presence of the Spirit.

It is also important to note what is *not* present in the outline presented above. If the Schleitheim Articles are taken as one of the earliest delineations of Anabaptist distinctives, we must note that only the first three articles (out of Schleitheim's seven) can be said to apply to Anabaptism as a whole at this early stage. Only Schleitheim's articles concerning baptism, the ban, and the Supper can be said to be universally "Anabaptist."[17] "Separation from the world," enjoined in Schleitheim's article 4, was being settled in the Swiss context by 1527, but the relationship between church, the world, and government was still being worked out in the South German and North German/Dutch movements until well into the last half of the sixteenth century. Schleitheim's injunctions against sword bearing and oath taking (articles 6 and 7) remained contentious issues in those contexts. We will document some of the discussion and disagreement among the Anabaptist groups on these questions below, when we examine "Anabaptism and Political Reality" in some detail. Likewise the recommendations for the election of pastors from the congregation (article 5 of Schleitheim) were not universally accepted, and in fact were ignored altogether in the Melchiorite stream.

In spite of the fact that the Schleitheim Articles, then, do not qualify as a pan-Anabaptist "confession of faith," nevertheless we see in early Anabaptism a movement with significant internal theological agreement and coherence. The shape of that "theological forest" was first outlined by the radical reformers, Karlstadt and Müntzer. Building on this common "radical reforming" approach to scriptural and pneumatological church reform, the Anabaptist movement established a new branch of radical reform because of its insistence on the ecclesiologically distinctive signs of adult baptism, the ban, a memorial Supper closed to all who had not taken the previous two steps of commitment, all of which was to lead to new social and economic relationships. Nevertheless, Anabaptist *ecclesiology* did not arrive complete and full-blown with believers' baptism, the ban, a closed Supper, and mutual aid. In early stages of its development Anabaptists could and did overlook numerous ethical and ecclesiological implications of their shared convictions which later would become divisive issues. In other words, in spite of the "theological core" at the heart of the movement, identifying the broadest of shared boundaries tells only the beginning part of the Anabaptist story.

The full Anabaptist story must be told within a framework that highlights not only diverse historical origins, but also deeply significant commonalities, differing rates of community self-definition within different regions (with attention being paid to the inevitable pressures of social, political and economic realities in those regions), the fluidity of movement between various Anabaptist groups during the various developmental phases, and the significance of cross fertilization, as ideas from various Anabaptist currents came into dialogue. It is this complex of "intramural" conversations that stands behind the development of an Anabaptist theological and ecclesiological *tradition*.

Perhaps in light of the evolutionary historical development of Anabaptism it would be best to say that what is needed is a "recovery of Anabaptist conversations," rather than a "recovery of *the* Anabaptist Vision." Of course, conversations about faith essentials are going on at present among the Believers' Church descendants of the Anabaptists; they have been going on non-stop since the sixteenth century.[18] My proposal as a Believers' Church historian is simply to suggest that the dialogue that shaped this faith tradition be allowed to inform contemporary Believers' Church conversations. There is much food for thought not only in the "origins" of Anabaptism, nor only in the eventual "traditions" that emerged, but perhaps especially in the "developmental" period in between. The author's own ideas about what would constitute the parameters of a fruitful contemporary "conversation" for Believers' Churches will become evident throughout, and will be made explicit in the concluding chapter. It bears repeating that the author's views are not being put forward as the "normative" way of reading Anabaptist history, of reading the Bible, or of engaging in present conversations. It is the author's hope that the views expressed here will be read as invitations to dialogue, and not as attempts at imposing one point of view.

Historically speaking, it was only at the end of the dynamic period of development that the rigid definition of boundaries for Anabaptist groups emerged. In spite of historical commonalities of belief and shared experiences of persecution and martyrdom, nevertheless the surviving Anabaptist communities came to the conclusion that salvation was to be denied even to the Anabaptist "brethren" outside their own groups. When we reach this final stage we have in a significant way reached the end of the "Anabaptist" story. It is at this point that we begin to tell the stories of the groups we call Swiss Brethren, Hutterites, and Mennonites.

End Notes

[1] All references are taken from the translation in H. Wayne Pipkin and John H. Yoder, trans. and eds., *Balthasar Hubmaier: Theologian of Anabaptism* (Scottdale, Pa.: Herald Press, 1989), 339-365. Subsequent page references will be identified within brackets in the text.

[2] See Jörg Maler's assertion in TA, Ostschweiz, #323, 238. For an early testimony from Switzerland, see QGTS, zu., pp. 161-2. The "articles of the faith" are exposited in the *Ausbund*, the Swiss Brethren hymnal (hymn 2 is a versification of the Creed). The most notable "Swiss" example of a confession built upon the credal pattern is Balthasar Hubmaier's "The Twelve Articles of Christian Faith," Pipkin/Yoder, 234-44, written in 1527; Leonard Schiemer exposited the Apostle's Creed in a letter to the congregation at Rattenberg, printed in Lydia Müller, *Glaubenszeugnisse oberdeutscher Taufgesinnter* (Leipzig: Heinius Nachfolger, 1938; reprint by Johnson Reprint Corp., 1971), pp. 44-58. For two later Hutterite examples, see Jeronimus Käls' exposition (1536) in Müller, *Glaubenszeugnisse*, pp. 205-10, and Peter Riedemann, *Account of Our Religion, Doctrine and Faith* (London: Hodder and Stoughton, 1950), written in 1542. In the Hessian context, Tasch's "Confession of Faith" of 1538 included the simple acceptance of the "twelve articles of the Christian faith." TA, *Hesse*, 255, art. VI. See also the later Swiss Brethren confession from Hesse in Theodor Sippell, ed., "Confession of the Swiss Brethren in Hesse, 1578," MQR 23 (Jan., 1949), 22-34; full text in TA, *Hesse*, 404-440. Jörg Maler wrote a confession based on the Apostles' creed (see the *Kunstbuch*, number 40) with the title "Ein bekanntnuss des gloubens, mach vermoeg heiliger gschrift zamengstelt..." TA, Ostschweiz, #599, 493. Menno did not exposit the Creed, but did paraphrase parts of the Creed in "A Brief Confession on the Incarnation," (1544), in CWMS, p. 428. In replying to Gellius Faber Menno said "I trust also that we ... agree not only as to the twelve articles ... but also as to all the articles of the Scriptures..." J.C. Wenger, ed., *The Complete Writings of Menno Simons*, (Scottdale, Pa.: Herald Press, 1956), p. 761. See Keeney, *Dutch*, p. 39. On the Creed generally, see also the discussion in Friedmann, *Theology*, 53-55.

[3] The best treatment is by Willimas. See *Radical*, chs. 11.2, 19.2c, 23.5, 28, 29, *et passim*.

[4] Later in his Catechism, Hubmaier inserts the following: "*Leonhart*: Which of the articles of the creed deal with baptism? *Hans*: The ninth and tenth articles, where we confess the universal Christian church, the fellowship of the saints and forgiveness of sins, just as the Lord's Supper is also included there." (351).

[5] On the development of Anabaptist/Mennonite confessions of faith, see C. J. Dyck, "The First Waterlandian Confession of Faith," MQR 36 (Jan., 1962), pp. 5-13; *idem*., "The Middelburg Confession of Hans de Ries, 1578," MQR 36 (Apr., 1962), pp. 147-161; *idem*., "A Short Confession of Faith by Hans de Ries," MQR 38 (Jan., 1964), pp. 5-19; James R. Coggins, "A Short Confession of Hans de Ries: Union and Separation in Early Seventeenth Century Holland," MQR 60(April, 1986), pp. 128-138. Also, Howard John Loewen, *One Lord, One Church, One Hope, and One God: Mennonite Confessions of Faith*, (Elkhart, IN: Institute of Mennonite Studies, 1985).

[6] Rempel, *Lord's Supper*, p. 96; on p. 109, Rempel notes Blough's contribution to this observation.

[7] On Anabaptist anticlericalism see especially Hans-Jürgen Goertz, *Die Täufer: Geschichte und Deutung* (Munich: C.H. Beck, 1980), pp. 40-76; *idem.*, *Pfaffenhass und gross Geschrei: Die reformatorischen Bewegungen in Deutschland, 1517-1529* (Munich: C. H. Beck, 1987), pp. 195-211. Note also the comments in Klaassen, *End of the Ages*, pp. 57-59; 62-65.

[8] "The whole Anabaptist movement believed itself to be under the immediate inspiration of God." Klaassen, *End of the Ages*, p. 101. On this theme, see especially pp. 95-105.

[9] Hubmaier's critique is clear in his preface to his "Freedom of the Will," written in 1527: "I ... find many people who to this point have learned and grasped no more than two pieces from all the preaching. First, one says: 'We believe; faith saves us.' Second, 'We can do nothing good. God works in us the desire and the doing. We have no free will.' Now, however, such remarks are only half-truths from which one can conclude no more than half-judgements." (427-28).

[10] In his 1525 writing, the "Summa of the Entire Christian Life," (Pipkin/Yoder, 81-89), Hubmaier notes that after repentance and belief "the sinner is enlivened again, comes to himself, becomes joyful, and henceforth surrenders himself entirely to the physician." (84). This "inward surrender" of the heart (85) is followed by an outward commitment in baptism to the church, "that he has surrendered himself already to live henceforth according to the Word, will, and rule of Christ..." (85). Later in this writing Hubmaier made an explicit connection between the Supper and the love of neighbour: "The person who practices the Supper of Christ in that way and contemplates the suffering of Christ in a firm faith will also give thanks to God for this grace and goodness. He will surrender himself to the will of Christ, which then is that we also should do to our neighbor as he has done to us and give our body, life, property, and blood for his sake." (88).

[11] See Pipkin and Yoder, *Hubmaier*, pp. 426-491.

[12] See especially Klaassen, *End of the Ages*. In his catechism Hubmaier limits himself to speaking generally about judgement day (pp. 363-4), with no particular anticipation that it was near at hand.

[13] The basic scriptural arguments for the baptism of believers were present already in Zürich in 1525, but they were elaborated most clearly by Hubmaier in what is probably his best piece of writing, "On the Christian Baptism of Believers." Pipkin and Yoder, *Hubmaier*, pp. 95-149.

[14] From "On the Christian Baptism of Believers," Pipkin and Yoder, *Hubmaier*, p. 147.

[15] The Anabaptist propensity for schism may be explained in part by the fact that Anabaptism was defined not so much its unique dogmatic or doctrinal content, but by the "life of obedience." Agreement is often easier to achieve at the level of "principle" than at the level of "practice."

[16] Karl Holl, "Luther und die Schwärmer," 1922, in *Gesammelte Aufsätze zur Kirchengeschichte*, I, (Tübingen: Mohr, 1948), p. 424, n. 1. James Stayer recently also emphasized this point in "The 'Radical Reformation' as 'Theology' and as 'History,'" paper read at the Anabaptist Colloquium, Conrad Grebel College, April 16, 1994.

[17] In contrast to Harold Bender's contention that Schleitheim "does, however, set forth seven major points on which the Anabaptists differed from the rest of Christendom, both Catholic and Protestant, and which remained characteristic Anabaptist emphases: baptism, ban, Lord's Supper, separation from evil, pastors, sword, oath." Harold Bender, Review of B. Jenny, *Das Schleitheimer Täuferbekenntnis* (Thayngen, 1951), in ARG 47 (1956), p. 136.

[18] Thanks to Shirley Showalter for her helpful observations on these questions.

Etliche schöne

Christliche Geseng/ wie sie
in der Gefengkniß zu Paſſaw im
Schloß von den Schweitzer Brüdern
durch Gottes gned gericht vnd geſun-
gen worden.

Pſalm. 139.

Die Stolgen haben mir ſtrick gelegt/Das garn haben
ſie mir auß ſulen auffgeſponnen / vnd dazen geben ſolt/
haben ſie mir Fallen zugeruſtet/Darumb ſprich ich zum
HERREN: Du biſt mein Gott ꝛc.

M. D. LXIIIL

Title page from the earliest Swiss Brethren hymnal,
the *Ausbund* (1564)

Chapter 7

The Communication of Anabaptist Ideas

Communication has been defined as an interaction that takes place between persons, utilizing verbal and nonverbal symbols, usually aimed at influencing the behaviour of others.[1] A study of communication processes was some time ago condensed into the formula: "Who says what in what channel to whom with what effect?"[2] The formula is a useful guide, particularly if we make clear that our interest is not in the "mundane" communication of daily life, but rather in the communication that aims to persuade. Persuasive communication is closely related to power. The more one is able to control the messenger, the message and the media (the who, the what, and the channels), the more influence one can wield over the recipients of the message (the effects upon whom).

The debate over whether the Reformation is to be considered "medieval" or "modern" has preoccupied historians for some time. The debate remains equally intense when communication becomes the focus. It is seemingly an undeniable fact that the Reformation was made possible by the widespread and ingenious use of Gutenberg's invention—the first application of modern mass communication. On the other hand, older and more traditional forms of communication did not suddenly and miraculously disappear because of the invention of movable type. The "oral/aural" communication systems were at least as crucial as was print in the communication of the original reform message to the *masses* of people, the vast majority of whom could not read the newly-printed pamphlets, broadsheets and vernacular Bibles. In the sixteenth century, ideas were being spread in the final instance primarily in nonliterate ways, even if writing and print were undeniably crucial intermediate steps in the rapid diffusion of new ideas.[3] The masses of people still were stirred by popular preachers, excited by the "news" read aloud from broadsheets at the market, informed and entertained by "news songs" (and slanderous ditties) sung in taverns, and introduced to new ideas by radical craftspeople in their places of work. And, rather than being read in silence, Reformation texts (and vernacular Bibles) also were most commonly read aloud to listeners; there is evidence that many Reformation pamphlets were deliberately composed with such oral performances in mind.[4] In other words, as Robert Scribner notes, in the sixteenth century, "even the printed word was most often mediated by the spoken word."[5]

Social conflict was sharpened by the evangelical reform because the Bible was cited as the source of ultimate authority. This was a brilliant way of undermining the interpretive privileges of the old guard, but the mass verbalizing, hearing, and interpreting of the Bible in the vernacular could not help but sharpen social and political conflict. The revolutionary nature of the appeal to "Scripture alone" in a predominantly oral culture was intensified by one further, crucial Reformation slogan: all Christians are in fact priests. From this affirmation one could deduce the right—even the duty—to interpret Scripture for oneself.

Particularly crucial in bringing together "Scripture alone" and the "priesthood of all believers" for the illiterate majority were the vernacularly literate, but not learned, commoners. Clerical and upper-class "literacy" in the sixteenth century remained the preserve of those who had had access to a Latin school and university education; such people were to be found in important pulpits and council chambers in the cities. But the commoner who had attained some measure of literacy in a vernacular tongue quite naturally related to the oral world of the lower classes, and exercised his or her literacy in that social context—among the craftspeople in the cities and villages and the peasants in the countryside. Thanks to print, vernacular reforming texts and Bibles could be bought and read aloud, and in this process the "literate" commoners played a crucial mediating role in bringing new ideas to, and promoting radical dissent among the people at the grass roots.

An early print shop

The contested nature of the "Word" in the sixteenth century reform, particularly between Radical Reformation interpreters and Mainline Reformers, often centred on the question of the nature of the True Word: was the True Word a written Word, or a spiritual Word? Appeals to the higher authority of the Spirit over the letter were impossibly egalitarian: those who had the Spirit, some said, could well claim to have access to the "Word" *even without being able to read the letter.* By hearing the "letter" of Scripture read aloud, remembering central passages, and living in accordance with its prescriptions, even the illiterate or semi-literate could claim to be true interpreters of the Word. Even further, truly "yielded" and spiritual people may well receive a direct Word from God in dreams or visions, and clearly literacy played no role in this. Thus the struggle over the nature of the Word in some cases reflected a very deep societal struggle between those in possession of the skill of learned literacy, who "owned" the traditional rights of interpretation of the Book, and those without the skill of letters (or with a mere vernacular literacy) who claimed a spiritual right to interpret the Book.[6]

Examining the communication processes at work in the Reformation is revealing, particularly for the light it sheds on the emergence and survival of a dissident grass roots reforming movement such as Anabaptism.[7] Looked at from a communications point of view we can see two distinct stages in the reform process we have outlined to this point. The first stage corresponds to the broad "evangelical" reforming movement that focussed its collective energies against Rome from 1517 to ca. 1525. At this initial stage the reformers happily utilized all available channels of communication, formal and informal, to convince political authorities to adopt a Reformation programme; part of the early strategy was to involve all levels of society in pressuring governments to reform; vernacular print communication as well as popular preaching played central roles here. The second phase in this process emerged when key reformers made alliances with the politically powerful, and gained control of the official communications channels—the church pulpits and the local presses. The broad "evangelical" coalition had begun to unravel already by 1521, when some reformers chose to remain with the papacy following Luther's excommunication. By 1522, as we have noted in the cases of Andreas Karlstadt and Thomas Müntzer, serious evangelical dissent also had emerged; by 1525 and the failure of the Peasants' War, the cleavage between the official or "magisterial" reform movements and the dissident grass roots movements was undeniable.

As we have seen, Anabaptism grew out of the general Reformation protest of the first phase, but more specifically, Anabaptism's roots lie firmly in the radical evangelical protest movement. The first adult baptisms in Zürich took place just as the Peasants' War erupted, and owed crucial ideological debts to the radical reformers, Andreas Karlstadt and Thomas Müntzer. But as soon as the peasants' movement collapsed the Anabaptists also found themselves (with rare exceptions) on the margins of power, limited for the most part to the informal, oral/aural channels of communication. As we will see, this did not mean that evangelization and the preservation of a theological tradition could not take place. To the contrary, Anabaptists utilized traditional, medieval communications systems very effectively indeed.

At this point we may identify the emergence of a third stage in the Reformation communication process. The consolidation of the Reformation was synonymous, in the sixteenth century, with the progressive elimination of religious dissent. An alliance of reforming clergy with political power, and control of the "official" channels of communication, were huge advantages in achieving religious and political hegemony in a given territory. But sixteenth century society—especially in the rural districts and villages, but also in the cities—still relied heavily on the traditional oral/aural means of communication. Locked out of the official channels of communication, the Anabaptists naturally continued to utilize the oral/aural channels of communication to proselytize and win adherents. What shaped up in some territories, then, was a virtual propaganda war to win the hearts and minds of the people. Urban/rural tensions played a role here, for the political consolidation of reform was a process of extending influence out to the peripheries from the urban centres of power. Once reformers and governments had won the battle for the official channels of communication in the cities, they continued to worry that they might lose the war because alternative and hostile communication was undermining them at the grass roots and in the countryside.[8] With very rare exceptions, the spread and development of Anabaptism throughout the sixteenth century took place under these latter conditions.

Anabaptist Communication and Evangelization

Events in Zürich provide an example of the way in which early reform encouraged proclamation, reading, and study of the Bible, followed by the progressive alienation and attempt to silence dissidents, culminating in the death penalty for disobedience.[9] The process that took place in Zürich was repeated (although not exactly) in several urban centres in the 1520s. St. Gall comes to mind, as do Nuremberg, Bern, Augsburg, and Strasbourg.[10] In territories that remained Catholic, of course, Anabaptism had been outlawed from the start, along with all other forms of evangelical reform.

The political marginalization of Anabaptism was matched by the limitation of communication possibilities. By 1530—and in most territories well before this date—Anabaptist evangelization took place of necessity in a clandestine, informal, oral/aural mode. On the one hand this posed difficulties, for Anabaptists were forced to live and travel in secret; they had little access to printing presses and even less to pulpits. All the same, the majority of Anabaptist members and leaders after 1527 were drawn from the working classes, and communication among the lower social order still was operating in a predominantly "medieval," communal, and oral/aural mode.[11] The fact that the Anabaptists often were mobile craftspeople and were operating in their own social milieu gave them an advantage over the learned and the powerful who often were viewed with suspicion by those in the lower social order.

If we return to the formulaic question posed earlier, namely "Who says what in what channel to whom with what effect?" we already can sketch a preliminary answer for the majority of Anabaptists throughout most of the sixteenth century. Persons drawn primarily from the lower social order called upon others (primarily from the same social order) to repent, be reborn, accept water baptism and church discipline, and henceforth to live regenerated lives unto death, even though they would be persecuted by "the world." The channel of communication was predominantly oral/aural, and the aim was the conversion of the hearers and their joining the "saints of God," "the elect," the "Body of Christ on earth" through water baptism. In what follows we will try to convey an impression of some of the ways in which this Anabaptist evangelization took place; the evidence is drawn from the court records of the time.

Evangelization in Daily Life

Anabaptist evangelization most often took place in the midst of the common round of daily activities. The first to be evangelized were kinship groups and friendship circles. The workplace often seems to have functioned as an informal "Bible school." Crafts such as weaving and spinning, for instance, often were carried out in large common rooms with a group of people present and occupied. Anabaptist evangelists thus had a good "cover" for their religious activities; Anabaptist women also proselytized and taught in such settings.

Jacob Groß, the travelling furrier and evangelist from Waldshut, was arrested early in 1526 in Aarau while present with a group of people who were "spinning and working" together in a large room. The authorities claimed, with some reason it appears, that these people were having an illegal religious gathering. Groß's defender claimed that it was no such a thing "since there was no reading or singing, either by the men or the women." But it turned out on further examination that Groß had celebrated the Lord's Supper with some of these people, and also had baptized one person, whether at the "workplace" or elsewhere is not said in the record. It is clear that Groß was doing more than just "spinning and working."[12]

Some crafts and vocations lent themselves extremely well to itinerant evangelism. Hans Hut, for example, was a travelling book salesman who was on the road constantly, and also constantly in conversation with people; his profession lent itself to evangelism and he applied himself to the task. His followers likewise were constantly on the move, evangelizing as they went. It is no surprise that some of the liveliest accounts of early Anabaptist evangelism come from the South German movement. Hut's predictions concerning the imminent return of Christ lent a special urgency to early South German Anabaptist proselytizing. Many who were baptized by Hut took to the road immediately on evangelistic missions and baptized many converts after only the most rudimentary instruction; time was short, they believed. The historical records have preserved interesting accounts of some of these encounters that provide us a glimpse into this early evangelistic activity.

Heinz Kestener of Schwerstedt was arrested in December of 1527 on suspicion of being an Anabaptist. In his testimony he described his meeting with three of Hut's "apostles." Heinz had taken onions to a neighbouring town, he said, and on his return trip he met three men walking on the road. They walked together and "talked about many things." As they were about to part company, one of the men asked his name and asked further if they could stay with him on their return. He agreed, and two weeks later they appeared in the evening. This time they told him that they were sent of God and that the world would end in eleven months. Then they spoke of the Word of God and the Holy Gospel, and finally one of them asked Heinz what he believed concerning baptism. Heinz was not interested in rebaptism, he said, and they all went to bed. The next day they left, warning about the cataclysm to come and blessing him as they departed.[13] In this case the chance encounter on the road did not lead to a baptism; in fact the men told Heinz that they had preached four days in a neighbouring town, but had not baptized anyone.

Anstad Kemmerer of Halle reported in detail about his meeting with some of Hut's followers and his subsequent baptism. He was away from home, having breakfast with a friend, when he noticed a short man going about here and there in the room; this man finally sat next to him and read from a book. The little man (*mennelein*) then asked him what he believed about baptism, and initiated a conversation on the subject. As Anstad remembered it, the small man read from the book of Jeremiah (?) about baptism and then told Anstad that there were those who had been chosen by

God to gain salvation by this baptism; furthermore, he told Anstad that he knew who the elect were and that there was very little time left for the elect to come to God. Those who received this baptism were not to worry about food, drink or clothing for there was enough for everyone; he then offered to include Anstad in the number of the elect through baptism. Anstad said that in view of the short time left, he did not want to run away from God's grace and so he requested baptism. This was done forthwith: someone brought a "little mustard pot" of pure water, and in the presence of three or more men and the same number of women (people Anstad did not know), they read from books that they carried, they prayed, and then asked him to kneel. Anstad did, and recited the Creed out loud, after which they poured water on him and made the sign of the cross on his forehead. Then they admonished him to be faithful, to treat others in the fellowship kindly, and not to be involved with usury. They told him further that the Lord would return in eleven months, that there were some 16,000 already in the company of the elect including "great and honourable people, margraves and others." Anstad, however, soon fell into doubt, repented of his baptism and returned to his old faith.[14] In some regions Hut's apostles, intent as they were on "sealing the 144,000 elect" with the sign of TAU (the cross on the forehead), were less concerned than were the Swiss and later South Germans with establishing communities. Time was short.

One of Hut's apostles, Hans Nadler, has left a fascinating record of his evangelistic method.[15] Nadler's profession also lent itself to itinerant evangelism: he made his living selling needles to cobblers and tailors in various cities. He was on the move constantly, he met very many people and, as he said, "whenever he met good-hearted persons in inns or on the street during his travels, he would give instruction from the Word of God."[16] This testimony is all the more remarkable because Nadler was illiterate; nevertheless, this handicap did not stop him from being able to defend himself with Scripture in debate, nor did it stop him from persuading people to join the Anabaptist movement.

After his arrest Nadler provided a detailed description of his *modus operandi*. Once he had struck up a conversation with someone he would begin "teaching" with a series of statements about the heavy consequences of faith, inquiring whether the hearer was disposed to suffer persecution and loss, and to "abstain from the joys of the world." If the hearer answered affirmatively, Nadler said, then he would outline what the hearer had to do to enter the Kingdom of God: "Yes, my brother or sister, you must receive the Word of God like a child and must be born anew," which Nadler then would proceed to demonstrate by citing various passages of Scripture on the subject which he had memorized in concordance-fashion. Secondly, Nadler warned that "as a new child of God, you must submit to the will of God and give your body as a sacrifice to God." In the third place, Nadler warned that "the world will hate you and be opposed to you—which you must suffer patiently."[17] If the hearer had not changed his or her mind after all of this, then Nadler proceeded to the "teaching," which consisted of an exposition of the Lord's Prayer. In a simple way which unlettered hearers could easily remember, Nadler reinterpreted for his listeners what each phrase of the prayer meant in an Anabaptist sense. After this followed a simple exposition of the Creed.

Nadler's personal, direct and simple approach seems to have been the norm in Anabaptist evangelization of people who were not part of one's own circle of friends and family. Notable in Nadler's method was the way that it was geared to the unlettered. The Lord's Prayer was known by virtually everyone; on this well-known structure Nadler built his Anabaptist teaching. Such memory aids were important in the evangelization of people who relied on memory rather than writing.

Preserving the Faith within the Group

It would seem to be the case that the oral/aural medium was well suited to evangelization, but not so well suited to the preservation of a "tradition" over several generations. The Anabaptists utilized a variety of means to overcome this difficulty, and to pass on their faith tradition to subsequent generations.

In the first place, given the importance of the Bible to their tradition, Anabaptist teaching subsequent to conversion and baptism seems to have consisted primarily in the teaching of key Bible passages that supported central Anabaptist teachings. This "concordance" approach to Anabaptist doctrine is evident in testimony after testimony in the court records, in which literate and illiterate Anabaptists alike cite virtually the same passages to defend adult baptism, the ban, etc. Many of the "booklets" carried by Anabaptist leaders, sometimes referred to in Anabaptist testimonies, were in fact small concordances—Hans Hut always carried one. Some of these concordances eventually got into print; they read almost like Anabaptist testimonies, minus the connecting sentences and phrases. Or said the other way, Anabaptist writings and testimonies most often read like prose concordances. More than one inquisitor was astounded by the "biblical knowledge" of "the simple" Anabaptists, including the illiterate, women, and peasants. Part of the explanation for this phenomenon was the "topical" approach to Scripture which made it possible for the unlettered and uneducated to remember impressive amounts of Scripture. The mnemonic structure was provided by the central Anabaptist theological "topics": baptism, ban, Supper, discipleship, suffering, martyrdom, apostasy, etc. Continuing biblical education easily added further passages and topics as time and opportunity permitted.

In the second place, the importance of song as a carrier and communicator of Anabaptist teaching has not been properly appreciated. The composition and singing of songs was a part of daily life in the sixteenth century. The Anabaptists applied the common sixteenth century tavern technique of composing rhyme to be sung to popular tunes—except that their rhymes encapsulated central Anabaptist teachings, kept alive the stories of Anabaptist martyrs, and taught such things as the Creed and the Lord's Prayer. Eventually these songs also were written down and eventually some of them were printed. The best known of these is the *Ausbund*, which was one of the first song collections to be printed (1564) and which still functions as a hymnal among the Old Order Amish in North America.[18]

In the third place, the Anabaptists composed a certain number of writings for edification, clarification and defense. In some cases we know of several manuscript copies of the same writing that have survived in archives, never having been printed. The multiple manuscript copies that survive indicate that these writings were considered important by the Anabaptists, copied by hand, and circulated in the communities. The production of manuscripts and codices was a natural technological alternative to print, which was expensive and out of reach in any case in the earlier years of the movement. Copying by hand was an older technique that served a small underground church perfectly well; there are many instances of earlier Anabaptist printed works being copied by hand, in whole or in part. In time some of these writings also were brought to print; others were not.[19] But communication by handwritten epistle, confessions, accounts of martyrdom, and exhortation was common among the early Anabaptists, whose leaders at least generally were literate in the vernacular. It was with this combination of topical biblical teaching, oral communication, musical composition, manuscript production, and print that Anabaptist teachings were preserved and passed on within the group itself.

An Underground Church in Augsburg, 1527-1528[20]

Events in Augsburg will be recounted in the following chapter; here we will outline the way in which the Anabaptists organized their fellowship in that city in 1527 and 1528. This sketch is possible because of the relatively rich records available in Augsburg for this period. John Oyer's study illustrates the way in which informal communication networks operated, making use of men and women in various social positions; notable is the prominent role of women (often hidden from view in other documentation). Although Anabaptist women did not usually preach publicly or baptize, they were crucial to the functioning of the "underground church" that operated in the city. The Anabaptist congregation in Augsburg was a large and thriving congregation by September of 1527, at the time of the first mass arrests in the city. Between that time and the second crackdown in April of 1528 Anabaptist women helped hold the movement together through a variety of covert activities.

Several women in Augsburg were instrumental in housing Anabaptists and hosting meetings. Susanna Doucher, wife of a prominent sculptor, testified to having been baptized in 1527 and to having attended several secret Anabaptist meetings, one of them in a forest outside the city walls. In spite of her husband's opposition, it turned out that she had housed and fed Anabaptist refugees and had contributed money and goods to the common Anabaptist treasury. Scolastica Stierpaur also came from the upper ranks of Augsburg society; her husband was the diplomat Crispin Stierpaur, who also joined the Anabaptists. Several Anabaptist ministers found lodging at their house, as did other Anabaptists, and several meetings were held there as well. She reported that "only" three people had been baptized in her house, including the grocer-woman Els Hegenmiller. Dorothea Frölich also was prominent among the Augsburg Anabaptists, present at many meetings and generous to the needy; she hosted and fed Anabaptists in her home.

At the other end of the social spectrum stood Katharina Wiedenmann, whose house was "almost constantly open to Anabaptist visitors." Katharina's husband Simprecht was a cobbler by trade; their shop and home became "a veritable center of clandestine Anabaptist activity," with people coming and going under the guise of having their shoes repaired. Many women also came together there to sew and "assemble around the distaff"—one of several subversive "sewing circles" that have come to light. Of course, under questioning both Katharina and her husband tried to make all this sound as innocent as possible, but besides providing a frequent meeting place, the Wiedenmann home also was an alms distribution centre—Simprecht had been elected one of the deacons or "purse keepers" for the congregation. Katharina distributed many of these alms personally and also served as a messenger to many other Anabaptists in the city, under the guise of routine business.

Two women grocers also were active in the Anabaptist congregation. Barbara Schleiffer was at the centre of Anabaptist coming and going, hosting at least one meeting and greeting and redirecting a steady stream of Anabaptist refugees from elsewhere. Oyer notes that "her steadfastness was a major factor in keeping the Anabaptist movement alive." Els Hegenmiller also was a grocer—it appears that the grocers' guild was uncommonly Anabaptist-minded.[21] Needless to say, a grocer's shop provided a perfect foil for covert communication. Els's testimony revealed the existence of a network of word of mouth communication by which Anabaptists informed each other about upcoming meetings and passed on other news. Els was generous to other Anabaptists, although she and her husband were of modest means. She routinely gave food to Anabaptists in need. For this—and because she shouted to the butchers who ran the neighbouring stall that the Catholic host was a "slimy idol"—the Augsburg authorities cut out her tongue and banished her for life.[22]

There is no doubt that the Anabaptist women of Augsburg were the mainstay of their underground church. They hosted meetings and subversive "sewing circles," provided a communications network, evangelized among their peers, housed and fed refugees and travelling Anabaptists, and provided support for the families of those in prison. Oyer suggests that the women were particularly active because they could move about less conspicuously than could the men.[23] And finally these women—like so many other Anabaptist women we come to know in the martyrologies—were amazingly steadfast when they were arrested and subjected to torture. Besides being routinely questioned while being tortured with thumbscrews, several recalcitrant women were branded on either cheek before being banished.

Oyer has extracted the following four "rules for operating an underground church" from his study of the Augsburg records, based on the techniques utilized by that congregation.

> 1. Do not ask or learn the name of your baptizer or of any traveling minister. Do not learn the name of the man or woman who provides free housing and food if you are a refugee. Then you will be unable to disclose their names if you are caught and hauled into court and tortured.

2. Hide the leaders at different places, even disguise them, have them remain anonymous or use pseudonyms. Move them out of town or village on their itinerant ways when it becomes dangerous to keep them longer.

3. Meet secretly: in a forest, a gravel pit, some isolated building at the edge of a village where the group could sing hymns without being heard, within the city in the more isolated houses which ought to be hung about with blankets etc. on the inside to block spying eyes, or in the city in very small groups in normal houses where people gather anyway for routine social purposes.

4. Greet each other simply so as to allay suspicion, but in some environments with an exchange that indicates to each party the Anabaptist inclination of the other. In this way strangers may recognize the Anabaptist in each other. One says "God greet thee, brother in the Lord." The other answers, "God thank thee, brother in the Lord." Some greetings are less elaborate, but very particular. (Some Anabaptists denied there was any special greeting, others declared that there was).[24]

The techniques described above were widely used within the Anabaptist movement; they recall similar techniques at work among the medieval heretical movements. In both cases the dissident religious communities relied heavily on personal contacts and oral/aural communication to win converts and to carry out their own religious activities.

Conclusion

The study of the process of communication in the Anabaptist movement is just beginning, and many questions are left to be answered. Nevertheless the dynamics of communication outlined above held true, in a general way, for the movement as a whole, even though print played a larger role in the Netherlands than it did for the Swiss Brethren and the South German movements. Since Anabaptist communication was most often carried on as invisibly as possible, under the cover of normal daily activity, the historian may catch a glimpse of the process only occasionally, when the authorities managed to detect, arrest, and question the participants. Through those occasional "windows," however, we see the stubborn resistance of predominantly "common people," intent on living out their faith against heavy odds, and zealous in their efforts to convert others to that faith. The heavy-handed response of the authorities to this grass roots religious dissent—which involved only a small percentage of the total population of any given territory—is explained in good measure by the fact that the oral/aural channels of communication lay mostly outside political/ecclesiastical control. The frightening prospect for civil authorities was that in this still predominantly oral/aural culture there were as many potential dissenting missionaries as there were speakers. For states intent on enforcing religious uniformity in order to consolidate political power, securing the pulpits and the presses was only a necessary first step. Religious hegemony would not be achieved until the more extensive oral/aural medium also came under control, for "the spoken word was power in the sixteenth century."[25] The fact that Anabaptism managed to survive in such a hostile context demonstrates the fact that although outlawed and persecuted, the Anabaptists were not silenced, and hence were not powerless.

End Notes

[1] Sophia Menache, *The vox Dei: communication in the Middle Ages* (New York: Oxford U. Press, 1990), p. 5.

[2] Harold Dwight Lasswell, "The Structure and Function of Communication in Society," in Lyman Bryson, ed., *The Communication of Ideas* (New York, 1948), p. 37.

[3] Elizabeth L. Eisenstein, *The Printing Press as an Agent of Change*, 2 vols. (Cambridge, 1979). A condensed version of this basic work is *The Printing Revolution in Early Modern Europe* (Cambridge: Cambridge University Press, 1983). Although Eisenstein urges that due attention be paid to the impact of print in making the Reformation possible, she also recognizes the key role played by oral transmission: "It is because the printed page amplified the spoken word and not because it silenced it that Luther regarded Gutenberg's invention as God's 'highest act of grace.' To set press against pulpit is to go against the spirit of the Lutheran Reformation." Eisenstein, *The Printing Press as an Agent of Change*, p. 374. See also Robert Scribner, *For the Sake of the Simple Folk* (Cambridge: Cambridge University Press, 1981), and the observations of William Graham, *Beyond the Written Word: Oral Aspects of Scripture in the History of Religion* (Cambridge: Cambridge University Press, 1987), especially chapter 12, "Hearing and Seeing: The Rhetoric of Martin Luther," pp. 141-54.

[4] Robert W. Scribner, "Oral Culture and the Diffusion of Reformation Ideas," in Robert W. Scribner, *Popular Culture and Popular Movements in Reformation Germany* (London: Hambledon Press, 1987), pp. 50-51; 54 ff. See the detailed study of Johann Eberlin von Günzburg's oral techniques in Monika Rössing-Hager, "Wie stark findet der nicht-lesekundige Rezipient Berücksichtigung in den Flugschriften?" in Robert Scribner and Hans-Joachim Köhler, eds., *Flugschriften als Massenmedium der Reformationszeit* (Stuttgart: Ernst Klett Verlag, 1981), pp. 77-137. Also Werner Kelber, *The Oral and the Written Gospel*, (Philadelphia: Fortress Press, 1983), p. 17.

[5] Scribner, "Oral Culture," pp. 50-51; Graham, *Beyond the Written Word*, pp. 39-41.

[6] The appeal to the Spirit as the legitimizing interpretive authority, which is evident in the Anabaptist movement from the start, was also common to the medieval sectarians. See Brian Stock, *The Implications of Literacy* (Princeton: Princeton University Press), pp. 106 ff.

[7] This chapter summarizes work previously published elsewhere. See Arnold Snyder, "Konrad Winckler: An Early Swiss Anabaptist Missionary, Pastor and Martyr," MQR (Oct., 1990); "Word and Power in Reformation Zürich," ARG (1990); "Biblical Text and Social Context: Anabaptist Anticlericalism in Reformation Zürich," MQR (April, 1991); "Orality, Literacy and the Study of Anabaptism," MQR (Oct., 1991); and "Communication and the People: The Case of Reformation St. Gall," MQR (April, 1993).

[8] Robert Scribner notes that the urban population numbered only 10 percent of the total at the time of the Reformation in Germany, and that the importance of the countryside has been underestimated. "It was rural,

rather than urban support which turned the reform movement into a mass movement..." Robert Scribner, *The German Reformation* (Atlantic Highlands, N.J.: Humanities Press, 1986), p. 30.

[9] See Arnold Snyder, "Word and Power in Reformation Zürich," ARG (1990).

[10] On St. Gall, see Arnold Snyder, "Communication and the People: The Case of Reformation St. Gall," MQR (April, 1993). The situation in Augsburg and Strasbourg will be sketched briefly in the chapters that follow.

[11] The parallels in the communication strategies of medieval heretical groups and those of Anabaptist groups in the sixteenth century are striking indeed. See Menache, *The vox Dei*, chapters 10 and 11.

[12] QGTS, 3, #26.

[13] Paul Wappler, *Die Täuferbewegung in Thüringen von 1526-1584* (Jena: Fischer, 1913), pp. 254-56.

[14] *Ibid.*, pp. 258-61.

[15] See Russel Snyder-Penner, "Hans Nadler's Oral Exposition of the Lord's Prayer," MQR (Oct., 1991), pp. 393-406.

[16] *Ibid.*, p. 395.

[17] *Ibid.*, pp. 396; 404-405.

[18] *Ausbund, Das ist: Etliche schöne Christliche Lieder...*, first edition 1564; second expanded edition 1583. Subsequent editions to the present essentially reproduce the 1583 edition, with a few additions. See Paul Yoder, ed., *Four Hundred Years with the Ausbund* (Scottdale, Pa.: Herald Press, 1964); Ursula Lieseberg, *Studien zum Märtyrerlied der Täufer im 16. Jahrhundert* (Frankfurt: Peter Lang, 1991); Rosella Reimer Duerksen, "Anabaptist Hymnody of the Sixteenth Century," Doc. Music dissertation, Union Theological Seminary, 1956. Crucial also for the subject of Anabaptist hymnody is Rudolf Wolkan, *Die Lieder der Wiedertäufer* (Nieuwkoop: B. de Graaf, 1965) [reprint of Berlin, 1903 edition], and Helen Martens, "Hutterite Songs: The Origins and Aural Transmission of their Melodies from the Sixteenth Century," unpublished Ph.D. dissertation, Columbia University, 1969.

[19] An interesting example comes from the seventeenth century. The Swiss Anabaptists around Zürich were subjected to severe persecution around 1639, at which time the authorities published a manifesto against them. A lengthy reply was composed and circulated in hand written copies; it was never printed. A copy arrived in the Netherlands, and a small part of the Swiss Anabaptist defense was subsequently printed in the *Martyrs Mirror.* As it happens, the *Martyrs Mirror* selection includes verbatim portions of Balthasar Hubmaier's booklet "The Opinion of the Ancient and New Teachers that One Should Not Baptize Young Children," (Nicholsburg, 1526). These were copied by hand by the Swiss around 1639, sent to the Netherlands as part of their *apologia*, and then translated into Dutch for the *Martyrs Mirror*. Readers can compare the resulting English versions in *Martyrs Mirror*, p. 1116 and Pipkin and Yoder, *Hubmaier*, p. 257ff.

[20] The following is drawn from John Oyer, "Anabaptist Women Leaders in Augsburg, August 1527 to April 1528," in Arnold Snyder and Linda H. Hecht, eds, *Profiles of Anabaptist Women* (publication forthcoming).

[21] Oyer counts at least six Augsburg grocers (all men) who became Anabaptists and at least three more "sympathizers" who met with the Anabaptists and provided help, but did not formally join. In addition there were at least seven grocer-spouses who joined the Anabaptists.

[22] Space does not permit the telling of more stories of prominent Anabaptist women Augsburg, such as those of Veronica (Albrecht) Groß, wife of Jacob Groß, and Anna Salminger who was married to the Anabaptist leader Sigmund Salminger. Veronica worked as a seamstress, met often with other Anabaptist women, and sometimes (she said) she "instructed" them. Veronica and Anna remained steadfast even though their husbands had been imprisoned.

[23] Historians are dependent upon, and are limited by, written records, and Anabaptist men were more often arrested—and hence were more often entered into the legal record—than were women. One suspects that the number of active Anabaptist women at least equalled, and perhaps surpassed the number of men, but this cannot be proven from the surviving sources.

[24] Oyer, "Women Leaders."

[25] Snyder, "Word and Power," p. 284.

Jan Wouterss and Adriaenken Jans moments before being burned at the stake

Anabaptist martyrs often used the occasion of their executions to proclaim their faith to the crowds assembled to watch the spectacle, and to exhort both spectators and their captors to repentance. Steadfastness in the face of torture, and a public, oral witness in the face of an imminent and horrible death (in this case, by fire) were powerful instruments of communication at the popular level. Rather than discrediting the movement, public executions only served to lend it credence. Authorities soon began silencing Anabaptist martyrs with gags, tongue screws, and other means to prevent their public witness. Anabaptists appealed to examples of heroic steadfastness as providing evidence for the genuineness of their movement.

Chapter 8

The Spread and Development of Early Anabaptism

It is not possible to detail the ebb and flow of early Anabaptism across southwestern Europe in the space of one chapter. The German portion alone of the Holy Roman Empire comprised more than three hundred principalities of varying size and importance, all of which could adopt their own practical approaches towards religious dissenters. There remained the various Swiss cantons, the particular cases of Moravia, Alsace, and a variety of free imperial cities. Every territory deserves to have its own story told in order to identify important changes in policy, as well as to detail particular events relevant to the development of the Anabaptist story in that city or region. In this chapter we will attempt to provide only the very broadest overview of the spread and some developments of the early Swiss and South German Anabaptist movement from 1525 to ca. 1540. We will sketch this development by means of a very general geographical description, some representative biographical sketches, and occasional concentration on crucial cities and territories. Our description will concentrate further on the more formative periods of interaction between the Swiss and South German Anabaptist movements.

Swiss and South German Anabaptism in Exile and Conversation

The political reality faced in the first decade of the movement (1525-1535) in Switzerland and the Holy Roman Empire was a swift narrowing of official tolerance for Anabaptism. With the first executions and official mandates Anabaptism became an increasingly "underground" movement, with adherents meeting in secret, travelling in disguise, and evangelizing and meeting at great personal risk. The "official" persecution of Anabaptists reached a climax of sorts with the events in Münster (1534-35), a story that will be told in more detail in a subsequent chapter. The Anabaptist kingdom of Münster was used to justify repression against Anabaptists in some territories that previously had been tolerant—such as in Moravia, for example. But early in the first decade of the movement, although some political authorities had moved decisively against Anabaptists with imprisonment, torture and death sentences, there remained places where, for a variety of reasons, Anabaptists were tolerated in practice.

In its areas of origin, the best chance for long-term Anabaptist survival lay in the countryside, where kinship networks and a general distrust of city-based magistrates made detection and enforcement difficult. Swiss Anabaptism, for example, would survive in small pockets of rural resistance in the northern cantons of Zürich, Appenzell, Bern and Basel well into the seventeeth century, and beyond. This same general pattern would be seen elsewhere: Anabaptism would come to survive more

and more in village and rural settings, where detection and enforcement were difficult for the authorities.[1]

Increased persecution also resulted in significant migrations of Anabaptists
from areas where there was active persecution, to those places where they were
tolerated outright or where legal enforcement was less severe. The relatively simple
story of Anabaptist origins, then, very soon becomes a complicated story of Anabaptist
migrations. One may say that after "genesis" came "exodus." The Anabaptism that
began in Zürich spread quickly west to Bern, Basel, Strasbourg and Alsace, into Baden
and Swabia, along the Neckar river in Württemberg, to eastern Switzerland (Appenzell,
St. Gall, Chur), and into the Tirol. But of all the places of refuge, Moravia provided the
best opportunities for freedom in the late 1520s, even though the distance and the
difficulty of travel were daunting. Several cities, such as Strasbourg, Augsburg, and
Esslingen also offered possibilities early on, and these cities in particular became
early Anabaptist centres of refuge. A few personal stories will illustrate the larger
pattern of movement among the Swiss Brethren in this first decade and a half of the
movement.

George Blaurock, Jakob Groß, and Margret Hottinger

George Blaurock (Cajacob) was from Bonaduz, a village in Grisons in eastern
Switzerland.[2] He studied at the University of Leipzig in 1513, and served as vicar in
the diocese of Chur from 1516 to 1518. He came to Zürich in 1525 and soon joined the
circle that had formed around Conrad Grebel and Felix Mantz. According to one account, Blaurock was the first to be baptized in January 1525, and soon he was active
in establishing an Anabaptist congregation in the village of Zollikon.[3] By all accounts
he was a fiery and passionate individual; he is well known for his public interruption of
a sermon in the village church in Zollikon; he told pastor Billeter "Not you, but I am
sent to preach."[4] On his second arrest by the Zürich authorities he was deported
back to Chur by boat, but after his release he worked to establish Anabaptism in Grisons
(where he and Mantz were imprisoned), and then returned to the Zürich area, working especially in the Grüningen district until yet another arrest in October, 1525.
After a second disputation on baptism in Zürich Blaurock was sentenced to life imprisonment (March 7, 1526), to be held in the Zürich tower until he either recanted
or died. Two weeks later the prisoners managed to escape. Mantz and Blaurock worked
again in Grüningen where they were arrested again in December, 1526. This time
Felix Mantz was sentenced to death, and George Blaurock was beaten out of the city
with rods.

Blaurock's movements are difficult to trace after this final expulsion from
Zürich: he made a trip to South Tirol in 1527, then appeared briefly in Bern, Basel and
Appenzell in 1528 and 1529, after which he returned to the Tirol. It is safe to assume
much itinerant pastoral activity (now hidden to us) was taking place during this period. By May 1529, Blaurock was active further east, in the Tirol, primarily in Clausen,
Guffidaun, Ritten, and towns near Bozen.[5] In August of 1529, Blaurock was captured
in Guffidaun along with Hans Langegger, subjected to extensive torture, and then

burned at the stake along with his companion in Clausen, September 6, 1529. It was through Blaurock's activity, and that of others like him, that Swiss Anabaptism entered the Tirol from the west and took root.

Jakob Groß, whom we have already met in our narrative, was a furrier from Waldshut who was introduced to Anabaptism by Conrad Grebel and baptized by Balthasar Hubmaier in Waldshut, sometime after April 1525.[6] He was expelled from Waldshut at the height of the Peasants' War for refusing to take arms in defence of the city; he immediately took up an itinerant ministry in Switzerland.[7] He worked in the Grüningen district in late summer of 1525, where he baptized 35 people in one day before being arrested and expelled.[8] He moved next to western Switzerland, to the Aargau, where he was active especially in and around the city of Aarau, leading Bible studies and baptizing Agnes Zender, for which he was arrested in Brugg in late February of 1526.[9] He worked next in the city of Lahr, was arrested and expelled, and then suffered the same fate in neighbouring Strasbourg, where he went on trial at the end of 1526.[10] Michael Sattler subsequently came to Strasbourg and pleaded with Bucer and Capito for the release of Gross and three more compatriots. It is very likely (although not certain) that Groß was present at the Schleitheim gathering in February, 1527.[11] Groß soon emerged as a leading Swiss Anabaptist leader in Augsburg, where he began baptizing soon after Easter of 1527;[12] he is known to have baptized some 22 persons in Augsburg.[13] Shortly after the Martyrs' Synod in Augsburg (end of August, 1527), Jakob Groß was arrested at a large gathering in the city. After suffering in prison some four years, he finally recanted his Anabaptist views on June 22, 1531.[14] We will return briefly to Jakob Groß when we look at the situation in Augsburg, below.

Margret Hottinger may be taken as representative of the more zealous Zollikon Anabaptists who, after Zürich cracked down on the movement, nevertheless sought ways to continue practising their faith. Margret Hottinger was baptized early in 1525 in Zollikon, probably by George Blaurock.[15] After being arrested, tried and sentenced with Grebel, Mantz, Blaurock and others, she suffered in prison for some months, finally accepting a recantation in May of 1526 in return for her freedom.[16] She remained active in neighbouring St. Gall in 1526; Johannes Kessler, chronicler of that city, described her as highly respected by the brethren for her piety and spiritual insight.[17] Although the Anabaptist movement in the village of Zollikon had virtually disappeared by the end of 1526, Margret Hottinger, her brother Felix, and their father, Jakob Hottinger the elder, continued in their Anabaptist convictions. Like many Swiss Anabaptists, however, they decided to flee to Moravia. In 1530 they were apprehended at Waldsee as part of a group of travellers who were making for the "promised land" of Moravia, the land of freedom. Jakob Hottinger was beheaded, and Margret was drowned, both refusing to recant; Felix was released because of his youth.[18] Very many refugees were to suffer a similar fate on their journeys to Moravia; but very many more managed the trip and arrived safely.

The three Swiss Brethren representatives profiled above offer a glimpse of how Swiss Anabaptism spread to the west, north and east, thanks to official persecution and the zeal of committed converts who took to the road. Should we think of this migrant Swiss Anabaptism as a homogenous movement, defined by the Schleitheim Articles? To a large degree this seems to have been true, but Swiss Anabaptist homogeneity can be overstated—as if after Schleitheim, all issues of importance had been settled for the Swiss Brethren. In fact, a number of issues still were being worked out among the Swiss, particularly relating to the sword of government, the oath, and community of goods, and the Swiss Brethren continued to dialogue actively with other Anabaptist groups throughout the sixteenth century.

Swiss Anabaptist homogeneity clearly was not achieved instantly at Schleitheim when we include—as we must—Balthasar Hubmaier in the "Swiss Anabaptist" grouping. In Nicholsburg, Moravia Hubmaier established an Anabaptist state church. He argued for the legitimate wielding of the sword by a Christian government and for the legitimate participation of Christians in all governing functions. Hubmaier gained a considerable following, but also present in Nicholsburg were Swiss Anabaptist refugees who had accepted Schleitheim separatism and nonresistance. As might be expected, the "sword bearers" and the "staff bearers"—both strictly speaking part of the same "Swiss Anabaptist" movement and "origin"—eventually came into conflict, although for some time the two views coexisted peacefully.

While differences concerning the sword of government may have simmered just below the surface among the Swiss refugees in Nicholsburg, the first overt division there occurred between the Swiss Anabaptist leader Balthasar Hubmaier and the South German Anabaptist leader Hans Hut.

Nicholsburg

By far the best possiblities of refuge for Anabaptists on the run between 1526 and 1528 lay in the city of Nicholsburg, under the lordship of Leonard of Liechtenstein. By the time Balthasar Hubmaier sought refuge there (ca. July, 1526) Nicholsburg had already moved in a Zwinglian evangelical direction thanks to the efforts of local pastors Hans Spittelmaier and Oswald Glaidt.[19] Although evangelical refugees knew about the freedom to be found in Moravia, the first Anabaptist contact apparently was established by Balthasar Hubmaier.[20] Details are missing, but within a few months Hubmaier had managed to turn Nicholsburg in an officially Anabaptist direction, baptizing Spittlemaier and Glaidt, as well as the city's lord, Leonhard von Liechtenstein. Within a short time the city had become an Anabaptist centre, with the number of baptized estimated at around 2,000.[21] Torsten Bergsten notes that although many Anabaptists with "differing shades of belief" from Switzerland, Germany and Austria came to Nicholsburg, nevertheless there was no initial trouble in the fall and winter of 1526-1527, such as would develop in the spring of 1527.[22]

There is indirect evidence that there were underlying tensions—as one might expect—between the Anabaptist followers of Hubmaier and more radically-minded Anabaptist refugees.[23] From later events, it appears that a separatist faction was led by "the one-eyed Swabian," Jakob Wiedemann, which gathered in the village of Bergen, outside the city walls.[24] Into this mix came Hans Hut in May, 1527, and won support not only among the more radical faction, but also among some important supporters of Hubmaier in the city.[25] The central point of contention seems to have been Hut's End Times calendar and preaching; some teaching on community of goods may have been involved as well, but this is not well documented.

Following a private meeting between Hut and Hubmaier, a public disputation was held between them (The Nicholsburg Disputation of 1527) in the church of the city, which was followed in turn by a private disputation at the castle, before Lord Leonard. The main points of contention appear to have been Hut's End Times calculations, opposed by Hubmaier, and Hut's accusation of Hubmaier's laxity in allowing too many unprepared people into the church.[26] Hut was thrown into prison by Lord Leonard—who himself was a baptized member of the Anabaptist community—and in spite of Hut's successful escape, the division of the Anabaptist community in Moravia was a foregone conclusion.

Hans Hut's interpretation of the signs of the times would create problems elsewhere in the Anabaptist movement, as we will see below: Hubmaier would not be alone in his opposition. The apocalyptic question, as Walter Klaassen has shown, was of concern to all sixteenth century persons and not just to Anabaptists. But Hut's Anabaptism was tending to define the movement as a whole in terms of a specific apocalyptic calendar of events—a view that appealed to many, but was opposed by many more. The departure of Hut and some of his supporters from Nicholsburg resolved some immediate tensions in the city, but there still remained the unresolved matter of the two contrasting Swiss Anabaptist views concerning the sword of government..

On June 24, 1527 Hubmaier published his last work, *On the Sword*. The evidence is persuasive that Hubmaier directed his writing on the sword to Swiss Brethren followers of Schleitheim, and against Schleitheim's article 6 specifically, as will be noted in chapter 13 below. This long-simmering issue had dogged Hubmaier since Waldshut (we may remember Jakob Groß's expulsion from Waldshut for refusing to bear arms) and continued to bother Hubmaier in Nicholsburg. The remarkable fact is not that open opposition emerged on this question, but rather that "sword bearing" and "staff bearing" Anabaptists managed to coexist for so long in Nicholsburg without first resolving this difference. The immediate objects of Hubmaier's *On the Sword* probably were the "brethren" gathered around Jakob Wiedemann in the village of Bergen.

Just one month after the publication of *On the Sword*, Hubmaier was arrested by Austrian authorities, and subsequently burned at the stake in Vienna on March 10, 1528; his wife Elsbeth was drowned three days later in the Danube.[27] Back in Nicholsburg, the Jakob Wiedemann group continued its separatist opposition to Lord Lietchenstein's Anabaptist state church, led by Hans Spittelmaier after Hubmaier's arrest. Early in 1528 a debate was held in Bergen between Spittelmaier on the one hand, and Wiedemann and Philip Jäger on the other. The Wiedemann group insisted on nonresistance in the manner of the Swiss followers of Schleitheim; Wiedemann and Jäger also seem to have incorporated some of Hut's End Times teaching—although obviously not Hut's views on the sword. Lord Leonard eventually asked the dissidents to leave, which they did in late winter, 1528. This particular crisis seems to have been precipitated because Liechtenstein had mobilized armed defence in the face of a threat by the Austrian provost.[28]

The "staff-bearing" group of 200 plus refugees from Nicholsburg found a political space in the Moravian city of Austerlitz where the local lords promised them freedom of worship. In the course of their journey there they did establish a common purse, based upon a seven point constitution which established community of goods in an eschatalogical context. It was to this group that Jacob Hutter came in 1529 from the Tirol.

Nicholsburg, attracting as it did Anabaptist refugees of all kinds, provides a window through which we can view early Anabaptist commonalities, differences, conversations, divisions, and compromises. Nicholsburg brought three distinct early "varieties" of Anabaptism into close contact: the "state Anabaptism" of Hubmaier that had emerged in the context of Swiss Anabaptism, the separatist Swiss Anabaptism of Schleitheim, and the South German apocalyptic Anabaptism of Hut. While some might argue that three "Anabaptisms" came into contact in Nicholsburg, such an interpretation overlooks the fundamental points of agreement that underlay all three Anabaptist "tendencies."

In terms of origins, Hubmaier and Hut represented two geographically and ideologically distinct points of beginning. Nevertheless, the disagreement between Hubmaier and Hut did not concern Anabaptist theological essentials regarding the nature of faith, repentance, regeneration, baptism, and a new life (in a word, soteriology), or the memorial Supper and the place of the ban in the congregation. They disagreed rather on the further interpretation of their shared Anabaptist distinctives. Hubmaier and Hut agreed on the centrality of Mark 16:16 in providing the biblical order pertaining to baptism, for example. But Hut also understood baptism as the eschatological "mark of TAU" that sealed the 144,000 elect of the Last Days—and this further interpretation of baptism Hubmaier could not abide.[29] Conversely, Hubmaier insisted upon church discipline, but supporters of Hut who had been in Nicholsburg testified later that in Hubmaier's church there had been no strict application of the ban or "proper" church order, by their definition.

It is beyond dispute that within the Anabaptist movement there emerged variant interpretations of the Last Days, the meaning of adult baptism, and the implementation of church discipline, explainable in part by the differing "origins" of the protagonists. However, the evidence from Nicholsburg suggests that on the basis of their *shared* beliefs, Anabaptist refugees of all sorts lived together as "brethren" for quite some time before variant interpretations of their shared Anabaptist principles led them to schism, in some cases, and to compromise in others.

To take another case in point, it would appear in retrospect that Hubmaier's "sword bearing" Anabaptism and the separatist Anabaptism of Schleitheim were fundamentally incompatible from the start. It has been assumed that Schleitheim marks an immediate and thorough consolidation. But pacifist brethren in Nicholsburg were still working out the full implications of their "two kingdoms" Schleitheim position. The problem for the nonresistant Anabaptists in Nicholsburg was that an *Anabaptist* ruler had granted them asylum and was protecting them with the sword against their enemies. Had Lord Leonard been a "non-believer" such protection undoubtedly would have been accepted, as it was later in other parts of Moravia, and presumably Lord Leonard could then have been comfortably (though quietly) consigned to hell along with all other members of "the world." But Lord Leonard was a "baptized brother." Thus the clash between "faithfulness to Christ" in nonresistance, and responsible governance (legitimate defence) could not be avoided by Anabaptists in Nicholsburg, in spite of an extended period of coexistence. In Nicholsburg, Schleitheim's "separatist nonresistance" proved ultimately divisive, but was not so initially.

It also is important to note that the various Anabaptist tendencies that met at Nicholsburg did not emerge unchanged from that setting. The pacifist "staff bearers" who went on to form communal settlements in other parts of Moravia demonstrated a fusion of the Swiss teaching of absolute separatist nonresistance with Hans Hut's apocalyptic expectations, to which eventually was added the ecclesiological distinctive of a legislated sharing of goods. This was a further refinement of the Anabaptist position which had not existed exactly in this form before, either in Hubmaier, the Schleitheim Swiss Anabaptists, or in Hut.

Hubmaier's state church Anabaptism did not long outlive him, and Hut's apocalyptic excitement waned quickly following his death in 1527. The separatist (but non-communitarian) Anabaptism of the Swiss Anabaptists and the separatist communitarian Anabaptism that emerged from the Nicholsburg experience, on the other hand, were interpretations and expressions of Anabaptism that would survive to the end of the sixteenth century and beyond.

Augsburg and the Martyrs' Synod, August, 1527

Until the mass arrests in April 1528, Augsburg was an important Anabaptist centre in southern Germany, as we have seen above. Along with Nicholsburg, it provides us a second "window" through which to view the interaction of various early Anabaptist "tendencies."

Pre-Reformation Augsburg was a city with a particularly strong tradition of lay piety and interest in mystical Christianity. Its active print shops had published many Bibles and religious works by the turn of the century. By 1524 several local reforming pamphlets had been printed there; Hans Hut peddled Thomas Müntzer's writings in the city in that same year.[30] Ludwig Hätzer was present in Augsburg for a few months in the summer of 1524, and returned to the city after his expulsion from Zürich in January, 1525. He may have introduced Anabaptist ideas to interested lay persons, but there is no hard evidence for this.[31] In any case, Hätzer was expelled from the city in September, 1525, but at just this time Hans Denck came to Augsburg as a teacher of Latin and Greek. It does not appear that Denck was yet baptized, for the issue of baptism did not emerge in Augsburg until 1526, and may well have been brought there in the person of Balthasar Hubmaier.

It appears that Hubmaier also arrived in Augsburg early in May, 1526 and may have stayed as long as two months; he had moved on to Nicholsburg by July of the same year.[32] The one piece of evidence pertaining to Hubmaier's activity in Augsburg points to contacts between Hubmaier and Denck; it is possible, although by no means certain, that Hans Denck was baptized by Hubmaier.[33] In any case, on May 20, 1526 Denck baptized Hans Hut in Augsburg; it is therefore possible that for a brief

A view of Augsburg, late fifteenth century

time in the late spring and early summer of 1526, Hubmaier, Denck and Hut may have been together in that city. By late summer, all three had moved on, although Denck and Hut would return: Denck moved on to Strasbourg for a time, Hut began his missionary journeys, and Hubmaier continued on to Nicholsburg.

The composition and leadership of the early Anabaptist community in Augsburg (from the summer of 1526 to the winter of 1527) remains hidden from view, but early in 1527 Hans Hut returned and baptized a large group of important Anabaptist leaders: the patrician Eitelhans Langenmantel, the former clergymen Jakob Dachser and Sigmund Salminger, the weavers Gall Fischer and Peter Scheppach, and many others.[34] At about the same time (ca. February, 1527) the Swiss Anabaptist leader and refugee, Jakob Groß, arrived in the city, and began baptizing as well. Rather than there being evidence of contrary "Anabaptisms" colliding at this point in Augsburg, the records show that Hut established a rudimentary church organization among the Augsburg Anabaptists which featured a common chest for relief of the poor, and which integrated Jakob Groß into the leadership structure: Sigmund Salminger was chosen "first minister" by lot, with Jakob Groß and Jakob Dachser as his assistants.[35]

The evidence from Augsburg suggests strongly that Hans Hut was working (in some places at least) for a broader Anabaptist movement without overtly linking adult baptism to his particular chronology of End Times events or his related understanding of the sword. The appointment of the Swiss Brethren pacifist Jakob Groß to a leadership position suggests as much; more striking still is the fact that Jakob Dachser, baptized by Hut himself, would become one of Hut's foremost opponents at the Martyrs' Synod later in 1527. The Swiss Brethren/South German distinctions (biblicist vs. mystical/non-apocalyptic vs. apocalyptic) which supposedly divided these two Anabaptist movements at their "origins" were not yet divisive in early Augsburg Anabaptism.

From the start, South German Anabaptism was not united on the apocalyptic question, promoted strongly as it was by Hans Hut, and more or less ignored by Hans Denck and Melchior Rinck. In May of 1527, Hubmaier had opposed Hut from a Swiss perspective; in August of that same year, in Augsburg, Hut encountered opposition from within the South German movement itself.

The "Martyrs' Synod" took place in Augsburg from August 20 to 24, 1527. The gathering has been given this name because very many of its participants would shortly suffer martyrdom.[36] There were at least 22 Anabaptist missionaries from outside the city in attendance at three successive meetings; the first and the last meetings had more than 60 people present. Hut and his End Times agenda dominated the meetings, and Hut was forced to agree that he would be less forward in presenting his End Times convictions and predictions.[37] Among those who opposed him was Jakob Dachser of Augsburg, who had been baptized by Hut.[38] Once the contentious apocalyptic question had been "settled" by means of compromise, the assembled brethren also commissioned apostles and missioners to various areas; they were drawn from both the Swiss and South German streams, although South German Anabaptists present at these meetings far outnumbered the Swiss.[39]

The Tirol

The general area of the Tirol provided another primary setting in which early Swiss and South German teachings met and combined for a time. The Swiss Anabaptist understanding appears to have been carried to the Tirol by George Blaurock, as already noted above; Hut's Anabaptism was brought there by followers such as Leonhard Schiemer, Hans Schlaffer, and Jakob Hutter.

With the coming of strong Austrian repression in the Tirol in the late 1520s, there were mass migrations of Anabaptist refugees out of the territory. The majority of these emigres would flee to the communal Anabaptist groups in Moravia. But it also was out of the Tirolean setting that Pilgram Marpeck and Helena von Freyberg, among others, emerged to carry their particular (non-communal) Anabaptist views to the Swiss and German territories north and west of the Tirol.[40] But in fact it was Moravia that would remain a focal point for a variety of Anabaptist groups until almost the end of the century. In Moravia would be found later not only communal Anabaptists (Hutterites), but also communities of immigrant Swiss Brethren (often living in the same towns and villages as the Hutterites) as well as a few smaller groups of Marpeckites.[41]

Central German Anabaptism

Central German Anabaptism took on various shades and forms, as different Anabaptist groups flourished and waned. The first Central German Anabaptist converts were baptized directly by Hans Hut in northern Franconia, and mirrored his enthusiastic apocalyptic expectation. This more militant and apocalyptic Anabaptist strand was subjected to some key arrests early in 1527; it came to a head in Hans Römer's aborted plans for an attack on Erfurt in January, 1528.[42] By the summer of 1528, Melchior Rinck was establishing a different kind of Anabaptism in western Thuringia, centred in the village of Sorga and in the vicinity of Hersfeld. The Anabaptist congregations he founded in this area survived his own incarceration and some mass arrests in 1533; many Anabaptists from this area also fled to Moravia. Hans Bott, a follower of Rinck who led a group of refugees to Moravia, got involved in some disputes between communal groups there.[43]

By 1534 Münsterite sympathizers and Melchiorite Anabaptists were making their presence felt in Hessian territory. After the collapse of Münster many refugees fled to Hesse, an area more notably tolerant than many others. In May of 1536 some thirty Melchiorites were arrested in Hesse, among them Georg Schnabel. As a result of this arrest and subsequent discussions with Martin Bucer, the Hessian state church instituted confirmation (in place of adult baptism) and introduced church discipline. In return the former Anabaptist leaders Georg Schnabel and Peter Tasch recanted their Anabaptist beliefs and led a general exodus of former Melchiorite Anabaptists into the Hessian state church under Bucer's tutelage.[44] By 1540, notes John Oyer, Anabaptism as a wide spread movement had disappeared from Central Germany.[45] After this time, Swiss Brethren did maintain small communities and Hutterite missionaries also recruited actively in the area, but the number of Anabaptist adherents remained small.[46]

Conclusion

In spite of distinct Swiss and South German "origins," the story of early Anabaptism is a story of mutual influence and interaction. Swiss Anabaptism, given its stronger emphasis on the literal word of Scripture, proved less susceptible to divergent interpretations than did South German Anabaptism, although the Swiss were open to apocalyptic ideas and supported voluntary community of goods—both of which have ample biblical basis. South German Anabaptism, in spite of its rootage in late medieval mysticism, certainly did not develop in any one predictable direction—or even just two! The continuation of a militant Hutian line (the apocalypticism of Bader) and a "Denckian" line (spiritualists like Bünderlin, Kautz, and Entfelder) points us back to some fundamental ideological differences in emphasis between Denck and Hut. The emergence of a moralistic, sectarian, and communitarian stream (the Tirol and separatist communitarian Anabaptism in Moravia) points us to Swiss Anabaptist influences on the South German movement. The emergence of a biblicistic and ethically oriented Anabaptism from Rinck suggests that strong leaders could "shape" Anabaptist essentials according to their own understanding and predispositions, regardless of who baptized them.

The point of these caveats is not to deny differences among early Anabaptists, or to posit some "homogeneous" movement. Hubmaier was well aware of differences between his interpretation of Anabaptist essentials and those of Hut on the one hand, and the pacifist Swiss on the other. Hut was well aware of differences between his own views and those expressed at Schleitheim. The point, however, is that in actual practice many of these differences were overlooked by the Anabaptists themselves, until a particular issue grew to be divisive, or a compromise was reached. In Nicholsburg, differences led to schism; in Augsburg they led to compromise. In both cases the initial Anabaptist communities were composed of brethren of different Anabaptist "orientation" and "origins."

It is worth noting that a "genetic" image of Anabaptist parentage (who baptized whom)—while it is a useful generalization at one level—does not bear up very well as an adequate paradigm explaining Anabaptist development. Groß was baptized by Hubmaier, but was a pacifist; Hut was baptized by Denck, but did not become a "Denckian"; Rinck was with Müntzer and was baptized by Denck, but his Anabaptism looks more Swiss than South German; Dachser was won for Anabaptism by Hut, but opposed Hut's "central" teaching concerning the End Times. All of these cases, and many more that could be mentioned, should lead us to question an "apostolic succession" approach to Anabaptist history. The bare fact of water baptism by a regional Anabaptist exponent did not entail a mysterious, direct transmission of that baptizer's beliefs to a recipient.[47] To the contrary: not only did the baptizing "agents" not always clarify the finer points of their own positions to baptismal recipients, the backgrounds and predispositions of the recipients also could prove decisive in the kind of Anabaptism that was appropriated, regardless of who did the baptizing. Perhaps "genetics" is not the best historical image to use when discussing a family composed exclusively of stepchildren.

There were broadly shared theological and soteriological principles that defined members of the "baptizing family" from the start, regardless of region; members could be won and baptized even though exact boundaries had not yet been defined with precision.[48] This latter process took place in a complex series of interactions, compromises, dialogue and schism that involved Anabaptists from all regions and "tendencies," as we will have reason to note also in the Strasbourg context to be examined in the following chapter. The Swiss and South German Anabaptist orientations would continue to interact, as would the various tendencies within each regional Anabaptist expression. However, the South German and Moravian cities which had provided the earliest centres of such interaction had all but closed to Anabaptists by 1530.

End Notes

[1] See Clasen, *Social History*, pp. 305-309.

[2] See the extended biography in ME, I, pp. 354-59.

[3] *The Chronicle of the Hutterian Brethren*, vol. 1, trans. and ed. by the Hutterian Brethren (Rifton, N.Y.: Plough Publishing, 1987), p. 45.

[4] QGTS, 1, p. 39.

[5] ME, I, p. 358.

[6] "Doctor Balthasar Fridberger hab ine zu Waltzhut widertawft und der Grebel hab ine dahin bewegt." Christian Meyer, "Zur Geschichte der Wiedertäufer in Oberschwaben" Part I: "Die Anfänge des Wiedertäufertums in Augsburg," *Zeitschrift des historischen Vereins für Schwaben und Neuburg*, I (1874), p. 246.

[7] See ME, II, pp. 598-99.

[8] QGTS, 1, pp. 108-109.

[9] QGTS, 3, nos. 26, 30, 31, 32, 33, 34. A profile of Agnes Zender is found in Snyder and Hecht, *Profiles*.

[10] His Lahr activity is only known on the basis of his later prison confession. TA, *Elsass*, I, #104, p. 129. His testimony of late December, 1526 in Strasbourg is found in *ibid.*, #67, pp. 63-64.

[11] See the discussion in Snyder, *Life and Thought*, pp. 89-97.

[12] According to the testimony of Hans (Krafft) Messerschmied: TA, *Elsass*, I, p. 180, n. 2.

[13] Hans Guderian, *Die Täufer in Augsburg* (Pfaffenhofen: Ludwig Verlag, 1984), p. 34.

[14] ME, II, p. 599.

[15] On Margret, see QGTS, 1, #30; #31, pp. 39-41; #135; #134, pp. 136-37; #170, p. 177; #170a, p. 178.

[16] QGTS, 1, #173, p. 183.

[17] See selection of Kessler's *Sabbata* in QGTS, 2, p. 618; translation in Harder, *Sources*, p. 548.

[18] In QGTS, 2, pp. 578-80, Johannes Rütiner reports on a conversation (in 1537) with Felix Hottinger, in which Felix describes the death of his father (Jakob) and sister (Margaret). In QGTS, 2, pp. 586-87, Fridolin Sicher recounts the execution at Waldsee in 1530.

[19] Torsten Bergsten, *Balthasar Hubmaier*, trans. and ed. by W.R. Estep (Valley Forge, Pa.: Judson Press, 1978), pp. 314-20.

[20] Jarold K. Zeman, *The Anabaptists and the Czech Brethren in Moravia, 1526-1628* (The Hague: Mouton, 1969), pp. 100-120. On Hubmaier, Hut and Nicholsburg, see Stayer, *Sword*, pp. 162-66; Packull, *Mysticism*, pp. 99-106.

[21] Bergsten, *Hubmaier*, pp. 320-24.

[22] *Ibid.*, p. 328.

[23] "The bold criticisms by Hans Hut in May 1527 did not introduce the controversy. They merely voiced tensions which must have been latent at Mikulov [Nicholsburg] since the earliest days of Anabaptism." So Zeman, *Czech Brethren*, p. 185.

[24] Williams, *Radical*, p. 340.

[25] Packull, *Mysticism*, pp. 100-101.

[26] On the belaboured question of the actual questions under debate, as compared with the "Nicholsburg Articles," I am guided by Stayer, *Sword*, pp. 162-66, and Packull, *Mysticism*, pp. 99-103. Compare with Bergsten, *Hubmaier*, pp. 365-370; Williams, *Radical*, pp. 341-344. Bergsten and Williams repeat the now untenable view

that Hut defended pacifism against Hubmaier. E.g., Williams, *Radical*, p. 342: "Hut pressed his pacifistic views with his wonted passion..."

[27] Bergsten, *Hubmaier*, p. 379.

[28] Stayer, *Sword*, p. 168; Bergsten, *Hubmaier*, p. 383.

[29] Bergsten concludes that the central disagreement between Hubmaier and Hut was found in eschatology. See Bergsten, *Hubmaier*, pp. 374-77.

[30] Packull, *Mysticism*, p. 92; more details in Guderian, *Täufer in Augsburg*, pp. 20-26.

[31] Guderian, *Täufer in Augsburg*, pp. 27-29.

[32] Bergsten, *Hubmaier*, p. 309.

[33] *Ibid.*, p. 310; Guderian, *Täufer in Augsburg*, p. 31. On this question, see especially Werner Packull, "Denck's Alleged Baptism by Hubmaier. Its Significance for the Origin of South German-Austrian Anabaptism," MQR 47(October, 1973), pp. 327-38.

[34] Guderian, *Täufer in Augsburg*, p. 35; Packull, *Mysticism*, p. 93.

[35] Packull, *Mysticism*, p. 93.

[36] See ME, III, pp. 529-31; Guderian, *Täufer in Augsburg*, pp. 40-44. Packull, *Mysticism*, pp. 118-19, cautions against considering "the goings-on in Augsburg" a "synod" in the usual sense of that word.

[37] A portion of the letter Hut circulated is reproduced in Guderian, *Täufer in Augsburg*, p. 43.

[38] Packull, *Mysticism*, p. 94.

[39] Guderian lists only Hans Beck, Jakob Groß, and Gregor Maler as Swiss Brethren representatives. Groß apparently was to remain in Augsburg; Beck was to travel with Denck to the Zürich and Basel areas; Maler was sent to work in the Voralberg region.

[40] On Helena von Freyberg, see Linda Huebert Hecht, "An Extraordinary Lay Leader: the Life and Work of Helene of Freyberg, Sixteenth Century Noblewoman from the Tirol," MQR 66(July, 1992), pp. 312-341, and Snyder and Hecht, *Profiles of Anabaptist Women* (forthcoming).

[41] In spite of its crucial importance to the Anabaptist story, historical sources from Moravia pertaining to the Anabaptists are virtually unavailable in published editions, such as exist for the German speaking territories (the *Täuferakten*). Zeman's *Czech Brethren* remains the only monograph treatment that has accessed Czech archives. There is much more to be learned about Moravian Anabaptism.

[42] See Oyer, *Lutheran*, pp. 47-50; Stayer, *Sword*, pp. 189-93. Römer also had been a follower of Müntzer, and had been a combatant at Frankenhausen.

[43] Oyer, *Lutheran*, pp. 65-6.

[44] See especially Werner Packull, "The Melchiorites and the Ziegenhain Order of Discipline, 1538-39," in Walter Klaassen, ed., *Anabaptism Revisited* (Scottdale, Pa.: Herald Press, 1992), pp. 11-28. Also Oyer, *Lutheran*, pp. 72-74.

[45] Oyer, *Lutheran*, p. 74.

[46] See Arnold Snyder, "The Confession of the Swiss Brethren in Hesse, 1578," in Walter Klaassen, ed., *Anabaptism Revisited* (Scottdale, Pa.: Herald Press, 1992), pp. 29-49.

[47] As against the conclusions of Hans-Jürgen Goertz, *Die Täufer*, pp. 26-27.

[48] Expressed well by Werner Packull who, in spite of recognized differences between Müntzer, Hut, and Denck, insisted that "the theological and soteriological differences between Hut, Denck, and Müntzer were differences of degree, and, in comparison with the presuppositional differences which separated all three from the Reformers, they were not fundamental." *Mysticism*, p. 66.

A view of Strasbourg in the late fifteenth century

Chapter 9

The Strasbourg Context

The city of Strasbourg occupies a unique and central place in the development of the Anabaptist movement.[1] The reasons are not hard to find: strategically located for trade and commerce on the Rhine—the central transportation link between north and south—in 1482 Strasbourg acquired considerable latitude when it became a free imperial city, under the jurisdiction of the Holy Roman Emperor alone. In 1524 it had a population of around 20,000, making it one of the largest cities in the Empire.[2] Already in the late medieval period Strasbourg had a well deserved reputation for toleration, and as a free imperial city it continued that tradition into the sixteenth century. Sebastian Franck, who as a religious dissenter experienced his share of difficulties with political authorities, wrote in his encyclopedic *Chronicle*: "Those who are hanged elsewhere are drived out of Strasbourg with rods."[3] In fact, Franck himself was expelled from Strasbourg (not hanged *or* beaten with rods, but nevertheless expelled) in December of 1531 for having published the *Chronicle* there.[4]

Sebastian Franck was one of a large group of religious dissenters, famous and not so famous, who resided in Strasbourg for varying lengths of time in the 1520s and 30s. Among the Anabaptist leaders who, at one time or another, were present in the city we may name Hans Denck, Michael Sattler, Jakob Groß, Wilhelm Reublin, Jakob Kautz, Pilgram Marpeck, Melchior Hoffman, Johannes Bünderlin, and Christian Entfelder. The list of non-Anabaptist radicals who were in Strasbourg for varying lengths of time is equally impressive: Andreas Karlstadt, Otto Brunfels, Martin Cellarius, Louis Hätzer, Caspar Schwenckfeld, Sebastian Franck, Michael Servetus, and John Campanus. When we add to this list representatives of an indigenous "radical" movement (Clement Ziegler and Fridolin Meyger, for example), an unusually irenic group of city clergy (Zell, Capito, Bucer), and a tolerant and deliberate city council we begin to appreciate why there was such an unusual breadth of reforming views represented in Strasbourg, at all levels of the social and political spectrum.

As occurred elsewhere during these early years of reform, very soon there appeared in Strasbourg an unofficial, grass roots movement for social and religious change that appealed especially to the "common people" of the city: the poorest guild members and the disenfranchised journeymen and unskilled labourers. This movement was not sanctioned by the magistracy at all but, because of Strasbourg's policy of toleration, it was allowed a wider scope of action than in most other cities of the Empire.[5] It was not the case that the city's evangelical preachers were standing still—by the end of January 1524, Matthias Zell had begun baptizing infants in German, by February his assistant Diebold Schwartz was conducting Mass in German, and later that year Zell married the remarkable Catherine Schütz Zell and was excommunicated by the bishop.[6] Still the grass roots movement agitated for more rapid and thorough change.

By the Fall of 1524 the city council had expressed open concern about "uproar." The concern was not unfounded, for along with matters of religious reform, social and economic questions also had come to the fore and would soon erupt in the Peasants' War. The Alsatian phase of the Peasants' War was over by May of 1525, and the city itself had avoided major upheaval by judicious trimming of taxes and other concessions.[7] But within a few months Balthasar Hubmaier's *On the Christian Baptism of Believers* had been printed in the city and before long Anabaptist refugees began to arrive.[8] In the case of Alsace in general, and Strasbourg in particular, there are few overt connections between the Peasants' War and the subsequent Anabaptist congregations. This does not mean that the various Anabaptist groups that emerged in Strasbourg were "apolitical" or "purely religious," but it does seem to have been the case that by the time Anabaptist communities emerged in the city, their aims excluded the larger social/political aims of the abortive Peasants' War.[9]

From the perspective of the city council and the city's preachers, however, the grass roots reforming appeal of Anabaptism posed some serious problems, both political and religious. Politically the problem was the same as elsewhere: political unity was decreed necessary for the effective defence of the city, and dissenting conventicles undermined such unity—especially when dissenters refused on principle to bear arms or to swear the civic oath. From a religious point of view, the reformers were faced in Anabaptism with a competing theological and ecclesiastical programme that put forward an alternative (and not unpersuasive) understanding of the central church ordinances of baptism, church discipline, and the Supper.

The problem was compounded in Strasbourg by the fact that two of the three most influential reformers, Wolfgang Capito and Mathias Zell (and his wife Catherine), were kindly disposed to dissenters and Anabaptists from the start; Martin Bucer was more attuned to political necessity and less convinced by the Anabaptist insistence on adult baptism, although initially he too was "sensitive to the moderate radicals on such matters as pedobaptism, moral reform, and the separation of the two swords."[10] By the time of the Strasbourg church synods of 1533 Bucer had managed to define Strasbourg's reform programme in a more restrictive way, and five years later managed to win virtually all the local Melchiorites back into the state church. In the meantime, however, Strasbourg became a haven for dissenters and Anabaptists of all kinds, many of whom were hosted personally by Capito and the Zells.

Anabaptism in Strasbourg to 1527

The beginnings of Anabaptism in Strasbourg no longer can be identified in the sources, although it is supposed that there were small groups of Anabaptists in the city already by late summer of 1525; with the fall of Waldshut in December and increased persecution in Zürich and elsewhere, refugees began to arrive in earnest. Among the first to be noted in the record was Wilhelm Reublin—former preacher in

Basel, then radical preacher to the peasants in the Zürich district and Hallau, part of the Grebel circle, baptizer of Balthasar Hubmaier, and later involved (for a time) in communal Anabaptism in Moravia.[11] Reublin stayed in the home of Jörg Ziegler, a tailor whose house would remain an important meeting place for Anabaptists; Reublin was not the originator of this small group, but rather came to visit a group already functioning.

Capito hosted discussions in his own home with Reublin in early Spring 1526, but Reublin refused to debate publicly and soon left the city. His host Jörg Ziegler was summoned to three discussions with the city's pastors, and the matter was laid to rest quietly.[12] Hans Wolff, a weaver who had arrived from Benfeld in April, was less inclined to be quiet. Although apparently he had not accepted adult baptism, he advocated some "Anabaptist concepts" including non-resistance and the separation of church and state. Following a series of talks and times in prison, Wolff imprudently interrupted a sermon by Matthias Zell in the cathedral, in the manner of George Blaurock in Zollikon, saying that the Spirit had called him to preach. He was jailed immediately and expelled in July, 1526. Like some others, Wolff was an evangelical lay "radical" who shared some ideas with Anabaptists, but did not become one himself.[13]

Although there was a report in July 1526 that preachers were subjected to insults when they baptized infants,[14] the preachers were hopeful that the Anabaptist movement was on the wane. But in November Hans Denck arrived, followed by Ludwig Hätzer, Jakob Groß and Michael Sattler in quick succession. Of these Hans Denck was the most active, and disturbed the city's preachers the most. He quickly gained a significant gathering in the city to the point that the reformers felt directly threatened. Following a private disputation in Capito's home with Cellarius, a public disputation was held on December 22, 1526 with the city's clergy, in front of 400 interested citizens. Martin Bucer carried the debate for the Strasbourg preachers; Denck was characteristically irenic and evasive. The end result was that Denck was banished from the city and departed on December 25.[15]

Probably as a result of the public disputation the civic authorities rounded up a group of Anabaptists: Jakob Groß, the itinerant Anabaptist evangelist from Waldshut; Jörg Tucher from Weissenburg Switzerland; Mathias Hiller, a furrier from St. Gall baptized by Groß in Strasbourg; Wilhelm Echsel, a cobbler from Valois baptized in Zürich; and Jörg Ziegler, the Strasbourg tailor who had given lodging to Reublin earlier.[16] Their testimony is interesting because it is one of the few glimpses we have of the emerging Anabaptist and radical conventicles in Strasbourg in late 1526 and early 1527. Besides emphasis on the obedience to the letter of Scripture and the admonishment to live a new life (love of neighbour), Tucher's testimony pointed also to a rudimentary teaching of community of goods and some uncertainty concerning the sword, both of which reflect the situation in Swiss Anabaptism at this time.

That Michael Sattler related to the "Swiss" Anabaptists in Strasbourg is clear from his connections to the individuals involved both before and after the arrest of

Groß and his compatriots. Jakob Groß and Sattler both missionized in Lahr, across the Rhine from Strasbourg, and both baptized converts there—Groß prior to coming to Strasbourg, Sattler after having been in Strasbourg; whether they worked in Lahr concurrently is no longer clear from the sources.[17] What, if any, Sattler's contacts were with the "Denckian" group in Strasbourg is no longer clear, but Ludwig Hätzer's negative comment concerning Sattler—that Sattler was "a sly evil lurker ... of whom we expected better things"—suggests an underlying tension with Hätzer at least, if not with Denck.[18]

There were, then, emerging "Swiss" Anabaptist conventicles in Strasbourg just prior to the composition of the Schleitheim Articles (February 24, 1527). They operated primarily among the craftspeople of the city: involved were furriers, tailors, tanners, coopers, weavers and cobblers. There were, in addition, persons who had associated more closely with Hans Denck and Ludwig Hätzer, such as the notary Fridolin Meyger, who continued to organize meetings in the city; and finally, local grass roots reformers like Clement Ziegler continued their activity.[19] But the lines of division between the grass roots radicals still were not firmly established. Clemens Ziegler (who never became an Anabaptist) was present at one Anabaptist meeting where a baptism took place, and continued to host Anabaptist meetings;[20] Jörg Ziegler claimed that he had been asked to lodge Anabaptists by Capito and Hans Denck. One would have to agree with Hans-Werner Müsing's observation that "the boundaries between the various groups were fluid" and probably not clearly visible to the participants themselves in early 1527.[21] Likewise the clergy were not of one mind as to how to deal with the various dissenting groups and individuals; Capito's vacillation and Bucer's growing determination point to either end of the spectrum.

The city council, while not yet declaring itself on doctrinal questions, "always based its actions on the preservation of peace and order."[22] On July 27, 1527, half a year after Zürich had drowned Felix Mantz for being an Anabaptist, the Strasbourg authorities promulgated their first decree against any who might reject a Christian government and destroy the unity of the community. With characteristic leniency, the penalties for disobedience to the mandate were not specified, but were to be applied in each particular case.[23] In light of increasingly harsh measures being taken elsewhere, this mandate encouraged, rather than discouraged the arrival of even more religious refugees.

Anabaptism to 1533

The boundaries and lines of division between the various radical groups in Strasbourg, including those between Anabaptists of differing tendencies, became increasingly visible from 1527 to 1533. Likewise by 1533, with the convening of the territorial synod, the city had consolidated its position doctrinally and with respect to the dissident groups in Strasbourg.[24]

The year 1527 saw a continuation of Anabaptist meetings in the city, the most notable of which revolved around Fridolin Meyger. Meyger, closely associated with

Denck and Hätzer, was baptized by Jakob Kautz most probably in the latter half of 1527.[25] The meetings involving Meyger and many others took place at the two syphilis hospitals and in Meyger's own home, and resulted in some expulsions. In the summer several hundred Anabaptist refugees from Augsburg came to Strasbourg, responding to the increasing repression there; among these would be found followers of Hans Hut.[26] An interesting mix of the visionary "Hutian" element and Swiss emphases is represented by the Anabaptist Michel Ecker, a cutler who had been exiled from Sterzing in South Tirol and resufaced in Strasbourg: he professed nonresistance and refused to swear oaths, but also offered to share his visions with the Strasbourg preachers and the council. He testified that every Sunday he and some 250 others would gather for worship at Fridolin Meyger's house.[27]

In September 1528 Pilgram Marpeck became a citizen of Strasbourg through the purchase of citizenship; his Anabaptist convictions and concerns for social justice led him to associate with Fridolin Meyger and Lukas Hackfurt, the latter of whom was responsible for poor relief.[28] These interests led to Marpeck's arrest in October 1528 for having allowed a meeting of Anabaptists in his house; arrested along with him were Meyger, Reublin, and Kautz, the latter two of whom had returned to Strasbourg in spite of having been banned earlier.[29] Meyger recanted and swore an oath at this time; Reublin and Kautz would not, and remained in prison; the record is silent concerning Marpeck's fate. Perhaps he was pardoned, for in his defense he argued that the meeting had taken place in order to help the many poor refugees that were to be found in the city, and there is no record of further hearings with him concerning this arrest. In any case he soon was in the employ of the city, supervising the purchase of forest land, the cutting of trees, and the construction of dams to transport the wood to Strasbourg.[30]

The arrest of Reublin and Kautz sheds some interesting light on how these two Anabaptists, representing the "Swiss" and "Denckian" streams respectively, understood each other in late 1528. In spite of some recognized differences—Reublin said that he did not agree with all of Kautz's points—nevertheless in January 1529, after some two and a half months spent in prison together, they composed a joint confession, written in the first person plural.[31] They confessed that they had lived disordered lives before they had been freed by God's grace and the hearing of the Word. But as soon as they had made a covenant of their good conscience before God through baptism, and had joined the Body of Christ, immediately they were persecuted as had been Christ, "hunted from one city to the next." They were agreed that baptism in water was the "inscription of believers into the outer community of God," and should be given to all who have repented and desire it from the heart; they opposed infant baptism. They also agreed that, because of the "lack of fruit" in Strasbourg, it was clear that the preachers had not been called of God. Reublin and Kautz, although representing two different Anabaptist origins and tendencies, still considered each other members of the same group, and agreed on essential teachings, including the existence of an "inner" or spiritual church called directly of God, which became the "outer" or visible church, recognizable through obedience to the commands of Christ and the practice of the apostles, particularly through water baptism.[32]

It would not be long, however, until the lines of division between the more "literal" Swiss Anabaptists and the "spiritualist" group—implicit already in Sattler and Denck and visible, though not divisive, in Reublin and Kautz—would be drawn clearly in Strasbourg. The year 1529 saw the arrival of Hans Bünderlin, Christian Entfelder, Sebastian Franck, and Caspar Schwenckfeld; all of them were, or soon became, defenders of a more "spiritual" Christianity.

Both Bünderlin and Entfelder were Anabaptists in the South German line of Denck and Hut. Hans Bünderlin was born in Linz, Austria and studied at the University of Vienna. He was in Augsburg in 1526, where he accepted baptism, possibly from Hans Denck, and soon was leading an Anabaptist congregation in Linz. At an unknown date he fled to Nicholsburg, but as the situation became more tenuous for the lords of Liechtenstein he fled to Strasbourg, where he had arrived by early 1529. Bünderlin led meetings in the city and, prior to his two arrests and expulsion later in 1529, had four books published there. The third of these, "Explanation through Study of the Biblical Writings," was directed against the Anabaptist practice of water baptism and celebration of the Supper. Bünderlin had moved to a purely spiritualist position, as we will see in more detail in chapter 21 below.[33]

Christian Entfelder likewise had solid Anabaptist credentials. Although it is not known who baptized him, he was in Nicholsburg with Hubmaier in 1526, and then served as Elder of an Anabaptist congregation in Eibenschitz, Moravia. At some point in 1529 he appeared in Strasbourg and, although there is no documentation of contact with Bünderlin, the first of Entfelder's three books, "On the Many Divisions in the Faith," is very close in spirit and content to Bünderlin's "Explanation." In this writing Entfelder distanced himself from all the disagreeing Reformation groups, including the Anabaptists, and called for internal spiritual unity instead.[34]

The move away from "external" Anabaptism to spiritualism by Bünderlin and Entfelder echoed Hans Denck's repudiation of "external ceremonies" just before his death in Basel. Bünderlin and Entfelder, both erstwhile Anabaptist leaders of some repute, brought to light a fundamental tension present in the theological underpinning of Anabaptism as a whole. Simply put, if the "essential" baptism is spiritual, to which the water is only a "witness," and if the essential Supper is also spiritual and the physical elements are incidental, why should mere "ceremonies" be observed—particularly since they are non-essentials that only serve to divide believers from one another? To this challenge Pilgram Marpeck responded with two booklets written in 1531: *A Clear Refutation* and *A Clear and Useful Instruction*.[35] Lending weight to these "spiritualist" defections from Anabaptism in Strasbourg were Sebastian Franck and Caspar Schwenckfeld, both of whom were influential spiritualists and prolific writers. The spiritualist option was presented in a variety of appealing ways in the year 1529 and following; it was made all the more attractive by unrelenting persecution, growing division within Anabaptism, and the spiritualist root at the heart of Anabaptism itself.

It was into this rich and volatile setting that Melchior Hoffman came in the summer of 1529. Prior to Hoffman's conversion to Anabaptism, which took place in Strasbourg in 1529, the internal development of the Anabaptist movement had revolved around Swiss and South German Anabaptism in their various settings. Now, at the same time that the latent tension between the spiritualist and separatist poles in Anabaptism was becoming overt and divisive, Hoffman developed yet a third expression of Anabaptism which, although it incorporated adult baptism, the ban, and a memorial Supper, nevertheless placed these ecclesiological ordinances in a visionary, apocalyptic context. From Hoffman would originate the Anabaptism of North Germany and the Netherlands, as will be described in the chapter to follow.

By 1533 the Strasbourg council and preachers set out to define their reformation in the face of the varied challenges posed by the religious dissidents in their midst. The mild mandate of 1527 against harbouring Anabaptists and other radicals had not had the desired effect, nor had the abolition of the Mass in 1529 brought religious unity to the city. Numerous dissident leaders had been jailed and exiled— Pilgram Marpeck was exiled early in 1532—but their various groups continued to meet nonetheless. There also were those among the city's clergy who opposed any civil interference in religious matters.[36] The end result of several synodal sessions in 1533 was the emergence of Martin Bucer as the pre-eminent pastor in Strasbourg— "the bishop of our church" in the words of Capito—and "the consolidation of the magisterial reformation" in the city.[37] The council now had the mandate to regulate not only law and order in the city, but also matters of church doctrine and discipline.

Strasbourg remained a tolerant city, and remained an Anabaptist centre important especially to small numbers of Swiss Brethren in the 1540s, after Bucer managed to win over the Melchiorite leaders Georg Schnabel and Peter Tasch, and most of their following, in 1538 and 1539.[38] Strasbourg's central geographical location and continuing relative toleration made it the site of Anabaptist gatherings in 1554, 1555, 1557, 1568, 1592, and 1607.[39]

Conclusion

By 1533 the boundaries dividing Anabaptist groups from each other were increasingly visible. The Anabaptist Hans Frisch, who lived in the city from 1529 to 1534, described the Anabaptists in Strasbourg as divided into three distinct groupings: those following the teachings of Hoffman, Kautz, and Reublin respectively, with the Hoffman and Kautz groups "a little mixed together."[40] Sebastian Franck, on the other hand, wrote in his *Chronica* that there were so many different varieties of Anabaptists that he could not possibly name them all, although he devoted many pages to delineating important, and not so important, differences between them.[41] Contrasting Franck's comment with Frisch's we are brought back again to the question of the forest and the trees in attempting to describe Anabaptism as a movement; but looking further at Franck's description of the Anabaptism he witnessed in Strasbourg also brings us back to the fundamental tensions underlying Anabaptist theology from the start.

As we have seen, there were indeed very many differences in detail among Anabaptist individuals and groups, many of whom Franck came to know during his time in Strasbourg. But Franck's comment and description must be taken for what it was: a systematic attempt to find and describe as many differences of opinion as possible. A detailing of Anabaptist differences served Franck's central point in this part of his *Chronica*, which was to demonstrate that the "heresy of the letter" (biblical literalism) inevitably led to disharmony and disunity, both among the reformers and among the dissidents. "The letter (of Scripture) ... always has produced heretics," wrote Franck, "for since the Scripture is divided and not unitary according to the letter, literalism must lead to heresy."[42] The answer to such literally-based divisiveness said Franck, repeating Bünderlin and Entfelder's points, was to establish a non-sectarian, spiritual Christianity that relied on the living Spirit rather than the outer word and empty "outer ceremonies."

Franck's description of the fragmentation within Christendom was part of his determined effort to oppose cantankerous, coercive, and divisive religion, and at the same time to promote a tolerant, peaceful, spiritual communion and fellowship among those who claimed to follow the Prince of Peace. But Franck was not merely describing; he also was participating in the debates of the day—and he was a persuasive and influential participant indeed, particularly from an Anabaptist perspective. The basic historical structure and argument of the *Chronica*, by describing an historical and heroic "church of heretics" alongside a fallen, coercive institutional church, served later Anabaptist writers well. Ironically, the massive *Chronica* soon became the indispensible sectarian encyclopedia, even though it was written to combat "sectarianism" and division.[43]

Franck's appeal to freedom of conscience and religious toleration also served later Anabaptists well. In the latter part of the sixteenth century, for example, the "literalist" Swiss Brethren freely utilized Franck's "spiritualist" argument for religious toleration, namely that faith, being a spiritual gift of God's grace, cannot be coerced by external means.[44] But Franck's message, after all, was a critique not only of coercion by those in possession of the sword, but also of *any* "external" coercion, including the Anabaptist ban used in support of water baptism, a memorial Supper, and external rules of behaviour. Franck's anti-sectarian critique and appeal to a tolerant spiritualism thus continued to pose a live option in Anabaptist circles, especially in the Netherlands after 1536.[45]

Early Anabaptism was a loose "movement" characterized by a plurality of views that more or less recognized a broad spiritual and theological kinship; it included both "spiritualizing" and "biblicist" tendencies, as we have seen, sometimes working together and sometimes at cross purposes. This tension did not last. By 1530 Anabaptists were defining their borders more and more strictly in their relationships with one another (a process Franck saw at work), according to increasingly exclusive scriptural criteria. Franck recognized the inherent tension within Anabaptism between the spirit and the letter and between the inner spiritual life (baptism of the spirit) and the outer manifestation of the inner life (baptism in water, the ban, and the Supper). In arguing for the essential priority of the spiritual, inner life, Sebastian Franck lent the weight of his erudition to a separation of the spiritual life from the "ceremonies" that defined the outer religious life.[46] In effect, he urged Anabaptists to follow the lead of Hans Denck, Hans Bünderlin and Christian Entfelder, and to leave behind the "outer" marks of church as non-essential.

In light of the fundamental presuppositions underlying the Anabaptist understanding of faith—as at once a free, inner, and spiritual gift of God, but requiring external "obedience"—it is not surprising that Franck's critique of Anabaptist divisiveness over "externals" and his spiritualist counter proposal would prove attractive to Anabaptists weary of persecution from without, and of acrimonious, boundary-defining controversy from within. Obbe Philips, who baptized Menno Simons, withdrew from Anabaptism under such spiritualist influence; his brother Dirk, who was instrumental in cementing Dutch Anabaptist boundaries, found it necessary to write directly against the errors of Sebastian Franck some twenty years after Franck's death.[47] Franck's tolerant, individualist spiritualism would remain an attractive option in the

Netherlands, particularly among the Waterlanders and later *Doopsgezinden* (baptism minded), who eventually came to adopt a broad-minded Anabaptism that Franck would have applauded.

End Notes

[1] For a good overview of events in Strasbourg, 1519-1535, see Williams, *Radical* (1992), chapter 10, part II; also John S. Oyer, "Bucer and the Anabaptists," in Christian Krieger and Marc Lienhard, *Martin Bucer and Sixteenth Century Europe* (Leiden: Brill, 1993), vol. 2, pp. 603-613.

[2] Stephen F. Nelson and Jean Rott, "Strasbourg: The Anabaptist City in the Sixteenth Century," MQR (July, 1984), p. 230. For a succinct overview of the social and political structure of the city, see Stephen B. Boyd, *Pilgram Marpeck: His Life and Social Theology* (Durham, N.C.: Duke University Press, 1992), pp. 43-44. On Strasbourg's political structure, see Thomas A. Brady, *Ruling Class, Regime and Reformation at Strasbourg* (Leiden: E. Brill, 1978); on the reform as such, see Miriam U. Chrisman, *Strasbourg and the Reform* (New Haven, Conn.: Yale University Press, 1967).

[3] Cited in Nelson and Rott, "Strasbourg," p. 232. See the brief biography of Franck by Steven E. Ozment, "Sebastian Franck: Critic of the 'New Scholastics'," in Hans-Jürgen Goertz, ed., *Profiles of Radical Reformers* (Scottdale, Pa.: Herald Press, 1982), pp. 226-33.

[4] Williams, *Radical*, pp. 395-96. Franck's publisher and printer in Strasbourg was Balthasar Beck, who inherited the print business through marriage to Margarete Preuss, daughter of the Strasbourg printer Johann Preuss. Balthasar and Margarete lent their press to radical causes and published several works by Melchior Hoffman. After the death of Franck's first wife Ottilie, he married Barbara Beck, daughter of Balthasar and Margarete. *Ibid.*, p. 702. For a profile of Margarete Preuss, see Snyder and Hecht, *Profiles*.

[5] It should be noted that the city's preachers enjoyed wide support among the common people of the city, and also acted on their behalf before the magistrates. See Boyd, *Marpeck*, p. 47, n. 24.

[6] Williams, *Radical*, pp. 364-65.

[7] Tom Scott and Bob Scribner, trans. and eds., *The German Peasants' War: A History in Documents* (London: Humanities Press, 1991), document #75, pp. 189-91.

[8] Hubmaier's *Von der christlichen Taufe* was printed in the Matthias Schürer shop in Strasbourg in July or August of 1525, and was distributed quickly in all parts of Switzerland. See HS, p. 117. English translation of this seminal writing in Pipkin and Yoder, *Hubmaier*, pp. 95-149.

[9] Stayer, *German Peasants' War*, pp. 75-7, who notes that the evidence for Alsace and Swabia shows "no significant connection between the two movements." p. 77.

[10] So Williams, *Radical*, p. 372; for the above, see pp. 369-77. Oyer, "Bucer and the Anabaptists," p. 613, argues against the view of Bucer as "a calculating politician," maintaining rather that "Bucer was irenic, generally mild toward Anabaptists, tolerant of their continued presence as much as he could be in his own assessment of the situation."

[11] See the compact biography of Reublin by James Stayer, "Wilhelm Reublin: A Picaresque Journey Through Early Anabaptism," in Hans-Jürgen Goertz, ed., *Profiles of Radical Reformers* (Scottdale, Pa.: Herald Press, 1982), pp. 107-117.

[12] For the account of events in 1526/1527 I am following Hans-Werner Müsing, "The Anabaptist Movement in Strasbourg from Early 1526 to July 1527," MQR (April, 1977), 91-126; for the information above, see pp. 91-93.

[13] *Ibid.*, pp. 94-97.

[14] TA, *Elsass*, I, p. 56.

[15] For a detailed account, see Müsing, "Anabaptist Movement in Strasbourg," pp. 101-107.

[16] The record is undated, but the arrests and questioning probably took place at the end of 1526. See TA, *Elsass*, I, pp. 62-7; and the excellent summary in Müsing, "Anabaptist Movement in Strasbourg," pp. 107-12.

[17] On Groß's Lahr activity, see TA, *Elsass*, I, p. 129; on Sattler's activity, see the testimony of Ottelinus, reformed pastor at Lahr, in *ibid.*, pp. 72-4, summarized in Snyder, *Life and Thought*, pp. 95-96. Groß's companion in Waldshut, expelled with him was Ulrich Teck; Sattler was arrested with Teck later in Zürich. See *ibid.*, p. 97.

[18] Cited in Müsing, "Anabaptist Movement in Strasbourg," p. 100.

[19] Müsing suggests a close connection between Meyger, Hätzer and Denck, "Anabaptist Movement in Strasbourg," p. 115; see also Boyd, *Marpeck*, p. 50.

[20] Müsing, "Anabaptist Movement in Strasbourg," p. 108.

[21] *Ibid.*, p. 119.

[22] *Ibid.*, p. 125.

[23] Summarized in *ibid.*, pp. 122-23; see TA, *Elsass*, I, pp. 122-23 for the mandate.

[24] For a detailed overview, see Williams, *Radical*, pp. 377-430.

[25] In March, 1529, Fridolin Meyger confessed to having been baptized by Jacob Kautz, who was converted to Anabaptism in Worms most probably by Denck. TA, *Elsass*, I, #179, p. 234. This baptism probably took place in Strasbourg sometime after Kautz's expulsion from Worms (June, 1527) and before Kautz's first expulsion from Strasbourg (June, 1528). On Kautz, see TA, *Baden und Pfalz*, p. 116, n. 1; TA, *Elsass*, I, p. 163.

[26] Boyd, Marpeck, p. 50. The numbers are not exactly known, but fall between 100 and 500 refugees.

[27] TA, *Elsass*, I, pp. 154-55. Ecker was arrested and expelled in April, 1528.

[28] See Boyd, *Marpeck*, pp. 52-56.

[29] TA, *Elsass*, I, pp. 184-86.

[30] Details in Boyd, *Marpeck*, pp. 56-9.

[31] Reublin's disclaimer is in TA, *Elsass*, I, p. 195; their confession is found in *ibid.*, pp. 197-99.

[32] Further writings from Reublin and Kautz are no longer extant, but more can be inferred from the lengthy writing submitted to the council by the preachers. There both Reublin and Kautz are said to hold to both an invisible and visible church, as described above. The preachers refer in more detail to Kautz than to Reublin in their refutation. TA, *Elsass*, I, pp. 201-18.

[33] ME, I, pp. 469-470; see also Packull, *Mysticism*, pp. 155-63 and Boyd, *Marpeck*, p. 59. On his baptism in Augsburg, TA, *Elsass*, I, p. 232.

[34] See Packull, *Mysticism*, pp. 163-75; ME, II, pp. 226-27. Entfelder remained sympathetic to Anabaptists after he had separated from them; he entered the service of Albrecht von Hohenzollern as councillor in 1536 and negotiated the first large settlement of Anabaptists from the Netherlands in East Prussia. So Packull, *Mysticism*, p. 163.

[35]Klassen and Klaassen, *Writings*, pp. 43-106. See Boyd's theological analysis of Marpeck's response to the "radical individualism" of Bünderlin and Entfelder in *Marpeck*, pp. 84-90. We will review the arguments in more detail in chapter 21.

[36] These were the so-called "Epicureans," led by Anthony Engelbrecht and including, among others, Otto Brunfels. See Williams, *Radical*, pp. 412-17.

[37] *Ibid.*, p. 422, and n. 187.

[38] See Packull, "The Melchiorites and the Ziegenhain Order of Discipline, 1538-39," pp. 11-28. Oyer notes that after 1538 "The Anabaptist threat had subsided. Their most able leaders, those capable of attracting and holding disaffected Reformed, had been exiled. Quirky leaders such as Hoffman posed no threat. Strasbourg held only small, dispirited groups of Swiss Brethren, erstwhile followers of Kautz who held themselves apart from all others, and a few stragglers who still believed Hoffman." Oyer, "Bucer and the Anabaptists," p. 608.

[39] John Oyer, "The Strasbourg Conferences of the Anabaptists, 1554-1607," MQR (July, 1984), pp. 218-29. Oyer notes that in the second half of the sixteenth century the city authorities still did not practice captial punishment, but relied on exile to control the Anabaptist movement.

[40] TA, *Elsass*, I, pp. 288-89; cited in Boyd, *Marpeck*, p. 61. The followers of Kautz we may take to be Anabaptists of a more "spiritualist" leaning; the followers of Reublin would be the more biblicist and rigorous Swiss Brethren, and probably also followers of Marpeck.

[41] In the 1536 Ulm edition of the *Chronica* the Anabaptists are discussed in the third "chronicle" concerning "Popes and spiritual matters, from Peter to Clement," pp. cxciii, recto to cci, verso. See especially Franck's concluding comments on p. cc, recto. (In the 1536 edition, the first two major sections or "chronicles" are numbered sequentially; the third "chronicle," while bound with the other two, begins numbering with Roman numeral i again). Franck was best acquainted with the South German Anabaptists. He names Hubmaier, Rinck, Hut, Denck, and Hätzer as key leaders in this section, p. cxciii, recto; the martyrdoms of Michael Sattler, Jörg Wagner, and Lienhart Kaiser are noted elsewhere (third chronicle, pp. clxxvi, verso-clxxvii, verso). The Melchiorite movement had really just begun at the time of the publication of the first, Strasbourg edition of the *Chronica* (1531), but by the time he prepared the 1536 edition Franck had inserted a separate description of events in Münster. He placed these events in the second "chronicle" whose overall subject was "Chronicle of the Emperors and World History." (second chronicle, pp. ccxci, recto to ccxciiii, recto).

[42] *Ibid.*, p. cci, recto.

[43] Franck's historical perspective, and citations from and allusion to his text, appear freely among the Hutterites (the *Hutterite Chronicle*, for example), the later Swiss Brethren (the lenthy and apologetic Swiss Brethren "Ein kurtze einfaltige erkanntnuß," ca. 1585, cites the *Chronica*), and the Dutch (the *Martyrs Mirror*).

[44] The argument surfaces in the second (1583) preface to the *Ausbund*, the Swiss Brethren hymnal, as well as in the lengthy apologetic writing "Kurtze einfaltige erkanntnuß" (anonymous, ca. 1585).

[45] Williams, *Radical*, p. 396, notes sixteen full editions of the *Chronica* in German, and seven in Dutch.

[46] After noting extensively how some Anabaptists (particularly Denck) emphasized the spirit and left outer things "free," while others got caught up in the letter and outer requirements, Franck argued against those

who have "their legal rules, monasticism, and regulated Christendom, which cannot be a Christian faith for (a Christian faith) tolerates no law or ordering and cannot be set down in rules; rather it is a freeing of the spirit in which the Holy Spirit alone wishes to be teacher and master..." *Chronica*, part III, p. cc, verso.

[47] See Obbe Philips' "Confession" in Williams, SAW, pp. 204-25; on Dirk's "Answer to Sebastian Franck," see Cornelius Dyck, William Keeney, and Alvin Beachy, eds. and trans., *The Writings of Dirk Philips*, (Scottdale, Pa.: Herald Press, 1992), pp. 445-467. Dirk Volkertsz Coornhert (1522-1590) of Haarlem was a promoter of Franck's views and influential among the Mennonites. *Ibid.*, p. 446.

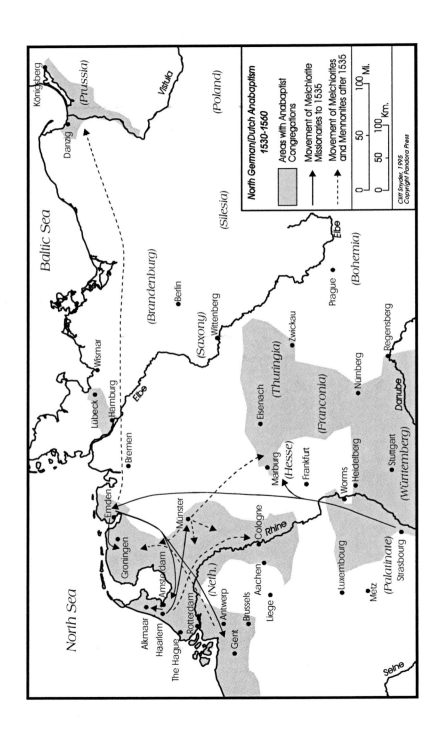

North German/Dutch Anabaptism
1530-1560

Areas with Anabaptist
Congregations

Movement of Melchiorite
Missionaries to 1535

Movement of Melchiorites
and Mennonites after 1535

Mi.
100

50

Km.
100

50

Cliff Snyder, 1995
Copyright Pandora Press

Baltic Sea

North Sea

Königsberg

(Prussia)

Vistula

Danzig

(Poland)

(Silesia)

(Brandenburg)

Berlin

(Saxony)

Wittenberg

Elbe

Wismar

Lübeck

Hamburg

Prague

(Bohemia)

Bremen

Elbe

Zwickau

(Thuringia)

Regensberg

Eisenach

Nürnberg

(Franconia)

Danube

Emden

Marburg

(Hesse)

Frankfurt

Groningen

Münster

Worms

Heidelberg

Stuttgart

Amsterdam

Cologne

(Neth.)

Rhine

(Württemberg)

Alkmaar

Haarlem

Rotterdam

Antwerp

Aachen

Luxembourg

The Hague

Gent

Brussels

Liège

Metz

(Palatinate)

Strasbourg

Seine

Chapter 10

The Origin and Spread of North German/Dutch Anabaptism

The Anabaptism of North Germany and the Netherlands, unlike the Anabaptism of Switzerland or that of South Germany and Austria, can be traced to the overwhelming influence of one man, who stamped the northern movement with very discernible features. That man was Melchior Hoffman, and his brand of Anabaptism proved to be both fruitful and unstable.

Melchior Hoffman

Melchior Hoffman was born between 1495 and 1500 in Schwäbisch Hall. He became a furrier by trade, he was literate, and a persuasive and powerful speaker.[1] By 1523 he was active as a Lutheran lay missionary in Livonia (1523-26). The work of the Holy Spirit was centrally important to Hoffman already in his early years as a Lutheran, and it appears that Karlstadt was more influential for him than was Luther.[2] His ministry concentrated on the poor, and had strong anticlerical tones, with resulting social unrest and violence in the city of Dorpat.[3]

Hoffman's attraction to apocalypticism was already evident in his early work: the Holy Spirit was being poured out on all people; the two witnesses of the Last Days (Elijah and Enoch) were already present in the world; but the sword was to be used only against evil doers, and not in the church.[4] Hoffman also came to believe in the progressive "divinization" of human beings: the spiritual battle was an inner one. What was needed was spiritual yieldedness (*Gelassenheit*), so that God could do what God willed.[5] Clearly Hoffman would have problems with Luther at key points: "at once justified and a sinner" did not fit Hoffman's pneumatology or anthropology, nor did predestination suit either. The background to Hoffman's teaching on *Gelassenheit* was the medieval mystical tradition, the Theologia Deutsch, and Andreas Karlstadt.[6]

Hoffman's career as a "Lutheran" was a rocky one. He missionized for a time in Stockholm, and then moved on to Schleswig-Holstein (1527-29). His open break with the Lutheran reformers came in the matter of the Lord's Supper, in which Hoffman denied a real presence. Following a disputation in April, 1529, after which Hoffman was banished, his break with the Lutheran stream was complete. Lutheran clergy now were added to the list of false prophets; henceforth Lutheranism was a "new popery."

Following a brief work in East Frisia in the Spring of 1529, Hoffman moved south to Strasbourg, where he came into contact with several varieties of Anabaptism and spiritualism. As noted above, present in the city were conventicles of Swiss Brethren, spiritualist followers of Hans Denck, followers of Pilgram Marpeck, the spiritualist Caspar Schwenckfeld, and a group of enthusiastic disciples of Hans Hut.[7] Visible in the writings Hoffman published in Strasbourg in 1530 was an overriding concern with prophetic Scripture and its interpretation. Hoffman later would be responsible for publishing the visions of Ursula Jost, which dealt with the End Times. These visions were destined to have a large impact in North Germany and Holland. Hoffman was convinced that God was speaking directly through such contemporary prophets.[8]

It is particularly difficult to identify specific Anabaptist influences on Hoffman, for he seems to have appropriated elements from different theological streams, as they suited him. We do not know who baptized him, but it is clear that he joined no existing group in Strasbourg. Rather, he formed his own.[9] Nevertheless his first Anabaptist writing, *The Ordinance of God* (1530), emphasizes Anabaptist distinctives noted elsewhere in the movement: sinners are called to unite with Christ through repentance and baptism; believers celebrate the Supper of unity (understood in a memorial sense); and believers submit to and practise discipline within the community of the covenant.[10]

Hoffman's teachings on the sword and government, so crucial to later developments in Münster, are hard to unravel, since he blended together elements that tended to fly apart. Hoffman's reading of biblical prophecy led him to the view that the ungodly clergy would be done away with before Christ's imminent return. On the other hand, along with this lively expectation of the imminent destruction of the ungodly mob, Hoffman also taught that the saints (individual Christians) were *not* to take up the sword. Apparently God would find other means of destroying the ungodly than through the direct participation of the elect. On still another front, when it came to political authority, Hoffman taught that there would be pious political rulers who would be God's instruments in bringing about the final victory of the saints.[11] Hoffman maintained his "high" view of political authority to the end.

The ambivalence visible in Hoffman's drastic anticlericalism, his rejection of the sword for individual saints, his prediction of the extermination of the ungodly before the second coming, and his expectation of holy intervention on the part of "godly" authorites proved to be problematic later. Hoffman's Anabaptist followers resolved the ambiguities in his views in a variety of ways, not all of them peaceful.

By April of 1530 the authorities in Strasbourg had heard enough and decided to arrest Hoffman, but he managed to leave town one step ahead of the police and resurfaced in the north, in the city of Emden. He is said to have baptized 300 in the church in Emden.[12] Much as did Hans Hut earlier, Hoffman baptized persons who became zealous evangelists and baptizers of others; in both cases the expectation that Christ's return was imminent seems to have provided a special impetus for evangelism. The way for Anabaptism in the Lowlands had been prepared by the Sacramentarian movement, and Anabaptism very quickly became a mass movement of religious resistance.[13] From the Emden beginnings, Hoffman's version of Anabaptism spread into the Netherlands, where it was to have its greatest success.[14] Among those baptized as a consequence of Hoffman's journeys to the north were Jan

Volkerts Trijpmaker, Sikke Snijder, Obbe Philips, Dirk Philips, Bartholomeus Boekbinder and Pieter Houtsagher.[15] But in December 1531, disaster struck when the Melchiorite apostle, Jan Volkerts Trijpmaker, was put to death along with nine others. Hoffman suspended baptism, and the Melchiorite movement in North Germany and the Netherlands went underground.[16] Melchior Hoffman remained at large, working both in Strasbourg and in the north, until May of 1533, when he allowed himself to be arrested in Strasbourg, sure that this event signalled a crucial turning point in the End Times scenario. He was to die in prison some ten years later.

Along with Melchior Hoffman's Anabaptist spiritualism and apocalypticism, his turn to Anabaptism in 1529 also resulted in a novel Christology that remained a discernible feature for almost a century among the Anabaptists of the Lowlands. As has been noted above, the spiritualist Caspar Schwenckfeld appears to have provided Hoffman with the basic elements of this Christology, although Hoffman and Schwenckfeld differed on some details. Hoffman's "monophysite" Christology remained the most visible heterodox Anabaptist teaching; it remained a point of contention within and without the Anabaptist movement for many decades. Menno Simons defended Hoffman's view to his dying day. We will return to Melchiorite Christology in chapter 25 below.

The Melchiorite Anabaptist movement took strong root in the Netherlands, particularly in the cities of Amsterdam, Leeuwarden and Groningen; the East Friesland region in the far north remained strongly Anabaptist from the start. The province of North Holland, directly north of Amsterdam, was soon evangelized (the cities of Alkmaar, Hoorn, and Enkhuisen) and Anabaptist conventicles and martyrs appear in this region from 1534 on. The southern area including Zeeland, Flanders and Brabant (with the city of Antwerp as an important Anabaptist centre) was reached later, beginning around 1534. And of course, outside the Netherlands proper, in nearby Westphalia, the city of Münster grew to become the Anabaptist focal point in the north in the years 1534 and 1535.[17]

Jan Matthijs

Soon after Melchior Hoffman was imprisoned in Strasbourg in 1533, the Melchiorite baker Jan Matthijs began his prophetic activity in Amsterdam.[18] Led by direct dreams and visions, he reinstated baptism on the basis of his authority as the "Enoch" of the Last Days.[19] The baptism which Matthijs resumed was reminiscent of Hans Hut's conception. Hut, Hoffman and Matthijs interpreted Anabaptist baptism in the sense of the TAU, following Revelation 7:3: a mark of the 144,000 elect.[20] Matthijs's message had three central components: 1) This is the time of the working of the Spirit, 2) God is about to return and judge, and 3) those who are baptized will be spared.[21] Among those baptized by Matthijs and sent out as apostles was Jan van Leiden, later to become the proclaimed "King of Münster and the world."

Jan Matthijs disagreed with Melchior Hoffman on some basic issues. On the question of the measure of obedience due the authorities (especially tyrants) and the role of outside "godly authorities" generally, Matthijs leaned toward action on the part of the saints as opposed to waiting for God or "pious magistrates" to act. Matthijs became convinced that God had given the sword to the elect, particularly after the Anabaptists won a political victory in the city of Münster. Matthijs also was convinced that he was the Enoch of the End Times, although Hoffman favoured Cornelis Poldermann as Enoch. And Matthijs was convinced that Münster, not Strasbourg, was the true New Jerusalem.[22] With Hoffman held increasingly incommunicado in the Strasbourg jail, Matthijs' interpretations came to be more and more accepted in the north.

To all accounts, Jan Matthijs possessed impressive persuasive powers. Obbe Philips, undoubtedly with some exaggeration, described how Matthijs reacted to challenges to his prophetic claim: "He carried on with much emotion and terrifying alarm, and with great and desperate curses cast all into hell and to the devils to eternity who would not hear his voice and who would not recognize and accept him as the true Enoch." The brethren, says Obbe, "became obedient" to Matthijs following "much negotiation."[23]

Jan Matthijs of Haarlem

Matthijs soon became prominently involved in the reform of the city of Münster.

Bernhard Rothmann and Münster[24]

Parallel to events in the Netherlands were the reforming activities in the city of Münster in Westphalia. The leader of the reforming party there was Bernhard Rothmann.[25] He was born around 1495 in Stadtlohn, received a master's degree from the University of Mainz, and by 1529 had begun to preach the evangelical gospel just outside Münster. By 1531 there were acts of iconoclasm in his church which pressed the Münster city council. The situation in Münster was not unlike that of many other Reformation cities. There were three social groups at odds: the ruling class of patricians who controlled the city council; the Guilds (popularly based) who wielded increasing power; and the clergy (headed by the Catholic bishop).[26]

The first effects of the Reformation were anticlericalism and iconoclasm.[27] Attempts to silence Rothmann did not work, primarily because the city council found such pressure advantageous in its struggle against the privileges of the Catholic clergy. The Bishop was forced to acknowledge the Reformation (the Treaty of Dülmen, 1533) and the laity came to exercise authority in the city, but it was not yet clear which party of the laity was to gain control, that is, the privileged patricians, or the guilds.[28] This situation gave Rothmann the power of leverage "in legitimating the position either of the council or the guilds."[29] In general, Rothmann leaned more in the direction of the guilds; with the arrival of Heinrich Rol, he had also received a Zwinglian conception of the Supper.

Heinrich Rol was an ex-Carmelite who came to Münster as an evangelical preacher following the council decision to make Münster an evangelical city. In his view, the sacraments were to function as the instruments for building the Christian community, not as the means for dispensing grace. When Rothmann also began leaning in this "Zwinglian" direction it posed a political problem for the city of Münster, for Münster needed Lutheran allies against the Catholic bishop. Futhermore, Rothmann and his fellow evangelical preachers began questioning infant baptism and recommending adult baptism, although they had yet to take the step of instituting the practice.[30] The city council saw clearly that this Reformed theology-in-the-making was severely limiting the political options open to the city. By 1533 there was an open struggle among three groups: the remaining Catholics (now outnumbered), the Lutherans (supported by council), and the reformed followers of Rothmann (backed by the guilds).[31] Observing this situation in May of 1533 was an interested onlooker and visitor to the city, Jan van Leiden, who had been baptized by Jan Matthijs earlier in the year.

By January of 1534 the situation had become a tense stalemate, exacerbated when Rothmann, Rol and other leading figures accepted rebaptism from Bartholomaeus Boeckbinder and Willem de Kuyper.[32] Anabaptism already was an imperial crime punishable by death, and the effect was to isolate the city even more within the broader political context. By the time Jan van Leiden arrived in January of 1534, sent as an apostle of Jan Matthijs, some 1,400 people already had accepted rebaptism in the city, including nuns who had left their cloister and accepted baptism.[33] The tide within the city had shifted in favour of the Anabaptist faction: those within the city who were most concerned to maintain the city's independence from the prince-Bishop came to support the Anabaptist party as the best option under the circumstances.

The elections for city councillors of February 23 fell to the Anabaptists—Bernhard Knipperdolling was one of two burgomasters elected. Many political opponents already had left the city, and the die was already cast, since the bishop had set up military headquarters in the nearby town of Telgte in preparation for a siege. On February 24, Jan Matthijs entered Münster, claiming prophetic authority, and three days later the bishop began the military siege of Münster.[34] On that same day, February 27, 1534, all non-baptized inhabitants of Münster were forced either to leave, or to accept rebaptism. It is estimated that out of a population of 7,000 to 8,000 people in Anabaptist Münster, approximately 5,000 were from the city itself, with about 2,400 immigrants, plus a few hundred professional soldiers fighting for the city. Around 300 men and 2,000 women were forced into accepting adult baptism against their will. The Anabaptists were to hold the city for sixteen months.

On the question of the sword, historians have asked when and how Melchior Hoffman's teaching of peace for individual believers was abandoned.[35] Karl-Heinz

Kirchhoff has demonstrated that a key historical eyewitness to the Münster events falsified his account in defence of the bishop's military actions, claiming the existence of a violent Anabaptist group in Münster already in early January 1534. The original Anabaptist group in Münster was predominantly pacifist in the Melchiorite sense; an aggressive crusading mentality was brought into the city by Jan Matthijs. It was Matthijs who, first of all, wished to slay the "ungodly" still left in Münster; it was Knipperdolling who voted for the more moderate course of explusion. It also was Matthijs who insisted on the forced baptism of all who were to remain.[36] As for the Münsterites themselves, political and End Times motives combined to lead them to the "militant theocracy" they came to support.

Soldier with crossbow

Following Jan Matthijs' arrival in Anabaptist Münster, Bernhard Rothmann's role within the city diminished. He now assumed the role of propagandist for the New Jerusalem under the leadership first of "Enoch" (Jan Matthijs), and then under "King" Jan van Leiden, defending the taking of the sword of righteousness and, in a later phase, polygamy. We will take up further aspects of Rothmann's theology in chapters 14 and 19 below.

The tragic result of the Münsterite establishment of the New Jerusalem is too well known to need much elaboration here. The city soon was established according to the guidelines seen in Acts, including the forcible institution of community of goods, with deacons appointed for the care of the poor. Those who would not listen to the prophet Jan Matthijs were to be expelled from the city.[37] He preached with confidence that the second coming of Christ would take place, at the latest, by Easter 1534. On the fifth of April, Easter Day, citizens lined the city walls in expectation of viewing the spectacle of God destroying the heathen. In what was perhaps an act of desperation, Jan Matthijs eventually decided to sally forth with a few companions, confident that God would come to their aid. He was quickly hacked to pieces and his head paraded on a lance by the besieging soldiers.

With the death of Jan Matthijs the way was clear for Jan van Leiden to assume power within the city. His credentials were not impressive: he was a tailor, a salesman, and an amateur actor, all of 24 years of age. Nevertheless, he claimed that God had told him in a dream that he was to be Jan Matthijs' successor, and such was his personal charisma and ability that he managed to assume that role. In July of 1534 he married Matthijs' widow Divara, and began instituting other changes in the city's organization, primarily along Old Testament lines.[38] By the end of that month he had instituted polygamy within the city (in which women now outnumbered men by four to one). There was some resistance on the part of women who were not willing to participate in the arrangement; some resistors were put to death. Jan van Leiden himself eventually took sixteen "concubines" as well as his "leading wife," Divara. In September of 1534 a prophet in the city proclaimed Jan to be "King over the New Israel and over the whole world."[39] King Jan now took on the role of the "new David," King of the righteous and castigator of the unrighteous.

The persistent call from Münster in 1534 and 1535 for other Anabaptists to come and be a part of the New Jerusalem had a profound effect on the Melchiorite movement in the Low Countries. It appears that the majority of Anabaptists in the north in fact supported the Münsterites, with a minority dissenting from the violent turn of affairs.[40] Added to the difficult economic conditions of the time, persecution of Anabaptists had begun in earnest in the Netherlands in 1534. One can only imagine the strong appeal of the Münsterite message "Flee out of Babylon ... for this is the time of the Lord's vengeance"—a message directed precisely to persecuted folk living in difficult economic conditions. In March of 1534, many thousands of people from North and South Holland answered the call to assemble near Hasselt in the province of Overijssel, where a prophet of God was supposed to be present to guide them to the New Jerusalem of Münster. Many travelled by land; some twenty-seven boats with 3,000 men, women and children arrived at the designated place on March 24. The unfortunate pilgrims were met by officers and soldiers, who had been forewarned. There was no armed resistance, although some of the pilgrims had arms and far outnumbered the government officers. The majority of the pilgrims were sent home; there also were a few executions.[41]

Other Melchiorites in the Netherlands became more aggressive, especially as the siege of Münster wore on and agents from Münster participated more actively in mustering armed resistance. Some three hundred Anabaptists managed to take over the monastery of Oldeklooster in Friesland in March of 1535 and held it for a week, finally succumbing to an all-out military attack; at least half lost their lives. This episode strongly affected Menno Simons, who was a priest in neighbouring Witmarsum at the time; it is possible that Peter Simons, who perished in the Oldeklooster attack, may have been Menno's brother.[42] Jan van Geelen, the Münster emissary responsible for leading the Oldeklooster adventure, planned an attack on the Amsterdam city hall for May 10, 1535. Only forty local Anabaptist supporters participated in the abortive attack, the end result of which was increased persecution by the authorities.[43]

Back in Westphalia, after two failed assaults on the city, the Bishop decided on the more expensive expedient of a total blockade. This was successfully accomplished, and by April of 1535 the situation inside the city was desperate: there was so much hunger that is was said that some people were eating grass. It is not known how many men, women and children died of starvation and disease in the beleaguered city, but it is estimated that in the three months prior to the taking of Münster, between 600-700 men lost their lives attempting to flee. The final taking of the city

began June 25, 1535. It was made possible
through the betrayal of the city by two of its citizens, and initiated a two day bloodbath. The
stench in the city was said to be overwhelming,
and the thousands of dead eventually were buried by neighbouring peasants. Rothmann's body
never was identified, and he may have managed
to escape the slaughter. If so, he never re-ap-
peared in the historical record. Jan van Leiden
was paraded around the countryside for show,
and finally in January 1536 he, Bernhard
Knipperdolling, and Bernd Krechting were publicly tortured for hours with red-hot tongs and
eventually executed before the cathedral. Their
remains were hung from the tower of St.
Lamberti Church in three iron cages.

The three cages still hang from
the tower of St. Lamberti Church

Melchioritism after Münster

After the fall of Münster, the Melchiorite
movement in the north disintegrated into several
factions, identified by James Stayer as follows:

1. The pacifist group, critical of Münster,
gathered around Dirk and Obbe Philips and David
Joris.

2. Followers of Jan van Batenburg in the
Netherlands, who continued to wield the "sword of righteousness."

3. Münsterite refugees in Westphalia grouped around Heinrich Krechting.

4. Rhineland and Hessian Melchiorites led by Georg Schnabel and Peter Tasch.

5. The remnants of the Melchiorites in Strasbourg, gathered around Lienhart
Jost.

The first attempt to gather these groups together was undertaken by David
Joris, who emerged as the most important Melchiorite leader in the days immedi-
ately following Münster's collapse.[44] For the purposes of this survey we will first
trace three post-Münster Melchiorite tendencies through their leaders, namely the
Münsterite continuation led by Jan van Batenburg, the spiritualist solution offered by
David Joris, and the "Obbenite" group that gathered eventually around Menno Simons.
We will conclude with an overview of the geographical spread and theological development of Dutch Anabaptism in the period from 1535 to ca. 1600.

Jan van Batenburg

Jan van Batenburg joined the Melchiorite movement in April, 1535, while
Münster was still under seige. Following the collapse of the New Jerusalem, he gathered around him frustrated Münsterites who still cherished the hope of punishing
the ungodly with the sword of vengeance.[45] The Batenburgers lived a secret existence, no longer baptizing converts but plundering churches, burning crops, and occa-

sionally executing the "ungodly." Although van Batenburg was arrested and executed in 1538, unrest of this type continued sporadically in Westphalia and the Netherlands. Some held the hope that in 1540, God would intervene and re-establish Münster again as the New Jerusalem, raising all the dead Münsterites from the grave and destroying the godless with heavenly fire.[46] As late as 1580 Jan Willems, a follower of Batenburg's disciple Cornelis Appelman, was burned at the stake. He had led a band of terrorists, reprinted Rothmann's "Restitution," and had taken twenty-one wives. The crusading ideals expressed at Münster, while no longer at the centre of the Melchiorite movement, lingered on here and there for a surprisingly long time.

David Joris

David Joris, along with Dirk and Obbe Philips, had been one of the few Melchiorite leaders opposed to the crusading interpretation of the Münsterites during the height of excitement in 1535.[47] In the summer of 1536 at a meeting of Melchiorite leaders at Bocholt, Westphalia, David Joris emerged as the most important leader of the post-Münster Melchiorites. His approach was conciliatory, emphasizing points of unity rather than points of difference.[48] In fact, as Gary Waite has demonstrated, a listing of active Anabaptist leaders from 1536 to 1540 shows Davidite leaders far outnumbering competing groups: in those years Davidite leaders outnumbered "Mennonite" leaders five to one.[49]

Joris' mediating approach stressed the message that the visible kingdom would come into being sometime in the future, as a result of God's action, rather than there being a visible kingdom established in the here and now established by human agency, as had been attempted by the Münsterites and was being continued by the Batenburgers. Joris' spiritualized pacifism allowed that Christians could be government authorities although, like Hoffman, he held that the authorities should be tolerant of religious differences and not interfere in the affairs of the church.

Joris' preeminence in post-Münsterite Anabaptism up to 1539 is undeniable. However, if Joris' conciliatory position won him a leadership victory at Bocholt in 1536, his failure in 1538 to convince the Strasbourg Melchiorites of his spiritual authority marked the beginning of the end of his dream to unite actual and erstwhile Melchiorites under his mantle. Joris continued to "spiritualize" his message to the point that eventually he was content to drop all external signs of Anabaptism. By 1544 he had disappeared from the Netherlands, re-appearing in Basel under a pseudonym. He died there in 1556, although his movement continued in his absence into the next century.[50]

Menno Simons

Menno Simons became an Anabaptist leader in the wake of the disastrous events of Münster. Menno (b. 1496) had been ordained a Catholic priest in 1524 at Utrecht and served in the parish of Pingjum near Witmarsum. His path to reform began with doubts about the sacramental claims relating to the Lord's Supper. According to his later account his doubts had begun almost immediately, but it took him twelve more years to move first to a sacramentarian position, then to the evangelical position, and finally to Melchiorite Anabaptism. He did not leave the Catholic priesthood until 1536.[51]

Two of the most important leaders of the non-Münsterite branch of Melchioritism were the brothers Obbe and Dirk Philips. It was this "pacifist" Melchiorite wing that Menno eventually would join. Menno had begun questioning the biblical basis for infant baptism following the martyrdom of the Anabaptist Sicke Freerks Snijder in 1530; he said later that he had found no word in Scripture concerning infant baptism. Nevertheless, he preached against the Münsterite kingdom during 1535, but in January 1536, he suddenly left the priesthood and "sought out the pious," either in Leeuwarden or Groningen. He received baptism at the hands of Obbe Philips, and married Gertrude, who would accompany him until his death in 1561. They became parents to two daughters and one son.[52] He was ordained an elder sometime early in 1537, again by Obbe Philips, and began a tireless mission of reorganizing the scattered Melchiorites. By 1542 the authorities had put a price of 100 guilders on his head but miraculously, in spite of constant travel and a life spent underground, Menno never was betrayed or apprehended.

Menno Simons clearly was not a Münsterite, but he was just as clearly a *Melchiorite* Anabaptist. The most visible evidence of this was Menno's adoption of Melchior Hoffman's "celestial flesh" Christology—a position he defended (with growing reluctance) until his death (see chapter 25 below). Menno also stood well within the Melchiorite tradition in his view concerning political authority, as we will see in chapter 15. Menno died at Wüstenfelde in January, 1561.

Dirk Philips and Leenaert Bouwens

Two "younger" leaders were to play central roles in the development of Dutch Anabaptism, beginning around 1550. Dirk Philips and Leenaert Bouwens were particularly instrumental in promoting a strict church discipline—an emphasis which resulted in a series of church splits and divisions among the Anabaptists of the north.

Dirk Philips, younger brother of Obbe Philips, was born in 1504; one source identifies him with the Franciscan Order prior to his joining the Anabaptists.[53] He was baptized at the height of the Münster episode, in December 1534 or January 1535, by Jan Matthijs' emissary, Pieter Houtsagher. Soon after Dirk's baptism, Houtsagher participated in a spectacular event: he and several others ran through the city of Amsterdam with unsheathed swords, proclaiming the day of the Lord. Houtsagher was arrested and then executed in Haarlem.[54] Not much is known of Dirk's activities following the fall of Münster, but he clearly had sided with his brother Obbe and formed part of the non-Münsterite Melchiorites. He probably was active in and around Emden. In 1538, Jan van Batenburg identified the three most important leaders of the movement as David Joris, Obbe Philips, and Dirk Philips; Menno was not mentioned by van Batenburg at all.[55] Beginning in the mid-1540s, Dirk took on a more prominent leadership position. He was present at the debate with the David Jorist Nicolaas van Blesdijk in 1546 and soon emerged as a central figure in the controversies surrounding the elder Adam Pastor and the question of the proper form of maintaining church discipline (chapter 24 below).

Leenaert Bouwens (1515-1582) became an Anabaptist at an unknown time;

he first appears in the historical record as a minister who attended the Lübeck conference in 1546; he was ordained an elder by Menno Simons in 1551.[56] He was present at the conference that adopted the "Wismar Articles" in 1554. Although he lived near Emden, Bouwens developed an amazing itinerant ministry stretching from Antwerp to Danzig. He kept a detailed record of his activities from 1551 to 1582 which is still extant. It records an astounding number of baptisms—10,386 individuals baptized by Bouwens alone, in 182 different locations, in the space of 31 years.[57] In spite of the valuable leadership qualities of both Dirk and Leenaert, both men were strict disciplinarians, which contributed to dissension and division among the Anabaptists in the Netherlands.

The Development and Spread of Dutch Anabaptism

As was also the case in Swiss and South German Anabaptism, there were evident differences in emphasis and practice among the North German/Dutch Anabaptists before, during, and after the Münster episode, particularly regarding the matter of the sword and the spirit and the letter. Nevertheless, there were also evident similarities and fundamental points of coincidence. It was on the basis of these commonalities that David Joris managed to forge a temporary pan-Melchiorite agreement at the Bocholt conference of 1536.[58] The militantly Münsterite faction (Batenburgers, followers of Bernd Krechting) represented a minority grouping that faded slowly but surely from the scene, especially after the death of Batenburg in 1538. The followers of David Joris, on the other hand, were more numerous and influential immediately following Münster, and remained a strong Anabaptist force until at least mid-century. Joris' removal to Basel under a pseudonym weakened his movement in the Netherlands, however, and after 1540 the "Mennist" party gained ground steadily. After 1550 the followers of Menno comprised the undeniable majority of North German and Dutch Anabaptists, with the competing factions in decline.

The geographical spread of Anabaptism in the Netherlands can only be described in cursory fashion. In spite of the Münsterite experience, there continued to be an Anabaptist presence in Westphalia; in neighbouring Hesse a Melchiorite faction led by Peter Tasch and Georg Schnabel gathered followers alongside the original Anabaptist followers of Melchior Rinck. East Friesland (especially the city of Emden and its vicinity) and Groningen remained strong centres of Anabaptism throughout the sixteenth century.[59] Not only did leaders like Menno, Dirk Philips, and Leenaert Bouwens find refuge in these northern territories, but many thousands of Anabaptist refugees also fled there when persecution became intense in other areas. In spite of persecution, Amsterdam remained an Anabaptist centre throughout some difficult years of persecution; these ended in 1578 with the taking of Amsterdam by Prince William I, and the church there entered a "golden age."[60] Many Anabaptists also lived in North Holland throughout the sixteenth century.

The situation in South Holland, or what is present-day Belgium, followed a different pattern thanks to the political situation there. In Flanders and especially in the city of Antwerp, Anabaptism grew very rapidly in the 1530s and 40s. It was countered by edicts enforced by the imperial government resident at Brussels.[61] There was a constant flow of emigration from Flanders not only to the northern Netherlands, but also to London.[62] From 1553 to 1565, Leenaert Bouwens' remarkable ministry also reached Flanders, where he baptized many hundreds.[63] The increased repression in the south that began in the 1550s resulted in the emigration of many Flemish Anabaptists, and the relocation of many more in other parts of Flanders.[64] The eventual takeover of the southern provinces by a Catholic regime (1585) led to much more emigration, especially to the northern Netherlands, and the virtual extinction of Anabaptism in Flanders. Some of the cultural differences between the Flemish Anabaptist refugees and their Frisian Anabaptist hosts contributed later to the stubborn Flemish/Frisian Anabaptist schism.

In the area of the lower Rhine, in Cologne and the surrounding territory, there had been Anabaptists since the early 1530s. Menno Simons himself missionized in this area beginning in 1544, as did Dirk Philips.[65] It was especially along the Rhine that Swiss Anabaptists moved north and met North German/Dutch Anabaptists moving south. Beginning in the 1550s there was increased interaction between these two groups. In 1555 a meeting took place in Strasbourg between Swiss and Dutch representatives in an effort to resolve the christological differences between them; in 1557 Swiss leaders met again in Strasbourg and this time the main topic under discussion was the ban.

It remains to mention the steady spread of Dutch Anabaptism in the far north, along the Baltic coast to the east into Schleswig-Holstein, Mecklenburg, and into the Vistula Delta and the city of Danzig. The Hanseatic cities, located as they were along well-travelled trade routes, also came to have Anabaptist congregations. Hamburg, Lübeck, Wismar and Rostock all had a documented Anabaptist presence by the 1530s. Further east, estimates are that some 3,000 Dutch refugees, the majority of whom were Mennonites, came to Danzig and East and West Prussia from 1527 to 1578. The link with the Netherlands was provided by Dutch shipping that connected the cities of the Baltic coast with the port cities of the Netherlands.[66] This general eastern migration of Dutch Anabaptists would continue into the next century, culminating in the settlement of Mennonite emigres in Russia in the 18th century.[67]

Conclusion

North German/Dutch Anabaptism, as this survey shows, was grounded in the Anabaptism of Melchior Hoffman; Swiss Anabaptism played no discernible role in its origins; South German Anabaptism played a role only insofar as it was mediated through Melchior Hoffman himself.

Melchior Hoffman's teaching included a strong preaching of repentance, rebirth, and a new life, an emphasis on the End Times, the possibility of direct revelations in dreams and visions, and the expectation of the physical punishment of the ungodly. His spiritualist emphasis and concern with the atonement resulted in his holding an unorthodox, docetic Christology which was passed on and accepted in Dutch Anabaptism. Like Hans Hut, Hoffman expected suffering to be the lot of true believers, until God brought about the restoration, soon to occur; unlike Hans Hut (who had no great hopes in the magistracy, and hoped rather that the Turks would execute vengeance on the powerful), Hoffman expected godly rulers to be God's instrument of vengeance. Hoffman's radical followers soon went beyond both Hut and Hoffman and embraced a "crusading" activity on behalf of God's restoration.

Much as was the case in South German Anabaptism, the discernible point of origin of the North German/Dutch Anabaptist movement is not in doubt. Nevertheless, Melchior Hoffman's Anabaptism proved amenable to wide interpretation, variation, and change, depending upon individuals and circumstances. The story of North German/Dutch Anabaptism after the fall of Münster is a story of competing Melchiorite points of view and emphases, vying for the support of the same group of people. It also is a story of increasing interaction, as the century wore on, with other Anabaptist groups.

End Notes

[1] "This Melchior was a very fiery and zealous man, a very smooth-tongued speaker who was celebrated for his great calling and commission..." Obbe Philips, "A Confession," in Williams, *SAW*, p. 208.

[2] Deppermann, *Hoffman*, pp. 45; 47; 49.

[3] Hoffman outlined his theology in Stockholm in 1526: The poor who were called in the spirit were more learned than the educated: "poor in the flesh—rich in the Spirit." He also applied some folk wisdom: the mountains (rich) were less fruitful than the valleys (poor). Deppermann, *Hoffman*, p. 59.

[4] *Ibid.*, pp. 65-66.

[5] *Ibid.*, p. 73.

[6] *Ibid.*, pp. 74-75.

[7] Cornelius Krahn, *Dutch Anabaptism*, (The Hague: Nijhoff, 1968), pp. 87-89.

[8] *Ibid.*, p. 89. Following his rejection by Bucer, Hoffman gathered together earlier followers of Denck, especially some "prophets." Among them were Katharina Seid, Andreas Klaiber, Lienhard Jost, Ursula Jost, Barbara Rebstock and Hans Rebstock. The Rebstocks had been banned from Esslingen and had been influenced by Hut. Deppermann, *Hoffman*, pp. 178-80. Selections from the 1530 publication of Ursula Jost's visions in Heinold Fast, *Der linke Flügel der Reformation* (Bremen: Carl Schünemann Verlag, 1962), pp. 298-308.

[9] See the detailed analyses of Deppermann in *Hoffman*, passim; Krahn, *Dutch Anabaptism*, pp. 89-91; 112-117.

[10] Krahn, *Dutch Anabaptism*, p. 95; English translation of the *Ordinance* in Williams, SAW, pp. 184-203.

[11] Deppermann, *Hoffman*, pp. 227-232. "Hoffman wanted a 'revolution from above' with the help of the already existing legitimate authorities. The military breakthrough was supposed to be accomplished by the current Christian governments of the Free Imperial Cities.... The Anabaptists should not unilaterally seize the sword, but remain passive even in the holy war of the Imperial Cities against the powers of Antichrist..." Stayer, *Sword*, p. xxvi. See also *ibid.*, pp. 213-223; xxv-xxviii.

[12] Krahn, *Dutch Anabaptism*, p. 96.

[13] *Ibid.*, pp. 118-19; Williams, *Radical* (1992), chapter 2.

[14] Krahn, *Dutch Anabaptism*, p. 100 suggests that Hoffman also worked in the Netherlands with some success during 1531.

[15] Deppermann, *Hoffman*, p. 284.

[16] *Ibid.*, pp. 285-87.

[17] See Krahn, *Dutch Anabaptism*, pp. 118-27.

[18] On Matthijs, Rothmann and events in Münster, see Stayer, *Sword*, pp. 227-80.

[19] Stayer, *Sword*, pp. 227-28.

[20] Deppermann, *Hoffman*, p. 289.

[21] Bornhäuser, *Leben und Lehre*, p. 15.

[22] Deppermann, *Hoffman*, pp. 292-93.

[23] Obbe Philips, "A Confession," in Williams, *SAW*, p. 214.

[24] It is now commonly accepted that the Münster episode belongs firmly within the Anabaptist story. James Stayer notes, "The Münster Anabaptists were genuine Anabaptists, not a corrupt sect misusing the Anabaptist name. The Anabaptist regime in Münster arose from a peaceful Anabaptist movement established in the town since the summer of 1533, and its survivors and successors became peaceful Anabaptists after the fall of Münster, except for a militant remnant." Stayer, *German Peasants' War*, p. 123. For a concise and excellent account of events in Anabaptist Münster, see *ibid.*, pp. 124-131.

[25] See Willem J. De Bakker, "Bernhard Rothmann: Civic Reformer in Anabaptist Muenster," in Irvin B. Horst, ed., *The Dutch Dissenters: A Critical Companion to their History and Ideas*, (Leiden: E.J. Brill, 1986), pp. 105-16.

[26] De Bakker, "Rothmann," pp. 106-07.

[27] Willem de Bakker, "Bernhard Rothmann: The Dialectics of Radicalization in Münster," in Hans-Jürgen Goertz, ed., *Profiles of Radical Reformers* (Scottdale, Pa.: Herald Press, 1982), pp. 191-93.

[28] *Ibid.*, pp. 193-94.

[29] *Ibid.*, p. 194.

[30] Rothmann's earliest "Anabaptist" writing, in which he attacked infant baptism and recommended baptism on confession of faith, is the "Wydder Andwurt" of July, 1533. Rothmann was not baptized until January of 1534. It must be assumed that Melchiorite influence was involved, although the early connecting links are no longer visible. Martin Brecht, "Die Theologie Bernhard Rothmanns," *Jahrbuch für Westfälische Kirchengeschichte* 78 (1985), pp. 64-65; Stayer, *Sword*, pp. 228-29.

[31] de Bakker, "Rothmann," p. 197.

[32] On Rothmann's theological development, see Brecht, "Theologie," pp. 49-82. Brecht argues that Anabaptist ideas were introduced into Münster first by the evangelical preachers, Rothmann, Roll, and the Wassenbergers, and not by Jan Matthijs' disciples. *Ibid.*, p. 66.

[33] Gerd Dethlefs, "Das Wiedertäuferreich in Münster 1534/35," in Hans Galen, ed., *Die Wiedertäufer in Münster*, (Münster: Aschendorff, 1986), p. 22.

[34] Dethlefs, "Wiedertäuferreich," pp. 24-25.

[35] Karl-Heinz Kirchhoff, "Gab es eine friedliche Täufergemeinde in Münster 1534?"*Jahrbuch des Vereins für Westfälische Kirchengeschichte* 55/56 (1962/63), pp. 7-21; English translation in MQR 44(October, 1970), pp. 357-70.

[36] "Eine friedliche Täufergemeinde in Münster bis zur Ankunft des Matthys bestand. Jan Matthijs war es, der 'anfänglich den Gebrauch des Schwertes und der Gewalt wider die Obrigkeit einführte', wie Bockelson bekannte." *Ibid.*, p. 21. Also Williams, *Radical* (1962), pp. 369-70.

[37] Dethlefs, "Wiedertäuferreich," p. 26.

[38] On Divara, see Snyder and Hecht, *Profiles* (forthcoming).

[39] Dethlefs, "Wiedertäuferreich," p. 30.

[40] "Only a minority of the Melchiorites remained true to the apoliticism of the founder during the revolutionary period. The Mennonites had to revive, rather than merely carry on, the tradition of Melchiorite apoliticism." So Stayer, *Sword*, p. 227; see also p. 280.

[41] See Krahn, *Dutch Anabaptism*, pp. 145-47. Some estimates put the number of pilgrims headed for Münster at between 14,000 and 16,000, which seems a clear exaggeration. The numbers, however, were astoundingly large.

[42] See Stayer, *Sword*, pp. 272-73; Krahn, *Dutch Anabaptism*, p. 152.

[43] See Stayer, *Sword*, pp. 275-77; Krahn, *Dutch Anabaptism*, pp. 153-55. Some sources suggest that there were anywhere from 3,500 to 5,000 Anabaptists in Amsterdam at this time; city authorities put the number of baptized in Amsterdam at around 100. See Stayer, *Sword*, p. 276. For a profile of Fenneke van Geelen (Jan's wife), martyred in Deventer, see Snyder and Hecht, *Profiles* (forthcoming).

[44] Stayer, *Sword*, p. 284, and more recently, Gary K. Waite, *David Joris and Dutch Anabaptism, 1524-1543* (Waterloo, Ont.: Wilfrid Laurier University Press, 1990), especially chapter 6.

[45] See Stayer, *Sword*, pp. 284-97 for an account of the "lingering, festering death" of Münsterite thought.

[46] *Ibid.*, p. 292.

[47] *Ibid.*, pp. 267-68.

[48] *Ibid.*, pp. 289-91.

[49] Waite, *Joris*, p. 114.

[50] Stayer, *Sword*, pp. 298-302; Waite's account of these crucial years clearly maps not only the rise and fall of David Joris' leadership fortunes, but also the stresses and strains experienced by Dutch Anabaptism following the collapse of Münster.

[51] Irvin B. Horst, "Menno Simons: The Road to a Voluntary Church," in Irvin B. Horst, ed., *The Dutch Dissenters: A Critical Companion to their History and Ideas* (Leiden: E.J. Brill, 1986), 194-203;); Krahn, *Dutch Anabaptism*.

[52] Bornhäuser, *Leben und Lehre*, p. 30.

[53] Dyck, Keeney, and Beachy, *Writings*, p. 19 and p. 44, n. 3.

[54] "Dirk Philips: A Biography," in Cornelius J. Dyck, William E. Keeney, and Alvin J. Beachy, eds., *The Writings of Dirk Philips* (Scottdale, Pa.: Herald Press, 1992), pp. 19-23.

[55] *Ibid.*, p. 25.

[56] "Leenaert Bouwens," ME III, p. 305. The editors of Dirk Philips' *Writings* say that Menno and Dirk ordained Bouwens and elder sometime between 1547 and 1553. Dyck, Keeney, and Beachy, *Writings*, p. 27.

[57] Krahn, *Dutch Anabaptism*, p. 229. Bouwens' wife appealed to Menno for help in curtailing Bouwens' travel; Menno's reply to her (1553) is found in CWMS, pp. 1038-1040. In a nutshell, Menno advised her to "strengthen your husband and do not weaken him... May the Almighty merciful Father ... guide the heart of my

beloved sister so as to be resigned to His holy will." p. 1040.

[58] Krahn notes that the Melchiorites, Münsterites and Batenburgers who met at Bocholt "shared views in matters of baptism, the Lord's supper, the incarnation of Christ and, to some extent, also in regard to the second coming of Christ." Krahn, *Dutch Anabaptism*, p. 167.

[59] See ME, II, pp. 119-122.

[60] See ME, I, pp. 101-108.

[61] There were strong anti-Anabaptist edicts promulgated in 1535, 1539 and again in 1541. A.L.E. Verheyden, *Anabaptism in Flanders, 1530-1650* (Scottdale, Pa.: Herald Press, 1961), p. 23. See also ME, I, pp. 270-271.

[62] See Krahn, *Dutch Anabaptism*, pp. 214-215.

[63] Also notable was the leadership in the south of Gillis van Aken, Joachim Vermeeren and Hans Busschaert (Hans de Wever). Verheyden, *Flanders*, pp. 38-39.

[64] *Ibid.*, pp. 50-51.

[65] Krahn, *Dutch Anabaptism*, pp. 182-189.

[66] "Many of the Amsterdam Anabaptists were sailors who made repeated trips to Danzig." So Krahn, *Dutch Anabaptism*, p. 220.

[67] For a concise account, see Cornelius J. Dyck, ed., *An Introduction to Mennonite History*, 2nd. edition (Scottdale, Pa.: Herald Press, 1981).

Chapter 11

Anabaptists and Scripture:
An Overview

Anabaptists understood themselves to be a part of the evangelical reform movement, which began with an appeal to the authority of Scripture. Since this was so, in order to understand Anabaptism as a movement we must understand how the "Scriptural issue" was addressed internally. Was there an "Anabaptist hermeneutics" (a specifically "Anabaptist" approach to interpreting Scripture)? Based upon the survey of Anabaptist origins above, the answer will have to be "yes and no." When we look at Anabaptist approaches to the interpretation of Scripture in a developmental framework we can mark three phases in the development of Anabaptist hermeneutics.

1. There was a limited common "core" of foundational texts and interpretations of those texts at the origins of the movement that in effect "defined" the movement as Anabaptist. We will mention that scriptural "core" briefly in this chapter. Anabaptism became a movement because of *agreement* on the meaning and centrality of a core of biblical texts relating to church reform.

2. There followed disagreements as Anabaptists worked out concrete implications based upon their common core of biblical texts and principles. These disagreements were worked out in the period from 1525 to ca. 1560. We will detail those various views, disagreements, and developments in this section as a whole. As we will see in our study of Anabaptist development in the sections that follow, Anabaptist differences concerning specific practicalities of the Christian life had their roots in contrasting assumptions concerning the interpretation of Scripture. On one level it is true to say that Anabaptism became a movement *in spite of* significant hermeneutical differences.

3. On the far side of interpretive differences emerged a narrower consensus on an interpretive approach, as well as a general agreement on practical questions relating to discipleship and church practice. We will outline this interpretive and practical "tradition" in chapter 26 below.

It is possible to overemphasize difference in telling the Anabaptist story, particularly if one concentrates on the second, developmental phase of Anabaptism. But in spite of significantly different interpretive approaches among the early Anabaptists, it bears repeating that the "baptizing" movement became a movement because there was a core of *agreement* concerning what the Bible required of believers. The core of Anabaptist beliefs surveyed in chapter 6 above reflects Anabaptist agreement concerning what were the essential biblical teaching and practices that defined a "reformed" church.

First, the early Anabaptists maintained that the "biblical order" concerning salvation was that teaching (hearing the Gospel), repentance, and faith (all the work of the Holy Spirit) *must* precede water baptism, and that water baptism and a commitment to a new life *must* follow hearing, repentance, and faith. The Anabaptist doctrine of salvation, as entailing both faith and obedience, implied an active pneumatology and optimistic anthropology, as well as a doctrine of free will in human beings (a rejection of predestination) and a call for active discipleship. This fundamental theological distinctive was not limited to one Anabaptist "tendency" or region, but is seen clearly in all Anabaptists, from Hubmaier, to Sattler, Denck, Hut, Hoffman, Rothmann, and Menno.[1] As Walter Klaassen notes, "Much Scripture even in the New Testament called for evangelical obedience and if God called for it, Anabaptists argued, it must be his will and it must be possible to do it. Works were the outward expression of faith and not simply the fruit of faith as Luther had said."[2] A variety of scriptural texts were used to argue the point, but a text commonly cited was James 2: faith without works is dead.[3]

Along with the insistence on faith and works in baptism came an early Anabaptist consensus on the biblical "works" that would mark the true, reformed church.[4] In the first instance, the fundamental biblical texts concerning adult water baptism were those relating the "Great Commission" of Jesus to the disciples, first to teach, and then baptize all nations (Matthew 28:18ff.; Mark 16:15ff.).[5] In the second place, the Anabaptists agreed that in Matthew 18 they had found the biblical church polity that would lead to a properly reformed, disciplined church: sin must be admonished and corrected, leading either to repentance and readmittance, or expulsion of the unrepentant. According to the biblical order, they believed, the church is to be a visibly reformed and visibly "pure body."[6] Third, Anabaptists agreed that those who had repented, believed, and been baptized on their confession of faith, and who thereby submitted to the community discipline of the ban, were to celebrate a "memorial Supper" together, symbolizing and pledging again their commitment to each other and to God (1 Corinthians 11:23, with its warning about celebrating "unworthily" was especially significant here).[7] Fourth, baptized believers would share generously of their earthly goods with other members of the Body of Christ (the church), according to the general pattern described in the Acts 2 and 4.[8]

There was widespread agreement among Anabaptists of all kinds (implicit if not explicit) that at least on these points the Spirit had illuminated the letter of Scripture and had outlined the proper ecclesial order of salvation. It was this agreement that established these biblical boundaries of belief and church practice as distinctively "Anabaptist." However, as we will see in more detail below, the question of further concrete practices of "discipleship" soon became battlegrounds on which competing interpretive currents vied for supremacy within the Anabaptist movement itself.

The interpretive question of what constituted a true spiritual reading of Scripture continued to cause the Anabaptists trouble. Granted that the Spirit had to inform the reading of the letter, just how was that Spirit interpreting the letter? There was, it is fair to say, considerable dissension on this question until later in the sixteenth century. A crucial developmental aspect of the Anabaptist story is the working out of more precise scriptural interpretive principles.

The Spirit and the Letter

Where the Anabaptists stood on the question of the authority of Scripture, and more specifically on the issues of spirit and letter, has long been debated in Anabaptist historiography and polemics. Lutheran interpreters, for example, traditionally maintained that Anabaptism was to be characterized by antinomian spiritualism, taking its origins from Thomas Müntzer. Mennonite apologists in this century argued to the contrary that "evangelical" Anabaptism, or "true" Anabaptism, was resolutely committed to the letter of Scripture.[9] The truth of the matter is not nearly so black and white, particularly when we look at the entire Anabaptist spectrum.[10] Anabaptist testimonies from all regions emphasize, in particular, that without the baptism of the Spirit there could be no understanding of the letter of Scripture.[11] In this important sense there were no "strict literalists" among the Anabaptists. Anabaptist egalitarianism and anticlericalism was rooted theologically and scripturally in the "spiritual" reading of the "letter" of Scripture. The first mark of an Anabaptist approach to Scripture, then, is the insistence that the Spirit must inform any true reading of Scripture. Anabaptist pneumatology was central to early Anabaptist hermeneutics, but there was no consensus on how far to extend the influence and activity of the Holy Spirit in the interpretive process.

In the second place, the true interpreter of Scripture is known by the outward witness of that interpreter's life. Anabaptist rootage in late medieval reforming sentiments is evident in the common critique of pastors who claim to be preaching the truth, but nevertheless continue to live dissolute and undisciplined lives. Negatively expressed, this attitude may be called anticlerical; positively expressed, the same attitude points to the Anabaptist insistence that inner regeneration and the presence of the Spirit must produce visible, outward good fruits. In the absence of such fruits there was reason to question the presence of the Spirit; and without that Spirit, there could be no true interpretation of the Bible. Thus the necessary reading of the letter by those in possession of the Spirit was tested in Anabaptist hermeneutics by the necessary outer manifestations of inner, spiritual renewal.

These spirit/letter and inner/outer tensions defined the outer boundaries of the Anabaptist approach to Scripture, but tremendous questions remained within those boundaries. Does the "letter" of Scripture stand in judgement over the "spirit," or should the order be reversed? How is Law related to Gospel; the Old Testament to the New? Does the Holy Spirit of the Last Days speak "extra-biblically"? Who is competent to decide the truth of spiritual and scriptural revelation: illumined "apostles," biblically learned teachers, congregations? Are there specific good fruits that give reliable evidence of the presence of the Spirit, and thus of a trustworthy interpreter of Scripture? These questions were debated within Anabaptism as the movement struggled to define its spiritual and biblical path of reform.

When leading Anabaptist representatives are plotted along the spirit/letter continuum, three positions emerge which in some ways do, and in other ways do not parallel the regional differences noted by polygenesis historiography: the more "literally" oriented approach; the more "spiritualistic" (mystically oriented) approach; and the "prophetic apocalyptic" approach.

Letter over Spirit

In this first group we find Anabaptists who came to emphasize the priority of letter over spirit—although they always affirmed the need for the spirit: e.g., Conrad Grebel, Michael Sattler, Balthasar Hubmaier, Jakob Hutter, Peter Riedeman, and Menno Simons. We may note that represented here are first generation Swiss Anabaptists (Grebel, Sattler, Hubmaier), second generation South German Anabaptists, specifically from the Hutterite group (Hutter, Riedemann, and other Hutterites), and second generation Melchiorites (Menno Simons, Dirk Philips). Developmentally speaking it is significant that the Swiss maintained their emphasis throughout, while the Hutterites and Menno evolved into their views against a backdrop of spiritualist and prophetic apocalyptic origins. By the late sixteenth century there would be a strong congruence between the Swiss, Mennonite, and Hutterite approaches to Scripture, but the paths that led there were not the same. It must be noted further that among these more "literal-minded" Anabaptists the work of the Holy Spirit was not rejected. Rather, these Anabaptists tended to limit the working of the Spirit to what was verifiable (or sometimes, communicable) in and through Scripture.

Some basic principles of interpretation were outlined by the Swiss Anabaptists at an early stage. One ruling exegetical principle, seen already in 1524 in Conrad Grebel's writings and visible also in Hubmaier, is that the reform of the church and the Christian life is to be ruled by what Scripture has *commanded*.[12] The principle that "whatever has not been expressly commanded in Scripture is forbidden," led to a closely literal exegesis of biblical texts which in the end came to define the Swiss Anabaptists. However, it is important not to lose sight of the fact that among the early Swiss Anabaptists there was a *progression* toward a more literal exegesis that began with appeals to the direct working of the Spirit. The Anabaptist sources from the Zürich area reveal that many of the first Swiss Anabaptists, some of them baptized by Grebel, appealed to direct revelations of the Spirit.[13] A second interpretive principle that played a central role in the Swiss Anabaptist movement was an emphasis on the New Testament over the Old. The words of Scripture are all words of God, but they do not carry the same weight or significance in guiding the life of believers. The Bible is not "flat"; the Old Testament has been superseded by the New, and within the New Testament Christ's words and example are definitive. This principle also emerged eventually in the Hutterite and Mennonite traditions, as will be noted later.

In the question of the spirit and the letter, Balthasar Hubmaier stood very much in the "Swiss" tradition, emphasizing strongly the letter of Scripture,[14] although he too appealed to the working of the Spirit in the believer.[15] In fact, Hubmaier held together the working of the Spirit to the hearing of the outer word: although the working of the Spirit was necessary for regeneration, "the Spirit comes with the Word."[16] For Hubmaier, the external word, written and preached, was the means by which the internal Word chose to work. Although Hubmaier would disagree with other

Swiss Anabaptists concerning the sword, as will be seen in chapter 13, he had no *hermeneutical* disagreement with them. In his statements at the Second Zürich Disputation (October, 1523)[17] Hubmaier agreed with Zwingli that all matters under dispute ought to be decided by "the clear Word of God as written in both Testaments," but he also outlined a more radical exegetical principle: "If they are not commanded, then they are worthless. For everything which God has not taught us either with words or deeds is worthless and in vain."[18] This principle—in complete harmony with Grebel's application in 1524—had as its consequence the rejection of all practices not explicitly commanded in the Bible (but especially in the New Testament), primary among which was the baptism of infants.

It must be noted that the more "literal" approach to Scripture was simply an interpretive *tendency* that provided no guarantee of particular ethical results. If we take the question of the sword as an example, we see that the literal interpretive emphasis could result in (a) a defence of Christians taking the sword (Hubmaier), (b) a moderate acceptance of the possibility of rulers also being Christian (Menno), (c) a strict division between nonresistant followers of Jesus and all others (Sattler, Riedeman), or (d) a rigorous biblicistic ethic of following New Testament commands (Grebel). Furthermore, it is not accurate to say that the central *Anabaptist* hermeneutical principle was the priority of the New Testament over the Old. This principle did emerge early in the Swiss Anabaptist movement, but took considerably more time to be accepted in other regions, where other principles of scriptural harmonization were applied. As an example of this we will review below Menno's disagreement with Bernhard Rothmann, on the one hand (chapter 15), and with the David Jorists on the other (chapter 22).

Spirit over Letter

In this group we find Anabaptists who stood at the other end of the spirit/letter tension, who emphasized the priority of the Spirit (inner Word) over the letter (outer word)—although as long as they remained in the Anabaptist camp they never denied the need for the letter of Scripture. In this grouping we find Hans Denck, Leonard Schiemer, Hans Schlaffer, Jakob Kautz, Hans Bünderlin, and Christian Entfelder. All of these leaders were, at least in their Anabaptist phases, rebaptizers in a more mystical mode. Leonard Schiemer and Hans Schlaffer died as Anabaptist martyrs; Hans Denck, Jakob Kautz, Hans Bünderlin, and Christian Entfelder, on the other hand, abandoned the "outward ceremonies" of Anabaptism and moved on to a more inward, personal religion.

Hans Denck

On the question of the relationship of the Testaments, Hans Denck set the tone for this group of Anabaptists: on his own testimony, Denck valued the "inner Word" above the "outer word."[19] On the spirit-letter continuum, Hans Denck stood at the opposite extreme from Grebel, Sattler, and Hubmaier.[20] For Hans Denck and those in the spiritualist stream, the harmonization of the Old and New Testaments was resolved, in the first instance, by an appeal beyond the letter to a higher spiritual unity.[21] The spiritualist Anabaptists thus appear to hold to a "flat" Bible, in which Old and New Testaments are of equal value. Nevertheless, for Denck and the others there was a "higher spiritual law"; it led them to value the New Testament over the Old in matters relating to the Christian life. It is *Christ*, said Denck, who has revealed the fundamental spiritual principle that underlies both Testaments, and this principle is the divine spirit of love.[22]

There was to be a visible "separation from the world" for Denck and the spiritualistic Anabaptists in their "baptizing" periods; separation was marked by water baptism and maintained by the ban, and so marked a division between "the children of God and the children of the world."[23] However, as distinguished from Sattler, Denck's fundamental principle was not this visible separation maintained by "ordinances," but rather the inner working of the spirit within each human being. Denck's hermeneutics was oriented to the principle of Christocentric love, not to a literal "following after Christ" (*Nachfolge Christi*). Said another way, Denck's "dualism" was anthropological, not ecclesiological.[24] Nevertheless, Hans Denck's well-known saying, that "the medium is Christ whom no one can truly know unless he follows him in his life, and no one may follow him unless he has first known him,"[25] demonstrates the interrelationship he maintained between the inner Word and ethical behaviour. But in the end, the outward signs of ecclesiological separation meant less to Hans Denck than did his spiritualistic beginning point, and this led him and other spiritualist Anabaptists after him out of the "adult baptizing" movement proper.[26]

One is tempted to create a further category for Pilgram Marpeck, for he fit somewhere between the two poles identified above, and shared some of each. Marpeck always worked to maintain a balance between spirit and letter, and carried out vigorous disagreements with more extreme representatives of both of the above tendencies, as we will note in chapters 21 and 23 below.

Prophetic Spirit and Prophetic Letter

In this grouping we find Anabaptists whose basic interpretive framework was provided by the conviction that they were living in the Last Days. Since the Last Days took place in the age of the Spirit, these Anabaptists expected to receive spiritual revelations (dreams, visions) and considered them to be complementary to prophetic scriptural revelation, in which the secrets of the divine were encoded. In this group are found Hans Hut, Melchior Hoffman, Jan Matthijs, Bernhard Rothmann, and David Joris. We will look in more detail at Hut and Hoffman here, as representatives of this interpretive tendency.

Hans Hut

Hans Hut's own writings contain few examples of his full exegetical method, but we find direct evidence in the testimonies of his followers.[27] Hut derived what he called "seven judgements" from Scripture, which he taught only to full initiates.[28] The seven judgments were: 1) The Covenant of God: (Gospel of Christ, faith and baptism), 2) The Body of Christ (Supper), 3) The End of the World, 4) Concerning judgment and the future of God, 5) The resurrection of the dead, 6) The Kingdom of God, and 7) Eternal judgment (punishment of the damned). These judgments were considered to be a summary of all biblical teaching in both Testaments, apparently revealed directly by the Spirit of God to Hut.[29] According to Hut's own testimony, the Christian of these "Last Days" was to act in accordance with the divinely revealed prophetic calendar and a prophetic ("Spirit-led") reading of the "signs of the times."[30] And, according to Hut's biblical calculations, Christ would return sometime before Easter, 1528.[31]

Although the Swiss Anabaptists also believed that they were living in the Last Days, Hut's prophetic spiritualism played an interpretive role in his reading of Scripture that is not to be seen in the Swiss stream. Certainly Hut also emphasized living a regenerated and holy life in his preaching and teaching; he could at times sound very "Swiss," emphasizing the union of believers into one body with Christ at its head,[32] but Hut's primary emphasis was not on a separated church following strict ethical guidelines, such as many of his followers would soon develop.[33] Rather, Hut was primarily concerned to gather together the elect who would be the Bride of Christ when the Lord returned within a few months; his "ethics" was thus governed by his understanding of the End Times calendar.[34]

The seventh seal is opened, four trumpets sound, and an angel announces "woe, woe, woe" to the inhabitants of the earth. Revelation chapter 8.

Melchior Hoffman

Melchior Hoffman's approach to Scripture, like Hut's, focused on the prophetic books of the Bible and a setting of dates for the return of Christ, and so placed the spirit/letter dichotomy within an apocalyptic context.[35] The emphasis on the heightened activity of the Holy Spirit in the Last Days also is visible in Hoffman: after 1530, probably under the influence of Hut's followers in Strasbourg, Hoffman also accepted extra-biblical prophetic revelation as authoritative.[36]

The most notable feature of Melchior Hoffman's interpretation of Scripture is, without a doubt, his allegorical and "figurative" method of interpreting biblical texts in relation to the signs of his times. Klaus Deppermann observed that Hoffman's "figurative" reading could mean either a "typological" or an "allegorical" reading. In a typological reading, certain pairs are bound together in meaning, e.g., Melchisedek and Christ. In an allegorical reading, the spiritual meaning of a past event is linked to a present reality, e.g., the Exodus is linked with the salvation of the soul, or the temple of Solomon with the Church. Hoffman was not very precise in his application of such distinctions, but the figurative method of reading Scripture allowed him and his followers to range widely beyond the strictly literal text, and then to apply the resulting "biblical" insights to contemporary events.[37]

Interesting as Hoffman's figurative reading of Scripture was (and it was by no means unusual in Anabaptist circles, where it was routinely used to interpret the Old Testament), it must be noted that he was, in essence, a preacher of repentance. At the heart of Hoffman's preaching of repentance stood the Gospel message of Christ's atonement for human sin, which all apostolic messengers were to preach.[38] Through Christ's perfect atonement for human sin, and by means of the proclamation of the Gospel by "apostolic messengers," God's grace and forgiveness was extended to all human beings. It remained for them only to accept that grace, repent, yield to God and enter into a new life.

The framework within which Hoffman preached repentance owed little to an allegorical or figurative reading of the Bible. Hoffman's explanation of salvation history, as revealed in the Bible, begins with the creation: God gave the word, and there was light, which was good, and then God separated light from darkness.[39] Light and dark functioned for Hoffman, as they do also in Scripture itself, as images representing good and evil: God created the light and the good; darkness, or evil, had a subsequent and derivative existence. The fall into sin by Lucifer, and subsequently by Adam and Eve, was a deliberate and self-conscious choosing of evil over good, of darkness over light. With the fall of Lucifer a "Kingdom of darkness" was established which continued throughout history to strive against God's "Kingdom of light."[40] The subsequent evil choices of Eve, Adam, and Cain demonstrate, said Hoffman, the self-willed nature of sin and the choosing of Satan's Kingdom of evil.[41]

A scriptural theme to which Hoffman returned often was the "pure fear of God" which he saw as the necessary first step—and a necessary continuing step—in the saving process.[42] Hoffman effortlessly collated scriptural references on this theme, from Isaiah to Malachi, Maccabees, and Matthew, and also made reference to numerous biblical figures as both positive and negative examples,[43] but here too his central point owed nothing to allegory: "The Scriptures are filled with such examples, of how the pious lived in the highest fear of God, preferring to lose everything in this world, life and limb, rather than renounce the fear of God."[44] Opposed to the pure fear of God was "fear" of the world, which was no more than idolatry, or the elevation of created things above the Creator.[45]

By 1530, Hoffman had associated God's grace in Christ, the preaching of the Gospel, repentance, *Gelassenheit*, and the acceptance of Christ's sacrifice, with the baptism of believers: "they also who have surrendered themselves to the Lord should lead themselves out of the realm of Satan and from the kingdom of darkness and from this world and ... they should purify themselves and lead themselves into the spiritual wilderness and also wed and bind themselves to the Lord Jesus Christ, publicly, through that true sign of the Covenant, the water bath and baptism."[46] Even though Hoffman's debt to the late medieval mystical tradition is evident, his treatment of these scriptural themes was straightforward, in no way peculiar, and thoroughly Anabaptist.[47] The same cannot be said, however, for Hoffman's treatment of End Times texts.

If Hoffman's understanding of the two kingdoms, free will, repentance, regeneration, baptism, and salvation was based on a fairly literal reading of Scripture, the same cannot be said for the manner in which he set out to discover the "hidden" prophetic messages which, he was convinced, were to be found in Scripture. Central to Hoffman's figurative approach to prophetic Scripture was his understanding of the relationship of Scripture to history. In a book written late in 1529 or early in 1530, dedicated to interpreting the prophecies of Scripture, Hoffman clarified that "God the almighty does nothing that he has not revealed beforehand and given in secret through his prophets."[48] Since this is so, "every God-fearing servant of Christ" ought to seek the Scriptures, for there will be unlocked "the door of the divine Word through the key of David."[49] History, thought Hoffman, is determined by God and furthermore, a description of the future course of history has been hidden in prophetic Scripture. Since this was so, a "figurative" interpretation of all of Scripture—Old Testament as well as New—was possible for those who, through the Spirit, possessed the crucial interpretive "key of David."[50] Those who held the interpretive key would be able to apply the principle of the "cloven hoof," which harmonized apparent scriptural contradictions.[51]

The crucial presuppositions underlying Hoffman's interpretive method certainly were not foreign to the Anabaptism that preceded him. Anabaptists of all persuasions were convinced that they were living in the End Times.[52] Hans Hut also had assumed that the secrets of history, particularly the events of the Last Days, were hidden in prophetic Scripture. Likewise the view that the Spirit would be poured out in the Last Days was a common theme, as was the view that those led by the Spirit would be the true interpreters of Scripture. What set Hoffman's scriptural approach apart was not the premise that the Spirit was directing his interpretive activity, but rather his amazing capacity to apply a figurative method of interpretation to Scripture passages that appeared, on the surface, to have no inherent relationship. Whereas Hans Denck, for example, also gave equal weight to both Old and New Testaments and applied a "spiritualist" exegesis to them, he took the comparatively simple interpretive step of reconciling scriptural differences by reading Old and New Testaments in light of the spiritual law of love, revealed in Christ. Hoffman, on the other hand, entered the labyrinth of allegorical, figurative, and numerical interpretation, with a view to extracting precise contemporary information. Nevertheless, it bears repeating that Hoffman's End Times speculation was not an end in itself, but rather always served his larger purpose of preaching repentance and salvation.

Typical of Hoffman's treatment of End Times texts is his exegesis of Revelation 16:17: "And the seventh angel poured out his vial into the air." Hoffman begins his exegesis of this passage by noting that the Spirit of God divides all peoples into four parts, like the elements, into parts that correspond to the Sea, the Earth, the Air, and Fire (or "Heaven"). This four-fold division corresponds, says Hoffman, to the different comparison that Christ made in Matthew 13(3ff.), in the parable of the sower. The "figure" for the rich and the proud is the earth covered in thorns, or in the book of Revelation, the sea; the figure for the ungodly or impious is the path, or the way side, which corresponds to the earth; the figure for the careless is the stony ground, which corresponds to the air; and the figure for the children of God is the good ground, which corresponds to fire or heaven.[53] Having established all of this,

The great winepress of God's wrath.
Revelation 14:19-20.
Images of impending judgment were powerful
motivators in the sixteenth century.

Hoffman then exegetes the passage: the messenger of the Lord (the "angel" signifies a preacher of the Gospel in the last days) pours out God's Word (the vial that is poured out is the Gospel) into the air; this means that "the teaching of God's Word out of God's Spirit and through the spirit and courage of the teacher is poured into the hearts of the careless ones, and becomes air, or is compared to the birds in the air."[54] Hoffman's point, in the end, was far simpler than the path by which he chose to make it: those who are careless and not mindful of God will miss the last proclamation of the Gospel and the Spirit of God, to their condemnation. Examples of this kind of "figurative" exegesis in Hoffman's writings could be multiplied many times over, with little difficulty.

Also crucial to Hoffman's "figurative" interpretive framework was his understanding of the different roles to be played by different members of the church. Since Hoffman expected the Spirit of God to be active in all believers, one might have expected him to support an egalitarian church in which all members would have equal interpretive ability. But although earlier in his reforming career Hoffman had held such a "democratic" conception, in Strasbourg he came to the conclusion that there were different spiritual offices within church, each with its particular function, namely apostles, prophets, pastors, and regular members. The Apostles were the overall leaders, for they possessed the greatest spiritual gifts of interpretation and leadership. To the Apostles was granted the power to "unravel" the mysteries of Scripture, as well as the mysteries contained in contemporary dreams and visions.[55] Concerning the interpretation of Scripture, Hoffman wrote: For all words of God are of equal weight, also just and free, to him who acquired the right understanding of God and the Key of David. The cloven claws and horns (only) the true apostolic heralds can bear, because (to explicate) the Scripture is not a matter for everybody—to unravel all such involved snarls and cables, to untie such knots—but only for those to whom God has given (the power).[56]

Hoffman considered himself to be an "apostolic messenger," rather than a prophet.[57] Nevertheless, the role of the prophets also was extremely important to his movement, since they conveyed directly the living words of God.[58]

The Dreams and Visions of Ursula Jost

The key to Melchior Hoffman's approach to Scripture lay in the fact that he was convinced that he was standing *in continuity* with the biblical prophetic tradition. It is in this context—as a continuation of spiritually inspired prophetic revelation—that direct dreams and visions came to play a role in Hoffman's movement. The role of the Strasbourg prophets in Hoffman's movement was very significant, particularly the role of the prophetesses Ursula Jost[59] and Barbara Rebstock.[60] The visions of Ursula Jost, which were published by Hoffman in 1530, do contain some interpretation by Ursula herself, and are prefaced and concluded by Hoffman, thus giving us some insight not only into the visions themselves, but also into how they were understood.

There is no good way, first of all, of conveying an adequate second-hand impression of the visual richness of Ursula Jost's visions, for they are panoramic, colourful, and full of exotic imagery in the manner of the book of Revelation. Contemporary woodcuts illustrating passages from the Revelation may convey some sense of the visions Ursula received. She described great wars, clouds dripping blood, rainbows, wreaths, toads, snakes, bishops, knights, virgins, and much more. Nevertheless, the basic framework can be seen immediately and easily grasped by the modern reader: it is one of two kingdoms at war with one another—the one clear, light, and good, the other dark and evil. Likewise the recurring images of wreaths and rainbows (on the side of good) and dark warriors, fearsome creatures, and black pits (on the side of evil) have obvious symbolic meaning. Even when the exact interpretation of specific visions is hidden from us, taken as a whole Ursula's visions powerfully convey images of a titanic struggle between the Kingdom of God and the Kingdom of Satan, images of the impending judgment from God, and images of hope for the elect after times of suffering and persecution.

Many of Ursula's visions are easily recognizable as elaborations on biblical themes. Thus the power and providence of God reappear throughout,[61] most often revealed in visions of God's ultimate judgment.[62] In her fifty-seventh vision, for example, Ursula saw a great and powerful hand, holding a great rod. Although she asked what it might mean, no answer was given to her at the time. In her following vision, however, "the clarity of the Lord" asked her if she knew what the hand meant. "Then I answered and said: 'Oh Lord, how can I know if it was not explained to me?'" Then the Lord explained that the hand was "the strong hand of the almighty, the God of Israel, and He will wreak vengeance on all people, and if they do not better themselves, He will punish them severely."[63] Along with the themes of judgment and repentance, the images of the narrow way leading to salvation, and the broad road leading to destruction also appear several times,[64] as does the theme of resurrection.[65] The cross, needless to say, appears in numerous visions throughout.

Along with the biblical themes present in Ursula Jost's visions are particular emphases which also appear in Melchior Hoffman's own writings. There are at least two visions rejecting a sacramental understanding of the Supper and images,[66] and several strongly anticlerical visions.[67] The poor play prominent roles in several visions, sometimes as victims of clerical greed. In her fourteenth vision, for example, Ursula saw a huge crowd of people hacking away at the earth, in heavy labour, with hoes. She then saw a huge crowd of "bishops and spiritual prelates and scribes (*Schriftgelehrten*)" all coupled together, standing and watching the workers work.[68] And there is judgment against the ungodly and idle clergy. In her twenty-first vision, Ursula saw a bishop brought along on a great chair, but then his head was split open and he was thrown into a dark pit. As in Hoffman's writings, the Turks also make an appearance as the instruments of God's vengeance,[69] as do the apostolic messengers who proclaim divine justice.[70] In short, the conceptual structure, biblical themes, and Melchiorite thematic emphases of Ursula Jost's visions place her solidly within the Anabaptist (and specifically Melchiorite) tradition. While the visual imagery is rich and sometimes overwhelming, the theological "grammar" standing behind the imagery can be read in Hoffman's own works.

There is no doubt that Melchior Hoffman and Ursula Jost both believed that these visions were directly revealed by God in the manner of biblical prophecies. Ursula, who appeared to have some doubts at one point, was reassured—in a vision of course—that she was not being deceived and that she would see great wonders and "the clarity of God."[71] The Holy Spirit, they believed, had never closed the canon of Scripture. But what is striking, both in Hoffman's figurative exegesis and in the interpretations of Ursula Jost's visions, is not that new revelations are added to Scripture, but rather the reverse. The figures extracted by Hoffman and the visions of Ursula Jost are often incredible, but the *meaning* extracted from them is commonplace, in essential continuity with, and in reinforcement of, the biblical prophetic tradition.

What may we conclude about Melchior Hoffman's manner of interpreting Scripture? In the first place, Melchior Hoffman's exegetical method was not always "figurative"; the core of Hoffman's Anabaptist repentance theology was based on a straightforward, literal exegesis. Hoffman's soteriology was not based on a "flat" Bible, but clearly placed the redemption of humanity through Christ at the centre. In the second place, Hoffman's emphasis concerning the End Times needs to be read within the context of his preaching of two kingdoms, sin, grace, repentance, baptism and salvation, as lending increased urgency to the message of salvation. In the third place, for all its flights of fancy, Hoffman's figurative exegesis was not an instance of a pure spiritualism divorced from the letter of Scripture. To the contrary, Hoffman referred to Scripture at every turn, in bewildering profusion. Insofar as Hoffman's own writings are concerned, the objection to his figurative method of interpretation cannot be that he ignored the text of the Bible in favour of direct spiritual revelations, for he fairly devoured biblical texts.

What would cause trouble in the Melchiorite movement later were the parallel interpretive assumptions first, that the same Holy Spirit that had "coded" prophetic Scripture had now "decoded" it accurately and decisively for those in possession of the interpretive Key of David; and second that this prophetic Scripture, once decoded, would yield precise contemporary information. The first assumption led to an undeniable concentration on the prophetic books of Scripture (those in which the "hidden" could be brought to light); the second gave a sharp social, economic, and political relevance to the prophetic secrets thus revealed. The greater part of Hoffman's Anabaptist literary production consisted of biblical exegesis of what he considered to be prophetically significant passages, but these interpretive exercises also were politically charged. They became occasions for a critique of social, political and economic conditions, along with calls for repentance, and promises of imminent justice and retribution for the unrepentant.

In an important sense Hut, Hoffman, Matthijs, Rothmann and Joris must be classed with the "spiritualists," but two new issues of biblical interpretation emerge at both the side of the "spirit" and the side of the "letter": the role of extra-biblical prophecy at the "spirit" side, and a predilection for interpreting the prophetic and apocalyptic books of Scripture at the "letter" side. For Hut, Matthijs and Rothman, the acceptance of both extrabiblical prophecy and a preference for exegeting apocalyptic Scripture (Daniel, Esdras, Revelation) opened the door to an acceptance of the sword of righteousness in the hands of the elect in the End Times scenario. Rothmann, in fact, came to locate more authority in the five books of Moses and the Prophets than in the New Testament; in this way he defended not only a holy crusade, but also polygamy in Münster.

Hut, Hoffman, Matthijs, Rothmann and Joris were radically spiritualist, but on the other hand, after their own fashion they also emphasized, read, and scrutinized the written letter of Scripture. This combination of prophetic spiritualism and prophetic biblicism was consonant with the core of Anabaptist theology, and grew out of the combined pneumatic and biblical emphases found there. The core of Anabaptist beliefs, with its strong pneumatological emphasis and generally shared conviction that the Last Days had arrived, encouraged the growth of the prophetic/apocalyptic interpretation of Scripture. The cases of Hut, Hoffman, Matthijs and Rothmann (less so for Joris) suggest not a "rejection of the letter" in favour of "spirit," but rather an interpretive system which held spirit and letter together in its own particular way.[72]

Conclusion

The three interpretive groupings identified here interpenetrated at many levels and developed in different ways, over time, in different historical settings. The Swiss Anabaptists happen to have reached an early consensus on a more literalistic, ethical interpretation of Scripture, with a decided emphasis on the New Testament witness to the life and words of Christ and the apostles; the spiritualistic and apocalyptic frames of interpretation did not become live issues for Swiss Anabaptist *hermeneutics*. This does not mean, however, that "Anabaptism" had settled the hermeneutical question at this early date. The South German/Moravian and North German/Dutch streams, for example, had to grapple with the spiritualist and apocalyptic interpretive frameworks for some decades more. A description of "Anabaptist hermeneutics" must take these larger processes into account.[73]

The major sections which follow will examine Anabaptist discussions and differences concerning political reality, socio-economic reality, and religious reform. In essence these Anabaptist discussions had to do with how God's revelation was to be understood, with Scripture and its "spiritual" interpretation at the centre of concern. We will see that the various "positions" we have noted above were subject to change over time, across the Swiss/South German-Austrian/North German-Dutch lines established by the polygenesis paradigm. As the Anabaptist movement progressed along the road to self-definition some interpretive positions gained strength, while others faded from view. Thus the apocalyptic and prophetic readings of Scripture and the signs of the times (the interpretive frameworks which characterized so much of the movement in the 1530s) had faded to minority positions by the 1550s, and had virtually died out by the end of the century. The predominance of the letter over the spirit became the most widely accepted Anabaptist interpretive position by the end of the sixteenth century, not only among the Swiss Brethren, but among all surviving Anabaptist groups, including the former Melchiorites.

End Notes

[1] See the fine introduction and the selections in Walter Klaassen, *Anabaptism in Outline* (Scottdale, Pa.: Herald Press, 1981), chapter 2, pp. 41-71.

[2] *Ibid.*, p. 42.

[3] As, for instance, by Hubmaier. See *ibid.*, p. 44.

[4] See Klaassen, *Outline*, chapters 5 and 6 for a sampling of Anabaptist views concerning the church.

[5] See Klaassen, *Outline*, chapter 8 for a wide range of Anabaptist statements on baptism.

[6] See Klaassen, *Outline*, chapter 10.

[7] See Klaassen, *Outline*, chapter 9.

[8] See Klaassen, *Outline*, chapter 11.

[9] Summarized in Bauman, *Gewaltlosigkeit*, pp. 130-34.

[10] Walter Klaassen, "Word, Spirit, and Scripture in Early Anabaptist Thought," Thesis submitted for the degree of Doctor of Philosophy, Oxford University, 1960; and Walter Klaassen, "Spiritualization in the Reformation," MQR 37 (1963), pp. 67-77.

[11] "It is not in the least surprising that Anabaptists have traditionally been regarded as enthusiasts and visionaries. The *Täuferakten* and their own writings are full of pneumatic language, of expressions of their conviction of the immediacy of God's working. They knew themselves to be under the direct command of God and could say without doubt or reticence that what they did was a result of God's direction." Walter Klaassen, "Word, Spirit, and Scripture in Early Anabaptist Thought," p. 98.

[12] See, for example, Conrad Grebel's letter to Thomas Müntzer, Sep. 5, 1524, in QGTS, 1, #14, pp. 13-21. For an English translation of the letter see Harder, *Sources*, pp. 284-294. At the Zürich disputation concerning the Mass and images (October 26-28, 1523), Hubmaier expressed his exegetical principle as follows: "If they are commanded, show us the Scripture and there will be no more question. If they are not commanded, then they should not exist. For everything which God has not taught us either with words or deeds should not be and is in vain." Harder, *Sources*, p. 241.

[13] Bauman, *Gewaltlosigkeit*, pp. 134-35, gives some examples. There are many others, especially from the St. Gall and Appenzell territories.

[14] At the second Zürich Disputation, Hubmaier echoed Zwingli in arguing that the "Word of God as written in both Testaments" is the only fitting judge in religious controversies. See Pipkin and Yoder, *Hubmaier*, pp. 23-24; also pp. 51-54. Furthermore, although Hubmaier was a trained theologian, he did not usually rely on scholastic methods to extract meaning from "plain" Scripture. Concerning skill in languages he noted: "Although I also do not reject tongues or languages for the exposition of dark passages, still for the sun-clear words one needs neither tongues nor lungs." "On the Christian Baptism of Believers," Pipkin and Yoder, *Hubmaier*, p. 99. Hubmaier was not entirely consistent here, however, as his exegetical work relating to the Lord's Supper demonstrates. See John Rempel, *The Lord's Supper in Anabaptism: a study in the Christology of Balthasar Hubamaier, Pilgram Marpeck, and Dirk Philips* (Scottdale, Pa.: Herald Press, 1993), pp. 57-65.

[15] "On the main themes of Word, Spirit, and Scripture there is no difference between the Swiss Brethren and Hubmaier." Walter Klaassen, "Word, Spirit, and Scripture in Early Anabaptist Thought," p. 68.

[16] In his "Theses ... concerning the instruction of the mass," 1525, Hubmaier underlines the predominant value of the spiritual and inward reality signified by external symbols, but he then says "the Spirit makes us

alive, and the Spirit comes with the Word." Pipkin and Yoder, *Hubmaier*, p. 75. Likewise in 1527, in his exposition of the Apostles' Creed, Hubmaier affirms that God "has restored to me, by his holy Word, which he has sent, the power to become thy child in faith." *Ibid.*, p. 235. Nevertheless, it is the Holy Spirit, not the Son, which conceives the "new man." *Ibid.*, p. 236. The role of the Holy Spirit is that of "sanctifier." *Ibid.*, p. 238.

[17] See Pipkin and Yoder, *Hubmaier*, pp. 21-29.

[18] *Ibid.*, pp. 23 ff.

[19] "The one who has received God's new covenant, i.e., in whose heart through the Holy Spirit the Law was written, is truly just. Whoever thinks he can keep the Law by following the good Book ascribes to the dead letter what belongs to the living spirit. He who does not have the Spirit and presumes to find it in Scripture, looks for light and finds darkness, seeks life and finds utter death, not only in the Old Testament but also in the New..." Hans Denck, "The Law of God (1526)," in Edward J. Furcha, ed. and trans., *Selected Writings of Hans Denck* (Pittsburgh: Pickwick Press, 1975), pp. 59-60. See the discussion in Bauman, *Gewaltlosigkeit*, pp. 135-37.

[20] Denck opposed the Lutheran (and, one would say, the Hubmaierian) association of Word of God with Scripture because it "undermined Luther's earlier pronouncements regarding the priesthood of all believers. It tended to reestablish a privileged position for the literate clergy." Werner O. Packull, "Hans Denck: Fugitive from Dogmatism," in Hans-Jürgen Goertz, ed., *Profiles of Radical Reformers* (Scottdale, Pa.: Herald Press, 1982), p. 63.

[21] In his earliest known writing, Denck said: "When I seek to plumb the depth of Scripture on my own, I do not understand a thing. But when (truth) drives me, I comprehend, not because of merit but on account of grace." Scripture, he maintained, cannot remove the darkness by itself, since "it is written by human hands, spoken with human mouth, seen with human eyes and heard with human ears," but light comes "when day breaks in our hearts." Hans Denck, "Confession to the City Council of Nürnberg, 1525," in Edward J. Furcha, ed. and trans., *Selected Writings of Hans Denck* (Pittsburgh: Pickwick Press, 1975), pp. 15-16; original in Baring and Fellman, *Schriften*, II, pp. 20-26.

[22] "He who honors Scripture but lacks divine love must take heed not to turn Scripture into an idol as do all scribes who are not 'learned' for the kingdom of God." Hans Denck, "The Law of God (1526)," in Edward J. Furcha, ed. and trans., *Selected Writings of Hans Denck* (Pittsburgh: Pickwick Press, 1975), p. 63.

[23] Baring and Fellmann, *Schriften*, II, p. 82.

[24] Peter C. Erb, "Anabaptist Spirituality," in Frank C. Senn, ed., *Protestant Spiritual Traditions*, (Mahwah, N.J.: Paulist Press, 1986), p. 102.

[25] Klaassen, *Outline*, p. 87.

[26] "The *Gemeinde*, as conceived by the Swiss Brethren and the later Hutterites and Pilgramites, was not central to his theology." Packull, *Mysticism*, p. 59. See also Hulshof, *Geschiedenis*, pp. 30-31.

[27] See especially the testimony of Ambrosius Spittelmaier, "Reply to Questioning," in Karl Schornbaum, *Quellen zur Geschichte der Wiedertäufer*, II. Band, pp. 47-56. Also the testimony of Hans Nadler, *ibid.*, p. 153.

[28] For Hut's own account of the seven judgements, see Christian Meyer, "Zur Geschichte der Wiedertäufer in Oberschwaben" Part I: "Die Anfänge des Wiedertäufertums in Augsburg," *Zeitschrift des historischen Vereins für Schwaben und Neuburg*, I (1874), p. 230.

[29] As noted by Hans-Dieter Schmid, "Das Hutsche Täufertum. Ein Beitrag zur Charakterisierung einer täuferischen Richtung aus der Frühzeit der Täuferbewegung," *Historische Jahrbuch*, XCI (1971), p. 331.

[30] In Hut's case, unfortunately, some key documentary evidence consists of testimony extracted under torture. Following repeated questioning on the matter, however, Hut's testimony remained consistent, and it coincides with the testimonies of his followers. See Hut's interrogation statement, translated in Klaassen, *Outline*, pp. 320-21.

[31] Deppermann, *Hoffman*, pp. 175-76.

[32] "All of these are one community and one body in Christ. All who are enemies of sin are members of this community, that is only those who desire and love justice (or righteousness)." Meyer, "Zur Geschichte der Wiedertäufer in Oberschwaben," p. 36.

[33] Claus-Peter Clasen, *Anabaptism: A Social History, 1525-1618* (Ithaca: Cornell University Press, 1972), p. 33.

[34] See the outline of Hut's timetable in Packull, *Mysticism*, p. 101.

[35] As Deppermann notes, Hoffman's apocalypticism depended on the Holy Spirit being poured out on all people; the two witnesses of the End Times were already present in the world. In his commentary on Daniel (1526) Hoffman interpreted the End Time as being present, which was central to his entire message. Deppermann, *Hoffman*, pp. 65-67.

[36] See Walter Klaassen, "Eschatalogical Themes in Early Dutch Anabaptism," in Irvin B. Horst, ed., *The Dutch Dissenters*, (Leiden: E.J. Brill, 1986), pp. 22-23.

[37] As noted by Deppermann, *Hoffman*, pp. 212-14.

[38] Hoffman, *Ordinance of God*, p. 186.

[39] Melchior Hoffman, *Warhafftige erklerung aus heyliger Biblischer schrifft / das der Satan / Todt / Hell / Sünd / und dy ewige verdamnuß im ursprung nit auß gott / sundern alleyn auß eygenem will erwachsen sei.* (Straßburg, Jakob Cammerlander), 1531, p. A I.

[40] *Ibid.*, p. A II.

[41] *Ibid.*, p. A IIII.

[42] See, for example, *Ein rechte warhafftige hohe und gotliche gruntliche underrichtung von der reiner forchte Gottes* ... (1533), and *Weissagung usz heiliger götlicher geschrifft* (1529/1530), pp. A III ff.

[43] In *Von der reiner forchte Gottes*, Hoffman listed Abel, Enoch, Noah, Abraham, Lot, Daniel, Susanna, and Joseph as positive examples; The fallen angel, Adam, Sodom, and the people of Egypt are examples of those who failed to fear God, whose reward was "unentliche todt." pp. A II-A III.

[44] *Weissagung*, p. A IV.

[45] *Weissagung*, p. A IV.

[46] Hoffman, *Ordinance of God*, pp. 186-87.

[47] See Deppermann, *Hoffman*, pp. 74-75.

[48] *Weissagung*, p. A I.

[49] *Ibid.*

[50] Using this interpretive key, Hoffman divided history into three periods: 1) That of the Old Testament (Law), 2) That of the New Testament (Free Will), and 3) That of the Holy Spirit (Power). Deppermann, *Hoffman*, p. 217.

[51] Deppermann, *Hoffman*, pp. 213-15. Deppermann notes that the "cloven hoof" approach has its roots in German mysticism. Hans Denck and Sebastian Franck shared Hoffman's thought, even if they did not use his language. *Ibid.*, p. 215.

[52] See Walter Klaassen, *Living at the End of the Ages* (Lanham, Md.: University Press of America, 1992).

[53] Hoffman, *Weissagung*, pp. C IV-D I.

[54] Hoffman, *Weissagung*, p. D I.

[55] As Hoffman notes concerning the interpretation of Ursula Jost's visions. Melchior Hoffman, *Prophetische Gesicht und Offenbarung der goetlichen würckung zu dieser letzten zeit / die vom XXIIII Jahr biß in dz XXX einer gottes liebhaberin durch den heiligen geist geoffenbart seind / welcher hie in diesem büchlin LXXVII verzeichnet seindt* (1530); reference from Heinold Fast, *Der linke Flügel der Reformation* (Bremen: Carl Schünemann Verlag, 1962), p. 306.

[56] Hoffman, *The Ordinance of God*, in Williams, SAW, pp. 202-03.

[57] So Deppermann, *Hoffman*, p. 213.

[58] Deppermann, *Hoffman*, pp. 233-34.

[59] Deppermann, *Hoffman*, pp. 181-84.

[60] Among the Strasbourg prophets were Katharina Seid, Andreas Klaiber, Lienhard Jost, Ursula Jost, Barbara Rebstock, Hans Rebstock, Valentin Dufft, Valentin Nessel, Gertrud Lorenz, Josef Lorenz, Wilhelm Blum the elder, Wilhelm Blum the younger, and Agnes Jost. The Rebstocks had been followers of Hut, subsequently banned from Esslingen. Deppermann, *Hoffman*, pp. 178-80.

[61] Hoffman, *Prophetische Gesicht*, e.g. visions 3; 48.

[62] *Ibid.*, e.g., visions 4; 21; 31; 32; 36; 37; 38; 39; 51.

[63] *Ibid.*, p. C II.

[64] *Ibid.*, visions 24, 27, 29. In her twenty-fourth vision, she saw a beautiful rainbow. Next to the rainbow were many animals on which sat men who looked like fire, and they were surrounded by blue fire. Then the fire divided and two roads appeared out of it. One was small and beautiful, but the other was broad and large, and it led into a great darkness.

[65] *Ibid.*, e.g., visions 18; 56; 70.

[66] *Ibid.*, visions 17; 65.

[67] *Ibid.*, e.g. visions 9; 14; 21; 41; 42.

[68] *Ibid.*, p. A V.

[69] As in, for example, her seventy-fourth vision. *Ibid.*, C IV.

[70] *Ibid.*, vision 20. In this vision, Ursula saw men sitting on a ship, but it was not ship, but rather was like a four-cornered cloth which bound up all four corners of the earth. She prayed to the Lord that he show her what this meant and it was revealed to her that they were apostles and proclaimers of divine justice.

[71] *Prophetische Gesicht*, vision thirteen, p. A V.

[72] Heinold Fast wished to deny that this group of people were "Anabaptist," preferring to classify them as "Schwärmer," marked by their appeal to "extra-biblical" revelation. Heinold Fast, *Der linke Flügel der Reformation* (Bremen: Carl Schünemann Verlag, 1962), p. xxviii. Regardless of how we may judge their interpretive efforts, it is clear that they themselves considered "dreams and visions" in continuity with biblically revealed truth (and in continuity with biblical examples), not as going "beyond" the Bible.

[73] As against J.H. Yoder's description, which traces the hermeneutics of the old "evangelical Anabaptist" grouping, but excludes important Anabaptist figures. See John. H. Yoder, "The Hermeneutics of the Anabaptists," MQR 41 (Oct., 1967), pp. 291-308.

Chapter 12

Anabaptism and Political Reality

The potential relationship of Anabaptism to the political powers of the day was dependent upon factors both internal and external to the movement. The core doctrines of Anabaptism did introduce certain limits and challenges to the political status quo: a church composed of those who freely chose baptism as adults would not be a "territorial" church in the conventional, sixteenth century sense. But there was the corresponding "external" factor of government reactions to Anabaptism: what kind of political space, if any, would be made available for the practice of Anabaptism?

Internal Factors: Toward an Anabaptist Political Ethic

Looking first at Anabaptist teachings that impacted on potential relationships with governments, we can trace the development of a succession of doctrines and practices that increasingly moved toward a principled separatism. There was first of all the requirement, universally shared by all so called Anabaptists, that baptism should be administered only to adults. This in itself, it turned out, was reason enough for sixteenth century political authorities to outlaw the "baptizing" movement. There would be those in any given political territory, perhaps many, who might choose not to be baptized, and no one knew what chaos or anarchy might result from such a situation. As long as Anabaptists were unwilling to abandon their defining principle of adult baptism on confession of faith they were in effect calling for uncoerced, voluntarily gathered believers' churches. This "internal" or theologically limiting factor thus came face to face with the "external" reality of political life in the sixteenth century. If Anabaptism was going to occupy a legitimate political space, there had to be rulers who accepted the existence of such believers' churches in their territories.

But in fact the core Anabaptist teachings went beyond the simple question of baptism and included church discipline for those who were baptized. In later discussions between Reformers and Anabaptists, the question of the ban often was a more difficult point of negotiation than was adult baptism.[1] Anabaptists sometimes were willing to grant that baptism could be left "free" (that is, they would be willing not to require adult baptism), but they found it harder to countenance a church without discipline. Baptism and the ban were intimately connected to each other, and they were likewise linked with the "closed" practice of the Lord's Supper: as a matter of church reform, the Anabaptist celebration of the Supper was to be limited to those who had submitted both to baptism and to the discipline of the community. And finally, a "reformed" economic behaviour also was required of Anabaptist members. In a word, the core of Anabaptist church reform principles called for a seriousness of purpose on the part of church members that proved an ill fit with the territorial church model.

Insofar as the "core" principles were upheld as necessary marks of the true church, the Anabaptist reform placed itself on the margins of what came to be acceptable politically in the sixteenth century, although that fact became increasingly apparent only over time. But there remained further points of clarification that the initial doctrinal and ecclesiological consensus had not addressed, particularly in terms of what constituted proper "outward" behaviour for Anabaptist believers. Would Anabaptism move in a direction of accomodation with civil society and governments, or would it move in a direction of separation from them? Movement in either direction was possible. We know this because there were Anabaptists who did, in fact, propose adjustments in both directions.

Two issues of crucial importance for defining the relationship of church to government came up for discussion in Anabaptist circles. Following the agreement at Schleitheim in 1527, Anabaptists elsewhere were confronted with brethren who insisted that a true Christian would not take the sword (and so would not serve in governments), and further, that a true Christian would not swear oaths of any kind. Accepting these teachings, of course, would mean an even further political marginalization of Anabaptism, and a stronger move towards separation from civil society and its government.

Because of the almost uniformly negative reaction by political authorities to the "core principles" of Anabaptist reform, it appears in hindsight that a strong separatism was implied in those principles from the start. But in fact, it is truer to say that Anabaptism as a whole *developed into* separatism. There were other roads taken and tried on the way to what eventually became a separatist tradition. The movement towards, and development of an Anabaptist "tradition" concerning church and government is the story that will concern us in the chapters which follow in this section of the study.

External Factors: Anabaptism and Political Reality

The largest political territory into which Anabaptism spread, if it may be called a "territory," was the Holy Roman Empire, which in the sixteenth century included in its scope a good third of western Europe. But the Holy Roman Empire was not a centralized or coherent political territory. It was ruled by an Emperor who was chosen by seven electors; the "empire" encompassed hundreds of territories, principalities, and cities of varying sizes, with a wide variety of freedoms and privileges.

With the election of Charles of the house of Hapsburg as the fifth Holy Roman Emperor (Charles V, emperor from 1519 to 1558), the Holy Roman Empire was added to Hapsburg holdings elsewhere.[2] Seen on a map of western Europe, the political area controlled by the Hapsburgs has the appearance of a large sandwich, with strength on the outside, but weakness in the middle, precisely in the Holy Roman Empire. Hapsburg political strength rested not in the Empire, but rather in Austria and Spain, the hereditary lands ruled directly by the royal house.

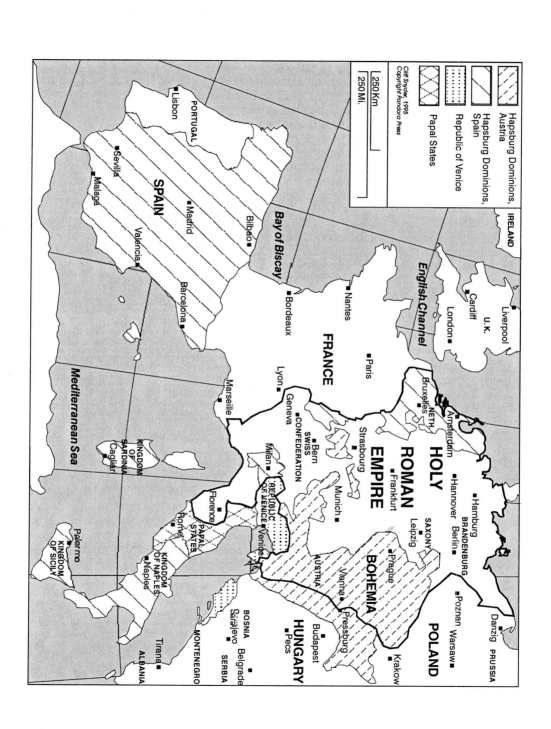

Legend:
- Hapsburg Dominions, Austria
- Hapsburg Dominions, Spain
- Republic of Venice
- Papal States

250 Km
250 Mi.

Cliff Snyder, 1995
Copyright Pandora Press

IRELAND

PORTUGAL
Lisbon
Sevilla
Malaga
SPAIN
Madrid
Bilbao
Valencia
Barcelona

Bay of Biscay

English Channel

U.K.
Liverpool
Cardiff
London

FRANCE
Nantes
Bordeaux
Paris
Lyon
Marseille
Geneva

Mediterranean Sea

NETH.
Bruxelles
Amsterdam
SWISS CONFEDERATION
Bern
Milan
Strasbourg
HOLY ROMAN EMPIRE
Frankfurt
Munich
Hamburg
Hannover
Berlin
BRANDENBURG
SAXONY
Leipzig
Prague
BOHEMIA
AUSTRIA
Vienna
Pressburg
HUNGARY
Budapest
Pecs
Poznan
Warsaw
POLAND
Danzig
PRUSSIA
Krakow

KINGDOM OF SARDINIA
Cagliari
Florence
Rome
PAPAL STATES
REPUBLIC OF VENICE
Venice

KINGDOM OF NAPLES
Naples
Palermo
KINGDOM OF SICILY

BOSNIA
Sarajevo
SERBIA
Belgrade
MONTENEGRO
Tirana
ALBANIA

To the east lay the traditional Hapsburg Austrian lands. They were ruled by Archduke Ferdinand, brother of Charles V and later to succeed Charles as Holy Roman Emperor (1558-64). These lands had grown to include Moravia and Bohemia in the sixteenth century (over which the Hapsburgs worked to establish tighter political control). The Austrian territories marked the eastern frontier of Christian Europe, for the Ottoman Turks had marched up the Danube and were threatening Vienna and the borders of Austria itself. The "Turkish threat," which created so much apocalyptic excitement, kept the emperor and his brother quite occupied militarily and strained financially. Hapsburg preoccupation with the Turks, in fact, provided crucial political breathing space for princes and cities intent on establishing Protestant reforms: as long as the Hapsburgs were occupied to the east, they couldn't enforce Catholic practice in dependent territories. Further to the west were scattered Austrian territories and dependencies that included the Tirol and isolated territories located here and there in areas as far west as Württemberg and Alsace. Anabaptists could fall into Hapsburg hands (and be tried in Austrian courts) in places as diverse as Rottenberg on the Neckar, the Tirol, Austrian territory proper, Moravia, and Bohemia.

Far to the west lay the Spanish dominions of the Hapsburgs. They were ruled directly by Charles (known to the Spanish as Charles I). These territories included the southern part of Italy (the Kingdom of Naples) and the Kingdoms of Sicily and Sardinia in the Mediterranean. Slightly further afield, the Spanish administration of the Hapsburgs also ruled over the Netherlands, including Luxembourg and what today is Belgium. This territory was politically more vulnerable, isolated as it was from other Hapsburg holdings. It was separated from Spanish dominions by France, and from Austrian lands by German territories. And, of course, beginning in 1492, Charles (as king of Spain) became the ruler of most of the American continents, whose vast size and wealth became known only gradually.

Looked at from the Hapsburg perspective, Anabaptism was virtually unknown in the Spanish territories proper; it made a strong appearance, as we have seen, in the Netherlands, which not coincidentally was making a bid for independence from Hapsburg control in the sixteenth century. In the east, Anabaptism was initially strong in the Tirol, where the peasantry had risen in revolt against Hapsburg rule in 1525-26. Anabaptism then spread up and down the Danube in Austria proper. Resolute Hapsburg persecution soon forced Anabaptists to flee from those areas to the toleration of nearby Moravia, where strong local lords successfully resisted Hapsburg pressure throughout much of the sixteenth century.

Hapsburg resistance to all "evangelical heresy" (which included Anabaptism in its scope) was legendary for its cruelty and thoroughness. Of the executions that can be documented in Swiss, German, and Austrian territories (not counting Spain and the Netherlands), about seventy occurred in Switzerland, about 360 in German territories of the Empire, and more than 400 in Hapsburg territories proper. Archduke Ferdinand in particular "distinguished himself by the amount of blood he shed in suppressing Anabaptism."[3] The inquisitorial process had been perfected in Spain in the late fifteenth century, and it was applied consistently (in direct proportion to local Hapsburg influence) in all Hapsburg lands.[4] It included routine torture and the most painful forms of inflicting death that could be imagined. All this is amply documented not only in martyrologies like the *Martyrs Mirror*, but also in official court records.[5]

Not surprisingly, these methods achieved their end: Anabaptism managed to survive long-term only in lands that were under more marginal imperial control, such as Moravia and the northern Netherlands. Swiss territories, Protestant and Catholic alike, also came to be uncompromisingly hostile to Anabaptists (although they executed fewer people). The natural result of high levels of political persecution in Swiss and Hapsburg territories was that the more persistent among the Anabaptists migrated to other areas; the political problem was not removed, but simply displaced elsewhere. Cities and territories in Alsace, the Palatinate, Württemberg, Hesse, and increasingly in the northern Netherlands and along the Baltic coast, became destinations for Anabaptist refugees and their communities. The pattern of migration in search of religious toleration, which continued into the twentieth century among Mennonites, Amish, and Hutterites is a phenomenon that began almost immediately following the first adult baptisms in Zürich.

Anabaptist Political Arrangements

Historically speaking, five different kinds of political arrangements *vis-a-vis* Anabaptism can be described. One of the earliest also was one of the rarest. Balthasar Hubmaier established Anabaptism as the official religion, first of the city of Waldshut (a Hapsburg dependency), and then in Nicholsburg Moravia, in the territories of the lords of Liechtenstein. Neither of these experiments lasted long enough for us to be able to discern how non-compliance in religious matters was dealt with in these "territorial" Believers' Churches. The case of Hubmaier is important, however, for he was influential in defining the early theological contours of Anabaptist baptism, the ban, and the Supper, and yet he also considered this "Believers' Church" to be compatible with "official religion" status. This indicates that the strong "separation from the world" ethic that pervaded later Anabaptism was not a *necessary* original component of Believers' Church ecclesiology, but was a further theological interpretation that was encouraged, in part, by the encounter with a decidedly hostile world.

The second "political arrangement" also was unique in Anabaptism, for it happened only once, in the city of Münster. We never will know what shape Anabaptist reform would have taken in Münster had political events not conspired against the city, and had apocalyptic excitement not overtaken Rothmann's Anabaptist reform. But the fact of the matter is that in Münster Anabaptist visionaries came to control the "state," and the results were much the same as in city state religions elsewhere in Europe: dissenters were expelled, executed, or forced to conform, in the name of God's will. The internal theological dynamic that led to the Anabaptist Kingdom of

Münster was prophetic apocalypticism. This reading of Scripture was done in light of prophetically interpreted "signs of the times," and led to the conviction that Münster was the New Jerusalem of the Last Days, and further, that in this time of "restitution of all things," unique social/political rules applied.

The third political arrangement was the "zero tolerance" approach to Anabaptism exercised, as noted above, in the Hapsburg territories, sporatically in some Protestant territories, eventually becoming the policy in Protestant Swiss territories as well (Zürich and Bern in the seventeenth century). Under these regimes Anabaptists were actively hunted down and rooted out by all available means. In the face of a determined political will to eradication, Anabaptism could not and did not survive.

A fourth and more widespread approach, especially in German territories at some remove from imperial pressure, was to proclaim an official policy of no tolerance, but to implement an unofficial policy of not looking for trouble. Many rural districts in Switzerland, Alsace, the Palatinate, and Hesse fit this model at different times during the sixteenth and seventeenth centuries, as did Augsburg and Strasbourg for a time; so did various cities and rural districts in northern Germany and the Netherlands at different times. In these settings Anabaptism could survive in "underground" fashion, but it was a very precarious existence. The appearance of a zealous local priest or preacher could unleash a wave of arrests, or the death of a tolerant prince could mean the end of the "unofficial" relationship of toleration. The result would then be forced flight or exile to a more "friendly" territory (if one could be found), or worse.

The fifth approach was adopted in the sixteenth century only in Moravia, and that was to tolerate Anabaptist settlers openly, although no thought was given to adopting Anabaptism as the "official" territorial religion. In the Moravian setting Anabaptists—virtually all of them refugees and immigrants—formed cultural/religious enclaves within the "host" society. It was in Moravia that the communitarian Anabaptism of the Hutterites flourished in the later sixteenth century, but there were communities of Swiss Brethren refugees living in Moravia too, as well as some communities who looked to Pilgram Marpeck for leadership. A strong motive behind the Moravian policy of toleration was economic: lands needed settling and developing, and the Anabaptists were industrious and good for local economies.

The economic motive underlying Moravian toleration would come into play prominently in subsequent centuries, and came to define Mennonite, Hutterite and Amish migrations into the twentieth century: rulers in search of industrious settlers would offer privileges to the descendants of the Anabaptists, all too often revoking those privileges once lands had been improved and were productive again. In this way beleaguered Swiss Anabaptists would find political space in the Palatinate after 1648, where they were invited to settle after the Thirty Years' War devastated the territory; Dutch Anabaptists were welcomed in the Vistula Delta, where their ability to reclaim land from the sea was valued; Mennonites in Prussia would be invited to settle in the Ukraine by Catherine II, who valued their agricultural skills; the British crown would offer generous land grants to Mennonites and Amish in Pennsylvania, and to Mennonites and Amish in Upper Canada following the American Revolution, for the same reason. In the sixteenth century, however, political space such as Moravia offered was rare indeed, and by the end of the sixteenth century, Moravia also proved inhospitable.

With almost negligible exceptions, Anabaptism was forced to develop in an openly hostile political environment. Even in the exceptional settings of Waldshut, Nicholsburg, Münster and Moravia, where some kind of official arrangement existed, the reality still was that in the sixteenth century climate, those political arrangements themselves virtually guaranteed political intervention from the outside. Even when we look at the exceptional cases, then, there was no escaping the fact that to be an Anabaptist in the sixteenth century meant that one had placed oneself on the margins of acceptable society. It is thus not surprising that a separatist interpretation of Anabaptism came to prevail, and that the biblical themes of the righteous having to suffer at the hands of the unrighteous, the persecution and exile of God's chosen people, and the final reward of the faithful remnant would become increasingly important in defining the movement. One strand that we wish to trace in the chapters which follow is the internal biblical and theological debate that accompanied the Anabaptist move towards a tradition of separatism.

Conclusion

Beyond the basic questions of adult baptism, ban, Supper, and mutual aid, there were no more critical political/ethical issues facing the Anabaptists than questions of "the sword" (which included the matter of governmental authority as well as personal pacifism) and the oath. In accordance with the reformational principle that the church was to be reformed acording to the norms of Scripture, the Anabaptists sought to discern and then establish a relationship between church and political authority as ordained by God in the Bible, read in light of the Spirit. It is not surprising that there was no early consensus on this question for, as we have seen above, there was no early agreement on interpretive approaches to Scripture.

Among the separatist Anabaptists (who generally followed the more "literal" hermeneutic approach), the most pervasive theological image used to describe Anabaptist political reality was that of the "two kingdoms." By the end of the century the "two kingdoms" image, read in a separatist mode, had come to prevail in the movement as the dominant interpretive context to be handed on to succeeding generations. But there were alternative interpretive frameworks that competed with the "two kingdoms" view in the developmental stages of Anabaptism. In what follows we will outline some of the views that were expressed among the Anabaptists concerning the sword and the oath, using as our frame of reference the three interpretive Anabaptist groupings (literalists, spiritualists, apocalypticists) outlined in chapter 11 above. As will be seen below, Schleitheim's position on both sword and oath was only one among several contrasting views in early Anabaptism.

End Notes

[1] As, for example, in Bucer's discussions with Hessian Anabaptists. See Werner Packull, "The Melchiorites and the Ziegenhain Order of Discipline, 1538-39," in Walter Klaassen, ed. *Anabaptism Revisited* (Scottdale, Pa.: Herald Press, 1992), pp. 11-28.

[2] See the discussion in Williams, *Radical* (1992), pp. 23-34.

[3] Claus-Peter Clasen, *Anabaptism: A Social History, 1525-1618* (Ithaca: Cornell University Press, 1972), pp. 371-72. See all of chapter 11 for an analysis of persecution of Anabaptism in Switzerland and South Germany.

[4] On the earlier developments in Spain, see Williams, *Radical* (1992), pp. 35-41.

[5] The *Martyrs Mirror* notes that up to 1556, Charles V was "chiefly responsible for the shedding of the blood of the saints in the Netherlands, as also for the most cruel tyrannies which, through the instrumentality of the Inquisition ... were inflicted upon them, by fire, water, sword and otherwise." p. 551. See further references to the "Spanish tyranny" on pp. 758, and esp. pp. 1095ff. The latter extended passage notes how God punished former tyrants, including the infamous persecutor, the Duke of Alva.

Chapter 13

The Sword and the Oath
in Swiss and South German/Austrian Anabaptism

The earliest "baptizing" movements, in Switzerland and South German/Austrian territories, were born in uncertain political circumstances, in the shadow of the Peasants' War, in a religious climate that encouraged church reform but had not yet defined the parameters of that reform. The variety of positions that were taken up by different Anabaptists on questions of the sword and the oath (we will outline six different views in this chapter alone) reflect the uncertain, exploratory nature of the time, when all things seemed possible. In the context of early Swiss and South German/Austrian Anabaptism, the Schleitheim Articles loomed large because they were a very early articulation of a clear political ethic. Anabaptists elsewhere had to elaborate their own views in dialogue with the defenders of the Schleitheim position. Without a doubt the importance of the Schleitheim Articles has been overrated by modern Mennonite interpreters: they *do not* represent the defining moment for Anabaptism as a whole. But it is also true that Schleitheim represented a strong articulation of an Anabaptist political ethic that needed to be countered by Anabaptists who were proposing alternative models. In this chapter Schleitheim will hover in the background, as we outline how Hans Denck, Pilgram Marpeck, Balthasar Hubmaier, Hans Hut, and finally the Hutterite tradition came into conversation with Schleitheim's views.

Sattler, Denck, and Marpeck: Law or Love?

One point of tension in the development of an Anabaptist political ethic lay between the more "literal" reading of the New Testament, represented early in the Swiss tradition by the Schleitheim Articles, and the "spiritualist" reading of Scripture as a whole, represented by Hans Denck. In this context, Pilgram Marpeck represented a mediating voice between the two tendencies.

Michael Sattler

Beginning at the "letter" side of the spirit/letter continuum, Michael Sattler's writings emphasized a Christocentric, New Testament measure of behaviour. The backdrop against which this ethic was formulated was that there were two separate kingdoms ruled by two separate "princes" (Christ and Satan); individual believers and the church as a collective must separate from the world, and follow the biblical ordering which Christ had outlined for his followers. Both the example of Jesus's life, and the commands Jesus gave his followers in New Testament Scripture thus set the norms of conduct for the church.

The central point concerning the oath (article 7 of Schleitheim) was made with reference to Matthew 5:33-37, where Jesus requires no swearing at all by way of "command": believers simply are to affirm "yea" or "nay."[1] A central point made by Sattler against swearing oaths was the inability of human beings to keep their promises.[2] The conclusion was straightforward, and required little by way of argument: Christ has commanded us not to swear, and we should therefore obey. The results of this "simple" conclusion were catastrophic in the sixteenth century political context, especially in city states where oaths of all sorts were routinely administered, ranging from the yearly civic oath required of all citizens, to oaths required on joining guilds. As Edmund Pries notes,

> For early modern Europeans, oaths defined and legitimated the relationships between governing authorities and their constituents or subjects, regulated the relationships between fellow citizens and fellow peasants, and served as the glue that held both urban and rural sociopolitical structures in place. The existence of a community without an oath was unthinkable. Thus the refusal of the oath seemed like a repudiation of society.[3]

Those who refused to swear any and all oaths were placing themselves outside the margins of acceptable civil society.

Schleitheim's well-known arguments against sword bearing (articles 4 and 6) began by making the point that Christ's command is "nonresistance," and argues further that believers must "follow after Christ" by doing as He did; this was followed by an appeal to Paul's injunctions that the church and the world operate according to different standards, and that Christians must be separate from the world. Scripture is cited in the following way:

a) Matthew 5:39. "Thereby shall also fall away from us the diabolical weapons of violence—such as sword, armor, and the like, and all their use to protect friends or against enemies—by virtue of the word of Christ: 'you shall not resist evil.'"[4] Significantly, this first mention of the sword comes at the end of Article 4, concerning separation: weapons and the like are of Satan and the world, from which the Christian has been freed and from which Christians must separate. Therefore, followers of Christ shall not resist. Members of the perfection of Christ are to yield before the world, and trust in God.[5] The descriptive name of "nonresistance" has been given to this position primarily because of the centrality of Matthew 5:39 in the argument as a whole.

b) Romans 13:1ff. "The sword is an ordering of God outside the perfection of Christ. It punishes and kills the wicked, and guards and protects the good."[6] Article 6 on the sword opens with the explicit citing of Romans 13, and immediately makes clear that the sword of government stands "outside the perfection of Christ." What that means for the church is clarified immediately, with reference to John 8.

c) John 8:11. "But within the perfection of Christ only the ban is used ... without the death of the flesh, simply the warning and the command to sin no more." The central point made initially, which would be developed in more detail throughout, is that two very different means of discipline apply: the ban is used within the Body of Christ; the sword outside the Body. Further, these two means of discipline are not related to each other in any way (Article 6), for what is outside Christ is "nothing but an abomination which we should shun."[7]

The remainder of Article 6 consists of a detailed clarification of how Romans 13 is to be understood within the setting of the two opposed kingdoms. The basic response to the question of whether a Christian may wield the sword of government against the wicked, in defence of the good, is that Christ is the example from whom we are to learn. Article 6 concludes:

> (Philipians 3:20; 2 Corinthians 10:4; Ephesians 6:13-17). The rule of the government is according to the flesh, that of the Christians according to the spirit. . . . The weapons of their battle and warfare are carnal and only against the flesh, but the weapons of Christians are spiritual, against the fortification of the devil. . . . In sum: as Christ our Head is minded, so also must be minded the members of the body of Christ through Him...[8]

The result of this emphasis on the New Testament Christocentric "letter" was a thoroughgoing separatism: the "letter of Scripture" read in this way provided a literal, objective "rule of life" and political ethic for believers, members as they were of the "Kingdom of Heaven and of Christ."

Hans Denck

Hans Denck did not accept the literalist interpretive framework that underlay Schleitheim's views on sword and oath, even though in many respects Denck arrived at ethical conclusions that closely resembled those of Schleitheim. In spite of his "spiritualism," Hans Denck emphasized a necessary congruity between the inner Word, the outer testimony of Scripture (particularly as the written testimony of Scripture witnessed to Christ's own spirit of love and life of perfect love), and the outward lives of believers. Hans Denck followed the mystical tradition in asserting that an inner spiritual change would result in a life in conformity with God's will, as revealed in Christ's life.[9]

Denck's treatment of the oath points to clear differences between his reading of Scripture and that of Schleitheim.[10] Where Schleitheim makes yea and nay into an ordinance to be obeyed by those who have "the mind of Christ," in *Concerning True Love* Denck launches into a subtle discussion outlining the difficulties of vowing what is possibly not in one's power to fulfill. The point, says Denck, is not simply avoiding oaths as such, for even saying yea or nay when one cannot fulfill what one promises amounts to perjury. And finally, Denck clarifies that calling God to witness for events that have occurred in the past is of a different order than promising something for the future; the former is permitted.[11]

In his so-called "Recantation" of 1527, Hans Denck spoke again to the question of oath-taking and concluded that Christ never meant to forbid affirmations of truth telling, whether one calls them oaths or not. When people swear oaths, says Denck, it corresponds to the Apostle Paul's calling God as a witness (2 Corinthians 1:23); that is, one is saying "I propose to do this or that, so help me God; that is to say, if I do not mean it, may God not help me." Thus for Denck, raising one's hand for solemn oath taking is not forbidden, although casual swearing is.[12] Denck's "recantation" concerning the oath really showed very little movement in contrast to his earlier position: he had little interest in an ordinance or biblicistic prohibition concerning oaths, but rather was concerned with the spirit of the text, which had to do with truth telling. Denck's analysis, standpoint and argumentation is plainly distinct from that of Schleitheim.

Denck's position on the "spiritualist" side of the continuum also led him to assert nonviolence as the norm for the Christian. His understanding was that there exists a "progressive revelation" of God's will in Scripture, but that this progressive revelation is a spiritual, not a literal one. An application of Denck's spiritualist, Christocentric hermeneutics of love is visible in his discussion of Moses's killing of the Egyptian.

> Thus it is with the works and teachings of Moses, David and any other of the patriarchs. However good they may have been, at the point at which this love, which is Jesus, surpasses them with something better, they must be considered evil because of the better teaching. . . . Thus the zeal of Moses in killing the Egyptian who had harmed an Israelite was in some sense good in that he was zealous for the right against the wrong (Ex. 2:11ff). But if Moses had known perfect Love or indeed possessed her, he would have allowed himself to be killed in place of the Israelite, his brother, rather than strangle the Egyptian, his brother's enemy.[13]

Old Testament guidelines "may have been good" in their time, but it is the higher law of love in Christ that provides the spiritual, hermeneutical, and ethical guideline for Christians.

On the matter of the sword, Denck was resolutely nonresistant, but the foundation for his stand was a spiritualistic emphasis on following Christ *in love*, and not the more literally biblicist argument deriving from Christ's commands and behaviour. The argument in *Concerning Divine Love* is striking.

> It is not that power in itself is wrong seen from the perspective of the evil world, for [the government] serves God in his wrath, but rather that love teaches her children a better way, namely to serve the graciousness of God. For it is the nature of love not to will or desire the hurt of anyone, but as much as is possible to serve for the betterment of everyone. . . . Insofar as it were possible for a government to act [in love] it could well be Christian in its office. Since however the world will not tolerate it, a friend of God should not be in the government but out of it, that is if he desires to keep Christ as a

Lord and master. Whoever loves the Lord loves him regardless of his station. But he should not forget what characterizes a true lover [of God], namely that for the Lord's sake he renounce all power and to be subject to no one but the Lord.[14]

Denck doubted that the world would tolerate Christ-like behaviour in a ruler.[15] But his nonresistance, as Stayer notes, emphasized not an ordinance legislating absolute separation, but rather the more flexible biblical norm of "the love of Christ."[16]

This observation is important, not only because it points back to Denck's "spiritual" ethic of love, as distinguished from Sattler's more literal biblicism, but even more so because of the legacy of each teaching. On the basis of the Schleitheim consensus, the Swiss Brethren very quickly moved to a legislative (not to say legalistic) attitude concerning the outward ordinances of oath, sword, separation, dress and conduct. Denck's legacy was continued by, on the one hand, outright spiritualists such as Bünderlin and Entfelder, but on the other by the Marpeck circle, whose members struck a middle course between the legislative approach of the Swiss and Denck's spiritualist approach.

Pilgram Marpeck

In the Marpeck circle we find people who, like Denck, would assume final positions which looked very much like Schleitheim's nonresistance, but who in reality had their interpretive roots in the more mystical South German Anabaptist stream. In fact, Marpeck set his path very carefully and deliberately between the spiritualist descendants of Hans Denck (such as Bünderlin and Entfelder), and the Swiss and the Hutterites. Against the spiritualists Marpeck stressed the incarnate Christ and the necessity of visible church ordinances, while against the more literal-minded Swiss and Hutterites, he stressed the freedom of the Spirit and the centrality of love.[17] Marpeck also insisted on "separation from the world," but he refused to judge prematurely concerning anyone's true "citizenship." Such judging belonged to the Holy Spirit, he said; in the meantime, believers were to hope and work for the repentance of those who manifestly erred.[18]

There is one striking similarity between Marpeck's approach and that of the Swiss Brethren: Marpeck argued strongly for the existence of "two kingdoms" with contrasting modes of behaviour pertaining to each. He argued for the separation of the heavenly and earthly kingdoms, and called unequivocally for the Christian to affirm citizenship in the heavenly kingdom, to the exclusion of all other loyalties.[19] This was very Sattlerian language and argument, and in fact such a polarity, taken to uncompromising extremes, was a hallmark of Sattler's thought.[20] Thus it is possible to conclude a direct line of "influence" from Sattler/Schleitheim to Marpeck. But in fact the differences in approach between them were substantial.

According to Marpeck, what prevents a magistrate from being saved is not (as Schleitheim argued) that simply being a magistrate violates a law of discipleship (Jesus refused this, and therefore we must refuse it as well). What prevents a Christian from being a magistrate, Marpeck insisted, are any "worldly" acts required by the office that go contrary to God's will and the rule of Christ's Spirit.[21] Marpeck wrote:

> It is thus clear that worldly rulers have a special wisdom for their service. For Christian wisdom is not suited to their office nor will it serve them since it brings about only grace, mercy, love for the enemy, spiritual supernatural things, cross, tribulation, patience and faith in Christ without coercion, killing of the body and the external sword, but only through the Word of God. The wisdom of the office of the worldly rulers is designed to work through the external sword in vindictiveness, mercilessness, hatred of the enemy, physical vengeance, killing of evildoers, worldly natural governments, judgments, and similar things.[22]

Pilgram Marpeck's conclusion, like Hans Denck's, was that insofar as a Christian would be able to govern according to the law of Christian love (something he thought was probably impossible, given what he knew of governing), serving as a magistrate was allowed to Christians. Certainly Marpeck's own employment as a civil servant, as well as his acceptance of exile when his principles were violated, demonstrated concretely how he understood benign, limited government service to be possible.

Pilgram Marpeck argued christocentrically, as did the Swiss Brethren and as would Menno Simons, but in effect he admonished the more literalistic Brethren to deepen their understanding of Christ's life and example, and to apply this deeper understanding both to the question of "the world" with its sword, and the church with its Ban. According to Christ's example, evil is to be resisted and overcome by means of good, by means of loving patience.

> With gentle patience, love, and truth He overcame evil with all goodness, love, faithfulness, truth, and mercy, and [for evil] returned passionate intercession for His enemies... This is the universally hallowed cross of Christ—and no cross of guilt—by which in the innocence of Christ all the followers of Christ overcome, and through which they have free access in and to God, provided their hearts do not accuse them in guilt.[23]

Insofar as the love of Christ dwells in the heart, that love maps out a new manner of "overcoming evil" in this life, be that evil within or without the church community. Thus the most fundamental reason Christians forego violence and coercion, within and without the church, is that they are ruled by Christ's law of love, a gift of grace which bears good fruit, in season and out.

This "loving resistance," first articulated by Hans Denck in the Anabaptist movement, played a role in Anabaptist discussions in the middle of the sixteenth century. But the centrality of love as the measure which was to guide the use of *both* the sword and the ban was not a theological position that was destined to survive. As will be seen, in the post-Münster Anabaptism of the North, Menno Simons' position of strongly emphasizing the "law of Christ" would end by holding not only to a rigorous doctrine of the ban, but would go well beyond the Swiss in requiring the shunning of banned members. This legalistic tendency of emphasizing purity in the congregation would result in church divisions in the north as well contributing to the Amish schism of the 1690s.

There is less textual evidence than one might wish for determining Marpeck's position concerning the taking of oaths, but the evidence is consistent throughout. It appears that sometimes Marpeck swore oaths, but at other times refused to take the civic oath and counselled others not to take it.[24] Only two further significant references to the oath appear in his writings. In the first, Marpeck leaves unchanged a discussion of the "oath-like" character of a sacrament in Rothmann's *Confession*.[25] This does not really speak to the question of either the oath as discussed in Schleitheim, or to Marpeck's own position on the question of swearing oaths. The other reference stems from a letter to the Swiss Brethren, dating from 1543. In that letter Marpeck begins a discussion on the oath, saying "Concerning your understanding of the oath on which we have sufficient clarity from you, we cannot bind anyone's conscience nor put a rope around anyone's neck, nor are we able to submit our consciences to your understanding."[26] Unfortunately, however, the rest of the discussion is missing, since the following page was torn out of the codex.[27] The beginnings of the argument, however, added to what we know of Marpeck's disagreements with the Swiss, allows us to fill in the rest of the reply with fair certainty. At the very least, Marpeck was not arguing for unreflective oath taking (since he had refused the civic oath in Strasbourg), but rather was arguing against a legislative approach to oath-taking, pro or con.

In conclusion, there are significant differences between Michael Sattler's foundation for a political ethic for Christians, and those of Hans Denck and Pilgram Marpeck. In a significant point of unity, however, all three looked to Jesus as the example, model, and foundation for political ethics. But Sattler looked to the New Testament words by and about Jesus, and His way of life, as providing a literal and concrete "rule of life" for the Christian. Sattler had been, after all, the prior of a Benedictine monastery and, although he left the monastery he seems to have remained most comfortable with the notion of a literal "rule" that would govern community behaviour. Denck and Marpeck, on the other hand, while placing Jesus at the centre of the ethical life, nevertheless emphasized the more flexible norm of the "law of love" in the hearts of believers as the foundation for Christian ethics. Here the influence of the late medieval mystical tradition (as represented, for example, by the *Theologia Deutsch*) is evident.

The problem for Christian ethics as outlined by these two distinct interpretive traditions remains with us today: is the image of "two kingdoms" the appropriate context in which to understand Christian ethics; and if so, are those "kingdoms" to be distinguished from one another by "law" or by "love"?

Sattler and Hubmaier: Lordship of Christ, or Lordship of God?

A second point of tension in the early Anabaptist movement emerged within the "literalist" Swiss Anabaptist camp itself. Michael Sattler and Balthasar Hubmaier agreed on basic interpretive principles. But they came to disagree in their respective biblical understandings of how God had "ordained" church and government to fit together. A crucial point of difference between them was that Sattler's political ethic was Christocentric, whereas Hubmaier's was theocentric.

Michael Sattler

In the Schleitheim Articles, Michael Sattler argued that there are two opposed kingdoms, and that the Christian belongs under the lordship of Christ. Once the two kingdoms are identified, the remaining argument flows logically. The scriptural argument is Christocentric, placing Christ at the heart of Scripture as the example which Christians are to emulate and follow, since they have now "died to self and risen in Christ" (Schleitheim article 1, on baptism) and pledged themselves to His kingdom. Schleitheim thus drives a firm wedge between the Christian life of the spirit (and the Christian's citizenship in heaven), and the life of the worldly citizen, who responds to the political demands of this world. Christians are no more to participate in the governmental order than they are to participate in any other works of the kingdom of darkness. Schleitheim's position can quite properly be called "separatist nonresistance."

Balthasar Hubmaier

Hubmaier's argument in *On the Sword*[28] was directed against Schleitheim's strict ethic of "doing what Jesus did." Hubmaier made three central points. First, he argued that at best we are Christians, not Christ; insofar as we remain human, our kingdom is still of *this* world: "Christ alone can say in truth 'My kingdom is not of this world.'" As far as Christ's followers and disciples are concerned, "we are stuck in [this world] right up to our ears, and we will not be able to be free from it here on earth."[29] Certainly this was one crucial point of the argument, for if Christians are considered fundamentally *incapable* of "living as Christ lived," then the appeal to His life loses its ethical force, and is relativized. Likewise if Christians are firmly lodged "in this world," and cannot appeal to an alternative "citizenship in heaven" (as Christ alone could), then separation from the "kingdom of this world" is not only ill-advised, it is impossible. Hubmaier would develop these points in more detail throughout the tract.

Hubmaier's second argument against Schleitheim's view stated that Christ's role was that of Saviour; Jesus Christ, being the Son of God sent on a mission of salvation, assumed one human body and one earthly function, and so could not possibly play all social roles (e.g., that of judge or magistrate). Therefore the example of His life cannot be universally binding on all persons in every conceivable social station and situation. Everyone, concluded Hubmaier, should thus continue in their proper "offices," performing the duties appropriate to those offices: "Just as Christ wanted to do justice to his office on earth, likewise we should fulfill our office and calling, be it in government or in obedience."[30]

To these arguments Hubmaier added a third: God, said Hubmaier, did not "ordain" two opposed kingdoms, but rather intended a harmony to exist between church and government. Hubmaier listed apparently contradictory passages of Scripture, such as "Melting the swords into plowshares and the lances into sickles and yet breaking the plow for swords and the hoes for lances, Isaiah 2:4; Joel 3:10," and "We should not judge and yet should install judges who judge among us, Luke 6:37; 1 Corinthians 6:4."[31] The proper way of harmonizing the command not to kill (Matthew 5) and the divine "ordering" of the sword of government (Romans 13), Hubmaier said, is to see the *personal* focus of the first command (which calls even more fundamentally for a lack of hate or anger on the part of individual Christians), and the establishment of government which "does not kill out of anger ... but by the order of God..."[32] Hubmaier concluded: "the judges, governments, and executors of justice are called servants of God in the Scripture and not murderers, Rom. 13:4. God judges, sentences, and kills through them, and not they themselves."[33] In fact, those who refuse to mete out justice through government are themselves guilty of killing, says Hubmaier, for they have failed to defend the innocent one and so are "guilty of his death as much as the one who does not feed the hungry."[34] Against an ethic based exclusively on the measure of Christ's life (a "Lordship of Christ" ethic), Hubmaier insisted on "the Lordship of God," who ordained both nonresistance and the "legitimate" use of force, each in its proper sphere. Not surprisingly, Hubmaier nowhere addresses the question of oath refusal; it is clear that in no way did he oppose the swearing of civil oaths. Such oaths belonged to the sphere of civil authority ordained by God for human governance and peace.[35]

The dilemma for Christian political ethics posed by the contrasting approaches of Sattler and Hubmaier remains pressing in our own day. There is no doubt that Jesus calls for a perfectionist ethic in the Gospels, but can Christians really fulfill those demands? Is even a "regenerated" human being capable of being a full citizen of heaven alone? Do all mechanisms of human governance therefore fall into the realm of Satan? Did God not also ordain government for good? To what extent can or should the ethic of Jesus influence and limit the public ethic of God's governance of the world?[36]

Sattler and Hut: Ordinances or Prophetic Calendar?

A third point of tension in the early Anbaptist movement emerged between the literalist and Christocentric Swiss reading of Scripture and the prophetic-apocalyptic interpretation. These divergent interpretive approaches led to differences on questions of the oath and the sword, as a review of Hans Hut's position makes clear.

Hans Hut

It is clear from Hans Hut's early following of Thomas Müntzer that he was no pacifist in his pre-Anabaptist career, nor did he become much of a "nonresistant" after his adult baptism. At his interrogation, Hut stated that he had unequivocally opposed the "pacifist brethren," those who had maintained that a Christian was not to bear the sword when the authorities so demanded it; likewise he had opposed those who did not wish to swear civil oaths.[37] Hut testified more specifically that he had opposed some Swiss brothers who had "made an ordinance" forbidding the participation of Christians in war—a clear reference to Schleitheim and to those who were following its ordinances. He, on the other hand, had argued that "this was not contrary to God, nor was it forbidden."[38]

Hans Hut had faced a dilemma after 1525: the Peasants' War had failed. The ungodly had not been rooted out, but rather the peasants had been thoroughly defeated and Müntzer and Pfeiffer put to death. How were these facts to be interpreted? Hut came to admit that the peasants had been mistaken, but even as an Anabaptist he did not abandon Müntzer's hope that the righteous would, in the end, be able to punish the ungodly by the sword. The essential adjustment had to to with timing, motivation, and personnel. After his arrest, Hut gave the following explanation.

> They now see that the peasants were not right about their uprising, for they had sought their own and not God's honour. ...A Christian may well have a sword but ... it must remain in the scabbard until God tells him to take it out. Before then they would all be scattered and tried. Finally the Lord would gather them all together again and himself return. Then the saints would punish the others, namely, the sinners who had not repented.[39]

Hut's understanding of the sword emerged in the context of his eschatological and prophetic calendar. According to his own testimony and that of his followers, Hut continued to identify Müntzer and Pfeiffer as the Elijah and Enoch of the Last Days; he eagerly awaited God's vengeance on the ungodly at the hand of the invading Turks, after which the elect would complete God's work of just vengeance, sword in hand. According to Hans Hübner, one of Hut's converts in Thuringia,

> The Turk will enter these lands and great war will come either from the south or Hungary, or from the north. When that happens, the gospel will be preached purely and clearly. When the Turk comes, the people will flee into the forests and hide themselves. But those who have bound themselves to Christ through this sign (of baptism) shall flee into the wilderness, and into Hungary. Then, if this judgement takes place, those who have accepted the covenant will root out all those who survive the Turks. Soon thereafter Christ will come and the last day. It is twenty-two months before the last day comes.[40]

Christ's return was expected sometime before Easter, 1528.[41]

Hut's understanding of the proper use of the sword was not in harmony with Schleitheim, Denck, Marpeck, or Hubmaier; it was guided and given shape by his previous commitment to Thomas Müntzer's apocalyptic hopes, the cause of the peasants, and his reading of prophetic Scripture. His interrogation statement, that he had taught obedience to governmental authority,[42] has to be interpreted in light of his expectation that Christ would come again very soon, after which the believers who had "obeyed" governments, and held their swords in their sheaths, would be called upon to wield them against the impious.[43]

Hans Hut, the most successful early Anabaptist missionary, was well acquainted with Schleitheim's separatist positions on the sword and the oath, and emphatically rejected them.[44] His own position could best be described as "provisional pacifism," based on a "dispensationalist" reading of history and Scripture: there would be different ethical requirements depending upon the particular period of history one happened to inhabit. And, the identification of a particular "dispensation" would be revealed to those in possession of an interpretive key, revealed by the Spirit of Christ. This "dispensationalist" manner of interpreting Scripture would appear again later in the Anabaptist movement, in the Kingdom of Münster.

Hans Hut's political ethic, tied as it was to specific historical occurrences such as the Peasants' War of 1525 and the Turkish military threat, may not seem relevant today, but the interpretive approach that led him to his conclusions is an option that continues to be exercised in the present. It could be argued that those who said that the New Testament represents a "higher" revelation than the Old adopted a "dispensationalist" reading of Scripture, but the "dispensationalism" generated by a prophetic-apocalyptic reading of Scripture was of a different order altogether. From an ethical perspective, the primary difference is that the ethic of Jesus can be relegated to an earlier "dispensation"; the ethical rules that will apply in "the Last Days" then come to depend entirely upon how interpreters understand the shape and the needs of the current "dispensation," usually understood to be the "final" or "penultimate" dispensation before the Lord's return. In the case of Hut (and later of Münster) the prophetic-apocalyptic reading of Scripture combined with a heightened spiritualism that expected direct guidance from the Holy Spirit in discerning these matters; contemporary prophecy (signs, visions, and their interpretation) became significant factors.

The historical results of this interpretive approach are clear enough in the history of the Anabaptist movement: for some Anabaptists, End Times ethics came to include not only Hut's provisional pacifism, but also Münster's "godly crusade" of aggression against the ungodly, coerced religious conformity, and legislated polygamy. Contemporary disasters following much the same interpretive approach are evident still in the last decade of the twentieth century, as the tragic, fiery end of the Branch Davidians in Waco, Texas illustrates. The historical specifics vary, but the interpretive paths leading there are strikingly similar.

Hutter and Riedemann: Return to Separatist Nonresistance

The emergence and development of communitarian Anabaptism in Moravia manifested a pattern that would be evident elsewhere in the Anabaptism movement: from spiritualistic and apocalyptic beginnings there evolved increasingly "separated" communities, defined by ethical boundaries set by external "rules of conduct" or *Ordnungen*.[45] As were the Schleitheim Articles, the communitarian "rules" of the Hutterites were based on a Christocentric, New Testament interpretive framework.

On reading later Hutterite statements on the sword and the oath, one would be hard-pressed to identify Hans Hut as the "father" of this movement, even though it was Hut's missionary activity that was primarily responsible for bringing it into existence. Whereas in 1527 Hut had disagreed with "pacifist brethren" who were making external prohibitions concerning the sword, the oath, clothing, and behaviour in general, within less than five years his erstwhile followers in Moravia had become "pacifist brethren" who became even more zealous legislators of "external ordinances" than had been the Swiss whom Hut criticized. No doubt the failure of Hut's predictions for Christ's return, and the necessity of maintaining a disciplined community life in a threatening political environment played important roles in this development.

The communitarian movement in Moravia within which Jacob Hutter worked, although still showing some faint signs of the apocalyptic hope that was Hut's legacy, was strongly separatist and thoroughly nonresistant in the manner of Schleitheim and the Swiss. In 1535 Jacob Hutter wrote:

> We desire to molest no one; not to prejudice our foes, not even King Ferdinand. Our manner of life, our customs and conversation, are known everywhere to all. Rather than wrong any man a single penny, we would suffer the loss of a hundred gulden; and sooner than strike our enemy with the hand, much less with the spear, or sword, or halbert, as the world does, we would die and surrender life.[46]

There is no hint of Hut's "provisional pacifism" here.

Hutter's nonresistant emphasis remained in Peter Riedemann's extremely influential later writing and teaching, with an even more marked emphasis on a legislated separation and absolute nonresistance.

> Now because in Christ our King is the full blessing of God ... all that was given in wrath must come to an end and cease in him, and has not part in him. But governmental authority was given in wrath, and so it can neither fit itself into nor belong to Christ. Thus no Christian is a ruler and no ruler is a Christian, for the child of blessing cannot be the servant of wrath.[47]

Riedemann elaborates this theme further when he addresses biblical counter-arguments, in particular the citing of Romans 13 in a "theocratic" sense, such as Hubmaier had done. How can it be that Paul calls government authorities "servants of God," and yet it is claimed (by Schleitheim as well as by Riedemann) that they are not true Christians? Riedemann answers that not all "servants of God" are God's chosen people, citing the Old Testament examples of Nebuchadnezzar and the king of Assyria: "For God hath two kinds of servants, servants of vengeance to execute wrath" and servants of Christ who "is not come for vengeance, but for blessing."[48] Rulers, Riedemann concluded, are as free to "come to Christ" as are subjects (although rulers will find it "more difficult" to do so, he says), but when they do come to Christ they "must surrender ... utterly to him." This means that rulers who become Christians will cease to rule, in imitation of Christ: "For Christ fled when men wanted to make him king."[49]

This very "Schleitheimian" two kingdoms polarity would remain a hallmark of the Hutterite community.[50] Included in this polarity was the requirement that Christians are to follow the "higher truth" revealed by Christ concerning the swearing of oaths: "Weigh up the words of Christ carefully. He said, 'To men of old was said: Ye shall not swear falsely, but I say unto you: Swear not at all.'"[51] Riedemann concludes, in militantly separatist fashion: "It is not our duty, for the sake of those who are outside, to copy them, but on the contrary to testify against their sin, for God hath given his Spirit for this purpose: to reprove the world for sin."[52]

Conclusion

The earliest baptizing movements in Switzerland, South Germany, and Austria were not of one mind in their interpretive approaches to Scripture, nor were they of one mind concerning the proper relationship of church to government. Their differences on the issues of the oath and the sword illustrate these points clearly enough. By 1530, however, some earlier questions had been settled.

—The "separatist nonresistant" ethic of Schleitheim soon became the accepted position of the Swiss Brethren, although the text of Schleitheim itself was cited only sporatically as the century wore on.[53] Nevertheless, the Christocentric and separatist "two kingdoms" foundation of Schleitheim's position on sword and oath did survive and came to define the political ethics of the Swiss Anabaptists.

—Denck's spiritualist emphasis on the "love of Christ" in the hearts of believers led some Anabaptists to leave the "baptizing" movement, with its emphasis on external rites and rules, to defend instead an inner, largely invisible religion of the heart. The individualist thrust of this ethic allowed for "loving" political service. The "spiritualist" stream, while not representing an articulated *political* ethic, remained a very live option for Anabaptists weary of battling "the world." An appeal to an inner religion of the spirit opened the door to various degrees of Nicodemism, the public appearance of conformity with outward religious practice while believers inwardly and secretly continued to practise their true convictions.

—Pilgram Marpeck's emphasis on an ethic based both on the love of Christ in believers' hearts, and the public and visible practice of a new life based on the New Testament, outlined a flexible political ethic that allowed for limited, benign government service. The documentation is sparce, but apparently this moderately separatist social and political ethic was the norm in the scattered communities of "Pilgramites" in Switzerland, South Germany, and Moravia. The "Pilgramites" were never numerous, and all trace of them is lost in the seventeenth century.

—Hubmaier's option, which closely resembled the church polity of the Reformed churches, did not survive as an Anabaptist option. Anabaptism found no "legitimate" political defenders anywhere in western Europe who wished to make Anabaptism the religion of their states.

—Hut's option of "provisional pacifism" faded away quickly after of the prophecies on which it was based proved to be mistaken. This view soon was transmuted by the majority of Hut's followers into a separatist ethic closely resembling the one articulated in the Schleitheim Articles.

—The Hutterite separatist political ethic, with its emphasis on nonresistance and the non-swearing of oaths, sprang from South German/Austrian beginnings (Denck and Hut), but soon came to resemble most closely the views expressed at Schleitheim. There is good reason to assume some direct influence from the Swiss Anabaptists in this development. George Blaurock had brought Swiss Anabaptism to the southern Tirol (1527-1529), and the text of Schleitheim was copied repeatedly by the Hutterites. Seven hand copies of the Articles have survived in various Hutterite codices.[54]

End Notes

[1] Yoder, *Legacy*, pp. 41-2.

[2] For a more detailed analysis, which tends to extend more influence to Schleitheim than seems warranted, see Heinold Fast, "Die Eidesverweigerung bei den Mennoniten," MGB, N.F. 17 (1965), pp. 18-32.

[3] Edmund Pries, "Oath Refusal in Zurich from 1525 to 1527: The Erratic Emergence of Anabaptist Practice," in Walter Klaassen, ed. *Anabaptism Revisited* (Scottdale, Pa.: Herald Press, 1992), pp. 65-84; citation from p. 65. Cf. Fast, "Eidesverweigerung," pp. 19-20.

[4] Yoder, *Legacy*, p. 38.

[5] See, for example, Sattler's reply at his trial to the question of what Christians should do in the case of invasion by an enemy: They should pray and trust in God's defense.

[6] Yoder, *Legacy*, p. 39.

[7] *Ibid.*, p. 38.

[8] *Ibid.*, pp. 40-41, *passim*.

[9] See the discussion in Packull, *Mysticism*, pp. 35-61. Packull describes Denck's views as "following the 'affective' mystical tradition with its concern for conformity to the will of God." *Ibid.*, 50.

[10] The case is more nuanced than Jan Kiwiet allows when he states that "One specific mark of the Anabaptists in their attitude toward the state was their refusal to take an oath. Denck also adhered to this concept during the time that he was an Anabaptist." "The Theology of Hans Denck," MQR 32 (Jan., 1958), 22.

[11] "Nor should anyone be overly hasty with [their] Yes and No because it is merely a promise, for, whoever wishes to assure and fully guarantee someone with his Yes, has already sworn..." Bauman, *Spiritual Legacy*, p. 199.

[12] *Ibid.*, p. 259.

[13] Hans Denck, "Concerning Genuine Love," (1527), in Edward J. Furcha, ed. and trans., *Selected Writings of Hans Denck* (Pittsburgh: Pickwick Press, 1975), 105-106; also in Bauman, *Spiritual Legacy*, pp. 183-203.

[14] Hans Denck, "Concerning True Love," cited from Klaassen, *Anabaptism in Outline*, 250-51.

[15] "And, insofar as it is possible for a government to act in similar fashion, it also might well be Christian..." Bauman, *Spiritual Legacy*, p. 201.

[16] Stayer, *Sword*, pp. 149-50.

[17] William Klaassen, "Pilgram Marpeck: Liberty without Coercion," in Hans-Jürgen Goertz, ed., *Profiles of Radical Reformers* (Scottdale, Pa.: Herald Press, 1982), pp. 169-70. Klaassen notes Marpeck's difficulties with

Swiss legalism: "For Marpeck, standing in the ethical tradition of Denck, the importance of love was increasingly stressed." *Ibid.*, pp. 171-72.

[18] See Marpeck's "Judgement and Decision," in Klassen and Klaassen, *Writings*, p. 324.

[19] William Klassen notes that Marpeck "kept intact a clear distinction between the realm of the Spirit and the realm of the world. For him separation from the world did not rule out the participation of Christians in political office, although he saw that such participation would be severely limited by the nature of the case." William Klassen, "The Limits of Political Authority as seen by Pilgram Marpeck," MQR, 56 (Oct., 1982), p. 360. Klassen notes further that the evidence goes "contrary to Klaus Deppermann who states that the Reublin-Marpeck circle remained with the Schleitheim Confession and 'denied that is was possible for any official of the state to be a Christian.'" *Ibid.*, p. 360, n. 60. At Strasbourg, Marpeck said "(There is) no Christian ruler except Christ himself. The title is too high for a human being, involves a belittling of Christ, although it is perhaps not intended in that way... But when people in political authority are Christians or become Christians (as I heartily wish and pray), they may not use their previous physical force, power and rule in the Kingdom of Christ." Stayer, *Sword*, p. 179. See TA, *Elsass*, I, pp. 505-06.

[20] Snyder, *Life and Thought*, 112 ff.

[21] See Stayer, *Sword*, p. 184 and W. Klassen, "Limits," p. 348.

[22] Klassen and Klaassen, *Writings*, p. 558.

[23] Klassen and Klaassen, *Writings*, p. 547.

[24] Klassen and Klaassen, *Writings*., p. 31. Cf. TA, *Elsass*, I, pp. 184; 275; 359 ff., and see the summary in Boyd, *Marpeck*, p. 164.

[25] Klassen and Klaassen, *Writings*, p. 170.

[26] *Ibid.*, p. 368.

[27] Cf. *ibid.*, p. 580, number 3, n. 6 and "Oath," in ME, IV, p. 7. In the latter, William Klassen suggests that Rothenfelder's one-page discussion of the oath may be the missing end of Marpeck's epistle. Klassen notes, "The position reflected in this statement deviates from the absolute rejection of the oath by Schleitheim by equating calling God as witness with swearing an oath, and making it legitimate since Paul and Peter did this." Klassen chalks up this difference as the difference in approach to Scripture between Denck and Sattler. *Ibid.*

[28] Translation in Pipkin and Yoder, *Hubmaier*, pp. 492-523.

[29] *Ibid.*, p. 497.

[30] *Ibid.*, p. 500.

[31] *Ibid.*, p. 513.

[32] *Ibid.*, p. 515.

[33] *Ibid.*, pp. 515-16.

[34] *Ibid.*, p. 516.

[35] Hubmaier's only mention of the oath is in positive, sacramental contexts, when for example he equates the "baptism of Christ" with "a public and outer confession or oath of faith" which enrolls one in the Christian community and functions as a sign and promise of one's desire to live under the Rule of Christ. *Ibid.*, p. 209. The same usage is repeated later, where baptism is called an "oath" which binds one to a conversion and bettering of one's life. *Ibid.*, p. 202; cf. p. 384.

[36] For a good contemporary discussion of these issues, see Rodney Sawatsky and Scott Holland, eds.,

The Limits of Perfection: A Conversation with J. Lawrence Burkholder (Waterloo, Ont.: Institute of Anabaptist-Mennonite Studies, 1993).

[37] At his trial, Hut noted that he had opposed Jacob Groß' contention that a Christian is not to swear oaths. See Christian Meyer, "Zur Geschichte der Wiedertäufer in Oberschwaben" Part I: "Die Anfänge des Wiedertäufertums in Augsburg," *Zeitschrift des historischen Vereins für Schwaben und Neuburg*, I (1874), pp. 227-28. It is evident that through Hut's contact with Groß, he had come become acquainted with Schleitheim's separatist ordinance concerning oaths, and had rejected it. The appearance of Groß in this testimony is significant, given his close connections with Michael Sattler in Lahr and in Strasbourg, just prior to the Schleitheim conference. For these connections, see Snyder, *Life and Thought*, p. 97.

[38] Concerning government, Hut is reported to have maintained that "there should be government and force among Christians, for this was ordained by God." Meyer, "Zur Geschichte," p. 229. Cf. *ibid.*, p. 231.

[39] Interrogation of Hans Hut, 1527, from Klaassen, *Anabaptism in Outline*, p. 273.

[40] Klaassen, *Outline*, p. 321.

[41] Deppermann, *Hoffman*, pp. 175-76.

[42] "sie halten, wie Paulus unnd Christus anzaigen, das man den oberkaiten gehorsamen sein solle." Meyer, "Zur Geschichte," p. 227.

[43] See *ibid.*, pp. 241-42.

[44] As Seebass says, Hut "rejected outright the 'Sermon on the Mount ethic' of the Swiss Brethren that had pervaded the 'Schleitheim Articles.'" Gottfried Seebass, "Hans Hut: The Suffering Avenger," in Hans-Jürgen Goertz, ed., *Profiles of Radical Reformers* (Scottdale, Pa.: Herald Press, 1982), 58.

[45] See Packull, *Communitarian Experiments*.

[46] Jacob Hutter, "Letter to the Vice-Regent," 1535, from Klaassen, *Anabaptism in Outline*, p. 275.

[47] Peter Riedemann, "Account," 1542, in *ibid.*, p. 261.

[48] Peter Riedemann, *Account of our Religion, Doctrine and Faith* (Rifton, N.Y.: Plough Publishing House, 1974), pp. 213-14. See the entire section "Concerning Governmental Authority and its Appointed Service," pp. 205-223.

[49] *Ibid.*, p. 217; cf. Schleitheim's use of this same passage and argument, in Yoder, *Legacy*, p. 40.

[50] See Riedemann, *Account*, esp. "Concerning Separation" and successive topics, pp. 91ff. On the topic of "separation," Riedemann's argument parallels Schleitheim's, and appeals to Paul.

[51] *Ibid.*, p. 201.

[52] *Ibid.*, p. 205. The discussion of the oath is found on pp. 194-205.

[53] See Arnold Snyder, "The Influence of the Schleitheim Articles on the Anabaptist Movement: An Historical Evaluation," MQR 63(October, 1989), pp. 323-44.

[54] See Snyder, "Influence of the Schleitheim Articles," p. 336, and n. 41.

Chapter 14

Melchior Hoffman and Bernhard Rothmann: Sword and Oath

With very few exceptions, Anabaptist scholars have come to agree that Melchior Hoffman represents a unique Anabaptist tradition, independent of the Swiss Brethren, with some links to South German Anabaptism.[1] In fact, later Mennonite understandings concerning separation, the sword, and the oath appear to have developed directly from Hoffman's teachings and in response to Melchiorite developments, with no visible connection to the Swiss tradition of Schleitheim.

Melchior Hoffman

By 1529 and Melchior Hoffman's conversion to Anabaptism in Strasbourg the question of "legitimate state Anabaptism," such as Hubmaier had attempted, had been resolved in the Swiss and South German/Austrian movements: the negative political reaction to Anabaptism decreed that there would be no "legitimate" Anabaptism, unless some cataclysmic event were to change the nature of politics altogether. There still remained four live options, however, all of which were represented among the Anabaptists of Strasbourg in 1529: the separatist option (Swiss Anabaptists), the spiritualist option (followers of Denck), Marpeck's moderate separatism, and the apocalyptic option (Hut's followers).

Hoffman, like Hut, had an overwhelming concern with the End Times that governed his reading of Scripture.[2] Hoffman's arrival in Strasbourg in 1529 would have marked the time and place for him to have absorbed Schleitheim's distinctive teachings, had he been ready to do so, for the Swiss Anabaptists were strongly represented there. But Hoffman was receptive, not to the Swiss Brethren, but to the representatives of the spiritualist and apocalyptic streams: Hans Bünderlin, follower of Hans Denck; Hans Hut's Augsburg followers and lay prophets; and eventually Caspar Schwenckfeld, to whom Hoffman came to owe his peculiar docetic Christology.

Apocalyptic expectation, although increasingly abandoned by the majority of Hans Hut's followers in Austria and Moravia, nevertheless remained a live option for those who continued to hope for the "reform" of society as a whole. The return of Christ as ruler over all the earth was certain to change the political map. There is no way to gauge the degree of apocalyptic expectation within the Anabaptist movement as a whole around 1530, but certainly many Anabaptists (perhaps most Anabaptists) continued to hope and wait expectantly for Christ's imminent return. Christ's coming would signal the establishment of Anabaptist communities as the faithful Bride of Christ who would rule with Him in the New Jerusalem. So it was that the political "miracle" of the Anabaptist takeover of the city of Münster, prepared for as it had been by Melchior Hoffman's apocalyptic Anabaptism, seemed to many thousands to indicate that political reality had been altered decisively, and that the End Times had definitely arrived.

The Sword

The tension that arises on a literal reading of Matthew 5 and Romans 13, so significant in the early Anabaptist debates concerning the sword, was less pressing for Melchior Hoffman; he tended to read all Scripture through apocalyptically tinted glasses. Indirect evidence of Hoffman's disagreement with the Swiss Brethren interpretation of Matthew 5 and Romans 13 is available in the form of Hoffman's exegesis of the book of Romans, published in Strasbourg in 1533.[3] In his exegesis of the first five verses of Romans 13, Hoffman emphasizes first of all the truth of the statement that "the authorities are ordained of God."[4] Nevertheless, Hoffman qualifies this statement in several ways: the earthly magistracy has no real authority over the spiritual Adam or the spiritual Mount of Zion, for example. Nevertheless, since order among the beasts of the earth must be kept, God has ordained that everyone be obedient to the authorities "in all that is not contrary to God."[5] As an example Hoffman notes that one must be obedient even if the Antichrist himself is set up as a king, so long as God gives the Antichrist this power. But the limits of obedience are reached when, as in the case of Daniel, the Antichrist demands idolatry.[6]

Are rulers then to be considered "antichrists" or "outside the perfection of Christ"? Hoffman answered with a definite "no." In a passage that recalls Hubmaier's more "theocratic" interpretation, Hoffman argued that the political authorities were ordained of God to punish evil and protect the good, and those who perform this function are "always God's servants and friends."[7] In a passage that appears to be directed specifically against the Schleitheim view, in his commentary on Romans 13:4, Hoffman laments the fact that "some today do not wish to acknowledge the authorities as Christians... [This] is a blindness such that they cannot tell the difference between offices, therefore we must bear their blindness for a time yet, until the true light dawns."[8] Hoffman considered Schleitheim's relegation of political authorities to "the world" and hell as a misguided "blindness," and he clarified the point further: "Although priests and Israelites in the New Testament were to use no other sword than the sword of the spirit, this was not a command that men should not trim an animal's claws, nor kill according to God's command or not take the sword, but rather such use of the sword is God's good will, as also the spiritual sword leads to spiritual death."[9]

Not only did Hoffman reserve a legitimate place for Christian authorities in the time before Christ's return, he reserved a special, God-ordained role for them in the calendar of End Times events. Although Hoffman insisted that the political authorities were not to coerce in the church itself, which was to be governed only by the ban, nevertheless the role of the political authorities in the world was to undergo a radical change once the seven trumpets of the Apocalypse had anounced the End. Here Hoffman's conclusion brings Hans Hut to mind: the role of the political authorities would be determined by the particular point that had been reached in the calendar of End Times events. Once the final events had begun to unfold, thought Hoffman, the "godly rulers" would take the sword in defence of the true faith, as a preparation for the coming of Christ.[10] In appealing to King Friedrich I of Denmark, for example, Hoffman notes that it is true, as Paul says, that God has not elected many who were powerful or noble [1 Corinthians 1:26], because they find it hard to achieve spiritual poverty. Nevertheless, "although only a few have been elected (by God), there will be some whom God will attach and implant into his people."[11]

Hoffman's direct appeal to various rulers, that they carry out their God-ordained functions now that the final trumpets had sounded, owed nothing to Schleitheim's radical "two kingdoms" view which placed political authorities "outside the perfection of Christ." On the question of the "two kingdoms" and of church and government, Hoffman resolved the tension between Matthew 5 and Romans 13 in a unique manner: the "office" of the ruler or governor was ordained of God and thus open to Christians (here one thinks of Hubmaier), but governments and individual rulers needed to *choose* to work on the side of the light, particularly in these dangerous Last Days. If they did not choose the light they were working on the side of darkness and the Antichrist. Into which "kingdom" particular rulers belonged would not be decided automatically by virtue of their governing "office," as per Schleitheim, but rather by their convictions, choices, and deeds.

There was thus a crucial ambiguity in Hoffman's political ethic that allowed for both pacifist and crusading interpretations. While Hoffman himself emphasized divine initiative, and denied that the elect would take the sword prior to the collapse of the forces of Hell and the establishment of the New Jerusalem,[12] nevertheless, as Deppermann maintains,

> with the idea that the extermination of the godless must precede the day of final judgment, and with the conception of an earthly reign of saints in a theocratic intermediate kingdom until the return of Christ, Hoffman had created the most important ideological presuppositions for the Anabaptist kingdom of Münster.[13]

In the end Hoffman stood at quite a distance from the Schleitheim Articles, and although much closer to Hubmaier in one respect, and Hans Hut in others, nevertheless represented a unique Anabaptist biblical interpretation and political ethic that was irretrievably linked to prophesied events of the Last Days.

The Oath

In his commentary on Daniel 12 Hoffman did maintain that oaths should not be sworn. That he arrived at this position independently of the Swiss Anabaptists (or at least, independently of Schleitheim) is demonstrated by the fact that he held such a position already in 1526, prior to the composition of the Schleitheim Articles.[14] Furthermore, Hoffman's line of argumentation does not parallel in any way the argumentation of Schleitheim's article 7.

The strongest parallel between Schleitheim's article 7 and Hoffman's argument lies in the fact that both positions were based on Matthew 5:33-36. Following this, however, the respective discussions diverged. Schleitheim's article 7 presents and rejects three counter arguments to the Matthew 5 passage: first that Abraham swore (Genesis 26:3); second that swearing is allowed, as long as one does not swear "by heaven" or by any of the words forbidden by Christ; third that the Apostles also swore (Romans 1:9; 2 Corinthians 1:23; 11:31).[15] Hoffman, by contrast, rejected different counter arguments altogether: that swearing is allowed "because of love of neighbour"; that the nobility are bound to swear oaths of loyalty; and that the swearing of oaths maintains civil order, since evil persons would feel free to do evil if they were not sworn to the good.[16]

To these objections Hoffman replied, first, that "love of neighbour" is not a sufficient cause for going against the clear commands of Christ. Such argumentation, he said, might also lead one to sleep with the neighbour's wife, or even to commit murder out of "love for one's neighbour."[17] Hoffman's "literalism" here is striking: there can be no relativizing of this command by an appeal to love. To the nobility, Hoffman argued that one cannot promise obedience to two masters (Matthew 7); and concerning the prospect of civil chaos if oaths are not sworn, Hoffman maintained that evil persons were not restrained by oaths in any case; but "for the Christian, 'yea' is his oath and he holds to it; those who do not keep their promises, will also not keep high oaths either. A Christian does no evil, oath or no oath. Therefore it is silly and dangerous to dig up oaths against God's Word."[18]

As this brief comparison makes clear, the positions of Hoffman and Schleitheim, while both based on Matthew 5:33-36, are nevertheless independently argued and address totally different objections in respectively unique ways. In particular, where Schleitheim rejects oaths because of the human inability to keep such promises, Hoffman *equates* the Christian "yea" with the oath. In a civil context, however, both positions would have been equally radical, for both forbade baptized adults to swear civil oaths.

Conclusion

In the end Melchior Hoffman's political ethic stood closest to Hut's within the Anabaptist camp. Like Hut, Hoffman interpreted baptism on confession of faith as signifying a thorough "yieldedness" to the Spirit of God—a dying to self and rising in Christ—and like Hut, Hoffman saw this baptism as a sealing of the elect of the Last Days.[19] Hoffman emphasized the working of the Spirit of God in "yielded" believers and, like Hut, also expected the poor and simple to be more ready to "yield" than the powerful; the established clergy were particularly singled out for criticism.[20] Like Hut, Hoffman expected the godless to be eradicated before Jesus' return partly by the agency of the Turks,[21] but unlike Hut, he expected the "godly magistrates" to play a major role in the final cleansing, not necessarily the "elect" themselves. And finally, Hoffman's approach to Scripture, like Hut's, focused on the prophetic books of the Bible and a setting of dates for the return of Christ, and so placed the spirit/letter dichotomy within a lively apocalyptic context.[22] The emphasis on the heightened activity of the Holy Spirit in the Last Days is also visible in Hoffman: after 1530, probably under the influence of Hut's followers in Strasbourg, Hoffman also accepted extra-biblical prophetic revelation as authoritative.[23]

A crucial question to be decided was how Anabaptism was to relate to political authority. In this respect, Melchior Hoffman bequeathed a volatile legacy to his followers in the north. Along with the conviction that these were the Last Days came the conviction that the secrets of Scripture and the signs of the times were being laid bare for the anointed apostles and prophets. Added to the mix was Hoffman's own conviction that there would be a purging of the godless before Christ's return, and a fatal ambiguity about who exactly would be responsible for the purging, and when the purging was to begin. All of these elements, taken together and heated to a fever pitch in the Netherlands, led to the establishment of the Anabaptist kingdom of Münster, an event which, sadly, belongs firmly within the history of Anabaptism as such and which ultimately owed its existence to the teachings of Melchior Hoffman.

Bernhard Rothmann on Sword and Oath

The issue of how the spirit was related to the letter, how the letter of Scripture was to be read, and what God was revealing with regard to the saints and government was nowhere more pressing than in Westphalia and the Netherlands during and after the establishment of the kingdom of Münster. The Münsterite "New Jerusalem" owed much to Melchior Hoffman's teachings concerning the Last Days and his openness to direct spiritual revelations; it also owed much to the direct spiritual "revelations" of Jan Matthijs, on the basis of which he claimed prophetic authority. At the other end of the spirit/letter continuum, Hoffman's exegetical instrument of the "cloven hoof" allowed for the very free, figurative interpretation of the Old Testament. In the hands of Hoffman's followers in the Netherlands, the "cloven hoof" came to allow for a more literal application of Old Testament practices in the context of the restitution of all things in the Last Days.[24]

Münsterite practices were defended and explained theologically by Bernhard Rothmann. The spiritual revelations of Jan Matthijs and other prophets were crucial beginning points for Rothmann's conviction that he was living in the Last Days, but it was a figurative exegesis (Hoffman) and the subsequent *literal* reading of the Old Testament that was central to Rothmann's ethics.

Bernhard Rothmann and the Sword

Standing behind Rothmann's justification for the taking of the sword in Münster was the exegetical principle of the "cloven hoof," which was for both Hoffman and Rothmann the way of resolving apparent contradictions in Scripture.[25] The most crucial point to be "resolved" in this way was, for Rothmann, the fact that Scripture pointed to different "times" in salvation history. Scripture and its "figures" could not be interpreted properly until one knew to which "time" (we might say, "dispensation") in history a particular passage referred. Rothmann believed that there were three primary "times" in salvation history: from creation to the flood; from the flood to Münster; and from Münster to the end of time, which Rothmann called the "time of Restitution."[26]

Rothmann was convinced that since the final age of salvation history had arrived, the letter of Scripture needed to be read differently. His "canon within the canon" became the Pentateuch and the Old Testament Prophets.[27] The Old Testament injuctions concerning God's vengeance on the ungodly at the end of time were to be applied once again, in a literal way, in the time of Restitution.[28] Thus the New Testament injuctions of Jesus (e.g. in Matthew 5) needed to be understood in a non-literal mode: the Mosaic rules of behaviour applied to the Christians of the Last Days. The time of suffering and "turning the other cheek" belonged to the second age, which had now passed. In the time of restitution, God's Kingdom would be established not by the spiritual sword alone, but by the exercise of the physical sword, in preparation for Christ's return.[29] Thus it was that in answer to the question of why Münsterite Christians seized the sword, when according to the New Testament, Christians were called upon to suffer, Rothmann replied that one must understand that it was now the time of restitution, when the true Kingdom was being erected, and the ungodly were to be brought to an end.[30]

One further step was necessary for Rothmann's explicit justification for taking up the sword, and this was the argument that the faithful *themselves* were to take up the sword in preparation for Christ's arrival, rather than waiting for God to initiate the final "cleansing." Although Rothmann defended the truth of his "insight" initially by appealing to visions and signs that had appeared to the faithful in Münster, his more fundamental argument was scriptural and revolved around the "throne of David." Here Rothmann used Melchior Hoffman's "figurative" exegesis, and turned it to his own purposes: he argued that the David of the Old Testament was not a "figure" for Christ (a common interpretation), but rather, it was King Solomon who must be understood to be the Old Testament "figure" for Christ.

> See! The Throne of David must be reestablished, the Kingdom prepared and armed, and all the enemies of Christ humbled by David. Then the peaceful Solomon, the eternal king and anointed God, Christ, will enter and possess the throne of his father, David, and his Kingdom shall have no end...[31]

With this step, Rothmann could apply all the Old Testament prophecies concerning the raising up of the fallen throne of David. Those prophecies applied, he argued, to the kingdom of Münster and to King Jan van Leiden—the second David.

Once Rothmann had established (to his satisfaction) that he was living in the time of Restitution, that the time of the "Gospel" was passed, and that the throne of David was being reestablished in Münster under the second David (Jan van Leiden), Rothmann could apply, in a literal way, the Old Testament prophecies concerning the judgment that would befall the "godless." In this way emerged some of the most remarkably aggressive passages ever pronounced in the name of the Prince of Peace. From the besieged city Rothmann wrote the following, to encourage supporting military actions elsewhere:

"Now, dear brothers, the time of vengeance is here. God has raised the promised David and armed him for vengeance and punishment over Babylon and its people. Therefore, dear brothers, arm for battle, not only with the Apostles' humble weapon of suffering, but also with vengeance, the magnificent armor of David, to stamp out the entire Babylonian power and the entire godless establishment with the power and the help of God. Think that you can do to them everything that they have done to you; indeed, they shall receive in the same measure with which they have measured out... Let God, the Lord of Lords, who has determined and through his prophets predicted this from the beginning of the world, awaken your heart with the power of his spirit and arm you and his whole Israel."[32]

Portrait of John van Leiden, dressed in his royal robes, holding the symbols of his office.

All the divine signs pointed to the fact that God was calling his elect to take up the sword. Although they had been ready to suffer death for the sake of the Kingdom, said Rothmann, God had other plans for His saints in these Last Days. God had made it clear that the "time of restitution" was at hand, the time of grace and mercy was over, and the time of divine vengeance had begun.[33]

The still-smoking remains of this Old Testament-based "glorious aggression"[34] confronted Menno Simons when he began working to reorganize the Melchiorite movement in the north, following the collapse of the Münsterite kingdom.

End Notes

[1] The role of some Hutian prophets in the Strasboug Melchiorite group may be the strongest link between Hoffman and Hut. See especially Klaus Deppermann, *Melchior Hoffman: Soziale Unruhen und apokalyptische Visionen im Zeitalter der Reformation*, (Göttingen: Vandenhoeck & Ruprecht, 1979); James Stayer, "Davidite vs. Mennonite," in Irvin B. Horst, ed., *The Dutch Dissenters: A Critical Companion to their History and Ideas* (Leiden: E.J. Brill, 1986), pp. 143-159; idem., *Sword*, pp. 203-329; Walter Klaassen, "Visions of the End in Reformation Europe," in Harry Loewen and Al Reimer, eds., *Visions and Realities* (Winnipeg: Hyperion Press, 1985), pp. 13-57; Helmut Isaak, "The Struggle for an Evangelical Town," in Horst, *Dutch Dissenters*, pp. 66-82.

[2] Deppermann, *Hoffman*, p. 67.

[3] Only a Dutch translation of the original writing survives: *Die eedele hoghe ende troostlike sendebrief / den die heylige Apostel Paulus to den Romeren gescreuen heeft / verclaert ende gans vlitich mit ernste van woort to woorde wtgelecht Tot eener costeliker nutticheyt ende troost allen godtvruchtigen liefhebbers der eewighen onentliken waerheyt.* 1533. Original in UB, Amsterdam.

[4] "Het is ymmers waer / dat die overheyt van God geordineert is." *Ibid.*, p. T7a.

[5] *Ibid.*, p. T7b, and p. T8a.

[6] *Ibid.*, p. T7b.

[7] *Ibid.*, pp. T8a-T8b.

[8] *Ibid.*, p. T8b.

[9] *Ibid.*, pp. T8b-V1a.

[10] See Deppermann, *Hoffman*, p. 232.

[11] Fast, *Flügel*, p. 312.

[12] "Hoffman described the cleansing as follows: during the final apocalyptic struggle the free imperial cities would defend the true gospel against the 'divinity of hell'—the emperor, pope, and false teachers. Although the Anabaptists themselves would not bear arms, they were to support the struggle by prayer and by building fortifications. After a testing period of a difficult siege, the attacking enemy would collapse. Led by the 'two witnesses' of the Apocalypse, the 144,000 'apostolic messengers' would then proclaim the joyous message of the universality of divine grace in the whole world, dispensing the baptism of faith. The entire host of false parsons, including the 'bloodsucking anti-Christian Lutheran and Zwinglian preachers,' would perish. A new theocracy would emerge after the destruction of Babylon. The pious king and the Spirit-filled prophet would work hand in hand as once in the old Israel under Solomon. This coming reign of peace was to be the necessary precondition for the return of Christ." Deppermann, "Hoffman," in Goertz, *Profiles*, pp. 186-87.

[13] *Ibid.*, p. 187.

[14] Deppermann, *Hoffman*, pp. 74-5.

[15] See Yoder, *Legacy*, pp. 41-2.

[16] Melchior Hoffman, *Das XII Capitel des propheten Daniels aussgelegt...* (Stockholm, 1526), e2v-e3v.

[17] *Ibid.*, e3r.

[18] *Ibid*, p. e3v.

[19] Hoffman wrote in 1530 that Baptism signifies that those baptized will obey "the will and pleasure" of the Father, the Son and the Holy Spirit, "and that their own will, life, desire, spirit, and passion be wholly slain ...

and that henceforth they live solely in the Spirit, and the mind, and the will and from the wisdom of God and the eternal Word of life, as a true bride, obedient to her dear spouse in all things..." Hoffman, *The Ordinance of God*, (1530), in Williams, SAW, p. 187.

[20] For Hoffman the poor who are called in the spirit are more learned than the educated; his view was summed up in the saying "arm in Fleisch—reich im Geist." Hoffman's teaching contained a good bit of bitter anticlericalism. Deppermann, *Hoffman*, p. 58.

[21] See Hoffman's *Weissagung uß heiliger götlicher geschrifft*, pp. B IV ff.

[22] As Deppermann notes, Hoffman's apocalypticism depended on the Holy Spirit being poured out on all people; the two witnesses of the End Times already were present in the world. In his commentary on Daniel (1526) Hoffman interpreted the End Time as being present, which was central to his entire message. Deppermann, *Hoffman*, pp. 65-7.

[23] See Walter Klaassen, "Eschatalogical Themes in Early Dutch Anabaptism," in Irvin B. Horst, ed., *The Dutch Dissenters*, (Leiden: E.J. Brill, 1986), pp. 22-3.

[24] The best description of Rothmann's appropriation of Hoffman, and his additions to Hoffman, is in Deppermann, *Hoffman*, pp. 296-302.

[25] In the "Restitution," Rothmann argued that all contradictory scriptural statements concerning free will (vs. bound will) are resolved "as long as one knows that the Scripture is 'two-hoofed' ("dat de Schrifft tweyklauich ys")..." Stupperich, *Schriften*, p. 254. Also in his "The Hiddenness of Scripture," *Ibid.*, p. 353.

[26] See Stayer, *Sword*, pp. 239-252, for a thorough treatment of this theme in Rothmann.

[27] Deppermann, *Hoffman*, p. 297; Bornhäuser, *Leben und Lehre*, p. 51; Cf. Stupperich, *Schriften*, p. 302.

[28] Deppermann, *Hoffman*, p. 296.

[29] As paraphrased by Deppermann, *Hoffman*, p. 299.

[30] "The Lord wishes ... that we and all true Christians in this time not only be allowed to turn away the power of the ungodly with the sword, but even more, that the sword be put into the hands of his people to avenge all that is unjust and evil in the whole world... The time is at hand." Bernhard Rothmann, "Restitution," 1534, in Stupperich, *Schriften*, p. 282.

[31] Supperich, *Schriften*, p. 366. Translation from Stayer, *Sword*, p. 250.

[32] Stupperich, *Schriften*, p. 297; translation from Stayer, *Sword*, pp. 251-52.

[33] "God will make for his people bronze claws and iron horns. They will make ploughshares and hoes into swords and spears. They shall choose a captain, fly the flag, and blow the trumpet. They will incite an obstinate and merciless people against Babylon. In everything they will repay Babylon with her own coin, yes, in double measure." Bernhard Rothmann, "Concerning Vengeance," Stupperich, *Schriften*, p. 292; translation from Klaassen, *Outline*, p. 335.

[34] Phrase from Stayer, *Sword*, p. 240.

"And I John saw the holy city, new Jerusalem, coming down from God out of heaven, prepared as a bride adorned for her husband." Revelation 21:2

The image of the church as the Bride of Christ, a foretaste of the New Jerusalem, was a powerful and defining image in all branches of the Anabaptist movement.

Chapter 15

After Münster:
The Sword and the Oath in the Melchiorite Tradition

Following the collapse of Münster David Joris attempted to reunite the dispersed Melchiorites under his own prophetic and spiritual leadership. He had opposed the Münsterite taking of the sword, and also had opposed Rothmann's "literal" reading of Scripture. Thus on the question of the interpretation of Scripture in ethical matters, Menno Simons was faced with Münsterite "literalism" on the one hand, and with David Joris' "spiritualism" on the other.[1] He attempted to keep to the middle ground between either side, although in the face of Joris's direct and continuing challenge, Menno undoubtedly came down more on the "literal" side of the question.

Menno Simons
The Sword

Menno Simons worked continuously to overcome the negative image that Münster had created. Nevertheless, in his early writings we find Menno to be solidly in the Melchiorite tradition, speaking the common Melchiorite theological language, but attempting to combat the "errors" of the Münsterites. Menno, unlike Rothmann, did not rest his interpretation of Scripture on a three-fold periodization of history, although he did make some central historical distinctions.[2] Menno's central point lay in the Christocentric foundation for binding ethical "laws."[3] "For no other foundation can be laid, than that which is laid, which is Jesus Christ" (1 Corinthians 3:11). This was the verse that Menno would inscribe on the title pages of all of his writings.[4] The Christocentrism pointed to by that verse also provided Menno's essential argument for the periodization of salvation history, for the evaluation of contemporary prophetic claims, and for the reading of Scripture. The most crucial distinction for Menno was that the Bible as a whole needed to be read from the Cristocentric perspective, that all prophecy had to be tested by Christ and, further, that the time of the Gospel would last until Christ himself came again in glory. For Menno the Old Testament was authoritative, but only in a "provisional" and exhortative sense. It could supply examples of true faith, for example. But in the crucial matter of commands and ethical behaviour, Christ's words, commands and examples were central.[5]

Menno's rejection of a literal reading of the Old Testament had its roots in an earlier disagreement among the Melchiorites concerning the proper use of the "cloven hoof." In the Fall of 1535, at the height of the Münsterite kingdom, a debate took place in Amsterdam between Jacob van Campen and Obbe Philips on this very question. Jacob van Campen defended the use of the "cloven hoof" as it was being interpreted in Münster, and insisted that "the Old Testament types must have both a literal and a spiritual fulfillment in the Christian era." Obbe argued, to the contrary, that Old Testament "figures" were to be applied only in a spiritual, figurative sense. Echoes of Obbe's spiritualized, "figurative" approach, which rejected the literal application of Old Testament practices to Münster, are found in Menno's writings, but they were expressed most fully in the later writings of Dirk Philips.[6]

The first writing we have from Menno's hand, "The Blasphemy of John of Leiden"[7] was written around April, 1535 as a direct refutation of the Münster events. From the beginning his argument places Christ at the centre of the matter; he must write, he says, "because we cannot tolerate the shameful deceit and blasphemy against God that a man be placed in Christ's stead..., and such deceit and abominable

Menno Simons, pictured with his crutch (he had trouble walking in his later years) holding a Bible open to 1 Corinthians 3:11: "For no othe foundation can anyone lay than that which is laid, which is Jesus Christ."

heresy concerning the promised David and other articles are defended with passages from the Bible."[8] Christ is God, and King of all the earth; since this is so, "how can John of Leiden call himself a joyous king of all...?"[9] Christ is the Lawgiver; "What then becomes of John of Leiden?"[10] Christ is the "true Melchisedec," the King of peace, the pious Isaac; "Christ is the true David."[11] Menno repeatedly attacked Rothmann's claim that Jan van Leiden was the "second David" preparing the way for

"Solomon" (Jesus). "Is this not an abomination standing in the holy place?" asks Menno. John van Leiden "claims to be the promised David of whom all the prophets testify and does not admit that Christ is the promised one."[12] "Greater antichrist there cannot arise than he who poses as the David of promise. This David is Christ as the Scriptures testify abundantly."[13]

In this earliest writing, Menno read the Old Testament as providing "figures" which pointed to Christ. The similarity to the "figurative" exegesis of Hoffman and Rothmann is striking.[14] But Menno was using what he considered to be the *proper* "figurative" interpretation in order to counter Rothmann's improper "figure" and the Münsterite "literal" reading of the Old Testament. "One should not imagine," Menno said, "that the figure of the Old Testament is so applied to the truth of the New Testament that flesh is understood as referring to flesh; for the figure must reflect the reality; the image, the being, and the letter, the Spirit."[15] Thus Menno read the Old Testament "figures" Christologically (or "spiritually," as he said), and argued against their literal meaning or application, as had Obbe against van Campen.[16] Since the Old Testament "figures" and prophecies point to Christ, who is the King and Master, "it is incontrovertible that we dare not accept any other doctrine but the doctrine of Christ."[17]

With Christ placed back at the centre of Scripture (and especially at the centre of the Old Testament), Menno insisted that one must look to what Christ had taught about warfare, violence and vengeance.

> If Christ fights His enemies with the sword of His mouth, if He smites the earth with the rod of His mouth, and slays the wicked with the breath of His lips; and if we are to be conformed to His image, how can we, then, oppose our enemies with any other sword?[18]

Christ left us an example, that we should follow, said Menno; He was minded to suffer, and so must all Christians be minded, overcoming their foes with the spiritual sword of the Word of God. The literal words and the concrete example of Jesus' life became the central ethical measures for Menno, as they had become also for the Swiss and the Hutterites.

There remained the matter of the End Times calendar, which had played such a central role for the political ethics of both Hoffman and Rothmann. Against the Münsterite argument that God wished to punish Babylon by means of His Servants (the "true Christians," meaning the Anabaptists), Menno said no: "leave to the Lord His works," for no one knows the "times nor the seasons." Babylon would indeed be punished, justly and soon, for its iniquities against the saints, but God would do the punishing, not Christians.[19] Menno, however, did spend some time assuring the Melchiorites that the enemies of Christ would receive their just reward (punishment), but Christ had first to return in glory: "Therefore when ye shall see Christ come in this manner you may rest assured that all the enemies of God will be punished."[20]

On the question of prophetic authority—a pressing matter in Melchiorite Anabaptism—Menno again set forward a Christological measure:

> even though Elijah himself were to come, he would not have anything to teach contrary to the foundation and doctrine of Christ and the apostles. But he must teach and preach in harmony with them if he would execute the office of the true preacher, for by the Spirit, Word, actions, and example of Christ, all must be judged until the last judgment. Otherwise the whole Scriptures are false."[21]

The foundation which is Christ cannot be moved, and is the measure by which all Scripture and all prophecy is to be measured.[22] Furthermore, that foundation remains "until the end of the world"; there is no "dispensation" remaining between the time of Jesus' birth and His second coming.[23]

Menno's linking of "spirit" to the "letter" of Scripture that points to Christ forms the essence of his counter both to Old Testament literalism and unbridled prophetic spiritualism. The spiritual sword (Word of God) belongs to the saints, the physical sword to the heathen; the divine Word teaches imitation of Christ and suffering, whereas satanic, blasphemous doctrine teaches vengeance and physical violence; vengeance is the Lord's, and Christians must follow Christ in nonresistance, through all manner of earthly tribulation. As Menno would repeat later, in his "Foundation" book (1539; revised 1558),

> They who are baptized inwardly with Spirit and fire, and externally with water, according to the Word of the Lord, have no weapons except patience, hope, silence, and God's Word. . . . Iron and metal spears and swords we leave to those who, alas, regard human blood and swine's blood about alike.[24]

This basic argument against Christian participation in warfare was to be repeated, with different nuances and accents, throughout Menno's writings.[25]

The sharp distinction that Menno thus drew between the spiritual and the earthly kingdoms puts one in mind of Michael Sattler, and the strict polarity seen at Schleitheim, which consigns all use of the sword (and hence all ruling and judging functions of the magistrates) to a realm "outside the perfection of Christ."[26] But Menno's position on the magistracy is closer to Hoffman's, and does not echo Schleitheim. Menno actively and repeatedly admonished princes and rulers to repentance, but he did not consider them non-Christian (outside the perfection of Christ) simply by virtue of their office, nor did he assume that if they became Christian they would have to abandon their ruling offices, in imitation of Christ (such as Schleitheim and Riedemann both argued).

Throughout his writings Menno assumed the possiblility that rulers could repent and become true Christian *rulers*.[27] In the "Foundation" book, for example, Menno described the ruler's task as "to chastise and punish, in the true fear of God with fairness and Christian discretion, manifest criminals..."[28] Thus Menno had a more "theocentric" political ethic, following the Romans 13 outline concerning the legitimate ("Christian") positive and negative functions assigned by God to rulers: protection of the good, punishment of the evil. But in his early writings Menno went beyond an ambiguous granting that God had so ordained the sword of government, and called on rulers to use their power for good, even in matters relating to the church.

In more than one place, Menno asked rulers to "restrain by reasonable means, that is, without tyranny and bloodshed" the "deceivers" (false priests, monks, preachers) "so that they may no longer detract from the power of the almighty majesty of God."[29]

> Help us to obstruct seductive teachers and false sects ... who oppose the Spirit, ordinances, Word, and life of Christ; not with violence, tyranny, or sword, as, alas, it is the custom with you; but with the Spirit of Christ, with doctrine, exhortation, and the proper services and kind means, so that they may turn from evil and hear and follow Christ.[30]

Menno cited the examples of Moses, Joshua, David, and other Old Testament rulers who "discharged their calling with reason, accommodated themselves to the Word of God, protected their subjects with solicitous care, obeyed the commands of the Lord, abolished the false prophets and priests of Baal."[31] As James Stayer has noted, Menno was "a bit confused" in his early thinking, concluding on the one hand that forcing beliefs on people with violence was devilish, but on the other hand expecting Christian rulers to abolish "false religion."[32]

Although Menno soon moved away from counselling rulers to legislate and enforce true religion, nevertheless he maintained to the end the possibility of the existence of pious Christian rulers.[33] Menno concluded that "there are but few of you, ... I fear scarcely a one, who seeks the Lord with all his heart; fears, loves and serves Him," but still Menno obviously hoped that princes and rulers would repent, and then *rule in a Christian manner*.[34] This understanding put Menno at a good distance from Schleitheim, much closer to Denck and Marpeck in his conclusions.[35] In spite of similarities in approach to Scripture between Menno and the Swiss (the priority of the New Testament; Christocentrism in personal and corporate ethics) Menno Simons remained a follower of Melchior Hoffman in his understanding of the sword of government (his political ethics).[36]

The Oath

Whether to swear oaths or not to swear oaths does not seem to have become an issue in Münster. In spite of Melchior Hoffman's rejection of oath taking, as outlined above, Bernhard Rothmann did not address the issue at all.[37] The swearing of oaths seems to have been assumed to be legitimate in the "New Jerusalem." This would stand to reason, given Rothmann's explanation that Jesus' commands in the New Testament had been superseded in the "time of restitution." That oaths were sworn in the Old Testament had never been in doubt, just as the fact that the Israelites had wielded the sword was never a debated issue. That oaths should no longer be sworn, and that the sword should no longer be wielded by Christians depended, in large measure, on the argument of a "progressive revelation," that a binding "higher" ethical standard had been revealed by Jesus. If now Jesus' commands were relegated to an "age" (or dispensation) whose time had passed, Old Testament guidelines concerning oath, sword, and even polygamy could be freely applied.

Menno Simons apparently did not consider the oath to be as urgent a matter as the sword, or perhaps he became convinced only gradually that oath taking should be forbidden. In any case, he took up the specific issue of the oath rather late in his reforming career and writings. Apart from a casual mention of "yea and nay" that *may* date back to 1541,[38] the earliest extended discussion dates from 1552 (sixteen years after Menno became an Anabaptist!), where an entire section of "Confession of Distressed Christians" is devoted to the question of the oath.[39] Addressing himself to those who continue to persecute Anabaptists, Menno argues that the oaths required by the magistracy are forbidden to Christians. Menno's argument is Christocentric, first of all: we must hear Christ, for "no emperor or king may ... command contrary to His Word."[40] In the second place, Menno traces the development of oath taking in the Bible, arguing for a progressive revelation perfectly revealed by Jesus: the treatment of oaths in the Old Testament has been superseded by Jesus' words on the matter. Menno concludes: "To swear truly was allowed to the Jews under the Law; but the Gospel forbids this to Christians."[41]

Menno recognized the political difficulties that oath refusal meant for the Anabaptists: the Gospel forbids oath taking, and yet the magistracy insists upon it. If the Christian swears, Menno noted, "he falls into the hand of the Lord. If he swears not, he will have to bear the disfavor and punishment of the magistracy."[42] Menno concluded by pleading first with the Anabaptists to "continue in the Lord's Word" and to refuse to swear oaths "whether life or death be your lot."[43] For Menno, disobedience to the literal words of Christ was cause for damnation; therefore the oath became a life and death issue. Menno pleaded with those in power, that they accept "yea and nay" as being as binding as oaths, "since we deem our yea and nay to be no less than an oath." In fact, Menno said, if a brother or a sister affirms yea or nay, and is then found to be lying, "let him be punished as a perjurer."[44] Menno's hope for relief from persecution lay with a tolerant attitude on the part of the magistracy, not with any non-literal interpretation of Matthew 5 or "hiddenness" or dissembling on the part of the faithful.[45] The Bride of Christ would be visibly "separate" according to the literal, Christocentric, New Testament Word.

David Joris and Menno

Menno Simons opposed the Münsterites by pointing resolutely to the letter of Scripture in the New Testament and to Christ, the only foundation stone. David Joris pointed rather to the Spirit and the "inner restoration" as the next step following the failure of Münster. Faced with Münster's collapse and the need to reunite dispirited Melchiorites, Joris explained the failure of Münster in terms reminiscent of Hans Hut after the failed Peasants' War: the Münsterites, said Joris, had tried to establish a physical restitution when they had not yet managed to attain a full spiritual restitution. What was needed was a postponement while the spiritual "third restitution" was taking place within true believers.

Immediately following the slaughter in Münster Joris (as had Hut after the Peasants' War) dwelt upon the joys of the eventual vengeance of the Lord on the impious. Joris wrote in 1535:

> Oh Behold, God's scythe will strike all of you
> And it shall violently cut you down to the earth,
> so that neither branch nor root will remain...
> His burnished sword will cut, yes indeed,
> it is grasped to hew, to strike all who are drunk,
> and who are unconcerned and glad.[46]

Joris usually maintained that it was "God and His angels" who would do the punishing, not the "saints," but occasionally he implied that believers (once perfected) also would be able to enjoy vengeance in their own person.[47] Joris spoke often and extravagantly about the "sword of the Spirit" in ways that could easily be misunderstood and misinterpreted. In writing about the struggle of spirit against flesh, he wrote concerning "the fleshly being of sin which hinders Christ and his Spirit." Believers were to "Repel and strike him, I say, to the death. Shed all his blood and do not hold back your sword."[48] As Gary Waite has noted, "Revolutionary-minded supporters with more concrete concerns might be excused for not understanding the finer points of Joris' allegory."[49]

If there was some ambiguity in Joris' earlier teaching concerning the sword, with some hints that he might be expecting followers to take up a physical sword in due course, his increasing move towards spiritualism from 1539 onward settled the question. Increasingly Joris became convinced of his own prophetic and spiritual authority as the "third David."[50] And he insisted more and more that all events of true significance would happen "spiritually" and internally, in the souls of believers. The restitution would take place there, as would the return of Christ.[51] External actions, so long as they did not harm the inward, spiritual person, were of little consequence. Thus he could write concerning "judges and commanders" that insofar as they "do all things correctly in the faith and do not hinder Christians nor the gospel," then "it is free to them."[52] Soon he would go further and take up a secret identity himself: in 1544 he moved to Basel under a pseudonym, publicly conforming to all required practices while secretly continuing to write treatises and letters of counsel for the spiritual edification of his followers. For Joris there were, emphatically, two kingdoms, but the visible and physical kingdom of darkness was so unimportant that actions performed in that kingdom were of very little consequence.

Menno Simons had not been present at the Bocholt conference of 1536, when David Joris had had some success in mediating between competing Melchiorite factions, but it became increasingly clear that he and Joris were working at cross purposes. The opening salvo in the dispute between Menno and Joris came from the pen of Menno Simons. In the first edition of his *Foundation Book* (1539/40) Menno included a section dealing with the "corrupt sects."[53] At the time of this early writing, just four years after the fall of Münster, Menno directed his comments primarily to the supporters of the Münsterites and the Batenburgers.[54] Menno argued that the Melchiorite prophets (and this included David Joris, of course) had gone beyond the testimony of Scripture, substituting their own authority for that of Christ. They taught that the time of the New Testament had passed and that a new era had begun, in which the revelations of the "false prophets" were to be believed as if they were true.[55] In the second place, Menno emphasized repeatedly that true holiness would be in conformity to the Gospel of Christ as revealed in the Word of God; true holiness is obedient to that Word. The righteous live by faith, and that faith "must be conformed to the gospel of Christ."[56]

Joris' reply to Menno came in the form of a sharp letter, pugnacious and conciliatory at the same time, entitled "Writing to Menno Simons, out of love, from one of the so-called corrupt sects."[57] It was Menno, said Joris, who had walked where angels feared to tread, and arrogated to himself the ability to judge what is spirit and what is flesh, to decide who will be saved and who will be damned.[58] Menno was acting like the Pharisee in judging the publican to be a sinner, which was a sign of the lack of Christ's Spirit;[59] Menno was judging only on the basis of appearances, which was exactly how the world judged, namely according to the flesh and not the spirit.[60] Joris judged Menno to have grasped only the letter of Scripture.[61]

From this opening exchange we see clearly the difficulties that confronted post-Münster Melchiorites on the matter of teaching authority. Menno and Joris, both baptized by Obbe Philips, not surprisingly were agreed on certain Anabaptist essentials. Both agreed (on the surface, at least) on what were the proper and biblical external ordinances (baptism, ban, Supper). Menno, no less than Joris, held that those who would understand the letter must have been "reborn" by the Spirit of God; the Spirit must accompany the reading of the letter of Scripture. Menno opposed the "literal" or "unspiritual" reading of Scripture of both the Münsterites and the Protestant clergy; both Menno and Joris had opposed the use of the sword. But Menno wished to set limits on the working of the Spirit by appealing to the life and teachings of Christ, thereby denying the possibility of scriptural interpretations that went beyond Christ, and denying the possiblity of contemporary prophetic revelations.

Against the background of Melchior Hoffman's teaching, which both Menno and Joris shared, Menno was the innovator; Joris was claiming little more than had Hoffman or Matthijs. Joris' claim to charismatic, prophetic authority placed him in continuity with the mainstream of the Melchiorite tradition, and placed Menno is the awkward position of appearing to be one of those "learned preachers" who appealed not to the Spirit, but to their own wisdom and knowledge in the interpretation of the *letter* of Scripture. In light of this fact, it is not surprising that Joris' *ad hominem* critiques of Menno had great currency among Melchiorite Anabaptists in the later 1530s.

On the substantive issue of spirit and letter Joris did add some further argumentation in reply to Menno's letter. Menno had written that obedience to Christ was central. Joris agreed, but added an important qualification: "All understanding must be taken captive under the obedience of Christ (not under the obedience to the letter of Scripture, but to the eternal truth), for so it is written." The fiery flame of the Spirit, said Joris, must come with power into one's mind and spirit, from which will come righteousness and truth with power.[62] It is obedience to this inner, spiritual

Christ and eternal truth that is true obedience; the fleshly, outer person reading the letter cannot attain to this truth. In fact, said Joris, he himself had received the spiritual power to know the truth. The same Lord who had authored the Scriptures had given him a learned tongue, had made his mouth into a razor in the spirit, and had given him knowledge of the right time to speak; the Lord had opened Joris' ears like a master does for a disciple.[63]

In a revealing passage found in a writing dating from around 1542—and most probably with Joris' criticisms in mind—Menno spoke to the question of prophecy and his own authority to teach. "Brethren, I tell you the truth and lie not. I am no Enoch, I am no Elias, I am not one who sees visions, I am no prophet who can teach and prophesy otherwise than what is written in the Word of God and understood in the Spirit."[64] In fact, said Menno, he did not desire "visions or angelic inspirations" lest he be deceived. "The Word of Christ is sufficient for me. If I do not follow His testimony, then verily all that I do is useless, ... even if I had such visions and inspirations..."[65] Likewise, said Menno, he was not a "third David as some have boasted and do even now boast." There are only two Davids in Scripture, namely the son of Jesse, and Christ, the spiritual David. "Whosoever poses as a third is a falsifier and blasphemer against Christ."[66] With this Menno declared against both Jan van Leiden (the "second David" of Münster) and David Joris, who was considered by his followers to be the "third David."

If, then, Menno claimed no prophetic authority, on what basis did he teach? For all his disavowals of prophetic illumination, when pushed to the limit Menno did not shy away from claiming spiritual authority. He acknowledged that in his natural person he was "nothing but unclean slime and dust of the earth," until, he said, "the clear light of grace and knowledge appeared unto me from high heaven. This has given me such a heart, will, and desire that I willingly seek after that which is good and strive with the holy Paul to follow..."[67] The difference between the true grace and knowledge which came to him from "high heaven," and the false visions and illuminations of the contemporary prophets, Menno suggested, could be proven in the objectives of their respective doctrines. The false prophets "are intent upon their own honor, fame, and gain," while Menno's own writing and preaching "is nothing else than Jesus Christ."[68] Nevertheless, in the final analysis Menno too had to rest his particular (Christocentric) reading and interpretation of Scripture on a "spiritual understanding" that had come to him through "the light of grace and knowledge from high heaven."

It is not stretching the truth to say that within the Melchiorite context, it was Joris who stood closest to the Melchiorite tradition of charismatic, prophetic authority; Menno was the innovator, whose appeal to a literal, scriptural measure in some ways seemed to move him dangerously closer to the Münsterite literalists and also to the "Lutherans," whom the David Jorists also accused of "literalism."[69] Certainly Menno's emphasis on the letter, and the outer signs of inner regeneration, led him to work for the establishment of *visible* outposts of the Kingdom of God on earth (again closer to the Münsterite ideal); Joris was content to gather together a largely invisible, "spiritual" church.

In the matter of sword and oath, David Joris' solution of internalizing obedience to a spiritual Christ while conforming outwardly to the demands of governments, was a solution Menno could not abide. He fought strenuously against the Nicodemism of the Jorists, as we will have occasion to note further, and insisted that the witness of the church must be a visible obedience, measured by the words and the life of Christ in the New Testament.

Conclusion: Sword, Oath, and Separatism

How was the true church to relate to the world? The lack of consensus among early Anabaptists on how Scripture was to be interpreted was visibly demonstrated in the various positions early Anabaptists assumed concerning the sword of government and the oath. The diversity of Anabaptist views during its developmental period, first brought to our attention by James Stayer's seminal *Anabaptists and the Sword* and sketched again in the foregoing chapters, is beyond dispute. Such historical diversity among the early Anabaptists should put an end to casual appeals to the so-called "normative" position of "Anabaptist nonresistance" as given expression in Schleitheim's article 6. At the time of its composition, Schleitheim expressed one view among many, based on one way among many of interpreting and reading Scripture in search of guidelines for the reform of the church.

When we turn our attention from the period of Anabaptist origins and development, however, and look instead to the ongoing "traditions" of the Swiss Brethren, the Hutterites, and the Mennonites, we do find that a separatist consensus did emerge concerning the world, government, the sword, and the oath. All three traditions appealed to a literal Christocentric hermeneutics, focused on the words and the life of Jesus; all three traditions read this Scripture as providing a "rule of life" to be followed obediently by disciples. In all three cases, sword and oath were forbidden to Christians, on virtually identical biblical grounds. There was agreement, then, in the Anabaptist traditions that had crystallized by the end of the sixteenth century, but it was a consensus about biblical and ethical norms that emerged only at the end of a sometimes bloody and often chaotic period. In fact, consensus on questions of the sword and the oath was achieved only after apocalyptic prophecy had failed and spiritualist Anabaptists had departed or been banned.

The general development in hermeneutics that is visible in the foregoing chapters will also be seen in the chapters to follow. The steady emergence and dominance of Christocentric, "literal" readings of Scripture, with the New Testament at the centre, will provide answers to many of the questions under dispute in the Anabaptist movement.

End Notes

[1] Christoph Bornhäuser, *Leben und Lehre Menno Simons'* (Neukirchen-Vluyn: Neukirchener Verlag, 1973), p. 50.

[2] In one of Menno's later writings he did divide salvation history into three parts, but they did not correspond to Rothmann's system. In his "Reply to False Accusations," Menno responded to the false charge of polygamy by pointing to three different periods in which different rules concerning marriage prevailed: the time before the mosaic law, the time under the law, and the time of the new covenant. Bornhäuser, *Leben und Lehre*, pp. 52-53; CWMS, pp. 560-61.

[3] In "Distressed Christians," Menno points to three different laws concerning oaths and oath taking in the periods before the mosaic law, under that law, and under Christ. Christ "points us now from the Law to yea and nay..." CWMS, p. 518. On Menno's Christocentric reading of Scripture and his understanding of the relationship between the two Testaments, see William E. Keeney, *The Development of Dutch Anabaptist Thought and Practice From 1539-1564* (Nieuwkoop: B. De Graaf, 1968), pp. 35-39.

[4] The citation of 1 Corinthians 3:11 appears also, appropriately enough, in the middle of Menno's writing against the "corrupt sects." CWMS, p. 218.

[5] Henry Poettcker, "Menno Simons' View of the Bible as Authority," in C.J. Dyck, ed., *A Legacy of Faith* (Newton, Kan.: Faith and Life Press, 1962), p. 35; Bornhäuser, *Leben und Lehre*, pp. 49-50, notes that the Old Testament has primarily an exhortative function for Menno.

[6] See Keeney, *Development*, pp. 35-39; also A. F. Mellink, *De Wederdopers in de Noordelijke Nederlanden, 1531-1544* (Groningen: Wolters, 1954), pp. 118-119; 245; and Douglas H. Shantz, "The Ecclesiological Focus of Dirk Philips' Hermeneutical Thought in 1559: A Contextual Study," MQR 60(April, 1986), pp. 115-127.

[7] CWMS, pp. 31-50.

[8] *Ibid.*, p. 34.

[9] *Ibid.*, p. 35.

[10] *Ibid.*, p. 36.

[11] *Ibid.*

[12] *Ibid.*, p. 37.

[13] *Ibid.* The point is repeated several times in the following pages.

[14] As time went on, Menno moved further away from the "figurative" exegetical method. See Bornhäuser, *Leben und Lehre*, pp. 48-49.

[15] CWMS, p. 42.

[16] In the later edition of the "Foundation" book Menno wrote against the Münsterites: "If you want to appeal to the literal understanding and transactions of Moses and the prophets, then must you also become Jews, accept circumcision, possess the land of Canaan literally, erect the Jewish kingdom again, build the city and temple, and offer sacrifices and perform the ritual as required in the law. And you must declare that Christ the promised Saviour has not yet come, He who has changed the literal and sensual ceremonies into new, spiritual and abiding realities." *Ibid.*, p. 217.

[17] *Ibid.*, p. 43. These arguments were elaborated again in Menno's "Foundation" book, especially in the fourth section written "To the Corrupt Sects." CWMS, pp. 215-221.

[18] *Ibid.*, p. 44.

[19] *Ibid.*, p. 46.

[20] *Ibid.*, p. 47.

[21] *Ibid.*, p. 220.

[22] "Menno insists that an interpretation must always be in keeping with (the) central place of Christ." Poettcker, "Simons," p. 35.

[23] CWMS, p. 216. Cf. Bornhäuser, *Leben und Lehre*, p. 52. "Menno meinte, es sei verwerflich, auf ein neues Zeitalter zu hoffen, da in Christus alles bereits erfüllt sei." Hans-Jürgen Goertz, "Der Fremde Menno Simons; Antiklerikale Argumetation im Werk eines mechioritischen Täufers," in Irvin B. Horst, ed., *The Dutch Dissenters: A Critical Companion to their History and Ideas* (Leiden: E.J. Brill, 1986), p. 168.

[24] CWMS, p. 198.

[25] Cf. *Ibid.* pp. 200, 347, 423 ff., 555-557, 715.

[26] To cite one example from Menno: "The Scriptures teach that there are two opposing princes and two opposing kingdoms: the one is the Prince of peace; the other the prince of strife. Each of these princes has his particular kingdom and as the prince is so is also the kingdom." *Ibid.*, 554.

[27] See *Ibid.*, pp. 193 ff., 357 ff., 549 ff.

[28] *Ibid.*, p. 193.

[29] *Ibid.*, p. 193.

[30] Menno Simons, "True Christian Faith" (1541, revised 1556), *Ibid.*, p. 362.

[31] *Ibid.*, 193.

[32] Stayer, *Sword*, p. 314.

[33] Stayer traces Menno's development in this regard in *Sword*, 314-319.

[34] CWMS, p. 197.

[35] The following citation from "True Christian Faith" sums up Menno's view. "Yes, dear sirs, if you could thus convert yourselves with all your heart; if you could change yourselves and humble yourselves before God, could deny yourselves and seek and follow Christ and His righteousness; if you could renounce the world and flesh and its lusts, as you have heard, then you would be kings and priests not only in natural things, but also in spiritual. You would possess your souls in peace, *rule your land in Christian wisdom*, in the pure fear of God; then you would be victorious against all harmful enemies of our souls, live in grace, die in grace, and *deserve to be called in truth, without hypocrisy, Christian kings and believing princes*." *Ibid.* p. 363 (emphasis mine).

[36] Irvin Horst sees Menno's stance on government as "a middle road between the reforms of Luther and Zwingli on one hand and the revolution of the Münsterites on the other." Menno stood to the "left" of Luther and state church option, but to the "right" of Schleitheim, that is, closer to Hubmaier. Irvin B. Horst, "Menno Simons: The Road to a Voluntary Church," in Irvin B. Horst, ed., *The Dutch Dissenters: A Critical Companion to their History and Ideas* (Leiden: E.J. Brill, 1986), p. 197. Cf. Bornhäuser, *Leben und Lehre*, pp. 122-28.

[37] A search of his collected writings failed to turn up any references. See Stupperich, *Schriften.*

[38] Menno's mention of the saints "with their simple yea and nay" appears in "True Christian Faith, CWMS, p. 360, written originally in 1541. Since the versions available to me all reproduce the heavily revised 1556 edition of this writing (see CWMS, p. 322), it is not clear whether the off-hand reference to the oath dates from the earlier or the later date. One would suspect the latter. Cornelius Krahn states that the 1552 discussion of the oath is the first discussion by Menno of the matter. *Menno Simons*, p. 175.

[39] The "Confession" is found in CWMS, pp. 499-522; the discussion of the oath on pp. 517-521.

[40] *Ibid.*, p. 518.

[41] *Ibid.*, p. 519.

[42] *Ibid.*

[43] *Ibid.*, p. 520.

[44] *Ibid.*, p. 521. This point in the argument is reminiscent of Hoffman's discussion, and directly at odds with Sattler's contention that "guarantees" of all kinds are beyond the power of human beings.

[45] Nevertheless, some dissembling was necessary and was allowed. The "Wismar Articles" of 1554 allow believers to carry "an honest staff or a rapier," all "according to the conditions of the land" in order to escape detection. See *ibid.*, p. 1042; cf. Krahn, *Menno Simons*, pp. 173-74.

[46] Waite, *David Joris*, pp. 101-102.

[47] "When you are advanced enough and know that your flesh is dead so that it seeks nothing for itself ... then [you may] burn with wrath as Moses, Phyneas, Ehud, Jahel, David, Christ etc., [burn] against the evil ones..." Cited in *ibid.*, p. 102. Waite notes that at the Bocholt conference, Joris "proposed that vengeance upon the godless was to be performed only by God and his angels. The identity of the latter remained open." *Ibid.*, p. 118.

[48] Waite, *Writings of David Joris*, p. 154.

[49] Waite, *David Joris*, p. 103.

[50] *Ibid.*, pp. 170-71.

[51] *Ibid.*, pp. 165 ff.

[52] Waite, *Writings of David Joris*, p. 154.

[53] English readers should know that the version of "To the Corrupt Sects" translated in CWMS, pp. 215-221, is a later edited version (1558) of the section Menno published under the same title in 1539. The 1539 edition, to which Joris responded initially and which will be surveyed here, was shorter, milder, more conciliatory to former Münsterites, and less explicitly anti-Jorist. A critical edition of the 1539 *Fundamentboeck* is found in Menno Simons, *Dat Fundament des Christelycken Leers*, H.W. Meihuizen, ed. (The Hague: Nijhoff, 1967). The section "Tot den vordorvene secten" is found on pp. 197-205. This particular writing also appeared in print as a separate tract. See Zijlstra, "Nicolaas Meyndertsz van Blesdijk," p. 27, n. 3.

[54] Cf. Stayer, "Davidite," p. 144.

[55] *Ibid.*, p. 200.

[56] *Ibid.*

[57] David Joris, *Christlijcke Sendtbrieven...* (n.p., n.d.). This volume is a published collection of Joris' letters (three volumes were published, of which this is the first). The first letter to Menno is found in Part 3, fol. 63b-66b: "Schrijft eener van die verdurven Secten genaemt / wt liefden an Menno Symons: die sich een veeraer tegen een yeder der ganscher Werlt beroept / om mit den Godtlijcken Swaerde te verwinnen / oder verwonnen te werden." (Hereafter *Sendtbrieven* I, 3.). The letter was written between 1540 (the publication of Menno's *Fundamentboeck*), and 1542, the date of Menno's direct reply to Joris.

[58] *Ibid.*, f64a.

[59] *Ibid.*, f.64b-65a. The "pharisaical" image was a recurring theme in Jorist arguments against Menno.

[60] *Ibid.*, f.65a

61 *Sendtbrieven*, I, 3, f.65b. See also Zijlstra, "Blesdijk," p. 28.

62 *Sendtbrieven* I, 4, f.2b.

63 *Sendtbrieven* I, 4, f.2b.

64 Menno Simons, "Why I do not cease teaching and writing," CWMS, p. 310.

65 *Ibid.*

66 *Ibid.*

67 *Ibid.* In his "Admonition to the Amsterdam Melchiorites," Menno identified the "true shepherds" as those "whom the Holy Spirit has sent." CWMS, p. 1022.

68 *Ibid.*, p. 311.

69 The first of the alleged "Articles of the Jorists" reads: "They are Lutheran clerics who prove their matters with Scriptures and who will not believe any articles which are not proven with biblical Scriptures." Waite, *Writings of David Joris*, p. 292.

Chapter 16

Anabaptism and Socio-Economic Reality

In this section of our study we will focus on the development of Anabaptist views concerning economics, equality between men and women, and Anabaptist marriage. The wider context for the continuing Anabaptist conversations on these topics was the social and economic reality of the sixteenth century which had been challenged (so it seemed) by the call to biblical reform. Sixteenth century society was built upon hierarchies of all kinds which were assumed to be "God given," that is, in the nature of divine order and creation. But it was a time of uncertainty and redrawing of boundaries. Some crucial hierarchical assumptions of dominant, cultural Christianity already had come under attack by the evangelical reformers, particularly the privileged social position of the clergy. It was only natural that social and economic relationships of all kinds would be re-evaluated and tested by the authority of "the Word of God" in Scripture.

One of the unintended effects of Martin Luther's reformation efforts was the appropriation of egalitarian social and economic principles by the "common people." A doctrine of "community of goods" could be, and was, based on a reading of Acts 2, 4, and 5. "Scripture alone" thus leapt the bounds of a strictly "theological" reading and fueled reformation movements that called for larger measures of equality in Christendom. As one example, we find Sebastian Lotzer of Memmingen, who later authored the "Twelve Articles" of the peasants, expressing socially radical reforming ideas already in 1523, based on the principle of "Scripture alone."[1] Likewise the "priesthood of all believers" was a "levelling" principle that contributed to the "laicization" of the pastoral role, especially in the Radical Reformation.[2]

Proposals for a restructuring of society along more biblical and egalitarian lines originated from the lower social orders, of which two notable examples were Johannes Hergot's "Concerning the New Changes in Christian Life," and Michael Gaismaier's "Constitution, the latter of which outlined the principles for a political re-ordering of the Tirol.[3] Many of these "levelling" ideas lived on in the Anabaptist movement. Reinforcing the egalitarian social and economic impulses that Anabaptism inherited from the early Reformation of the common people were the basic theological principles that were common to all branches of the Anabaptist movement.

Primary among these socially challenging theological principles was the emphasis on the work of the Holy Spirit, so much in evidence in early Anabaptism. The Spirit seemed to be blind to conventional social hierarchies: it did not choose to speak primarily to the educated, to aristocrats, or only to men, but rather spoke to *all* those who humbled themselves in obedience to God, who "yielded" themselves to that

Spirit. This understanding stood behind Anabaptist challenges to the social and economic realities of sixteenth century society. Furthermore, the Anabaptists believed, the "inner" change wrought by the Spirit in "every person" had to be manifested in concrete "outer" actions that were in conformity with the social and economic "ordering" of Scripture.

Economic Questions

Economic practice must be placed in the midst of the tension between the "two kingdoms," for how the opposition between spirit/flesh, church/world, heaven/earth is resolved will determine, in large part, how economic activity will be understood and valued. Is the economic activity that is peculiar to human life in "this world" an impediment to salvation, is it a positive means to salvation, or is it essentially "neutral" in the process?

Economic activity within the medieval church as a whole was both restricted by canon law, and blessed (when used properly) as a positive aid in the saving process (although the ascetic ideal within monasticism followed another path). Some secular economic activities were controlled by "legal" requirements in medieval canon law—most notably, the forbidding of Christians to charge "usury,"[4] but property itself, and the ownership of property, was not considered sinful or an impediment to salvation. In fact, the proper use of physical resources and wealth (within the Catholic penitential system) could be of considerable help in the salvation process. For example, the wealthy often endowed monasteries with property and thereby ensured the saying of perpetual masses for the salvation of their souls.

For the laity (as opposed to the monastics) in the medieval church, one's salvation did not depend on a rejection of earthly life and its economic activity, but rather on one's participation in the physical means of grace mediated by the church—including the mechanisms of confession, penance, forgiveness for sins committed, and prayers for souls in purgatory. The proper or "graced" living of one's earthly life, and the proper use of one's wealth, particularly within the context of the system of penance, aided the believer in attaining eternal life.

In the mainline Protestant tradition, the line separating heaven from earth became essentially an invisible one, drawn in the heart, and known to God alone. Salvation was attained by the gift of faith in Christ; no life of "discipleship," no physical "works of mercy"; no financial endowments within a system of penance could aid in the matter of salvation, or give certain evidence of one's eternal status. Conversely, then, in the Protestant tradition life in "this world," along with its economic activity, was largely cut free from the restrictive demands of spirituality, eventually coming to occupy a position virtually independent of religious constraint. As one prime example of this, in the case of the charging of interest, so crucial for the emergence of capitalism, Protestant casuistry progressively allowed Christians to charge "interest" of other Christians—a practice forbidden by canon law in the medieval church.[5] In this sense Protestantism was leaning towards the coming "modern" (secular) economic world, based as it would be on the accumulation of surplus capital.

　　The Anabaptists, on the other hand, looked back to medieval social and ascetic economic ideals, rather than anticipating the coming capitalist revolution. In the first place, Anabaptists did not agree that the economic life of Christians was "neutral" in matters of salvation. It is because the Anabaptists echoed many elements of the monastic understanding of the "holy life" that was supposed to follow true faith that they related social, economic, and ethical matters directly to the "spiritual life." Justification demanded a fundamental change in one's actual spiritual condition, and thus a corresponding change in the visible life of the sinner on this earth. The living of a life of discipleship thus became paramount, just as it had been in the monastic traditions. This meant that the economic activity of the regenerated believers needed to be carried out according to the norms of the Kingdom of Heaven. And, the Anabaptists believed that these "norms" were sufficiency (not surplus) and the sharing of surplus with those in need, the justification for which they were convinced could be found in the Bible.

　　Many of the same religious, social and economic impulses that fueled the so-called Peasants' War remained issues within the Anabaptist movement well after the peasant uprising had been suppressed.[6] Many of the first Anabaptists were active participants in these protest movements "from below"; thus reflection on the proper relationship of economics to church structure was integral to the Anabaptist protest from its inception. The development of the Anabaptist movement, however, demonstrates a significant shift in the way questions of economics and social justice were addressed.

　　Early Anabaptism in Switzerland and South Germany, given its close connections with grass roots reform movements for social change, vacillated for a time on the question of whether all of society was to be reformed "according to the biblical pattern," or whether only the true church could be expected to reform. As long as all of society was considered "Christian," then biblical standards could be applied to society at large. For the South German and Melchiorite Anabaptists, the apocalyptic events of the Last Days would play a central role in this final "reform" of society. The tone was less apocalyptic in Switzerland, but there are many significant examples from the early Swiss Anabaptist movement that illustrate an initial desire to reform all of society, and not just a minority church of the baptized, in isolation.[7]

　　In the end, of course, the Peasants' War did fail, as did Münster, and reform principles came to be applied by the surviving Anabaptist groups only to the "regenerated" who "separated from the world," as Schleitheim would state unequivocally in 1527.[8] Insofar as the separatist principle was accepted, economic reform was directed inward, to the church, and society was left to its own devices. With two important exceptions—Balthasar Hubmaier in Nicholsburg and the Münsterite experience—the bulk of Anabaptist writing concerning economic matters was composed within this later, "separated" framework, written for the church of the faithful, not for society at large. The most fundamental points of discussion reflected in Anabaptist writing on economic matters thus have to do with the question of how the "true church" ought to incarnate biblical economics.

The broad shape of this Anabaptist thinking on economic matters is generally recognized and has been noted above as one of the "core" Anabaptist beliefs: All Anabaptists agreed that the reborn, baptized and regenerated believers made up a *sharing community* by virtue of their re-birth, baptism, participation in the Supper, and manner of life obedient to Christ's commands. It was inconceivable to the Anabaptists that there could be reborn and regenerated Christians, baptized into the one Body of Christ, who would cling to surplus goods or wealth when they saw a fellow member of the Body in need. Such an understanding was universally Anabaptist, present in the Swiss, South German, and North German/Dutch manifestations.[9]

In its "weakest" manifestations (Swiss Brethren; Mennonite), this understanding expressed itself in a form of economic organization that could be described as a voluntary community of goods, moving eventually into a doctrine of "mutual aid"; in its "strongest" manifestations (Hutterite; Münsterite), the Anabaptist form of economic organization could be described as a legislated community of goods.[10] We will look in more detail at the development of these differences below, for they came to drive a wedge between surviving Anabaptist groups. Nevertheless, on the basic principle there was no disagreement: economic relations within the church, the Body of Christ, were to be governed according to the distributive principle of sufficiency for all.[11]

The Equality of Persons Before God

Many Anabaptists expressed their socially egalitarian views by citing the text "God is no respecter of persons" (Acts 10:34-35), which appears repeatedly in the court testimonies and other places. A Swiss Brethren biblical concordance dating from around 1550 devotes twelve pages to this theme, collating and citing a variety of Scriptures to make the point.[12] The collection of texts and references begins with lengthy verbatim citations from the Old Testament: 1 Samuel 2,[13] 1 Samuel 16 (Eli's anointing of David),[14] 2 Chronicles 19,[15] and others; the citations are interspersed with further references which are not cited. The central point made by the Old Testament citations is that God calls whom God will call, looking to true piety and not worldly status.

The texts cited from the New Testament continue the theme: Matthew 11(:25-27): Jesus thanks God for hiding the truth from the wise, and revealing it to the simple; Matthew 12(:49-50): Jesus says that his brothers, sisters and mother are those who do God's will; John 7(:47-48): the Pharisees say that no rulers, but only the rabble believe in Jesus; Acts 10(:34-35): God has no favourites; 1 Corinthians 1(:17-31): the wisdom of the wise is destroyed; divine folly is stronger than human strength; God has chosen what the world despises.[16] The message conveyed by this collection of Scripture passages is plain. In matters of faith and salvation, the way in which the world views "the person" is immaterial. Every person stands equally accountable before God. But, to what extent did "spiritual equality before God" translate into equality in social relationships?

The three-fold understanding of baptism in the Anabaptist movement gave visible expression and form to the idea of personal equality before God. The "baptism of the Spirit" placed the inner working of God's Spirit at the beginning of the process of repentance, conversion, faith, rebirth, and obedience. It was the *sine qua non* of Anabaptist baptism, for the "baptism with water" was simply an outward confirmation of the inner reality. Both the inner baptism of the Spirit and the outer baptism in water were, in a very important sense, radically *individual* events: no priest, wife, husband, parent, or godparent could take these steps for anyone else; salvation was not granted by a powerful church with its clergy, but rather was a matter between the believer and God. For the Anabaptists, all individuals were required to pass through the same process of "yielding" personally to the Spirit of God, and of exercising their free will either to accept God's grace and its consequences—above all, obedience (water baptism, community discipline, economic sharing)—or to reject grace and its visible, communal consequences. And, of course, the acceptance of water baptism meant not only a visible commitment to a radical new community of brothers and sisters in the Lord; it also signified a willingness to "bear the cross" of persecution and possible martyrdom—the baptism of blood.

All of these steps—from an openness to the Spirit, to the acceptance of water baptism, to the steadfastness unto death called for by state persecution—were steps that could be taken only by individuals who had freely chosen (and who continued to choose) the "narrow way" by means of God's grace. Nevertheless there was a tension between the individual and the communal in Anabaptism. In the Anabaptist understanding, individual choice (that is, openness to the Holy Spirit) led inevitably and ineluctably to a binding of oneself to others: the Body of Christ on earth. This two-fold movement, from radical individual choice to the limitation of choice by the community of believers framed the question of "equality" in the Anabaptist community of saints.

One might suppose, on the basis of these frequently-repeated principles, that Anabaptist communities were radically egalitarian in practice, offering full religious equality to women and men as well as to peasants and aristocrats.[17] Some historians have drawn this conclusion, among them Roland Bainton and George Williams.[18] Harold Bender wrote that, "The Anabaptist emphasis upon voluntary membership, adult baptism, and personal commitment inevitably opened up new perspectives for women,"[19] a view that was expressed even more strongly by Wolfgang Schaeufele. According to Schaeufele, "The woman in Anabaptism emerges as a fully emancipated person in religious matters and as the independent bearer of Christian convictions."[20]

Such conclusions have not gone unchallenged. Claus-Peter Clasen's groundbreaking work in the Swiss and South German Anabaptist sources led him to conclude that, "Revolutionary as Anabaptism was in some respects, the sect showed no inclination to grant women a greater role than they customarily had in sixteenth century society."[21] Likewise, Joyce Irwin claimed to have found no evidence for religious equality in Anabaptism, nor did she find evidence of women preaching, missionizing, or taking leadership roles in Anabaptist congregations.[22]

Perhaps the most important reason underlying these radically opposed evaluations is the nature of the sources used in each case, and the way in which those sources have been evaluated. At one stage in the historiography of Anabaptism it was the practice to extrapolate from theological ideas and conclude that "true" Anabaptist practice corresponded generally to those ideas. Social historians, more interested in what actually was the practice in Anabaptist communities, have revised the earlier "ideal" picture. Nevertheless, even some of the more recent detailed studies have tended to rely on a narrow selections of sources—for example the readily accessible martyrologies[23] and the writings of male Anabaptist leaders—to the exclusion of court records and testimonies—or to rely on a narrow spectrum of court records from one locale or historical period.

It may safely be said that a reliable and comprehensive account of the role of women in the Anabaptist movement has yet to be written. In order for such a task to be accomplished, much more intensive work in the Anabaptist court records (*Täuferakten*) is needed, for it is in these court records that the full extent of the involvement and activity of Anabaptist women is most clearly seen. The immensity of this task should not be minimized, but serious efforts in this direction have already begun.[24] Preliminary results of these meticulous, gender-specific studies fall somewhere between the two extreme positions noted above: While Anabaptist women were usually not given equal status with men in the formal leadership of the movement,[25] they did experience far more freedom of individual choice than was the social norm, as will be seen below. This was especially so in the earlier more pneumatic stages of Anabaptist development.[26]

In the second place, in citing evidence purporting to shed light on the role of Anabaptist women, particular attention must be paid to the developmental stage from which the sources are drawn. Harold Bender recognized a significant change when he noted that "after the creative period of Anabaptism was past, the settled communities and congregations reverted more to the typical patriarchal attitude of European culture."[27] Linda Huebert Hecht has restated this same point using Max Weber's analysis of the "religion of the disprivileged classes," which in its early stages of development tends to "allot equality to women," particularly in allowing them prophetic roles. In later stages of development, "as routinization and regimentation of community relationships set in, a reaction takes place against pneumatic manifestations among women."[28]

These latter observations are particularly relevant to a study of the roles played by Anabaptist women for, as we have seen, the tension between spirit/letter and inner/outer in Anabaptism was resolved increasingly in a steady movement away from pneumatic manifestations. As Harold Bender noted, and as preliminary work in the *Täuferakten* confirms, the early Anabaptist movement was far more open to manifestations of "the spirit," and thus allowed wider roles to women than would be the case in the later communities. In the survey that follows we will look particularly to the role allowed to women in the religious communities as such. We will look in par-

ticular to the roles assumed or not assumed by women in church leadership (proselytizing, preaching, prophesying, baptizing) and the role of women in congregational
life generally (e.g., votes in congregational decisions). In connection with this latter
question, we also will note briefly the development of leadership patterns within the
movement.

Anabaptist Marriage

From the very beginning of the Anabaptist movement fundamental questions
were raised concerning the marriage relationship.[29] Marriage in the Roman Catholic
tradition had come to be viewed in a two-fold manner. On the one hand, celibacy had
long been esteemed as a "higher" state of life, required of those who had vowed
themselves totally to God. For monks and nuns, the profession of monastic vows had
been seen as a "second baptism" which signified a marriage to Christ, and an enter-
ing upon the path of perfection; celibacy for secular clergy had been strictly enjoined
from the eleventh century onward. On the other hand the religious significance of
marriage itself also was bolstered: by the thirteenth century, Peter Lombard's listing
of marriage as one of the seven sacraments had been accepted generally in the Roman Catholic Church. Thomas Aquinas, for example, taught that marriage conferred
sacramental grace to the laity.[30]

The Protestant Reformers simultaneously elevated and lowered the religious
status of marriage. Marriage was elevated by the Protestant denial of the salvific
value of celibacy and asceticism in general; nevertheless, marriage in the mainline
Protestant tradition was also "devalued," since it was not considered a sacrament, or
a means of grace. In matters of salvation, marriage as such played no particular role
in mainline Protestantism.[31]

Thomas Müntzer critiqued Luther and Melanchthon at precisely this point
already in 1522.

> By your arguments you drag men to matrimony although the bond
> is not yet an immaculate one, but a Satanic brothel, which is as harmful
> to the church as the most accursed perfumes of the priests. Do not
> these passionate desires impede your sanctification? How can the
> spirit be poured out over your flesh and how can you have living
> colloquy with God when you deny such things?"[32]

Müntzer's central point, that marriage had to be considered part of the "sanctification" process, and thus a part of the salvation process, was not what Luther had
in mind at all. For Luther, "outward things" had no essential role to play in salvation as
such, which depended upon God's imputing righteousness to sinners. The essential
point of Müntzer's critique would appear again in various guises in the Anabaptist
movement.[33]

As in so many other matters, the Anabaptist views concerning marriage can
be distinguished from both the Catholic and the Protestant views, while sharing some
features of each. Following the Protestant and early Radical Reformers, the
Anabaptists rejected vows of celibacy,[34] were critical of the immorality of the clergy,[35]

and also rejected the elevation of marriage to the status of sacrament as part of their rejection of sacraments generally.[36] Nevertheless, in keeping with their more ascetic understanding of spiritual regeneration, the baptismal commitment to Christ, and the life of discipleship that was to follow, marriage was seen to have spiritual and salvific consequences. For the Anabaptists, all actions "in the world" could affect one's salvation. This was true of political, social and economic activity, and was true also for marriage. Furthermore, these consequences applied to men and women alike.[37]

When we consider Anabaptist marriage in light of Müntzer's widely accepted point that marriage should not impede the sanctification or salvation process, we see that there would be serious tensions here in the Anabaptist movement as a whole. What was to be done when a person who was already married "in the world," was then "reborn of the Spirit" and joined the community of saints by water baptism? Was marriage essentially a "spiritual" union, or a "physical" one? Was a former marriage still valid if the spouse of an Anabaptist remained an "unbeliever?" If it was granted that the unbelief of one marriage partner constituted adequate grounds for separation, was unbelief also grounds for divorce? Might one remarry after having separated from an unbeliever? How was marriage between two Anabaptist believers to be understood and carried out? These questions and many others would be resolved in a variety of ways in the Anabaptist movement, generally depending upon where particular Anabaptist groups stood on the spirit/letter and inner/outer questions, and depending also on where in the developmental process a particular community found itself.

On the central question, however, there was broad agreement. The fundamental principle applying to Anabaptist marriages of all kinds was the insistence that one's *primary* allegiance (or "marriage") was to Christ. In fact, this recalls the ultimate commitment to Christ symbolized in the "second baptism" of the monastic vows. For the Anabaptists, if there were a conflict between one's commitment to one's spouse and family, and one's commitment to Christ, there was no question but that believers were expected to decide in favour of their "higher" commitment. As the Anabaptist movement established firmer community boundaries, however, the communities themselves exercised increasing authority in regulating marriage matters.

The chapters that follow will trace the development of Anabaptist discussions concerning economics, the role of women in the church, and marriage. Our primary focus again will be on a narrative of historical developments within the movement, with special attention paid to the scriptural lines of argumentation that emerged.

End Notes

[1] See Barbara Bettina Gerber, "Sebastian Lotzer: An Educated Layman in the Struggle for Divine Justice," in Hans-Jürgen Goertz, ed., *Profiles of Radical Reformers* (Scottdale, Pa.: Herald Press, 1982), pp. 72-87.

[2] As noted by Goertz, *Die Täufer*, p. 53.

[3] Johannes Hergot was a Nuremberg printer and book peddler, who wrote only this one book. He was arrested in Zwickau, in Saxony, and executed in Leipzig on May 20, 1527. See Ferdinand Seibt, "Johannes Hergot: The Reformation of the Poor Man," in Hans-Jürgen Goertz, ed., *Profiles of Radical Reformers* (Scottdale, Pa.: Herald Press, 1982), 97-106. On Gaismair, see Walter Klaassen, "Michael Gaismair," in Hans-Jürgen Goertz, ed., *Profiles of Radical Reformers* (Scottdale, Pa.: Herald Press, 1982), pp. 88-96. For a more comprehensive treatment, see Walter Klaassen, *Michael Gaismair: Revolutionary and Reformer* (Leiden: Brill, 1978). A translation of Gaismair's *Landesordnung* (Constitution) is found in an appendix in this latter book.

[4] In the patristic and medieval periods, "usury" indicated the charging of *any* interest on money lent, and was forbidden to Christians. The distinction between "interest" (the charging of a "reasonable" rate for money lent) and "usury" (the charging of an unreasonably high rate for money lent) was a later casuistic distinction (beginning in the sixteenth century) made by the church to allow for Christian banking activity and capitalistic enterprise. See "Usury," F.L. Cross, ed., *The Oxford Dictionary of the Christian Church*, (London: Oxford University Press, 1961), p. 1401. For a fascinating and detailed study, see Benjamin Nelson, *The Idea of Usury*, 2nd. ed., (Chicago: University of Chicago Press, 1969).

[5] "By the middle of the seventeenth century the traditionalist forces had been thoroughly routed in Protestant lands. The Jewish hardness of heart .. is gradually generalized to allow usury among Christians.... All men are assumed to have equally hard hearts." Nelson, *Usury*, p. 95. See *ibid.*, pp. 29-72 for a detailed discussion of the German reformed theologians and developments concerning the question of usury.

[6] Arnold Snyder, "The Schleitheim Articles in Light of the Revolution of the Common Man: Continuation or Departure?," *Sixteenth Century Journal*, 16(1985), pp. 419-30.

[7] As noted above (chapter 4). See also James Stayer, "Die Anfänge des schweizerischen Täufertums im reformierten Kongregationalismus," in Hans-Jürgen Goertz, ed., *Umstrittenes Täufertum, 1525-1975* (Göttingen, 1977), pp. 19-49, and his "The Swiss Brethren: An Exercise in Historical Definition," *Church History* 47(1978), pp. 174-195. Most recently, see Stayer's *The German Peasants' War and Anabaptist Community of Goods* (Montreal and Kingston: McGill-Queens University Press, 1991). On the Swiss, see pp. 61-75, and all of chapter 4.

[8] See Snyder, *Life and Thought*, pp. 114-123; the Articles themselves are found in Yoder, *Legacy*, pp. 34-43. Stayer notes that the Swiss Anabaptist attitude could be called "a disillusioned radicalism, no longer innocently hopeful about a general commoners' Reformation." *German Peasants' War*, p. 99.

[9] "The notion that property might exist solely for the selfish interest of the possessor was totally foreign to Anabaptism." So Klassen, *Economics*, p. 36. See pp. 28-49 for a full discussion.

[10] See Sommer, "Rideman and Menno."

[11] See, for example, the introduction and selections of the chapter on economics in Walter Klaassen, ed., *Anabaptism in Outline* (Scottdale, Pa.: Herald Press, 1981), pp. 232-243.

[12] *Concordantz und Zeiger der namhafftigsten Sprüch aller Biblischen Bücher alts und news Testamentss / auffs kürtzest verfasset und zusamen gebracht* (n.p., n.d.[ca. 1550]), pp. 189-202: "Gott ist nicht ein anseher der Person." Only known copy in Mennonite Historical Library, Goshen, Indiana.

[13] The concordance cites vs. 27-30. The central verse is: "I will honour those who honour me, and those who despise me shall meet with contempt." I Samuel 2:30.

[14] I Samuel 16:1-13. The point is that God's choice is not necessarily the one human beings would make.

[15] Cited: 2 Chronicles 19:6-7: Jehosophat admonishes the judges to fear God, and be no respecter of persons: "bey dem Herrn unserem Gott ist kein unrecht, noch ansehen der person..." *Ibid.*, p. 195.

[16] Noted, but not cited are: Matt. 4; 9; 16; 22; Mark 1; 3; 12; Luke 1; 2; 8; 10; 20; Acts 4; Romans 2.

[17] The following overview of the literature is drawn from Linda Huebert Hecht, "Faith and Action: The Role of Women in the Anabaptist Movement of the Tirol, 1527-1529," (Cognate essay, Master of Arts, History, University of Waterloo, 1990), pp. 7-12. See also her published summary, "Women and religious change: The significance of Anabaptist women in the Tirol, 1527-29," *Studies in Religion* 21(1992), pp. 57-66.

[18] See Roland Bainton, *Women of the Reformation in Germany and Italy* (Mineapolis: Augsburg, 1971); Williams, *Radical* (1962), pp. 506-07.

[19] "Women, Status of," in ME, IV, p. 972.

[20] Wolfgang Schaeufele, "The Missionary Vision and Activity of the Anabaptist Laity," MQR 36(April, 1962), p. 108. Similar positive assessments were made by Sherrin Marshall Wyntjes, "Women in the Reformation Era," in *Becoming Visible: Women in European History*, ed. by Renate Bridenthal and Claudia Koonz (Boston, Houghton Mifflin, 1977), pp. 165-91; and Elise Boulding, *The Underside of History: A View of Women through Time* (Colorado, 1976), esp. p. 548. After noting that in Lutheranism, patriarchy, hierarchy, and mysogyny remained the rule, Robert Scribner noted cautiously, "Perhaps only Anabaptism, with its strong emphasis on the fellowship of all Christians, male and female, managed to break out of this mould." Robert Scribner, *The German Reformation* (Atlantic Highlands, N.J.: Humanities Press, 1986), p. 59.

[21] Claus-Peter Clasen, *Anabaptism: A Social History, 1525-1618* (Ithaca: Cornell University Press, 1972), p. 207.

[22] Joyce L. Irwin, *Womanhood in Radical Protestantism, 1525-1675* (New York: Edwin Mellen, 1979). See the comments of Hecht, "Faith and Action," p. 11. Keith L. Sprunger, "God's Powerful Army of the Weak: Anabaptist Women of the Radical Reformation," in *Triumph Over Silence: Women in Protestant History*, ed. by Richard L. Greaves (Westport, Cn.: Greenwood Press, 1985), pp. 45-74, also concludes that Anabaptist women were not active in preaching or leadership roles. A. Jelsma concludes that leadership positions were "seldom" open to women, even in the Radical Reformation. A. Jelsma, "De positie van de vrouw in de Radicale Reformatie," *Doopsgezinde Bijdragen*, nieuwe reeks 15(1989): 25-36. "Ook in de radicale reformatie waren zulke posities zelden voor vrouwen weggelegd." *Ibid.*, p. 29.

[23] See Jenifer Hiett Umble, "Women and Choice: An Examination of the Martyrs' Mirror," MQR 64(April, 1990), pp. 135-145; Sprunger, "God's Powerful Army"; Wayne Plenert, "The Martyrs Mirror and Anabaptist Women," *Mennonite Life* 30(June, 1975), pp. 13-18.

[24] The work of Linda Huebert Hecht has already been mentioned. Her intensive work in the Tirolean court records spanning just three years has yielded impressive results. Marion Kobelt-Groch's work also has been based on intensive work in the *Täuferakten*. See her "Aufsässige Töchter Gottes: Frauen im 'Bauernkrieg' ind in den Bewegungen der Täufer," (Ph.D. dissertation, Hamburg University, 1990).

[25] "Equality" clearly is an anachronistic criterion when applied to sixteenth century social and religious movements. Lois Barrett notes that "One cannot really ask about Anabaptist 'feminism.' Feminism is an anachronism when applied to 16th-century Europe. . . . The question which Europeans in the 16th century asked was whether the Spirit of God could so fill a woman or give her such an extraordinary vocation that she would be authorized to prophecy and preach." Lois Barrett, "Women's History/Women's Theology: Theological and Methodological Issues in the Writing of the History of Anabaptist-Mennonite Women," *The Conrad Grebel Review* 10(Winter, 1992), pp. 12-13, *passim*. Cf. Barrett, "Wreath," p. 114.

[26] See Marion Kobelt-Groch's conclusion in "Why did Petronella Leave Her Husband? Reflections on Marital Avoidance Among the Halberstadt Anabaptists," MQR 62(January, 1988), p. 40. On p. 40, n. 57 Kobelt-Groch cites corroborating work that also "raises substantial doubts about Clasen's sweeping conclusion..."

[27] ME, IV, p. 972.

[28] Max Weber, *The Sociology of Religion* (Boston: Beacon, 1922), p. 104; cited in Hecht, "Faith and Action," p. 82, n. 50; cf. her discussion on pp. 22-23.

[29] See "Marriage" in ME, III, pp. 502-511.

[30] "Matrimony," *Oxford Dictionary of the Christian Church*, ed. by F.L. Cross (London: Oxford University Press, 1961), p. 873.

[31] James Stayer speaks of Luther's "naturalistic" view of marriage, as opposed to the ascetic, platonic view which devalued women and marriage. Thus marriage was considered an "outward" thing, like food or clothing. James Stayer, "Vielweiberei als 'innerweltliche Askese,'" *Mennonitische Geschichtsblätter* N.F. 32(1980), p. 27.

[32] Matheson, *Works*, p. 44.

[33] "Thomas Müntzer hatte eine Kritik an Luther und den Wittenbergern vorgebracht, die später unter den 'Radikalen' Widerhall finden sollte." Stayer, "Vielweiberei," p. 29.

[34] In 1524 Balthasar Hubmaier wrote: "To forbid marriage to priests and then tolerate their carnal immorality is to free Barabbas and to kill Christ. To promise chastity in human strength is nothing other than to promise to fly over the sea without wings." Pipkin and Yoder, *Hubmaier*, p. 34.

[35] Johannes Brötli, who played an influential role in Swiss Anabaptist beginnings in and around Zürich, broke his clerical vow of celibacy and married already in 1523. He protested that he and his wife should not be persecuted, but rather the authorities should be prosecuting adulterers and prostitutes, and insisting that priests enter into honourable marriages. QGTS, 2, #682, pp. 558-62.

[36] The only exception to this that I have found is in an early testimony (November, 1525) of a Swiss Anabaptist, who listed marriage as a sacrament. "Rudolf Ruotsch Wiss of Wesen confesses that of the three faiths, namely our true old faith [Catholicism: the reporter is Catholic], the Lutheran and the Anabaptist, the Anabaptist faith is the best. He will stay in that faith and will also die in it. He also confesses that there are only four sacraments: baptism, the altar (Lord's Supper), marriage and ordination. He also believes there is no purgatory nor (does he believe) in the intercession of the holy saints and the dead." Wiss was executed by drowning November 4, 1525, in Schwyz. QGTS, 2, #685, pp. 563-64.

[37] The Hutterite bishop Peter Walpot wrote: "The husband cannot give account for his wife, nor the wife for her husband, but rather each must render account personally on that day, and bear their own burden." Lydia Müller, ed., *Glaubenszeugnisse oberdeutscher Taufgesinnter* (Leipzig: Nachfolger, 1938; New York: Johnson Reprint, 1971), p. 256.

A depiction of a Hutterite family in Moravia, standing in front of their communal dwelling (*Haushaben*).

This woodcut was the cover illustration for a Jesuit polemic written against the Hutterites:
Christof Erhard, *Gründliche kurtz verfaste Historia von Münsterischen Widertauffern: und wie die Hutterischen Bruder so auch billich Widertauffer genent werden...*
(Munich: Adam Berg, 1588).

Chapter 17

Anabaptism and Economics

The most consistent early Anabaptist pattern, seen among the Swiss as well as the South German Anabaptists, was an attempt to put into practice the apostolic pattern of sharing described in Acts 2, 4 and 5.[1] This early principle, while accepted virtually across the board in the Anabaptist movement, became a point of contention because Scripture provided no guidelines for the concrete implementation of the principle. Thus it was that the strongest disagreements about economics within the Anabaptist movement came on the question of patterns of production and ownership, not on general principles of distribution. These disagreements, as James Stayer's recent detailed study confirms, emerged only over time.

The crucial issue that emerged as a point of contention among the Anabaptists was whether the sharing of possessions was to be a "voluntary" expression of one's inner regeneration, or whether a certain level of external "yielding" of claims to economic goods needed to be "ordered" or "legislated" by the true church, the Body of Christ. This question was argued early in the Moravian communitarian context, then between the Swiss Brethren and the Hutterites (where it continued as a central point of contention), and was addressed indirectly by Pilgram Marpeck, in his revision of Rothmann's *Confession concerning the two Sacraments*.[2] It is important to emphasize a point made by Stayer: it is a mistake to define the "Anabaptist" stand on "community of goods" by later Hutterite practice. The Hutterite position, in which a crucial external measure of the true church was its adherence to a legislated community of goods, was a later development, a further definition of the relationship of inner regeneration to outer behaviour.

Early Swiss Views

James Stayer has argued convincingly that the ideal of "community of goods" (that is, the application of Acts 2, 4 and 5 as a rule of Christian conduct) was a strong feature in Swiss Anabaptism from its inception.[3] Although under questioning the Swiss Brethren almost always denied that they taught "community of goods," what they meant by their denial was that they did not teach a coerced community of goods for society at large—i.e., that they did not teach that property should be forcibly taken from landowners and generally redistributed. When asked to explain what they did believe, the answers provided by the Swiss Brethren were suprisingly uniform in content. Felix Mantz's reply is typical. Mantz admitted in 1525 that he had taught those whom he baptized "about love and unity and community of all things, as in Acts 2." Just before his execution in 1527, however, he denied that he had taught "community of goods"; he had taught, rather, that "whoever is a good Christian should share with his neighbour when he is in need."[4] As Stayer notes, "A deadly semantic game was in progress here": Mantz was on trial for his life on what were, essentially, charges of sedition. His clarification of what he had taught, namely the sharing of goods by true Christians with those who had need, was an application of the principles of Acts 2, 4 and 5 to the community of the regenerate.[5]

A passage from Hubmaier's important book, "On the Christian Baptism of Believers," points to the regenerationist underpinnings of the Swiss Anabaptist view.

> The flesh must daily be killed since it wants only to live and reign according to its own lusts. Here the Spirit of Christ prevails and gains the victory. Then the person brings forth good fruits which give testimony of a good tree. Day and night he practices all those things which concern the praise of God and brotherly love. By this the old Adam is martyred, killed, and carried to the grave. This is a summary and right order of a whole Christian life which begins in the Word of God.[6]

Hubmaier clarified in a later writing—in language that closely paralleled that of other Swiss Anabaptists—just what the regeneration meant in the matter of "community of goods."

> I have ever and always spoken thus of the community of goods: that one person should always look out for the other, so that the hungry are fed, the thirsty given drink, the naked clothed, etc. For we are not lords of our goods, but stewards and distributors. There are certainly none who say that one should take what belongs to the other and make it in common. Rather, much more that one should give the coat besides the mantle.[7]

Hubmaier wrote these lines in Nicholsburg, Moravia, before the south German strand of thought, influenced indirectly by Thomas Müntzer and directly by Hans Hut, had split away to begin its experiments in communal living. His point, and that of the Swiss Anabaptists generally, would remain a central Anabaptist position: because of their rebirth and possession of the Holy Spirit, the regenerate will share with the needy *voluntarily*. By mid-century, however, the Swiss would in fact "legislate" certain principles of economic behaviour, even though they did not abolish private property as such or attempt to establish communal living arrangements.[8]

South German Views

A contrasting early Anabaptist position emerged from the South German Anabaptist stream. Although Thomas Müntzer's own position concerning community of goods is virtually hidden to the historian, his mystical doctrine of *Gelassenheit* and his apocalypticism lent impetus to Hans Hut's later Anabaptist teaching.[9] Stayer concludes that an "anti-materialistic piety" was "the most important thing south German-Austrian Anabaptists inherited from Thomas Müntzer."[10]

In the matter of community of goods, as in many other matters, Hans Hut taught rank and file converts one thing, and close initiates a more esoteric teaching.

Hut's own prison testimony (which was without a doubt self-serving) echoed the Swiss position: "I did teach that anyone who had more than enough should help the needy. Thereupon some people of means sold fields, vineyards or other properties and distributed the proceeds to the poorer brothers."[11] That Hut taught such a principle of help for the needy is confirmed by the testimonies of his converts. However, a second level of teaching by Hut concerned the state of affairs that would prevail once the events of the Last Days had proceeded further: after the Turks had wreaked vengeance on the godless, and the elect had finished the job, private property would be abolished.[12]

Hut's hopes for the abolition of private property, like his expectation that the regenerate would wreak vengeance on the ungodly, were thwarted by the failure of his apocalyptic predictions. Nevertheless among his followers the mystical notion of *Gelassenheit* and freedom of attachment from material things remained a powerful motivation in economic questions. The writings of Leonhard Schiemer and Hans Schlaffer, for example, reflect a mystical piety of suffering and yieldedness, without Hut's enthusiastic apocalypticism. In a characteristic sentence from his 1527 letter to the church at Rattenberg, Schiemer wrote, "this is blessedness and God himself that I love nothing save God alone and seek joy and comfort, security and life in nothing else than in the one God alone, and that my heart no longer depends on the creatures."[13] Schiemer expected the true church to be a persecuted, suffering church; but even more, he expected it to be a "yielded" and "apostolic" church, as described in Acts 2, 4 and 5.[14] Just how this church was to be organized in concrete practice Schiemer did not elaborate; the emphasis in his writings was on the necessary preliminary steps of losing attachment to creaturely things and cleaving only to God.

The Rise of Communitarian Anabaptism in Moravia

The mystical piety of South German Anabaptism readily lent itself to a sharing of possessions among those who had need, but a stronger communitarian emphasis soon became evident in the atmosphere of relative political toleration found in the Moravian territories. The beginnings of the communitarian movement in Moravia have been examined in detail by Werner Packull; his detailed study sheds new light on a history that usually has been read in a "Huttero-centric" way.[15]

The emergence of the first documented communitarian grouping in Moravia has been described above: 200 refugees, expelled from Nicholsburg in March 1528, chose two "servants of needs" and pooled all of their possessions. As Stayer notes, at the time "it was just another schism. All Anabaptists were committed ... to the implementation of Acts 2, 4 and 5."[16] From this beginning emerged the Hutterite communities—but not before other parallel Anabaptist communitarian experiments had been attempted. A second group of communitarian Anabaptists in Moravia originated in Silesia and were called Gabrielites, after their leader Gabriel Ascherham; a third communitarian group, the Philipites, had roots in Swabia and were led by Philip Plenner. Neither of these latter groups managed to survive the 1535 expulsion from Moravia, although a significant number of Philipites did join the Swiss Brethren, and some also joined the Hutterites.

The origins of Silesian Anabaptism are obscure, and bound to remain so; what evidence remains suggests that there were Anabaptists in Silesian territories at least by 1527.[17] Gabriel Ascherham probably became an Anabaptist in 1528, quite possibly baptized by Wolfgang Brandhuber who also established a communitarian Anabaptist group in Linz.[18] Sometime in 1528, a community led by Ascherham was established in Rossitz, Moravia; it came to number some 1,200 members, considerably larger than the proto-Hutterite group established in Austerlitz that same year. The Gabrielites were joined at Rossitz sometime in 1529 by Swabian Anabaptist refugees led by Philip Plenner, but differences arose between them; these were resolved amicably, and the Philipites settled in their own community in Auspitz in 1529-30.[19] Before long the Gabrielites and Philipites were joined by a splinter group from Austerlitz, led by the well-travelled Swiss Anabaptist Wilhelm Reublin and Jörg Zaunring. From 1530 to 1533 these three communitarian Anabaptist groups lived peacefully together, recognizing Gabriel Ascherham as their "primary shepherd" or bishop (*Oberhirte*). A major schism in 1533 led to the founding of the Hutterites as such.[20]

Werner Packull has described the practice of these groups in the following way.

> Gabriel and his followers practised a voluntary form of community of goods with a common treasury. Members of the community were divided over a number of households (*Haushaben*) led by deacons and elders. . . . The community quickly developed certain rituals and practices which involved, besides baptism and celebration of the Lord's Supper, weekly services of admonition, greeting each other with the 'brotherly kiss', the use of the ban for discipline and the refusal to pay war taxes.[21]

This communitarian practice, if one is to judge by Gabriel's own writing, was founded principally in a spiritualist theology of illumination and regeneration by the Holy Spirit.[22]

Central to Gabriel's thought was the distinction between human understanding and divine wisdom; Gabriel (as one might well imagine) emphasized the latter. Packull notes that "The 'internal house of understanding' took priority ... and had to be set in order first. The external would then follow naturally and unforced."[23] Gabriel's treatise, written sometime after the 1533 schism, was directed against the Hutterite requirement that all members of their community relinquish possession of all their earthly goods. Gabriel criticized those who ran about "with great commotion proclaiming: you can't be saved with your property. You must sell it and leave it and move under the cross because without suffering you cannot be saved!"[24] Gabriel opposed this practice on spiritualist and regenerationist grounds, and pointed to its soteriological implications.

> I tell you, if you can be saved only through community of goods, then you will never be saved. For salvation does not lie in good works, but

in the grace of God. And he who is saved, in him the desire for community of goods is uncoerced. It cannot be hidden because the heavenly mind determines the temporal and natural one.[25]

Gabriel Ascherham established, led and fostered communitarian Anabaptist groups, but he insisted that "Uniformity of practice ... should grow voluntarily out of oneness in spirit and *Gelassenheit* toward material things. It should not be solicited and extorted as a mandatory sacrifice."[26] This voluntaristic emphasis corresponded more closely to early and later Anabaptist practice than would the legislated community of goods that came to define the Hutterite community.

The Philipite community at Auspitz, prior to its expulsion from Moravia in 1535, had grown to number approximately 400 members and included two other communties as well. Although the one estimated membership figure of 5,000 Moravian Philipites is clearly an exaggeration, Packull notes that "the Philipites, one year before their expulsion from Moravia, were still a dynamic, growing community, still drawing recruits from as far away as the Rhineland and Swabia."[27] Nevertheless, after their expulsion the Philipites very quickly disappeared as a separate community, remembered primarily for their contribution of hymns to a collection of "Swiss Brethren" hymns first published in 1564. This core of Philipite hymnody grew and eventually was published as the *Ausbund*, hymnal of the Swiss Brethren. Two hymns, both extolling community of goods, were dropped in the second "Swiss" collection of hymns— by 1583, "community of goods" was associated with the Hutterites, with whom the Swiss had serious disagreements. Nevertheless, the Philipites in Moravia, like the Gabrielites, had held to a voluntary community of goods "as the natural outgrowth of fraternal love..."[28]

The story of the division that occurred among the communitarian brethren in Moravia is told (from a decidedly Hutterian perspective) in the Hutterite *Chronicle* "in much unedifying detail," as Stayer notes.[29] Not surprisingly, Jakob Hutter emerges as the heroic figure in the *Chronicle* account, opposed by the lying, deceitful and avaricious trio of Simon Schützinger, Gabriel Ascherham, and Philip Plenner. Apart from the obvious personality conflicts brought to a head by Hutter's arrival, at the heart of the trouble lay Hutter's vision of a stricter practice of community of goods. Early in the proceedings, with the Auspitz leader Simon Schützinger sick in bed, Hutter "held a meeting in which he admonished and taught in the power of God, exhorting the people to the true community of Jesus Christ." This "true community" as preached by Hutter clearly involved a total giving over of possessions to the community. Instrumental in the process of schism was the discovery of several cases of "Ananias and Sapphira" (Acts 5:1-11), including Schützinger himself, who was found to have hidden forty *Gulden* in the roof of his room.[30] The end result, besides mutual recrimination, excommunication and schism, was the establishment of a strict and legislated community of goods in the Auspitz community under Hutter, which has characterized the Hutterian fellowship ever since.

In this move to outward legislation (*Ordnungen*) concerning behaviour in the community, the previous emphasis on *Gelassenheit* was retained, but now linked indissolubly to an outward condition of total yieldedness in economic matters. This linkage is common in subsequent Hutterite writings; one particularly clear example is found in the "Cherished Instructions," a writing by Ulrich Stadler, dating from around 1537.[31] Stadler begins his discussion of "the true community of the saints" with the memorable sentence: "There is one communion (*gmain*) of all the faithful in Christ and one community (*gmainschaft*) of the holy children called of God." Since this one communion and community has one Father, one Lord Christ, one baptism, one Spirit, one mind, one cross, and one hope, "in this community everything must proceed equally, all things be one and communal, alike in the bodily gifts of their Father in heaven, which he daily gives to be used by his own according to his will."[32]

Two crucial features of this "one community," according to Stadler, were an inner condition of *Gelassenheit* and an outward communal life.

> They have also yielded themselves and presented themselves to (Christ) intimately, patiently, of their own free will, naked and uncovered, to suffer and endure his will and, moreover, to fulfill it and thereafter also to devote themselves in obedience and service to all the children of God. Therefore, they also live with one another where the Lord assigns a place to them...[33]

Furthermore, Stadler made clear, a lack of readiness to give over one's possessions to the community provides irrefutable evidence that such a person is not truly "yielded" to God in spiritual things. In fact, such a person (it appears) will not be saved.

> Therefore, where there is ownership and one has it, and it is his, and one does not wish to be one (*gmainsam*) with Christ and his own in living and dying, he is outside of Christ and his communion (*gmain*) and has thus no Father in heaven. If he says so, he lies.[34]

With this step (implicit already in the 1533 excommunications) the Hutterites drew an impermeable boundary between themselves and other Anabaptists: salvation would be attained only by those who submitted their possessions to the Hutterite community (or one like it) and submitted to the *Ordnungen* established for the running of that community.[35] For the Hutterites, true spiritual "yieldedness" and regeneration by the Holy Spirit must, if it is genuine, lead of necessity to a Christian community in which no individuals made claims to possession of material things. Here the inner life of believers was linked to a very specific outer behaviour on which there could be no compromise.

Swiss Brethren and Hutterites

With the disappearance of the Gabrielites and Philipites after 1535, the Hutterites remained the sole communitarian Anabaptist fellowship in Moravia. Nevertheless, communities of Swiss Brethren and followers of Pilgram Marpeck were still to be found in Moravia at the end of the century, and there was continuing contact between all these Anabaptist groups. Also, because of the active Hutterite mission-ary and recruiting efforts, which seem to have been directed consciously to areas where other Anabaptists lived, Hutterites were in constant friction with the Swiss Brethren. There are records of contact, conversation and disagreement between these groups.[36] In 1567 some Swiss Brethren in Moravia wrote a 160 page book to the Hutterites, in which they raised seven basic points of disagreement. Although the original book has not survived, the substance of Swiss Brethren concerns can be reconstructed from the 376 page reply (!) composed by Peter Walpot.[37]

The first article addressed by the Swiss, and the only one that concerns us directly here, had to do with community of goods. The Swiss position, supported by scriptural argumentation, was that "because all Christians are free in Christ they do not need to give up temporal goods or live in community; they can earn their own livelihood, raise their own children, and give to the church as often and as much as they deem correct."[38] Variations on this argument would reappear in later discus-sions, namely that while property and possessions were to be shared freely and vol-untarily by the regenerated with the needy, still it was not necessary for salvation to live within a community that legislated community of goods.

Peter Walpot composed a seventy page reply to the first article alone, basing Hutterite communal practice in the common purse Jesus used with his disciples, as well as using many other scriptural arguments and texts. Walpot's conclusion, as summarized by Leonard Gross, maintained that

> Christian love and unity, integral in the Christian faith, could be ful-filled only within the confines of close brotherhood sharing. Such a community of believers ... had been established by God in New Tes-tament times, had continued up to the time of Augustine, had been reinstated by the Hutterites, and would endure as long as God would have his community endure...[39]

In concluding his book (which the Swiss appear to have ignored) Walpot noted that the Swiss Brethren "were simply not true followers of Christ. The world re-mained the world, and the Hutterites avoided it; since the Swiss were part of this world, the Hutterites were therefore to avoid them in eating, drinking, working, buy-ing and selling."[40] The lines of division between these two Anabaptist fellowships, once drawn in this fundamental way, were not easily dissolved, and remain to this day.

Bernhard Rothmann, and Marpeck's Response

There was only one other major instance of legislated community of goods outside of Moravia, and that was in the years 1534 and 1535, in the city of Münster. James Stayer has identified three distinct phases in the development of community of goods in Münster. Prior to the arrival of Jan Matthijs, economic practice among the Anabaptists in Münster had corresponded closely to non-communitarian Anabaptist practices elsewhere: there was to be no "usury" among the brethren, and the poor were to be cared for by voluntary contributions.[41] The second phase lasted from Februry 1534 to Easter of that year. It corresponded to the height of apocalyptic excitement under the prophetic leadership of Jan Matthijs and featured the "official" abolition of private property. Nevertheless, only money, some food, and some clothing was actually redistributed. The third phase, from April 1534 up to the fall of the city in June, 1535 was carried out under the leadership of Jan van Leiden. In this final phase the communal sharing of goods became less and less a reality, as the siege began to take its toll within the city.[42]

Bernhard Rothmann was the official apologist for Münsterite communalism. He was disposed in a communitarian direction already before Matthijs arrived, and defended the practice with increasing enthusiasm as the reality became less and less evident in the besieged city.[43] Rothmann wrote his "Confession concerning the two Sacraments" in August of 1533, before Münster had turned in an Anabaptist direction.[44] It is particularly interesting because of Pilgram Marpeck's later editing of Rothmann's comments.

In a section of that book entitled "On the Practice of the Apostles in Breaking the Bread and Their Observance of the Communion of Christ," Rothmann cited Bullinger as his source for how the Apostles practised the Supper. After prayer and the reading of Scripture, communal admonition was practised by use of the ban. Following this, Rothmann notes,

> Each individual would be given what he needed. As indicated in Acts 4, they shared all things in common, 'so the community was united in heart and soul, so that no one said concerning his goods that they were his own, but rather they had all things in common.' This practice was current for some time. Not only was it described by Clement, the Roman bishop, in his epistles, but Augustine also makes it sound as if it was prevalent even in his day.[45]

Rothmann's connection of "sharing things in common" with the practice of the Supper was consistent with Anabaptist emphases elsewhere, which understood the Supper not only as a memorial, but also as a sign and seal of unity and equality in the Body of Christ.

Marpeck's edition of Rothmann's work did not challenge this basic understanding at all, but Marpeck did interpolate an extended comment at this point in Rothmann's treatise, clarifying the question of "community of goods," and interpreting further the events recounted in Acts 4. Marpeck made two central points in his interpolation of 1542, the first concerning freedom and coercion.

> Here we go beyond Bullinger's writings for a better understanding. No coercion or commandment, however, made them share all things communally. Rather, the sharing was done simply out of a free love which caused the community to be of one heart and soul.[46]

The point, said Marpeck, was that individuals in the Jerusalem community *could* have kept their goods for themselves (Acts 5:4). "Such a practice," said Marpeck, criticizing both the Münsterite experience and Hutterite practice which he also knew first hand, "is unlike the practice of some who, desiring to have common property more out of greed than of love, coerce others into giving."[47] Here Marpeck echoed earlier critiques of a legislated community of goods by the Gabrielites in Moravia, a critique that was echoed as well by the Swiss Brethren.

Marpeck's second objection ran exactly counter to the further point Rothmann had made (which surprisingly, was not removed from the text edited by Marpeck), namely that "this practice was current for some time." Marpeck noted to the contrary that "The Corinthians, Macedonians, and Romans *did not* share their possessions, as Paul clearly shows in 1 Corinthians 16." The proof was that Paul had appealed to those churches for "contributions to the saints." Marpeck concluded, "it can be clearly seen that community of possessions was not practiced in all churches."[48]

Marpeck ended his interpolation by putting forward his own vision concerning a proper Christian attitude toward possessions.

> Even though they control their possessions, such true believers do not say in their hearts that these are theirs; rather, their possessions belong to God and the needy. For this reason, among true Christians who display the freedom of love, all things are communal and are as if they had been offered, since they have been offered by the heart.[49]

Here Marpeck returned to the spiritual underpinning of community of goods seen early in the South German movement, especially in the writings of Leonhard Schiemer and Gabriel Ascherham. Possessions must be "yielded" to God in the heart, along with all earthly things, but no external or legal "coercion" can be demanded.

Menno on Economics

Always looming in the background of Menno Simons' writings, especially early in his Anabaptist career, were the events in Münster, among which a legislated "community of goods" had played a major role. In 1552 Menno wrote a "Reply to False Accusations" in which he devoted one section to refuting the charge that he taught "community of goods." Menno said unequivocally "We do not teach and practice community of goods"; nevertheless he went on to explain (in language reminiscent of Stadler) that since all believing Christians are baptized into the one Body, and partake of one bread, and have one Lord, therefore "it is Christian and reasonable that they piously love one another, and that the one member be solicitous for the welfare of the other..."[50] The one sign of true Christianity, said Menno, is the demonstration of love (John 13:35). Those who are truly reborn by the Spirit

> show mercy and love, as much as they can. No one among them is allowed to beg. They take to heart the need of the saints. They entertain those in distress. They take the stranger into their houses. They comfort the afflicted; assist the needy; clothe the naked; feed the hungry; do not turn their face from the poor; do not despise their own flesh. Isa. 59:7,8. Behold, such a community we teach.[51]

Menno, like the majority of other Anabaptists, denied that there should be (or was) an external order which legislated the sharing of property among all people. He exegeted the crucial Acts passages in much the same way as had Marpeck, namely that the early apostolic practice "was not permanent with the apostles, therefore we leave things as they are and have never taught nor practiced community of goods." Nevertheless Menno expected the economic fruits of regeneration to be evident within the Body of Christ: "we diligently and earnestly teach and admonish assistance, love, and mercy, as the apostolic Scriptures abundantly teach."[52]

Interestingly enough, Menno revealed his own propensity to a strong interpretation of "community of goods" when he added, "even if we did teach and practice community of goods as is falsely reported, we would be but doing that which the holy apostles full of the Holy Spirit did in the previous church in Jerusalem—although as was said they discontinued it."[53]

The ground of Menno's teaching concerning economic questions was the work of the Spirit in regenerating believers. Some of Menno's most impassioned passages concerning economics emerge in his writing on "True Christian Faith." These passages form a part of a brief meditation on the faith of Zacchaeus, the Publican. Zacchaeus, said Menno, provides an example of true repentance followed by true reformation: "He received Christ into his house with joy. He believed and was renewed; he reformed his life; he walked no more in his evil ways."[54] Zacchaeus presents a lesson for all of this world who are tempted by the lure of wealth, and subsequently go on to lead un-Christian lives: the Lords and princes, the judges, the soldiers and mercenaries, the preachers who preach for pay, the wicked merchants and retailers. What they need is the "faith, spirit, and converted life of Zacchaeus."[55]

> All who with Zacchaeus receive Jesus Christ in the house of their consciences, with him rightly believe the Word of Christ and are truly born by it, these are also given the Spirit of Christ and are of the same mind with Him. Therefore it is impossible for them to defraud anyone of so much as a farthing.

It was axiomatic for Menno and other Anabaptists that being a believer meant that one had received the "Spirit and mind" of Christ. Believers will not defraud others; believers will care for the needs of others, not because they are ordered to do so, but because they have been regenerated by the living Spirit of God. Becoming a Christian meant, for Menno, passing from being a person concerned with self-advancement—a condition of sinfulness that would have clear and concrete economic manifestations—to being a person ruled by the Spirit of Christ, which is a spirit of love of God and neighbour—a condition of grace that also would have clear (and contrasting) economic manifestations.

In Menno's understanding, then, accepting God's offer of salvation by grace, through faith and the power of the Holy Spirit, concretely transfered one's mind, life and kingdom citizenship from the former kingdom of self-will and death, to life in Christ's Kingdom of joyful self-sacrifice, service and love. But even more, since the process was essentially a spiritual one, there could be no question of external coercion, or the taking and possession of the land and property of another.[56]

Conclusion

It would be a mistake to minimize the differences between the Anabaptist economic models of community described above. Certainly the Anabaptists themselves considered their differences on economic questions to be significant, as their internal polemics and eventual schisms demonstrate.[57] Still in all, in the eyes of contemporaries the Swiss Brethren, Pilgramites, and Mennonites, no less than the Hutterites, presented a very threatening critique of contemporary economic practices.[58] This was because, in the end, the Anabaptist critique of contemporary economic practices was not simply directed within, to other church members, but also was directed without, implicitly and explicitly, against all those who wished to call themselves Christians. Given Anabaptist soteriology, in the end there could be no decisive severing of one's economic practice from the process of salvation.

In the first place, the Anabaptists were critical of the poverty they saw around them, particularly since the poor were supposedly also "members" of Christ's Church, whether Protestant or Catholic. Menno Simons said eloquently,

> Is it not sad and intolerable hypocrisy that these poor people boast of having the Word of God, of being the true Christian church, never remembering that they have entirely lost their sign of true Christianity? For although many of them have plenty of everything, ... yet they suffer many of their own poor, afflicted members (notwithstanding their fellow believers have received one baptism and partaken of the same bread with them) to ask alms; and poor, hungry, suffering, old, lame, blind, and sick people to beg their bread at their doors.[59]

The sign of true Christianity, Menno and other Anabaptists believed, involved the avoidance of riches, and had to include the care of those who had need within and outside of the baptized Body of Christ.[60]

In the second place, all Anabaptists were extremely suspicious of trade and commerce as means of earning one's livelihood. In their Confession of 1578, for example, the Swiss Brethren in Hesse maintained that Christians should be engaged in "honest hand labour," avoiding merchandising and the like. In this they were repeating earlier Swiss sentiments.[61] Menno thought that there perhaps *could* be "God-fearing merchants and retailers," but he was certain that they were in grave danger of being overcome by avarice.[62] Peter Riedeman, on the other hand, expressed the Hutterite opinion that the work of a trader or merchant "is a sinful business." Therefore, said Riedeman, "we allow no one to buy to sell again." It is wrong "when one buyeth a ware and selleth the same again even as he bought it, taking to himself profit, making the ware dearer thereby for the poor, taking bread from their very mouths and thus making the poor man nothing but the bondman of the rich." Riedeman echoed the Swiss (and Menno would repeat the point) when he argued that Christians "should labour, working with their hands what is honest, that they may have to give to him that needeth."[63]

Finally, the Anabaptists uniformly rejected the charging of interest on money at loan. Such interest, according to the understanding of the time, was most often simply described as "usury" or even "theft." In St. Gall, Switzerland in 1532, Hans Marquart argued that Christians should lend without any hope of recovering the principal; much less, then, might a Christian be allowed to collect usury on money lent.[64] The sentiment was echoed by the Swiss Brethren in their Confession of 1578. They argued that the reborn children of God should not invest their money to get interest, but should use their surplus to help the poor, "to lend and give to them, and expect the reward from God."[65] The charging of interest was so far from Hutterite economic life that Riedeman did not even mention the subject, but Menno Simons openly opposed the charging of interest and the making of money with money: there were to be no Swiss Brethren, Hutterite, or Mennonite financiers or entrepreneurs![66]

In contrast to Christian groups outside the Anabaptist movement, the fundamental uniformity of Anabaptist teaching on economic matters is striking, from the common "spiritual" underpinnings, to the concrete manifestations of economic community that were expected to emerge as a result of rebirth and baptism. The understanding also was common that the celebration of the Lord's Supper was a recommitment to the community in all things, including economic necessity.

However in the end, the practical specifics governing the economic life of the reborn came to divide the Anabaptist fellowship, driving a permanent wedge between the Hutterites and other Anabaptists. In terms of the inner/outer relationship which was crucial in this disagreement, we may end with an observation by the great Hutterite bishop Peter Walpot. His comment takes us back to Anabaptist soteriology, and the decisive linking of inner regeneration with outer behaviour.

> It should be realized that where there is genuine spiritual communion, there is also external community of goods; the one cannot exist without the other and it does not endure without the other. Otherwise it would also follow that the interior baptism of the Spirit were sufficient and the external confirmation of water baptism unnecessary, although here, too, the one cannot exist without the other.[67]

If the "outer" and the "inner" lives of believers are indissolubly linked and are determinative in the process of salvation, as the Anabaptists maintained, will a spiritual union of believers also result necessarily in a shared life of radical economic sharing?

End Notes

[1] "When the early Anabaptists (or Thomas Müntzer) referred to community of goods, they were citing Acts 2 to the effect that the first Christians in Jerusalem 'had all things in common' and that 'they sold their possessions and goods and distributed them to all, as any had need.'" Stayer, *German Peasants' War*, p. 9.

[2] This was Marpeck's *Vermanung* of 1542. See Klassen and Klaassen, *Writings*, pp. 159-302.

[3] "In fact, there is good evidence of a major preoccupation with Acts 2 and 4 at the very beginning of the Swiss Anabaptist movement, as might be expected of a religious group entangled with the contemporary peasant resistance to the established order." Stayer, *German Peasants' War*, p. 96. One might also add that the same preoccupation might be expected of a group that was looking to Scripture for concrete reforming guidelines.

[4] *Ibid.*, p. 97.

[5] See *ibid.*, pp. 96-105 for other examples from the early Swiss Anabaptist movement (e.g. Heini Frei, Hans Krüsi, J. Brötli, Heini Seiler, etc.).

[6] Balthasar Hubmaier, "On the Christian Baptism of Believers," in Pipkin and Yoder, *Hubmaier*, p. 147.

[7] "Dialogue with Zwingli's Baptism Book," in *Ibid.*, p. 183.

[8] See, for example, Harold S. Bender, "The Discipline Adopted by the Strasburg Conference of 1568," MQR 1(January, 1927), p. 65.

[9] Stayer surveys the evidence on Müntzer in *German Peasants' War*, pp. 107-111. Müntzer's only explicit statement to the effect that "all things should be held in common" was extracted under torture. Nevertheless, as Stayer notes, Müntzer had a "truly ascetic vision": "Salvation came not with ... pleasant, materially satisfied lives but through the inner turmoil of a struggle for faith that led to the renunciation of all material attachments." *Ibid.*, p. 110.

[10] *Ibid.*, p. 121.

[11] Cited in *ibid.*, p. 114.

[12] Stayer reviews the evidence in *ibid.*, pp. 114-15.

[13] Translation from Klaassen, *Outline*, p. 54.

[14] "Among us you will find the life of the church of the apostles. But whenever it is found it is called a new sect, and its members are killed even as they did the apostles. . . . This church you will find clearly described in Acts 2, 4, and 5." *Ibid.*, p. 105.

[15] See Werner Packull, *Communitarian Experiments during the Reformation. A Narrative History of Hutterite Beginnings: 1525-1545* (forthcoming, Johns Hopkins University Press). In chapters 4 and 5, Packull examines the Philipite and Gabrielite movements, shedding important new light on non-Hutterian communitarianism in Moravia. The Huttero-centric reading of this history is virtually inevitable, since the Hutterite writings (especially the great *Chronicle*) are by far the most important historical sources available. My thanks to Werner Packull for allowing me the use his manuscript prior to its publication.

[16] Stayer, *German Peasants' War*, p. 142.

[17] The evidence is exhaustively surveyed by Packull, *Communitarian*, chapter 5.

[18] Evidence in *ibid.*, chapter 5.2.

[19] On the establishment of the Philipites, see Packull, *Communitarian*, chapter 4.2.

[20] *Ibid.*, ch. 5.2.

[21] *Ibid.*

[22] Again, Packull's recent work is fundamental here. See his discussion of Gabriel's "On the Distinction between Divine and Human Wisdom," in *Communitarian*, ch. 5.2.

[23] *Ibid.*

[24] Cited in *ibid.*

[25] Cited in *ibid.*

[26] *Ibid.*

[27] *Ibid.*, Ch. 4.2.

[28] So Packull, *ibid.*

[29] Stayer, *German Peasants' War*, p. 143; see *The Chronicle of the Hutterian Brethren, I* (Rifton, N.Y.: Plough Publishing House, 1987), pp. 97-146. These events are recounted and analyzed in detail in Packull, *Communitarian*, chapter 9.

[30] *Chronicle*, pp. 103-04.

[31] Most of the "Cherished Instructions on Sin, Excommunication, and the Community of Goods" is translated in Williams, *SAW*, pp. 274-284. Original in Lydia Müller, *Glaubenszeugnisse oberdeutscher Taufgesinnter* (Leipzig: Nachfolger, 1938; New York: Johnson Reprint, 1971), pp. 215-227.

[32] Williams, *SAW*, p. 277.

[33] *Ibid.*, pp. 277-78.

[34] *Ibid.*, p. 278.

[35] A description of Hutterite economic organization is found in Robert Friedmann, "Economic Aspects of Early Hutterite Life," MQR 30(October, 1956), pp. 259-266.

[36] In June 1578, Hans Pauly Kuchenbecker of Hatzbach, author of a Swiss Brethren Confession of faith, distinguished himself and his brothers from the Hutterites because the latter "take the property of their brethren, separate marriages, love their leaders better than their brother, have all things in common. Also that they have no ban, and that they do not restore anything to those who leave." To the contrary, "he and his group are Swiss Brethren." TA, *Hesse*, p. 393. Swiss Brethren-Hutterite polemics had already assumed fixed forms by this time. See Claus-Peter Clasen, *Social History*, pp. 38-42. Kuchenbecker's objection concerning the ban may refer to a perception of laxity in its application among the Hutterites.

[37] The author has not yet had a chance to see or read this document. The following is taken from Leonard Gross, *The Golden Years of the Hutterites* (Scottdale, Pa.: Herald Press, 1980), chapter 8, and Amos B. Hoover, "Übrigen Brocken (The Extra Crumbs): A Review," *Pennsylvania Mennonite Heritage*, 4(1981), pp. 10-15.

[38] *Ibid.*, p. 170. Hoover notes that the Swiss reproached the Hutterites for seeming to imply "that salvation depends on community." Hoover, *Übrigen*, p. 11.

[39] Gross, *Golden*, p. 171.

[40] *Ibid.*, p. 184. Earlier in the 1567 writing the charge is levelled by the Hutterites that the Swiss "gave loans to their brethren." *Ibid.*, p. 12. See the interesting articles concluding the Hutterite writing, translated in Hoover, *Übrigen*, p. 15. The Hutterites there criticize a number of Swiss economic practices. As a result of the Swiss lack of community, "unbelieving children may eventually inherit the property that actually belongs to God..." (point 2). The Swiss are said to "have self-gain (money) to use just as the worldly people do" (point 3). "They hire to heathen and worldly people their own children..." (points 5 and 6). "One continuously buys (or sells) with another just as the unbelievers and heathen do" (point 7). "When one brother has eaten with another among

them, the host often prepares the leftovers ... and accepts money for it" (point 8). "If one teaches another a trade, the apprentice must pay the other (the master) the same as unbelievers" (point 9). Also criticized is the Swiss practice of paying war taxes and "the priests' interest and tithes" (points 11 and 12).

[41] According to the testimony of Jakob Hufschmidt, who left in February 1534, "the Anabaptists taught that usury and zins contracts were unchristian. They were not to be extracted by Anabaptists from others, nor were they to be paid by the Anabaptists themselves. The congregation had two officers concerned with the care of the poor. These reported cases of need, received voluntary contributions and administered poor relief." Stayer, *German Peasants' War*, p. 133.

[42] "Community of goods ... was shaped increasingly by the military necessities of the siege and by the need to appease a leadership-group in which notables were prominent." *Ibid.*, p. 132.

[43] "In his *Restitution* Rothmann proclaimed that the Anabaptist realm had abolished human exploitation: 'the eating and drinking of the sweat of the poor, that is, to use our servants and our neighbours, so that they must work so that we may feast.' In practice, Anabaptist communism in Münster fell far short of Rothmann's ideal. It reached its high point in the heady weeks following the 'February miracle.' Afterwards it showed its tawdry reality as a dreary 'war communism...'" *Ibid.*, p. 138.

[44] Critical edition in Robert Stupperich, *Die Schriften Bernhard Rothmanns* (Münster: Aschendorffsche Verlagsbuchhandlung, 1970), pp. 138-195.

[45] Klassen and Klaassen, *Writings*, pp. 278-79; Stupperich, *Schriften*, p. 184.

[46] Klassen and Klaassen, *Writings*, pp. 278-79.

[47] *Ibid.*, p. 279.

[48] *Ibid.*

[49] *Ibid.*

[50] CWMS, p. 558. On this general subject, see William E. Keeney, *The Development of Dutch Anabaptist Thought and Practice From 1539-1564* (Nieuwkoop: B. De Graaf, 1968), pp. 135-36.

[51] *Ibid.* See also the selections from Menno translated in Klaassen, *Anabaptism in Outline*, pp. 241-42.

[52] CWMS, pp. 559-60.

[53] *Ibid.*, , p. 560.

[54] *Ibid.*, p. 367.

[55] *Ibid.*, p. 369.

[56] *Ibid.*, p. 558.

[57] See Gross, *Golden*, pp. 164-193.

[58] As Walter Klaassen has noted, the Anabaptists were persecuted for "economic" reasons not because they were "misunderstood," but because they were understood all too well. Walter Klaassen, "The Nature of the Anabaptist Protest," MQR 45(October, 1971), pp. 302-303.

[59] CWMS, p. 559. The same sentiments were expressed by Swiss Brethren at various times and places. For example, in Hesse in 1578: It is the duty of "believing, re-born Christians" to keep their needy fellow members from want and poverty. See TA, *Hesse*, p. 435, no. 33, "Von den Armen." See also Hans Marquart's testimony, QGTS, 2, p. 466.

[60] Sommer, "Rideman and Menno," pp. 210-212.

[61] TA, *Hesse*, p. 436. In the Strasbourg Discipline of 1568, the Swiss agreed that "No brother shall engage in buying or building or other large (unnecessary) business dealing without the counsel, knowledge, and consent of the brethren and bishops." Harold S. Bender, "The Discipline Adopted by the Strasburg Conference of 1568," MQR 1(January, 1927), p. 65.

[62] "True Christian Faith," CWMS, pp. 368-69.

[63] Peter Rideman, *Account of our Religion, Doctrine and Faith* (Hodder and Stoughton, 1950), pp. 126-27. See also Claus-Peter Clasen, *Anabaptism. A Social History, 1524-1618* (Ithaca and London, 1972), pp. 195-96.

[64] QGTS, 2, p. 467. The same argument was used at the Zofingen disputation in 1532, between Swiss Brethren and Reformed pastors. See Stayer, *German Peasants' War*, p. 102.

[65] TA, *Hesse*, p. 437.

[66] "Yes, good reader, the whole world is so affected and involved in this accursed avarice, fraud, false practice, and unlawful means of support; in this false traffic and merchandise, with this finance, usury and personal advancement that I do not know how it could get much worse." "True Christian Faith," CWMS, p. 369. See Sommer, "Rideman and Menno," p. 214.

[67] Cited in Stayer, *German Peasants' War*, p. 157.

Chapter 18

Equality in the Community of Saints

In the sixteenth century context, the Anabaptist appeal to the working of the Holy Spirit in women and men alike, buttressed by appropriate biblical references of course, was potentially an avenue of liberation leading away from the accepted social hierarchies of the time. The authorities took this threat absolutely seriously, and regarded it as rank sedition, especially when marriages were threatened. Nevertheless, we must not distort the Anabaptist appeal to the Spirit by applying the individualist measures of our century: being "informed by the Holy Spirit" did not mean to the Anabaptists what we mean today by "individual freedom of choice." The presence of the Holy Spirit for the Anabaptists meant "submission to the one true Lord." For the Anabaptists, the work of the Holy Spirit did not do away with hierarchy, but simply *reestablished* the proper, biblical, divine "order," with God as Lord over all. The attitude was thus not "liberation" for all—although in the context of the time, elements of liberation were present—but rather the attitude called for was "yieldedness" to the proper, divine ordering (*Gelassenheit*), with God as Lord of one's life.

Obedience to God was the first step, but it was followed by the requirement of obedience to the Body of Christ on earth, the church. This two-fold obedience frames the development of "equality" within Anabaptism. Concerning "obedience to God," a crucial question was whether the emphasis fell on the *Spirit* of God working within individual believers, or on the written word of Scripture which was interpreted by the gathered community, led by men of authority. The former emphasis opened wider leadership possibilities for women because the Spirit bloweth where it listeth; the latter limited leadership possibilities for women by appealing to community standards (which tended to mirror societal norms) and textual Pauline restrictions. In fact, the early Anabaptist movement was far more open to manifestations of "the Spirit," and thus allowed wider roles to women than would be the case in the later Anabaptist communities.

Women in Swiss Brethren Congregations

Of all the Anabaptist groups, the Swiss Anabaptists most quickly established community guidelines governing the election of pastors and restricting individual action. These guidelines were put in place by the Schleitheim Articles in 1527, slightly more than two years after the first baptisms in Zürich. Nevertheless, within that initial two-year period Swiss Anabaptism manifested many of the "spiritual" characteristics that can be seen also in the South German and North German/Dutch movements.

The first Anabaptist congregation was established in the village of Zollikon, just three kilometres from Zürich. While all of those involved in the first stage of the movement were men, very soon women joined the movement in large numbers. Margret Hottinger testified that "when Grebel and Mantz had come to them in Zollikon and read to them and spoken to them about these things, no one had yet been baptized, until Blaurock came; he was the first to begin baptizing."[1] George Blaurock was a charismatic, fiery leader who based his baptizing ministry on a direct call from God.[2] In the early phases of the movement in Switzerland, direct calling from God and individual proclamation and action were the rule, not the exception.

In April of 1525 the Zürich authorities sent an official to Zollikon to collect fines from those who had been rebaptized. He reported that he had encountered a group of very angry and stubborn women. The wife of the local overseer had been rebaptized, but she refused to pay her fine saying that she would wait until the others had paid. While she was refusing to pay, an older woman standing nearby joined the discussion: "If I," she said, "were involved in this thing like the others, then we women would stick together and we would see if we had to pay the fine or not." She continued for some time to give the official a tongue lashing "with many nasty words." The wives of Wishans Hottinger and Jacob Unholtz "spoke evil and shameful words" to the official, "as if milords were doing them an injustice; they also refused to answer whether they intended to pay their fines or not." After some resistance, Regula Lochman finally did give something as security on her fine, but Elsy Lochman refused to pay. So did Elsy Boumgartner, who added a common reproach of the peasants that "God created the earth for her as much as for milords."[3]

Although there was very active involvement of many women in the early Anabaptism of Zollikon, there is no evidence that these women took on "official" leadership roles within the congregation. Leadership in preaching, baptizing, and presiding over the Lord's Supper was exercised by men in all the recorded testimonies. Nevertheless, it is safe to say that the Anabaptist women of Zollikon were involved in more informal proselytization for the movement; they were not reticent in expressing their views!

One young woman from Zollikon, Margret Hottinger, stood out for her zeal and determination; she appears to have exercised some prophetic gifts as well.[4] She came from a family of religiously radical farmers and artisans. Her uncle, Klaus Hottinger, was an early partisan supporter of Zwingli's reforms, and a close friend and confederate of Conrad Grebel.[5] After being banished from Zürich in November 1523 for destroying a public crucifix, he was arrested and martyred in March 1524, in Catholic Lucerne. Heinrich Bullinger lauded Klaus Hottinger as the "first martyr" of the evangelical faith in Switzerland.[6] Klaus' brother Jakob, Margret's father, is described in one testimony as an "old, bearded peasant." He also was involved early in reforming agitation, with at least two documented cases of public argumentation with clergy.[7] Jakob also was close to Conrad Grebel, and it was no surprise when he was in the first group to be arrested in Zollikon for being an Anabaptist. Jakob Hottinger was a peasant farmer, but he could read German, and he functioned as one of the leaders of the Zollikon Anabaptist group; two of his sons were baptized before February 1525 and Margret shortly received baptism as well.[8]

In November 1525 Margret Hottinger was arrested also as part of a general crackdown by the Zürich authorities. The list of prisoners sentenced on November 18 reads like an early Anabaptist "who's who": Conrad Grebel, Felix Mantz, George Blaurock, Michael Sattler, Ulrich Teck, Martin Linck, *and Margret Hottinger*. Michael Sattler and Martin Linck, both notable leaders later on, demonstrated at this time much less determination than did Margret: they swore oaths that they would desist from rebaptism, and were released from prison. Margret, on the other hand, refused to recant and was imprisoned in the tower along with the rest of the "stubborn ones."[9] Margret was still in prison in March of the next year; when questioned and urged to recant, her testimony was even stronger: the court scribe noted that Margret held that whoever opposed adult baptism "such a one is a child of the devil."[10]

The following day the court pronounced sentence on a large group of recalcitrant Anabaptists, Margret among them.

> [The prisoners are] to be placed together in the New Tower and are to be given nothing more than bread and water to eat, and straw to lay upon. And the guard who watches them must swear an oath not to allow anyone in or out. Thus let them die in the tower. Let it be so until one is willing to desist from opinion and error and be obedient.[11]

But finally, after six months of harsh imprisonment Margret, along with a group of other Anabaptists, agreed to a recantation written by some court official. It read:

> Margret Hottinger confesses that she erred; she holds infant baptism to be correct and rebaptism to be useless and incorrect. She asks milords that they be merciful to her and do the best; she wishes to be obedient to them from now on. The judgement was read to her, and she accepted it. Done this first day of May, 1526.[12]

In spite of this recantation, Margret Hottinger was not yet done with "rebaptism," nor did she display much "obedience" to the authorities in her subsequent activity.

Sometime later in 1526 Margret travelled to neighbouring St. Gall, in the company of her brother Jakob Hottinger (the younger). Johannes Kessler of St. Gall described Margret in a remarkable, if hostile, vignette in his chronicle, the *Sabbata*.

> There arose wild and arrogant error through the women of the Anabaptists, particularly one young woman from Zollikon in the canton of Zürich named Margret Hottinger ... who lived a disciplined way of life, so that she was deeply loved and respected by the Anabaptists. She went so far as to claim that she was God. And many other Anabaptists believed this and defended it against opponents, protecting and sustaining it with the words of Christ, 'Have you not

read in the law, you are gods, etc.' [John 10:34]. And also: Whoever keeps my commandments abides in me and I in him, etc. [John 15:10]. Moreover, this Margret forgave and absolved the sins of those praying and would say nothing about it nor give further judgment, but abide by the words. Following that she undertook to speak of things that nobody could understand, as if she were so deeply raised up in God that nobody could comprehend her speech, and then began to say, 'Is it not written, cursed is he who is hung upon a cross?' [Galatians 3:13]. But still [she] would say nothing further to anyone. She lived an austere life and overcame many obstacles, so that many of her followers declared that whoever speaks the most or can do the unusual which nobody can comprehend or evaluate, those were held to be the most devout and most immersed in God.[13]

Even allowing for undeniable hyperbole and exaggeration on Kessler's part (it is highly doubtful, for example, that Margret claimed to be God!), still the picture emerges of a charismatic and prophetic young woman who exercised considerable influence among the early Swiss Anabaptists. Kessler reported further on other prophetic activities and pneumatic manifestations on the part of Anabaptist women in St. Gall in 1526—a story which cannot be told here.[14] Suffice it to say, however, that in the first two years of the Anabaptist movement in Switzerland, appeals to the Holy Spirit as well as spiritual manifestations among Anabaptist women were not uncommon.[15]

The Schleitheim Articles of 1527 mark a turning point in Swiss Anabaptism. The preface notes that "A very great offence has been introduced by some false brothers among us, whereby several have turned away from the faith, thinking to practice and observe the freedom of the Spirit and of Christ."[16] In light of events in St. Gall in 1526, these words appear to be directed in the first instance against unbridled pneumatic manifestations of the kind Kessler describes. Among other things, the Schleitheim Articles now prescribe how leadership among the Swiss congregations is to be structured: the "shepherd" of the church must be a morally upright person (1 Timothy 3:7); the shepherd will preside in the congregation in reading, exhortation, teaching, warning, admonishing; in prayer and the Lord's Supper.

Clearly there was no thought of electing a woman to such a position: "*He* shall be supported ... by the congregation which has chosen him," say the Schleitheim Articles.[17] There is further evidence that corroborates this early exclusion of women from official leadership posts in the Swiss congregations following Schleitheim. At his trial in December 1529, Konrad Winckler (who had baptized a large number of women into the movement) testified that "it was forbidden for women to teach and to baptize."[18] And of course, there is no mention of "prophecy" nor any place given in the

Schleitheim Articles to ecstatic utterance. It appears that the charismatic leadership of women such as Margret Hottinger was marginalized, if not negated completely, by the year 1527 in Swiss Anabaptism.

The tension between prophetic egalitarianism and Pauline "church order" is evident in Balthasar Hubmaier's "Theses against Eck," written in September 1524. One would expect this to be the case, given Hubmaier's understanding that the Holy Spirit "comes with the Word." Nevertheless Hubmaier initially seemed to lean toward granting women an equal pneumatic status. Hubmaier's first thesis against Eck reads "Every Christian is obligated to give account for his hope and thereby of the faith which is in him to whoever desires it."[19] That "every Christian" might be read to include women is suggested by two subsequent theses. Thesis 17 reads *"All persons* may prophesy one by one, so that everyone may learn and all may receive encouragement; thesis 21 reads similarly: "In this spiritual combat *everyone* must apply himself to prophesy and be armed with the armor of the Holy Spirit..."[20] But Hubmaier clarifies in thesis 22 that there are gender limits on such prophecying in the congregation: "In this gathering women shall be silent and at home they should learn from their husbands..."[21] Having said this, however, Hubmaier enters an interesting caveat.

> But where the men are afraid and have become women, then the women should speak up and become manly, like Deborah, Hulda, Anna the prophetess, the four daughters of the evangelist Philip, and in our times Argula.[22]

In his early pre-Anabaptist writings, Hubmaier already relied on the Pauline texts calling for women not to speak in the congregation, but at the same time he encouraged women to step forward prophetically in cases of need.

Writing three years later Hubmaier called on early church examples in describing a further teaching role for women in the congregation.

> One article among others of the Seventh council at Carthage, held by the Latins, Africans, Europeans, and others, provided that the widows and nuns, who were endowed for that reason, were elected to the office and ministry of women. They should teach the women the art of writing and in addition should instruct the uneducated farmers' wives as to the time at which the girl catechumens should be admitted to baptism, how they should answer the baptismal minister, and then how they should live after baptism.[23]

Although Hubmaier says no more about this educative role for women in his writings, it appears that he was ready to allow women a restricted teaching function in his congregations—at least in theory. There is no evidence of the actual implementation of female catechists in his churches.

There is only one other reference by Hubmaier pertaining to the role of women in the congregation. In outlining the practice of the Lord's Supper in 1527, Hubmaier repeated his earlier citation of Paul: "Let women keep silence in the congregation. If they want to learn anything, they should ask their husbands at home, so that every-thing takes place in orderly fashion, 1 Corinthians 11; 14."[24] The evidence from Hubmaier's writings leads to the conclusion that, apart from exceptional cases when women are to become prophetically "manly," and with the exception of a possible catechetical role for qualified women in the congregation, Hubmaier allows women no leadership possibilites. Hubmaier's earlier calls for prophetic utterance and the his-torical teaching role of women in the church are not mentioned again in his Nicholsburg writings.

Although the movement from pneumatic enthusiasm to the congregational election of male leaders took place among the Swiss in only two years (1525-1527), the same general pattern would be repeated over a longer span of time elsewhere in the Anabaptist movement, for the same basic reasons: direct spiritual revelations and pneumatic manifestations came under suspicion, and were replaced by the rev-elation of written Scripture, interpreted by a male leadership. And as Anabaptist groups moved steadily away from spiritualism toward biblicism, the words of Paul came ever more into play. The diminished role of women in Anabaptist congregations was thus roughly proportional to the victory of letter over spirit in Anabaptism.

Nevertheless, it would be a mistake to overstate the inequality of the undeni-ably patriarchal congregational polity outlined at Schleitheim. In spite of the exclu-sively male leadership outlined at Schleitheim, women were granted considerable disciplinary authority as members of the congregation. According to Schleitheim, the *congregation* was to have the final say over the pastor: if a shepherd does something "worthy of reprimand" which is confirmed by two or three witnesses, shepherds are to be disciplined. Women were not excluded from excercising this disciplining func-tion. In the second place, there are individual cases of informal female "leadership" that continue among the Swiss Brethren, particularly instances of active proselytization. In a spectacular example of such activity, Margaret Hellwart was so active in persuading other women to join the movement that frustrated local authori-ties chained her to the floor of her house.[25] And finally, there was banishment, impris-onment, torture, and martyrdom for Anabaptist men and women alike—the ultimate tests of an individual's commitment to Christ. The final choice of sacrificing one's life was one in which women and men were equally "free."

In 1530, Margret Hottinger paid with her life for her convictions when she was drowned as an Anabaptist. According to one account,

> She was graciously pulled out of the water and asked again to re-cant, but in no way did she wish to do that. Rather she said: "Why did you pull me out? The flesh was almost defeated." With that the judge-ment was carried out [i.e., she was drowned].[26]

The call of the Spirit was heard by men and women alike and led them *individually* to commit their lives to Christ and the "Body of Christ on earth." This individual call of the Spirit may have been dampened, but it was not extinguished by Swiss Brethren congregational polity.

Arrest of Catherine Müller in Zürich, 1637

Women in Tirolean and Moravian Anabaptism

The appeal to a direct and spiritual "call from God" as the basis for preaching, teaching and action was even stronger in Hans Hut's circle than among the Swiss.[27] Systematic examination of the role of women in Hut's movement has only begun, but Linda Huebert Hecht's study of one volume of published court records for the Tirol revealed a high percentage of female participation in the early Anabaptist movement from 1527 to 1529. Out of 455 Anabaptist members who appeared in the court records for these years in Tirol, 210 were women (46%).[28] In this earliest period of Anabaptist growth in Tirol, Hecht counted seven lay leaders, ten lay missioners, and 49 martyrs from among the 210 Anabaptist women identified.[29]

There is good evidence for the proselytizing activity of Anabaptist women in the Tirol in this earliest period, but very little evidence shedding light on the spiritual "calling" of these women because of nature of the surviving evidence.[30] Ursula Binder and her husband had been baptized by Hans Hut, who then sent them to missionize in Salzburg; the court record suggests that she was as active in this as was her husband, but gives no further relevant details.[31] One would like to know more about the woman who, it was reported, said that she had "made six new Christians in a short time," but again no further information is available.[32] Helene von Freyberg (about whom more will be said below), was a member of the lower nobility who used her castle at Münichau to give refuge to Anabaptist preachers and also gathered and led an Anabaptist conventicle there.

Kinship and friendship networks clearly were important in the spread of Anabaptism in the Tirol, with women participating actively in proselytization within those networks and beyond. In several cases the court records name women as "principal baptizers and seducers."[33] However, there really is no compelling evidence that women in the Tirol were involved in the actual baptizing of believers into the movement.[34] Thus the "profile" of involvement by Anabaptist women for this early phase of the Anabaptist movement in Tirol matches closely what we have noted for the Swiss Anabaptists around Zürich: although women do not appear to have performed the "formal" rites of baptizing believers and leading in the Lord's Supper, they made up almost half of the Anabaptist membership and were extremely active in missionizing and proselytization, particularly through their networks of family and friends. As such they were actively sought out for arrest by the Austrian authorities and were all-too-often tortured and martyred along with the men.[35] The records are silent concerning explicit prophetic activity on the part of Tirolean Anabaptist women—whether because there was no such activity, or because the record is deficient is impossible to say.

As persecution increased in the Tirol, and life for Anabaptists became untenable in that land, many fled to Moravia, joining the communal groups that had emerged there. What is significant for our topic is the very different social ethos encountered by the Tirolean refugees when they entered the Moravian communities, especially the Hutterite communities. The strong emphasis on a biblical "rule of life" necessary to sustain a communal endeavour soon restricted the scope of activity for women.

The implicit contradiction between a democratic theological "ideal" (spiritual equality before God) and a hierarchical (and patriarchal) ordering of the community was nowhere more in evidence than in the Hutterite communities.[36] Spiritual equality was even more strongly stressed by the communal Anabaptists (following in Hut's footsteps), given their emphasis on individual *Gelassenheit* which was expressed concretely in a renunciation of private property and a shared communal life. Paradoxically, this spiritual equality of yieldedness resulted in a highly structured community life ordered by strict legislative guidelines (*Ordnungen*).[37] In establishing the "God-ordained" order for their communities, the Hutterites appealed to familiar biblical examples. In 1545 the Hutterite leader Peter Riedeman wrote in his *Rechenschaft*

(Account of our Religion):

"Since woman was taken from man, and not man from woman, man hath lordship but woman weakness, humility and submission, therefore she should be under the yoke of man and obedient to him, even as the woman was commanded by God when he said to her, "The man shall be thy lord." Now, since this is so she should heed her husband, inquire of him, ask him and do all things with and naught without his counsel. For where she doeth this not, she forsaketh the place in the order in which she hath been set by God, encroacheth upon the lordship of the man and forsaketh the command of her Creator as well as the submission that she promised her husband in the union of marriage."[38]

In this way did "spiritual equality before God" become a practical inequality within the community: men, as those "in whom something of God's glory is seen" were to have compassion on the "weaker vessels" even as men "went before" and exercised spiritual and physical leadership and authority;[39] women, for their part, were to be humble, submissive, and obedient.

Activity within the Hutterite community was, according to later witnesses, strictly segregated, with women working at their own particular tasks. Jakob Christoph Grimmelshausen offered the following description around the middle of the seventeenth century.

> Nowhere did I see men and women together but everywhere each sex was performing its own work apart from the other. I found rooms in which there were only nursing mothers who, without the supervision of men, were abundantly supplied, together with their infant children, with the necessary attention by their sisters. The duty of caring for the nursing mothers and children was committed to the widows alone. Elsewhere I saw over a hundred women with distaffs. One was a washerwoman, another a bed-maker, a third a stable-maid, a fourth, dishwasher, a fifth, linen maid, and so all other also had a particular work to do. . . . Also each sex had a physician and an apothecary...[40]

Women also worked as cooks, nurses and weavers, as well as helping with field work (in charge of gardens, orchards and berry patches). Particularly interesting is the role of women in Hutterite education where a niche was open to them as schoolmistresses.[41] Nevertheless, even here it was suggested that their teaching activities (which were restricted to the youngest children) needed to be supervised and directed by male overseers. Peter Walpot, for example, suggested that "the [male] schoolmaster is to be present ... to give aid and advice to the sisters, for they need your oversight just as much as the children — since women are women and the weaker vessel..."[42]

The patriarchal frame of mind was pervasive in Hutterite community organization, and extended even to the most basic participation in decision making processes: the men alone exercised voting power within the congregation, and excluded women from such votes. Thus, in spite of the "levelling" appearance of communities which held "all things in common," the Hutterites were even less "egalitarian" than were the Swiss.[43]

The one area in which women had exercised considerable initiative and leadership in the early Tirolean period, that is as lay leaders, missioners, and proselytizers, also was closed to them once they joined the Hutterite community—if the extant documentation tells anything like the full story. The Hutterites were the most active "missionaries" of all the Anabaptist groups, but their systematic and extensive activities were to be undertaken by duly appointed and commissioned men.[44] Occasionally the "duly appointed men" would be accompanied by their wives on missionary journeys, but the work of proselytization does not appear to have been shared equally by men and women.[45] In short, leadership within the Hutterite church and community was in exclusively male hands; individual choice for women remained in the initial commitment to baptism and the community, in the freedom to leave "unbelieving" spouses (as will be noted in the following chapter), and in the ultimate testimony of martyrdom.

Women in Pilgram Marpeck's Communities

The communities led by Pilgram Marpeck were notable for the active roles taken by several remarkable women, among them Anna Marpeck, Helene von Freyberg, Magdalena Marschalk von Pappenheim, Walpurga von Pappenheim, Kunigunda Schneider, and Anna Schmidt. Marpeck never spoke explicitly concerning the "proper" role of women in his congregations, but the evidence suggests that certain women in his circle exercised their leadership and teaching skills.[46] This is particularly true of two noble women who were part of that circle: Magdalena von Pappenheim and Helene von Freyberg.[47] It may be that their status as aristocratic women—unusual in the Anabaptist movement—allowed them more freedom of action than was the norm.

Magdalena Marschalk von Pappenheim was born into an aristocratic South German family descended from an imperial *Hofmarschall*; in the sixteenth century the von Pappenheims were manorial lords of Kalden.[48] At an unknown date Magdalena entered the Benedictine convent at Urpring in Swabia, near the city of Ulm, but by 1541 she had left the convent and was in correspondence with both Pilgram Marpeck and the aristocratic Silesian spiritualist, Caspar Schwenckfeld von Ossig. With Magdalena acting as go-between, Marpeck and Schwenckfeld intitiated a correspondence in which they attempted to convince each other—along with Magdalena, Helene von Freyberg, Helena Streicher and others—of the correctness of their respective views. Magdalena von Pappenheim and Helene von Freyberg sided with Marpeck and took the Anabaptist position in the controversy. Both women initiated correspondence and participated actively in the theological discussion. Magdalena continued to be a part of the Marpeck circle: two letters written by Marpeck to her, dated 1545 and 1547, have survived.[49]

It is not known when Magdalena died, but by 1571 her niece, Walpurga von Pappenheim, noted that both Magdalena and Pilgram Marpeck had passed to their final rest. Walpurga von Pappenheim was Magdalena's niece, and also a part of the Marpeck circle. In 1571 she copied and corrected Marpeck's lengthy answer to Caspar Schwenckfeld (the *Verantwortung*), using a manuscript bequeathed to her by Magdalena—a task that, as Walpurga noted in the margin, she did "for the sake of God's glory." Walpurga's manuscript has been preserved to this day.[50] Walpurga also is known to us as a hymn writer: hymn 75 of the *Ausbund* is attributed to her—the only hymn in the collection explicitly credited to a female composer.[51] Another relative, Sophia von Bubenhofen, born Marschalkin von Pappenheim, is known to have been part of the Marpeck Anabaptist circle.[52]

Helene von Freyberg was a member of the lower nobility in the Tirol. She was baptized into the Anabaptist movement in 1527, but unlike the majority of Tirolean Anabaptists, her path did not lead to the Hutterite communities in Moravia. Her family lived near Kitzbühel at Münichau, and there were early family connections with the Marpeck family: in 1491 her father bought "mining and grazing rights" from Heinrich Marpeck, father of Pilgram Marpeck. Perhaps because of this early family connection Helene had continuing contact with Pilgram Marpeck after both Pilgram and Helene had been forced to flee the Tirol for being Anabaptists. Although both Pilgram Marpeck and Helene were introduced to Anabaptism in the Tirol by followers of Hans Hut, their respective paths of exile led to the South German territories to the north-west, rather than to the Moravian territories to the north-east.

From the beginning Helene took initiatives appropriate to her station in life: by 1528 the authorities had received word that she had been baptized and that her home was a centre of Anabaptist activity. Helene's "castle church" at Münichau was active from the Fall of 1527 to December 1529, when a recanting Anabaptist furnished the necessary incriminating evidence against her. When orders for her arrest came down, Helene fled, finding refuge in the city of Constance in 1530. There she continued to host Anabaptist meetings in her home and to maintain contact with Marpeck, who now was in Strasbourg. Her activities were too much for the civic authorities at Constance, and she was dispossessed and exiled as an Anabaptist in 1532. After a time back in the Tirol, during which she offered a private recantation, she left her homeland for good, settling in Augsburg where she lived the last eleven years of her life. While at Augsburg she continued to host small Anabaptist meetings in her home and took an active role with Magdalena von Pappenheim, as noted above, in the dispute between Marpeck and Schwenckfeld. In 1542 it came to light that she had led her tailor, Hans Jacob Schneider, into the Anabaptist faith; we may assume that his was no isolated case. He later became a central Anabaptist leader in Augsburg and also an associate of Pilgram Marpeck. Helene passed to her final rest in 1545.

Although there are no "typical" instances of women's participation in Anabaptism, the cases of Magdalena von Pappenheim and Helene von Freyberg are especially unusual because of the sustained leadership they undertook, even if that leadership was at the "informal" level. Their aristocratic status undoubtedly gave them more political space than was granted to commoners—the political authorities proceeded more carefully with the nobility, as the case of Schwenckfeld demonstrates. Their noble standing—unusual within the movement as a whole—also may have had something to do with their readiness to assume leadership within the movement. God may have been no respecter of persons, but within the Anabaptist family of "communities of saints," noble birth seems to have lent a stronger voice to women. Perhaps it was no accident that these noble women were attracted to Pilgram Marpeck's Anabaptist communities, rather than to the "communities of artisans" that had been established in Moravia.

Women in the Melchiorite Movement

Nowhere in the Anabaptist movement did women achieve and maintain as lofty a pastoral and leadership role as in the Strasbourg Melchiorite community. As noted above, Hoffman distinguished four roles for members of his congregations, namely those of Apostles, Prophets, Pastors, and Regular members. It was in the second category that a place of leadership open to women was "institutionalized" in Hoffman's congregations.[53] Although no female "apostles" are known to us, it was quite otherwise in the leadership category of "prophets." Of the 18 active prophets in Hoffman's community, 8 were women.[54] Lois Y. Barrett was able to find no explicit theological justification for the involvement of women in these positions, apart from Hoffman's citing of Joel 2:28-29 and Acts 2:17-18: "In the last days ... I will pour out my Spirit upon all flesh, and your sons and your daughters shall prophesy..."[55] Given Hoffman's conviction that he was living in the Last Days such scriptural justification undoubtedly was considered self-evident and not requiring further proof.

Two of the most prominent of all the prophets in Strasbourg were Ursula Jost, whose visions have been described above, and Barbara Rebstock. Ursula is perhaps the best known because of the publication of her visions in 1530; beyond this, however, we do not know much more about her; she died sometime between 1530 and 1537.[56] Barbara Rebstock, on the other hand, seems to have been considered by contemporaries the more important of the two prophetesses. She was widely renowned for her prophetic powers. In November of 1534 Melchior Hoffman testified that "Hannß Rebstock's wife from Eßlingen [Barbara] is a leading prophetess of all the [Melchiorites]."[57] In a testimony dating from April 1534, Franz from Hazebrouck in Flanders testified that he had been baptized in Münster by Bernhard Rothmann. He had come to Strasbourg specifically to see Barbara. The court reporter noted that "He had heard of her in the Netherlands, how she performed wonders, and therefore he had come to see her."[58]

Barbara also led regular gatherings in her place of residence in the "Kalbgasse." In 1533 the Strasbourg authorities identified four people within the city who were holding "special meetings." Two of the four were women: the "prophetess in the Kalbgasse" (Barbara Rebstock), and "Schenken's wife."[59] And, as will be noted in the following chapter, Barbara also pronounced against the bigamy of Claus Frey, and admonished him to return to his first wife. It is thus abundantly clear that Barbara Rebstock exercised direct leadership in the Strasbourg Melchiorite congregation, not only through visions and prophecies, but also as an inspired counsellor and teacher. The cases of Ursula Jost and Barbara Rebstock demonstrate again how—under certain conditions—sixteenth century gender barriers could be overcome in the Anabaptist movement by demonstrations of spiritual inspiration. What was remarkable about Barbara Rebstock in particular was the long-term pastoral leadership and counsel she continued to provide to the Strasbourg Melchiorite community, as will be seen below.

Melchior Hoffman's openness to female prophetic leadership was not transferred wholesale to the Netherlands; although there were also some notable prophetesses in the north, their activity took place mostly in the pre-Münsterite period.[60] The institutionalized avenue open to Ursula Jost and Barbara Rebstock was considerably restricted in the Münsterite context. Although there were also some instances of prophetic inspiration and initiative in Münster on the part of women—the case of Hille Feicken[61] would come to mind—the prevailing theology and mood in the "New Jerusalem" was patriarchal and restrictive. Bernhard Rothmann wrote: "God has placed the woman below the man, that she be submissively obedient to her husband and honour him, and follow and hear him only."[62] This attitude culminated in a male-dominated polygamy, justified in Old Testament biblical terms.

This patriarchal attitude was carried forth by David Joris after the fall of Münster, although he numbered many women in his following.[63] Joris was concerned—in matters of marriage as well as in general terms—that men reassert leadership and that women take a subservient place in the community of saints.[64] Joris liked to advise men to "let your beards grow."[65] He wrote to the Melchiorites in Strasbourg:

> The wife should listen to her husband, and she must follow him. Just like the husband must hear and follow the Lord, Christ. This is God's will. If he follows her, he castrates himself and loses his beard. He thereby dishonors God's glory and despises his order. He becomes effeminate and is called a woman. For he is one with the wife, which is not proper for a true Christian man. This has gone on so long, and still does among most Christians, not to mention those of the world who act like women. But God will not bear this any longer, but desires that they become like men. This will be a new thing upon the earth. As it is written.[66]

How would such teaching concerning men and women be heard in the original Melchiorite setting (Strasbourg), and by Barbara Rebstock, whose husband clearly occupied a spiritual role second to hers in the congregation? The question came to a head in 1538, when David Joris came to Strasbourg in an effort to convince the Melchiorite "elders" of his prophetic and leadership authority.[67] One of those elders was Barbara Rebstock.

On the morning of the first day of meetings, David Joris made a concerted effort to impress the Strasbourg Melchiorites. He assumed what can charitably be called a bullying manner: "Christ counselled us to leave ourselves. . . . Now I ask, have you taught and understood all of this well? If not, then learn from me in his name."[68] Jan Pont, speaking for the group, was reluctant to step aside to "be taught" unconditionally by Joris, but he appeared to be wavering. Joris pressed his point repeatedly, and concluded with a challenge: "Do you now know well the fear of the Lord—humility, meekness, longsuffering, friendliness, mercy, chastity, truth, simplicity and innocence? Even more, do you have them? Give now your answer."[69]

A long silence fell on the gathering which was broken by none other than Barbara Rebstock. This "caused a disorder" since, Joris noted, "she prevented the answer which they were now supposed to give." An argument ensued over whether she should be allowed to speak at all. Barbara said "Might I too speak a word? For my spirit impels me." Jan Pont answered "Yes, since the Spirit impels you, why should you not speak?"

> **Barbara:** I will proceed as the Lord has uttered to me. I think that some who are here desire to pluck the fruits of our tree before they are ripe. Therefore the Lord warns us that no one speak further, for they will account for it.
>
> **David:** Do you speak this by the Lord?
>
> **Barbara:** I am compelled to do so.
>
> **David** (spoke to the brothers): I ask you if I have spoken against the truth. Give me an answer. I ask you, Barbara, if you know indeed what I have said and if you understand me.
>
> **Barbara:** No, I firmly believe that it is still necessary to talk further about it. For we have been of the fear of the Lord for over ten years, do you believe that we are godless?
>
> **David:** Now I can say that you have not spoken from the Lord, but from the devil. For you have interrupted our speeches here and have thus disturbed the Spirit (by hindering the answer)...
>
> **Jan Pont:** ... But she is of such a mind that it is necessary to speak of this matter. For she has been of the fear of the Lord for many years. Therefore she has not needed such rebuke.
>
> **David** (stood right up and spoke to the brothers): I say to you, that you are not small nor poor, but your understanding is veiled, so that you do not see. I would be pleased to let you know how you might serve God further. But the will of Satan has its way, for he comes to disturb the Spirit and to plug the ears of the oppressed by the serpent's deception. . . . See, I warn you that you not let yourselves be misled. Men, regard yourselves above the women, then you will not be deceived. Understand correctly.[70]

This remarkable exchange puts into sharpest focus the high esteem in which the Strasbourg congregation held Barbara Rebstock's prophetic counsel; her continuing leadership in that congregation is beyond dispute. Her position of leadership in the congregation was secured by Melchior Hoffman's institutionalization of the prophetic office, which was open to men and women alike, and depended only on the prophetic gifts of the individual in question. David Joris, on the other hand, was primarily working to cement his own prophetic authority as the "third David." His views on the necessary subordination of women served that purpose well enough; but in fact, he had no place for "prophets" of *either* gender who did not bow to his authority. Nevertheless, given his views on the "proper" subordinate role of women, it must have been particularly galling to Joris to have his authority undermined by a woman "speaking in the Spirit." Joris' concluding diatribe, with its references to the serpent and Satan (thus heakening back to the Genesis account, and Eve's role in the "Fall"), summed up his frustration in unmistakable biblical language: had Barbara not intervened, he might well have swayed the "bearded" leadership in Strasbourg.

Women in Menno Simons' Movement

While the Strasbourg Melchiorites and David Joris disagreed about the gender limits of the prophetic office, Menno simply denied Melchior Hoffman's "prophetic office" to men and women alike. Not surprisingly, in light of the prophetic disasters that occurred in the 1530s, Menno turned resolutely to Christ and the letter of Scripture, to be interpreted by duly called preachers and teachers. Menno's denial of prophetic authority was a qualified one for as we have seen above in Menno's debate with David Joris, the fundamental call to preach and teach had to come, in the final analysis, directly from God. Nevertheless, Menno left no room in the church for Melchiorite "prophets," male or female.

Menno taught the "biblical submission" of women to their husbands "in all reasonable things," but did not belabour the point; rather he wrote as though the matter were self-evident.[71] Menno, Betti Erb has noted, "cannot be considered a champion of women."

> Some of his writings suggest that women are equal in every way and must live responsibly before God every bit as much as men. Other passages give evidence of a conviction that biology determines function: that men are authoritatively superior to women who in turn surrender their wills to their menfolk and that women, excluded from leadership in spiritual matters, should live inconspicuously, create a pleasant home atmosphere, and concentrate on motherhood. . . . The female, as the well-known argument went, had been first to disobey God and women thereafter have paid with their position of subordination.[72]

Menno's stance was buttressed by his erroneous understanding of the woman's "passive" role in biological procreation: men provide the fertile seed of regeneration; women (so he believed) are the passive "fertile fields," but contribute nothing essential to the process.[73] All this aside, Betti Erb notes that Menno's writings give evidence of a warmly pastoral concern for women, even if the patriarchal and patronizing attitudes of the age also are much in evidence.

Menno's closing of the prophetic office to men and women alike certainly eliminated a potential position of leadership for women such as had been exercised in the early Melchiorite movement by Ursula Jost, Barbara Rebstock and others. Certainly the progression away from the prophetic office to a more literal biblicism had the effect of restricting pastoral and leadership possibilities for women.[74] Nevertheless there is evidence that women continued to exercise informal leadership in the Mennonite setting, as they did also in the rest of the later Anabaptist movement. The case of Elisabeth Dirks, who appears to have functioned as such a leader, is well-known to readers of the *Martyrs Mirror*.[75] In some cases women were better-educated than their husbands and were able to give them help in reading Scripture.[76] Women in the north also became notable hymn writers. Soetjen Gerrits of Rotterdam, who was blind, composed an entire book of hymns that was published in Haarlem in 1592; the hymns of Vrou Gerrets of Medemblick also were published together in 1607.[77] Numerous individual hymns composed by Dutch Anabaptist women also were sung, collected, and printed.[78] Finally, it was among the descendants of Menno that the office of "deaconess" was established. Elisabeth Dirks may have been an early deaconess (although the evidence is not conclusive); by 1632, however, the office was established well enough that the ninth article of the Dordrecht Confession, section 5, described the pastoral duties of women chosen to be deaconesses.[79]

Conclusion

In spite of the preliminary and incomplete nature of this study we may still draw some general conclusions concerning equality in the Anabaptist community of saints. One must agree with Linda Huebert Hecht's observation that "at no time was the ideal of full equality achieved" in the Anabaptist movement.[80] At the same time it must be noted that within the sixteenth century social context, full gender equality was hardly a live option for the Anabaptists or anyone else. The question is not how well or badly the Anabaptists measure up to our current ideas about the equality of men and women, but rather, how Anabaptist theological principles worked themselves out in the sixteenth century social context.

In its broadest outlines a fundamental tension can be seen within Anabaptism because of the crucial role played by the Holy Spirit in "calling" men and women *alike* to lives of costly discipleship. The initial call of the Spirit was never considered to be gender-specific; furthermore, the Spirit was to accompany believers throughout their walk on the narrow way "in this world," right up to the moment of death. How then did it come to be decided that it was beyond the power of the Spirit to call women to preach, teach, or baptize? How was the Spirit restricted to calling men alone to "official" leadership positions? Societal norms undoubtedly played important roles here, but part of the answer also was the steady movement away from pneumatic beginnings to increasing reliance on literal Scripture as providing the "rule of life" for the Body of Christ on earth. Although the pouring out of the Spirit upon all of humankind also has scriptural backing, turning to Scripture in search of ecclesiological guidelines appealed to very different texts—Paul's injunctions concerning the proper role of women in the congregation came to the fore, as did the biblical tradition ascribing to Eve the lion's share of the blame for the Fall.[81]

All surviving Anabaptist groups arrived eventually at very similar (paternalistic) leadership structures, with the Swiss maintaining the highest degree of participation by rank and file members. The Hutterite and Mennonite communities, on the other hand, were led by even more restricted groups of male elders. Nevertheless, a crucial part of the Anabaptist story lies in the movement on the way to that eventual church structure, when the tensions between spirit/letter and inner/outer were being worked out.

In the end, societal assumptions about the "proper" role of women and men lent the weight of cultural legitimacy to the establishment of a "biblical" patriarchal church order. But even in the earlier, more pneumatic phases of development there were clear restrictions on the activities of women. There may have been very isolated cases of women baptizing, for example, but such an event (and I have yet to locate one solidly documented case) would have been an extraordinary exception to the general rule. There were gender limits from the very start. Even in Melchior Hoffman's community, it appears that women did not function either as "apostles" or "teachers"; their leadership possibilities were restricted to the prophetic role—although Barbara Rebstock's remarkable ministry certainly expanded the pastoral horizons of that role. But it would be a mistake to characterize early, pneumatic Anabaptism as a "golden age" of pure spiritual equality that opened up the same leadership possibilities for men and women alike. Such was not the case.

At the same time it is evident that the early pneumatic phase of Anabaptist development opened up many more possibilities of direct participation and leadership for women than was the social norm in the sixteenth century, or than would become the norm in later Anabaptism. As individuals called by the Holy Spirit to faith and discipleship, women needed to respond personally to that call; no husband or guardian could take that step.[82] If their faith commitment was threatened by an "unbelieving" spouse, women were free to leave that relationship, as we will see below. Women exercised remarkable "informal" leadership in proselytization, Bible reading (in some cases), in occasional teaching and hymn-writing, and (in the early movement) in prophetic utterance.[83] And finally, women chose of their own volition to suffer imprisonment, torture, and death for their faith. From available figures, a third or more of all Anabaptist martyrs were women. In all of these ways Anabaptist women were empowered to choose for themselves, contravening common societal restrictions on their gender.

End Notes

[1] QGTS, 1, #124, p. 126.

[2] QGTS, 1, #29, p. 39.

[3] QGTS, 1, #69, pp. 76-77.

[4] A. Nüesch and H. Bruppacher, *Das alte Zollikon* (Zurich, 1899), p. 72 correctly identify Margret as the daughter of Jakob Hottinger the elder of Zollikon; Klaus Hottinger of Zürich was therefore her uncle. In 1526 she travelled to St. Gall with her brother, Jakob Hottinger, the younger, of Zollikon. Harder, *Sources*, p. 548, confuses Jakob Hottinger the elder with Jakob the younger, coming to the mistaken conclusion that Margret Hottinger was the sister of Jakob Hottinger the elder and of Klaus Hottinger.

[5] Thomas Schärli, "Die bewegten letzten zwei Jahre im Leben des Niklaus Hottinger, Schuhmacher, von Zollikon, enthauptet zu Luzern 1524," in Emil Walder, et al., eds., *Zolliker Jahrheft, 1984* (Zollikon: Baumann, 1984), p. 28. Bullinger called Klaus a "shoemaker," and praised him as a "wolbeläßner und der religion wol berichter redlicher man." J.J. Hottinger and H.H. Vögeli, eds., *Heinrich Bullingers Reformationsgeschichte*, 3 vols. (Frauenfeld: Ch. Bepel, 1838-1840), vol. I, p. 127.

[6] See Bullinger, *Reformationsgeschichte*, I, pp. 149-51.

[7] In June 1523, Jakob confronted Dr. Lorenz in the Zollikon parish church. See Emil Egli, *Aktensammulng zur Geschichte der Zürcher Reformation in den Jahren 1519-1533* (Zurich, 1879; reprint Nieuwkoop: B. de Graaf, 1973), #369, pp. 133-34. On Jakob's public dispute with Kaspar Großmann in January, 1525, see QGTS, #23, p. 33; translation in Harder, *Sources*, pp. 331-32.

[8] See QGTS, 1, #30; 31, pp. 39-41.

[9] "Concerning Margret Hottinger it is our decision that she be spoken to, and asked whether or not she will persist in rebaptism and the teaching of Grebel, Mantz, etc. And if she persists, she should be placed in the Wellenberg." QGTS, 1, #133, p. 136. Part of her testimony read: "She asked milords that they prove infant baptism to her; if they can prove to her that infant baptism was correct, then she will desist." *Ibid.*, p. 137.

[10] QGTS, 1, #170, p. 177. Testimony of March 5, 1526.

[11] QGTS, 1, #170a, p. 178.

[12] QGTS, 1, #173, p. 183.

[13] See selection of Kessler's *Sabbata* in QGTS, 2, p. 618; translation from Harder, *Sources*, p. 548, with minor changes.

[14] See QGTS, 2, pp. 618-22. Kessler's apologetic intent is clear in his *Sabbata*; it is a source that must be used with care. Nevertheless, he cannot on that account be discredited completely as an historical source, as John Horsch attempted to do. See "An Inquiry into the Truth of Accusations of Fanaticism and Crime Against the Early Swiss Brethren," MQR 8(January, 1934), pp. 18-31.

[15] Agnes Linck of Biel testified in Solothurn in 1528 that she had been baptized in the Spirit; she denied having been instructed by any Anabaptist, but rather she had been instructed "by Christ her Lord." She was literate and confessed to having "instructed" two younger people. See QGTS, 3, #844, 845, 846; #350.

[16] Yoder, *Legacy*, p. 35.

[17] Yoder, *Legacy*, pp. 38-39.

[18] "es sige och den wybern zu leren und zu touffen verbotten." QGTS, 1, p. 313. See Arnold Snyder, "Konrad Winckler: An Early Swiss Anabaptist Missionary, Pastor and Martyr," MQR 64(October, 1990).

[19] Pipkin and Yoder, *Hubmaier*, p. 51.

[20] *Ibid.*, pp. 54; 55. Emphasis mine.

[21] *Ibid.*, p. 56. The texts noted are 1 Corinthians 14:34; 1 Timothy 2:2; Joel 2; 1 Corinthians 11.

[22] *Ibid.* Judges 4-5; 1 Chronicles 34:22ff.; Luke 2:36ff.; Acts 21:9; Acts 18; Deut. 1:28ff. Argula of Grumbach was a Bavarian noblewoman who wrote evangelical pamphlets. See *ibid.*, p. 56, n. 15.

[23] *Ibid.*, p. 273.

[24] *Ibid.*, p. 396.

[25] See Walter Klaassen, "Margaret Hellwart," in Snyder and Hecht, *Profiles*, forthcoming.

[26] QGTS, 2, p. 587.

[27] As noted by Goertz, *Die Täufer*, p. 51.

[28] Hecht, "Faith and Action," pp. 33-34. Hecht is working with Claus-Peter Clasen's figures, as well as her own. Figures from Augsburg from 1526 to 1529 show that 43% of documented Anabaptists were women. This dropped to 29% after 1532. Noted on p. 33. Hecht's evidence is drawn from Grete Mecenseffy, ed., *Quellen zur Geschichte der Täufer, Österreich, II. Teil* (Gütersloh: Gerd Mohn, 1972).

[29] Hecht, "Faith and Action," Table 1, p. 33a.

[30] The colourful information provided by chroniclers in St. Gall is not replicated in the Tirol; the result is a fairly one-dimensional portrait of Tirolean Anabaptist women, based almost exclusively on official court documents.

[31] The evidence is suggestive, but not overwhelming. Cf. Hecht, "Faith and Action," p. 53, with QGTS, 7, p. 26.

[32] QGTS, 7, #330, p. 229. Cf. Hecht, "Faith and Action," p. 56.

[33] Hecht, "Faith and Action," pp. 62ff.

[34] The evidence concerning Peter Egger's one-eyed sister is equivocal; the court record does identify her as someone who is travelling about (with two men) as a missioner and proselytizer, but the reference to "baptizing" in the record is a general one (referring to the three together) that does not single her out. One would think that a woman baptizer would have warranted special mention in the record. Cf. QGTS, 7, #120, p. 119 with Hecht, "Faith and Action," pp. 64-65. "Compelling" evidence would be the testimony of an imprisoned Anabaptist who would identify a woman as the person baptizing. Such evidence did not come to light in this volume of court records.

[35] Women comprised 40% of Anabaptists put to death in the Tirol between 1527 and 1529. Hecht, "Women and Religious Change," p. 61.

[36] Clasen, *Social History*, p. 255. Clasen's lack of gender analysis is critiqued by Julia Roberts, "Hutterite Women in the Sixteenth Century: The Ideal and Aspects of the Reality (unpublished paper, University of Waterloo, 1990), p. 2. Also helpful is Marlene Epp, "Women and Men in the 16th Century Hutterite Community" (unpublished paper, University of Toronto, 1991).

[37] The Hutterite *Chronicle* notes: "So there has to be an order in all areas, for the matters of life can be properly maintained and furthered only where order reigns..." *The Chronicle of the Hutterian Brethren*, vol. 1 (Rifton, N.Y.: Plough Publishing House, 1987), pp. 406-07. Roberts' observation is apropos: "The communalness of Hutterite society ... was not anarchistic or even libertarian in form. Rather, it depended upon a rigid authoritarian structure to maintain order, obedience, and an acceptance of duty. Roberts, "Hutterite Women," p. 5.

[38] Peter Riedeman, *Account of our Religion, Doctrine and Faith* (Rifton, N.Y.: Plough Publishing House, 1970), pp. 98-99.

[39] A man is to "go before his wife and guide her to blessedness." Riedeman, *Account*, p. 101.

[40] Cited in John Horsch, *The Hutterian Brethren, 1528-1931* (republished: Cayley, Alberta: Macmillan Colony, 1985), p. 67.

[41] "Women taught the children, and cared for their biological needs until the age of six, at which point a male schoolmaster furthered their education." Roberts, "Hutterite Women," p. 16; cf. Epp, "Women and Men," pp. 18-19.

[42] John Hostetler, Leonard Gross and Elizabeth Bender, *Selected Hutterian Documents in Translation, 1542-1654* (Philadelphia: Communal Studies Center, Temple University, 1975), pp. 6-7; cited in Roberts, "Hutterite Women," p. 16. The education given to boys was different than the one given to girls, preparing each for different

roles within the community. According to a visitor in 1578, "children remained with their mothers until they were two, at which age they were placed in the school. The girls learned to pray and to read; the boys learned to read and write, and when they grew older they would learn a trade." Cited in Gross, *Golden Years*, p. 39.

43 "None of the leadership positions were open to women nor did they have a voice in filling them as women were not allowed to vote or speak at community meetings." Marlene Epp, "Women and Men," p. 7, with reference to Mary Ault Harada, "Family Values and Child Care During the Reformation Era: A Comparative Study of Hutterites and Some Other German Protestants," (PhD dissertation, Boston University, 1986), p. 130. The practice among modern Hutterites reflects sixteenth century practice: male members nominate potential preachers (all male) who are then chosen by lot. Elders are elected directly by "the voting body," which consists of "the male members of the church." Horsch, *Hutterian Brethren*, p. 148.

44 Riedeman is most explicit: "It is not for all and sundry to take upon themselves such an office, namely that of teaching and baptizing... ...none must take upon himself or accept such power, unless he be chosen properly and rightly by God in his Church and community..." Riedeman, *Account*, p. 80.

45 See Clasen, *Social History*, pp. 215-16. Marlene Epp notes some possible exceptions in "Women and Men, pp. 10-12. Some informal proselytizing may have occurred when women accompanied their husbands on missionary journeys, as in the case of Apollonia, Leonhard Lanzenstiel's wife, who was arrested and drowned in 1539. *Ibid.*, p. 11. Nevertheless, such cases (which are, unfortunately, poorly documented) would have been exceptions, rather than fitting the usual Hutterite pattern.

46 Stephen B. Boyd, *Pilgram Marpeck: His Life and Social Theology* (Durham, N.C.: Duke University Press, 1992), p. 96, n. 132. Marpeck's only explicit remark is equivocal: it reflects the prevailing view of women as "weak members," but notes the positive role they played in proclaiming the good news. In spite of their weakness, says Marpeck in arguing against the spiritualists, Christ chose them to announce the resurrection, and the apostles believed them. Pilgram Marpeck, "A Clear and Useful Instruction," in Klassen and Klaassen, *Writings*, pp. 91-92.

47 On Helene von Freyberg, see Linda Huebert Hecht, "An Extraordinary Lay Leader: the Life and Work of Helene of Freyberg, Sixteenth Century Noblewoman from the Tirol," MQR 66(July, 1992), pp. 312-341; on Helene von Freyberg, as well as on Magdalena, Walpurga, and Sophia von Pappenheim, see the respective chapters devoted to them in Snyder and Hecht, *Profiles of Anabaptist Women*, forthcoming.

48 On Magdalena von Pappenheim, see ME, IV, "Pappenheim," pp. 114-116; Boyd, *Pilgram Marpeck*, pp. 104-106; Williams, *Radical Reformation* (1992), pp. 703-716.

49 For the writings of Marpeck that relate to Magdalena, see Klassen and Klaassen, *Writings*, pp. 376-389; 407-411; 466-483.

50 See Johann Loserth, *Quellen und Forschungen zur Geschichte der oberdeutschen Taufgesinnten im 16. Jahrhundert* (Wien: Fromme, 1929).

51 There is some question whether Walpurga actually composed the hymn in question, since it was published in 1531 in the "Songbook of the Bohemian Brethren." Since the compiler of that songbook, Michael Weisse, in other cases did use hymns composed by others (and did not attribute authorship to them), the possibility remains that Walpurga wrote the hymn. See *Ausbund, Das ist: Etliche schöne Christliche Lieder...* (numerous editions), hymn 75; Philipp Wackernagel, *Das deutsche Kirchenlied*, III, (Leipzig: Teubner, 1870), pp. 290-91; Michael Weisse, *Gesangbuch der Böhmischen Brüder* (1531); Facsimile edition (Kassel: Bärenreiter, 1957); Rudolf Wolkan, *Die Lieder der Wiedertäufer* (Berlin: Behr, 1903; reprint edition Nieuwkoop: B. de Graaf, 1965).

[52] Nothing more is known about Sophia, beyond what can be gathered from a letter preserved by the Marpeck circle. She may well have been a sister or a cousin of Walpurga. See Number 36, *Kunstbuch*. (Page 347 in the Geiser transcription of the Kunstbuch, at the Mennonite Historical Library, Goshen, Indiana).

[53] In light of this one might want to modify slightly Sprunger's statement that "Article IX [of the Dordrecht Confession] on officers in the church for the first time in Mennonite theology made a recognized place for women officers, the deaconesses." Keith L. Sprunger, "God's Powerful Army of the Weak: Anabaptist Women of the Radical Reformation," in Richard L. Greaves, ed., *Triumph over Silence: Women in Protestant History* (Westport, Cn.: Greenwood Press, 1985), p. 51.

[54] See Lois Y. Barrett, "Wreath of glory: Ursula's prophetic visions in the context of Reformation and revolt in southwestern Germany, 1524-1530," (Ph.D. diss., The Union Institute, 1992), p. 202.

[55] *Ibid.*, p. 203.

[56] Ursula's husband, Lienhard, had married again by 1537. See Barrett, "Wreath of glory," pp. 174-75.

[57] *Ibid.*, #617, p. 393. "Hannßen rebstocks haußfrau von Eßlingen, die sei ein hauptprophetin jr aller..."

[58] TA, *Elsass*, 2, #533, p. 300. "und im Niderland von ihr [Barbara] gehört, wie sie wunder thue, darumb sey er auch zu ihr kommen."

[59] TA, *Elsass*, 2, #400, p. 110.

[60] Lois Barrett notes the cases of Bernhartz Maria of Niederrollesbroich, who was a visionary, and Aeffgen Lystyncx of Amsterdam, the latter of whom "organized Anabaptist conventicles at Limmen in 1533 [and] travelled to Münster where she functioned as a prophet for a time." Barrett, "Women's History/Women's Theology," pp. 7-8. Cf. Sprunger, "Army of the Weak," p. 54, n. 39; ME I, pp. 18-19.

[61] Hille Feicken received a "call" to emulate the Old Testament example of Judith. She went forth in an attempt to assassinate the bishop of Münster but was discovered and executed. See Marion Kobelt-Groch's profile of Hille in Snyder and Hecht, *Profiles of Anabaptist Women*, forthcoming.

[62] Stupperich, *Schriften*, p. 262.

[63] See Gary Waite, "Prominent Women Supporters of David Joris," in Snyder and Hecht, *Profiles of Anabaptist Women*, forthcoming.

[64] Joris' view of women's "proselytizing" to unbelievers was interesting in that he assigned them an explicit preliminary role. "Also, let everything in the church be handled under man and woman, so that whoever is not faithful to the Word might be won through the obedience of the good woman's conversation, without having to speak the Word [1 Pet. 3:1-2]. See, all manner of fruit will be produced among us through the conversation of the women; through their humble, honorable ways and obedient ears and hearts. Then let the man come to the fore." Waite, *Writings*, p. 118.

[65] "You men, let your beards grow and your strength increase in Christ which you, in the first Adam, have allowed the woman (your own flesh) to shave off [cf. Judg. 16:4-21; Lev. 19:27]. By this you have lost the seven Spirits of God, namely, the entire strength and power of God in every manner. You have gone the way of Samson, being bound with bands and straps of darkness, and you will be defeated by death, that is certain [Judg. 16:21,30]. Therefore, each of you watch what you are doing." Waite, *Writings*, p. 117.

[66] Waite, *Writings*, p. 162.

[67] See Waite, *Writings*, chapter 7, for a translation of the record of these proceedings.

[68] Waite, *Writings*, p. 199.

[69] Waite, *Writings*, p. 200.

[70] *Ibid.*, pp. 220-201. Also cited in part in Barrett, "Women's History/Women's Theology," pp. 10-12.

[71] In one of the few direct references, Menno says "Be obedient to your husbands in all reasonable things so that those who do not believe may be gained by your upright, pious conversation without the Word, as Peter says." CWMS, p. 383.

[72] Betti Erb, "Reading the Source: Menno Simons on Women, Marriage, Children, and Family, CGR 8(Fall, 1990), p. 302. Cf. CWMS, p. 113.

[73] *Ibid.*, p. 306.

[74] "De radicale reformatie bood in principe meer openheid voor verdergaande veranderingen; het biblicisme blokkeerde echter het ontwikkelen van een nieuwe zienswijze op de positie van de vrouw." A. Jelsma, "De positie van de vrouw," p. 34.

[75] See ME, II, p. 185; *Martyrs' Mirror* (Scottdale, Pa.: Herald Press, 1950), pp. 481-83; retold also in Sprunger, "God's Army of the Weak," pp. 53-54.

[76] "Claesken of Workum (1559) was better educated than her husband who could not read or write, and gave a much better account of her faith before execution. Her prosecutors accused her, because of her good education, of seducing her husband into Anabaptism. Claudine le Vettre's husband, himself a minister of the Word, praised her astonishing knowledge of Scripture. 'For whenever he could not find a passage, he would ask his wife Claudine, who would at once clearly indicate to him what he sought.'" Sprunger, "God's Army of the Weak," p. 59.

[77] See ME, IV, p. 570; ME, II, p. 502. Also the survey of Dutch Anabaptist hymnody in pp. Rosella Reimer Duerksen, "Anabaptist Hymnody of the Sixteenth Century," (unpublished D. Music dissertation, Union Theological Seminary, 1956), pp. 50-64.

[78] As, for instance, the poems of Judith Lubbertsdochter. See ME, III, p. 410. See Sprunger, "God's Army of the Weak," p. 56.

[79] Deaconesses were to "visit, comfort, and take care of the poor, the weak, the afflicted, and the needy, as also to visit, comfort, and take care of widows and orphans; and further to assist in taking care of any matters in the church that properly come within their sphere, according to their best ability." Cited in ME, II, p. 22. See the entire article on "Deaconess," in *ibid.*, pp. 22-25.

[80] Hecht, "Faith and Action," p. 11.

[81] Keith Sprunger's conclusion is essentially correct: "Anabaptism was both legalistic and spiritualistic. Where legalistic doctrines prevailed, Anabaptist women were the quiet sisters; but in communities where the Spirit broke forth abundantly, women grasped many opportunities. Following the heroic Reformation era, the "Mennonite sister" (*Menniste zusje*) settled into an unprominent place in church and home." "God's Army of the Weak," p. 69.

[82] There was no ecclesiological "cuius regio, eius religio" in Anabaptism; the husband or father was not the "ruler" of a woman's conscience or faith.

[83] Future studies need to focus much more on the area of the "informal" leadership of Anabaptist women. It is only by sifting carefully the *individual* stories of Anabaptist women, as they emerge in the court records and other sources, that we will gain an adequate picture of how women actually functioned in the emerging Anabaptist communities. Concentrating only on the later stages, or access of women to the "official" leadership offices—while it is a pressing question currently—misses a crucial and dynamic dimension in the story of Anabaptist women.

Chapter 19

Anabaptist Marriage

Anabaptism required a spiritual commitment with concrete results "in the world." Marriage was not exempt, as Anabaptist writings and court records demonstrate, but rather was re-evaluated as the movement developed. In what follows we will look first to the questions of separation, divorce and remarriage, and will then outline how marriage between Anabaptist believers came to be understood.

Separation, Divorce, and Remarriage

It was not uncommon early in the sixteenth century for Anabaptist women to leave their "unbelieving" spouses, and even their families, in order to be "obedient to God." Although statistics are not available, one has the impression that more Anabaptist men than women left "unbelieving" spouses and families.[1] This very fluid situation called for community guidelines concerning marriage, separation, and remarriage, and these came to be established over time. In the matter of separation for reasons of faith, Anabaptist men and Anabaptist women were considered to be equally "free" on the basis of their higher commitment to Christ, although much internal discussion was generated on what this higher commitment was to mean in practice.

Swiss Anabaptism
The Case of Adelheit Schwarz

The case of Adelheit Schwarz of Watt may be taken as a typical early Swiss Anabaptist case of marital separation.[2] It is unusual only in that we have more documentation in her case than for that of many others.[3] Adelheit Schwarz was married to Balthasar Spilmann and in the year 1529 lived with her husband and their combined family of thirteen children in the Swiss village of Dällikon, near Zürich. In the Spring of 1529 she came to the notice of the Zürich authorities because of her attendance at an Anabaptist "reading," at which there were a number of other women present. As a result she was arrested but soon released again: she had not yet accepted adult baptism. Nevertheless, it was soon reported that she was no longer attending the state church. In December of 1529 Adelheit was arrested again, along with eleven other women and an equal number of men. Some of these women eventually were subjected to torture with thumb screws in an effort to extract information from them, but to no avail. Adelheit remained in prison with her Anabaptist friends for a little more than a year, even though she still had not been baptized with water: when questioned she said that she still did not know what God's will was concerning baptism. She was finally released in the second week of January, 1530, on her promise to be "obedient" to the authorities.

Sometime in the next year, Adelheit did accept baptism and took the drastic step of leaving her family. We know this because in March of 1531, Balthasar Spilmann appeared in "marriage court" in Zürich, asking for a divorce from Adelheit. She was, he said, an Anabaptist who had twice been arrested. She had borne him seven children. But one night she had packed some things and left, and he did not know where she was. He wished to divorce her, he said, because he had to care for his thirteen children, and he needed a wife for that purpose! He had suffered much with Adelheit, but to no avail. The court told him to be patient, but gave him a letter setting forth the facts in the case. He was to find his wife and ask her to appear before the court, with safe conduct, so that the court could hear both sides in the case.

On April 27, Balthasar Spilmann was back before the court. He said that he had made inquiries and had located Adelheit, and had then sent a daughter to fetch her. Adelheit had come back with the girl, and had stayed overnight, but had left again immediately. And although he had shown her the letter from the court, and had asked her to appear with him before the judges, she had said insulting things and would not agree. She said furthermore that "she wished to be obedient to God, and not to the earthly authorities" (Acts 5:29). Two days later the court granted Balthasar a divorce from Adelheit. We know little more about Adelheit or her family, except that a testimony from 1548 still names her as a worshipping member of the Anabaptist community north of Zürich.[4]

Adelheit's appeal to Acts 5:29 as the justification for leaving her husband and family was commonly accepted among Anabaptists as legitimate cause (applying equally to men and women) for such separations: One's highest obedience is due to God, not human beings. This raised the question, however, of divorce and remarriage for those who had left "unbelieving" marriage partners and had joined Anabaptist communities. Was the "spiritual marriage" to Christ something that negated a "natural" marriage that had been contracted before repentance and conversion?

The tract "On Divorce"

The Swiss spoke early to this matter, as reference to the tract "On Divorce" (before 1533) reveals.[5] The guidelines concerning separation, divorce, and remarriage were based primarily on Jesus' words in Matthew 5:31-32. The tract notes that "we do not permit that one divorce ... unless it be for fornication, i.e. because of adultery. . . . He who divorces without fornication, the only reason, and remarries, commits adultery..."[6] Nevertheless, the Swiss tract offers the interpretation that if the partner of a believer has committed adultery, this act is a *de facto* divorce and "one who finds herself thereby divorced may now marry, whom she will, only let it be in the Lord..."[7] The tract goes on to note that although believers may well be "pressed and driven out" by unbelieving spouses, this fact does not constitute a "divorce" or grounds for remarriage.

The Swiss Brethren tract on divorce stated emphatically that a separation that comes about because of the faith is part of the test of discipleship which believers may expect. On a more positive note, the tract went on to emphasize the "higher" spiritual marriage of believers with Christ and the ascetic renunciation that must accompany that higher "marriage."[8] The strong emphasis on the spiritual marriage of believers to Christ—a bond that outweighs all earthly commitments—would remain a central principle underlying the conception of marriage for both men and women in all Anabaptist groups. The stronger emphasis on "spiritual marriage" in the Melchiorite tradition is undeniable, as will be seen below, but in the context of the Anabaptist movement as a whole, it was a difference in degree, not a difference in kind.

The principles outlined were clear enough; they all referred to New Testament scriptural passages. But only by examining the court records with care can we know how they were in fact implemented. Although careful work on this question is still being done, it is clear from the Swiss court records that there were numerous anomalies that did not fit the "ideal" prescriptions outlined in the tract on divorce. For example, in October 1543, Margaret von Ringgenberg (near Interlaken in Bernese territory) told the court that she had married Ulli Bucher eight years before. He had become an Anabaptist, had left her six years ago (ca. 1537), and had taken another wife, as he himself had told her four years previous (ca. 1549). She testified that she had behaved honourably. The court decided to announce the suit, wait a month, and then grant her a divorce if nothing had changed.[9] Further details are not known, but on the face of it, Ulli Bucher's behaviour toward his wife did not fit the ideal prescribed for Swiss Anabaptist behaviour concerning separation, divorce, and remarriage.[10] There was an undeniable tension that arose for Anabaptists in "mixed marriage" situations. The evidence suggests that Anabaptist groups made serious attempts to resolve these questions, although not always successfully.[11]

From preliminary work in the court records, it appears that the problem of marital separation was handled in various *ad hoc* ways in the early, more chaotic years of the movement. Marital separation, however, became particularly pressing when set communities formed, and the boundaries between "church" and "world" were patently visible, as they became in the Hutterite communities, or when stronger community boundaries were established by strict banning practices, as can be noted among the Dutch beginning in the 1550s. In these cases the question of cohabitation with an "unbelieving" spouse threatened the "pure" nature of the closed community.

Hutterite Practice

In the Hutterite tradition, marital separation was particularly contentious because of the requirement that Hutterites live in community, governed by the rules of that community. What then was to be done with the unbelieving spouse and family of a believer? In 1567 some Swiss Brethren wrote a lengthy letter to the Hutterites in which, among other things, they accused the Hutterites of breaking up marriages. In his reply, Peter Walpot argued that mixed marriages were in fact allowed among the Hutterites, with the hope that the "unbeliever" would be won over. But if spiritual harm was noted, or if the unbeliever did not allow the arrangement to continue, then God must be obeyed above human beings.[12] Since, for Walpot and the Hutterites, "obeying God" meant committing oneself to living in the Hutterite community, the communal test of obedience put tremendous pressure on mixed marriages and family ties.[13]

In his response to the Swiss, Walpot critiqued them for not acting forthrightly enough in cases when separation from an unbelieving spouse should have been carried out.

> Look at the tanner's wife at Oberwisternitz, who had an ungodly evil husband who hit her nine times in one day. When she came to complain to your people as a member and sought counsel, she was sent home without any other judgment.... Ought you not to have exercised a judgment?[14]

Apparently by the 1560s, the Swiss were less ready to separate from "ungodly" spouses than they had been in the early years of the movement.

Furthermore, in Hutterite eyes some of the Swiss were irresponsible concerning the rearing of their children. Walpot noted in particular the case of "ungodly wives" of Swiss "believers," who raised children who "stick feathers on their hats, [and] carry weapons, and all this before their father's eyes. If he wants to have peace in the house, he dare not utter a peep. He has the name of the head of the household, but the unbelieving wife and the children rule."[15] Walpot found this completely wrong, although his argument was a bit peculiar: strictly speaking, in Hutterite communities fathers also abdicated most of the usual roles of the "head of the household." But his critique had a point: as we know from other sources, by mid-century "mixed marriages" among the Swiss were not uncommon and resulted less and less in automatic "separation." In such situations, the education of the children into the Anabaptist faith was problematic; remaining in such marriages undeniably meant compromise. The Hutterites, to the contrary, expended great efforts in educating their children "into the faith," that being one point at which there was to be no compromise.[16]

Probably because of their strong community emphasis, the Hutterites adopted a stronger stand than the Swiss on separation and divorce from unbelievers. Adultery, of course, was accepted as cause for divorce, as with the Swiss (1 Corinthians 7). But Peter Walpot argued further that "where she is endangered in her faith or is hindered by the unbelieving husband in the training of her children in the true faith, she may divorce her husband, but must remain unmarried as long as her husband lives."[17] Not only was marital separation thus encouraged (sometimes from Swiss Brethren spouses, who were treated as "unbelievers" by the Hutterites), but the prohibition against remarriage was not, according to critics, always enforced by the Hutterites, further adding to the tension between the Hutterites and other Anabaptist groups.[18]

For both Swiss Brethren and Hutterites "obedience to God" was to be placed higher than marriage or family ties.[19] Nevertheless, over time the community boundaries appear to have weakened for the Swiss, while at the same time they grew less permeable among the Hutterites. These differences contributed to the growing estrangement between these two Anabaptist groups. The weakening of community boundaries among the Swiss Brethren who managed to survive in Switzerland contributed also to the controversy over banning and shunning which led to the Amish schism in the last years of the seventeeth century, as will be seen below.

For the Swiss and South German Anabaptists, the institution of marriage was considered to be a "natural" union that needed to be respected. The binding character of that union was recognized implicitly in the strictures against divorce and remarriage that the Swiss and the Hutterites attempted to institute in the cases of unavoidably "mixed" marriages. Thus it is not entirely fair to say that the Anabaptists had a *strictly* religious, ascetic view of marriage.[20] In the less-than-ideal cases of mixed marriage, the "natural" bond of marriage was recognized as binding—at least in theory, and (we may suppose) most often in practice as well. It was in the Anabaptist "ideal" understanding of marriage between believers that the "otherworldly" aspects were highlighted.

North German/Dutch Anabaptism

Two characteristics of Melchiorite Anabaptism raised further questions concerning marriage, separation and divorce: Melchior Hoffman's "high" view of the regeneration of believers, and his openness to direct spiritual revelations.

The "higher commitment" of believers to Christ, present in all branches of the Anabaptist movement, was raised to a new qualitative level by Melchior Hoffman. In his *Ordinance of God* (1530), Hoffman described the "spiritual marriage" of believers with Christ.[21]

> The bride has now so covenanted herself with the Lord under the sign of the covenant [baptism] and so given herself over to him, and he to them, through his Word and again with the bread, that many brides are become one congregation and bride of the Lord, and he the husband and the Bridegroom.[22]

For Hoffman this "spiritual marriage" was more than a metaphor; it was a reality that resulted in a totally remade person, to the point that sin itself was conquered. "Such victors," said Hoffman, "cannot sin any more, for [a] new, true rebirth maintains them..."[23]

At the base of Melchior Hoffman's understanding of the spiritual rebirth of believers stood his Christology: just as Christ the Redeemer did not take on human flesh, and so was able to overcome the sin of Adam and Eve for all humanity, so likewise believers also could overcome sin by uniting with Christ. They had come to partake of the "heavenly flesh" of Christ when they united with Him in spiritual marriage. In this way "The Word becomes Flesh."[24] Thus Hoffman's Christology pushed his regenerationist anthropology to a qualitative level not often seen among the Swiss.[25] Klaus Deppermann noted that for Hoffman, "Divinization was not an exception that only a few saints could hope for, but rather it must be the goal of all Christians."[26] Furthermore, possession of the Spirit of Christ by believers meant that the "law of the Spirit" now dwelt within them and that they thenceforth were bound to no external law.[27]

Although Hoffman himself never took this theoretical antinomianism in a radical, practical direction, the drastic possibilities offered by Hoffman's view are plain enough, especially with respect to marriage. If the "spiritual marriage" to Christ is the true marriage; if believers have the spiritual law within, then is this not an invitation to overlook a "natural" marriage undertaken "in unbelief?" This possibility was even more likely when prophetic spiritualism was added to the mix. When the notorious case of Claus Frey emerged in Strasbourg in 1533, however, Melchior Hoffman staunchly rejected spiritualist and antinomian consequences concerning marriage. But the Frey incident prefigured, in an uncanny way, problems that were about to emerge among the Melchiorites in the north.

Claus Frey and Elßbeth Pferdsfelder

Claus Frey and Elßbeth Pferdsfelder were arrested in May, 1533 by the Strasbourg authorities on charges of bigamy.[28] Claus Frey had begun his Anabaptist career in the Swiss camp: he was baptized in Windsheim by Julius Lober of Zürich, but soon was arrested for being an Anabaptist. When he refused to recant he was forced to leave his home territory, which he did with his wife's consent, leaving both her and their eight children behind. But when she later refused to follow him into exile, he separated from her, and divided his goods with her. He emerged as an Anabaptist teacher in Franconia, where he appears to have come under the influence of spiritualist visionaries. While living in the home of the Anabaptist Georg Groß, called Pfersfelder, he came to know Georg's sister, the widowed Elßbeth Pfersfelder.[29]

Beginning with instruction concerning rebirth and baptism, their relationship grew through a series of visionary experiences. One night Elßbeth experienced a power or impulse that told her that she should subject herself to Claus with all of her earthly goods, and that he should do with her what he willed.[30] Elßbeth wrote that the next morning, after the "power" had left her, she went to Claus and told him everything, upon which "he received me and united himself with me."[31] At his first hearing in Strasbourg in May 1533, Claus testified that it had been 31 weeks since "God had joined them." He maintained that Elßbeth was his wedded sister, even though he had a wife and children at Windsheim.[32]

A central text to which Claus Frey referred in justifying his separation from wife and family was none other than the familiar Luke 14:26, used universally in the Anabaptist movement as a call to costly discipleship: "If anyone comes to me and does not hate his father and mother, wife and children, brothers and sisters, even his own life, he cannot be a disciple of mine." Claus wrote to Elßbeth: "What I am supposed to hate I cannot also love, since it is against the adoption by God; now as you can well see, I must be dead to the previous, old life and rather take on the spiritual and blessed life..., therefore I must hate [my wife]."[33] And further: "Now note the Word of God which comes from faith: unbelief must be trodden underfoot, which is my wife. All this took place of necessity, for I did not do it, rather [it was done] by God who lives in me, and I in him."[34]

It is to the credit of Melchior Hoffman and his Strasbourg group that the "revelations" of this couple were tested and found wanting. Not only did Hoffman and the prophet Valentin Dufft urge Claus Frey to leave his "spiritual wife" Elßbeth and return to his family, so too did Barbara Rebstock.[35] In the end Claus Frey and Elßbeth Pfersfelder found themselves excluded by all the Anabaptist groups in Strasbourg;

Hoffman himself denounced Frey as a thief of God's glory and a satanic whoremaster.[36] Nevertheless, within Melchiorite teaching itself, the elements were freely available for recurrences of the Claus Frey kind, and they were not long in coming.

The arrest of Claus and Elßbeth in May, 1533 had dire consequences for Hoffman. Frey denounced him to the authorities as one who was stirring up rebellion among his followers through prophecies. Hoffman was arrested instantly—an event which he welcomed.[37] Hoffman had predicted the end of the world for 1533, and an "old Frisian" had prophesied that Melchior's arrest would last only half a year, after which the Melchiorite movement would cover the earth.[38] With Hoffman in jail the Melchiorite movement in the north was set in a new direction thanks largely to the "revelations" of Jan Matthijs—a man who in many respects fit the Claus Frey profile.

Jan Matthijs and Divara, the Brewer's Daughter

Obbe Philips, writing many years after he had left the Anabaptist movement, described what took place in the north less than half a year after Hoffman's arrest in Strasbourg.

> There arose a baker of Haarlem named John Matthijs, who had an elderly wife whom he deserted, and he took with him a brewer's daughter who was a very pretty young slip of a girl and had great knowledge of the gospel. He enticed her away from her parents with sacred and beautiful words and told how God had shown great things to him, and she would be his wife. He carried her secretly with him to Amsterdam and brought her to a clandestine place.[39]

Less than a year after Hoffman had denounced Claus Frey as a satanic whoremaster for abandoning his wife and taking another in "spiritual marriage," Jan Matthijs did exactly the same thing.[40] But Matthijs, rather than being excluded from Anabaptist circles, came to be accepted in the north as a great prophet—the Enoch of the Last Days.[41] Matthijs' importance in the establishment of Münsterite Anabaptism has been described sufficiently above.

Münsterite Polygamy

The polygamy that was established in Münster can be traced back to a complex of causes, none of which is sufficient of itself to explain the phenomenon. The theological elements were provided by Melchior Hoffman, particularly his understanding of the "spiritual marriage" of believers with Christ and their subsequent divinization. The implications of this view for earthly marriage, however, were developed further by Bernhard Rothmann. The "prophetic" elements which opened the door to novel interpretations of marriage were provided by Jan Matthijs and Jan van Leiden. And finally, the establishment of polygamy also must be attributed in part to desperate conditions in beleaguered Münster.[42] Most relevant to our purposes here is Rothmann's theological justification for separation and "spiritual" remarriage.

In his "Confession of the Faith and Life of the Christian Church at Münster" (1534), written well before the institution of polygamy in the city, Bernhard Rothmann interpreted the meaning of marriage using Hoffman's basic categories.[43] Although

Rothmann defended monogamy in this writing (one man and one wife), and cited the usual Anabaptist text concerning divorce (what God has joined let no man put asunder), nevertheless he reversed the usual understanding of this latter text: "In the same way, what has not or will not be joined by God ... is no state of marriage, but rather plain whoredom in God's eyes."[44] Building on this logic Rothmann concluded that marriage between unbelievers "is sin and is unclean, and is no marriage before God... For what does not come from faith is sin..." Since God had not joined "heathens" together, they were therefore not truly married.[45] Even further, in the case of a "mixed" marriage between a believer and an unbeliever, Rothmann said, a believer "is not bound to the unbeliever, but rather is free."[46] The way was thus open for a rather easy separation and (in fact) "divorce" from unbelieving spouses, and remarriage among believers.

In October 1534, Bernhard Rothmann published his important "Restitution of the true Christian teaching," in which he provided the theological justification for, among other things, the institution of polygamy in Münster.[47] In outlining the requirements of a "true marriage," Rothmann now placed the commandment to go forth and multiply in first place: men must not misuse or waste the "seed and gift of God" in intercourse with pregnant or barren women. Furthermore, those who had accepted baptism and so had been washed of all sin, were to renew their marriage vows accordingly in order to proceed henceforth in all purity.[48]

The justification for polygamy came, appropriately enough, in a chapter outlining the "proper," predominant place of the man in marriage.[49] "A man's freedom in marriage is that he may very well have more than one wife," wrote Rothmann, in the first place because of the command to be fruitful. Since the man, the carrier of the divine seed, is able to "fructify" more than one woman "he is therefore left free, especially because of need, to take more than one fruitful woman in marriage..." Rothmann appealed, furthermore, to the polygamous examples of the patriarchs in the Old Testament, namely Lamech, Abraham, Jacob, David, etc.[50] Rothmann's appeal to the Old Testament as a behavioural guideline in the "time of Restitution," already seen above in the matter of the sword, is here applied in justification of polygamous marriage.

Münsterite polygamy, for all its lascivious undertones, was hardly a celebration of human sexuality or an invitation to a love-fest; its outlines, in fact, sound rather grim. James Stayer has aptly noted the "innerworldly ascetic" character of Münsterite polygamy: no "fleshly lust" was to play a role; sexual relations were for the purpose of procreation only. There was a strongly patriarchal cast given to these polygamous relationships—doubtless in an attempt to maintain some order in what must have been a chaotic network of relationships.

After the fall of Münster, Melchiorite teaching on marriage flowed in three different directions: in some circles (e.g. Jan van Batenburg and his followers) there was an attempt to maintain Münsterite polygamy; David Joris retained the elements of Hoffman's "spiritual marriage" (and Rothmann's interpretation of Hoffman's view) in a novel "spiritualized" fashion; Menno and his followers arrived at a position concerning separation, divorce, and remarriage most closely resembling that of Melchior Hoffman. In what follows we will trace only the positions of Joris and Menno.

David Joris

David Joris, in an effort to expand his authority, attempted to persuade the Melchiorite leadership in Strasbourg of his prophetic calling to leadership.[51] This was no small task, for the "elders in Strasbourg" were widely respected in the north, and were not disposed to accept Joris' extravagant claims to be the "third David."[52] Two other issues also stood in the way: the prominent role played by the prophetess Barbara Rebstock in the Strasbourg Melchiorite community and that community's view concerning the nature of marriage.

In 1537 David Joris wrote a long reply to Johannes Eisenburg, who had emerged as a leader of the Strasbourg Melchiorites during Melchior Hoffman's imprisonment.[53] Eisenburg, in a writing now lost, had written to Joris concerning separation, divorce and marriage. Reading between the lines of Joris' reply, it is clear that Eisenburg and the Strasbourg Melchiorites had remained with Hoffman's view: they opposed divorce even in cases of "mixed" marriages, and opposed polygamy as well.

Central to Joris' view of marriage was the logic and argumentation that had been used earlier by Rothmann: what God has joined together cannot be separated, but what God has not joined together may be separated.[54]

"See, what God has brought together, no person can separate. Observe this correctly in every way. But what Satan, or the fleshly nature, or the evil world, or human reason brings together, God or his Spirit may indeed separate. Is this not so? Yes..."[55]

Since marriages between believers and unbelievers are not true marriages (in God's eyes), believers may leave unbelievers freely. In fact, urged

"The New Man." Engraving after David Joris' illustration in the *Wonder Book*

Joris, it is not *fitting* for the pure to remain with the impure.[56] Appropriating "two kingdoms" language, Joris argued:

> Now the difference between the people of God and the heathen, between the flesh and the spirit, has been well enough explained or

> heard. For how does the wheat accord with the chaff? The grapes
> with the brambles? The lies with the truth? Light with darkness?
> The believers with the unbelievers? The righteous with the unrigh-
> teous? Christ with Belial? Therefore, there must be a separation so
> that the good will not ultimately be expelled by the evil, nor the pure
> by the impure. Thus the many who are born for sin's sake perish,
> says the Lord. But my grapes will be saved in my planting. For I
> have perfected them with much labor.[57]

The only true marriage, argued Joris, is a spiritual marriage. Those then who are truly "spiritual" will be committed to no marriage (certainly no "earthly" or "fleshly" marriage) other than the spiritual one.[58]

It is apparent from Joris' reply that Eisenburg had appealed to 1 Corinthians 7:12: "If a Christian has a heathen wife, and she is willing to live with him, he must not divorce her..." Here Joris appealed to his own prophetic authority over that of Paul: "I have knowledge from the Spirit of God: Of this I am certain. Listen to it, for it is better than the fat of rams [1 Sam. 15:22]. For this reason, I say that what was the good advice of Paul was not a command of the Lord in this matter."[59] Paul was giving the Corinthians "milk" rather than solid food, said Joris. Furthermore, Paul allowed a "mixed" couple to stay together, but only if the unbeliever did not wish to "rule" the believer. The "solid food" of the Gospel, which the Corinthians (and the Strasbourg Melchiorites) were not prepared to receive, was that separation from all impurity is necessary.[60]

Like Rothmann, Joris argued for a patriarchal view of marriage and, like Rothmann, he also argued that the only "pure" union of a man and a woman is one in which lust or sexual desire plays no part. The only aim of a truly spiritual marriage, said Joris, could be the production of regenerate children. Here Joris' unorthodox approach to sexuality becomes evident, for not only did he speak eloquently about "spiritual intercourse," he also had high expectations for the children resulting from such unions.

> They go to their wife not from the love of the flesh, nor from the
> lusts of the flesh, nor from the desires or burning of the flesh, but
> instead only from the love of the true Spirit, with lust in the Spirit
> and not a burning spirit; only for the sake of the breeding of healthy,
> blessed children, who are holy in their nature, just like Samson,
> Samuel, and John the Baptist.[61]

Joris was convinced that those who had truly been regenerated spiritually would be able to overcome the "lusts of the flesh" completely; in fact, the true test of a man's regeneration was the ability to lay naked with a woman and to feel no lust.[62] At this point we certainly have reached the outer limits of optimism regarding inner regeneration and outer behaviour, where the number of the "elect" would be few indeed. One also suspects, given the nature of children, that the "holy" progeny resulting from this pure "lust of the Spirit" may also have fallen short of the lofty goal set by Joris.

Bernhard Rothmann had argued for polygamy in Münster using the same basic principles as did Joris. Did David Joris also favour polygamy? The evidence is mixed, and Joris' writings are very guarded on this question. He nowhere forbids the practice, nor does he explicitly allow it—although he did allow the former Batenburgers who joined him in 1538 to continue their polygamous practice. Gary Waite concludes, "At the most, Joris was indifferent, but not hostile, to polygamy."[63] Given Joris' emphasis on the inner state of *Gelassenheit,* the outer manifestations may well have been a matter of indifference to him. His Nicodemism makes it virtually impossible to know with certainty what his teaching in fact was; it may well have been a "graduated" teaching, depending on whether individuals were to be fed "milk" or "solids."

On the general question of separation and remarriage, Joris did offer one way out for Melchiorites following Münster. The basic Melchiorite tenets of "spiritual marriage" were retained, with a heightened emphasis on the inner,

"The Image of the Bride of Christ"
**Engraving after an illustration by David
Joris, from the *Wonder Book***

spiritual aspects of marriage, sexuality, and child bearing. If, as James Stayer has argued convincingly, Münsterite polygamy can be seen as an instance of "innerworldly asceticism," David Joris continued the emphasis and raised it to an even higher ascetic plane. One is reminded of St. Anthony's temptations, with this difference: Joris was attempting to overcome the "demon of lust" not in a solitary desert cave, but in the marital bed itself. Whether the untenability of Joris' hopes in this area contributed to the decline of his movement is not clear, but the high demands of his extreme asceticism would have argued for a limited following.[64]

Menno Simons

Menno Simons, as has been noted above, defined his own position over against the Münsterites and the David Jorists, openly criticizing the Münsterite use of the sword and polygamy, as well as David Jorist teachings and practices concerning sexuality and marriage.[65] Menno's appeal to the authority of Scripture, most especially to the New Testament as a guide to behaviour, governed his approach to the question of marriage as it did in other matters. Thus the radical dimension introduced by Melchiorite prophetic spiritualism was negated by Menno's Christocentric biblicism. Men and women are to be married to only one spouse from whom they can be divorced only in cases of adultery.[66]

Nevertheless Menno's "high" doctrine of regeneration, which he sometimes described in Melchiorite terms as a marriage between believers and Christ, opened the door to further questions concerning separation and divorce.[67] We will look further at this development in Menno's thought in chapter 24, in connection with the ban. Suffice it to say here that the Melchiorite concern for the purity of individual believers (which was threatened, thought Menno, by mixed marriages), coupled with a growing concern for the purity of the Body of Christ (the church), combined to lead Menno to recommend the shunning of banned spouses.

Although Menno denied that such shunning was a "divorce" (the latter to be allowed only in cases of adultery), the distinction was a fine one indeed: marital shunning was a *de facto* divorce—a divorce in all but name.[68] The fundamental rationale for such marital separation and shunning was the common Anabaptist teaching: one's highest commitment is to Christ, not to one's spouse. But in contrast to the Swiss, for example, Melchiorite emphases extended this necessary separation to banned spouses.

We return in conclusion to the question posed when we first looked at Melchior Hoffman's teaching: If the "spiritual marriage" to Christ is the true marriage, then is this not an invitation to overlook a "natural" marriage undertaken "in unbelief?" As we have seen, Hoffman introduced elements that had the potential to devalue "natural" marriage, although he himself was not willing to take this step, as the Claus Frey case shows. With Jan Matthijs, Jan van Leiden, and Bernhard Rothmann that further step was taken: the only "true marriage" was one that had been contracted between believers. David Joris continued this tradition after Münster.

The Strasbourg Melchiorites and Menno Simons returned to Hoffman's earlier view, with Menno moving closer to the Swiss because of his New Testament biblicism. Nevertheless, the stronger Melchiorite regenerationist and ascetic view remains visible in Menno. The controversy surrounding banning and marital avoidance would demonstrate Menno's basic grounding in Melchiorite thought.

Marriages between believers

It should be clear by now that in light of the wide variety of individual cases and examples, it is difficult to generalize about the "Anabaptist" view of marriage. The higher commitment of believers to Christ meant that Anabaptist men and women were extended more freedom to leave spouses and families than was the social norm in the sixteenth century. These people sometimes remarried "believers" later. In the earlier, formative years of the movement there were questionable cases of abandonment, bigamy, and polygamy.[69] Nevertheless, as the Anabaptist movement began to establish community boundaries, it also began to establish norms of conduct governing marriage. This historical progression towards settled communities was paralleled by a collective movement towards Christocentric, New Testament biblicism; it also corresponded to increasing official pressure from ecclesiastical and state authorities. As Anabaptist communities established firmer boundaries (and as dissenters were separated from those communities), the standard biblical texts enjoining monogamy were cited and applied; scriptural norms of conduct were applied to marriages between believers, and these scriptural norms also were expected to govern relationships between husband and wife within marriage.

The marriages that were performed in the Anabaptist communities themselves were predominantly religious unions in which the commitment of believers with God in Christ was held to be primary over their union to one another. A very frequent way in which Anabaptists referred to their marriage partners was to call them "wedded brother" or "wedded sister" in the Lord.[70] The language is significant. The brotherhood/sisterhood bond of faith was considered primary; the "wedded" aspect was secondary.

Clearly, marriage between two people who shared Anabaptist religious principles was the preferred ideal; the problems of "separation" posed by mixed marriages would be avoided thereby, and the group would be strengthened by the addition of children raised in the faith. It is not surprising that there are increasing injuctions for believers to marry only within their communities.

Since marriage between Anabaptist believers was understood as an essentially spiritual union, such marriages quickly came to be performed by the Anabaptists themselves. There are numerous reports in Swiss and South German sources of such Anabaptist marriages in their clandestine meetings in forests and other places.[71] The Swiss authorities in particular acted quickly to condemn such marriages as illegal.[72] The Zürich *Sittenmandat* or "Mandate concerning Morals" promulagated in 1530 made it obligatory for there to be a public proclamation of marriage from the state church pulpit.[73] The 1532 Synod in Bern decreed that henceforth marriages were to be performed in the state church, not only as a religious rite, but also as a civic requirement.[74] Later in the sixteenth century, both Zürich and Bern took the further step of denying inheritance rights to children of couples who had not been married in the state church.[75]

The establishment of state churches in Protestant Swiss Territories meant that pastors of local parishes became, to a certain extent, state agents. By 1525 the Zürich authorities were beginning to keep systematic parish records concerning marriages, births, baptisms and burials; these were monitored and recorded by local state church ministers. The Anabaptists in these territories made every effort to avoid being entered into these registers, for obvious reasons: it was all too easy to check up on the baptism or non-baptism of infants with this information readily at hand.

Besides the explicit legal disadvantages of being an Anabaptist and marrying "illegally" in an Anabaptist community, there were also more subtle legal disadvantages that emerge in the Swiss "marriage court" records. In February of 1526, Katharina Hottinger brought a suit against Klaus Unholz before the marriage court in Zürich.[76] Katharina claimed that Klaus had promised marriage. Klaus denied such a promise, and swore an oath to that effect. Part of his defence was that "Only God knows what ideas the spirit, which she and other Anabaptists boast of, gave her." His defence stood up, and her claim was denied.[77]

The majority of Anabaptists had no scruples about avoiding state-sanctioned marriages, but we do know of one case in which a disagreement arose over whether the avoidance of the state in these questions was justifiable or not. Jörg Maler, a member of the Marpeck circle living in Switzerland around mid-century, disagreed with the Swiss practice of simply making marriages known "among themselves." He believed that the authorities also should be involved since part of their God-ordained governing function included the punishment of marital misdeeds.[78]

Although Jörg Maler's view was a minority opinion among the Anabaptists, perhaps he was reacting to actual and potential abuses of the *ad hoc* practice of marriage among various Anabaptist groups. There are known instances of misuse and abuse, and it is certain that the vulnerability of spouses and families was increased tremendously when Anabaptist marriages could be conducted at the will of any particular Anabaptist group. Maler apparently felt that in such cases, the government should take appropriate legal steps to punish wrong-doers. There were other cases far less notorious than those of Claus Frey and Jan Matthijs.[79] Perhaps for these reasons, Anabaptist groups made increasing efforts to regulate marriage from within their groups.

Charges of bigamy, polygamy and sexual impropriety were directed against the Swiss Anabaptists from the start, beginning with Ulrich Zwingli in Zürich. On occasion, as we have seen, these charges had a basis in fact. When Hans Seckler was questioned in 1527 in Bern about whether the Anabaptists had "wives in common" he said that it was true that some Anabaptists did, but he did not agree with the practice.[80] It was more often the case that the charges were simply denied by those accused. Heinrich Seiler of Aarau was asked if the Anabaptists shared wives in common. This he denied, saying that "Whoever would do that would go against the community of God."[81]

An interesting case came to court in Bern in 1536 when Anni Flückinger publicly confronted the local preacher for having said from the pulpit that the Anabaptists held "all things in common." Anni denied that the Anabaptists to whom she and her husband belonged taught such a thing. The pastor apparently had intimated that wives were included in the "common things," for Anni went on to say that "she was not a common woman (or wife) and her husband was not a common man." In his defence, the pastor maintained that he had been maligned, since the Anabaptists did teach these things. The court awarded him the decision, apparently considering him a more reliable source concerning Anabaptist teaching and practice than were an Anabaptist husband and wife.[82]

By mid-century, the Swiss appear to have moved to regulate marriage in a more systematic way. Jörg Maler said at his hearing in 1550 that the Swiss would not allow their members to marry unbelieving spouses, and that they disciplined anyone who did not comply. He was not in agreement with this practice since it went against Paul (1 Corinthians 7:12); but again, Maler's view appears to have been a minority opinion.[83] Later Swiss Brethren practice was outlined more explicitly in two articles of the "Discipline" adopted by the Swiss in Strasbourg in 1568.

> 12. Those who wish to enter the state of matrimony shall do so with the knowledge and counsel of the ministers and bishops, and it shall be undertaken in the fear of God; and since it is fitting they should inform and report to their parents.
>
> 13. If believers are persecuted and driven from their homes by unbelieving husband or wife, they shall be encouraged to continue in earnest prayer to the Lord for patience until He shall show a way out; in order to avoid this danger believers shall marry only in the Lord, and not in unbelief, whether they be maidens, youth or widows (or widowers).[84]

In these articles can be seen the increasing community control and legislation concerning marriage among the Swiss: marriage was to be carried out in an orderly fashion, under the direction of bishops and elders, who would see that members married only "in the Lord." The agreement adopted in Cologne in 1591 was even more explicit, stating that "believers do not have the freedom to marry, except among those who through faith have become a member of the body of Christ, who are thus a spiritual brother or sister..." Those who transgressed this injunction were to be disciplined with the ban.[85] The visible lines between church and world came to be drawn with increasing precision among the Swiss, with marriage as one of the crucial boundaries.

The Hutterite view was correspondingly more precise at an earlier date. Community boundaries were even more important to the Hutterites, given their communal living arrangements; the role of the elders and leaders in maintaining Hutterite communal boundaries is most evident in marriage questions.[86] By 1540, Peter Riedemann could write that "one should not ask his flesh but the elders that God might show him through them what He hath appointed for him. This, then, one should take with real gratitude as a gift from God, whether young or old, poor or rich, even as God hath shown through their counsel."[87] According to an eyewitness who observed the following in 1578, the elders would call together the single young men and women on a given Sunday, place the men on one side and the women on the other. "Two or three boys are then suggested to each girl, one of whom she has to accept. Of course they are not really compelled, but on the other hand there is not much chance to act against the counsel of the elders."[88]

Some of the Hutterite principles underlying this practice can be seen in the articles concerning marriage and divorce in the "Great Article Book," most likely written by Peter Walpot in 1577.[89] It is not surprising that Walpot emphasized Paul's injunction not to become "unequally yoked" to unbelievers (2 Corinthians 6:14ff.). Believers are the "temple of the living God," and so are called to separation from the world and all impurity.[90] Marriage, says Walpot, is not excluded from this demand for separation from the world. To the objection that such separation is a "spiritual" one that takes place in the heart, Walpot answers that whoever has truly separated from the world spiritually will exhibit this by physically joining the people of God: outer behaviour (including marriage) must conform to the inner spiritual change.[91]

Among the later followers of Menno the pronouncements at Wismar (1554) set the tone for later developments, placing marriage under the authority of the congregation and the elders. The first article maintains that those who marry outside the community of believers are to be banned "until they manifest a proper Christian life before God and the brethren."[92] Matters concerning separation and remarriage are "subject to the advice of the elders of the congregation"; likewise in the matter of marriage between the children of believers, congregational consent is required, with the proviso that the parents of the couple also give their consent. The congregation and the elders, however, have the final word.[93]

The fundamental justification for these marriage practices was set forth by Menno, following the common Anabaptist and Melchiorite Pauline image: "the heavenly marriage bond between Christ and our souls ... must be kept unbroken in willing obedience to the only and eternal Bridegroom."[94] As community boundaries became increasingly important among the Dutch, however, the elders and congregations became the arbiters of the limits of external obedience. This led to schism and church divisions. Among the Frisians, marriage outside the church was a matter of unalterable excommunication; among the Waterlanders, the more moderate position of Wismar was adopted, which allowed the possibility of re-entry into the congregation following appropriate contrition.[95] The Dordrecht Confession of 1632, influential also among the Swiss Brethren in the later seventeenth century, would allow only "marriage in the Lord," with no caveats or exceptions.[96]

Marriage practices in the settled Anabaptist communities, then, were surprisingly uniform. The establishment of separated communities of believers dictated marriage within that group, and placed the control of marriage under the authority of the congregations and, especially, the elders and leaders of those congregations. An increasing concern to maintain the purity of the separated church is evident, as is also the concern to raise children "in the faith." The continued existence of those communities was at stake. Under these later, more settled conditions the matter of "separation" became less and less a question relating to "mixed" marriages. What

came to the fore were either separations because of the banning of a marriage partner (a contentious issue, as will be seen below), or separations that occurred because
of persecution.

As so many martyr accounts demonstrate, the natural human ties to parents,
spouse and children were certainly not considered sinful, but rather were treasured
gifts of God. Nevertheless, these same family bonds often were the strongest ties
"of the flesh" that needed to be overcome in order to remain "obedient unto death."[97]
In just one example of this tension, taken from the *Ausbund*, the exiled songwriter
Hans Büchel carries on a Job-like dialogue with God.[98] Büchel cries out in his misery
to God: although his dear wife and child have been given to him by God, still he has
been driven far away from them by the persecution of the authorities. God's answer
comes in the form of Christ's words: Whoever begins to construct a building should
calculate the cost before commencing (stanza 5). The commitment to Christ's way,
sealed in baptism, was the narrow way of the cross from the start. Büchel's lament
continues, with parallels drawn between the sufferings of Christ and those that must
be endured by the true followers of Christ. Finally the songwriter asks God for patience: "Forgive the sin and fault of all who do hateful things to me, and who do not
care what happens to my wife and child" (stanza 28); and, in the penultimate stanza
of the song, he remains hopeful: "Lord, be gracious and watch over my wife and small
child; keep them in your protection; and if it be your gracious will, give them back to
me" (stanza 31).

Büchel's song demonstrates—as do numerous other testimonies—that he did
not consider there to be anything intrinsically "sinful" or "unspiritual" about marriage or family attachments as such: they were good gifts and blessings of God. Still,
if it were to come down to a choice between obedience to Christ or allegiance to
family bonds, obedience to Christ and the Body of Christ had higher claims. Büchel's
view would appear to represent the majority of Anabaptist opinion, although as we
have seen above, more radically ascetic views also were not uncommon at certain
stages of the movement.

Conclusion

The question of Anabaptist marriage is one that brings to the fore both the
unity and the diversity of Anabaptist thought and practice. On the one hand, there is
undeniable diversity in Anabaptist practice which corresponds roughly to the Swiss,
South German, North German/Dutch divisions identified by polygenesis historians.[99]
This is particularly true when one surveys Anabaptist thought and practice from
1525, including the events in Münster, until around 1550. On the other hand, there is
a surprising uniformity in the theological argumentation used to support Anabaptist
views about marriage—even when the more radical marriage views are included.
The essential argument, pre-figured by Thomas Müntzer, was that believers are
those who have committed themselves spiritually to Christ above all else; all earthly
relationships thus fall into second place, including the marriage relationship. The biblical image of a spiritual "marriage to Christ" in connection with marriage was used in

all the Anabaptist groups, in the same situational contexts, and with the same essential meaning. Underlying different Anabaptist practices, then, were shared assumptions about the primary Christian commitment to Christ which recalled the commitment of monastic profession. There is an "ascetic" substratum to all Anabaptist thinking about marriage that marks it as Anabaptist and nothing else.

The primacy of the inner, spiritual commitment to Christ—of which water baptism was the outward witness—meant that Anabaptist men and women alike were "freed" from earthly attachments that stood in the way of their relationship to Christ. This too was universally true in all Anabaptist groups and it led to some chaos, especially in the early years of the movement. Just how "free" such previously married believers were to enter into new relationships was, as we have seen, a contested issue until community boundaries and guidelines were established by the different Anabaptist groups at differing points during the sixteenth century. But the issue was the *extent* of freedom such believers were to have; the principle itself never was disputed among the Anabaptists. What did become a disputed issue among them was the extent of regeneration implied by one's "marriage to Christ," and what this might mean for outer life and practice.

The "inner/outer" tension was taken in the most radically spiritualist direction in the Melchiorite tradition, based as it was on Hoffman's high Christology and doctrine of regeneration. Melchiorite perfectionism, openness to antinomianism, and acceptance of direct spiritual revelations made possible the polygamy of Münster, the "spiritual marriages" of the David Jorists, and also prepared the way for the shunning of marriage partners in the Mennonite tradition. The distinctive nature of the Melchiorite tradition is not in doubt, but there is likewise good reason to say that the differences between the Melchiorites and the rest of the Anabaptists in marital teaching and practice were in fact differences of degree along a shared inner/outer continuum. It is for this reason that, in the end, there is so much uniformity of marital teaching and practice among the settled Anabaptist groups.

Finally, it must be noted that the freedom granted to all believers to leave unbelieving spouses moved further into the background as Anabaptist communities formed and established more stringent marital guidelines. The freedom to separate in certain cases of unworkable mixed marriages was never removed, but the reality for the settled communities was the legislation of marriage practices among *believers*. In this situation the earlier, pneumatic "freedom" to separate that was based on "obedience to God rather than men," was replaced by obedience to community norms. These norms were based on oft-repeated biblical texts pertaining to the marriage relationship, in particular the Pauline injunctions concerning the husband-wife relationship. In the settled community context the patriarchal patterns of marriage were adopted, following closely the social norms and patterns of the sixteenth century: Christ is the head of the husband, the husband the head of the wife, the wife is to be submissive and obedient to the husband, and the children are to be submissive and obedient to their parents.

Were the Anabaptists "radical" in their understanding of marriage? One's answer will depend in large part upon the historical sources one chooses to read. An historian studying the early, chaotic phase of the movement may be excused for concluding that the Anabaptists granted radical freedom to men and women alike; an historian reading the theological writings pertaining to marriage (written exclusively by men) may be excused for concluding that the Anabaptists simply mirrored the patriarchal patterns of sixteenth century society. Both conclusions are partially right, and partially wrong, but taken together provide a reliable picture of the tension underlying Anabaptist marriage relationships. It was a tension that emerged because of the ultimate claim made by Christ upon believers. It was a claim that simultaneously freed individuals to respond as individuals to God's call in Christ, but then bound them to lives of obedience to Christ (and by extension, to the Body of Christ, the church) in their outward lives.

End Notes

[1] Many male Anabaptist leaders in particular abandoned their wives and children while they did the "work of the Lord." Claus-Peter Clasen summarizes: "Many of the early apostles did not concern themselves too greatly over the fate of their families. Hut's family was reduced to utter chaos. The wives of Kruesi, Kellermann, Gross, Salminger, and Nespitzer wandered from place to place for weeks and even months, earning meager livings as seamstresses and maidservants. Repeatedly they were arrested, imprisoned, driven out. Sattler's wife was even executed." Clasen, *Social History*, pp. 59-60. For a Dutch example, see Menno's letter to Leenaert Bouwens' wife, CWMS, pp. 1038-1040.

[2] See, for example, the case of Erhard Suter of Schaffhausen (1530), whose wife had left him at least three times, and was currently not with him, since she was with the Anabaptists. He filed for divorce, but there is no further information in the sources. QGTS, 2, #61, p. 58. Hans Hoffman's wife of twenty years left him and their three children in late summer of 1529, in the company of several Anabaptists. He filed for divorce. QGTS, 1, #413, pp. 398-99. In May 1531 four men complained to the Zürich magistrates that their wives were Anabaptists and had abandoned them and their children. QGTS, 1, #339, pp. 358-59. In Bernese territory, Hanns Lüscher put out a warrant for the arrest of his wife Anni "who is an Anabaptist and has run off." QGTS, 3, #223. In May of 1555, Hans Locher of Appenzell was ordered arrested "because he does not wish to live with his wife." QGTS, 2, #333 (1555), p. 243. Among others, see QGTS, 3, #766 (1544): Hans Meyer, Anabaptist, abandoned Margaret Schwyter and their six children in 1540. The last time he saw his wife (apparently in Fall of 1543), he told her not to allow their children to go to church. Cf. *ibid.*, #770; 771; QGTS, 2, #373 (1548), p. 292-93, esp. n. 19. Cf. Paul Peachey, *Die soziale Herkunft der Schweizer Täufer in der Reformationszeit* (Karlsruhe: Schneider, 1954), pp. 71-72.

[3] This story, along with numerous others, is told in more detail in Snyder and Hecht, *Profiles of Anabaptist Women* (forthcoming). A parallel case is discussed in Kobelt-Groch, "Petronella," pp. 26-41.

[4] The sources documenting Adelheit's story are found in QGTS, 1, #293, 294, 302, 304, 330, 338; STAZ, EI, 7.2, nr. 94. In June, 1531, the Zürich government responded to the problem of spouses who left families (perhaps in response to Adelheit's case) by proposing a common mandate (with Bern, Basel, Freibourg, Solothurn, and Schaffhausen) that would punish deserting Anabaptist spouses "in life and goods, without mercy." The

Second Kappell War prevented the adoption of the mandate. See QGTS, 2, #4, pp. 8-9. See also the recommendation of the "marriage court" to the Zürich magistracy that strong punishment be meted out to the Anabaptists who simply left spouses and families, and "respect neither the bond of marriage, the laws of the government, nor oath and honour, etc." QGTS, 1, #415, p. 399.

⁵ See "On Divorce," in John H. Yoder, *The Legacy of Michael Sattler* (Scottdale, Pa.: Herald Press, 1973), pp. 100-107.

⁶ *Ibid.*, p. 102.

⁷ *Ibid.*, p. 103. The feminine pronoun is in the original. See *ibid.*, p. 106, n. 17.

⁸ See *ibid.*, pp. 103-104.

⁹ QGTS, 3, #760.

¹⁰ Many other relevant examples could be culled from the Anabaptist court records. These concrete cases need to be weighed against the "ideal" described in published tracts more carefully than can be done here. In 1534 in Bernese territory, a Swiss Anabaptist weaver named Högerly was arrested for Anabaptism. It then came to light that he had recently married, even though it was known that he had another wife. When the local overseer questioned him about the matter, he answered that he had once had a wife but that they had separated some five years earlier, and he did not know if she were dead or alive. He then was asked whether he had been divorced from her, and he answered "Yes. God has divorced us." QGTS, 3, #182, 183, 184. Cf. also *ibid.*, #768, b. Cf. the case of Hermann Gereume, of the Halberstadt Anabaptist group, who left his wife of 22 years, and their 15 children. He took an Anabaptist widow as his wife. When she left the faith, he recanted and returned to his first wife. Kobelt-Groch, "Petronella," p. 31.

¹¹ Even in light of the numerous anomalies, it is an overstatement to say that "It was usually considered legitimate to enter into marriage with one of the faithful, leaving the relationship with one's first spouse unresolved, or, to put it more precisely, unconsidered." So Kobelt-Groch, "Petronella," p. 31. I would agree with Claus-Peter Clasen's conclusion that among the Swiss and South German Anabaptists, the majority held that spousal abandonment was permissible only in cases of adultery. Clasen, *Social History*, pp. 204-05.

¹² Leonard Gross, *The Golden Years of the Hutterites* (Scottdale, Pa.: Herald Press, 1980), p. 174. Cf. Walpot's "Five Articles," in Müller, *Glaubenszeugnisse*, pp. 253-57. Walpot cites Old Testament evidence concerning the purity required of the people of Israel, and a variety of New Testament verses concerning marriage and separation. He concludes with this sentence: "The covenant with God is worth a thousand-fold more than the covenant of marriage between human beings." *Ibid.*, p. 257. For Walpot's more extended argumentation on this subject, see Robert Friedmann, ed. *Glaubenszeugnisse oberdeutscher Taufgesinnter*, II (Gütersloh: Gerd Mohn, 1967), pp. 299-317.

¹³ "Marriage, child-rearing, living arrangements and work practices—all had the same result: the community was everything, and the family was as weak as it could be without disappearing entirely." So Stayer, *German Peasants' War*, p. 146.

¹⁴ Cited in Gross, *Golden Years*, p. 175.

¹⁵ *Ibid.*

¹⁶ See the interesting educational guidelines in Müller, *Glaubenszeugnisse*, p. 237, n. 1.

¹⁷ Cited in "Divorce from Unbelievers," ME, II, p. 75.

¹⁸ Stayer, *German Peasants' War*, p. 145; 215, nn. 34 and 35; Cf. Clasen, *Social History*, p. 205.

¹⁹ Peter Riedeman noted that marriage had three "steps": "First is that of God with the soul or spirit, then that of the spirit with the body, and thirdly that of one body with another, that is, the marriage of man with

woman; which is not the first but the last and lowest grade..." Peter Riedeman, *Account of our Religion, Doctrine and Faith* (Rifton, N.Y.: Plough Publishing House, 1970), p. 98.

[20] Cf. Stayer, "Vielweiberei," p. 30.

[21] *Ibid.,* p. 31.

[22] Williams, *SAW,* p. 196.

[23] *Ibid.*, p. 201.

[24] Deppermann, *Hoffman,* p. 212. Cf. Stayer, "Vielweiberei," p. 31.

[25] Perhaps the closest comparable examples among the Swiss Anabaptists occurred among the Anabaptists of St Gall in 1526. The stories of Margaret Hottinger, Magdalena Müller, Barbara Mürglen, and Frena Buman are told by Johannes Kessler. See QGTS, 2, p. 618ff; brief summary in Keith L. Sprunger, "God's Powerful Army of the Weak: Anabaptist Women of the Radical Reformation," in Richard L. Greaves, ed., *Triumph over Silence: Women in Protestant History* (Westport, Ct.: Greenwood Press, 1985), p. 55.

[26] Deppermann, *Hoffman,* p. 208.

[27] Argued by Hoffman in his exegesis of Romans. See Deppermann, *Hoffman,* pp. 208-09.

[28] ME, II, p. 396, has a short entry on Frey. Deppermann gathers more evidence in *Hoffman,* pp. 254-56.

[29] She testified that she was a widow, having lost two husbands. After having been arrested for Anabaptism in Bamberg, and having managed to leave prison "with God's help," she went to Nuremberg where "God had joined her to this Claus Frey." TA, *Elsaß,* 2, pp. 11-12.

[30] According to Wolfgang Capito's account of the affair, published in June, 1534. Capito claims to be citing Elßbeth's own written words in describing this experience. See TA, *Elsaß,* 2, pp. 321-342 for Capito's book; Elßbeth's vision is on p. 324.

[31] *Ibid.*, p. 324: "do nam er mich an und vereinbaret sich mit mir."

[32] *Ibid.*, p. 12.

[33] *Ibid.*, pp. 326-27; reported by Capito.

[34] *Ibid.*, p. 327; again, as reported by Capito.

[35] *Ibid.*, p. 13.

[36] Deppermann, *Hoffman,* p. 255.

[37] Obbe Philips recalled: "When Melchior saw that he was going to prison, he thanked God that the hour had come..." Philips, "Confession," in Williams, *SAW,* pp. 209-10. Hoffman was arrested May 20, 1533. TA, *Elsaß,* 2, pp. 14-15; Deppermann, *Hoffman,* p. 255.

[38] Recalled by Philips; Williams, *SAW,* p. 209.

[39] Williams, *SAW,* pp. 213-14. The brewer's daughter was Divara, who after Matthijs' death became the wife of Jan van Leiden, and Queen of Münster.

[40] A point brought out by Deppermann, *Hoffman,* p. 290.

[41] A fascinating description of Matthijs' persuasive powers is found in Philips' "Confession," in Williams, *SAW,* p. 214.

[42] These reasons are outlined in Stayer, "Vielweiberei," pp. 31-34.

[43] Rothmann also uses the pauline image of Christ and the church as a model for Christian marriage. Stupperich, *Schriften,* p. 204.

[44] *Ibid.*, p. 204.

[45] *Ibid.*

[46] "Und ales non gescheg, dos der man oder die frow eins gleipig werde und das ander ungleibick plipe,

wolde der worheit Gotes nicht gehorsam sein, sonder ungleipigh, ein seliche ist dan nit gepunden an den ungleipigen, sonder frei." *Ibid.*, p. 205.

[47] "Restitution Rechter und Gesunder Christlicher Lehre," in Stupperich, *Schriften*, pp. 208-283. On marriage in general, see "Van den rechten unde christliken Ehestande," pp. 258-262.

[48] *Ibid.*, pp. 260-62.

[49] "Van Behör und Herlichkeit des mans in der Ehe," *Ibid.*, pp. 262-268.

[50] *Ibid.*, p. 264. "Hyrumme so ein man ricklicker van Godt gesegent were, dan eine frouwe tho befrüchtigen, unde he en moit van wegen des Godtlicken gebades, sodanen segen nicht mißbruken, so ys em fry gelaten, ya van nöden, meer fruchtbare frouwen in de Ehe tho nemmen..."

[51] See Gary Waite, *David Joris and Dutch Anabaptism, 1524-1543* (Waterloo, Ont.: Wilfrid Laurier Press, 1990), pp. 129-144.

[52] See Gary Waite, trans. and ed., *The Anabaptist Writings of David Joris, 1535-1543* (Scottdale, Pa.: Herald Press, 1994), p. 155.

[53] Translation of this letter in Waite, *Writings*, pp. 157-175.

[54] Deppermann, *Hoffman*, p. 317.

[55] Waite, *Writings*, p. 158.

[56] "... there are teachers, who will say that it is pure (let them dispute among themselves as much as they want) or fitting to remain with the impure. But their childish understanding will, I hope, be ultimately revealed to them." *Ibid.*, p. 159.

[57] *Ibid.*, p. 162.

[58] "You believe about this that two will be one flesh and, therefore, one should not separate one flesh [Gen. 2:24; Matt. 19:5-6]. But two must be one spirit, therefore, they can indeed be separated." *Ibid.*, p. 167.

[59] *Ibid.*, p. 165.

[60] *Ibid.*, p. 166.

[61] *Ibid.*, p. 173; cf. p. 169.

[62] See Waite, *David Joris*, appendix V, pp. 203-09.

[63] Waite, *Writings*, p. 156. See also Samme Zijlstra, "Nicolaas Meyndertsz van Blesdijk; Een bijdrage tot de geschiedenis van het Davidjorisme," (doctoral dissertation, Rijksuniversiteit Groningen, 1983), p. 32.

[64] Joris himself considered the inner struggle to be so mighty that those who successfully conquer are to be praised more highly than flesh and blood martyrs. "...their hands grasp their loins in pain on account of the old nature's evil and strife. Therefore, their crowns will be more valuable than those who have been physically killed or those who have not approached or handled women. Yes, in this way many more will be especially blessed above those who are killed, whom the fire has taken away and protected. But those who are left behind, these have the strongest works and faith. For although they are still alive, they are continually dying." Waite, *Writings*, pp. 173-74.

[65] See Menno' "Sharp Reply," CWMS, pp. 1020; 217; 301; 412. Also Zijlstra, "Blesdijk," pp. 32-44.

[66] See Betti Erb, "Reading the Source: Menno Simons on Women, Marriage, Children, and Family, CGR 8(Fall, 1990), pp. 301-319; esp. pp. 308-12. On these topics, see CWMS, pp. 94; 217; 479; 560-61; 970.

[67] See, e.g., CWMS, p. 972, for a reference to the "spiritual marriage" of believers. Menno's anthropology is also very optimistic, with obvious Melchiorite echoes: "It is also the nature of those who are in God not to sin, as John says: Whosoever abideth in God sinneth not..." CWMS, p. 415.

[68] In his 1550 writing on the ban, Menno said "we do not speak of divorce but of shunning... To shunning Paul has consented, although this is not always coupled with adultery, but not to divorce. For divorce is not allowed by the Scriptures except for adultery." CWMS p. 479. Menno says, "Therefore our view is that the husband should shun his wife, and the wife her husband... We must consent with the church to their sentence, we must seek their Scriptural shame unto improvement of life, and take care lest they be leavened by them, as was said above." *Ibid.*, p. 479.

[69] Although there were questionable cases in the Swiss and South German movements, one must agree with Claus-Peter Clasen that there is no evidence that "Anabaptists in Switzerland, Austria, and south and central Germany ever thought of abolishing monogamy." Clasen, *Social History*, p. 201.

[70] As one example among many, Hans Heune of the Halberstadt Anabaptists "remarked about his wife that he looked upon her 'according to Christ's ordinance as his spiritual sister.'" Kobelt-Groch, "Petronella," p. 32.

[71] See Clasen, *Social History*, pp. 202-03; also p. 468, n. 120. In 1548 Hans Fischer described a "forest" marriage this way: "Concerning the marriage which had taken place recently, he said that approximately four weeks ago they, the Anabaptists, held a meeting near Winingen. Hans Bechi Fridli, a blacksmith from the Bernese territory, working at that time in Dietikon, and a young woman from Utlikon near Würenloß, were given to each other (zusamen geben), since each of them wished this." STAZ, EI 7.2, #94, p. 3r.

[72] The Zürich authorities noted the problem already in 1526, and forebade any married person to separate from their spouse on their own decision (eigens gewallts) for any reason. The mandate concerning marriage is printed in J.J. Hottinger und H.H. Vögeli, eds, *Heinrich Bullingers Reformationsgeschichte*, I. Band (Frauenfeld: Ch. Beyel, 1838; reprint Zürich: Nova-Buchhandlung, 1984), pp. 377-80. In 1527 Zürich attempted to coordinate action with other cantons. See QGTS, 2, #1, p. 3. Rumours were rampant, especially that the Anabaptists had two or more wives, "one here, another one there." This was reported at the Zürich Synod of 1529. QGTS, 1, #292, p. 307.

[73] Cornelius Bergmann, *Die Täuferbewegung im Kanton Zürich bis 1660* (Leipzig: H. Nachfolger, 1916), p. 24. This move had been prepared by the requirement that marriages be declared in the state church and duly entered in a registry book by the clergy. See Bullinger's *Reformationsgeschichte*, I. Band, p. 381.

[74] Samuel Geiser, *Die Taufgesinnten Gemeinden*, 2. Auflage (Jura, 1971), p. 113. Cf. the Synod resolutions at Scaffhausen, taken May 10, 1555. QGTS, 2, #195, pp. 169-70.

[75] Bergman, *Täuferbewegung*, p. 29. Bern followed suit in 1567. See Gratz, p. 12.

[76] This is undoubtedly "Trini" Hottinger, daughter of the early Anabaptist Conrad Hottinger of Zollikon. See QGTS, 1, #48, pp. 58-59.

[77] QGTS, 1, #405, p. 393. See the suit of Dorothea Äberlin against Heini Rüegg. Part of his defense was that "she is an Anabaptist." The court decided that she had seduced him, and not otherwise, and freed him from a marriage commitment. QGTS, 1, #407, pp. 394-95. For a reverse case, see the complaint of Engeli Furrer against Martin Egli. Engeli, 18 yrs old, claimed that Martin had seduced her and promised marriage. He was an Anabaptist, but she had trusted him. QGTS, #408, p. 395. According to Zürich's marriage mandate of 1526, if one had "promised" marriage to another and a physical relationship had begun, this constituted a marriage, and all legal strictures applied. See Bullinger, *Reformationsgeschichte*, I. Band, p. 380.

[78] QGTS, 2, #323, p. 239 (April 28, 1550).

[79] For example, in 1573 in the Grüningen territory near Zürich, the son of Heini Walder was said to have taken three wives through Anabaptist marriages—whether simultaneously or sequentially is not clear from the record. STAZ, EI 7.2, #123.

[80] Ernst Müller, *Geschichte der Bernischen Täufer* (reprint: Nieuwkoop: de Graaf, 1972), p. 43.

[81] QGTS, 3, #306. Printed in Steck und Tobler, #2306.

[82] QGTS, 3, #584 (July, 1536). The court reported Anni's words as "sy wer nit ein gemein wib, er nit ein gemein man..."

[83] QGTS, 2, #323, p. 238.

[84] Harold S. Bender, "The Discipline Adopted by the Strasburg Conference of 1568," MQR 1(January, 1927), p. 65.

[85] Leonard Gross, "The First Mennonite Merger: The Concept of Cologne," in *Mennonite Yearbook*, 1990-1991, p. 9.

[86] A useful overview of Marriage and Separation in the Hutterite movement is found in Marlene Epp, "Women and Men in the 16th Century Hutterite Community" (unpublished paper, University of Toronto, 1991), pp. 12-18.

[87] Rideman, *Account*, p. 100. Cited also in ME, III, pp. 510-11.

[88] ME, III, p. 511.

[89] See Gross, *Golden Years*, pp. 200-02; Walpot's writing is edited and published in Friedmann, *Glaubenszeugnisse*, pp. 49-317. See also Riedeman, *Account*, pp. 97-102.

[90] *Friedmann, Glaubenszeugnisse*, p. 313.

[91] *Ibid.*, pp. 313-14.

[92] CWMS, p. 1041.

[93] *Ibid.*, p. 1042.

[94] *Ibid.*, p. 970; cf. p. 221 ff.; p. 1023.

[95] ME, III, p. 504.

[96] "There is no other liberty allowed to believers under the New Testament Dispensation, than to marry amongst the 'chosen generation,' or the spiritual kindred of Christ; that is, to such—and none others—as are already, previous to their marriage, united to the church, are of the same faith and doctrine..." Cited from Howard John Loewen, *One Lord, One Church, One Hope, and One God: Mennonite Confessions of Faith in North America* (Elkhart, In.: Institute of Mennonite Studies, 1985), p. 67, article 12.

[97] Kobelt-Groch sees in Anabaptism "a ... fundamental antagonism toward any pleasure whatever," with a correspondingly "unsensual" understanding of marriage. The conclusion is overdrawn, particularly in light of her admission that she "cannot furnish any sources as verification..." "Petronella," p. 32. There is much evidence, to the contrary, of very warm relationships between Anabaptist couples "wedded in the Lord." One would hardly expect such relationships to develop in marriages grudgingly undertaken primarily for progeny and prevention of lust.

[98] Hymn 45, "Es b'gab sich auf ein Zeite, Als ich vertrieben war..."

[99] "Die Trennungslinien, die zwischen den verschiedenen täuferischen Traditionen verlaugen, können an der Einstellung zu Fragen der Geschlechtlichkeit und Ehe markiert werden." So Stayer, "Vielweiberei," p. 30.

Chapter 20

Anabaptism and Religious Reform:
The Inner and the Outer

The preceding two sections of our study have focused on contentious and debated issues within Anabaptism, and have traced the way in which those differences were worked out over time. We have seen that the core principles that defined the "baptizing" reform movement beginning in 1525 had nevertheless left undefined how Anabaptism would relate to the political reality of the sixteenth century. In section C.1. above (chapters 12-15) we have traced the resulting discussions concerning the sword and the oath within the movement. Likewise the regenerationist and egalitarian principles inherent in the core Anabaptist principles left undefined how social and economic relationships would be structured *vis-a-vis* society and within the Anabaptist communities. Section C.2. above (chapters 16-19) has traced Anabaptist discussions and developments concerning economics, social equality, and marriage. In this section of our study (Section C.3, chapters 20-25) we will return to the question of church reform "in head and members," looking especially at the fundamental "inner/outer" tension that is visible in the core Anabaptist principles. We will trace some further theological and ecclesiological developments within those core principles.

There was a crucial tension in the core Anabaptist principles that became visible because of the necessary relationship that Anabaptists insisted had to exist between the inner, spiritual lives of Christians and their external lives and witness. We have seen already that, on one level, this "inner/outer" tension was expressed in debates concerning the proper relationship of Spirit to Letter. The "spirit/letter" tension we have noted throughout took as its point of departure the reality and activity of the Holy Spirit in the life of believers. Further debated issues that arose among the Anabaptists always related to how the letter of Scripture, the Word of God, was to be interpreted, for the measure of both the inner and the outer lives inevitably was scriptural.

In retrospect, it seems unavoidable that differences in approach to the interpretation of Scripture would manifest themselves in differences and disagreements concerning ethical questions and matters of "discipleship." Which scriptural/spiritual approach would provide the correct guidelines for how the "community of heaven" should relate to "the world" and the governing authorities? According to what biblical and spiritual principles should social relationships and economic activities be organized? And, what were the essential marks of the true church, the Body of Christ? The answers to these further questions were not obvious, even if there was general agreement from the start that the Bible was clear concerning how the truly reformed church would understand and practice baptism, the ban, the Supper, and economic sharing.

Most recent descriptions of Anabaptism have concentrated on the "outer marks" of the movement, and not without reason. Anabaptist insistence that "salvation by faith" of necessity entailed a "life of discipleship" was a most visible part of the movement. But somewhat obscured in all of this has been the inner, spiritual dimension without which Anabaptism would never have come to exist at all. It was the renovating power of the living God, the power of the Holy Spirit, that provided the fundamental groundwork for subsequent Anabaptist spirituality and discipleship, which created a church reform movement, and which eventually came to define the Believers' Church ecclesiological *tradition*. This "spiritualist" substratum, however, created tensions and ambiguities within the movement that needed to be resolved over time.

The Spiritualist Challenge

The "inner" emphasis noted in early Anabaptism was not typically Protestant, but rather had significant roots in several related strands of late medieval piety.[1] Nevertheless, while the Anabaptists shared the more optimistic anthropology of late medieval Christianity, they faced a very significant question as a result of their "evangelical" critique of that tradition: what role, if any, were the "external ceremonies" to play in *making possible* the "life of the spirit"? The inherent connection in late medieval Catholicism between the reception of the sacraments and growth in holiness was severed by the Anabaptists, following as they did the initial Protestant (and more specifically, Zwinglian) lead in these questions.

The difficulty raised by the anti-sacramental legacy was this: If the external elements contained no saving power of themselves, and the primary saving action was internal, being the work of the Holy Spirit in the heart, then what rationale could there be for keeping "external" ordinances *at all*? This was the central question posed by the "spiritualist" faction within Anabaptism, and how it was answered would have significant consequences for how the "true church" was conceived. The more "spiritualist" Anabaptists naturally played down the importance of the "outer" marks of the church, especially the "ceremonies" of baptism and the Supper. They found such ceremonies divisive and, given their secondary nature, saw no problem in dropping them altogether under certain circumstances. The more "literalist" Anabaptists naturally emphasized obedience to the words and commands of Christ—and there are clear "commands" in the New Testament to baptize, discipline, be nonresistant, not swear oaths, celebrate the Lord's Supper, and share with those in need.

There was, however, a third option represented in the "developmental" Anabaptist period. Pilgram Marpeck argued for a "middle way" between the spiritualist rejection of the outer "ceremonies" and the literalist insistence on "obedience to the letter." Although no ongoing "Pilgramite" branch managed to survive to the present, Marpeck's insightful perspective provides a useful Believers' Church commentary still today. We will devote a chapter below to a description of these debates in the Swiss and South German branches.

The tension that arose concerning the necessity of the outer marks of the church was no isolated phenomenon within the Anabaptist movement. It became visible in Melchior Hoffman's readiness to abandon the "outer sign" of baptism, in the debate between Pilgram Marpeck on the one hand, and Hans Bünderlin and Christian Entfelder on the other, in the insistence by some Anabaptists that true, inner *Gelassenheit* must of necessity result in adherence to a legislated community of goods by the Hutterites, and it would surface again later in the Netherlands in the debate between Menno Simons and Dirk Philips, on the one hand, and David Joris, Nicolaas van Blesdijk and other spiritualists on the other.

The "inner" dimension of the Anabaptist understanding could be understood as an invitation to Nicodemism, and had the potential of moving the Anabaptist fellowship away from being a visible and martyred community to becoming an invisible spiritual fellowship, indistinguishable (on the surface at least) from the surrounding world.[2] The temptation to Nicodemism was particularly strong in the sixteenth century, when failure to conform publicly to accepted religious ritual often resulted in torture and death. Even more so was the temptation reinforced if outer religious observances were held to be of no essential spiritual significance. Although there were degrees of outward conformity allowed by virtually all Anabaptist groups living in hostile territories, the central issue of the necessity or non-necessity of a particular outward life (and hence martyrdom) occasionally emerged as a full-fledged debate. One particularly vivid debate on this question occurred between Menno Simons and Nicolaas van Blesdijk, follower (and son-in-law) of David Joris. We will devote one chapter below to this debate.

The Depth of Sin, the Limits of Discipleship, and Church Discipline

The manner, means, and thoroughness of regeneration became crucial questions within the Anabaptist movement. Did the Holy Spirit regenerate believers directly, through no "outward" means except perhaps the hearing of the Word? And was this regeneration thorough and complete to the point that the regenerate could expect to remain essentially free from sin, unless "inadvertently overtaken"? All Anabaptists agreed that saving grace was efficacious, but how far and how deep did this efficacy extend? This question was focused especially by the Anabaptist consensus that Christians should submit to fraternal discipline in cases of sin. How was "sin" to be understood and what measures of sin would be applied? A "high" view of regeneration, when joined to a literalistic ethic of "discipleship," would necessarily involve a strict application of the ban, whereas a more pessimistic view of regeneration would tend towards a more lenient application of the ban. On occasion there also appeared a "high" view of regeneration coupled with a reliance on direct, extra-scriptural revelation that could and did lead to antinomianism, the view that the "spiritual law" had superseded the "written law" and that "to the pure all things are pure." David Joris took this particular road.

Debates on the thoroughness of regeneration can be seen in Hubmaier's critique of some Swiss Brethren (in his "On the Sword"), Marpeck's disagreement with some Swiss concerning the ban, and later Dutch disagreements concerning marriage and the enforcement of the ban. We will devote one chapter below to Marpeck's disagreements with the Swiss Brethren concerning the ban, for his observations raise relevant points about sin, regeneration, and the place of discipline in the congregation. We will devote a further chapter to the banning controversy that emerged around mid-century among Menno's followers.

The Church as the Body of Christ

The conception of the church itself as the visible Body of Christ was significant. It pointed to a very "high" ecclesiology indeed. We may say for Anabaptism, the identification of the church as the "visible Body of Christ" was the theological expression of the sociological phenomenon of sectarianism. Because of the understanding of the church as the Body of Christ, Christological conceptions had far-reaching implications. In the same way that Christ was "in this world," but not "of this world," so also would His Body be "in this world." The tendency to emphasize the spiritual, divine nature of Christ (expressed in quasi-docetic terms in the Melchiorite tradition), had significant repercussions for ecclesiology. It is within the context of a "high" Christology, linked to an optimistic doctrine of regeneration, that we must understand the strenuous efforts of the Dutch Anabaptists to define the limits of this true church, this visible Body of Christ. In the final chapter of this section we will conclude by making some general observations about Anabaptist ecclesiology, such as it had assumed shape by the time of the death of Menno Simons (1561).

The working out of the inner/outer tension inherent in the core of Anabaptist theology (in close relationship to the spirit/letter tension) was one of the significant factors that determined the eventual "denominational" shape of Anabaptist groups, although not always in simple or predictable ways. The more biblicistic Swiss Brethren, for example, in fact held to a more optimistic pneumatology and anthropology (and hence to a stricter understanding of the ban) than did either Hubmaier or Marpeck. The Hutterian branch of the South German/Austrian Anabaptists, in spite of its more spiritualistic beginnings (Hans Denck and Hans Hut), indissolubly linked the inner condition of *Gelassenheit* to an outward legislation of community of goods, drawing community boundaries *vis-a-vis* other Anabaptists on that point. In the north the struggle between an inner versus an outer interpretation of Anabaptist essentials was decided in favour of "outer" marks of regeneration by Menno Simons and Dirk Philips. The basic tension, however, continued well beyond Menno, and shaped later divisions. But the general pattern of Anabaptist development on the inner/outer questions is clear. As we have seen in questions of the sword and the oath and in socio-economic questions, Anabaptism increasingly moved away from the spiritual, experiential, inner side of the Christian life and increasingly emphasized the outer, legislated marks of the "true church." The emphasis came to fall less and less on repentance, faith, and regeneration, and more and more on the "obedience of faith."

End Notes

[1] Kenneth Davis, *Anabaptism and Asceticism* (Scottdale, Pa.: Herald Press, 1974).

[2] Nicodemism is a word that denotes the secret holding of one belief, while outwardly practicing, and appearing to believe another.

HET
BLOEDIGH TOONEEL
DER
DOOPS-GESINDE,
EN
WEERELOOSE
CHRISTENEN.

Die / om het getuygeniſſe JESU hares Salighmaeckers /
gelenen hebben / en gedoodt zijn / van CHRISTI tijdt af /
tot deſe onſe laetſte tijden toe.

Mitſgaders:

Een beſchrijvinge des H. DOOPS, ende andere ſtucken van den Gods-
dienſt, door alle de ſelve tijden geoeffent.

Begrepen in Twee BOECKEN.

Zijnde een vergrootinge van den voorgaenden MARTELAERS-SPIEGEL, uyt
vele gelooſweerdige Chronijcken / Memorien / Getuygeniſſen / &c.

DOOR
T. J. V. B.

Gedruckt tot DORDRECHT, by Jacob Braat.

Voor Jacobus Savry, woonende in 't Kaſteel van Gendt.
In 't Jaer 1660.

Title page of the first edition of the *Martyrs Mirror (1660)*,
compiled by Thieleman van Braght

Chapter 21

The Challenge of Spiritualism:
The South German/Austrian Stream

One possible way of developing the implications of the Anabaptist stress on the "inner" life was to insist that, in comparison to the inner, spiritual reality, the outward marks of the church (the "ceremonies") were strictly secondary. The ceremonies were simply witnesses, or signs, "pointers" or "reminders" of the true essence within. This point was made with particular force by Hans Denck, and was taken up by several influential Anabaptists after his death, notably Hans Bünderlin and Christian Entfelder. Two contrasting responses emerged to this spiritualist challenge. The "literalist" response simply reiterated the necessity of "obedience" to the words of Scripture as evidence of one's inner renewal. This was the approach of the Swiss Anabaptists and, later, of Menno Simons. A second approach was taken up by Pilgram Marpeck, who developed a more sophisticated rationale for the celebration of the "external" ceremonies of the church.

Hans Denck

Hans Denck took a contemplative and mystical approach to the Christian life, but in his writings we recognize the same crucial turning points we have noted in the writings of other Anabaptists. Denck joined other Anabaptists in opposing the Protestant understanding of justification by faith alone, imputed righteousness, and "at once justified and a sinner."[1] He opposed Luther's understanding of predestination and the "bound will" and (along with Erasmus, Hubmaier, and Hoffman) wrote an original treatise against Luther, defending free will.[2] Denck's concern was to place the responsibility for sin squarely on the shoulders of human beings, rather than attributing sin to God. In doing this, Denck also emphasized the ethical responsibility borne by human beings which could not be excused by appealing to an irresistible predestination. The ethical emphasis emerges as strongly in Denck's thought as in that of other Anabaptists: salvation is not dependent on "imputed righteousness" on the basis of faith in Christ alone, but rather salvation involves living a sanctified life, in the power of Christ's Spirit.[3]

The life of yieldedness played an even more major role for Hans Denck than it did for Hubmaier or the Swiss Anabaptists generally. In their yieldedness, believers are simply following the example of Jesus himself.

> All Christians are in some sense like Christ, for, as he offered himself up to the Father, so they are ready to offer themselves. Not, I say, that they are so perfect, as Christ was, but rather that they seek exactly the perfection which Christ never lost.[4]

To believe meant, for Hans Denck, that one was willing to obey. That very willingness already is the result of grace, and indicates that one is ready to set aside self-will in favour of doing God's will.[5] This means a life of "mortification" of the old Adam.[6] The general shape of Denck's understanding of the spiritual life is clearly Anabaptist, with its emphasis on inner regeneration, an outward commitment of water baptism, and a call for a new life in conformity with the life of Christ lived within the community of baptized believers, and involving continued mortification of the "old Adam." All the same, the special emphasis which Denck gives to the inner life of the spirit gives a unique colour to his spirituality, in contrast to that of other Anabaptists.

In spite of the "spark of the divine" present in human beings, and the necessity for human yieldedness to the divine, Denck made perfectly clear that the process of conversion, regeneration and salvation depended in no way upon *human* goodness, but rather was purely a gift of divine grace which (thanks to God's grace) had not been rejected.[7] Having said this, however, it must be said immediately that Denck had a very high pneumatology: he expected the living Spirit of God to be efficacious, and he expected the elect to be *able* to allow the Spirit of God to reign in their lives. Thus Denck could speak of the work of progressive "deification" within the elect;[8] in the same way he could expect believers who were ruled by Christ's Spirit, to live as Christ lived.[9] Although Denck did not expect believers to attain perfection in this life,[10] nevertheless he definitely sided with the Swiss, against Hubmaier, in maintaining that believers must say with Christ, that their kingdom is not of this world. For this reason no Christian may use force or hold a post in government, but rather all "students of Christ" simply admonish and teach evildoers.[11] In the matter of the regeneration of sinful human nature, in the possibility of the regenerated human beings living as Christ lived, and in matters of violence and coercion, Hans Denck very much sided with the Swiss Brethren against Hubmaier.

Although Denck sided with the Swiss, insisting that the process of regeneration demands a life of following after Christ and living as He did,[12] nevertheless his emphasis on the inner Word and inner life led him to a very non-Swiss evaluation of outward, written laws and ceremonies. The same "inner" emphasis that we have noted above, concerning the priority of the living, inner Word over that of the outer, written word of Scripture, emerges again in Denck's understanding of the value of external ceremonies. The essential distinctions were drawn clearly in Denck's "The Law of God," written in 1526, after he had accepted water baptism. In that writing Denck distinguished between commandments, customs, and laws.

The highest observances ordered by God are the "commandments," which are "those that flow from the love of God and neighbour. To overlook them is to incur sin."[13] The highest command to love God and neighbour is thus the most fundamental "command" that the Christian must obey. In fact, it is an inner commandment, with ethical implications. Denck made a further distinction between God's "commandments" (which have to do with love), and "customs." The latter were "external ordinances, geared to natural and daily habits of men by which they were to be reminded of the things which are divine and eternal."[14] Into this category fell all outward observances and "ceremonies" which might be ordered by Scripture, such as circumcision, baptism or the Supper. For Denck, such outer ceremonies were strictly secondary to the highest commandment to love.

> Ceremonies are an outward order, given for their improvement to the common people of Israel to whom all spiritual language was foreign. Thereby they were to be reminded of the simplicity of all laws which had been revealed to Adam in paradise from the beginning, namely to love God above and to hate whatever may hinder love.[15]

To the one who has the "law of love" written in the heart, such outward ceremonies or "reminders" were not only secondary, they were useless: "Whoever fulfils the law of love, truly fulfils all ceremonies also, even though he may never give them a thought."[16] On the other hand, however, such outward ceremonies may have a secondary usefulness insofar as they "hasten the advancement of said love in others."[17] In such a case the "spiritual" believer may well keep the outward ceremonies, for the sake of the highest commandment to love.

Finally, Denck spoke of the "laws," which are "judgments that are established between brothers to protect the innocent and punish the unjust."[18] What Denck had in mind here were civil ordinances, instituted to maintain social order. These laws, while they have been instituted as part of God's order, do not point beyond themselves to God's highest commandment, as do customs, but have a merely practical function in human society.

How were these various levels of "observances" related to one another? Hans Denck had no doubt whatsoever.

> All commandments, customs and laws which are laid down in writing in either the Old Testament or the New are abrogated for a true student of Christ. In other words, he has written upon his heart the one word, which is that he loves God alone. He knows how to govern his every deed by this, even though he may have nothing written in front of him.[19]

The inner reality of God's love living in one's heart is the absolutely primary command.

The incarnation was central to the rule of love, for it was in Jesus that Denck saw love most perfectly manifested.

> Such Love could not be comprehended by flesh and blood but for the fact that God demonstrates it in some people who are called godly persons and children of God, because they take after God, their spiritual Father. The more fully such Love is demonstrated, the more fully it may be known by men; and the more it is known, the more Love is practiced. Therefore it has pleased the eternal Love that the man in whom it was most fully revealed, ought to be called a redeemer of his people.[20]

Hans Denck affirmed his faith in the redemption wrought by Christ, but he insisted further that "divine love" was meant to be appropriated by all "friends of God," who follow after Christ: "All those who are saved are of one spirit with God. But he who is the most perfect in this love, is also a forerunner of those who are to be saved."[21] Salvation for Denck depended less on Jesus' historic atonement on the cross, and much more on a faithful following of the risen Christ, in love.

Given that God's love was fully revealed in Jesus, the customs and laws given to the Old Testament patriarchs have been superseded. Denck hastened to say that the customs and laws set up between God and the Israelites were not wrong, but rather that something better had been revealed through Christ, the first-born of the children of the Spirit. Thus the Old Testament customs and laws could be disregarded through the "freedom permitted by Love," a freedom allowed to children of God, even though forbidden to servants under the law.[22]

If Old Testament customs and laws thus become secondary to one who has yielded to divine love, what of New Testament ceremonies instituted specifically by Christ, particularly the external marks of the church such as baptism, the Supper and fraternal admonition? Denck maintained a central distinction between the Old Testament customs and laws that were ordered to be kept as laws, and New Testament ordinances, which are "free and uncompelled." Baptism and the Supper are celebrated, not because they have been "ordered" by some scriptural "law," but rather they are celebrated as "testimonies," "remembrances" and "witnesses" among God's children, whereby they "recall from what and for what end they have been called, namely out of the world to God to serve Him throughout their lives in holiness and righteousness..."[23] In all of this, Denck made clear, the primary teaching and reality is divine love, dwelling in the heart of believers. "Everything we have written above," he wrote in conclusion, "flows from the perfect Love of Christ from which one may clearly discern who has the spirit of the Lord."[24]

It was a particular strength of Hans Denck's thought that he insisted on focusing continually on the living character of God's presence with human beings. By contrast to the Swiss Anabaptist approach, Denck could not allow the historical written text, or the "externals" of religious ceremony to steal centre stage from the work of the living Spirit of God. By repeatedly pushing back to this point, that the Christian life is, most fundamentally, a life immersed in the living Christ, Hans Denck was repeating a venerable theme in Christian spirituality. Nevertheless, Denck's rejection of the medieval sacraments removed a crucial lynch pin of earlier spirituality, which had linked together the inner and the outer worlds, and had provided outer, visible, and tangible mediators of grace.

In philosophical terms, Hans Denck and the spiritualists assumed a dualistic universe in which the "outer," physical world was of no essential use in the saving process; it had a secondary significance only. The only reality to be heeded was "spiritual"; the physical reality could, at best, provide the "proving ground" for inner regeneration (discipleship) and provide reminders and pointers to that "more real" spiritual world.

It must be noted, however, that the "literalist" Anabaptism of Grebel, Sattler, and Menno Simons (which called simply for "obedience to Scripture") actually assumed the very same dualistic philosophical premises as did the spiritualists. The literalist Anabaptists agreed: the "spiritual" world is the "higher" one; the physical world shares nothing essential with it. To the obvious question of why one would continue with divisive "secondary" ceremonies, the literalists could only add the proviso "we do it because Jesus said so." The literalist Anabaptists could provide no more reason than could the spiritualists for why outer ceremonies were connected to the spiritual life that leads to salvation; the only link was provided by simple "obedience" to the letter. Pilgram Marpeck recognized this difficulty, and attempted to re-establish the essential centrality of the "outer ceremonies" of the church as necessary for the spiritual life of its members. He did this, as we will see below, by reformulating the dualistic philosophical and Christological premises that had been taken for granted by both spiritualist and literalist Anabaptists.

Although Hans Denck died early, his influence continued to be felt. Some Anabaptists, inspired by Denck, were led to reject all outward church ordinances and ceremonies as useless and even positively harmful. Hans Bünderlin was one such Anabaptist.

Marpeck and Bünderlin

Although many details concerning Hans Bünderlin's life and activities are missing, it is clear that this educated Austrian reformer came in contact with spiritualist Anabaptists, and subsequently became one himself.[25] He was baptized in Augsburg in 1526, and then worked as an Anabaptist missioner in and around Linz, in Austria.[26] He spent some time in Nicholsburg, Moravia in 1527, and by 1528 he had moved on to Strasbourg. There he published three of his four known writings. In his first writing, published in 1529,[27] Bünderlin dealt with four main articles: the inner and outer Word, concerning the two Testaments, concerning Moses, the Law and ceremonies, and finally concerning Jesus and the New Testament. In his treatment of all of these themes, Bünderlin showed himself to be a faithful follower of Hans Denck.[28] By 1530, however, and the publication of his third book, Bünderlin's position had shifted even further in the spiritualist direction. The title of the work, in Bünderlin's typically long-winded style, sets out his central thesis: *Explanation, by means of biblical comparisons, that water baptism and other external ordinances used in apostolic churches are restored again by some in our time without God's command or testimony of Scripture.*[29] With this writing Bünderlin abandoned external "ceremonies" and the Anabaptist congregations that continued such usages.[30] It was against this specific writing by Bünderlin that Pilgram Marpeck composed his "Clear Refutation" in 1531.[31]

In his "Clear Refutation," Marpeck highlighted three issues or points of view held by "certain spirits" that needed specific replies. First Marpeck wished to argue against the conclusion that "ceremonies are to be shunned because they have been abused and destroyed by the Antichrist (i.e. the papacy)."[32] In the second place, Marpeck argued against the conclusion that "because of the death of the apostles, there is no longer any command or witness of the Scriptures concerning ceremonies such as baptism and the Lord's Supper."[33] Finally, Marpeck argued against the conclusion that there had been no legitimate bishop appointed since apostolic times.[34]

We will follow Marpeck's points below in detailing the expressed differences between Bünderlin and Marpeck.

Ceremonies have been abused, and are therefore invalid.

Central to Bünderlin's "Explanation" was the historical argument that throughout biblical history, the true, spiritual worship of God had been perverted,[35] culminating in papist sacramentalism. The Roman Catholic error, said Bünderlin, was that the bishops "completely united the spirit and God himself to actual breath or speaking, making a holy word or consecration of it, as occurred in the Lord's Supper, in the same way that the Jews or Israel perverted God's meaning in the Law."[36] To this argument rejecting the Roman Catholic sacraments Pilgram Marpeck replied that he was in partial agreement: ceremonies had been abused and misused, both by the Israelites and in the Roman Catholic church.[37] Nevertheless, said Marpeck, such misuse "cannot invalidate them for the believer who understands, uses, practices, and promotes them in a correct and pure manner." For such a believer outward ceremonies are "performed in a Christian manner and spiritual form."[38]

At the base of this difference of opinion was a very different reading of God's intention in the biblical and historical process. Bünderlin's argument was that God's Word and order were, and always had been, secret and spiritual.[39] It was Cain who began outer ceremonies,[40] and God, in response to human self-will and stubbornness, attempted to speak to humanity in a variety of ways, some of necessity, external. The divine message, however, was that the external was only a secondary sign pointing to the inner, spiritual essence itself.[41] With the coming of Jesus, God's secret was fully revealed: the earlier ceremonies were only external signs, and had no validity in themselves.[42] With Jesus' coming, Bünderlin said, God revealed the desire for the establishment of a purely spiritual Israel, without outward ceremonies.[43] The true Israelites were those who had the Word in their hearts, and performed the true sacrifices "in spirit and in truth."[44]

Marpeck had a different reading of this scriptural history. Marpeck agreed that believers were those who were "inspired by Christ's mandate of faith, spirit, and truth," and that many had misused ceremonies. Nevertheless, Marpeck did not agree that God's secret will and order from the beginning was to do away with external observances altogether. Rather,

> just as the Israelites, rescued out of Babylonian captivity, restored the ancient ceremonies, so too does Christ today, through His servants rescued out of the prison of the Antichrist, restore and renew His instituted ceremonies by means of His inner command and His bestowal of the certainty of His Spirit.[45]

Christ was bestowing his Spirit on the elect, not to do away with the external "commands, laws, and ceremonies," but rather to purify them by means of His messengers. The "purely spiritual" kingdom was not instituted with the birth of Christ, but rather would arrive only when Christ returned at the end of the age.[46]

There no longer is any command to practice Baptism and the Lord's Supper.

A central and necessary point in Bünderlin's argument for the cessation of baptism and the Supper was the explanation of how it was that Jesus ordered both to be carried out, as well as an explanation of the fact that the apostles had baptized with water and celebrated the Supper with physical elements. Bünderlin's explanation was, first of all (as we have seen above), that the true celebrations of baptism and the Supper were spiritual, not physical. In the second place, however, he argued that the apostles had been specially commissioned by Christ to carry out these ceremonies, but that such a commission was intended only for them. Furthermore, their special commission was sealed with signs and wonders. Those who later carried out water baptism and a physical celebration of the Supper were neither appointed directly by Christ or the Holy Spirit, nor was their office confirmed by signs or wonders; they were ignorant of the spiritual significance indicated by Christ, and clung only to the external shell.[47]

Against these arguments Pilgram Marpeck countered that prophets and messengers of Christ were to be recognized not by miracles, but "by their fruits (Matthew 7)." Furthermore, Scripture had no testimony of Philip or Apollos receiving a direct command or commission, and yet they preached, baptized and testified, having been "sent inwardly by Christ's Spirit."[48] And finally, the expressed testimony of Scripture itself argued that the Supper and preaching, teaching, and baptism were to be carried out, not only in Christ's time, but also in "the world which will remain and the nations which will exist until the end or the last day."[49] Marpeck concluded, "These spirits speak with neither discernment nor the support of the Scriptures, and think that, because the ceremonies of the Old Testament have been abrogated ... the ceremonies of the New Testament have also been abrogated. They are mistaken. . . Today these spirits desire to make the kingdom of Christ far too spiritual, and make too great a leap, just as, on the other hand, the Antichrist has made it too physical."[50]

Embedded in Marpeck's detailed scriptural argument is yet another significant argument, drawn from the same Denckian spiritual roots he shared with Bünderlin. He could not agree with "these spirits," he said, because of their "shying away from the discipline of God." "I sense," he continued, "that they lack the Holy Spirit dedicated to the common good (1 Corinthians 12), who uses the gifts of the Holy Spirit for the edification of others (1 Corinthians 14; Ephesians 4), and thus serves them (1 Peter 4)."[51] The radical *individualizing* of the Spirit indicates, said Marpeck, that the "erring spirits" did not have the Spirit of Christ: "If they are members of the Body of Christ, they will speak differently." Quite simply,

> The fruit of the Spirit is love and faithfulness. Faith must manifest itself in witness, fruit, and work. So love is faith in action; it edifies and improves. If they do not love the neighbor, how can they fulfill the law, for such love is the fulfillment of the law. . . . Thus, the gifts of the Spirit manifest themselves not only for private but also for common benefit, service, and improvement.[52]

Against the radical spiritualist individualism advocated by Bünderlin, Pilgram Marpeck returned to the note sounded by Hans Denck in his most Anabaptist writings: love of neighbour cannot lightly be set aside.

With this note, Marpeck anticipated a second crucial point to be made in his following observations, namely that the inward, individual spiritual life (the love of God) cannot be so neatly separated from the outward, social and physical life (the love of neighbour). The two are linked together in the highest commandment of the Lord. In sum,

> The salvation of the soul depends upon love for the neighbor. Whoever does not love his neighbor does not love his own soul, and foolishly seeks his own profit to his highest damage.[53]

The highest spiritual command, love, demands external "preaching, teaching, or action toward others," and not simply attention to one's own internal spiritual condition.

There have been no legitimate bishops appointed since apostolic times.
We have already noted Bünderlin's argument to the effect that following the apostolic age, the bishops of the church continued a "spiritually barren" celebration of external ceremonies. Against this conclusion Pilgram Marpeck argued—borrowing a page from the spiritualists—that the passing on of the authority to teach and preach did not depend on any external transmission (or "apostolic succession"), but rather on a spiritual mandate thrust into the heart of the recipients. Furthermore,

> Christ left, until the end of the world, His external authority and command in the Scriptures to all His disciples, brothers, and members who possess His Spirit or mind.[54]

The spiritual authority to teach and proclaim did not come to an end in the apostolic era, but rather remains until Christ's return.[55] Again, two very different understandings of the movement of divine history are in evidence here.

Of more significance is Marpeck's accompanying argument. The spiritualists "seek even to abolish all external order and means of God, through which and in which His invisible being is seen." However, the "external order" cannot be dispensed with, said Marpeck, for *through it* human beings are "led from the visible into the invisible."[56] The outward ceremonies, although they can be misused, nevertheless "have been instituted by Christ for our service and benefit" in the same way that Christ took on a human body in order to serve humanity.[57]

Marpeck's point led away from radical spiritualism, back towards the Catholic sacramental tradition in a significant way. While Marpeck agreed that there was a higher "spiritual" realm and a lower "physical" realm, nevertheless he insisted that the two were *indivisibly linked*. Marpeck refused to deny spiritual significance to the physical realm: the outward ceremonies instituted by Christ were *means* by which believers would be "led from the visible to the invisible." This is not late medieval Roman Catholic sacramentalism, to be sure—Marpeck did not accept that physical elements blessed by ordained clergy somehow "contain" and transmit grace *ex opere operato*—but Marpeck did hold that physical elements were visible signs pointing to, *leading to*, and thus participating in God's economy of grace. Such a point could not be made by the spiritualists, who at best (as in the case of Denck's final statement) merely allowed external ceremonies to be carried out as memorials or "reminders," for the sake of love, for those not yet perfected in the inner life. Marpeck argued, to the contrary, that the physical side of creation was a crucial and necessary *way to* the divine. And, conversely, Marpeck argued that where invisible grace had come to be present in the heart, there the visible ordinances established by Christ would be "practiced externally and practiced according to love."[58]

Conclusion

It is important to note that in the debate between Marpeck and the spiritualists, the primary role of the Spirit of God was not at issue. Marpeck, no less than Denck and Bünderlin, maintained that a personal experience of the renewing Spirit of God was necessary in order for one to become a Christian believer.[59] Pilgram Marpeck recognized the validity of Hans Denck's insight: the Christian life of the spirit is rooted in the reality of the living God, made present in one's life. Furthermore, the living reality of God must be described as a "law of love" dwelling in the heart. The Christian is one who, in some significant measure, is ruled by the personal and living appropriation of the highest commandment to love God above all things, and one's neighbour as oneself.

Thus Pilgram Marpeck also would agree with Hans Denck on questions of coercion, maintaining that it was on the basis of the living Spirit of God in the heart that Christians could live out a life of love. Since this was so, the Christian life would be above all a life devoted to peace and growth in Christ-likeness. The fundamental reality leading to a life of love and peace was not a series of external New Testament "commands" that were to be obeyed to the letter, but rather a life of spiritual growth informed by the living reality of Christ's presence. Pilgram Marpeck agreed with the spiritualist critique of "mechanical," outward church observances. Such mechanical, external "worship" missed the point, which is that worship must both express and lead to the spiritual reality of the living God.[60] These "spiritualist" insights remained central for Marpeck, and informed his discussions with other Anabaptist groups.

But Pilgram Marpeck could not agree with the conclusion that, since personal spiritual renewal was primary, therefore it was the *only* reality leading to life and salvation. Pilgram Marpeck argued, to the contrary, that individualist spiritualism actually is a denial of love, because it is a denial of community. Said another way, an exclusive concern with the state of one's personal and internal "love of God" actually can lead to a denial of love for one's neighbour. Marpeck's pithy observation is worth citing once again: "If they do not love their neighbor, how can they fulfill the law, for such love is the fulfillment of the law."[61] The highest commandment is two-fold: it points not only "above," but also points simultaneously to the incarnation of love in this world. Furthermore, as we will see in a later chapter, Marpeck did not agree either on philosophical or Christological grounds, that physical reality was in fact unconnected from spiritual reality.

For all of his agreement with the starting point of the Anabaptist spiritualists, then, Pilgram Marpeck rejected what he perceived to be two fundamental dangers in Christian spiritualism: a doctrine of salvation that excluded the neighbour, and a Christology that ignored the human nature of Christ. That is, insofar as "spiritualism" concentrated attention on one's own inner condition of grace, to the exclusion of the love of neighbour, it could not be, said Marpeck, the Spirit of Christ that was ruling the heart. Second, as will be seen in more detail below, insofar as such spiritualism focused attention on the divinity of Christ, to the exclusion or detriment of His humanity, it could not be the Spirit of Christ that was ruling the heart.

End Notes

[1] "Indeed, he has made satisfaction and has levelled the path which no man could otherwise find that one may walk therein and reach life. Whoever does not walk it, does not reach life; for him the path is useless. He has fulfilled the Law, not to place us above it, but to give us an example to follow Him." Hans Denck, "The Law of God (1526)," in Edward J. Furcha, ed. and trans., *Selected Writings of Hans Denck* (Pittsburgh: Pickwick Press, 1975), 49. "They (the Protestants) say thoughtlessly and without making any distinctions ... 'Peace, peace; simply believe and you are accepted and everything is in order.' O you miserable little people; how readily you entrust your soul to dangerous foxes; but you do not trust even for the smallest bit of bread, the shepherd and guardian who can protect you." Hans Denck, "Divine Order," in *ibid.*, p. 97.

[2] Hans Denck, "Whether God is the Cause of Evil," (Augsburg, 1526), in Williams, SAW, pp. 88-111.

[3] "Through His suffering Christ has made satisfaction for the sin of all men. Otherwise no man could be saved... He who depends on the merits of Christ, but continues, nonetheless in a carnal, animal-like existence, holds Christ in utter disregard... As long as we are in the old life, we do not yet truly believe, nor do we want to be good and innocent." Hans Denck, "Recantation," (1528), in Edward J. Furcha, ed. and trans., *Selected Writings of Hans Denck* (Pittsburgh: Pickwick Press, 1975), pp. 124-25.

[4] Hans Denck, "Whether God is the Cause of Evil," in Williams, SAW, p. 99.

[5] *Ibid.*, p. 109.

[6] "The poisoned selffulness of the flesh which man has taken on himself against God and without God ought and must be mortified." *Ibid.*, p. 108.

[7] See *ibid.*, p. 93.

[8] "The Word was in human beings for this purpose that it might divinize them, as happens to all the elect." *Ibid.*, p. 101.

[9] "Christians, that is, they who have received the Holy Spirit, are in God, like unto Christ and equal to him, in such a way that what refers to the one refers also to the other. As Christ does, so do they also." *Ibid.*, p. 100.

[10] "This does not mean that (the believer) is perfect and without afflictions..." *Ibid.*, p. 90.

[11] See Hans Denck, "Concerning Genuine Love," (1527), in Furcha, *Selected Writings*, p. 116.

[12] "(The) Means is Christ, whom none may truly know unless he follow after him with his life." Williams, SAW, p. 108. "(The believer) obeys not of his own account. Rather, he has learned to do so from his leader Jesus of Nazareth so that the Word born of the Father from eternity which has wrought in the same Jesus grace amidst

highest disgrace may also work in him according to the measure of his faith." Hans Denck, "Divine Order," in Furcha, *Selected Writings*, p. 84.

[13] Hans Denck, "The Law of God (1526)," *ibid.*, p. 66. The central importance of Jesus' "highest commandment" to love remains fundamental for Denck throughout his writings; he expounds the centrality of love most eloquently in "Concerning Divine Love," written in 1527.

[14] *Ibid.*, p. 66.

[15] *Ibid.*, p. 51.

[16] *Ibid.*, p. 52.

[17] *Ibid.*, p. 51.

[18] *Ibid.*, p. 66.

[19] *Ibid.*, pp. 66-67.

[20] *Ibid.*, p. 103. Or again, in a passage that brings Marpeck to mind, Denck writes: "God's love toward man and man's love toward God cannot be manifest in a better way than in this Jesus in whom God had such compassion with the world that he was willing to forego all justice in dealing with our sins, provided we did not disdain it. This has been amply shown in the humanity of Jesus, but not as coming from men, but as taught by God. To wit, man is to stand in the highest degree of love toward God and as far as is possible he should help his neighbour toward this aim also, so that he too may know and love God." *Ibid.*, p. 104.

[21] *Ibid.*, p. 104.

[22] *Ibid.*, pp. 109-110.

[23] *Ibid.*, p. 110.

[24] *Ibid.*, p. 117.

[25] ME, I, pp. 469-70.

[26] TA, *Elsaß*, 1, p. 232.

[27] Hans Bünderlin, *Ein gemeyne berechnung uber der heyligen schrifft innhalt...* (Strassburg, 1529). Claude R. Foster's study of Bünderlin concludes that the "gemeyne berechnung" was Bünderlin's second book, and presents an English translation of "Aus was Ursach" which, Foster argues, was Bünderlin's first publication. See Claude R. Foster, Jr. and Wilhelm Jerosch, trans. and ed., "The Reason Why God Descended...", MQR 42 (October, 1968), pp. 260-284.

[28] Some examples will suffice: God's Word is spirit and life; the kingdom of God is in us and all human hearts, and not outside us. (Aiiii r.) Flesh, which is against spirit, opposes God, and seeks to do its own will. (Aiiii v.) The outer word serves only to admonish and comfort; the real Word of God is within. (Bi r.) Sin comes from us; righteousness from God. (Bvii r.) The Word of God can be heard within, by all, and doesn't depend on outer preaching. (Civ v.) Predestination is opposed, (Fviii v.) Conversion and daily sacrifice are called for. (Gii r.) Outward ceremonies must become inward sacrifices of the spirit. (Nvi r.) See also the detailed argumentation in Claude R. Foster, Jr., "Hans Denck and Johannes Buenderlin: A Comparative Study," MQR 39 (April, 1965), pp. 115-124. Foster argues for a very close relationship between Denck and Bünderlin.

[29] Hans Bünderlin, *Erklerung durch vergleichung der Biblischen geschrifft, das der wassertauff sampt andern eüsserlichen gebreüchen...* etc. (Strasbourg, 1530).

[30] The noted spiritualist Sebastian Franck spoke highly of Bünderlin in a letter to Johannes Campanus, February 4, 1531. He also sent along a "booklet" by Bünderlin, most probably the *Erklerung*. See TA, *Elsass*, 1, p. 317, n. 5.

[31] Pilgram Marpeck, *Ain Clarer vast nützlicher unterricht, wider etliche trück und schleichendt geister, so jetzt in verborgener weis ausgeen dadurch vil frommer hertzen verirrt und verführt werden...* (1531). This book was once thought lost. The text is translated Klassen and Klaassen, *Writings*, pp. 44-67. Note the relevant literature, *ibid.*, p. 569, nn. 1-3. Boyd, *Marpeck*, pp. 62-63, and Neal Blough, "Pilgram Marpeck and Caspar Schwenckfeld: The Strasbourg Years," in J. Rott and S. Verheus, eds., *Anabaptistes et dissidents au XVIe siecle* (Baden-Baden: Koerner, 1987), pp. 371-75, note that Marpeck also directed this writing against Christian Entfelder.

[32] Klassen and Klaassen, *Writings*, p. 45.

[33] *Ibid.*, p. 47.

[34] *Ibid.*, p. 55.

[35] Bünderlin, *Erklerung*, Biv r and following.

[36] *Erklerung*, Ev verso.

[37] Klassen and Klaassen, *Writings*, pp. 45-46.

[38] *Ibid.*, p. 45.

[39] *Erklerung*, Avi r-Avii r.

[40] *Ibid.*, Avii v.

[41] *Ibid.*, Bv v.

[42] *Ibid.*, Bvii r-v.

[43] *Ibid.*, Cii v.

[44] *Ibid.*, Cv v.

[45] Klassen and Klaassen, *Writings*, p. 46.

[46] *Ibid.*, p. 47.

[47] See Bünderlin, *Erklerung*, Div r; Ei r and ff. See his comments concerning baptism, Evi r.

[48] Klassen and Klaassen, *Writings*, p. 51.

[49] *Ibid.*

[50] *Ibid.*, p. 52.

[51] *Ibid.*, pp. 52-53.

[52] *Ibid.*, p. 53.

[53] *Ibid.*, p. 54.

[54] *Ibid.*, p. 56.

[55] *Ibid.*, pp. 58; 60.

[56] *Ibid.*, p. 57.

[57] *Ibid.*, pp. 58-59.

[58] *Ibid.*, p. 65.

[59] "The outpouring of the Spirit of God on the apostles or on another man next to me does not profit me, a coarse, crude man, except it also be poured into my heart for common good unto salvation." *Ibid.*, p. 60.

[60] Marpeck notes: "Whoever practices or receives such ceremonies and matters (i.e., baptism, the Lord's Supper, Scripture) without true faith, because of an external urge or other reasons, errs even though there is, externally, correctness of words and procedures." *Ibid.*, p. 64.

[61] *Ibid.*, p. 53.

Chapter 22

The Challenge of Spiritualism:
Menno Simons and Nicolaas van Blesdijk

The debate we have traced above, between Pilgram Marpeck and the spiritualists, would be repeated again among the Anabaptists in the north with slightly different emphases, within the Melchiorite Anabaptist tradition. The recurrence of these issues should not be surprising for, as we have seen, the basic points of tension were present in the Anabaptist movement from the start. Given the fact that the essential rebirth, baptism and worship took place inwardly, in the spirit, how was the relationship between the inner life (faith and regeneration) and outer life (the "obedience of faith") to be understood and defined?

Apocalypticism heightened spiritualistic elements within Anabaptism, but End Times questions were notably absent in the debate between Marpeck and Bünderlin. In the north it would be otherwise, for the basic elements for that discussion were provided by Melchior Hoffman. Thus the central scriptural issues had to do with the role of the Spirit in the utterance and interpretation of prophecy (both biblical and actual), while the inner/outer debate had to deal with Hoffman's spiritualized Christology, his optimistic anthropology, and subsequent Melchiorite attempts to establish a visible kingdom of righteousness on earth. After 1535 in the north, Anabaptists had to take into account the disaster at Münster and the dramatic failure of Melchiorite prophetic interpretation. The matter of outer manifestations, versus inner spiritual regeneration thus presented a very real problem. Why, if outer elements were secondary to a spiritual and inner rebirth and true faith, was it necessary to separate from the world in a visible way?

Complicating the picture in the north was Melchior Hoffman's own equivocation concerning external ordinances. Although he had argued that baptism, the Supper, and the ban were divinely ordained and should be followed,[1] nevertheless in the face of the persecution and martyrdom of followers in the north, he suspended water baptism, perhaps following the lead of South German spiritualizing Anabaptists. Hoffman was willing to allow the external ordinances to lapse, if the "time" in the prophetic calendar was not right for them to be carried out. It was only under the prophetic leadership of Jan Matthijs that water baptism was taken up again in the north, as a necessary outer sign of election. For Matthijs the resumption of baptism was related to his eschatological convictions: like Hut, he baptized in order to mark the 144,000 elect of the Last Days.

After 1535, the brethren in the north had to contend with the fact that in the forefront of those who had insisted on the outward, physical signs of inner regeneration had been those who had set out to establish a highly visible kingdom of God on earth, and had taken the sword as a means to this end. Was not one of the failures of Münster precisely the fact that too much had been made of externals, when in fact the kingdom of God was spiritual, not physical? Would not the way of peace be served best by emphasizing the essential inner rebirth and life of the Spirit, allowing only secondary importance to the outer manifestations of religious life?

Menno and the David Jorists

The issues raised in the debate between Menno and Joris—in particular the questions concerning the proper outer evidences of an inner rebirth—were addressed by Menno in several writings between 1541 and 1546. At that latter date Menno, along with Gillis van Aachen, Dirk Philips and Leenaert Bouwens, participated in a debate with Nicolaas M. van Blesdijk, David Joris' son-in-law who, during Joris' secret exile in Basel, had become the most able and visible defender of Joris' position in the north.[2] It is from Blesdijk's writings that we gain the clearest view of the next series of arguments between the followers of Menno and those of Joris. Blesdijk, unlike Joris, continued the direct dialogue with Menno and his followers, replying to the charges of idolatry and Nicodemism raised by Menno and others in Menno's camp.[3]

In 1545 or possibly even earlier, Menno wrote Blesdijk a letter which has since been lost; we know of its contents thanks to Blesdijk's summary.[4] In that letter Menno cautioned Blesdijk not to "turn into the wide path of idolatry, toward pomp and ostentation, to violation of the word and the ordinance of Christ, and to damnable conformity to this world," under the appearance of humility.[5] There are many, Menno said, who "turn away from obedience to the Holy Word and return to all sorts of disgraceful idolatry, avarice, presumptuous curiosity, flight from the cross, denial or repudiation of the word of Christ, to drunkenness, baptismal feasts, false preachers without a calling, infant baptism, worldly communion, etc." Although they bragged of freedom in these things, such a claim was contrary to Scripture, where "such things are forbidden and pushed aside in full clarity." Therefore, advised Menno, Blesdijk would do well to "forsake all such good-for-nothing, frivolous, cross-fleeing, loud-mouths and to remain with the simple, wretched congregation of Christ, which is hated by all, etc."[6]

The line of argument taken by Menno in Blesdijk's summary is well attested in Menno's extant writings. In what follows we will trace the points of disagreement between Menno and Blesdijk, supplementing Blesdijk's sketch of Menno's arguments with selections taken from other writings of Menno dating from this time.

The Issue of "Idolatry"

Already in 1539, in his writing against the corrupt sects, Menno had alluded to the evil of Nicodemism; he brought up the issue again explicitly in his reply to David Joris and also in a writing published around 1542.[7] In his letter to Blesdijk, Menno charged that participating in the public services of Catholics or Protestants was "idolatry," and it was this statement that Blesdijk took up immediately in reply.

Blesdijk agreed with Menno that idolatry was always a sin, but he insisted that the true nature of idolatry must be understood.[8] God is Spirit, and must be worshipped in spirit and in truth; thus true worship, or conversely idolatry, can be measured by no outward words or deeds.[9] Since loving God in the heart above all things is the highest law, idolatry must be defined as loving created things above God.[10] If Menno understood idolatry in this way, then Blesdijk agreed that Menno's judgment was true. But, if Menno wished to label infant baptism, attendance in other churches, or participation in the Supper of other churches as "idolatry" then, Blesdijk said, this was "a false, heathen judgement that has no foundation in Holy Scripture, nor can it be defended with any word or understanding of the Spirit."[11]

Blesdijk's opening line of defence followed, as one might expect, the logic of David Joris' emphasis on the inner spiritual life, but Blesdijk proceeded next to take up Menno's arguments on Menno's own grounds, namely Scripture itself. Menno had asked: Why did God command certain outward ceremonies, and forbid other ceremonies, temples, etc. in the Old Testament?[12] Menno's appeal to the Old Testament was falsely put, answered Blesdijk, for the New Testament knows nothing of such commandments and prohibitions. The Old Testament ceremonies were shadows of the true essence, which was brought to light by Christ's death.[13] The "evangelical, apostolic teaching" shows the true way to serve God, namely by means of righteousness, purity and truth in one's heart which *cannot be brought about by any ceremonies or outer things*, but rather are the fruit of faith in the heart.[14] Such a heart cannot be attained by outer ceremonies, repeated Blesdijk, but only through faith in Christ, through the Holy Spirit, and when this occurs, "then one is freed from the laws and darkness of all ceremonies."[15]

Blesdijk's essential proof for Christian freedom was not based on David Joris' prophecies or visions, or on an appeal to a pure spiritual rebirth (although it presupposed both), but rather was argued with the writings of Paul. In Colossians 2, Paul had said that faith in Christ frees believers from ceremonies and the penalty of sin.[16] Eating, drinking, and the use of any earthly thing (*elementisch dinck*) were thus made free in Christ, that is, "in the Spirit and mind of Christ, which is preached and confessed in the Gospel."[17] In fact, holding to ceremonies as though they were necessary demonstrated an unclean heart, and condemning others (who professed the same faith in Christ) on the basis of their use of outer ceremonies alone was a greater abomination than any use of ceremonies could be. In short, Blesdijk admonished Menno to look to himself, and beware that he not be missing the log in his own eye, or straining a gnat in order to swallow a camel.[18]

The case of Baptism

A case in point for Menno was the question of baptism. Holding to the necessity of this external ordinance in fact had been a central defining characteristic of the movement from the start—except of course that its necessity had been challenged by the spiritualists and (at least temporarily) by Melchior Hoffman himself. Menno argued that Christ had most clearly *commanded* the church to baptize believers on their confession of faith. "If now I do not believe and do not suffer myself to be baptized in accordance with God's Word, but allow my little children without Scriptural warrant to be baptized, am I then obedient unto the voice of the Lord? Can I then inherit the promise given to the believers? The answer is no."[19]

For Blesdijk, on the other hand, the issue was not one of literal obedience to Christ's command, but rather a needless argument over a secondary and unessential question. To argue over whether to baptize a child that is two days old, or rather wait until the child is twelve years old, is an argument over nothing more important than the timing of an outer ceremony—as if salvation depended on the ceremony.[20] Better simply to put up with the misuse of outer ceremonies for a time longer, as did Paul and Peter with the Jewish Christians, in order to win over those who are weak to the true, inward faith. For Blesdijk water baptism of adults was fine, insofar as it served to strengthen the inner baptism of the Spirit; beyond such a function, the water had no essential meaning.

It is worthy of note that Blesdijk agreed with Menno that the "proper" and biblical mode of baptism was water baptism of adults on confession of faith: on this point, said Blesdijk, "we have no disagreement." The question was, rather, whether Christians were free to use or not to use outer ceremonies such as baptism.[21] Blesdijk's argument implied that he and his group would follow the proper or biblical ceremonies whenever possible, but ceremonies really were not of the essence, since ceremonies did not *lead to* a change of heart.[22] Here one might have expected Menno to argue, as had Marpeck against Bünderlin and Entfelder, that the outer ceremonies of the church community did in fact lead to and build up the inner life of faith, and that the outer testimony of the church was essential to the church being church. But Menno did not take up this line of argumentation, preferring rather to reiterate the necessity of obedience to the "commands of Scripture" in the maintenance of purity.

External Appearances and Visible Separation

One of Menno's critiques in his letter to Blesdijk concerned the use by David Jorists of "gold, silver, and expensive clothing."[23] Blesdijk replied that all things created by God, such as wife, children, houses, etc., were given by God for human use, "and therefore are not evil in themselves, but rather are God's pure handiwork."[24] Misuse of created things was sin and abomination, but such sin stemmed not from the mere use of created things, "but rather from the hearts of those who use them. It is the heart that makes works good or evil."[25]

Blesdijk's reliance on the "inner essence" argument was predictable but, borrowing a page from Menno, Blesdijk went further and did a literal exegesis of James 2:2ff. The problem James was addressing in that chapter was not the fact that someone wearing costly clothing had entered the church to worship—for that in itself was not castigated or forbidden by James—but rather the sin consisted in the fact that wealth was honoured when it should not have been.[26] Of course, said Blesdijk, if created things were threatening to distance one's heart from God, or threatening to join one's spirit to the world, they should be avoided for those reasons.[27] If this was Menno's teaching, then it was good. But, said Blesdijk, appealing again to Paul on Christian freedom—1 Timothy 4, in this case—if Menno's teaching was that costly clothing and outer things could not be used at all, then this was "a teaching of the Devil."[28] Such a teaching was nothing but superstition and monkery, an attempt to appear holy that missed the essence of holiness, the spirit, and truth itself.[29]

Martyrdom and the Cross

In Menno's letter to Blesdijk, as well as in other writings, Menno had alleged that David Jorist dissimulation was in fact an attempt to "flee the cross" by conforming to the outward rites of the state-sanctioned churches.[30] Blesdijk noted, to the contrary, that the David Jorists also had been true to their faith unto death. In 1538 in Delft, for example, thirty-eight David Jorists were put to death by sword and water, and he noted some hundred more who had suffered the same fate elsewhere.[31] If it were argued that these people were put to death because of their evil deeds, Blesdijk said that the authorities and the common people alike recognized that the David Jorist martyrs had died for their faith, primarily over the issues of Supper and baptism.[32] But the essence of the matter for Blesdijk was, simply put, that suffering death by persecution could provide no proof of true martyrdom: Jews, Mohammedans, Catholics in England, and followers of Luther and Zwingli in Italy, France, Spain, and Upper and Lower Germany all likewise died for their beliefs, the Christians among them all being ready to defend their positions with Scripture.[33] It simply could not be the case that such manifestly opposed positions and opinions could all represent the true mind of God.[34] The long and the short of it is, asserted Blesdijk, that God is the only possible judge in these matters, for God sees the heart.[35] Unless those who suffered and died for their beliefs had the spirit of love in their hearts (Blesdijk quotes I Corinthians 13:1-4 here), the offering of their bodies was in vain.[36] True wisdom and religion is a gift from God that enlightens the inner person, and especially gives the gift of love towards all, including enemies.[37]

Just as Blesdijk denied that evangelical freedom was a David Jorist cover for sinful licence, so also did he deny that emphasizing the inner nature of true faith (and holding outer ceremonies as secondary) was an escape from martyrdom and the cross. The community of which he was a part was made up of people "who believe in Christ and follow in His footsteps in love, ready and even eager to testify to their faith and to seal that testimony with their goods and their blood."[38] In a subsequent writing Blesdijk clarified his criteria for accepting martyrdom: If the matters in question are so important that the salvation of the soul is involved, then it is right and proper to lay aside all earthly goods and even one's life. Such is the case, for example, when one is pressured to deny one's faith in Christ, or to say that one may be saved by any other name; or when one is pressured to say that ceremonies of themselves have the power to forgive sin or to save outside of Christ; or to deny that God has the power of judgement to eternal life or death.[39] In all such cases, Blesdijk said, he and his fellow believers would die in defense of their beliefs, and honour God above men, just as had the apostles.[40]

Principles of Scriptural Interpretation

The exchange between Menno and Blesdijk made clear some essential points of difference that were not addressed in Menno's debate with Joris concerning spiritual authority. Writing around 1542, Menno asserted that the true congregation of Christ is made up of those who are genuinely converted, born from above of God, who have a mind regenerated by the Holy Spirit "through hearing of the divine Word." Such have become children of God and so "have entered into obedience to Him, and live unblamably in His holy commandments."[41] The key concepts for Menno, in distinction to Joris, were the coming of the Holy Spirit through the Word, and a life of visible obedience to Christ's commandments.

The worldly church, said Menno, had abandoned obedience to Christ. In particular the "corrupt sect of the third David" (David Joris) had the idea that "to the pure all things are pure so that it is permissible to show outward reverence toward images, to baptize children..." But, Menno objected, giving voice to his principle of scriptural interpretation, all things which are "not implied, expressed, nor commanded in the Word" are false. "The Holy Spirit of God has abundantly testified through Paul and John that those who commit these things shall not inherit the kingdom of God."[42]

That the true church would be made up of those who have been spiritually reborn Menno held with Joris, but he insisted that those who have been reborn in the inner spirit will live outward lives in visible separation from the world, in conformity to the life and commandments of Christ. Just as the Holy Spirit is tied to the literal Word (particularly as it reveals Christ, His life, and His commandments), so also the outer lives of the regenerate are necessarily tied in obedience to the testimony of the Word—in particular the "commandments" of the New Testament.

Blesdijk, for his part, returned repeatedly to Paul's writings in his reply to Menno,[43] in order to reinforce his basic position: if Paul allowed believers to eat food sacrificed to idols, how could Menno say that outer ceremonies were "commanded"? There was no eternal law given in Scripture concerning ceremonies, but rather only one eternal law, "namely to believe, fear, thank and love God with all one's heart, with all one's strength, etc., and one's neighbour as oneself. This is an eternal decretal, commandment, and eternal law...which no one can or is able to change."[44] All the ordinances of Moses, the apostles, and even those given and used by Christ were given and established "only to instruct human beings, in order to lead and bring them to the mind and spirit of the only Law."[45] Since faith in Christ was entirely in the hearts of believers, there could in fact be no such a thing as idolatry for them.[46]

Menno, in his letter to the Amsterdam church, refused to grant the scriptural argument concerning Christian freedom, and opposed Blesdijk's citing of Paul with Pauline citations of his own. The pure bride of Christ is espoused to one husband (2 Corinthians 11:2); it is a pure church, which separates from drunkards, the covetous, fornicators, the idolatrous, and the proud, as the apostle said: avoid them and don't eat with them (1 Corinthians 5:11). Any who preach another gospel are accursed (Galatians 1:8). Likewise, Paul said that those who taught circumcision were dogs (Philippians), and also gave counsel on whom to avoid (Philipians 3:2, 17, 19). "The apostle would have the bride so pure that no dissension was allowed; no drunkards, bandits, idolaters, nor those that taught any other doctrine than he taught."[47] In short, says Menno, "How then can some say this is a matter of liberty? Of this liberty any sensible Christian may judge. Shall we who declare that we defend the glory of God talk of a matter of liberty where God is blasphemed and His ordinances broken?"[48] There was no inner, spiritual obedience for Menno apart from outer obedience and a visible witness of nonconformity to the world.[49]

For Blesdijk, however, Menno's attempt to prove that outward actions are idolatrous was an instance of literal proof-texting. "There is nothing so evil," noted Blesdijk, perhaps thinking back to the Münster experience, "but that people will find some letter of Scripture that appears to command or defend it."[50] But Blesdijk also defended the David Jorist position against the charge of antinomianism: some might say that since idolatry is only of the heart, then one may do what one wishes, including murder, robbery and the like. But, Blesdijk objected, such things could not be done without the consent of one's heart, and therefore they remained the fruits of idolatry. But allowing children to be baptized in a state church, or attending services in such churches, are not matters of the heart, and so are not idolatrous.[51]

Blesdijk's response to Menno's literal approach was even more specific in a later writing. Against the argument that Christ had commanded believers to be baptized, thus not leaving baptism "free," Blesdijk answered: "Scripture is a rule which instructs us concerning what we ought to do and avoid doing; it is not a rule which instructs us concerning what is free or not free. Rather, what is not forbidden is free; infant baptism is not forbidden, therefore it is free."[52] Here Blesdijk's broader exegetical beginning point was clarified. The cause of the many disagreements between Christians, concluded Blesdijk, was the fact that so many in his day held to literal words of Scripture, and did not grasp the meaning of the whole.[53] The summary and foundation of all Scripture, said Blesdijk, could be summarized in a short sentence: a faith which is active in love, or love which comes from a pure heart and sincere faith. "All other words of Scripture must be explained and understood according to this rule of faith and love."[54] In fact, the Devil finds it impossible to hide himself behind the law of faith and love, the way that he so easily can under the appearance of outer ceremonies.[55]

Conclusion

What are the limits of Christian freedom, and what does the "obedience of faith" demand? The debate between Menno Simons and Nicolaas van Blesdijk is particularly interesting because Blesdijk took up the argument on Menno's ground, namely that of Scripture itself. Further, he acknowledged the priority of the New Testament over the Old and did not disagree with the Christocentric reading of the Bible. But Blesdijk and Menno approached Scripture with very different attitudes and presuppositions. Blesdijk's rejection of literal prooftexting was based on his conviction that love was the "highest summation and foundation of all the Scriptures" (*die Hooftsomma ende gront aller Schriftuyren*), by which all other scriptural statements must be measured.[56] Menno continued to insist that Christ's "commands" must be obeyed. For Menno, what was not "implied or commanded" in the New Testament was forbidden and false; for Blesdijk, what was not forbidden in the New Testament, was allowed.

In the disagreement concerning idolatry, Blesdijk cited Paul to good advantage. Pauline texts arguing for freedom from the law could be applied extremely well as a counter to Menno's literalistic position, which emphasized "obedience to the law" even in his reading of the New Testament. Blesdijk's biblical point is worth recalling for those in the Believers' Church tradition, for that tradition has tended to follow the logic of Menno's position. The danger of Menno's view is that outward conformity can easily be mistaken for spiritual reality. Blesdijk's counter reminds us that ultimately, God judges the heart; furthermore, outward conformity can just as easily be pharasaic as it can be revelatory of the condition of one's heart.

While this critique of a legalistic attitude is well taken, Blesdijk and the spiritualists wished to push the logic of Christian freedom even further: since the inner is what really matters, the outer is practically inconsequential. Thus they came close to severing the link between the inner and outer lives of believers; furthermore, this radical individualizing of the Christian life also left little room for the community of believers as such. Blesdijk could grant that the proper biblical procedure was water baptism for those who have been baptized inwardly, but he would argue further that infant baptism was simply of no consequence (since it did not pertain to the inner life of the infant), and that water baptism was optional, serving only to confirm or perhaps strengthen the true baptism of the Spirit.

Menno's answer, although expressed in a more legalistic mode than that of some other Anabaptists, nevertheless reiterated a central point made in other parts of the movement: Baptism is administered following confession of faith because that is the biblical order, and believers are and ought to be obedient to the commands of Scripture.[57] Thus Menno in effect sidestepped the deeper philosophical question concerning the essential relationship of the inner lives of believers and the outward ceremonies of the gathered community, such as baptism and the Lord's Supper: the ceremonies, said Menno, are essential because they are commanded.

End Notes

[1] Especially in Melchior Hoffman, *The Ordinance of God*, (1530), in Williams, *SAW*, pp. 182-203.

[2] Stayer, "Davidite," in Horst, *Dutch Dissenters*, p. 147.

[3] Joris did reply indirectly to those charges in David Joris, *Onschuldt David Jorisz* (1540). See Zijlstra, "Blesdijk," p. 35. Adam Pastor in particular attacked Joris' teaching in twenty-five articles in a booklet published in 1542. Although the book apparently received wide circulation in the Netherlands, and was translated into French and Latin, no copies have survived. Gillis van Aachen also wrote a anti-Jorist tract in 1546, which also has not survived. Menno made passing comments against Joris' teachings in several writings, and addressed one letter in 1545 to Amsterdam Melchiorites who were wavering on the matter of Nicodemism. See Stayer, "Davidite," pp. 146-7; Zijlstra, "Blesdijk," pp. 37-8 on Pastor's booklet; *ibid.*, 43ff. on the Lübeck debate.

[4] On this letter, see Stayer, "Davidite vs. Mennonite," in Horst, *The Dutch Dissenters*, pp. 157-159. CWMS, following K. Vos, *Menno Simons*, 1914, p. 280 supposedly reproduces this "letter" from Menno following Blesdijk's description in, *Christelijke Verantwoordinghe*, 1607, "voorreden." In fact, this was a mistake that

apparently originated with Vos. As Stayer notes, "What appears ... in the *Complete Writings* is not Blesdijk's paraphrase of a letter of Menno but rather an excerpt from his foreword, in which he outlines the contents of his tract *against* Menno." Stayer, "Davidite," p. 157. Blesdijk's reproduction of Menno's letter, found a few pages later in Blesdijk's book, is reproduced and translated by Stayer, *ibid.*, pp. 158-59.

[5] Stayer, "Davidite," p. 158.

[6] Stayer, "Davidite," pp. 158-59; original in Blesdijk, *Christelijke Verantwoordinghe*, A4v-A5v.

[7] Menno Simons, "Why I do not cease teaching and writing," CWMS, p. 300.

[8] Blesdijk, *Christelijke Verantwoordinghe*, f.6a.

[9] *Ibid.*, f.6b.

[10] *Ibid.*, f.7a.

[11] *Ibid.*, f.8a.

[12] Menno also argued in this manner, quoting liberally from Numbers and Leviticus, in his letter to the Amsterdam community that apparently was tempted by the Nicodemite solution. See Menno Simons, "Admonition to the Amsterdam Melchiorites," CWMS, pp. 1023-1024.

[13] Blesdijk, *Christelijke Verantwoordinghe*, f.10b-11a.

[14] *Ibid.*, f.11a. Emphasis mine. The contrast with Marpeck is striking, for Blesdijk explicitly denies what Marpeck asserts.

[15] *Ibid.*, f.11b.

[16] *Ibid.*, f.12b-13a.

[17] *Ibid.*, f.13a.

[18] *Ibid.*, f.13a-14a.

[19] CWMS, p. 1025.

[20] "Die twist is alleene om den tijt der Doope." *Ibid.*, f.18a. See further f.18b-19a.

[21] Blesdijk, *Weder-antwoort Nicolaes Meynaertsz van Bleesdijck op zekeren Brief by Gellium onderteeckent / waer in hy sijne meyninge unde oordeel stelt op eenich Tractaet geintituleert Een Christlijcke verantwoordinghe unde billijcke wederlegginghe etc. Geschreven in't Jaer 1545.* (1607), f.5b-6a.

[22] *Christelijke Verantwoordinghe*, f.17a.

[23] *Christelijke Verantwoordinghe*, f. 21b-28b. Menno repeated the charge in his revised (1558) version of the Fundamentboeck section "To the Corrupt Sects": "This kingdom is not a kingdom in which they parade in gold, silver, pearls, silk, velvet, and costly finery, as is done by the haughty, proud world; matters which your leaders defend and allow with this meaningless provision; just so you do not desire these things and live for them in your heart." CWMS, p. 217.

[24] "is derhalven in hem selven niet quaet / dan Godes reyne heylige handtwerck." *Christelijke Verantwoordinghe*, f.21b.

[25] *Ibid.*, f.22a. Note Blesdijk's exegesis of I Tim. 2; 8, *Ibid.*, ff. 23a-b. His concluding point is that Paul does not forbid the use of creatures, but rather looks to attitude of the heart. *Ibid.*, f.24a.

[26] *Ibid.*, f.26a.

[27] *Ibid.*, f.26b.

[28] *Ibid.*, f.27a.

[29] *Ibid.*, f.28b.

[30]In "Admonition on Church Discipline," Menno critiques "a doctrine that contradicts the cross of Christ." CWMS, p. 412. In his revision of the Fundamentboeck (1558) Menno noted that in Christ's kingdom "Nor does anyone lay aside the cross of Christ as you do, but here the requirement is ... to testify to Jesus Christ with the mouth, conduct, possessions, and blood, if divine honor requires it." CWMS, pp. 217-18.

[31] *Verantwoordinghe*, f.30a. Anna Jansz of Rotterdam, one of the best-known martyrs in the Anabaptist tradition, was a David Jorist. Her story, testimony and writings were preserved in Thielemann J. van Braght's *Martyrs' Mirror* and in the Swiss Brethren hymnal, the *Ausbund*. See her profile in Snyder and Hecht, *Profiles of Anabaptist Women*, forthcoming.

[32] *Ibid.*

[33] *Ibid.*, f.32b-33a.

[34] "Dat niet sijn en conde / so sy beyde den eyghentlijcken sin godes kenden ende volchden." *Ibid.*, f.33a.

[35] *Ibid.*, f.30b.

[36] *Ibid.*, f.32a-b.

[37] *Ibid.*, f. 34b-35b.

[38] *Ibid.*, f.16a.

[39] Blesdijk, *Weder-antwoort Nicolaes Meynaertsz van Bleesdijck op zekeren Brief by Gellium onderteeckent... Geschreven in't Jaer 1545.* (1607), f.11a-b.

[40] *Ibid.*, f.11b.

[41] Menno Simons, "Why I do not cease teaching and writing," CWMS, p. 300.

[42] *Ibid.*, p. 301.

[43] In the *Weder-antwoort* Blesdijk refers to I Cor. 8 (f.14b.), and Gal. 5 (f.15a), for example.

[44] *Ibid.*, f.16b.

[45] *Ibid.*, f.17a.

[46] *Ibid.*, f.17b.

[47] CWMS, p. 1023.

[48] *Ibid.*

[49] "It behooves the true Christian to be pious externally and internally, glorifying God both in body and spirit." CWMS, p. 184.

[50] *Ibid.*, f.9b.

[51] *Ibid.*, f.10a.

[52] "...die Kinder-doop is niete verboden / Ergo so is sy vry." Blesdijk, *Weder-Antwoort*, f.6b. (The argument is repeated, f.8b).

[53] Blesdijk refers here to the disagreement concerning the Lord's Supper between Luther and Zwingli, as an example. *Ibid.*, f.20b.

[54] *Ibid.*, f.20b-21a.

[55] *Ibid.*, f.21a.

[56] Blesdijk, *Christelijcke Verantwoordinghe*, 20b.

[57] See Bornhäuser, *Leben und Lehre*, pp. 82-90.

Chapter 23

Pilgram Marpeck and the Swiss Brethren:
Regeneration and Discipline

The Swiss Brethren position on the ban was premised on the two kingdom understanding: Christians have been called out of the world, and now have their citizenship in heaven. The church is the community of heaven, living now according to the pattern and model of Christ. But the Swiss understanding of the two kingdoms was premised further on the possibility and actual fact of spiritual regeneration: obedience to the command to "go and sin no more" depends on the ability of believers to carry out that command. Balthasar Hubmaier, as we have seen, believed that sin was too deeply rooted in human reality for such a command to be perfectly effective in particular "visible" churches. Christians are regenerated, said Hubmaier, and they must strive to do their best by struggling against sin and the flesh, but in the final analysis, only Christ can say "My Kingdom is not of this world."

Between the position of the Swiss Brethren, which was strictly separatist, and that of Hubmaier, which tended to bless Christian participation in many activites of the world according to one's office, stood that of Pilgram Marpeck. Although his argument concerning the proper exercise of the ban was directed primarily against the Swiss and what he viewed as their excessive legalism, his outline of the proper Christian ban in effect mediated between the Swiss and the Hubmaierian positions, and opened new avenues of understanding.

The Swiss Brethren and the Ban

Article 2 of Schleitheim deals with the ban, basing itself entirely on Matthew 18:15ff.[1] The ban applies to those who have "given themselves over to the Lord" in baptism, and who have thereby pledged obedience to Christ's commandments. If any such regenerated brothers or sisters "still somehow slip and fall into error and sin," they are to be admonished and corrected, according to the pattern outlined in Matthew 18. The concern in Article 2 is that such admonishment take place before the Supper of the Lord is celebrated, so that "we may all in one spirit and in one love break and eat from one bread and drink from one cup."[2]

If spiritual unity is the focus of Article 2 on the ban, the emphasis on separation comes in Article 4. The Scripture passage alluded to here, 2 Corinthians 6:14ff., would remain central in the subsequent Swiss Brethren understanding of the ban. In this passage Paul admonishes the Corinthians to separate from those who do the works of darkness. In the Schleitheim understanding of the two kingdoms, those who had accepted rebaptism had thereby passed into the Kingdom of Christ; if they subsequently sinned, were admonished three times according to Matthew 18, and refused to confess and repent, then they were to be excommunicated. In other words, the spiritual sword was used in a disciplinary fashion to bring about repentance and confession, but failing that, it was then used to remove the diseased member from the Body; thenceforth, that member was again part of the kingdom of Satan to his or her damnation, for what had been bound by Christ's church on earth was also bound in heaven. Of course, readmittance was possible following confession of sin, repentance and acceptance by the church community.

Michael Sattler's letter to the church at Horb[3] contains repeated admonitions to maintain the holy conduct that "befits and becomes the saints of God." As he awaited his trial and likely execution, Sattler's expressed hope for his little flock was that the grace of the Holy Spirit "keep you flawless, without sin, and present you joyous and pure at the coming of our Lord Jesus Christ."[4] Above all Sattler echoed Schleitheim's concern for the maintenance of purity in the Body of Christ by means of a "strict attentiveness and excommunication" from those who "act against the command and law of God." Sattler's letter emphasized, then, two central themes seen at Schleitheim: the membership of Christians in the pure Body of Christ, which demands holy and sinless living according to "God's law," and the exhortation to strict separation from those who do not so live.

Sattler's letter to the Horb congregation, however, added one note not heard in the Schleitheim Articles. In a moving section of his letter, Sattler devoted significant time to the theme of love, "without which it is not possible that you be a Christian congregation." Sattler not only paraphrased 1 Corinthians 13, he went on to point to the "highest commandment" of Christ, the love of God and love of neighbour (Matthew 22:37-40), and applied these verses immediately to the practice of the ban:

> But if you love the neighbor, you will not scold or ban zealously, will not seek your own, will not remember evil, will not be ambitious or puffed up, but kind, righteous, generous in all gifts, humble and sympathetic with the weak and imperfect.[5]

Michael Sattler was not abrogating the necessity of separation from the unrepentant, for he emphasized repeatedly in his letter that such separation is commanded in Scripture and must be rigorously applied. Nevertheless, Sattler recognized the human propensity to zealous self-righteousness and the necessity for a generous and sympathetic attitude of love towards those who, through weakness, fall into sin.

It is clear from this that Sattler did not hold that regenerated Christians would be forever sinless, otherwise there would have been no need for a ban. Nevertheless, his optimism concerning the possibility of regenerated believers remaining without sin is striking. Although sin may occur in the regenerate, Sattler expected this to be a rare and "inadvertent" event, befalling the "weak and imperfect."[6] The ban, therefore, was for extraordinary cases, not a commonly-used instrument for spiritual growth or nourishment. That is to say, Sattler understood the ban primarily in its excommunicatory function of maintaining purity in the Body, not in its admonishment function of encouraging spiritual growth. The reason for this was Sattler's very optimistic view of the power of regeneration by the Spirit of God.

In the monastic setting from which Michael Sattler emerged, growth in the spiritual life was conceived as "a slow progress upward toward God, a climb of the hill by spiritual exercise—prayer, mortification of the carnal lusts, growth in the knowledge of God—until the soul has become Christ-like, God-like."[7] Thus communal prayer, the liturgy, obedience to a superior, and communal tasks all became vehicles through which the monks were to grow in the spiritual life. Michael Sattler's writings, while reflecting a strong ascetic emphasis on the renunciation of the flesh in favour of the life of the spirit, contained no hint of the monastic scheme of progressive sanctification. Rather, "Sattler spoke as if his hearers had already arrived, had already received the 'spirit of Christ' in its fullness."[8]

Sattler believed that those chosen by God to be God's children received Christ's Spirit at the time of election, and thereafter were to wage the ascetic battle against the temptations of flesh and world in order to maintain their purity. For Sattler, and for the Swiss Brethren, believers already were the saints, although they had to be on the watch lest Satan overtake them through temptation. This perfectionist understanding of the spiritual life had very definite consequences for the way the church's function was conceived and carried out. In Sattler's understanding, the assembly of believers was to be a place of unity, free from the impurity of unbelief.

> Apply yourselves to coming together constantly and that you may be united in prayer for all men and the breaking of bread, and this all the more fervently, as the day of the Lord draws nearer. In such meeting together you will make manifest the heart of the false brothers, and will be freed of them more rapidly.[9]

Seen in light of Jesus' coming, which Sattler was convinced was soon to occur, the church's central concerns were unity, prayer, and purity, in separation from all sinfulness.[10]

We can see here a crucial distinction between Michael Sattler's conception of the spiritual life and that of Balthasar Hubmaier. For Hubmaier, sin was not so readily conquered. In fact, sin remained rooted in the very being (flesh) of the regenerate and so perfection in this life was impossible. Nevertheless, for Hubmaier growth in the spiritual life was possible and necessary. In the end Hubmaier remained closer to the medieval church's conception of gradual sanctification, in that he structured the worship life of the church with a view toward spiritual growth; Sattler remained closer to the Roman Catholic understanding that a measure of "perfection" was possible in this life—but Sattler would hold that this high degree of perfection had arrived with the Spirit of Christ and was sealed by believers' baptism.

As a consequence, the Swiss Brethren position concerning church ordinances generally, the ban included, was that the ordinances served to emphasize the purity of the congregation, and its separation from the world. What was less clear among the Swiss, in spite of Sattler's appeals to the application of love when discipline was administered, was how the church and its communal worship activities could function to promote the spiritual growth of "the weak and imperfect." Hubmaier's understanding, focused as it was on a continual work of sanctification within the church, contained more constructive possibilities, especially for the second generation of believers who were to grow up within the Anabaptist churches.

That the Swiss Brethren after Schleitheim continued to hold Sattler's basic position concerning the ban is made clear from the disputations held in Swiss territories between the Swiss Brethren and local Reformed preachers.[11] At the disputation held in Bern in 1538, for example, the Reformed preachers were quick to point to what they perceived as the destructive aspects of the Swiss Brethren understanding of the ban.[12] The Swiss Brethren defended their practice by appealing to Matthew 18 and a variety of Pauline texts that enjoined separation from the ungodly, prominent among which was 1 Corinthians 6.[13] In all of this, they said, they were simply being faithful to the letter of Scripture and the "Rule of Christ" in Matthew 18.

When the Reformed preachers argued on the basis of Matthew 22:37-40 that the ban needed to be ruled by love of God and love of neighbour,[14] the Brethren replied that the violence approved of by the preachers against so-called heretics was no Christian ban. Furthermore, said the Brethren, emphasizing their literal approach to Scripture, "the love of God is in the keeping of His commandments."[15] The Reformed preachers replied that the Brethren were being too literalistic, servants of the "dead letter"; their use of the ban within the church should be ruled by Matthew 13:30. The heart of the matter, argued Erasmus Ritter, Reformed preacher at Bern, was that "Christ established the ban for building up and not for tearing down, as he says in Matthew 13: 'let both (weeds and wheat) grow together until the harvest.'"[16] Furthermore, argued another preacher, you also have sinners in your midst; you are trying to do the impossible, namely build a perfect church—something that will never be accomplished on this earth.[17] Further, if you follow Jesus' own example, you have to eat with sinners, not separate from them. Christ came for the sick, not the healthy.[18]

Throughout this onslaught, the Swiss Brethren maintained their basic position: the teaching of Scripture was clear and unequivocal and demanded obedience. Christians were called to admonish sinners to repentance according to Matthew 18, and to separate from those who persisted in sin and so maintain the purity of the Body of Christ. Such was Christ's teaching and the practice of the apostles. Love meant separating from evil.[19]

Pilgram Marpeck's Position on the Ban

Although the Bern disputation took place with Reformed preachers, and so was operating under different assumptions than would hold in discussions between Anabaptists, still the essential issues concerning the ban seen at the Bern Disputation of 1538 are also visible, in slightly different form, in Pilgram Marpeck's contemporaneous disagreements with the Swiss.[20]

Pilgram Marpeck's critique of Swiss Brethren practice centred on three points. First of all, Marpeck echoed Hans Hut's criticism of the legalism of the Swiss Brethren and their focus on external ordinances. In the second place, although Marpeck would not go so far as did Hubmaier, he sided with Hubmaier in criticizing Swiss Brethren optimism about the ability of the regenerated to conquer sin. In the third place, Marpeck insisted that the function of the ban was not primarily for the maintenance of purity in the Body, but rather the ban, properly understood, was an instrument for the building up of the Body of Christ in love. As a result, Pilgram Marpeck arrived at an alternative understanding of how discipline should function in the community of the faithful.

The Question of Legalism

It is no coincidence that at the beginning of his first letter to the Swiss Brethren, Pilgram Marpeck would immediately place the question of the ban in the context of the Lord's highest commandment.

> It happens easily that we depend more on our own knowledge and understanding than on love, which should be preeminent in all things.
> All knowledge of God subsists in this love of God and the neighbor.[21]

Marpeck was in good company on this point. Michael Sattler himself was concerned that the ban be carried out in the context of Christ's highest commandment to love, as was Hans Denck, and the Reformed preachers likewise were quick to point to the issue in their debates with the Swiss. But where Sattler did not develop the more positive aspects of his few statements on love (perhaps because he did not survive to write further on the matter), and the Reformed preachers used the argument from love to negate appeals to obedience to Christ's example, Pilgram Marpeck took the argument in a different direction.[22] The crux of the matter, said Marpeck, was that the "hasty judgements" of the Swiss contradicted both the words and the way of Christ.

A central distinction that the Swiss were missing, said Marpeck echoing Luther's insight, was that between law and Gospel. The law contains the threat of punishment, instils fear of God, and functions for the bringing about of repentance. As such, law is preliminary to Gospel. But the law, be it divine (scriptural) or human (ordinances), was not meant to, nor can it bring about the true peace of God.

> Everything that commands, forbids, institutes, orders, drives, or produces anything against this freedom [of Christ] brings quarreling, wrong understandings, zeal, strife, and unrest in heart and conscience.[23]

By contrast, the living Gospel is a setting free from the imprisonment of the law which condemns.

> [Christ] erases the handwriting of the devil so that it is no longer the law that reigns, but grace and freedom in Jesus Christ, according to the nature of the true love of God and neighbor. This love in God is the real freedom. Without any coercion, this love truly fulfills all commands and prohibitions of the whole pleasure of God. That is the true freedom in Christ Jesus. He thus set free is truly free, for whoever remains in His words is His true disciple...[24]

Echoing Hans Denck, Marpeck maintained that the law cannot rule in the Kingdom of Christ, but rather freedom in Christ must rule there. This is possible because "It is Christ Jesus Himself who is in the hearts of such liberated people."[25]

The Swiss Brethren, argued Marpeck, had turned the Christian life into one of obedience to law, and even if that law were based on Scripture (or more narrowly, the New Testament), it remained external law nonetheless. When the focus fell rather on the spiritual regeneration that occurs in the hearts of believers, then the ban took on a different dimension. The measure of Christian obedience was not then adherence to law or the maintenance of purity according to a legal standard, but rather adherence to the mercy, patience and love of Christ, whose Spirit had come to rule regenerated hearts.

On the other side of the issue, however, the Christian church should maintain its responsibility in administering discipline, but with the caution that no one should judge individuals "before the time of the fruit." Such hasty judging is premature, and ought to be left to the Lord.[26] Excommunication, insisted Marpeck, needed to be applied with extreme caution, for many who have appeared evil have turned out to be good, and vice versa.[27] Only God knows what lies in the hearts of human beings, and thus the church must take care not to "run ahead of Christ" in judging prematurely.

Towards the end of his first letter to the Swiss Brethren, Marpeck summed up his primary disagreement with them, and asked them to reconsider their practice and understanding.

> It is my fervent prayer that for the sake of Christ, you get your judgments from Christ, and learn long-suffering, forebearance, and meekness from Him. . . . My greatest contention in my conscience with you is that nowhere do I find such precipitate, superficial judgments and verdicts on every little matter in Christ and His apostolic church as I find with you.[28]

A true understanding of Christ's life and commands would put "long-suffering, forebearance, and meekness"—in a word, love—at the centre of the Christian life, and not a quick and strict application of excommunicatory discipline according to a legalistic reading of Scripture.

The question of Sin and Regeneration

A second point of contention between Pilgram Marpeck and the Swiss Brethren concerned Marpeck's understanding of the "freedom of the spirit in Christ" which, Marpeck noted, some had accused him of stretching too far.[29] In defending himself against this charge, Marpeck emphasized his understanding of the rebirth and regeneration that every believer must undergo. This rebirth is the result of grace, and a manifestation of the love of God. The same regeneration continues in all believers: "All who have, in baptism, died to the law of sin (Colossians 3:3) and have been buried with Christ (Romans 6:4), do not themselves live. Rather Christ lives in them, through the law of grace and the voluntary spirit in Christ Jesus."[30]

Nevertheless, even the reborn and regenerated believers are subject to attacks of the flesh, as Paul testified (Romans 7:25). This calls for vigilance.

> For whoever submits to the rule of the free Holy Spirit of the Lord Jesus Christ keeps his flesh and blood in obedience, and keeps it so against the will of flesh and blood until death. Indeed, Christ Jesus the Lord Himself, although his flesh was weak and His Spirit willing, prayed the Father to take the cup from Him. But His Spirit was willing and ready. He obediently subjected the flesh to death, and said to the Father: "Not my will, but yours be done."[31]

In these lines we recognize Marpeck's acceptance of the ascetic struggle of spirit against flesh. Thus, said Marpeck in his own defence, he was not a libertine: he recognized the absolute need for a spiritual rebirth, regeneration, and continuing subjugation of human self-will. However, he maintained that the central distinction was not a legalistic one, but rather a spiritual one between the freedom of the spirit in Christ, which is life, and the freedom of the flesh, which is death.

On the other hand, however, Satan retains a hold even on regenerated believers, because of the weakness of the flesh. "Even among men who possess the salvation given by the Son of God, there can be no cessation of sin."[32] Therefore the anthropological distinction Hubmaier made between Christ and the Christian was deemed valid by Marpeck: "In Christ the fullness of Godhead dwells bodily; in us, in this time, it is only in part."[33] To repeat, for Marpeck the crux of the problem was not so much in external behaviour, as in internal disposition. In Christ, love was complete and had no defect; human beings, on the other hand, "are full of weakness."[34]

Besides the human propensity to outward, sinful acts, human beings have an equally great capacity for self-deception: "Liars and hypocrites can also do the external work Christ already commanded and ordained to His church, and they can change their external appearance to angels of light."[35] Marpeck thus sounded a note of caution: "Ah, my brethren, how diligently and carefully we have to take heed that we do not consider our own impulse the impulse of the Holy Spirit, our own course the course and walk of Christ."[36] The most fundamental root of sin is in the heart, not in external actions—even though actions eventually reveal what is in the heart—and therefore even the regenerate must realize just how difficult a battle is the struggle of the "spirit" against the "flesh."

Given the reality of human frailty which, to the extent that it is overcome, is overcome by God's gift of grace, Marpeck warned the Swiss Brethren of the dangers entailed in "quarreling and strife."

> Therefore it behooves us to watch over our souls, our own and each other's, especially to observe and search out whether the enemy has secretly started a fire in our inmost heart, conscience, and soul in order to consume soul, conscience, and heart in the wrath of God. There is among you a hidden fire which has an evil, stinking smoke and taste of fire, which the enemy of truth is seeking to conceal in order that he may ignite, destroy, and burn to ashes many hearts before it is discovered...[37]

The Ban as Spiritual Medicine

In Pilgram Marpeck's view, the answer to the profound problem of human sinfulness lay in converting *the heart* away from "self-fullness" in an on-going and thorough way. The emphasis thus fell on spiritual growth through grace, not the keeping of literal commands. In this as in many other matters, Marpeck appears to be following in Hans Denck's footsteps.

> It does not depend on our willing or running, but rather on the mercy of God and on His grace in and with Christ. He gives the will, He can also do and accomplish it in His own. We must simply in all of our actions stand idle ourselves, as dead in ourselves, if Christ is to live in us, which life and walk alone are pleasing to the Father.[38]

These simple "standing idle in ourselves," and "dying to self" were anything but "simple," as Pilgram Marpeck well knew. Nevertheless, he maintained that such "yieldedness" lay at the very heart of a truly Christian life, and must lie at the heart of Christian discipline and admonishment.

Pilgram Marpeck was convinced that sin is most fundamentally a matter of inward rebellion and disobedience, regardless of outward behaviour; likewise, Christian purity is also most fundamentally a matter of the heart. For this reason he could not countenance the Swiss Brethren "rush to judgement" on the basis of some external negative evidences. People in such a hurry apparently had not experienced either the stubborn depth of their own sin and self-deception, or the loving mercy of God which was extended to those who, with true contrition, repented of their willfulness. Thus he wrote, with no little wisdom, to the Swiss Brethren:

> No one may judge except he who has first judged and sentenced his own life through the grace and mercy of God, whereby he has pulled the beam out of his eye. Then, very properly, in patience, humility, meekness, and love, he may with the greatest care pull the sliver out of his brother's eye without hurting or irritating the eye. That is, after all, how he has been treated by God.[39]

Love, patience, and forbearance most befit forgiven sinners who still struggle against the flesh, with the help of God's grace. Those who have been broken to contrition and brought back to life by Christ the Physician will be anxious to live out that same mercy and gentleness in relationships within the Body of Christ.

Conclusion

It should be evident from the foregoing that while the Swiss Brethren and Pilgram Marpeck agreed on many crucial issues concerning the ban, their disagreements also were extremely important for the way in which the inner change of regeneration would express itself outwardly in the church. On the question of grace and sin Marpeck steered a middle course between the Reformed preachers and the Swiss. Against the Swiss Brethren understanding, Marpeck insisted that God's work of grace was not completed or brought to perfection with initial repentance and rebirth. With this rebirth one had not yet arrived, rather one had begun. God's grace continued to be needed throughout the Christian life, and this not merely for the maintenance of initial purity, but for growth in the Christian life. Human sin, Marpeck noted, is not so easily displaced.

On the other hand, against the position of the Reformed preachers, Marpeck also insisted on obedience, growing from grace, according to the model of Jesus Christ.[40] Love may cover a multitude of sins, but love does not cover willful disobedience.[41] Those who wish to avoid obedience by appealing to God's all-forgiving grace are, in fact, denying and resisting the working of God's grace in their own lives. On the matter of "discipleship" or *Nachfolge* (following after) Marpeck was insistent: the Christian is to live as Christ lived, for Jesus' life is the highest example and model of how his disciples are to manifest the love of God and the love of neighbour.[42] Nevertheless, Pilgram Marpeck wished to push the question of discipleship to a deeper level. What makes it possible for followers of Christ to live as disciples? At the simplest level, Marpeck answered that discipleship is possible insofar as the heart has been regenerated by the love of God in Christ. Thus the obedience of faith is possible, not because the Sermon on the Mount is Jesus' Word and so ought to be obeyed. As Marpeck observed, not even the divine law can convert the heart; only God's grace can change one's very being. Thus one might be able to achieve a certain measure of outward conformity without inner regeneration, but true discipleship will be the result of a fundamental change in one's being.

It was Marpeck's image of Christ the Physician which provided the richest positive content for his understanding of the ban. What is crucial about the ban is its medicinal function, not its separating function.

> Certainly, the true shepherds will not drive a patient, humble, meek, and loving heart any further than the chief Shepherd, Christ has driven and bound it, but will let it go out and in, find full and sufficient pasture, and be and remain victorious over all temptation in Christ Jesus.[43]

Insofar as the Body of Christ is a true Body, it recognizes the pain involved in "cutting off" a member. If a member of one's body is "failing or weak," medicine is first lovingly applied, and then one waits, and hopes for improvement. "As long as [the member] is not dead and is only painful, the body bears it with patience and long-suffering, and delays the penalty to allow for improvement."[44] Of course, Marpeck concluded, if the medicine did not work, excommunication might have to be undertaken as a last resort.

Pilgram Marpeck was more pessimistic than were the Swiss concerning the possibilities of regeneration of the human heart. Marpeck recognized that Christians must combat the idolatry of self, growing continually in yieldedness, practising the external and internal disciplines that lead to Christlikeness. These insights are significant because they re-vision the Christian life as a process of spiritual growth into Christlikeness. Discipleship, Marpeck said, will not come easily, given the deep roots of self love that dwell in the human heart. Thus the Christian life for Marpeck was not the desperate defence of a perfect state, but rather a growing continually into the divine nature by means of individual and communal spiritual disciplines. The result was that Marpeck had a less militantly sectarian vision of the church. He conceived of the church less as a pure body, and more as the place where those in need of the "Great Physician's medicine" come for healing and wholeness. And, as we have seen, Marpeck insisted further that the "ceremonies" of worship were essential *means* to spiritual healing and wholeness.

End Notes

[1] Yoder, *Legacy*, pp. 36-37.

[2] *Ibid.*, p. 37.

[3] *Ibid.*, pp. 55-65.

[4] *Ibid.*, p. 63. See the discussion in Snyder, *Life and Thought*, pp. 124-25.

[5] *Ibid.*, p. 59.

[6] See the comments in Snyder, *Life and Thought*, p. 235, n. 100.

[7] Owen Chadwick, *John Cassian*, (Cambridge: University Press, 1950), p. 77; cited in Snyder, *Life and Thought*, p. 165.

[8] Snyder, *Life and Thought*, p. 166.

[9] Yoder, *Legacy*, p. 62.

[10] "Michael Sattler suggests a ... defensive image of a community of warriors, hand-picked to defend the divine citadel, waiting expectantly for the king and his army to return and end the siege." Snyder, *Life and Thought*, p. 167.

[11] See John H. Yoder, *Täufertum und Reformation in der Schweiz, I. Die Gespräche zwischen Täufern und Reformatoren 1523-1538* (Karlsruhe: Mennonitischen Geschichtsverein, 1962), for a historical survey; John H. Yoder, *Täufertum und Reformation im Gespräch* (Zürich: EVZ-Verlag, 1968), for a study of the theological issues that emerged from these disputations.

[12] *See QGTS,* 4, pp. 439-467.

[13] Among others, Galatians 5:17; 1 John 1:6; 2 Corinthians 6:15.

[14] "The ban should be used in the manner of faith and the rule of love, so that we may be made better by it." *Ibid.*, p. 446. For a discussion of how the "rule of love" played a role in the disputations, see Yoder, *Gespräch*, pp. 44-55.

[15] QGTS, 4, p. 447.

[16] *Ibid.*, p. 454.

[17] *Ibid.*, pp. 456 ff.

[18] *Ibid.*, p. 460.

[19] E.g. "Unnd sitt Christus selbs angebenn Mathei 18, wie man den bann bruchenn, das ouch der liebe am aller gemessesten, von bösem abzewysenn. Item die apostell zun Corinthern unnd annderswo eben nach derselbenn regell, wie es Christus angebenn, alls dem evangelio unnd der liebe gemessß, innharganngen sind, wüssent wir, das söllichs recht ist." *Ibid.*, p. 450.

[20] Marpeck's disagreement with the Swiss Brethren has been studied and put into the perspective of

his theology as a whole by Walter Klaassen, "Church Discipline and the Spirit in Pilgram Marpeck," in I. B. Horst, A. F. de Jong, and D. Visser, eds., *De Geest in het geding* (Alphen an den Rijn: Tjeenk Willink, 1978), pp. 169-180.

[21] Klassen and Klaassen, *Writings*, p. 312.

[22] In Marpeck's "Confession of 1532," he rejects Martin Bucer's argument concerning love in classic "Anabaptist" fashion. "When you say the commandment of love is the principal tenet and work of Christians which accomplishes every improvement (in human beings), I agree, but with this difference: In Christ we have a true God, and we must remain in His teaching and order. Whoever does not remain in the teaching of Christ has no God. Thus, the beginning of love is to believe in and hold to God and His Word as John 8(:21f.) advises: If you remain in my words, you will be my true disciples and you will know the truth, and the truth will make you free. Here is the love of the believers rooted." *Ibid.*, p. 156.

[23] *Ibid.*, p. 313.

[24] *Ibid.*, p. 315.

[25] *Ibid.*, p. 316.

[26] *Ibid.*, p. 345.

[27] Marpeck gives historical and biblical examples, *ibid.*, pp. 347-351.

[28] *Ibid.*, p. 360.

[29] *Ibid.*, pp. 322-23.

[30] *Ibid.*, p. 320.

[31] *Ibid.*, p. 322.

[32] *Ibid.*, p. 430.

[33] *Ibid.*, p. 532.

[34] *Ibid.*

[35] *Ibid.*, p. 422.

[36] *Ibid.*, p. 511.

[37] *Ibid.*, p. 501.

[38] *Ibid.*, p. 510.

[39] *Ibid.*, p. 326.

[40] "All the chosen of God must strive to follow the pattern and example given to us by the Lord Himself. The servant is not, nor ever will be, above his Lord, nor will the disciple be above his master, or the apostle above Him who sent him. The Lord Himself has tested this principle; so, too, will it also be tested in His servants." *Ibid.*, p. 438.

[41] See, for example, Marpeck's discussion of the varieties of sinfulness in "Men in Judgement and the Peasant Aristocracy (1547)," *Ibid.*, pp. 464-483.

[42] Pilgram Marpeck said that since Christ is known more clearly since he has come, "we can pattern ourselves after Him, and more fully partake of the divine nature and spiritual good. Thus revenge is no longer permitted in the New Testament for, through patience, the Spirit can now more powerfully overcome enemies than it could in the Old Testament. Therefore, Christ forbade such vengeance and resistance, and commanded the children who possessed the Spirit of the New Testament to love, to bless their enemies, persecutors, and opponents, and to overcome them with patience." *Ibid.*, p. 63.

[43] *Ibid.*, p. 346.

[44] *Ibid.*, p. 356. "Le but de la discipline est le réconciliation et non l'exclusion." So Blough, *Christologie*, p. 211.

Swiss Brethren in Alsace, from a later century

Chapter 24

Menno Simons:
The Church of the Regenerate

Anabaptist teaching on the ban hearkened back to the late medieval call for a moral reform of the church "in head and members"; it pointed also to the expectation that the outer behaviour of the Anabaptist churches would accurately reflect the inner state of grace and regeneration of its members. Because of the ban's importance as a principle of reformation, discipline, and sanctification within the community of saints, controversies among Anabaptists on serious issues routinely utilized the ban as the mechanism for purifying the church and reforming it again. However, there were differences in approach. In the Swiss and South German traditions, Anabaptists who emphasized the spirit/inner life tended to emphasize love, and the healing, reconciling, and redemptive potential of community discipline; those more disposed to the letter/outer life tended to emphasize unity, purity, and obedience to the Word. The contrasting manner of interpreting community discipline, as seen in the disagreement between Marpeck and some Swiss Brethren, was no isolated case.

The same pattern would be evident virtually everywhere. Nevertheless, over time the more literal, legalistic, "outer" emphasis became increasingly prominent. This tendency emerged with particular seriousness in the North after 1546, where it was fueled on the one hand by a particularly optimistic Melchiorite anthropology and doctrine of regeneration (based in Hoffman's docetic Christology), and on the other, by the propensity of Menno, Dirk Philips and Leenaert Bouwens to emphasize conformity to the letter of Scripture and purity in the community of saints. These elements led to a stricter definition of the ban itself which divided the Anabaptist communities in the north, and then travelled back South and led to the Amish schism among the Swiss toward the end of the seventeenth century.

The Melchiorite legacy had led to its fair share of internal tensions. In particular, the David Jorist emphasis on inner, spiritual purity carried with it the threat of an "invisible" church, to the point that (as Menno described it) the Jorists believed that "to the pure, all things are pure." But by 1546 an opposite trend had become evident.[1] The problem of extreme legalism became a pressing issue among Menno's followers. Without a doubt two younger and more rigorous leaders, Dirk Philips and Leenaert Bouwens, played a role in this development, although in important ways they simply emphasized to a greater degree, points made by Menno himself.

The "Banning" Controversy in the North: An Outline of Events

Early signs of what would become a full-fledged problem for the followers of Menno emerged in 1547. At a debate held in Emden in that year one of the questions concerned the place of avoidance in marriage. That is, if one's spouse were placed under the ban, was it necessary to avoid all physical contact with that person? The question of the manner and limits of church discipline increasingly became crucial topics, as subsequent events and writings attest.

Sometime before 1549, Dirk composed a short writing on the ban to which Menno referred in his own "Clear Account of Excommunication," written in 1549.[2] Following this came the important meeting and the Wismar Articles (1554) which outlined the proper procedures for church discipline; these included provisions for the shunning of the banned "apostate one."[3] Nevertheless, in light of developments yet to come, the Wismar Articles soon came to define the more moderate Dutch position.

In 1555 an open crisis erupted when Leenaert Bouwens banned the husband of Swaen Rutgers, and then demanded (although she was a pious woman and had herself done nothing worthy of discipline) that she shun all contact with her husband, under threat of excommunication. In a letter written to the church at Franeker, Menno addressed the matter of marital avoidance and "referred to a decision which he and Dirk had arrived at in 1547 and to the articles drawn up at Wismar."[4] Menno was asked to intervene in the case of Swaen Rutgers and her husband, and wrote a letter in 1556 to the church at Emden, in which he took up a moderate position, apparently on the side of Swaen Rutgers, against Bouwens.

By 1557 the lines had hardened between the "moderate" and the "strict" parties concerning the ban. Menno was now old and weak, nevertheless he travelled first to Franeker and then to Harlingen in order to try to find a solution. He managed to gain some agreement with the leaders in Franeker, but on arriving in Harlingen he was overcome by Dirk and Leenaert who insisted on a stricter position regarding the ban. According to the report of an eyewitness, Menno was threatened with excommunication by Leenaert Bouwens if he did not support the strict view.[5] Menno capitulated on the central question of whether shunning should be strictly enforced within families. The official position now became that shunning was a necessary accompaniment to banning. Within the Netherlands, those not in agreement with this decision soon left to form the "moderate" party of Waterlanders.[6] Further divisions on this issue also resulted with the Swiss Brethren and the "High German" Brethren of the lower Rhine.

In April of 1556, evidently in response to the Wismar Articles and subsequent events, three High German leaders (Zylis, Lemke, and Heinrich Krufft) visited Menno at Wüstenfelde to discuss the matter of the ban. After two days of discussion they left, apparently dissatisfied; Menno was left with the opposite impression, and seems to have expected the Anabaptists of the Lower Rhine region to follow the lead of

Wismar.[7] The following year a meeting of Swiss Brethren leaders took place at Strasbourg; gathered there were around fifty elders and leaders from Switzerland, Moravia, Württemberg, and Alsace. Among them were Zylis and Lemke. The conference took up three issues: the type of work or business permissible to a Christian, original sin, and the question of banning and shunning. The latter issue dominated the document that was sent to the Dutch.

The communication from Strasbourg was not well received in the Netherlands. It was felt that Zylis and Lemke had betrayed Menno, and had misrepresented the Dutch position. Dirk and Menno now took pen in hand once again, Dirk composing "The Ban" in 1558, Menno writing the lengthy "Instruction on Excommunication" and "Final Instruction on Marital Avoidance," both in 1558.[8] Zylis and Lemke responded with an anti-Menno tract, which has since been lost, and Menno replied again in 1559 in a writing directed specifically against these two High German leaders.[9] Zylis and Lemke were excommunicated by Dirk Philips and Leenart Bouwens in 1559.[10]

The split that developed between the Dutch Anabaptists and the Upper Germans (Swiss Brethren) took some time to heal. It was complicated by the further schism that had taken place in the Netherlands when the Waterlanders separated, and then by the split between the Frisians and the Flemish, the latter of which apparently had more to do with personalities and temperaments than with doctrinal issues or the ban as such. Menno Simons died in 1561, just four years before the Frisian/Flemish split took place. Dirk Philips died in 1568, at the height of that particular controversy, after having failed to reconcile the two parties. The Frisian/Flemish division was a particularly stubborn one in which the manner of banning was not an issue, but the ban itself was unmercifully implemented by both sides; the split was not ultimately healed until 1811, with the founding of the *Algemeene Doopsgezinde Societeit* (ADS, or General Society of the Baptism Minded).[11]

Menno and the Pure Church

Historians have long observed that Menno Simons' writings reflect a shift as one moves from the concerns of the "early Menno," to those of the "later Menno." In his earlier writings, Menno was concerned with placing Christ at the centre of Scripture, and with individual faith, regeneration, and the new life, all of which would lead to the community of saints. In a recent study, Sjouke Voolstra noted that a central theme in Menno's early theology "is the traditional, effective teaching on justification which aims at sanctification, and it has the Melchiorite teaching on the incarnation as a christological basis."[12] Thus one finds in the "early Menno" an emphasis on the mortification of the flesh, which results from and makes visible the spiritual rebirth that is witnessed to in baptism. The "later Menno," by contrast, became much more concerned with the "pure community."[13] This shift in accent from Christ to community has often been attributed, not without reason, to the influence of Dirk Philips and Leenaert Bouwens.[14] W. J. Kühler goes so far as to say that "In fact, after his defeat (at Harlingen), Menno was little more than a tool in the hands of Dirk and, above all, of Leenaert."[15]

These observations are undoubtedly correct in their general thrust. The agenda Menno had to face from 1546 until the end of his life, and which increasingly dominated his writings, seems to have been set in large part by the concerns for church purity that were primary for Dirk and Leenaert. Nevertheless, when we look at the issue of the ban in particular, we find that virtually all of the themes which became divisive later are to be found in Menno's earliest writings on the subject.[16] The difference on the ban which can be noted from the early to the later Menno was more one of tone and emphasis than one of content. It appears that Dirk, Leenaert and others simply appropriated themes visible already in Menno's earlier writings and brought them to the fore in such a single-minded fashion that they virtually determined the course of later developments.[17]

Dirk Philips

Menno's earliest writing on the subject of church discipline, "A Kind Admonition on Church Discipline" (1541) carefully set the theological context for the practice of church discipline: Menno spent more time discussing the new birth and the new life which results than he did discussing the ban as such.[18] Those who have been reborn and regenerated by God the Father, Menno stated, will live blameless lives, conformed to Christ.[19] But church discipline, Menno emphasized again and again in this writing, is undertaken out of love, because one values the soul and salvation of the brother or sister.

> If you see your brother sin, then do not pass him by as one that does not value his soul; but if his fall be curable, from that moment endeavor to raise him up by gentle admonition and brotherly instruction, before you eat, drink, sleep, or do anything else, as one who ardently desires his salvation...[20]

It is this warmly pastoral concern, this desire to make church discipline an instrument of reconciliation and salvation, that marks this early writing above all.[21]

On the other hand, the seeds of later conflicts are evident already in 1541. Menno was unsparing when it came to the "apostate ones," namely those who at one time had voluntarily accepted baptism and then "through false doctrine or a vain and carnal life" had turned their backs on that baptism. "Do not eat" with such apostates, counsels Menno. In fact, have nothing to do with them "no matter whether it be father or mother, sister or brother, man or wife, son or daughter, no matter who he be, for God's Word applies to all alike and there is no respect of persons with God."[22] Menno immediately mitigated this judgement by counseling patience, forbearance, and reconciliation with the fallen brother or sister; but he did not back away from his central point: if no repentance and amendment of life are forthcoming, then the sinner must be "put forth from us," but "not without great sadness and anguish of soul."[23]

In spite of the pastoral tone, the elements of later controversies are evident already here: an optimistic anthropology and doctrine of rebirth and regeneration which led to an expectation of a holy and blameless life;[24] a doctrine of obedience to the "law of Christ," which included the command to ban and to separate; an ecclesiology which emphasized purity in the Body of Christ. Likewise specific injunctions, such as the requirement to shun "apostates" within the family, would become central issues of contention later. What would be missing in the later controversies would be the caring and pastoral tone and emphasis which was central to Menno's views on the ban in 1541. The redemptive aim of the ban faded into the background as concern to maintain church purity assumed more and more importance.

By 1550 the situation within the Dutch Anabaptist churches had changed, and the manner and means of practising the ban had become contentious issues. The particular issues wracking the church are evident in the specific questions and the rules of conduct that both Menno and Dirk addressed in the writings dating from around 1550. May church members eat common meals with someone who has been banned? The answer from both Menno and Dirk was "no": banning means exclusion not only from the Lord's Supper, but from all eating.[25] May one buy and sell with a banned member? Answer: Only in exceptional cases, and not as a general rule.[26] May one greet or receive a banned member? Answer: Beyond common courtesy, no.[27] May one do acts of mercy for a banned member in need? Answer: Yes, although Dirk's reply suggested that he was suspicious about the possibilities of leniency or abuse.[28] Must banned family members be shunned? Answer: Yes. Menno and Dirk used virtually identical language here: "the ban is a general rule, and excepts none; neither husband nor wife, neither parent nor child."[29] Nevertheless both Menno and Dirk urged "modesty" and "restraint" in this matter, recognizing the dangers that lay ahead, with Menno voicing more overt concern than did Dirk. In an admonition that soon proved its truth, Menno said, "Brethren, it is a matter fraught with great danger."[30]

Of the nine articles agreed to at the Wismar conference in 1554, five dealt with marriage and the ban, giving evidence again of the divisiveness caused by these issues within the Dutch Anabaptist churches. Although the Wismar Articles went somewhat beyond the guidelines established in the writings of Menno and Dirk, especially in laying down explicit rules of behavior concerning marriage (Articles I, IV, V and VI), the essential position on shunning a banned marriage partner was a reiteration of the earlier position. Article III of Wismar stated that "the apostate one is to be avoided and shunned, whether it be husband or wife"; however, it went on to stipulate that "if it be a case of a weak conscience which is unable to grasp this, against this the Scriptures concerning marriage militate."[31] Although Leenaert Bouwens was among the elders present at Wismar, and so presumably subscribed to its contents, it was his own practice of "strict" banning and shunning within marriage that precipitated the next crisis.

Leenaert Bouwens' demand that Swaen Rutgers shun and separate from her banned husband became a test case of the limits of the ban. When Swaen refused, Bouwens banned her as well from the Emden congregation. Menno rendered his judgement in the Swaen Rutgers case, and spoke also to similar problems that had emerged in the church at Franeker. He pleaded for a middle course: "Be not too severe nor too lenient," he begged.[32] "I beseech all the pious for God's sake to pursue peace," Menno added, and returned in conclusion (almost in desperation, one senses) to his earlier themes of rebirth in Christ, unity, and reconciliation.

> Purify your hearts and be reconciled in Christ Jesus. . . . If you are baptized into one Spirit, then fulfill my joy and be of one mind with me in Christ. Build up, and destroy not. Let one instruct the other in love, and do not disrupt, so that blessed peace may be with all the children of God...[33]

In spite of Menno's statement concerning Swaen Rutgers that "My heart never shall consent to such indiscreet extremism or agree to such plans," he soon was moved to support the strict position in 1557 at Harlingen, as has been noted above.

The Strasbourg Conference of 1557, and the Waterlander Division

The Swiss Brethren leaders who gathered at Strasbourg in 1557 took up the issue of the ban in evident response to events in the Netherlands. They attempted to take a mediating position.

> Concerning shunning of brothers and sisters that have fallen away we should act as follows. First, the nature of the sin ought to be considered, and that any action be compatible with the Word of Christ and his apostles. We must make determined efforts for the purity and preservation of the church, and that the fallen brother and sister is prepared for repentance. This must be done with moderation according to the witness of Scripture, with aid, mercy, and helpfulness to them when necessary.[34]

Thus far the Swiss Brethren at Strasbourg could almost have been citing Menno himself, but in fact they subscribed to a view that was even more moderate than that of the mild Dutch party. A few lines later the Swiss Brethren wrote:

We also fervently desire that the brothers in the Netherlands do not counsel husband and wife to separate in the ban. Damage and vice will follow from it rather than God's praise and the welfare of souls. The commandment regarding marriage outweighs the one regarding shunning.[35]

This, as we have seen above, was not the position of Menno, Dirk, or Wismar, for although moderation and gentleness were counselled, still marital shunning as such was not a negotiable issue.

Back in the Netherlands, disagreement concerning the strictness of banning and shunning led to division, and the formation of the Waterlander party. Their position on this question appears to have corresponded closely to the one taken by the Strasbourg conference. The first Waterlandian confession contains an article describing avoidance.

Concerning the avoidance of an apostate brother, we confess that one should avoid all deliberate sinners who have been cut off from the church and who persist in carnal living, neither eating nor drinking with them, that they may be shamed and corrected. Nevertheless, since the ban should lead to healing, we do not wish that this fellowship should be denied him in time of need, or when the apostate, through such eating and drinking, might be converted and won again.[36]

While this appears to agree closely with Menno's position, a subsequent article on marriage points to the crucial difference between the Waterlander position and that of Dirk, Leenaert, and Menno. Marriage is so binding, says the Waterlandian confession, "that it may not be separated or broken for any reason except adultery, according to the words of Christ, Matthew 18."[37]

Both Menno and Dirk responded to the growing crisis in 1558. Dirk composed "The Ban," later included in his *Enchiridion*; Menno wrote his lengthy "Instruction on Excommunication," and "Final Instruction on Marital Avoidance." On the burning issue of marital avoidance, Menno spoke with less reservation than he had before. Adopting a familiar Melchiorite theme, he wrote that the essential reason why married believers had to shun a banned partner was that "the heavenly marriage bond between Christ and our souls" must be maintained in obedience; it carries a higher priority than any earthly, familial relationship. Furthermore, the danger of "infection" was ever-present:

I have known not much less than three hundred spouses in my day who did not observe between them and their mates the ordinance ... of the Lord and His apostles concerning shunning, and have so run together into perdition.[38]

The "external marriage bond" must give way to the "spiritual marriage bond made with Christ through faith." If one truly loves one's spouse, Menno added, then shunning will be observed so that the banned and shunned spouse may be shamed unto salvation. Although Menno concluded by admonishing elders and pastors to "prudence and paternal care," the thrust of his presentation was "willing obedience unto Christ."[39]

In 1560, Menno responded yet again with one of his last writings, and certainly not one of his best, his "Reply to Zylis and Lemke." Far more moderate in tone had been Menno's "Final Instruction on Marital Avoidance," written in 1558 to "certain brothers." There Menno had again allowed as an exception to marital shunning one who "is able to live out his faith without being hindered by his excommunicated mate," and included other extenuating circumstances as well.[40] In replying to Zylis and Lemke such measured judgement was absent: "None under heaven can practice his faith while living with his apostate consort," thundered Menno in this writing.[41] Subsequent to this, Dirk Philips and Leenaert Bouwens travelled to Germany and pronounced the ban against the "Overland" Swiss Brethren in 1559.[42]

The Dutch/Swiss Brethren split in the north finally was overcome in 1591, at a conference at Cologne. Two of the articles adopted there, on "Congregational Discipline and Marriage," took the milder view, discouraging (though not eliminating) marital shunning and emphasizing the reconciliatory aspect of church discipline. After citing the favourite text in Paul (1 Corinthians 5:9-13) enjoining the avoidance of open sinners, its strict interpretation of the text was mitigated immediately.

> To be sure, in carrying out such strict discipline, there is to be no misuse, which unfortunately has taken place many times, through which the misuse of marital avoidance and other such disorders also followed. Much more, according to the anointing of the Holy Spirit, one is to act with love in working with those being disciplined, that they may mend their ways.[43]

The "Concept of Cologne" was adopted by the High German Anabaptists and the Frisians; the Waterlanders also adopted the statement a few year later.[44] Nevertheless, the Dordrecht Confession of Faith of 1632 reiterated strict shunning. The subsequent adoption of Dordrecht by some Swiss Brethren ministers from the Palatinate and Alsace in 1660 was one of the factors that precipitated the Amish division among the Swiss in 1693.[45]

Conclusion

If it be said that Menno and his followers avoided the shoals of spiritualist antinomianism in overcoming the David Jorists, it appears that they did so only to run aground on the rocks of legalism. The combination of an optimistic doctrine of regeneration ("marriage to Christ"), a strong emphasis on obedience to the external Word, and an equally strong emphasis on a church maintained "without spot or wrinkle" by strict church discipline, was particularly disastrous for church life among the Dutch Anabaptists. As time went on, more and more legal distinctions were needed: What sins were serious enough to demand banning? Which of Christ's commands take precedence when there is a conflict between commands (e.g., between shunning and marriage)? Through all of this the inner regeneration, by God's grace, that enables discipleship faded further and further into the background, replaced by external measures of faithfulness and obedience.

The Moravian and Dutch schisms point us back to the fundamental spirit/letter and inner/outer tensions, crucial within Anabaptism from the start. We see in these controversies the victory of the letter of the law over the spirit of the law. Of course the disputants recognized the danger of the legalistic tendency too, and strove to overcome its negative consequences. But the repeated appeals to love, humility, forbearance, and patience—all desirable, if elusive, Christian virtues—inevitably had to give way before the more brittle obedience to "thus saith the Word of the Lord." It was as if once the basic presuppositions of regeneration, obedience to the Word, sinless living, the pure community, and community discipline were in place, the very logic of those assumptions drove to legalistic conclusions and results.

On following the course of the events in Dutch Anabaptism in particular, one is reminded of medieval Catholic practices, and the classifying of sins into mortal and venial categories, each having correspondingly severe penances. If there is no salvation outside the Church; if the Church holds the keys to "bind" and to "loose" the sinner; if the measure of sin is obedience to external law; then salvation becomes a matter of satisfying the eternal judge and (even more importantly) that judge's earthly representatives. Law engulfs Gospel. Regardless of how one ultimately judges the David Jorists, Blesdijk had a relevant point to make when, in his admonition to Menno, he stressed freedom from the law in Christ.

End Notes

[1] For a succinct overview, see Cornelius Krahn, *Dutch Anabaptism: Origin, Spread, Life and Thought* (The Hague: Martinus Nijhoff, 1968), pp. 229-237.

[2] Menno's tract is found in CWMS, pp. 455-485. CWMS identifies the year of publication as 1550; the editors of Dirk's *Writings*, p. 27, state that it was written in 1549. Dirk's first tract on "Separation" is his "Confession About Separation," *Writings*, pp. 611-617. There is some confusion in the scholarly apparatus of *Writings* concerning the order of Dirk's writings on the ban. Cf. *ibid.*, p. 27, n. 32 with p. 588, n. 3. In the latter note the editors identify, in order of composition: a) "The ban," included in the *Enchiridion* (*ibid.*, pp. 238-253); b) the "Evangelical ban and Avoidance" (*ibid.*, pp. 579-80); c) "Regarding the Evangelical ban and Avoidance" (*ibid.*, pp. 580-586); and d) "A Confession About Separation" (*ibid.*, pp. 611-616). The proper chronological order would place d) first, then a), b) and c). See *Writings*, pp. 611-612 for the dating of "Confession About Separation" (before 1550).

[3] CWMS, pp. 1041-1042.

[4] Dyck, Keeney, and Beachy, *Writings*, p. 28. Menno's letter is found in CWMS, p. 1043-1045.

[5] *Ibid.*, p. 29. More details in J.G. De Hoop Scheffer, "Eenige opmerkingen en mededeelingen betreffende Menno Simons," *Doopsgezinde Bijdragen* (1894), pp. 42-43. Bouwens is said to have told Menno: "If you cannot follow us, we will do with you just as we have done with the other leaders."

[6] A reply representing the position of the Waterlanders against both Dirk and Menno was written Hermann Timmerman, *Een verklaringhe: hoe en in wat manieren de Heere Jesus zynen Jongeren inder af-zonderinge / macht gegeven heeft* (1560). Timmerman was martyred in Antwerp in 1569; see *Martyrs' Mirror*, p. 766B.

[7] Krahn, *Dutch Anabaptism*, p. 235.

[8] *Ibid.*, p. 237. Dirk's writing came to form part of his *Enchiridion*; it is found in *Writings*, pp. 238-254. Menno's tracts are found respectively in CWMS, pp. 959-998, and 1060-1063.

[9] "Reply to Zylis and Lemke," CWMS, pp. 1001-1015.

[10] Scheffer, "Opmerkingen," p. 59.

[11] On the divisions and efforts at reconciliation, see Dyck, *Introduction*, pp. 124-135; 150-154. N. van der Zijpp notes that by 1590, the primary divisions among the Dutch were the Waterlanders, the "High Germans," the Old Flemish, the Flemish, the Old Frisians, and the Young Frisians. N. van der Zijpp, *Geschiedenis der Doopsgezinden in Nederland* (Arnhem: van Loghum Slaterus, 1952), p. 80.

[12] Sjouke Voolstra, "Themes in the Early Theology of Menno Simons," in Gerald R. Brunk, ed., *Menno Simons: A Reappraisal. Essays in Honor of Irvin B. Horst* (Harrisonburg, Va.: Eastern Mennonite College, 1992), p. 49.

[13] "The contours of the congregation without spot or wrinkle are still extremely vague in Menno's early theology." So Voolstra, *ibid.*, p. 49.

[14] Bornhäuser notes the growing influence of Dirk Philips, and maintains that by 1550, Dirk was no longer close to Menno. He also agrees with Meihuizen's appraisal of Menno's "shift": "Meihuizen stellt zu Recht eine Akzentverschiebung 'van de Heer (Christus) naar de gemeente' fest. Auf diesem Weg entfernt sich Menno—mit Ausnahme weniger Passagen—von dem Zentrum, von dem aus er zu Anfang seines Amtes das Wesentliche vom Unwesentlichen unterschieden hatte. Alle Kraft gilt jetzt dem Bemühen, den Bestand einer reinen Gemeinde zu sichern." Bornhäuser, *Leben und Lehre*, p. 160; cf. pp. 148-50. See also Krahn, *Dutch Anabaptism*, p. 230.

[15] "Inderdaad was Menno na zijn nederlaag weinig meer dan een werktuig in de handen van Dirk en vooral van Leenaart." W. J. Kühler, *Geschiedenis der Nederlandsche Doopsgezinden in de Zestiende Eeuw*, second printing (Haarlem: Willink, 1961), p. 324.

[16] William Keeney cautions that "Contrary to an impression which Vos and Kühler might give, the Dutch Mennonites were in general agreement on the need for church discipline, and a broader application of it than mere exclusion from the Lord's Table." *Development*, p. 162. He adds later, "Modern Dutch historians may have exaggerated Dirk's contribution to the difficulties." *Ibid.*, p. 166. Note his treatment of the relationship of Menno and Dirk on the matter of the ban, in *ibid.*, pp. 162-166.

[17] Well noted by Cornelius Krahn, *Menno Simons*, (Karlsruhe: Schneider, 1936), pp. 96-97: "Die Beeinflussung durch L. Bouwens und D. Philips hatte somit weniger eine Veränderung der Grundidee über den bann zur Folge, sie verschärfte aber die pracktische Auswirkung derselben."

[18] CWMS, pp. 409-418.

[19] "Those who are begotten of the living, saving Word of our beloved Lord Jesus Christ are by virtue of their new birth so joined to Christ, are become so like unto Him, so really implanted into Him...that they do not teach nor believe any doctrine but that which agrees with the doctrine of Christ..." CWMS, pp. 409-410.

[20] CWMS, pp. 411-12.

[21] Some examples: "we do not want to expel any, but rather receive; not to amputate, but rather to heal; not to discard, but rather to win back..." CWMS, p. 413. "Be not angry in your hearts, nor sharp in your speech concerning others... But always remember the patience of our beloved Lord Jesus Christ." *Ibid.*, p. 417.

[22] CWMS, p. 412.

[23] CWMS, p. 413. Characteristic of Menno's combination of brusqueness and pastoral concern is his warning to believers that "inasmuch as you must shun the apostate in accordance with the Word of God, take heed that while you shun them as diseased, foul, and unprofitable members unfit for the body of Christ, you yourselves may be found to be sound, fit, and profitable members in Christ Jesus." *Ibid.*, p. 415.

[24] "It is also the nature of those who are in God not to sin, as John says: Whosoever abideth in God sinneth not..." CWMS, p. 415. "In a word, the birth of earth makes earthly minded, and the birth of heaven makes heavenly minded." *Ibid.*, p. 416.

[25] Dyck, Keeney, and Beachy, *Writings*, p. 612; CWMS, pp. 473-74.

[26] *Ibid.*, p. 613; CWMS, p. 482.

[27] Dirk cites 2 John 10ff. Dyck, Keeney, and Beachy, *Writings*, p. 613; CWMS, p. 479.

[28] Dyck, Keeney, and Beachy, *Writings*, pp. 614-16; CWMS, pp. 480-81. Menno seemed more concerned that too much severity would result: "I sincerely hate this heartlessness. Nor do I wish to be considered a brother of such unmerciful, cruel brethren..." CWMS, p. 481.

[29] CWMS, p. 478; "Since the ban was given and left to us as a general command from the Lord, ... so the husband must also avoid his wife; the wife, her husband..." Dyck, Keeney, and Beachy, *Writings*, p. 613.

[30] Menno wrote: "beware that in this matter of matrimony you press none further than he is taught of God and than he and his conscience can bear..." CWMS, p. 479. He also tried to minimize the "command" to discipline when he asked that the brethren "make a difference between commandment and commandment, and not consider all commandments as equally weighty. For adultery, idolatry, shedding of blood, and the like shameful and abominable works of the flesh will be punished more severely than a misunderstanding in regard to the ban." *Ibid.*

[31] CWMS, p. 1041.

[32] CWMS, p. 1044. On the Matthew 18 question, Menno says that certain gross, public sins do not require a three-fold admonition. He then argues against the forcible disclosure of confessed sins.

[33] CWMS, p. 1045.

[34] Translation from Klaassen, *Anabaptism in Outline*, p. 231; original in Abraham Hulshof, *Gescheidnis van de Doopsgezinden te Straatsburg van 1525-1527* (Amsterdam: J. Clausen, 1905), pp. 227-228.

[35] Translation from Klaassen, *Anabaptism in Outline*, p. 231; original in Hulshof, *Geschiedenis*, p. 228. Cf. Krahn, *Dutch Anabaptism*, p. 236.

[36] Cornelius J. Dyck, "The First Waterlandian Confession of Faith," MQR 36(January, 1962), p. 12.

[37] *Ibid.*, p. 13.

[38] CWMS, p. 972.

[39] This section is entitled "The True Apostolic ban Makes No Exceptions," and is found in CWMS, pp. 970-974.

[40] CWMS, pp. 1060-63; esp. 1061.

[41] CWMS, p. 1007.

[42] Scheffer, "Opmerkingen," p. 59. See also the "Fragment" written by Dirk against the "abominable bitter slanders of some ... Swiss brothers," in Dyck, Keeney and Beachy, *Writings*, pp. 586-87.

[43] Leonard Gross, trans. and ed., "The First Mennonite Merger: The Concept of Cologne," *Mennonite Yearbook, 1990-1991*, p. 9.

[44] The Waterlanders united with the other two groups in 1601. Kühler, *Geschiedenis*, p. 459. A translation of the "Concept of Cologne" is found in the *Mennonite Yearbook, 1990-1991*, pp. 8-10. On these events, see C.J. Dyck, ed., *An Introduction to Mennonite History*, 2nd. ed. (Scottdale, Pa.: Herald Press, 1981), p. 132.

[45] See John D. Roth, trans. and ed., *Letters of the Amish Division: A Sourcebook* (Goshen, In.: Mennonite Historical Society, 1993).

Chapter 25

The Church as Sacrament

There was no easy way to reconcile the tension between the inner and the outer lives in the Anabaptist movement; dangers for the church lay in either direction, as historical events amply demonstrated. In fact it was in the midst of the uneasy tension between spirit and letter, inner and outer, invisible and visible, gospel and law, church and world, heaven and earth, that the Anabaptists were sure they were meant to live as believers, as pilgrims, and as a church. Towards the end of the sixteenth century, the surviving Anabaptist groups had achieved consensus on the central point that baptism was a necessary outer witness to the fact that they were living members of the visible Body of Christ on earth, the only true church. Another way of saying this is that "spiritualist" Anabaptism was excluded as a viable option by the groups that survived as identifiable Anabaptist descendants. The church "tradition" which the surviving Anabaptist groups passed on (their ecclesiology) was a very optimistic one indeed. The concrete and visible church was where the physical presence of Christ (in His members) would be incarnated in the world.

The apparently simple insistence that the physical members of Christ's Body somehow "incarnated" the Christ who had risen and was now sitting next to God the Father rested upon crucial theological and philosophical presuppositions. For the vast majority of Anabaptists these presuppositions were, it is safe to say, simply assumed as truths, rather than being the result of any systematic theologizing. There is good reason, then, to trace first the history of the development of Anabaptist practice and now, in a retrospective way, reflect upon some of the theological issues that were implied by that practice. Anabaptism developed "on the road." This is not to say that its development was "unreflective," but only to say that theological issues emerged in a secondary way. The Anabaptists were not "theologians" in the sense that they first worked out an intellectual framework and then put those principles into practice. Nevertheless, as the foregoing survey has demonstrated, there were implicit as well as explicit theological principles at work throughout.

There was, first of all, the question of regeneration. Debates concerning the ban brought out Anabaptist differences concerning pneumatology and anthropology very clearly indeed, although Anabaptist discussions did not deal with these differences as theological issues as such. There was, in the second place, the Christological question: What did it mean to say that regenerated members, being part of Christ's Body, would also incarnate the truth *as Christ had*? How had Christ been incarnated? What exactly were believers supposed to "mirror" in their own lives? Christological debates pointed to a further philosophical question that, although rarely acknowledged explicitly, underlay many of these discussions: Is the nature of reality essentially dualistic, with an impregnable division between the worlds of spirit and matter? If so, what will "incarnation" mean in such a world? How these questions were answered had significant implications for Anabaptist ecclesiology.

Sin, Regeneration, and the Ban

Anabaptist developments concerning the ban, as we have seen, moved increasingly in the direction of strict and immediate exclusion of those who had "fallen," and who were not repentant. The Swiss attained an early consensus on strict banning, shortly after Schleitheim; the Hutterite communities had followed by 1533; the Dutch Anabaptists cemented their insistence on strict banning around 1550 by insisting upon shunning as well as banning those who had violated or disobeyed the behavioural guidelines of the community, and who refused to repent.

When we analyze these developments, we see that the Anabaptists who supported the strictest positions on banning were, first of all, those who read the New Testament as providing a literal rule of life. The supporters of strict banning agreed upon a hermeneutic approach that appealed to "obedience to the commands of Christ," literally interpreted. Among those who shared this interpretive approach, however, differences emerged on what exactly Christ had commanded, and what to do when biblical "commands" conflicted in concrete situations. Had Christ commanded a legislated community of goods (Hutterites)? Had Christ commanded the shunning of marriage partners as well as the banning of the unrepentant (Mennonites)? As we have seen in previous sections of this study, these same "rule oriented" groups (Swiss Brethren, Hutterites, Mennonites) also came to share essentially the same positions (with some differences in detail, of course) on the sword, the oath, the place of women in the communities, and marriage. Again, agreement on a literal, Christocentric hermeneutic (and a resulting enforceable rule of life based in the New Testament) lay at the heart of the very similar ecclesiologies that came to be seen among the Swiss, Hutterite, and Dutch Anabaptist traditions.

In the second place, those who supported the strict maintenance of community boundaries by means of the ban assumed (usually without explicitly recognizing the fact) that regeneration by the Holy Spirit would be quite thorough, and that the human propensity to sin could be resisted successfully by the regenerate saints most of the time. This latter assumption is worth analyzing further, even though the Anabaptists themselves generally did not examine this question explicitly.

On the side of the Swiss Anabaptists who followed Schleitheim's guidelines, later called Swiss Brethren, there is precious little evidence of systematic reflection on the question of how a thorough regeneration was supposed to take place. The barest outline is evident in the Schleitheim Articles: believers are those who have "the mind of Christ," and they therefore live out an "obedience of faith." Looking at the evidence provided by the debate over the sword between followers of Schleitheim and Hubmaier, the debates between the Swiss Brethren and the Reformed preachers at Bern, and the debate between Pilgram Marpeck and the Swiss Brethren concerning the ban, we may say that the Swiss Brethren of the 1520s, 30s, and 40s simply assumed the regenerative premise as a given fact.

Balthasar Hubmaier's reservation concerning the thoroughness of regeneration in believers was anthropological: human beings remain stuck in this world "up to their ears," and only Christ can say "My kingdom is not of this world." Regeneration only marks the beginning of a process of overcoming sin, not its completion. Marpeck's objection was raised with respect to the ban. He made much the same anthropological point as had Hubmaier, but added a further point (raised also by the Reformed preachers at Bern): the "mind of Christ," he said, is reflected not in legislation and swift banning, but rather in humility, patience, and love of neighbour. Taken together, Hubmaier and Marpeck thus argued that the Swiss Brethren had not appreciated the stubborn nature of human sinfulness, and the difficult process involved in the regeneration of sinners.

Marpeck's further point, resting as it did on Christ's highest commandment, to love God and neighbour, reflected a deeper question about the visible evidence of regeneration. Would those who had accepted the power of the Holy Spirit in their lives be recognized visibly by "love," or by a life that manifested "obedience?" Marpeck attempted to say "by both," although emphasizing love over law.

It is fair to say that the emphasis on the individual reception of the Holy Spirit, repentance, faith, and regeneration, strongly present at the beginnings of the movement, began to fade in importance for the groups that were establishing stricter community boundaries by means of literal "rules of life" (*Ordnungen*), enforced by the ban. This process is visible for the Swiss Brethren and the Hutterites, but it is perhaps most apparent in Menno. The challenge posed by the spiritualists was taken up by the Swiss, Hutterites, and Mennonites not on anthropological or regenerative grounds, but rather on the ground of what must be the visible evidences of regeneration. In point of fact, the "literalists" and the "spiritualists" *agreed* that regeneration could be successfully accomplished, but the spiritualists simply could not agree that the measure of regeneration would be obedience to the letter of the New Testament. The debate between Menno Simons and Nicolaas van Blesdijk illustrates this point. Both shared an optimistic Melchiorite view of regeneration, but Menno insisted that genuine regeneration would be manifest in obedience to the "law of Christ"; Blesdijk insisted rather upon freedom from the law, and obedience to the law of love.

The contrasting answers given to these questions had significant ecclesiological consequences.

—The spiritualists were optimistic about regeneration, but they safeguarded the individual and subjective nature of the Christian life. The spiritualists resisted a communal, legislative restriction of the Spirit. Their insistence upon freedom from all law, except the law of love as manifested in Christ, meant that the boundaries of their communities were amorphous, and over time tended to become virtually invisible. The spiritualist Anabaptists preserved the individual, regenerative emphasis of early Anabaptism, but were ever more ready to abandon (or at least, compromise broadly) the visible, communal measures of that regeneration.

—The Anabaptists who insisted upon linking regeneration with obedience to a literal New Testament "law" were, by that step, elevating community guidelines above the individual reception of the Holy Spirit. The baptism of the Spirit would entail, they said, very *specific* visible evidences of regeneration, as defined by the true church, that is, by the true church's reading of Scripture. Increasingly, the visible guidelines defining the true church (which were the measures of having been renewed by the Holy Spirit) were drawn by smaller and smaller groups of male elders. Ecclesiology threatened to render pneumatology superfluous: the Spirit was present in tightly governed communities, it appeared, and nowhere else. The legislative tendency in fact came to define the subsequent ecclesiological tradition, handed on in the Believers' Churches descended from the Anabaptists, with the inner dimension of yielding to the Spirit presupposed, but not overtly emphasized or nourished.

It was characteristic of the more literally-minded Anabaptists that they believed that outside of their particularly defined visible church, there would be no salvation. They were not strict legalists on the finer points, and if pushed, remained true to their spiritualist, anti-sacramental origins: if someone became a believer and wished to be joined to the Body of Christ by water baptism, but was prevented by an untimely death, the lack of a baptism in water was no impediment to salvation. The water was just water. But they also firmly believed that true, saving faith would lead to an overwhelming desire to *obey* the literal "commands of Christ." Thus they believed that water baptism and a visible commitment to the Body of Christ on earth would naturally follow faith; outside of this progression there would be no salvation. This was the "narrow way" of commitment, discipleship, and suffering which Christ Himself had walked, and which all true disciples also must walk. Salvation would be granted to those who, through grace, became visible members of Christ's Body on earth; those who had the opportunity, but rejected it and took the broad road instead, were on the sure path to perdition.

—Hubmaier and Marpeck were among the few Anabaptists who took up positions between those of the spiritualists and the literalists on questions of regeneration. Their questioning of the actual thoroughness of regeneration was a significant objection, from an ecclesiological point of view. It was no coincidence that Reformed and Lutheran objections often focused on this same point, for a broader ecclesiology is the result of a more pessimistic anthropology.[1] If human beings remain in need of significant further regeneration after repentance and coming to faith, then the church will be structured not so much to preserve purity among the regenerate saints, but rather to encourage growth for the "weak and imperfect," which will include all members. Both Hubmaier and Marpeck pointed away from an understanding of the church as the only pure Bride of Christ, and saw the church rather as a gathering of people still in the process of regeneration. Pilgram Marpeck in particular attempted to hold together the poles that the spiritualist and literalist Anabaptists were driving apart. Marpeck called for freedom from the law, as well as a visible community of faith.

The Church as Sacrament: Christology and Ecclesiology

All Anabaptists—excepting perhaps Pilgram Marpeck—were in essential agreement with Ulrich Zwingli in their radical rejection of the sacramental mediation of grace. That the Anabaptists were radical anti-sacramentalists is clear from all of their statements on the subject. Again and again we read that "the water is just water"; "the bread is just bread"; "the wine is just wine." There is no divine power in the priestly blessing of these physical elements that can render them sacraments. The physical elements cannot become the visible signs of invisible grace. We have noted above that one logical outcome of this radical anti-sacramental view is to deny any value to the outer elements altogether, a point pressed by the spiritualists. In fact, the non-spiritualist Anabaptists (those who continued to insist upon and practise the visible, external church ordinances) were not as thoroughly anti-sacramental as we might be led to think. The sacramental substratum underlying the Anabaptist insistence on the visible signs of the church was made evident in the debates with the spiritualists.

The Anabaptists were living in the late medieval religious and intellectual world. The incarnational question was very much alive for them as a result: In what way may God be said to be present here and now to humanity, in Christ? Is God made present in the Spirit, in the Word, in the church, or in all three? The medieval church had claimed that the Body of Christ was made physically present to humankind in the elements of the Mass. This the Anabaptists denied. They argued that Christ had "ascended into heaven and sitteth at the right hand of God the Father." But all the same, many Anabaptists insisted that there *was* a physical presence of Christ on earth, and that was the true church itself, present in Christ's members. When we read Anabaptist statements describing the church as the Body of Christ, and individual believers as members or limbs of that Body, we tend to take this as an extended metaphor, not a literal description. There is much evidence to suggest, to the contrary, that for many Anabaptists it was intended as a literal description, and not a metaphor at all. As ecclesiology assumed more importance, so too did a sacramental conception of the church.[2]

Once we understand that for increasing numbers of Anabaptists, the gathering of the regenerate saints was itself to be a sacrament, a visible sign of invisible grace, we can begin to appreciate the ecclesiological pressures for a Christ-like life in all things. Individuals were "members" (unavoidably, bodily members) of Christ Himself because of their heavenly rebirth, regeneration, and incorporation into the Body of Christ on earth. Therefore, just as Christ was persecuted, so His Body on earth would be persecuted. Just as Christ forgave, rendered unto Caesar, refused to judge or take the sword, so His Body would also do. The Body of Christ on earth, the true church, would incarnate in a visible way, the mind and the spirit of Christ, by lives that conformed to His life.

It was in this peculiarly sacramental framework, then, that Christology became a pressing issue, although more pressing for the Dutch Anabaptists than for the Swiss and the Hutterites. The Swiss Anabaptists and the Hutterites were not given to Christological speculation, and were content with orthodox formulations. Jesus Christ, said the Hutterite elder Peter Riedemann, is the Eternal Word and Truth, the Saviour and Christ, fully human and fully divine, the only begotten Son of God.[3] The versification of the Apostles' Creed in the Swiss Brethren hymnal, the *Ausbund*, stuck even closer to orthodox language. Jesus Christ is the true Son of God, the only begotten Saviour, present with the Father before the world began, begotten not created, of the same substance (*Wesen*) as the Father through whom all things were made; conceived by the Holy Spirit of the Virgin Mary, he was born "a human being like any other common person."[4] There is no hint among the Swiss Brethren or the Hutterites of unorthodoxy in Christology.

Nevertheless, Riedemann's exposition of the Creed points to the particular Anabaptist interpretation (or extension) of orthodox Christology. After confessing that Christ alone "has the power to overcome death," Riedemann adds "and to quicken whom he will and to give his fullness to whomsoever and in what abundance he will. And those who take from and receive of him become through him likewise 'God's anointed' or Christians—failing this, they have the name in vain."[5] For the Anabaptists, the point of Christological formulations was not simply to affirm who Jesus Christ was and is, in a linguistically correct manner, but to insist further that "confessing Christ as Lord" can only be done by one who, in Riedemann's words, "experience(s) such a victory in himself, namely that Christ has overcome the devil in him also, and rent and removed his snare, that is sin." To confess Christ as the Son of God means, for Riedemann, that this "brightness of the glory of the Father ... has now taken us captive into his obedience and leads us in his way, teaches us his character, ways, and goodness..."[6] In typically Anabaptist fashion, for Riedemann Christological affirmations became quite naturally affirmations about the necessity of regeneration, obedience, and discipleship in Christ's human members.[7]

Swiss Brethren and Hutterite Christological statements, affirming as they do the joint divinity and humanity of Christ, can quite naturally go on to affirm both the "divine birth" of the Spirit of Christ in believers, and the concrete life of discipleship that must issue from rebirth and regeneration. As we have seen, it was the life of Jesus that provided the model for discipleship. The Dutch Anabaptists, however, had to deal with a slightly different set of problems, for they were heirs to Melchior Hoffman's very spiritualized Christology and heightened expectation for regeneration. In what follows we will outline Hoffman's view, inherited and modified from Caspar Schwenckfeld, consider Pilgram Marpeck's response to Schwenckfeld's Christology (which served as an indirect response to Hoffman's view), and conclude by looking at Menno's appropriation of Melchiorite Christology.

Schwenckfeld and Hoffman

Hoffman's Christology has been described as docetic and monophysite. His central point was soteriological: He believed that Satan's hold on human beings could only be loosed by a perfect sacrifice, for "if Christ had taken part of Mary's nature, we would have to await another saviour."[8] Hoffman's rejection of the two natures of Christ also was related to his understanding of the Supper. He believed that the orthodox two-natures Christology led to a false teaching concerning the real presence in the Eucharist. The key text for Hoffman was "the word *became* flesh," rather than "the word *took on* human flesh."[9] By means of this distinction, Hoffman believed that Christ's essentially pure and spiritual nature could be maintained, both in soteriology and in eucharistic theology.

Hoffman and Schwenckfeld had come to know each other in Strasbourg beginning in 1529. They shared some important commonalities, both having begun reforming careers in the Lutheran camp, both having rejected Luther's soteriology and anthropology, and both holding to a similar spiritualized understanding of the Lord's Supper.[10] From these similarities grew a similar Christological concern: Hoffman, no less than Schwenckfeld, became convinced that Christ's atonement for human sin would not have been valid if Jesus had been a mere creature. Hoffman's solution paralleled Schwenckfeld's very closely—Deppermann concludes that Schwenckfeld was the source of Hoffman's teaching, but that Hoffman was less careful than was Schwenckfeld about the danger of docetism.[11] Hoffman, like Schwenckfeld, held that God alone must be considered the progenitor of Jesus, but unlike Schwenckfeld, he did not agree that the Virgin Mary played any essential role in providing Jesus with human flesh—even of a unique and distinctive kind of human flesh.

Hoffman disavowed any "creaturely" addition to Jesus' nature, and held that Jesus had "passed through Mary like water through a pipe."[12] The differences in Christology between Schwenckfeld and Hoffman thus come to rest in their respective Mariologies: Schwenckfeld held to Mary's immaculate conception; Hoffman denied the immaculate conception of Mary.[13] Thus for Hoffman, any essential motherhood attributed to Mary would taint Jesus with "creatureliness"; Schwenckfeld attempted to avoid the problem by holding to Mary's own immaculate nature. In spite of the close similarities in their Christologies, then, Schwenckfeld resolutely combatted Hoffman's view, and considered it a gross mistake. He said later that Hoffman had "sucked [his] error out of our truth, as the spider sucks poison out of a precious flower."[14] Hoffman's rejection of sacramentalism—in both its Roman Catholic and Lutheran forms—was complete and in accord with the Anabaptist view. It was strengthened by his Christology: Salvation could not be mediated by a real, physical presence of Christ in physical elements, but would be mediated by a spiritual process leading to repentance, regeneration, and baptism, a process Hoffman described as a "spiritual marriage to Christ." Hoffman likewise rejected the Reformers' view of forensic justification, joining other Anabaptists in emphasizing rebirth in the Spirit, regeneration, and a life of actual righteousness. "The elect" were those who had yielded to the living Spirit of their own free will. True believers were those in whom the Spirit of Christ had come to dwell, and they would live visibly new lives according to the Spirit, not the flesh. As a consequence of his spiritualistic Christology, Hoffman's regenerative anthropology was extremely optimistic, for just as Christ had conquered the flesh perfectly by means of an immaculate, spiritual conception and pure birth, so those who had been regenerated by Christ's Spirit were thus "wedded" to Christ and joined by Christ to His spiritual Body, the church. The regenerate had, through Christ, conquered the flesh by the Spirit.

Hoffman's marked optimism concerning regeneration, based on his spiritualized Christology, made even more explicit the inner/outer tension already present in the movement. Hoffman's stronger emphasis on the Spirit is evident in his acceptance of contemporary prophecy, in his willingness to allow water baptism to lapse when persecution intensified, and in his spiritualized understanding of "discipleship." Hoffman's understanding of *Nachfolge*, which was as central to his Anabaptism as it was for the Swiss Brethren and Hutterites, differed from theirs primarily because he understood the following after Christ in more figurative than literal terms. The life of Jesus Christ was the "figurative model" believers were to follow, particularly Jesus' example of yieldedness to the Father's will, which led to the establishment of a new covenant sealed in baptism, and a time of testing in the wilderness.[15] In the second place, Hoffman (like Hut) understood *Nachfolge* within a calendar of End Times events, in which the actions of believers—especially those of the "pious rulers"—would be carried out in accordance with the demands of God's final justice. The yieldedness of believers, and their willingness to suffer as Jesus had suffered, was thus tempered in Hoffman by the expectation that God's justice would avenge that suffering before Christ's return, and that this vengeance would be carried out very soon.

Schwenckfeld and Marpeck

Pilgram Marpeck did not enter into a written debate with Melchior Hoffman, but he did engage Caspar Schwenckfeld's Christology at some length. As a result of this debate, Marpeck was forced to clarify his own Christology and understanding of the Lord's Supper, from an Anabaptist perspective.[16] Marpeck's views, although unique to Anabaptism and not destined to survive in an ongoing tradition, nevertheless remain valuable theological perspectives as such, given his Anabaptist presuppositions. Furthermore, because of the close similarity between Schwenckfeld's and Hoffman's Christologies, Marpeck's objections to Schwenckfeld applied equally well to Hoffman, and to the Dutch Anabaptists, like Menno and Dirk, who accepted Hoffman's views.

Already in 1531 Marpeck had made the connection between the two natures of Christ and his view that the physical and the spiritual formed one essential reality. The debates with Schwenckfeld in 1538 and 1539 forced him to clarify and refine his views.[17] Against the Melchiorite view that seemed to deny Christ's humanity Marpeck had spoken already: "He was a true natural human being ... the true seed of Abraham ...*fruit of the body of Mary*, therefore he can truly be called our brother... with all our weaknesses except sin..."[18] But by 1538 Schwenckfeld had come to the conviction that even Christ's human nature was "uncreated," and so came to oppose Marpeck's further elaboration of the meaning of the two natures of Christ. In his *Vermahnung* of 1542 Marpeck argued not only that Christ's nature was an essential union in one person of the human and divine natures, but also that this union continued after Christ's death, resurrection, and ascension. The "physical" part of the union was carried on, through Christ's spirit, by the church: the baptism, the Supper, and the acts of mercy of the gathered community are "prolongations of the incarnation."

Schwenckfeld, in reply, accused Marpeck of mixing the spiritual and the bodily, to which Marpeck answered in his *Verantwortung* of 1543. Marpeck argued there that Christ has two bodies, "the transfigured body of Christ (which is not yet perfect) at the right hand of the Father and the untransfigured body of Christ (composed of earthly members gathered by his Spirit)."[19] Marpeck argued that Christ's Spirit "secures" the human spirit, which then carries out physical acts and deeds in conformity with Christ's Spirit. "The new human being is one integrated entity which enjoys participation in ... the divine Spirit." Just as regenerated human beings are integrated spiritual and physical beings, empowered to act by Christ's Spirit, the community of believers "is constituted by the Spirit through the concrete acts of believers."[20]

Marpeck could thus maintain not only the full divinity and humanity of Christ, but also the essential unity of the spiritual and the human in individual believers and in the Body of Christ, the church. Because of this essential unity, which included the physical and the human dimensions as essential parts of the reborn Christian, the perfectionist strain was mitigated for Marpeck. Believers are being regenerated; they have not yet sloughed off their humanity nor been perfectly wedded to Christ. Furthermore, because of this unity, the ceremonies and acts of love in which that community participates reveal the divine in an essential way, rather than being simply physical signs pointing to another reality. As such, the ceremonies cannot be done away with, for they are of the essence of God's revelatory order as prolongations of the incarnation. In fact, Marpeck would argue against the spiritualists that "a person can neither know nor be saved by the transfigured Christ apart from the concrete life of [the] community."[21]

Menno Simons, Melchiorite Christology, and the Church

Menno Simons inherited Melchior Hoffman's docetic Christology, and consistently defended it.[22] Two writings in particular outline Menno's Christology: the *Brief Confession on the Incarnation* (1544),[23] and *The Incarnation of Our Lord* (1554).[24] In these writings Menno reiterates and defends the essence of Hoffman's spiritualized Christology as being in accordance with the letter of Scripture. Against the orthodox position that holds two undivided natures in one person, Menno wrote: "The Lord Jesus Christ is not an impure and divided Christ of two persons or sons, but an undivided and pure Christ, a single person, God's own first-born Son and only begotten

Son."[25] Granting that Menno misrepresents the orthodox position here (which does not hold that Christ was "two persons"), the key words are "impure" and "divided," as against "undivided" and "pure." Menno appeals to the words of John, and repeats the motto adopted by the Münsterites: John, he insists, "says, The Word became flesh. He does not say, *The Word assumed a man of our or of Mary's flesh and dwelt in this*, as our opponents say."[26] Menno argues further:

> Recall that Christ calls Himself the Son of man, and says that this Son of man descended from heaven. But *the son of Mary, whose flesh is of Mary* did not descend from heaven, did He, but must have *sprung from Adam's flesh*, if the position of the learned ones is correct.[27]

And so Menno concludes, in good Melchiorite fashion: "It follows irresistibly that the entire Christ Jesus, both God and man, man and God, has His origin in heaven and not on earth. . . . Fast and immovable is the testimony, The Word became flesh."[28]

In his earlier writing on the incarnation, Menno made it clear that he drew the same regenerationist conclusion from this Christology as had Hoffman. The "true brethren and sisters of Jesus Christ" he describes as

> the well-disposed children of God, who with Christ Jesus are born of God the Father and the powerful seed of the divine Word in Christ Jesus, who are regenerated by Christ, partake of His Spirit and nature, who have been made like unto Him, are Christian and heavenly minded...[29]

Menno then described the collected members of the "rightly believing, Christian church" as follows:

> They are the body and bride of Christ, the ark, the mount and garden of the Lord, the house, people, city, temple of God, the spiritual Eve, flesh of Christ's flesh and bone of His bone, children of God, the chosen generation, the spiritual seed of Abraham, children of the promise, branches and trees of righteousness, sheep of the heavenly pasture, kings and priests, a holy people which is God's own.[30]

Menno held with Hoffman that the Body of Christ, made up of those regenerated and "married" to Christ spiritually, would partake of the essential divinity of Christ in its sojourn on this earth.

As we have seen, however, Menno was not willing to draw all the same spiritualist conclusions from this Christology as had Hoffman and other Melchiorites. Whereas Hoffman had been willing to suspend outer ceremonies, Menno linked the performance of those ceremonies with obedience to Scripture. Where Hoffman had spoken of following after Christ in an essentially figurative way, Menno insisted upon a literal discipleship, based on the testimony of the New Testament. Whereas Joris and Blesdijk continued further down the spiritualist path outlined by Hoffman and his Christology, Menno attempted to hold on to Hoffman's spiritualist Christology *while at the same time* applying literal measures of spiritual regeneration. The result for Menno was a heightened emphasis on the visible purity of the Body of Christ, for the

Body of Christ would of necessity need to manifest in word and deed, in the world, the spiritual perfection of having been united to the essentially divine Christ.[31] It is in this way that the controversy concerning the ban in Dutch Anabaptism had significant roots in Melchiorite Christology.

Conclusion

The debates between Marpeck and the spiritualists, and Menno and the David Jorists provide two contrasting Anabaptist responses to the challenge of spiritualism. It is important to note that the primary role of the Spirit of God was not at issue in either debate. Marpeck and Menno, no less than Denck, Bünderlin, Schwenckfeld and Blesdijk, maintained that a personal experience of the renewing Spirit of God was necessary in order for one to become a Christian believer. Furthermore, both Marpeck and Menno maintained resolutely that the true church must be a visible church, in which the ceremonies and ordinances were practised and which showed forth, in an unmistakable and visible way, the inner regeneration which both they and the spiritualists held to be primary. Nevertheless, the contrasting responses of Marpeck and Menno are instructive.

Marpeck worked consciously to avoid a legalistic and literalistic response to the spiritualist challenge, while yet not losing touch with the demand for a renewed life of discipleship and following Jesus. Marperck's insistence on the integrity of the spiritual and physical dimensions of creation was grounded in an appreciation for the deeper meaning of the incarnation. Not only did a good God bring a good creation into being, the centrality of the physical side of creation in the saving process was revealed, confirmed, and cemented by the incarnation. The only way to salvation, Marpeck would affirm in many of his writings, is through the *humanity* of Christ; consequently, the human dimensions of the Body of Christ also form a crucial and continuing part of Jesus' mission to the world.[32]

Pilgram Marpeck insisted further against the spiritualists that the practice and expression of divine love must take place within the community of love, and cannot exist in splendid spiritual isolation. The ceremonies which define the community, and which are practised within the community of love are, said Marpeck, remembrances, pledges and memorials of Christ's historic love for humanity. Nevertheless, the ceremonies are much more than mere memorials, performed out of a blind obedience to the law. They are also, said Marpeck, physical means of growth into divine love and the mature spiritual life: "If these false teachers were correct, the ceremonies of Christ would become responsible for our condemnation, but they have been presented by Christ as a medicine and as a means to our salvation in order that we strengthen our human weakness."[33] With this insistence, Pilgram Marpeck moved the Anabaptist discussion back again towards the Catholic sacramental insight: the physical ordinances and ceremonies commanded by Christ and celebrated by Christians in communal worship are necessary means of grace, physical windows and doors that participate in and open the way to the divine, and without which the way to the divine will not be known.

Marpeck challenged the dualist presupposition of the spiritualists; Menno, the Swiss, and the Hutterites did not. But Menno had inherited a Melchiorite Christology which was built upon the stark division, and even enmity, between the spiritual and the physical dimensions of reality. Christ could only atone for human sin by not being tainted with "creatureliness." Having accepted this spiritualist Christology, Menno still faced the need to move beyond the prophetic apocalypticism and spiritualism that had accompanied it in Melchiorite Anabaptism. He did this, as we have seen, by appealing to the words and the example of Christ as witnessed to in Scripture, but he built this New Testament biblicism on the Christology he had inherited from Hoffman. That is, Melchiorite Christology simply heightened Menno's optimism concerning the ethical possibilities of the spiritual rebirth of believers, and thus heightened his expectations for the obedience of the pure Bride of Christ, the church.

As a result, the community of believers played several crucial roles in Marpeck's understanding of the process of redemption and salvation that are missing in Menno, the Swiss and the Hutterites. For Marpeck the church as the Body of Christ was a sacramental offer of God's grace, mercy, and salvation to all. As in the incarnation, God's grace continues to be offered through the physical Body of Christ to individuals and to the world by means of external and visible testimonies, ceremonies, and acts of love. On this Marpeck was in agreement with the Swiss, the Hutterites, and with Menno. But Marpeck took the "incarnational" point further: The Body of Christ is also the place where believers are expected to grow in Christian love *by means of* the practice of the disciplines of worship, love and service. For Marpeck, Christian worship was crucial for evangelization, and also for the spiritual development of believers, for it was through the church that believers were to be challenged and helped in the process of growing into the nature of Christ.

Such pastoral concerns were not lacking in Menno, the Swiss, or the Hutterites, of course. But for them, the church was to be, above all, "without spot or wrinkle," as Christ also was. It was the divine Christ, not the incarnate Christ, that inspired the Anabaptist tradition of the "Body of Christ"; consequently, it was above all divine purity, not human growth, that was expected to be "incarnated" by of believers. It was separation and purity, not evangelism, that defined the true church. Here Marpeck's Christological emphasis on the humanity of Christ, along with his less optimistic anthropology, tempered the perfectionist, sectarian tendency that had been part of Anabaptism from the start and that asserted itself increasingly in the ongoing Anabaptist ecclesiological traditions.

There was an uncanny parallel between Marpeck's critique of Swiss Brethren legalism and Blesdijk's critique of Menno's reading of Scripture. Menno's strongest argument against Blesdijk for the continuation of a visible church was to insist that Christ's commands must be obeyed. Blesdijk's objection was based on his Pauline appeal to Christian freedom, and his conviction that love was the "highest summation and foundation of all the Scriptures" by which all other scriptural statements must be measured.[34] One suspects, from other statements he made, that Marpeck would have agreed with Blesdijk, against Menno. While Marpeck would have disagreed with Blesdijk's conclusions regarding the visible marks of the church, he shared an appreciation with Blesdijk for the spiritual freedom of a Christian that Menno, the Swiss Brethren, and the Hutterites did not.

Historically speaking, it was the conception of the church without spot or wrinkle that became the consensus view in the surviving Anabaptist groups, and that was passed on to succeeding generations as the ecclesial tradition. Marpeck's answer to the spiritualist challenge, in spite of its rich ecclesiological possibilites, was not passed on to succeeding groups. Among the followers of Menno, the Christology that had provided the theological support for the emphasis on the pure Body of Christ on earth faded during the seventeenth century, although among the more conservative descendants of Menno defences of Melchiorite Christology were still being reprinted as late as 1825. The majority of Dutch Mennonites no longer held to Menno's Christology by 1800,[35] but the emphasis on the church without spot or wrinkle survived and flourished nevertheless. The Swiss Brethren and the Hutterites, while they elaborated more sophisticated scriptural defences of their ecclesiologies as the sixteenth century proceeded, maintained their views of the church as the pure Body of Christ, untroubled by Christological speculation. Marpeck's view disappeared, to be recovered only as a result of modern historical investigations.[36]

End Notes

[1] For a Lutheran example, see the written reply of the Hessian preachers to Hans Pauli Kuchenbecker and other Swiss Brethren (1578). Against Kuchenbecker's optimistic view of regeneration they argued that forgiveness of sins doesn't extend so far as to "tear out sin with its roots from human beings." And even if human beings receive the Holy Spirit in baptism, "this is only a beginning work, in this world." TA, *Hesse*, p. 447.

[2] See the important and insightful work of John D. Rempel, *The Lord's Supper in Anabaptism* (Scottdale, Pa.: Herald Press, 1993), for this and subsequent points.

[3] Klaassen, *Outline*, pp. 28-31.

[4] *Ausbund*, hymn 2, pp. 6-7.

[5] Klaassen, *Outline*, p. 29.

[6] *Ibid.*, pp. 30-31.

[7] Balthasar Hubmaier, after affirming orthodox declarations concerning Jesus Christ, adds "I believe and trust that the Holy Spirit has overshadowed my soul like Mary's, and that I was conceived a new man, and born again of your living immortal Word, and in the Spirit." Klaassen, *Outline*, p. 25.

[8] "Wenn Christus teilgehabt hätte an der Natur Mariae, dann müssten wir auf einen anderen Erlöser warten." So Deppermann, p. 199.

[9] "He did not take flesh upon himself but became himself flesh and corporal, in order that he might himself give salvation and pay for the sin of the whole world by means of his guiltless suffering, dying, and the pouring out of his blood." Melchior Hoffman, *The Ordinance of God*, (1530), in George H. Williams and Angel M. Mergal, eds., *Spiritual and Anabaptist Writers* (Philadelphia: Westminster Press, 1957), p. 198. See also Deppermann, *Hoffman*, p. 200.

[10] On this latter point, see Deppermann, *Hoffman*, p. 189.

[11] The view that Jesus was essentially divine, and only took on a human appearance.

[12] *Ibid.*, p. 190: "Christus...durch Maria hindurchgegangen war wie Wasser durch ein Rohr."

[13] *Ibid.*

[14] Cited in Maier, *Schwenckfeld*, p. 59.

[15] Hoffman notes Jesus's baptism by John, which was a betrothal through water, signifying Jesus' detachment from his own will; by this covenant of God Jesus was absorbed into God's will, and then led for 40 days into the wilderness, overcoming Satan in the end. Hoffman notes, "Such a figurative meaning the Lord Christ Jesus intends (when) he goes before his flock at the head to be a model," and concludes "In just such a manner *all* children of God and brothers of the Lord Jesus Christ should imitate him and also covenant and betroth themselves..." Melchior Hoffman, *Ordinance of God*, pp. 189-90.

[16] See especially Rempel, *Lord's Supper*, chapter 3.

[17] See Boyd, *Marpeck*, pp. 115ff.

[18] Cited in Boyd, *Marpeck*, p. 117; emphasis mine.

[19] *Ibid.*, p. 123.

[20] *Ibid.*, p. 124.

[21] *Ibid.*, p. 125.

[22] One must agree with Cornelius Krahn's observation that Menno's defense of the Melchiorite position on the incarnation was no mere "bagatelle," but rather was tightly integrated with his own soteriology and ecclesiology. This must be said over against the comments of J.C. Wenger, translator of Menno's works into English, who tends to dismiss the importance of Menno's defense. Cf. Krahn, *Menno Simons*, p. 156 with CWMS, pp. 420-21. See also Krahn's article on the "Incarnation of Christ" in ME, III, pp. 18-20.

[23] CWMS, pp. 422-454.

[24] CWMS, pp. 785-834.

[25] From *The Incarnation of Our Lord* (1554), CWMS, p. 793.

[26] Italics in original; CWMS, p. 795.

[27] CWMS, p. 797.

[28] CWMS, pp. 797-98, *passim*.

[29] CWMS, p. 423.

[30] CWMS, p. 448.

[31] See Krahn, *Menno Simons*, pp. 158-61.

[32] See, for example, Pilgram Marpeck, "Concerning the Humanity of Christ (1555)," in Klassen and Klaassen, *Writings*, pp. 507-515.

[33] Pilgram Marpeck, "A Clear and Useful Instruction," in Klassen and Klaassen, *Writings*, p. 105.

[34] Blesdijk, *Christelijcke Verantwoordinghe*, 20b.

[35] ME, III, p. 20.

[36] See above all the work of William Klassen, Neal Blough, Stephen Boyd, and John Rempel.

Chapter 26

The Continuing Anabaptist Tradition

This chapter will revisit the doctrinal and ecclesiological core of early Anabaptist teachings, contrasting that core with the tradition that came to survive in the Swiss Brethren, Hutterite, and Dutch Anabaptist groups. The traditions of the Swiss Brethren and the Hutterite branches are most easily described, for these groups had assumed fairly stable forms by the last quarter of the sixteenth century. For the purposes of this summary we will refer to Swiss Brethren and Hutterite writings dating from around 1570. The Dutch tradition is difficult to treat in cursory fashion, for the Waterlander division around the time of Menno's death in 1561 was followed quickly by the Frisian/Flemish division, which in turn resulted in further sub-divisions.[1] Rather than catalogue these doctrinal and ecclesial splits, we will refer to the Dordrecht Confession of Faith (1632), which was an ultimately unsuccessful effort to heal Dutch divisions. Although Dordrecht represents a conservative Dutch confession, its influence was extensive among Dutch Mennonite refugees that settled along the Baltic and to the east and, after 1660, was influential among the Swiss Brethren. In that year it was adopted by Swiss Brethren pastors in Alsace and the Palatinate; its emphasis on shunning as well as banning contributed to the Amish schism (1693), the one major division among the Swiss Brethren which has persisted to this day.

Anabaptist Views shared with Other Christian Confessions

The Creed

By the last quarter of the sixteenth century, mainline Protestant denominations had begun to enter a period of orthodoxy, in which their particular doctrines were elaborated in Confessions of Faith. These were based, first of all, on the ecumenical creeds of Christendom. Because of repeated contact and disputations with Lutheran and Reformed pastors and theologians, it was perhaps only natural that the Anabaptists also began composing confessions of faith which outlined distinctive Anabaptist beliefs in more detail. In some cases, the ecumenical creeds formed the background of these confessions. The Dutch took the lead here, but there are examples as well from the Swiss Brethren and Hutterite traditions of apologetic confessions.[2]

The primary Anabaptist developments over the sixteenth century with respect to the creed were the controversies generated by Melchiorite Christology, both within and outside the Anabaptist movement. Menno Simons was drawn into repeated debates on this question.[3] On occasion, such as at the Frankenthal Debate of 1570, Reformed pastors debating with Swiss Brethren wished to argue Christology, only to find that the Swiss agreed with them.[4] The Hutterite *Great Chronicle*, in describing Hutterite life up to 1560, noted simply that "All Twelve Articles of the Christian apostolic faith were confessed and observed."[5] As noted in the previous chapter, Melchiorite Christology, as defended by Menno, faded slowly to the point that by 1800 it no longer was considered a central doctrinal point in that tradition. The Anabaptists considered themselves adherents of the ecumenical creeds from the start, even though their soteriological and ecclesiological emphases on a lived faith decreased the practical importance of correct theoretical creedal statements within their traditions.[6]

Views shared with Evangelical/Protestant groups

Anti-Sacramentalism

Concerning the central ceremonies of baptism and the Lord's Supper the later Anabaptist tradition continued unbroken the anti-sacramental insistence seen from the beginning: physical elements remained just that, and could have no sacramental power. The attempt by Pilgram Marpeck to move Anabaptism back towards a more sacramental appreciation of the outer ceremonies of the church (and an essential link between the inner life and outer ordinances) did not have a permanent impact on the later traditions. The Swiss Brethren of Hesse argued in 1578, against Lutheran preachers, that the Supper was a "spiritual" celebration, dependent on faith, that confirmed the union of believers with Christ.[7] The Hutterite "Five Articles," composed at about the same time and directed primarily against Catholic opponents, held that the Supper was a "remembrance," and marshalled scriptural evidence against a teaching of a real presence in the elements.[8] Likewise Dordrecht affirmed that the Supper is observed "in *commemoration* of the death and sufferings of the Lord," to "*remind* us of the benefit of the said death and sufferings of Christ, namely the redemption and eternal salvation which he purchased thereby..."[9] In short, the stance of the ongoing tradition concerning the ceremonies of baptism and the Supper was that they are "signs" or "outward testimonies" of inward events which have their basis in faith.

Anticlericalism

The anticlericalism that early Anabaptists shared with evangelical Reformers was directed against the Catholic clergy, but quickly came to include all the "learned ones" (*Schriftgelehrten*), Protestant and Catholic alike. Early Anabaptist anticlericalism often was based on the true, spiritual call of Anabaptist preachers, contrasted with the worldly call of the mainline clergy. This was augmented by the argument that the preaching of the "false prophets" was proven false because of the "lack of fruit" in their churches. Thus both inner (pneumatic) and outer criteria (moral reform) fed early Anabaptist anticlericalism. Although the spiritual election of pastors faded as the century proceeded, pastors in the later Anabaptist tradition continued to be lay pastors, rather than salaried clergy, and were subjected to discipline. By these measures, pastors outside the Anabaptist tradition fell short. Finally, the continuing persecution of Anabaptists, in which Protestant and Catholic clergy participated (often in attempts in prison to get Anabaptists to renounce their beliefs) confirmed

Anabaptists in their anticlericalism. Clergy outside the Anabaptist communities continued to be described as "ravening wolves in sheeps' clothing" throughout the sixteenth century.

Priesthood of all Believers

As the appeal to the Holy Spirit faded in Anabaptism, replaced by an emphasis on the true church, the Anabaptist communities established their own ways of choosing and installing "shepherds," that is, their own clergy. The priesthood of all believers, which continued for a time in early Anabaptism, was replaced in later Anabaptism by a clergy/laity distinction. Nevertheless, differences may be observed between the Swiss Brethren, Hutterites, and Mennonites. The Swiss Brethren, following Schleitheim, chose pastors from within the congregation, with the congregation (as far as we know, men and women alike) participating in that election. The Hutterite communities, on the other hand, were led by elders who controlled the appointment of subsequent elders. Furthermore, the Hutterites instituted the practice of "double honour" for their elders: the elders, being "first among equals," received better food, clothing, housing, and transportation than did rank and file members. This became a heated point of contention between Swiss Brethren and Hutterites in the later sixteenth century.[10]

For the Dutch Mennonites, the question of legitimate pastoral leadership came up repeatedly. Menno had to contend with the fact that the Melchiorite tradition had been strongly spiritualistic: from Hoffman to Matthijs to van Leiden and David Joris, Melchiorite leaders had emphasized their spiritual call and "prophetic" authority as the basis for ministry and leadership. Menno felt the need to repudiate that tradition.

The alternative to a direct prophetic call—the calling of preachers and teachers by the community of believers and their commissioning by the elders of those communities—was open to question in the Melchiorite context. How could the commissioning by elders be legitimated if the Melchiorite "apostolic succession" of pastoral commission rested on prophets whose prophecies had proved to be false, and if elders (e.g., Obbe Philips) who had commissioned Melchiorite preachers and teachers (e.g., Menno and Dirk) had since turned to apostasy? This latter problem was crucial for Menno, since he had been commissioned by Obbe Philips, who had been baptized by Melchior Hoffman, and who later left the faith. In fact, the main thrust of Obbe's later "Confession" was to question the legitimacy of the Melchiorite pastoral call.[11]

Menno spoke to these questions in several sections of his "Foundation" book: "Some are called by God alone without any human agent as was the case with the prophets and apostles. Others are called by means of the pious as may be seen from Acts 1:23-26."[12] In both cases, however, the legitimacy of a preacher's call is to be measured by the "doctrines and customs of the apostles" and by the rule of Scripture.[13] The office of a preacher is to teach sound biblical doctrine[14] and to "admonish, rebuke or reprove, and comfort" the pious; they administer baptism and the Lord's Supper "rightly"; they must be of unimpeachable conduct and be ready to exclude the "incurable" from the church.[15] The inner call of God, Menno maintained, was a necessary first step; the commissioning by "the pious" was a second step; but the continued testing of the legitimacy of the pastoral call was the undeniable third step. This was accomplished by the measure of Scripture which provided the apostolic criteria of true doctrine, church practice, and conduct befitting a shepherd of the flock of Christ.

In light of Swiss practice (Schleitheim), Hutterite practice, and early Melchiorite practice, how was the "community of saints" constituted in Menno's following? There was, first of all, no thought of either the Holy Spirit or congregations commissioning women to the office of preacher, teacher, or elder: the "pious preachers and teachers" are "*men* whom the Holy Ghost has ordained bishops and overseers in His church."[16] But, are these male elders elected by the congregations (the Schleitheim model) or by other elders? Scholarly opinion is divided on this question, for the evidence is equivocal. Christoph Bornhäuser concludes that there was little "democracy" of the Schleitheim kind in the Dutch Mennonite congregations: there are no regulations laid down for congregational elections of pastors in the two decades following 1536, and the Wismar Articles of 1554 equivocate, speaking of pastoral election by communities *or* elders. Bornhäuser concludes that Menno supported the rule of elders over the flock; the elders, he says, in fact formed an oligarchy.[17] James Stayer suggests that "the greater authority of Mennonite elders over their flock seems to have been a watered-down continuation of the charisma of the early Melchiorite prophets."[18] Certainly in some disciplinary cases Mennonite elders appear to have exercised unilateral authority, without the counsel, vote or approval of congregations.

Pastors in the continuing Swiss, Hutterite, and Mennonite traditions were known not primarily by a prophetic call, or by formal education or training, and not at all by being "called" by government authority. They were legitimated by the measures of doctrine, practice, and personal conduct, and usually chosen and confirmed in processes controlled by community elders.

Anabaptist Doctrinal Emphases
Pneumatology: the activity of the Holy Spirit.
There is a marked change in pneumatological emphasis when the later Anabaptist traditions are compared with early Anabaptism. It is not only that appeals to the work of the Holy Spirit are muted in the later traditions, but more that the early individual emphases of the Spirit's work become, in the later traditions, communal emphases. Early Anabaptism was, as we have seen, a very "charismatic" movement, with some parts of the movement outlining in detail the process of individual yielding to the Spirit (South German Anabaptism). Other parts of the movement expected the Spirit to reveal God's will in the form of prophetic dreams and visions. The later Anabaptist traditions continued to insist upon the inner work of the Spirit which produces faith, but in contrast to the early movement, the emphasis fell on increasingly specific ethical and communal results of the Spirit's work, and ap-

plied Scriptural measures to test the genuineness of that work. Those Scriptural measures were defined by elders within communities, and enforced by the ban. In short, we may say that in the Swiss Brethren, Hutterite, and Mennonite traditions, ecclesiology came to contain and define pneumatology.

Spirit and Letter

Closely related to changes in pneumatology, the Anabaptist understanding of how God's will is revealed to humanity also underwent significant changes. Of the three interpretive tendencies outlined in chapter 11 above, only one survived in the ongoing tradition, namely the emphasis on the letter of Scripture, read Christocentrically, and emphasizing the priority of the New Testament within the canon. The spiritualist reading of Scripture continued to pose challenges to the Anabaptist movement long after the prophetic/apocalyptic tendency had been discredited, but in the end both of those tendencies were excluded from the Swiss, Hutterite, and Mennonite traditions of interpretation. Or perhaps it is more accurate to say that the spiritualistic and prophetic readings of Scripture were "subsumed" (for they did not disappear completely) under a literal, New Testament reading.[19] The later Swiss Brethren (ca. 1570), for example, continued to appeal to the presence of the Spirit for the proper interpretation of Scripture. The concluding argument to an article concerning the relationship of the Old to the Testament says: "Only the Holy Spirit and a spiritual person, taught by God, knows how to seek the witness of Christ and His Kingdom in the Old Testament, and to extract the truth from the figures by means of a spiritual judgment, harmonizing these with Christ."[20]

The question of how Scripture was interpreted and used over time in the Anabaptist movement is one that (surprisingly!) has yet to be addressed comprehensively or adequately in the scholarly literature. Anyone who reads the Anabaptist sources from the last quarter of the sixteenth century, however, knows that it is a mistake to conclude that the Anabaptist traditions simply abandoned the Old Testament, and only read the New Testament literally in search of ethical guidelines. This latter kind of reading certainly formed the centre of later Anabaptist hermeneutics, but there is ample evidence of *increasing* use of the Old Testament in the apologetic literature of the later Swiss, Hutterite, and Mennonite traditions. More interesting still, the Old Testament was very often read "figuratively" in these traditions. Did Melchiorite figurative exegesis exert its influence upon the entire surviving tradition, as the century progressed? It is possible, but this is only one of many questions for which we still have no answers.

Undoubtedly this return to the Old Testament can be explained in part by the continuing reproach on the side of theological opponents that the Anabaptists read only half the Bible, and by the need of the Anabaptists to defend themselves in debate.[21] But the Old Testament also provided the later Anabaptists with many relevant examples, especially when Israel was interpreted as the Old Testament "figure" for the pure church, as it generally was. In looking to the history of the people of Israel, the later Anabaptists could appeal to an exclusive, chosen community, a people of God, who were enjoined to purity. A few examples will have to suffice.

The confession submitted by Swiss Brethren in Hesse (1578) contains ample references to the Old Testament with, unfortunately, little commentary. However, the unpublished Swiss Brethren reply to the Frankenthal Debate, "A Short, Simple Judgment" (after 1571), which circulated in manuscript copies in Switzerland, contains an article comparing the Old and the New Testaments[22] and also utilizes a "figurative" reading of the Old Testament throughout. The central harmonizing principle is that the Old Testament presents only "shadows, figures, and earthly" pointers to the "clear, eternal, heavenly" realities realized by Christ and His church.[23] In this way the Old Testament is not ignored (indeed it is mined assiduously for relevant "figures"), but it nevertheless is placed in a secondary revelational position to the New. Thus Noah's Ark and the Temple of Solomon are called preliminary figures of Christ's church. Just as the threshhold of the king and that of the Temple were not to be too close together, and just as no foreign fire was to be brought into the Temple, so also magistrates do not belong in the church of Christ.[24] Examples of this kind of exegesis in this later Swiss Brethren writing could be multiplied many times over.

At the centre of the "Five Articles" of the Hutterites stands a biblical defence of community of goods, as one might expect. Also, as one might expect, there are abundant references to the words of the Gospel that have to do with giving up everything and following Christ, as well as references to Acts 2 and 4. But in the manner of the later Swiss Brethren apologies, the article begins with citations from Exodus, Leviticus, Deuteronomy, Numbers, Joshua, Isaiah, and Zechariah, all of which are said to support community of goods as God's will for the church. The prophecies of Isaiah "point to" the "church gathered in Christ," for example. Thus Isaiah 23:18 is taken as an indication of the coming community of goods of the Hutterites.[25] Likewise concerning whether Christians may wage war, the *Chronicle* exegetes Old Testament "figures" freely, and applies them to the church. For example, appealing to 1 Kings 6:7, the writer notes "When Solomon built the temple (which was to symbolize the church of Christ in the New Testament), it was made of blocks of undressed stone, and no hammer or axe or any iron tool was heard in the house while it was being built. This shows clearly that the church of Christ should not be built up with tumult..."[26] Such "figurative" Old Testament exegesis functioned as a support for the central point, which continued to be based in the New Testament, and the life and words of Jesus.

There are few examples of this kind of Old Testament exegesis in the Dordrecht Confession, but the writings of Menno Simons and Dirk Philips give ample evidence of the tendency. At the beginning of the banning controversy, Menno composed "A Clear Account of Excommunication" (1550) in which he spent a considerable amount of time appealing to Old Testament examples: the Jews did not admit the uncircumcised to their Passover, and open sinners were condemned to death according to the Law. The church is now "the holy Israel of God," and although "the Holy Spirit does not teach us to destroy the wicked, as did Israel," still the wicked must be expelled with sorrow from the church.[27]

Dirk displayed more skill than did Menno in the figurative exegesis of the Old Testament. Dirk's central theme in his booklet "The Ban" (1558)[28] was the purity that God demands of His Bride of the Last Days, a demand which is evident throughout the Old Testament as well as the New. In more ways than one, Dirk's approach is reminiscent of Melchior Hoffman's "The Ordinance of God." In Leviticus 11, 12, 13 and 14 Dirk found "many and manifold beautiful figures about the purification of Israel." Through these figures "is portrayed for us how holy and pure the congregation of the Lord must now be," for "since he who has called you is holy, be also holy yourselves in all your conduct."[29] And, Dirk concludes with Menno, if among the Israelites the willful sinners were excluded and even killed according to the Word of God in the Old Testament, how much more should such sinners be banned and shunned in Christ's church?

In the absence of a careful study of the development of "Anabaptist hermeneutics" (which, it is hoped, some enterprising scholar will soon undertake), these few observations will have to suffice. The variety of interpretive approaches in early Anabaptism did give way in the surviving traditions to an increasingly legalistic reading of Scripture, with the New Testament at the centre. The title of the fifth article of the Dordrecht Confession says it plainly. The article deals with "The *Law of Christ*, which is the Holy Gospel, or the New Testament."[30] Law was conflated with Gospel in the later traditions, and the figurative reading of the Old Testament provided support for this tendency.

Soteriology

The characteristic Anabaptist insistence that salvation is granted to those whose inner change (faith, regeneration) is manifest in outward behaviour (a new life) remained unchanged throughout the sixteenth century. But, as has been sufficiently noted in the preceding chapters, the emphasis increasingly came to fall on the outward signs of regeneration (and legislation concerning outward behaviour), rather than the process of regeneration as such. In questions of anthropology, the later Anabaptists continued to hold a doctrine of free will, following God's grace: human beings could choose to accept or reject God's regenerating grace. Likewise the call for *Gelassenheit* did not disappear, but was transferred increasingly to the outward realm where at times yielding to God's will meant something akin to what we might call "accepting Providence." Many later testimonies of the martyrs speak about "yielding" to God's will in accepting the world's persecution.

The historical records allow us to chart this general movement away from an early pneumatic/spiritualist emphasis on personal regeneration, to a more external and communal emphasis, but the records say very little about other matters which interest us very much today. We know very little, for example, about the actual conversion/regeneration process experienced by individual Anabaptists. Accounts describing these seminal experiences were not written or recorded. We are told that such conversions occurred, and we see undeniable evidence in the prison testimonies and martyr accounts, but there are no records to tell us more. Likewise we would like to know much more about the prayer and worship life that sustained the Anabaptists in their periods of trial and testing, as they strove to remain faithful to the end. From testimonies, letters, and songs we know that imprisoned Anabaptists prayed together, sang, and discussed Scripture. That these activities nourished a deep spirituality for those who persevered in prison, exile, and martyrdom must be assumed, since we see the evidence, but we have no revealing personal diaries that can shed specific light on how the inner life of the spirit was sustained throughout. How was the spirit of individual *Gelassenheit* nurtured and maintained in the later Anabaptist communities? There is evidence of the presence of such an attitude, but outside of a call to obedience to biblical/community norms, there is no evidence of a spiritual discipline designed to sustain and nourish a deep, personal yieldedness to God's will.

The historical record suggests that the most significant change in Anabaptist soteriology was not in the *principle* of an inner/outer correspondence (which remained constant), but rather in the various outward signs that the different groups came to hold as *necessary* evidences of inward regeneration, and upon which salvation rested. The Swiss Brethren had made this shift already in 1527, when other Anabaptists complained about their "legalism" in many things, including (according to Hans Hut) in matters of outward dress. Menno's shift from inner regeneration to community purity has already been noted. A dramatic instance of the later Anabaptist tendency to define the inner state by particular outward evidence can be seen in the "Five Articles" of the Hutterites. The heading for the central article reads: "True *Gelassenheit* and Christian Community of Goods." The conclusion to be drawn, after copious Scriptural references, is that true spiritual yieldedness to God *must* result in community of goods.

The insistence that the true church would be known by particular outward acts of obedience was not simply a later development. Anabaptism as such had insisted from the start on the necessary outer marks of baptism, the ban, a closed Supper of remembrance, and sharing of possessions within the community of believers. What was new was the increasing precision with which the outer marks of the true church came to be defined. The nebulouly defined "fruits of the Spirit and works of love" (Hubmaier) came to be measured by obedience to the various community norms, which then became the determinative measures of grace and salvation. In the surviving Anabaptist groups, ecclesiology circumscribed soteriology: outside the church, as defined by particular outward marks of obedience, there was no salvation.

Eschatology

By the end of the sixteenth century the enthusiastic apocalypticism of the early Anabaptists was muted and restrained. The later Anabaptist literature looks forward not so much with expectation to the End Times as it does to the resurrection. The tone among the Swiss Brethren in the 1570s is sober, directed toward purity and patience, looking to the resurrection of the dead and life everlasting.[31] Much the same tone can be read in the "Five Articles" of the Hutterites. Among the Mennonites, expectations of the End are even more restrained some sixty years later. In the Dordrecht Confession, "these dangerous Last Days" do not come into play at all. Instead there is a separate article on "The Resurrection of the Dead and the Last Judgment."[32]

Walter Klaassen has noted that in the End Times excitement of the early sixteenth century, Anabaptist ecclesiology, with its rigorous discipline, is best understood as a "short-range holding action." The emphasis fell on purity in view of the imminent return of the Head. "That would mean," he concludes, "that the concentration on the forms of congregational life and holiness never did, in their minds, constitute an alternative ecclesiology for the future, but that it became such when the apocalyptic expectations were not fulfilled."[33] This observation is important given the increasing role played by ecclesiology in defining the later traditions.

Anabaptist Ecclesiology

Later Anabaptist ecclesiology, when contrasted with the incipient ecclesiology of the early core, is notable primarily for the increasingly specific answers that were given to the question "What are the marks of the true church?" Thus the proper manner of interpreting Scripture, the proper stance regarding the sword and the oath, the proper role of women in the community, the proper form of marriage, correct economic relationships, and the biblical form of binding and loosing all came to be rigorously defined in the later Anabaptist communities. As we have seen in sufficient detail in the foregoing chapters, on some of these issues a consensus was reached; on other issues, differences among the various Anabaptists resulted in permanent schism. In what follows we will revisit the core marks of the true church in light of later developments.

Baptism

Two factors may be noted concerning baptism in the later Anabaptist groups. First, the apocalyptic tone given to baptism by Hans Hut, and later by Melchior Hoffman, faded in importance as the expectation for the imminent arrival of the End Times also faded. Although the peculiar form of baptism on the forehead seems to have persisted among some of the Dutch Anabaptists (Dirk Philips appears to have baptized in this way), the enthusiastic expectation had faded that the 144,000 elect, so marked, would soon reign with Christ.[34] In the second place, baptism was the rite in which the later Anabaptists continued to recognize the interior work of the Holy Spirit. Concerning rebirth, the later Swiss Brethren described the process as hearing the Word of God and believing it. Faith was sealed "with the power of God in the Holy Spirit." The power of the Holy Spirit then renewed and enlivened the believer, who died to sin and became righteous before God. The believer becomes "a new creature, a new person made in the image of God." To such as these water baptism belonged as a sign of rebirth, an outward seal that "one has committed oneself and united oneself with God and all the saints, no longer to live for oneself, but as a person obedient to God and His community, insofar as God gives grace."[35] Likewise the seventh article of the Dordrecht Confession, on baptism, notes that "all penitent believers, who through faith, *the new birth and renewal of the Holy Ghost,* have become united with God ... must, on such scriptural confession of their faith, and renewal of life, according to the command and doctrine of Christ ... be baptized with water."[36] There is little apparent movement from early Anabaptism to the later traditions in the matter of baptism.[37]

The Ban

The emphasis on community discipline also remained unchanged in the period of Anabaptist development. Changes concerning the ban had to do first with the increasing willingness to utilize excommunication in order to keep the communities pure. Insofar as more specific external measures of faithfulness were adopted by Anabaptist groups, by so much more did it seem that the ban needed to be put to use. Secondly, among the Dutch Mennonites, the ban itself became a contentious issue and a cause for division, as differences emerged concerning the degrees of shunning that were biblically appropriate for the "apostates" who had been banned.[38] The milder possibilities suggested by the approaches of Denck, Marpeck, and the spiritualist Anabaptists were not heeded in the later movement, and faded from view.

The Supper

As John Rempel has demonstrated, some interesting alternative theologies of the Supper were proposed in the developmental period of Anabaptism. The understanding of the Lord's Supper in the Swiss, Hutterite, and Mennonite traditions, however, reflected the broad, anti-sacramental view visible in the early movement. Dordrecht's statement may serve as a summary: The Supper was instituted by Christ, who commanded that it be observed "in commemoration." It also serves as an exhortation to believers "to love one another—to love our neighbor—to forgive and absolve him—even as Christ has done unto us—and also to endeavor to maintain and keep alive the union and communion which we have with God, and amongst one another." All this is "shown and represented" in the breaking of bread.[39]

Mutual Aid

The early Anabaptist insistence on mutual aid in the Body of Christ remained visible as a general ecclesiological principle in the later traditions. The one noteworthy development concerning mutual aid was the divisiveness caused by the question of whether a full and legislated community of goods was necessary, or not. This matter, more than any other, came to divide the Hutterites from the Swiss Brethren and Mennonites. Nevertheless, the tradition of economic sharing continued to be strongly held, even when other aspects of the Anabaptist heritage had dropped away. There are stirring examples of mutual aid across the Anabaptist "denominational" lines. The later Dutch Mennonites, especially in the seventeenth and eighteenth centuries, extended copious material aid to needy Swiss Brethren and Hutterite refugees, as well as establishing homes for orphans and the elderly.

Foot Washing

The later Dutch Mennonite tradition incorporated the ordinance of foot washing in addition to baptism and the Lord's Supper. The article on foot washing in the Dordrecht Confession follows after the article on the Supper. Foot washing was instituted because of Jesus' example; it was to be performed "as a sign of true humiliation; but yet more particularly as a sign to remind us of the true washing—the washing and purification of the soul in the blood of Christ."[40] With the adoption of the Dordrecht Confession by the Swiss Brethren in the seventeenth century, foot washing was accepted among the Swiss as well. It has fallen into disuse in the Netherlands, but continues to be practised particularly among the Amish.

Conclusion: The Quiet in the Land

The doctrinal and ecclesiological developments noted above, when added to the later Anabaptist consensus that the true church would be separate from the world in matters of the sword and the oath, gave a decidedly separatist ecclesiological "shape" to the surviving Anabaptist traditions. The concern with moral reform and ethical purity or, said another way, the concern with obedience to the Law of Christ, coupled with community mechanisms to enforce purity, resulted in a disciplined and regulated body of believers. Furthermore, the fading of apocalyptic expectation removed a strong motivation for evangelism and the conversion of the 144,000 elect. It was enough to look to purity within and to persevere to the end, whenever that might come. The internal strength of these tightly structured later communities was demonstrated throughout the sixteenth century and beyond, as they endured exile, persecution, and martyrdom. There is no better source than the *Martyrs Mirror* to shed light on this aspect of the surviving tradition.

External political factors continued to play a role in the development of the later Swiss, Hutterite, and Mennonite traditions, as did the internal separatist (or "sectarian") theological tradition of the two kingdoms. In particular, the need to emigrate forced itself upon those communities repeatedly. Very often the relocated communities were tolerated on the condition that they would not proselytize. The later Anabaptist groups were characterized by tightly-knit communities, supported by a separatist ecclesiology, usually living in conditions of exile in a world invariably hostile to them, although in varying degrees. The evangelizing fervour of early Anabaptism did not survive under these conditions. The price to be paid for survival in a hostile world was that Anabaptists needed to agree to be "the quiet in the land."

The notable exception to this rule occurred among the Dutch Mennonites who remained in the Netherlands. Religious toleration came first to the Netherlands and the Mennonites there were beneficiaries of that benign political atmosphere. Dutch Anabaptism always had been a strongly urban, as well as a rural phenomenon, and thus was in closer touch with the economic currents of the day. By the mid-seventeenth century, Dutch Mennonites were experiencing social and political acceptance, and came to enjoy a golden age of prosperity that mirrored the emergence of the

Dutch as a world economic power. The story of the development of this tradition in a more spiritualist, pietist, and liberal direction cannot be told here.[41] Suffice it to say that after acrimonious church splits and eventual reconciliations, the Anabaptists who remained in the Netherlands adopted, not the name of the rigorous disciplinarian Menno Simons, but rather came to call themselves the "baptism-minded" (*Doopsgezinden*). In a pattern that would repeat itself among Swiss and Mennonites elsewhere, at different times and places, toleration and prosperity wore down the walls of separation that had divided the Anabaptists and their descendants from the rest of unredeemed humanity. The surviving Hutterite communities and the "old order" Amish and Mennonites, on the other hand, continue to live in secure communal islands, in the world but not of it.

End Notes

[1] For a succinct overview, see C.J. Dyck, *An Introduction to Mennonite History* (Scottdale, Pa.: Herald Press, 1993), chapter 7, and Douglas Shantz, "The Ecclesiological Focus of Dirk Philips' Hermeneutical Thought in 1559: A Contextual Study," MQR 60(April, 1986), pp. 115-127.

[2] On the development of Anabaptist/Mennonite confessions of faith, see C. J. Dyck, "The First Waterlandian Confession of Faith," MQR 36 (Jan., 1962), pp. 5-13; *idem*., "The Middelburg Confession of Hans de Ries, 1578," MQR 36 (Apr., 1962), pp. 147-161; *idem.*, "A Short Confession of Faith by Hans de Ries," MQR 38 (Jan., 1964), pp. 5-19. Also, Howard John Loewen, *One Lord, One Church, One Hope, and One God: Mennonite Confessions of Faith*, (Elkhart, IN: Institute of Mennonite Studies, 1985). See the later Swiss Brethren confession from Hesse in Theodor Sippell, ed., "Confession of the Swiss Brethren in Hesse, 1578," MQR 23 (Jan., 1949), 22-34; full text in TA, *Hesse*, 404-440. This confession included an affirmation of the Apostles' Creed. In the Hutterite tradition, Peter Riedemann's, *Account of Our Religion, Doctrine and Faith* (London: Hodder and Stoughton, 1950), written in 1542, exposited the creed. For a later "confession" based on Hutterite distinctives, see the "Five Articles of Faith" (probably written by Peter Walpot, ca. 1570), in *The Chronicle of the Hutterian Brethren*, Vol. I. (Rifton, N.Y.: Plough Publishing House, 1987), pp. 251-294.

[3] See, for example, the "Reply to Martin Micron," CWMS, pp. 838-913.

[4] In debate, the Swiss Brethren leader Diebold Winter stated that "we have never before confessed, nor do we confess now, that the Lord brought his flesh from heaven." *Protocoll, Das ist Alle handlung des gesprechs zu Franckenthal inn der Churfürstlichen Pfaltz / mit denen so man Widertäuffer nennet / Auff den 28. May angefangen / und den 19. Junii dises 1571 jars geendet* (Heidelberg: Johann Mayer, 1571), p. 145.

[5] Cited in Leonard Gross, *The Golden Years of the Hutterites* (Scottdale, Pa.: Herald Press, 1980), p. 246; see the *Chronicle*, p. 404.

[6] The Swiss Brethren commentary (after 1571) on the Frankenthal Disputation says, concerning the article on the Trinity, that the article is "without a doubt a necessary one," but goes on to note that many people who confess its truth do not "know either God the Father, God the Son, or God the Holy Spirit in the proper way." John's epistle is then cited: those who say they know God and do not keep His commandments, are liars. *Ein kurtze einfaltige erkanntnuß uff die dryzehen artickell so verlouffens 1572 (sic) Jars zu Franckenthal in der Pfaltz*

disputiert worden... (Manuscript in the Berner Bürgerbibliothek; microfilm copy in the Mennonite Historical Library, #203), p. 164.

[7] TA, *Hesse*, pp. 426-27.

[8] *Hutterite Chronicle*, pp. 258-265.

[9] Article 10, in Loewen, *One Lord*, p. 67; emphasis mine.

[10] See Gross, *Golden Years*, chapter 8 for Swiss/Hutterite encounters; pp. 172-74 for a Hutterite reply of 1567 to the question of "double honour." Hutterite practice was based on a reading of 1 Timothy 5:17.

[11] After noting the commissioning of Melchiorite apostles and the disasters that followed, Obbe says pointedly: "See, dear friends, so did it come to pass with the first commission among us and such was the reliability of their prophecies." Williams, SAW, p. 219. Obbe notes his commissioning of his brother Dietrich, of David Joris, and Menno Simons, and says that he is still "miserable of heart" because of it. *Ibid.*, p. 223; cf. p. 225.

[12] CWMS, p. 159.

[13] *Ibid.*, p. 160.

[14] "Nothing may be preached in Christ's kingdom, house, and church except her King and husband's own commands and words, according to which the entire household must govern itself." *Ibid.*, p. 165.

[15] *Ibid.*, p. 161. "The shepherds who are sent of God and have been rightly called, teach the Word of God unfalsified, keep in its holy ordinances, live unblamably in their little power, for they are born of God, are taught and moved by His Holy Spirit..." *Ibid.*, p. 168.

[16] *Ibid.*, p. 171. Emphasis mine.

[17] Bornhäuser, *Leben und Lehre*, pp. 104-110. It is not clear whether women in Mennonite congregations were allowed equal rights to vote in those cases where a pastor was chosen from among the congregation, or whether women were allowed a vote in disciplinary cases that came before the congregation.

[18] Stayer, *German Peasants' War*, p. 131.

[19] The later Swiss Brethren (ca. 1570) continued to appeal to the presence of the Spirit for the proper interpretation of Scripture. The concluding argument to an article concerning the relationship of the Old to the New Testament says: "Only the Holy Spirit and a spiritual person, taught by God, know how to seek the witness of Christ and His Kingdom in the Old Testament, and extract the truth from the figures by means of a spiritual judgement, harmonizing these with Christ." *Ein kurtze einfaltige erkanntnuß*, p. 110.

[20] *Ein kurtze einfaltige erkanntnuß*, p. 110.

[21] Concerning the Old Testament, Swiss Brethren apology cited above says "we have been unjustly slandered (*gschmützt werdend*) by the lying pens of the learned ones, who say that we dismiss the Old Testament without discernment and give it no value." *Ibid.*

[22] *Ein kurtze einfaltige erkanntnuß*, pp. 89-110.

[23] See *ibid.*, p. 99, for example.

[24] *Ibid.*, p. 117 ff.

[25] See the *Chronicle*, pp. 265-67.

[26] *Chronicle*, p. 277.

[27] CWMS, pp. 457-485, *passim*.

[28] Cornelius J. Dyck, William Keeney, and Alvin Beachy, eds. and trans. *The Writings of Dirk Philips* (Scottdale, Pa.: Herald Press, 1992), 238-53; Shantz, "The Ecclesiological Focus."

29 *Ibid.*, p. 244.

30 Loewen, *One Lord*, p. 64; emphasis mine.

31 See *Ein kurtze einfaltige erkanntnuß*, pp. 347 ff. for a restrained discussion of the "end times"; pp. 197 ff. for an article on the resurrection of the body.

32 Loewen, *One Lord*, p. 69.

33 Klaassen, *Living at the End of the Ages*, pp. 117-18.

34 In his book on the ban, Dirk reminds his readers that they are the faithful Bride of Christ, "sealed with the seal of the living God on their forehead." Dyck, Keeney, and Beachy, *Writings*, p. 239.

35 *Ein kurtze einfaltige erkanntnuß*, p. 254.

36 Loewen, *One Lord*, p. 65; emphasis mine.

37 The first of the "Five Articles" of the Hutterites deals with baptism, but is directed primarily against the practice of infant baptism. The emphasis there is on faith, with only an implicit recognition of the work of the Holy Spirit in bringing about faith.

38 Dordrecht, article 17, deals with "The Shunning of those Who are Expelled." Loewen, *One Lord*, p. 69.

39 Loewen, *One Lord*, p. 67.

40 Dordrecht, article 11, in Loewen, *One Lord*, p. 67.

41 A concise account can be found in James R. Coggins, "A Short Confession of Hans de Ries: Union and Separation in Early Seventeenth Century Holland," MQR 60(April, 1986), pp. 128-138.

Chapter 27

Epilogue:
The Continuing Conversation

This concluding chapter will reflect further on selected issues framed by sixteenth century Anabaptist conversations, in hopes of encouraging a continuation of those conversations in the present. Leaping across some five centuries of history while clutching conclusions for the present is a hazardous process; important historical qualifiers need to be added at every point to be made here. Granting the dangers of addressing contemporary issues "historically," still it is important for the faith children of the Anabaptists to begin to reflect on how some issues have been defined by their theological tradition. With such an examination comes the possibility of a conscious acceptance of the presuppositions of one's inherited tradition, or of re-evaluation and conscious change. The intent of this chapter is only to encourage conversation. It does not pretend to draw normative conclusions about the proper content of an Anabaptist/Believers' Church theology and ecclesiology.

What might be learned by contrasting the core of Anabaptist theology with the dogmatic and ecclesiological tradition that had emerged by the end of the century? This tradition, which came to define the subsequent Believers' Churches, in fact made critical modifications to the earlier broad core beliefs. Given the tensional nature of those core beliefs, further definition and elaboration was altogether necessary. The most significant modification, from our perspective, was the gradual disappearance of the early pneumatic emphasis. Given the importance of pneumatology to Believers' Church soteriology, anthropology, and ecclesiology, it is fair to ask what might have been lost as well as gained in the sixteenth century process of defining the ecclesiological limits of the Believers' Church tradition.

Pneumatology

It is not an overstatement to say that early Anabaptist pneumatology was the *sine qua non* of the movement. The appeal to an active working of the Holy Spirit in believers was the bedrock upon which rested anticlericalism and anti-sacramentalism, for example. The emergence of Anabaptism as a church renewal movement would not have taken place apart from the pneumatological rationale and impulse that underlay its more "visible" features. But it is no mystery why the pneumatic/spiritualist side of Anabaptism fell out of favour within the movement: the spectacular failures of specific prophecies and apocalyptic projects certainly led to sober second thoughts; and, the more individualistic and spiritualistically oriented Anabaptists lost the battle to convince others to make their Anabaptism a predominantly interior one, and withdrew (or were expelled) from the movement. As the sixteenth century progressed, the general tendency in the surviving movement—the part of the movement that passed on the Believers' Church tradition—was thus to limit or even suppress pneumatic expression: letter took priority over spirit; conformity to outer ecclesial rules of behaviour took priority over experiences of inner regeneration; visible lines of demarcation separating church from world were defined with increasing precision.

Scripture: Spirit and Letter

There are some obvious negative lessons to be learned from the Anabaptist experience, as has been amply pointed out by church historians since the sixteenth century. One need only recall some of the concrete historical results of "prophetic" Anabaptism to see how an expectation of immediate visions, dreams, and revelations can lead to self deception and disaster. Apocalyptic excitement and appeals to direct revelations have led, and will continue to lead it appears, to tragedy upon tragedy. There is a "spiritual" manner of reading and interpreting the "hidden secrets of Scripture" that remains a live temptation in every generation, in spite of the fact that the misbegotten fruits of such interpretations litter every generation of our church's history.

The corrective that was passed on in the Anabaptist tradition was to emphasize the letter of Scripture, read with Christ at the centre, as we see in the writings of the Swiss, the Hutterites, and Menno Simons. In the context of the events that had overtaken the Low Countries, Menno's response may seem self evident. Certainly to those who carry the name "Mennonite," Menno's appeal to a New Testament biblicism does seem self evidently correct. Menno's insistence that Christ must be placed at the centre of Scripture and the Christian life remains a valid and helpful heuristic principle, and even more so when contrasted to the revelatory claims of his contemporary prophets. Menno had a point: the witness of canonical Scripture, read with the life and words of the incarnate Christ at the centre, is the bedrock of divine revelation for Christians. David Joris' visions and "revelations" did, in an important sense, usurp the place of Scripture; and in the end, Joris turned out not to be the "third David" after all.

Even if we agree that Scripture with Christ at the centre must be the revelatory measure for Christians, important questions remain: How is the New Testament witness to Christ to be interpreted? Does the New Testament witness to Christ provide a rule of life for believers? What might the freedom of the Gospel signify? What specific Christology underlies the appeal to Christ?

These questions take on more urgency if we can agree that not all that was planted along Menno's path can be said to have borne good fruit. Legalism became the response to the danger of antinomianism; obsessive purity the answer to the danger of libertinism. The pendulum swung to the opposite side of its arc, and brought with it not only solutions, but also a fresh set of problems. The Swiss, the Hutterites, and Menno tended to make a new "law" of the Gospel, making of Christ a new law giver, and making of the church (more specifically, the church elders) the enforcers of the "divine law." This legalistic, Christocentric reading of Scripture and definition of community boundaries became the norm for all surviving Anabaptist groups, whose descendants (not coincidentally) have had a long history of schism and division.

There were other approaches to the spirit/letter issue in the sixteenth century that we would do well to recall. Hans Denck's attempts to hold together spirit and letter provided an alternative Anabaptist Christocentric example, as did Pilgram Marpeck's efforts. In both of their cases, it was the love of Christ in the hearts of believers (always measured against the scriptural witness to Christ) that provided the crucial measure for the Christian. A "Christocentric" reading of Scripture for Denck and Marpeck meant that the law of love must take precedence over the legalistic application of commands—even the those of the New Testament. We may think here too of Marpeck's Christological formulations, forged in the midst of his debates with the spiritualists.

Looked at historically, the appeal to the highest commandment of love, in dialogue with the witness of Scripture, appears to be the more profound answer. Arguing, as did Menno, the Swiss, and the Hutterites, that the spirit will *necessarily* be linked to particular understandings of literal scriptural commands has more than once proved to be misguided. We may think of shunning as one such example, or the North American Mennonite issue of a particular head covering for women as another. From our vantage point at the end of the twentieth century, it appears that the love of Christ as revealed in His words and His life provides a heuristic principle that survives the interpretive predilections of any age—although the principle of itself does not prescribe behaviour in the appealing, normative fashion that humanity on the whole seems to desire.

The problem with an appeal to "the love of Christ" as an heuristic principle would seem to be primarily sociological and ecclesiological: it weakens visible, enforceable community boundaries. The strong assertion of biblical laws of conduct, to the contrary, makes clear who is "in" and who is "out." Perhaps for this reason neither Denck nor Marpeck founded groups that survived. Nevertheless, is historical survival an adequate measure of truth? Believers' Churches today must face the sixteenth century reformational question: To what extent must "traditions" be confronted anew by the Spirit and the Word?

Regarding the question of the spirit and the letter, it must be said that in the historical experiences of the Anabaptist movement, positions at either end of the continuum revealed their limitations and dangers. Individualist spiritualism resulted in a severely weakened ecclesiology; prophetic spiritualism opened the possibility of undue interpretive freedom by those who claimed prophetic insight; literal biblicism carried the danger of a new legalism. In view of this, the obvious "lesson" is to suggest a healthy *via media*—but this would be to give far too glib a reply to what is in fact a very difficult question. Nevertheless, one lesson of history is hard to miss: Christians should exercise a profound dose of humility concerning what they claim to know, biblically and spiritually. This humility needs to be exercised especially in our relations with those who disagree with us. In this sense Hans Denck ultimately may have more to teach us than do Michael Sattler or Menno Simons.

A particular *tradition* of biblical interpretation has been part of the Believers' Church inheritance: it is not as if every generation in the Believers' Church tradition has come to Scripture afresh, has read the text with new eyes, and still come to the same interpretations as did the late sixteenth century Anabaptists. To the contrary, to be part of the Believers' Church tradition has meant to have received a well established "canon within the canon" that already provides the answers to what a "pure and simple" reading of Scripture should conclude. These interpretations have been passed on as traditional (self-evidently true) teachings. Part of the conscious reappropriation of the Believers' Church tradition must be ready to include a fresh reading of Scripture that is prepared to test the received tradition not only against Scripture, but also against other theological traditions. It will no longer do to operate under the fiction that the Believers' Church tradition is "purely biblical" whereas other readings of Scripture are tainted with "human tradition." The Believers' Church reading of Scripture is also a human tradition. Those who doubt that this is so are invited to consult the emerging volumes of the "Believers' Church Bible Commentary" series.

The question may well be: How far are Believers' Churches today willing to trust the Spirit of God in the interpretation of Scripture? The tendency towards "biblicism" in the Believers' Church tradition is well explained as a reaction against spiritualistic excesses in the sixteenth century, but the resulting tendency to formalism and legalism, and the largely unexamined acceptance of a received tradition of biblical interpretation, all beg for a breath of the Spirit. It may well be that the broadest Anabaptist "scriptural principle," namely that spirit and letter must be held together in order to be revelatory, could prove helpful in our own time. The further recognition that all readings of Scripture are shaped by humanity should open the doors even further to ecumenical dialogue with other Christian traditions.

Priesthood of all Believers

The question of interpretive authority was a critical one in the Anabaptist movement, as we have seen. It was made all the more critical because the Protestant Reformation had removed the doctrine of interpretive authority through apostolic succession (from Christ through Peter to the Bishops of Rome). In its place, the Reformers had placed Scripture—but who was then vested with the authority to interpret Scripture? One answer of the mainline Reformers—that this authority rested only with those who had been called and then sent to preach by a legitimate political authority—was rejected by the Anabaptists, and continues to be rejected by Believers' Churches today. Historical events since the sixteenth century, particularly the genocidal insanities sponsored by "legitimate political authorities" in the twentieth century, have proved the truth and worth of the Anabaptist insight: the Gospel cannot be handed over to the "world" to use as it pleases. But who, then, will decide when an interpreter of Scripture is genuine?

When pressed, the early Anabaptists said that they had been called by *God* to preach the Gospel. It is no surprise, then, that in all varieties of early Anabaptism, we return in the end to the working of the Spirit of God as the fundamental basis for teaching and interpretive authority. As William Keeney has noted, this was the unrecognized "subjective factor" that caused so many problems for sixteenth century biblicists. Since the assertion was that "ultimately the appeal could not be to the letter alone but to the convincing power of the Holy Spirit in the heart of the believer, no objective test could finally resolve the differences. Each also had an unswerving belief that the correct understanding had been given to him by the Holy Spirit."[1]

It was the "convincing power of the Holy Spirit in the heart of the believer" that led to something approximating the priesthood of all believers in early Anabaptism, but this "pneumatic democracy" (to the extent that it actually functioned) was not destined to last. With the growing emergence of a tradition of textual interpretation came also a different kind of leadership: rather than looking to charismatic prophets and evangelists, congregations now looked to bishops and elders—a movement in Anabaptism that parallels almost exactly developments in the first century of Christianity. Although anticlericalism was crucial in Anabaptist origins, by the end of the sixteenth century the settled Anabaptist groups had drawn clear lines of distinction between their own clergy and laity. Bishops or elders were those empowered to baptize, to preside over the Lord's Supper, to perform marriages, make definitive interpretations of Scripture and, in more than one instance, bishops and ministers decided disciplinary matters and saw to the ordination of other pastors and elders.

The leadership tradition that was handed on, then, had moved well beyond emphasizing and legitimizing the individual call of the Spirit of God to believers that had provided the early foundation for a priesthood of all believers in Anabaptism. The qualifiers entered first at Schleitheim, then by the Hutterites, and finally by Menno Simons were decisive: the only true pastors would be those who were commissioned or chosen by the elders and/or the congregation. This insistence in fact rendered the priesthood of all believers functionally obsolete, even if in comparison to mainline Protestant churches, the "Anabaptist denominations" allowed for higher participation of the laity in church life.

Present-day theory and practice in the less conservative Believers' Churches reflects some confusion. In what appears to be a fairly straightforward development out of the received tradition of pastoral leadership, Believers' Churches now routinely train professional pastors (clergy, in other words) in seminaries, recognizing that theological and pastoral education is helpful in the task of pastoral ministry. At the same time, at a rhetorical level at least, many Believers' Churches extol the virtues of an idealized Anabaptist priesthood of all believers—all members are pastors, it is said, and minister in a variety of ways. But in practice, most Believers' Church members today do not function as "priests" who interpret Scripture within the congregation or who carry out other traditionally pastoral tasks. Although most Believers' Church members do participate directly in the "calling" or election of a pastor, the selection process generally draws from a pool of available candidates who have been trained at seminaries. In a majority of cases, the end result seems to be that a congregation becomes the employer of a professional Believers' Church minister.

The sixteenth century situation suggests that pastoral questions are settled in tandem with the settling of ecclesiological questions. If the church is understood as the faithful remnant expecting Jesus' return momentarily, the emergency election of leaders may well suffice (Schleitheim). If the church is understood to be a longsuffering minority in a persecuting world, pastors are needed who will instruct, strengthen and maintain community boundaries, and nurture succeeding generations (Menno). What is the pattern of leadership needed when a Believers' Church is accepted as part of the social/cultural landscape in a pluralistic, secular, and democratic society? Or conversely, what does the current pattern of pastoral leadership say about the state of Believers' Church ecclesiology?

Soteriology

A sure way of inviting open dispute is to attempt to identify what lay at the heart of Anabaptism: Was it discipleship, ecclesiology, existential theology? I will grant, even before I am challenged, that my own reading is partial, and may well be wrong, but in my view the heart and soul of the Anabaptist movement is found in its *soteriology*; and central to that soteriology is the integral linking of the inner and outer lives of believers which the Anabaptists were sure was true to the witness of Scripture. This inner/outer integration lay at the theological heart of the Anabaptist movement from the start, and was prefigured in the writings of Andreas Karlstadt, Thomas Müntzer, and other radical reformers. Certainly Anabaptism as a church reform movement was defined by ecclesiological distinctives (baptism of adults, the ban, the Supper), but these practices rested upon a prior commitment to this distinctive soteriological vision. Salvation, said the Anabaptists, is by grace through faith; but saving faith must be expressed in works of love, or it is no faith at all. Human beings must yield to the inner working of the Spirit of God (*Gelassenheit*), they must assent to this grace (exercise human free will) and, thanks to the regeneration by the Holy Spirit, they will live lives of visible obedience and discipleship. The church is thus the Body of Christ, visibly composed of these saints of the Lord. What happened to this soteriological vision as conversations progressed in the sixteenth century?

Regeneration

Beginning at the personal level of individual regeneration, we may ask whether Anabaptist optimism in this regard was in fact justified. Historically considered, the answer seems to be "no," in spite of some astounding examples to the contrary. On the whole, Anabaptist optimism concerning the extent and throroughness of regeneration was not borne out in ecclesial practice over the long run. This is not to say that there were not faithful disciples in the tradition, or that the ideals of regeneration and discipleship should be abandoned, but only to say that human sin was not as easily overcome as most Anabaptists had anticipated. A negative way of saying this would be: the Anabaptist "regenerationist" tradition did not take sin seriously enough. Optimism concerning regeneration became part of the received tradition; the Melchiorite stream, resting as it did on a docetic Christology, went even further than did the Swiss and Hutterite traditions.

Some modern appropriations of the "Anabaptist Vision" have argued that the Anabaptists were not "perfectionists," for if they had been, they would not have instituted the ban and used it. This caveat misses an important point: of course at times the ban did mirror the Roman Catholic practice of confession and absolution, but increasingly the Anabaptists utilized the ban in order to maintain community purity. Failure to live up to visible and external measures of discipleship meant that the one who had thus failed had given evidence of a lack of inner regeneration and so must either repent and be regenerated again, or be expelled as an "unfruitful member." The Anabaptist practice of the ban, far from negating a perfectionist attitude towards sin and the law, was the primary example of that attitude, and the instrument used to maintain a theoretical ideal of sinless perfection in the Body of Christ. This perfectionism was not incidental to the received tradition, but rather was central to it; the personal and ecclesiological implications for Believers' Churches have been profound.

One of the drawbacks of the perfectionist tendency has been the lack of an adequate means for dealing with personal failure and sin in Believers' Churches. As long as a perfectionist regenerational principle was accepted as the sum and substance of the Christian life, one had either visibly failed at discipleship or was visibly (or at least adequately) succeeding. The grey areas in between—where, quite frankly, the majority of Christians reside—was theologically and pastorally inaccessible. Yet it is precisely in the grey areas of life that Christians need mentoring, admonition, and help in order to grow and progress in the spiritual life. The "successful" disciple does not need the help; the disciple who has failed does not get attention until it is obviously too late.

The ban in the later Anabaptist tradition was an ecclesiological instrument attuned to spiritual failure, not spiritual growth. In such a setting the danger of hypocrisy—long a reproach on the side of mainline Protestants—could not be avoided completely, especially in close knit communities, where appearances could be as important as realities. Part of the continuing theological conversation for Believers' Churches is to return again to the question of sin, regeneration, discipleship, admonition, forgiveness, and growth. The entire package of pastoral issues related to sin and regeneration needs to be thought through with some care, particularly in light of the importance of discipleship in the received theological tradition.

It was Pilgram Marpeck who insisted on the importance of the distinction between law and Gospel as one that provided a crucial counter balance for those who tended to emphasize literal obedience to the commands of Scripture. The Gospel of Jesus Christ, Marpeck maintained, is a setting free from the law, which we were not able to keep perfectly in any case. Marpeck emphasized, from a thoroughly Anabaptist perspective, human dependence on God's love and grace; recognition of our dependence on grace, he maintained, acts as a hedge against human presumption.

A further related point made by Marpeck is well worth repeating: the law is not now, nor has it ever been, *capable* of changing the heart. Only God and God's

gracious Spirit can do that. Discipleship, then, is not fundamentally an issue of obedience to the law, but rather it depends upon God's grace and regeneration; true discipleship grows from the heart, and not as a result of an external legal code or the
threat of punishment. If regeneration is not perfectly accomplished in this life (as
Hubmaier and Marpeck argued), and if the church is not the spotless Body of Christ
on earth (as historical evidence amply suggests), what then becomes of the ban?
Either the ban must be abandoned altogether as a misguided attempt at maintaining
legalistic perfection, or radically reconceived as an instrument of admonition, growth,
and spiritual medicine.

It is this author's conviction that the integration of the inner and outer lives of
believers was a spiritual insight of great worth that lay at the heart of the Anabaptist
theological tradition. But the external, ethical, and legalistic dimensions of discipleship that came to be stressed in the tradition, coupled with a very optimistic
regenerationist conviction, have not worn well. A possible avenue to explore further
in the present day may well be the path indicated by the more mystical and spiritualist Anabaptists, who explored in some depth the process of *Gelassenheit* and growth
in the interior, spiritual life. Early Anabaptism suggests that there are inner dimensions of regeneration that must precede and accompany any genuine outward walk
of discipleship; these dimensions can and should be cultivated by means of the spiritual disciplines—of which obedience is one. Perhaps focusing again on the spiritual
life as a walk, a progression, a practice in obedience, a pilgrimage of growth—rather
than focusing on the perfect obedience to be expected from the baptized—will allow
Believers' Churches to develop a humane and realistic pastoral understanding of the
admonition and discipline that can offer positive aid to disciples on their pilgrimage.

Ecclesiology: Sect or Church?

Inner/outer matters show themselves immediately in ecclesiology. At the corporate level, we can see in Sattler and Hubmaier two very different visions of how
the church is to be structured: either in a separated, sectarian fashion, or along mainstream, church lines. Has God responded to human sin in such a way that the world is
allowed to proceed under the dominion of Satan for the time being, with governments
necessarily ruling according to violence and coercion as befits the kingdom of darkness? Or has God ordered the world in the best way possible, ordaining government
as a benevolent servant, the best means available for restraining sin? The New Testament provides crucial texts in both cases. If the latter is the true understanding,
then Christians who participate in the governmental restraining of sin and the pro-
motion of good are doing God's will; if the former is the case, Christians have no
business furthering Satan's work, but should rather separate from it. Is the image of
the two kingdoms one that still ought to be applied to Believers' Church ecclesiology?

Many present-day Believers' Church members in North America seem to have
concluded that the Anabaptist understanding of the two kingdoms no longer serves
as an adequate framework for our church life. In sociological terms the Anabaptist
understanding of the two kingdoms expressed itself in sectarianism. Today the Be-

lievers' Churches, including the Mennonite denomination, are moving rapidly away from the counter-culturalism of "sects" and much closer to the culture-embracing position of "churches."[2] What this means is that Believers' Churches generally no longer call their members out of "the world" to an exclusive citizenship in Christ's Body, which takes precedence over all else, to the point of death if necessary. The visible line separating the two kingdoms, which the Anabaptists drew at the church door, so to speak, has been progressively erased.

Sociological adjustments, such as the one described above, require theological adjustments. It is my impression that in the Believers' Churches of our day, the line separating the two kingdoms is becoming increasingly invisible and subjective—an anthropological dualism rather than an ecclesiological dualism. Salvation is now often understood in mainline Protestant terms of a forensic justification by means of Christ's vicarious atonement, and not necessarily related to a life of discipleship; fraternal admonition is no longer practised, adding to the invisibility of the saving process; economic activities are seen as essentially personal and neutral, not matters which the church at large need consider (except perhaps in extraordinarily embarassing cases, which never seem to include cases of excessive wealth). In short, the progressive sociological move towards a culture-affirming "church" has called for theological adjustments to match. And there are Christian spiritual and theological traditions, readily at hand, that can accommodate the move.

As the strict division between the two kingdoms is erased it may appear that the very nature of the Believers' Church also is erased, since so much of traditional Believers' Church ecclesiology was formulated in a two kingdoms context. Nevertheless, there are historical ecclesiological options in the Anabaptist experience other than the stark extremes of Hubmaier's culture affirming church and Michael Sattler's sectarianism. Just as there were a variety of views concerning spirit and letter among the Anabaptists, so too there was more than one interpretation of the two kingdoms. Hans Denck (in his early writings) and Pilgram Marpeck both maintained that the line between the two kingdoms, while real, was not to be marked by law, but rather by Gospel. That is, they insisted on the crucial point that the inner life of faith will have visible manifestations: there will be a visible distinction between the two kingdoms of church and world. But at the same time, they insisted that the visible Kingdom of Christ on earth will be visible because its members live according to the norms of Christ's love and mercy. There is, then, at least this third Anabaptist ecclesiological response to a two kingdoms view, standing between the better-known extremes of church and sect. Can there be a Believers' Church marked by love rather than law? Or is such an appeal simply the "slippery slope" leading to the practical extinction of Believers' Church boundaries?

The Sword

Reflection on questions of the sword may also be informed by reference to the sixteenth century conversations, although in a Mennonite context it may be helpful to begin with interpretations of this present century.

The articulation of a normative vision for the North American Mennonite church by means of a historical "recovery of the Anabaptist Vision" was carried out in the "Old Mennonite" conference (now officially called the "Mennonite Church" conference) early in this century. In 1927, John Horsch published *The Principle of Nonresistance as held by the Mennonite Church* in which Schleitheim's Article 6 on the sword was prominently displayed.[3] As the title of Horsch's book demonstrates, the historical position purportedly held by the Mennonite Church from its origins was described as nonresistance, drawing upon the non-retaliatory command of Matthew 5:39 and a host of sixteenth century Anabaptist examples. In subsequent books and articles, nonresistance of a strongly separatist variety came to occupy an ever more prominent place in "Old Mennonite" thought. The crowning achievement of this interpretation was Guy F. Hershberger's *War, Peace, and Nonresistance*, published in 1944. In a brief historical section, Hershberger documented the nonresistance of the "early Mennonites" (i.e., the Anabaptists) by extensive paraphrasing of Horsch's earlier work.[4]

By contrast, in the "General Conference" branch of the Mennonite Church, pacifist thinking in the early part of the twentieth century focused very little on Anabaptist roots, and the term "nonresistance" was used sparingly. Henry P. Krehbiel's *War, Peace, and Amity*, published in 1937, referred to the Anabaptists only in passing, as victims of persecution and as one in a list of minority church groups who refused to participate in war.[5] Krehbiel's focus was on "Christ's peace doctrine of love—love of enemy."[6] Far from calling for separation or non-involvement in affairs of the world, such as the "Old Mennonite" nonresistants did, Krehbiel hoped that renewed, pacifist Christians would go out into the world and help to shape a truly Christian state: "As godly spiritual life is deepened, the devoted patriotic Christian citizen sees where he ... can do something toward improving moral, economic, social or political conditions in the direction of Christian ethical standards."[7] Although Krehbiel argued strenuously for separation of church and state, he saw individual Christians playing a very positive role within the state, and even spoke positively of the "truly Christian state," words that would have echoed differently in Goshen, Indiana than they evidently did in Newton, Kansas. "General Conference" readiness for cultural engagement was far removed from the "Old Mennonite" insistence on non-involvement with the state, the latter of which was expressed historically in the Schleitheim insistence that all that falls outside the perfection of Christ is of Satan.

Had Krehbiel and others been interested in investigating the Anabaptist sources for themselves, rather than relying on John Horsch's summary, they would have found some historical backing in the early Anabaptist movement for their position of constructive Christian engagement with the state (e.g., Marpeck, Menno). But as it was, the historical "recovery" of Anabaptism was undertaken primarily by the historians of the "Old Mennonite" conference. This has had important consequences for subsequent Mennonite thinking about peace: the position of Anabaptists concerning matters of the sword has come to be described as one of nonresistance which, by extension, is held to be the historic "Anabaptist/Mennonite" position.

It is my view that the term nonresistance is of limited historical and descriptive usefulness, for several reasons. It is, first of all, a description of an ideal, generalized "Anabaptist" position, and is therefore inaccurate as a description of the historical reality of the movement. The early Anabaptists were not united in promoting "nonresistance." In the second place, even when we turn to the post-Schleitheim Swiss Brethren and exclude all other Anabaptists, "nonresistance" still is inadequate to describe their position as a whole. Matthew 5:39 certainly was applied by the Swiss to the "evil" of government and the sword of government. The sense was that governments were to be obeyed, not resisted, insofar as they did not command something contrary to God's Word; likewise, armed resistance was excluded in all cases— *Wehrlosigkeit* (being weaponless) was the term often used. Nevertheless, this nonresistance had very definite limits for the Swiss, precisely when governments (as they consistently did) commanded "evil" things: that the Anabaptists attend state churches, participate in the Lord's Supper in those churches, swear oaths of loyalty, bear the sword in defence of territories, or abjure their belief in believers' baptism.

Nonresistance had definite limits: there were very many issues on which the Swiss Anabaptists resisted evil in the world, even to the point of martyrdom. Their nonresistance meant primarily that they refused to participate in a reformation of society, which they saw as bound and delivered to Satan, and that they refused to participate in any governing function. Nevertheless, when the integrity of their own witness was jeopardized by what they saw as evil, resist they did. A re-appropriation of Anabaptist nonresistance which portrays the ideal Anabaptist position as an apolitical passivity simply does not fit the historical facts. There is an important sense in which "nonviolent resistance" is a descriptive term that fits even the Swiss Brethren reaction to governments much more accurately than does the term "nonresistance." The Anabaptists of the first few generations were anything but passive or free from resistance.

There is a further sense in which the word nonresistance is inadequate to capture the full Anabaptist position. All Anabaptists emphatically did "resist evil" in their own midst, by means of the ban. Nonresistance did not apply when evil needed to be opposed by the "sword of the spirit." It was by means of the ban that believers were to be admonished and disciplined. The spiritual danger represented by the ban, the spiritual sword, was that it could quickly become legalistic and coercive, as unChristian an example of resistance as physical violence itself.

Pilgram Marpeck's comments concerning the ban provide us with helpful guidance here. As we have seen, he insisted that the crucial principle was loving patience, and it applied equally inside and outside the church; it was a principle that applied in both kingdoms. Followers of Christ must obey and be faithful; they must "resist" any attempts that promote disobedience and evil actions, in the church or outside it. It was not a question of *whether* to resist or not; there simply *is* evil which must resisted. But it was rather the *manner* in which evil was resisted that made one's faithfulness Christian, or un-Christian.

Pilgram Marpeck's observations extend the question of the sword and the two kingdom understanding in helpful ways: not the automatic, culture-blessing acceptance of government calls to warfare; not the non-engaged passivity implied by "non-resistance"; not the focussed political action often implied in our day by "nonviolent resistance" (all too often without deep spiritual roots); but rather Christ's patient, loving resistance which recognizes and names evil, wishing to overcome it with good, ever depending on God's grace for the final victory. This loving resistance, furthermore, focuses not only on the violence and coercion that takes place *outside* the church, but looks with equal urgency to the manner in which all human relationships are carried out, most particularly *within* the church, where the flame of love should burn the brightest.

Economics

A further dimension that arises from the inner/outer linkage has to do with the economic activity of Christians. Some of the most moving passages describing *Gelassenheit* to be found in all of Anabaptist literature emerge from the communal South German tradition, and make most explicit the necessary connection between inner yieldedness to the Spirit and yieldedness in economic matters. While not all agreed that legislated community of goods was a necessary sign of *Gelassenheit*, the early Anabaptists did agree that economic questions were, in the end, spiritual questions. This observation has a pressing contemporary relevance, need it be said, in a context in which the relationship between one's Christianity and one's level of prosperity is increasingly being severed—that is, in a culture which tempts Christians continually to separate the inner life of faith from the outer life of discipleship.

Perhaps, given the theological trends we may note in the Believers' Churches, we are witnessing in our time the definitive "protestantization" of the Anabaptist remnant, in which social and economic activity will be divorced fundamentally from spirituality. Or perhaps, given the way in which our church institutions covet and encourage large donations from our wealthier members, we are witnessing a return to the late medieval Catholic system, in which the "churchly" use of one's wealth is valued as a positive aid to salvation. Or perhaps we are seeing the emergence of a "two track" system in which those who are specially called do the work of missions, evangelism, relief, and peace witness (much like religious in the Catholic system), are supported by the financial largesse of the "less religious" laity who remain fully immersed in "the world."

Are these developments a good thing? In my view the answer is "Maybe yes, but most probably no." It is true that there were some destructive ways in which the two kingdoms distinction came to be lived out in Believers' Church denominations. Insofar as the descendants of the Anabaptists lost sight of the truly spiritual foundations of the two kingdoms doctrine; insofar as the Kingdom of Christ came to be reduced to a narrow ethical path of outward observances; insofar as an overemphasis on ethics darkened the recognition that salvation is a gift of grace, then perhaps the passing of the old two kingdoms doctrine can be seen as a good thing. If "protestantization" means a recovery of the true spiritual foundations of the Christian life (as opposed to an ethnic, formal or legalistic understanding), then we may well celebrate what we are witnessing around us.

On the other hand, if "protestantization" means a fundamental divorce between the "life of the spirit" and a life of discipleship in this world (as if the two could ever be separated!), then this cannot be a good thing. The early Anabaptists (and the mainstream Christian spiritual tradition that preceded them) had it right: the Christian life in this world grows out of, and is an integral expression of, the new life in Christ; where there is true love of God, there must needs be a radical love of neighbour. What kind of "discipleship" is left when the economic dimensions of the love of neighbour are passed over in polite silence?

Equality

On this topic much can be said that is painful to hear. One way of continuing the conversation begun in the sixteenth century would be to ask again whether we believe that the Holy Spirit calls all of humanity to salvation, and that the response of faith will entail a pilgrimage of discipleship. If the Holy Spirit in fact does call men and women alike to faith and to lives of costly discipleship, what will be the outer, ecclesiological manifestations of this call? At what point in the Christian walk may we suppose that the Holy Spirit begins to recognize gender, begins to restrict the activities of women in the church, and proceeds to grant more and more ecclesial power to men alone? How are we to discern when we have arrived at such a delimiting case? Do males have some special "spiritual" receptivity that makes them uniquely suited to interpreting the purposes of God? If a woman were to think that the Holy Spirit had called her to ministry, is it true that her "call" cannot be considered legitimate until male elders have bestowed their confirmation of the presence of the Spirit of God?

Here we have, without a doubt, returned again to questions of the Spirit's role in the interpretation of the letter of Scripture. The role played in the church by the literal exegesis of selected Pauline verses needs no elaboration. Those few words about "women remaining silent" are as threadbare from overuse and misuse as are Paul's words in Romans 13, concerning governments and obedience. Is this what the Holy Spirit had in mind? Is this the Gospel?

As in all cases involving power and the imbalance of power, there is good reason for Believers' Churches to apply the "hermeneutics of suspicion" not only to the appropriation of the Gospel by governments, but also to the appropriation of the church by men. All human beings stand equally before God. So said the early Anabaptists, and they were right. As in the political question, so also in the matter of women and men in the church: We would do well to focus on how the Holy Spirit actually calls human beings and works in human history, rather that rehearsing endlessly the few lines of Pauline advice that have so dominated our conversation on these issues. The words "God is no respecter of persons" provide more profound guidance than do the needs of traditional oligarchies.

Church Ordinances

Sixteenth century developments that led to the establishment of an Anabaptist theological tradition had implications for the most visible church ordinances, namely baptism, the ban, and the Supper. The progressive weakening of Anabaptist pneumatology in the sixteenth century had implications for the way in which visible church ordinances functioned and were conceptualized.

Baptism

The solidly biblical rationale for adult baptism was one of the most visible parts of the theological/biblical tradition that was passed on in Believers' Churches. Biblical references buttressing the practice of believers' baptism were among the first that new converts learned; the standard verses are repeated interminably (to our ears) in thousands of court records. At one level this inherited literalist biblical rationale worked well: there is a biblical order that states, first teach, then baptize. On strictly biblical grounds the Anabaptists had a very strong case indeed for the baptism of adults following confession of faith. But when pressed beyond some literal limits, the rationale begins to weaken.

Would we agree with the later Anabaptist tradition that *salvation* depends upon obedience to the particular, literal "biblical order" concerning baptism? Should we be willing to excommunicate from our churches those who question the *salvific* necessity of following the "proper order"? Should we be willing to suffer martyrdom for the sake of this particular order of "first teach, then baptize"? Do we believe that infants who are baptized with water, but who are then confirmed in their faith as adults (in "mainline" churches) nevertheless are damned because they did not undergo the step of consciously chosen *water* baptism as adults? How far are we willing to push our inherited traditional literal reading of Scripture? Probably not nearly so far as were the later Anabaptists.

We may be able to learn something from a Pilgram Marpeck or even a Nicolaas van Blesdijk. They argued that the central point of water baptism following confession of faith was not "obedience to the biblical law" but rather an outward pledge to a community of an inner conversion by the Spirit of God. Without the inner change, the outer was to no avail, be its observance "biblical" or not, because the water is just water and has no power. When the focus mistakenly falls on the outer obedience to the rite of water baptism, does this not give undeserved salvific power to the water and the rite? Did not the original Anabaptist critique of the Roman Catholic sacrament oppose precisely this point?

Part of the difficulty here was the fact that first generation Anabaptists actively converted from one faith to another; freely chosen adult baptism sealed that inner conversion. But what would be the pattern in the second generation of Anabaptist believers and beyond? From what, and to what, would the children of Anabaptist parents convert? Although Ulrich Zwingli's argument attempting to link infant baptism to Old Testament circumcision was not convincing biblical exegesis, his point that the children of believers ought to be recognized as a part of the people of God was an argument that proved to have some historical force. With the coming of adult confirmation to some mainline churches, the practical distinction between those traditions and the Believers' Church tradition was drastically reduced.

Being of the second generation Anabaptist leadership, and also because he had the freedom to think and write over a longer period of time, Pilgram Marpeck was able to conceive of the church not only in its apocalyptic role as the "pure Bride" awaiting the Groom's coming, but also as a place of growth, where children of Anabaptist parents could be nurtured in the faith, and the weak (that is, *all* believers) could be strengthened. Already in 1532, Marpeck described a ceremony of infant dedication in which the congregation gives thanks for its children, prays for them, and admonishes the parents "to do whatever is needed to raise the child up to the praise and glory of God, and to commit the child to God until it is clearly seen that God is working in him for faith or unfaith."[8] The current practice of infant dedication in Believers' Churches has an Anabaptist referent; more importantly, the practice of infant dedication recognizes the different initiatory needs of children who are born and raised in the faith.

The other part of the problem of second generation children has been more difficult to address, namely "What will 'conversion' mean to children who have been raised in the faith?" The danger, especially when the outward rite is stressed as a point of salvific obedience, is that the water is received even though a spiritual transformation or inner commitment has not really taken place—again, the very critique the early Anabaptists made of infant baptism, namely that water was being applied without a genuine inner change. The fundamental theological rationale underlying believers' baptism certainly is not being addressed when entire Sunday school classes dutifully receive the waters of baptism simultaneously, at an "appropriate" age. For a time, in the North American Mennonite experience, revival meetings provided a context for public repentance, conversion, and commitment, which could then be followed by baptism into the church. This approach worked for some, but not all; it was an approach that claimed its share of psychological victims. How may the practice of baptism on confession of faith be rejuvenated in the Believers' Churches? How might the inner dimensions related to this powerful symbol of dying and rising in Christ be recaptured in churches long accustomed to fairly "automatic" performances of the outward rite?

The Ban

Sufficient attention already has been given to a critique of the kind of "discipline" exercised in the later Anabaptist tradition. Here we wish to make only one point: while the conception and practice of the ban was, on the whole, literalistic and legalistic in the sixteenth century, and became even more so as the century proceeded, there are dimensions of the ban that call for thoughtful reconsideration. The linking of the ban to believers' baptism cemented an important factor of accountability between church members that emphasized the communal nature of the fellowship. The inner spiritual change led not only to individual water baptism, but led necessarily to community and to a mutual accountability within that community. Can there be "Believers' Churches" in the absence of such accountability? How might this dimension be recovered in a secular and individualistic age such as our own?

There also were confessional, penitential, and absolutionist (forgiveness) dimensions in the early Anabaptist practice of the ban that need to be considered in our own time: there must be positive and helpful ways of confessing human sin and failure, and ways of being forgiven and of accepting forgiveness, within Believers' Churches.

The Supper

In this concluding discussion we have made much of the inner side of the Anabaptist conversations as possible correctives to the strong traditional emphasis on the outer dimensions of the Christian life. Our point has not been to urge a spiritualist or subjective reading of Anabaptism to the detriment of the outer expressions of inner renewal. Our point has been, rather, to suggest that there is wisdom in maintaining a balanced inner/outer integration. Nowhere is that balance, or lack of balance, more evident than in sacramental teaching, especially as it relates to the Lord's Supper. In the ancient Christian tradition, the Eucharist was a thanksgiving and celebration of the mystery of God's incarnation in Christ. What was defined precisely as transubstantiation in the late medieval period was earlier simply regarded as a mystery: in an inexplicable way, God became present to humanity again in the celebration of the Supper. In the celebration of the "sacrament of the altar" there was a "communication" between God and humanity in which God's grace was again offered to the communicant.

This is not the place to elaborate necessary historical and theological details. Interested readers are encouraged to consult John D. Rempel's excellent study *The Lord's Supper in Anabaptism* (Herald Press, 1994). Suffice it to say here that Anabaptist sacramental theology was based on a common philosophical critique of the day which denied the possibility that material things could mediate the divine. It is evident that two kingdom thinking fits within this philosophical universe very well: Christians are those who dwell in heaven, not on earth; they live according to the spirit, not the flesh; the Body of Christ, the church, is of a different "order" than "the world." But the Anabaptists did not completely sever the divine/human link. It was precisely concerning the "Body of Christ" that Anabaptists made a bold claim: God continues to be made present to humanity in the Body of Christ as late medieval Catholicism taught, but the Body of Christ is not the eucharistic host, but rather is the visible congregation of saints. As John Rempel notes, the Anabaptists "portrayed Christ as present in the church in his humanity,"[9] which in a sixteenth century context was a radical sacramental and christological claim indeed—and remains so! Underlying the necessity for visible purity in the Body of Christ was a late medieval understanding of what the Body of Christ is: a pure and holy sacrament.

We have suggested above that this optimistic ecclesiology made excessive anthropological, pneumatological and regenerationist demands. In the context of the Lord's Supper there is here a serious reversal of traditional eucharistic theology: rather than sinful humanity coming to the table to receive grace and forgiveness, in the Anabaptist tradition believers were to bring pure and regenerated selves to the table as an offering. The Supper thus became a celebration of grace already given and accepted, a remembrance of Christ's sacrifice which had offered forgiveness once and for all, a Supper of solidarity between "pure members" of the Body of Christ on earth.

Pilgram Marpeck stands out as one of the few Anabaptists who thought systematically about sacramental questions. He was troubled by the spiritualist critique, namely that if outward ceremonies are simply reflections of inner conditions, they then have no essential, spiritual reason for being. As we have seen, Marpeck argued that the ordinances of worship are powerful and efficacious *vehicles* which lead others to the divine reality, and which lead believers to deeper lives of love, yieldedness, and obedience.[10] The Christian life, as Pilgram Marpeck understood it, was not the expression of perfection, attained at the time of repentance, conversion and regeneration. Rather, the Christian life was one of continual growth, within the community of faith and by means of communal worship, ever deeper into the profound mystery of Christ's love and peace.

Pilgram Marpeck did not agree with the image of perfectly regenerated believers bringing that perfection together to constitute a pure church. The ecclesial image he used more frequently was the church as a place where the broken could be healed. "We do not ... do wrong," said Marpeck, "if we, who are weak and ill, employ the Great Physician's medicine, and if we extend it to one another, to those who are hungry ..."[11] The "Great Physician's medicine" comes to us, said Marpeck, in the forms of outward worship, in ceremonies and ordinances. They were meant to lead us to a deeper and more profound understanding of the love of God and neighbour; they can and ought to be sacraments for us, that is, "visible signs of invisible grace," or physical ways in which we may receive grace. Marpeck's appreciation for the spiritual power of communal symbols and ceremonies led him to an almost sacramental position in which external ordinances and actions were seen as physical means of growth into love and the mature spiritual life.[12]

Marpeck's observations may well be helpful for Believers' Churches today, as they work their way back from radically "non symbolic" forms of worship to ones that are beginning to recognize again the spiritual power of visible ceremonies, symbols and rituals. Marpeck's vision of the church as the place where the Great Physician's medicine is lovingly (and visibly) dispensed outlines an ecclesiology that still speaks powerfully in our century, particularly in a Believers' Church context. His alternative Anabaptist conception of the Christian life as one of growth "through instruction and knowledge of Christ's mind," and of the church as the place where the healing of Christ the Physician is made manifest, is a "vision" for believers who fall short of perfection, and yet believe that Christ's call to discipleship was meant to be followed.

The concluding comments made above undoubtedly concentrate too much on a critique of the received Anabaptist theological tradition, particularly focusing on the external aspects of that tradition. These comments were not meant to suggest that there was only externalism there, or that there was little of worth passed on by that tradition—far from it! It is because they stand on the solid foundation of what was passed on that the Believers' Churches have the luxury of being able to look back over a theological and ecclesial tradition that now spans almost half a millenium, and reflect critically upon it. In reflecting upon the historical development of Anabaptism, one central point spoke repeatedly to this observer: the vitality of early Anabaptism and of the received tradition rested upon an encounter with the living Christ. It was the grafting of lifeless twigs onto the living vine that, in the final analysis, brought into being a "church of believers." Believers' Churches are now venerable old plants, with deep and strong roots. May the caretakers and labourers in this corner of God's garden have the courage and wisdom to prune with care and patience, all that may hinder a life rooted in the living God; and may they have the foresight and wisdom to cultivate lovingly all that encourages that same life-giving rootedness.

End Notes

[1] Keeney, *Dutch*, pp. 42-43. Keeney is describing differences between Anabaptists and Reformed, but the point applies equally well, as he notes later, to scriptural differences within Anabaptism itself.

[2] For an incisive outline of the "modern" issues, see Rodney J. Sawatsky and Scott Holland, eds., *The Limits of Perfection: A Conversation with J. Lawrence Burkholder* (Waterloo, Ont.: Institute of Anabaptist-Mennonite Studies, 1993), especially Burkholder's "Autobiographical Reflections."

[3] John Horsch, *The Principle of Nonresistance as held by the Mennonite Church,* (Scottdale, Pa.: Mennonite Publishing House, 1927), pp. 14 ff.

[4] Guy F. Hershberger, *War, Peace, and Nonresistance*, (Scottdale, Pa.: Herald Press, 1946), pp. 73-77.

[5] Henry P. Krehbiel, *War, Peace, and Amity*, (Newton, Kan.: Published by the author, 1937), pp. 241; 291-92. Krehbiel footnotes Horsch's book, cited above, as the source of his information on the Anabaptists.

[6] *Ibid.*, p. 292.

[7] *Ibid.*, p. 271.

[8] Klassen and Klaassen, *Writings*, p. 147.

[9] See the perceptive discussion in Rempel, *Lord's Supper*, pp. 32-37; citation from p. 35.

[10] "Nor can an inward testimony be recognized, except when it is preceded by such outward teaching, deeds, commands, and ceremonies of Christ, which belong to the revelation of the Son of God in the flesh, and which are like a new creation in Christ. These things must be received and employed in a physical manner before the inner testimony can be felt and recognized." Klassen and Klaassen, *Writings.*, pp. 78-79. As Blough notes, Luther's influence may be visible here, and it seems to have led Marpeck "away from the Zwinglian Spiritualism which characterized many of the Swiss Anabaptists in relation to the sacraments." Neal Blough, "Marpeck, Luther," p. 211; *Christologie*, pp. 184-90.

[11] Klassen and Klaassen, *Writings.*, p. 87.

[12] "[The] ceremonies of Christ ... have been presented by Christ as a medicine and as a means to our salvation in order that we strengthen our human weakness." Klassen and Klaassen, *Writings*, p. 105.

Appendix

A Review of Anabaptist Historiography

The earliest attacks on Anabaptism, already in 1525, use the term *Wiedertäufer*, a German translation of Anabaptists or re-baptizers.[1] Johann Faber (Roman Catholic), writing in Latin, used the term "Anabaptista" in 1528. In 1527 Ulrich Zwingli, following a suggestion from Oecolampadius, had adopted the term "Catabaptist," which was supposed to carry "the additional connotation of 'anti-baptist,' i.e. attempting to destroy the true baptism."[2] Zwingli employed this term in his major attack on the Anabaptists of 1527, *In Catabaptistarum Strophas Elenchus*, but the term was not destined to great popularity, and quickly fell into disuse. The most important decree against the Anabaptists was the imperial mandate published at Speyer in 1529 which explicitly linked the sixteenth century Anabaptists with the "old sect of Anabaptism, condemned and forbidden many centuries ago." The Speyer mandate thus "renewed" the ancient imperial law, identified sixteenth century Anabaptism with the venerable heresy of Donatism, and decreed that "every Anabaptist and rebaptized man and woman of the age of reason shall be condemned and brought from natural life into death by fire, sword, and the like, according to the person."[3]

By 1530 the term *Anabaptista* or *Wiedertäufer* was the accepted designation for the group of Christians who baptized adults on confession of faith, as reference to the Augsburg Confession of that year demonstrates. The death penalty as applied in Protestant and Catholic territories, however, used various legal arguments, not simply those of the ancient code. In light of these responses it is not surprising that those who practiced adult baptism on confession of faith refused the label of "Anabaptists," and preferred to be called "brethren."[4]

The shocking events in the city of Münster in Westphalia in 1534 and 1535 simply reinforced the connotations of fanatical heresy already associated with the term Anabaptist. The polygamy and other excesses carried out in the city under siege gave a permanent lurid, violent, and sinister tone to Anabaptism as a movement. With very few exceptions subsequent majoritarian historiography in the seventeenth and eighteenth centuries continued to define Anabaptism as such a movement, following both Luther's description of Anabaptism as "fanaticism" and Bullinger's contention that the Anabaptists were children of Thomas Müntzer.[5] John Oyer has characterized this majoritarian historical point of view as follows.

> They regarded the Zwickau Prophets and Thomas Müntzer as the instigators of the movement. The Radical disturbances caused by the Prophets and Müntzer in Wittenberg and the Saxon lands spread to Switzerland, there to plague Zwingli and his following. In both re-

gions a radical spiritualism was the dominating element of the movement. Anabaptism reached its peak of development in the forceful establishment of the Kingdom of Münster. . . . After the rebellion was suppressed a rather pious but nonetheless harsh converted priest named Menno Simons collected the dispersed elements and attempted to direct them into more peaceful channels.[6]

The historiography of the victors distorted the Anabaptist movement, and a corrective was needed. Just what ought to be denoted by the term "Anabaptist," however, has remained a contentious issue.

Historiographical Overview

The outlines of Anabaptist historiography have been ably described by many modern authors.[7] At the risk of drastic oversimplification, here we will only outline the broadest developments within that historiography.

The first phase of Anabaptist historiography, lasting virtually from 1525 to the middle of the nineteenth century, can be described as an exercise in repetition of well-worn formulae, as has been noted. Nevertheless, there existed a minority current of historical writing that was the reverse-image of the mainstream view. Already in 1531, Sebastian Franck wrote a narrative of church history in which he extolled the "heretics" as the true Christians. The Anabaptists were cited as an historical example.

> (The Anabaptists) taught nothing but love, faith, and the need of bearing the cross. They showed themselves humble, patient under much suffering; they broke the bread with one another as an evidence of unity and love. They helped each other faithfully and called each other brothers. . . . They were persecuted with great tyranny, being imprisoned, branded, tortured, and executed by fire, water and sword. . . They died as martyrs, patiently, and humbly endured all persecution.[8]

Granted that Franck was a spiritualist, and critical of what he saw as the Anabaptist reliance on external ceremony, their Biblical literalism, and their judgmental tendency, nevertheless his positive portrayal of the movement stands in stark contrast to that of the Protestant theologians and historians.

Franck's tendency to trace church history by following the so-called heretical line of descent was adopted in Thieleman van Braght's *Martyrs Mirror*, long a spiritual resource in Mennonite and Amish homes, and finds echoes in the Hutterite Great Chronicle.[9] Beginning with Gottfried Arnold in 1699, in his *History of the Church and Heresy*, some Pietist writers also traced a "heretical" line of descent through Anabaptism on into Pietism. The same general apologetic approach continues among a minority of interpreters into the nineteenth and twentieth centuries, both within Mennonite circles and outside the Anabaptist denominations.[10]

A second significant phase of Anabaptist historiography, beginning around 1850, opened the door to new interpretations through the publication of archival sources.

With the appearance of these records, the possibility was opened of allowing the Anabaptists to speak for themselves, even though the published archival testimonies usually were confessions and court records, all too often extracted under torture. The growing availability of these critically edited archival sources, however, much advanced the historical description of Anabaptism.

By the late nineteenth and early twentieth century, the historical and theological descriptions of Anabaptism fell into at least four categories:

a) Representatives of the older mainstream apologetic historiography, that continued repeating the received wisdom of Anabaptists as "fanatical heretics." The theological description of Anabaptism, thus conceived, emphasized spiritualism and antinomianism.[11]

b) Minority apologetic interpretations of Anabaptism that saw in the movement significant continuations of earlier medieval traditions. Added to the apologetic views now came historical works that proposed that "Anabaptists" were a continuation of late-medieval heretical traditions (particularly the Waldensians), that they represented a continuation of mystical and spiritualist traditions, that they continued the ascetic tradition of the radical Franciscans, or that Anabaptists continued humanist sentiments.[12]

c) Socialist historiography (e.g., Friedrich Engels), that saw in Thomas Müntzer and the Anabaptists the beginnings of a popular German revolution. The socialist conception of Anabaptism tended to see "Anabaptists" as Müntzer's secret shock troops, and to read theological language as a "code" for social revolution.[13]

d) Sociological historiography (Max Weber and Ernst Troeltsch), that interpreted Anabaptism in sociological categories as a "sect type." The theological characteristics of Anabaptism highlighted by this interpretive grid tended to be those which outlined relationships to society and the ruling authorities.[14]

In North American circles, the most fruitful of the above models was that of the sociologist Ernst Troeltsch. In his great work *The Social Teaching of the Christian Churches* Troeltsch identified three distinct sociological "types" in the history of the Christian church: the church, sect and mystical types. A key element of this typology for the writing of Anabaptist history was the differentiation it provided between Anabaptism (understood as a "sect" type) and the "spiritualistic types" such as Thomas Müntzer and the Zwickau Prophets. This differentiation resulted in an immediate conflict between Troeltsch and the champions of the Lutheran concept of Anabaptists as "spiritualist Fanatics," but it endeared Troeltsch to North American Mennonite and Believers' Church historians.[15]

So it was that in the first decades of the twentieth century North American Mennonite historians began to "rehabilitate" Anabaptism in a vigorous and public way, building on the work of Troeltsch and interpreting and publicizing the now-available primary sources. Although such apologetic work never had been completely absent in Mennonite ranks, the quantitative and qualitative leap to be noted in North American Mennonite historical writing beginning in the 1920s marks a new era.

Although no one person can take the credit for this development, in North America no one did more to further a reinterpretation of Anabaptism than did the Mennonite church leader and historian Harold S. Bender (1897-1962).[16] Bender took exception to the mainstream apologetic historiography that depicted Anabaptism as fanatical heresy; likewise he rejected earlier efforts at rehabilitating placed it within a continuous stream of "pious heretical groups" or as a semi-monastic continuation of medieval movements. Marxist historiography was, of course, rejected out of hand. To the contrary, in his well-known "Anabaptist Vision" statement Bender argued that

> Anabaptism is the culmination of the Reformation, the fulfilment of the original vision of Luther and Zwingli, and thus ... a consistent evangelical Protestantism seeking to recreate without compromise the original New Testament church, the vision of Christ and the Apostles.[17]

According to Bender, "Anabaptism proper" was not to be "obscured by Thomas Müntzer and the Peasants War, the Münsterites, or any other aberration of Protestantism in the sixteenth century." *True* Anabaptism, or "Anabaptism proper," maintained "an unbroken course in Switzerland, South Germany, Austria, and Holland throughout the sixteenth century."[18] Given the limited historical reach of this "genuine Anabaptism," Bender had little trouble identifying its central theological features, namely, "first, a new conception of the essence of Christianity as discipleship; second, a new conception of the church as a brotherhood; and third, a new ethic of love and nonresistance."[19]

The project of recovering the "original" and "genuine" Anabaptist vision was pursued energetically in the pages of *The Mennonite Quarterly Review*, the scholarly journal Harold Bender founded and edited until his death in 1962, and came to fruition with the publication of the *Mennonite Encyclopedia* in 1955. As it happened, this North American Mennonite approach fit in extremely well with church history trends taking place elsewhere in North America, which increasingly worked to classify the broad movement of Reformation dissent. Such a broad classification would include, but was not limited to Anabaptists. Roland Bainton, church historian at Yale University, coined the phrase "Left Wing of the Reformation" to describe, distinguish, and circumscribe the radical wing of sixteenth century reform.[20] But it was George Williams' term "Radical Reformation" that won the day, with its classification of the broad movement for Reformation dissent into three distinct camps.

According to Williams' classification, the Radical Reformation included the Anabaptists (named for their insistence on adult baptism, following confession of faith), the "Spiritualists" (individuals who stressed the inner working of the Spirit, rather than unimportant outward ceremonies) and the "Evangelical Rationalists" (who located the source of divine truth in human reason).[21] Williams' encyclopedic classification followed Troeltsch's basic division between the "sect" type (Anabaptists) and the "spiritualist" type, but added a further compartment to include the "evangelical rationalists." Williams made even further divisions within these three classifications, dividing each of the three major divisions into three more subdivisions. Anabaptists, for example, were divided into "Evangelical," "Contemplative," and "Revolutionary" types.[22] Harold Bender's description of "true Anabaptists" being those who remained true to the original "evangelical Anabaptist" line that began in Zürich (monogenesis) thus fit very well as one compartment within Williams' classificatory scheme.

Because of the scope, quality, and sheer number of Anabaptist and Radical Reformation studies in North America an impression was formed that a kind of "consensus" had been reached. In fact, from a European perspective certain key assumptions had been questioned from the start. Writing in 1932 in the Dutch *Doopsgezind* (Mennonite) tradition, W.J. Kühler saw in Swiss Anabaptism not a pure form to be emulated, but rather a movement whose full development was prevented through persecution and which then ossified into externalism. The full historical development of the movement's potential took place only in the Netherlands; thus, the Anabaptist movement as a whole was best understood from that long-range view.[23]

Perhaps thanks to the necessity of understanding and explaining the Swiss, South German, and Dutch movements from an integrated perspective, Kühler's approach to the varieties of Anabaptist beliefs was developmentally oriented. Rather than positing a normative Anabaptist theology at the source, Kühler instead traced the theological development of Anabaptism according to the tension between individual and community, and between the spirit and the letter, which he said characterized the movement from the start. The working out of these tendencies responded to different conditions in different regions, responding to local circumstances.[24] Kühler's general approach can still be commended as a useful way of shedding light on Anabaptism as a relatively coherent movement which, nevertheless, manifested much diversity in its geographical expressions. What we have proposed in this book is in fact quite similar.

Dutch Anabaptist studies revealed further a critical fault line running through Harold Bender's "monogenetic" paradigm (namely that "true" Anabaptism began in Zürich, and spread from there): although it was crucial to include Menno Simons among the genuine Anabaptists, Menno's own historical connections to Swiss beginnings were virtually non-existent. To the contrary, his connections with Melchior Hoffman and the Melchiorite tradition were patently obvious—but Hoffman had been marginalized as an unsound radical, and no true Anabaptist, in the "Anabaptist Vision" scholarship. From the perspective of *Doopsgezind* scholarship in the Netherlands, the "Anabaptist Vision" paradigm never was very convincing.[25]

The North American "consensus" view did not go unchallenged in North American circles either. Robert Friedmann,[26] Hans J. Hillerbrand,[27] John Oyer,[28] and Walter Klaassen[29] all challenged the view that Anabaptism could be interpreted as "Protestantism taken to its proper ends." Hillerbrand and Oyer highlighted in particular the different soteriological emphases evident in the Lutheran and Anabaptist movements, respectively.[30] Friedmann and Klaassen, both of whom worked extensively with South

German/Austrian sources, highlighted among other things the importance of the Spirit in early Anabaptist thought, in distinction to the supposed "Anabaptist biblicism" that characterized "genuine" Anabaptists.[31] The way had been well prepared for Walter Klaassen's description of Anabaptism as "Neither Catholic nor Protestant" and the proposal of a new historical paradigm by Stayer, Packull and Deppermann.

The great advantage of the typological approaches of Troeltsch and Williams was that they had provided comprehensive structures within which the wide diversity of dissident reform could be placed. Nevertheless, the task of historical description according to "types" also posed limitations. Already in 1932, at the same time that Troeltsch was being cited with approval and appropriated in North America, Kühler had made a trenchant critique of Troeltsch's typological method. "My objection is," said Kühler, "that with Troeltsch the facts must conform themselves too much to the [typological] scheme."[32] The same basic objection has since come to be applied to Williams' classificatory scheme.

Concerning Williams' Radical Reformation classifications, it has been noted that the doing of history according to typological models tends to predetermine the results of historical investigation—an echo of Holl's and Kühler's critiques of Troeltsch. For instance, the existence of revolutionary impulses among "evangelical Anabaptists" was difficult to see given the classification itself—which defined the "evangelicals" as sectarian pacifists—and by the existence of the parallel category of "revolutionary Anabaptists." Thus, for example, members of the Swiss Brethren who argued in favour of taking the sword would, by definition, be classed as revolutionary Anabaptists, obscuring the historical dynamics within the geographical movement.[33] Likewise, the importance of the work of the Holy Spirit in the "evangelical" stream of Anabaptism was difficult to see, since such an emphasis, by definition, would tend to place its adherent in the "spiritualist" or "contemplative" stream.

In the second place, Williams' historical method traced the development of ideas and based its classification on the grouping of those ideas, with less attention paid to the social, political and economic aspects underlying the emergence of the ideas.[34] This meant that on occasion, specific historical circumstances in given locales became less significant than typological similarities or dissimilarities. And finally, the typological approach did not foster close attention to the development of ideas within the movement. Typologies, given their static nature, in fact make a developmental description extremely difficult to carry out.

Polygenesis and Beyond

It was in response to, and in critique of the North American "consensus" view that the "polygenesis" description of Anabaptism emerged. There were critiques which preceded the formulation of "polygenesis," of course, but the scope of the new descriptive paradigm was more sweeping than that of previous critiques; "polygenesis" (multiple origins) was formulated as a comprehensive interpretive alternative to the "monogenesis" assumptions concerning Anabaptist origins which had characterized much earlier North American scholarship. "Hillerbrand and Bender (like Holl and Troeltsch)," noted James Stayer, while they disagreed on certain points, "were in agreement that there was a single dispersion of Anabaptism—a single *successio Anabaptistica*, which certainly ran through Zurich. The only question was whether or not it went back further to Saxony."[35] Stayer's thesis, in a nutshell, argued as follows:

> The assumption of the *monogenesis*, as opposed to *polygenesis*, of Anabaptism was never really established. . . . It is an unexamined assumption which simply does not bear rigorous examination. The connections between Melchior Hoffman and the Swiss Brethren were no closer than those between Clemens Ziegler and the Swiss Brethren. Are we to assume, then, that the sectarian tradition stemming from Hoffman, including its Mennonite branch, was not genuinely Anabaptist, because it did not run through Zurich? It appears, furthermore, that in the beginnings of South German Anabaptism there is a certain parallel to Hoffman's independent initiation of adult baptism in Strassburg or Emden in 1530.[36]

In short, the polygenesis paradigm described Anabaptism as composed of three movements with distinctly individual origins: the Swiss, the South German/Austrian, and the North German/Dutch.[37] It was a fruitful corrective that has directed subsequent historical studies to limited geographical areas and has resulted in more carefully differentiated conclusions. No longer could historians speak simply of "Anabaptism" without first making careful distinctions concerning which branch of Anabaptism was under consideration.[38]

Although the "polygenesis" description of Anabaptist origins is indispensable for understanding Anabaptist beginnings, it was not intended as a comprehensive, developmental paradigm. It emerged as a model concerned with historical "genesis," or beginnings, articulated as an explicit alternative to, and rejection of, Harold Bender's "Swiss Origins" theory. The approach has proved extremely fruitful in the study of early Anabaptism, and must be retained. Nevertheless, the identification of diverse *origins* did not and does not of itself explain change and *development* within the movement as a whole.

Some original lines of distinction between Anabaptist groups proved stubbornly divisive over time; others disappeared without a trace; yet others proved permeable and malleable. From the perspective of the "baptizing" groups that survived the trial by fire in the sixteenth century one may ask: What were the developmental dynamics that led from Hut to Hutter, from Hoffman to Menno, from Grebel to Andreas Gut? Polygenesis studies have painted the beginnings of this larger portrait with bold strokes; more recent studies are beginning to fill in the subsequent, more comprehensive, developmental picture.

It must be noted that the two leading North American exponents of the polygenesis paradigm, James Stayer and Werner Packull, have already moved beyond the question of origins into a more developmental mode, with surprising and refreshing results.[39] Our survey has drawn heavily on this later work. James Stayer's recent monograph on the development of Anabaptist community of goods comes to the conclusion that from the start there was broad Anabaptist agreement on economic principles, based on Acts 2 and 4. This broad but fundamental agreement cut across the regional "faultlines" indicated by polygenesis, and defined an early "pan-Anabaptist" position on these questions.[40] Against this broader backdrop of Anabaptist agreement the eventual Hutterite definition must be seen as a later elaboration (and an ultimately divisive one) of shared *Anabaptist* economic principles.

Likewise Werner Packull's detailed study of the origin and development of communitarian Anabaptism in Moravia points repeatedly to surprisingly permeable boundaries between communities of different historical origin. In the development of Moravian communitarian Anabaptism the by-word was dialogue, interaction, and mutual influence, not simply the emergence of separate Anabaptist groups based solely (or even primarily) on disparate "origins."[41] Walter Klaassen's recent study of apocalyptical expectation in the Radical Reformation also found broad and fundamental commonalities in the way End Times themes were appropriated and used, in spite of individual differences in detail.[42]

How exactly the "Anabaptist story" will be told in the future cannot be predicted. The movement was complex, and there are far too many areas that remain unexplored. Added to this are the questions, still unasked, that future historians will direct to the sources. One can only hope that careful regional and local studies will continue, and that the original sources will continue to be discovered, read, and evaluated. Without such original scholarship there can be no advances in the telling of the broader story. At the same time it is hoped that general narratives also will continue to be written. Historical studies, like any other products of culture, invariably become historical artifacts themselves. When the old quilt gets threadbare, the only decent thing to do is to piece and sew a new one. Best wishes to those who will take on the task.

End Notes

[1] For example, Ulrich Zwingli's *Von der Taufe, von der Wiedertaufe und von der Kindertaufe*, May, 1525; also Oecolampadius' *Ein Gespräch etlicher Predicanten zu Basel...*, 1525.

[2] Harold Bender, "Catabaptist," ME, I, p. 524.

[3] Cited from Williams, *Radical*, p. 359.

[4] See the challenge to Luther in stanzas 22 and 23 of Hymn 54 of the *Ausbund*, pp. 301-02.

[5] Bullinger, after describing how Thomas Müntzer was captured, how he recanted and was executed, continues by saying: "Note well, you pious believers: here is the true parentage and the first beginning point of the Rebaptizing sect. And Müntzer, the rebel, is its patriarch or the first of its authors who indeed, before his end, confessed his error and misdeeds. Nevertheless his followers and disciples, the Anabaptists, continued in them

hard and fast." Heinrich Bullinger, *Der Widertöufferen Ursprung, Fürgang, Secten, Wäsen, fürnemme und gemeine irer leer Artickel, auch ire Gründ, und warumm sy sich absünderind, etc.* (Zürich: Froschauer, 1561; photoreprint, Leipzig, 1975), p. 3.

[6] John S. Oyer, *Lutheran Reformers Against Anabaptists* (The Hague: Nijhoff, 1964), p. 1.

[7] Parts of this chapter were published previously in Arnold Snyder, "Beyond Polygenesis: Recovering the Unity and Diversity of Anabaptist Theology," in H. Wayne Pipkin, ed., *Essays in Anabaptist Theology* (Elkhart, In.: Institute of Mennonite Studies, 1994), pp. 1-33; used with permission. A few of the better general treatments are: Harold Bender, "The Historiography of the Anabaptists," MQR 31(April, 1957), pp. 88-104; H.-J. Goertz, ed., "Introduction," *Profiles of Radical Reformers*, (Scottdale, Pa.: Herald Press, 1982), pp. 9-25; Klaus Deppermann, *Melchior Hoffman: Social Unrest and Apocalyptic Visions in the Age of the Reformation*, trans. by M. Wren (Edinburgh: T. and T. Clark, 1987), pp. 1-33; James Stayer, *Anabaptists and the Sword* (Lawrence, Kan.: Coronado Press, 1976), pp. 1-23; James Stayer, Werner Packull and Klaus Deppermann, "From Monogenesis to Polygenesis: The Historical Discussion of Anabaptist Origins," MQR 49(1975), pp. 83-122.

[8] Cited in John Horsch, *Mennonites in Europe* (Scottdale, Pa.: Mennonite Publishing House, 1942), p. 293.

[9] "It is expressly stated that the Waldenses, from ancient times were designated by the papists by the name of Anabaptists; doubtless, because they baptized those who had been baptized in their infancy again, or, at least, aright, afterwards, when they had attained to the faith; for these are words of the Waldenses themselves, as has been shown above. . . . It is certainly clearly and plainly said, that the Waldenses were anabaptists, as the ungodly now call the Christian baptists..." Thieleman J. van Braght, *The Bloody Theater or Martyrs' Mirror*, trans. by Joseph F. Sohm (Scottdale, Pa.: Herald Press, 1972), p. 279. Cf. *The Chronicle of the Hutterian Brethren*, Vol. I (Rifton, N.Y.: Plough Publishing House, 1987), p. 33 ff.

[10] See, for example, Leonard Verduin, *The Reformers and Their Stepchildren* (Grand Rapids: Eerdmans, 1964).

[11] Many examples could be cited. One will suffice. "[The Anabaptists] proposed to reach a state of perfection worthy of the early church; the members communicated to each other their visions and prophecies. The spiritual temperature gradually rose, recalling that of certain contemporary sects such as the pentecostists... Here a popular, fervently mystical and anti-social religion was being opposed to that of the reformers. . . . Opposition to the baptism of infants entered rather late into their programme and then doubtless under the influence of Thomas Müntzer." J. Rilliet, *Zwingli, Third Man of the Reformation* (London: Lutterworth Press, 1964), p. 140.

[12] See, for example, Ludwig Keller, *Die Reformation und die älteren Reformparteien* (Leipzig: Hirzel, 1885) and Ernst Müller, *Geschichte der Bernischen Täufer* (Nieuwkoop: B. de Graaf, 1972; original edition, Frauenfeld, 1895), both of whom argue for Waldensian continuity. Albrecht Ritschl, *Geschichte des Pietismus*, I (Bonn, Adolph Marcus, 1880) argues for radical Franciscan origins. Humanist influences are posited by Walther Koehler, "Wiedertäufer," *Die Religion in Geschichte und Gegenwart*, 2nd. ed. (Tübingen, 1931), V, 1918, and Leonhard von Muralt, *Glaube und Lehre der Schweizerischen Wiedertäufer in der Reformationszeit* (Zürich, 1938), pp. 6-7. For a recent appraisal of Ludwig Keller's influence, see Abraham Friesen, *History and Renewal in the Anabaptist/Mennonite Tradition* (North Newton, Kansas: Bethel College, 1994).

[13] "In the so-called religious wars of the Sixteenth Century, very positive material class-interests were at play, and those wars were class wars just as were the later collisions in England and France. If the class struggles of that time appear to bear religious earmarks, if the interests, requirements and demands of the

various classes hid themselves behind a religious screen, it little changes the actual situation, and is to be explained by the conditions of the time." So Friedrich Engels, *The German Revolutions; "The Peasant War in Germany" and "Germany: Revolution and Counter-Revolution"* (Chicago: University of Chicago Press, 1967; original editions 1850 and 1851), p. 34.

[14] "The Anabaptist movement broke out in 1525, in Zurich, in radical Reform circles, to whom Zwingli's application of the principles of Scripture seemed inadequate. The following were its main characteristics: emphasis on Believers' Baptism, a voluntary church, the precepts of the Sermon on the Mount, the rejection of the oath, of war, law, and authority, and, finally, the most far-reaching mutual material help, and the equality of all Church members, the election of elders and preachers by the local congregations, and, to a large extent, the unpaid character of the pastoral office; these principles were in close agreement with the democratic tendencies of the masses." So Ernst Troeltsch, *The Social Teaching of the Christian Churches*, 2 vols., trans. by Olive Wyon (Chicago: University of Chicago Press, 1981; reprint of the 1931 edition, Allen and Unwin), vol. 2, p. 703.

[15] See Karl Holl, "Luther und die Schwärmer," 1922, in *Gesammelte Aufsätze zur Kirchengeschichte*, I, (Tübingen: Mohr, 1948), pp. 420-67. Holl noted, "But even insofar as the sketch is intended only as a working out of the 'Types,' I cannot agree with it. What Troeltsch explains precisely ... is indeed abstractly clearly thought, but it corresponds not at all to reality. There is no Anabaptism which did not support mysticism however simply. Above all the Anabaptists placed the weight on the 'Spirit,' in contrast with mere learning and a literal understanding. . . . When Troeltsch freed the [spiritualists] as a group from the others, by means of the uniform 'Type,' he immediately destroyed what characterized the movement as a whole. And this is that in this movement, seeming opposites stand in a reciprocal relationship: a mysticism raised to a fine spiritualism, (along with) a determined will to renew the world. Thus at one point mysticism appears as the source of power, and at the next moment as the refuge for the disappointed..." p. 424, n. 1.

[16] For a retrospective look at the life and work of Harold Bender, see the entire issue of MQR, 37(April, 1964).

[17] Bender's original address was published in MQR 18(April, 1944), pp. 67-88. For this citation see Harold Bender, "The Anabaptist Vision," in Guy F. Hershberger, ed., *The Recovery of the Anabaptist Vision* (Scottdale, Pa.: Herald Press, 1957), p. 37.

[18] *Ibid.*, pp. 35; 36.

[19] *Ibid.*, p. 42.

[20] Roland Bainton, "The Left Wing of the Reformation," *Journal of Religion*, 21 (1941). See also the Introduction to Heinold Fast, *Der linke Flügel der Reformation* (Bremen: Carl Schünemann Verlag, 1962).

[21] George H. Williams, *The Radical Reformation* (Philadelphia: Westminster Press, 1962), pp. xxiii-xxxi. Williams speaks of the Radical Reformation as a "three-pronged movement ... which, besides Anabaptists of various types, included Spiritualists and spiritualizers of varying tendencies, and the Evangelical Rationalists, largely Italian in origin." *Ibid.*, p. xxiv. A substantially revised edition of Williams' great work was published in Spanish: *La Reforma Radical* (Mexico, D.F.: Fondo de Cultura Economica, 1983). His definition of the Radical Reformation remained unchanged in that edition. In a third edition of that work, Williams retains the classifications but acknowledges that individuals might move from one classification to another. See *The Radical Reformation*, 3rd. ed. (Kirksville, Mo.: Sixteenth Century Journal Publishers, 1992), pp. 10-11; 14 ff.; p. 1280, n. 69, for Williams' further reflections on the typology utilized.

[22] See the "Introduction," in George Williams and Angel Mergal, eds., *Spiritual and Anabaptist Writers* (Philadelphia: Westminster Press, 1957), pp. 19-38.

[23] Speaking of the Swiss and South German movements, Kühler writes "Het Anabaptisme blijft dan in beide gebieden voortbestaan, maar zijn beginselen groeien niet meer uit in nieuwe levensvormen, men gaat zich aan oude tradities vastklemmen, en het overblijfsel wordt meer en meer een eerbiedwaardige antiquiteit. Eerst in Nederland komt, in weerwil van niet minder zware vervolging, de volle ontplooiing; eerst hier toont de doopersche beweging, in een ontwikkelingsgang van eeuwen, welke krachten in haar scholen. Vandaar, dat veel van de geschiedenis in Nederland licht werpt op die daarbuiten." W.J. Kühler, *Geschiedenis der Nederlandsche Doopsgezinden in de zestiende eeuw* (Haarlem: Tjeenk Willink, 1932), p. 6.

[24] *Ibid.*, pp. 3-6.

[25] See James M. Stayer, "Was Dr. Kuehler's Conception of Early Dutch Anabaptism Historically Sound?," MQR 60(July, 1986), pp. 261-88; and Walter Klaassen, "Menno Simons Research, 1937-1986," MQR 60(Oct., 1986), pp. 483-496.

[26] Robert Friedmann, "Anabaptism and Protestantism," MQR, 24(1950), pp. 12-24; *idem., The Theology of Anabaptism* (Scottdale: Herald Press, 1973).

[27] Hans Hillerbrand, "Anabaptism and the Reformation: Another Look," in Stayer and Packull, *The Anabaptists and Thomas Müntzer* (Toronto: Kendall/Hunt, 1980), pp. 46-53.

[28] "The Lutherans and Anabaptists did not regard Christ in person and work in the same manner." John Oyer, *Lutheran Reformers Against Anabaptists* (The Hague: Nijhoff, 1964), p. 215. And again, "On the importance, indeed the absolute necessity, of works in the Christian life the Anabaptists of Central Germany spoke with rare unanimity. They did not always emphasize the same activities as works, but most of them included separation from the world, the sharing of material goods with the brother and suffering for the sake of the gospel. . . . This discipleship, this following of Christ by the new creature, had a distinct relation to salvation, so that one could not say it was unnecessary for salvation. . . . Unanimously (the Anabaptists) held that faith and obedience to the commands of Christ could not be separated in the salvation process." *Ibid.*, p. 221.

[29] "It is time to raise the question again as to whether it is sufficient to say that all they wanted was a little more of what Luther and Zwingli had to offer. It is the thesis of this paper that the matter went deeper than that. It was not simply a question of playing one-upsmanship with the Reformers. The Anabaptists started farther back religiously, economically, and politically. They not only agreed with the necessity for correcting abuses, but they raised questions about the basic assumptions of European religion and culture." Walter Klaassen, "The Nature of the Anabaptist Protest," MQR 45(October, 1971), pp. 293-94.

[30] Friedmann noted that the Reformers "concentrated on the individual and his predicament *qua* sinner." By contrast, "Nothing of this kind belongs to the Anabaptist vision. It is therefore not allowable to interpret Anabaptism as a sort of radicalized Protestantism or even as 'Protestantism plus more emphasis on ethics.'" Friedmann, *Theology*, p. 159.

[31] See Walter Klaassen, "Spiritualization in the Reformation, MQR 37(1963). Friedmann notes that "the first generation of Anabaptists shows ... a reliance on the spiritualistic or semimystical awareness of the presence of the Holy Spirit in the believer which enables him to understand the Scriptures without special learning, and also to interpret them afresh, independently from other teachers." It was only later that this was abandoned "in favor of a stricter biblicism." Friedmann, *Theology*, pp. 19-20.

[32] "Mijn bezwaar is, dat bij hem de feiten zich te veel naar het schema moeten voegen. Om zijn 'Sektentypus' terug te vinden beperkt hij het Anabaptisme willekeurig tot de strenge richting. Mannen als Denck en David Joris behandelt hij afzonderlijk en veel later. Zoo komt hij tot de ongerijmdheid, dat de uitdrukking 'freie Täufer' een 'contradictio in adjecto' is. In Nederland hebben de 16de-eeuwsche Doopsgezinden ander geoordeeld: zoowel bij hen als bij hunne vijanden vinden wij de gewraakte benaming van den oudsten tijd af." Kühler, *Geschiedenis*, p. 15, n. 2. There is, of course, a certain echo here of Karl Holl's earlier critique.

[33] An illustration of the limitations of the typological approach is found in Fast, who in *Der linke Flügel der Reformation* argued that, by definition, there could be no "revolutionary" Spiritualists or Anabaptists. "Spiritualismus kann nicht revolutionär sein. Ihm ist an einer sichtbaren Umwälzung grundsätzlich nicht gelegen. Ähnliches gilt von dem Begriff 'revolutionäres Täufertum'. Gewiß ist die Wiedertaufe von Melchior Hoffman und in Münster geübt worden. Insofern kann man hier von Täufern sprechen. Aber theologisch gesehen haben sie doch mehr gemein mit dem 'revolutionären Spiritualisten' Müntzer als mit den Täufern in Zürich. Sie sollten deshalb nicht mit den genuinen Täufern unter einem Namen zusammengefaßt werden, sondern mit Müntzer." pp. xxx-xxxi.

[34] As noted by Klaus Deppermann, *Melchior Hoffman: Soziale Unruhen und apokalyptische Visionen im Zeitalter der Reformation*, (Göttingen: Vandenhoeck & Ruprecht, 1979), p. 11: "der soziale und politische Kontext, in dem die Ideen ihren Sitz hatten, blieb weitgehend ausserhalb der Betrachtung."

[35] James Stayer, Werner Packull and Klaus Deppermann, "From Monogenesis to Polygenesis: The Historical Discussion of Anabaptist Origins," MQR 49 (April, 1975), p. 84.

[36] *Ibid.*, 83-85, *passim*.

[37] "Leaving aside the three movements which established themselves on the ruins of early South German Anabaptism, we see that the three more or less independent points of departure for Anabaptist history were South German Anabaptism, the Swiss Brethren and the Melchiorites. The Zurich baptisms of 1525 have priority in point of time, but the South German Anabaptism which began in Augsburg in 1526 and the Low German-Dutch Anabaptism which Melchior Hoffman began in Emden in 1530 cannot be regarded as 'derived' from the Swiss Brethren." *Ibid.*, p. 86.

[38] For summaries of the new "polygenesis" historical consensus, see Hans-Jürgen Goertz, *Die Täufer: Geschichte und Deutung* (München: Beck, 1980); J. Denny Weaver, *Becoming Anabaptist* (Scottdale, Pa.: Herald Press, 1987), the first three chapters.

[39] For James Stayer's most recent judgment, see his excellent article on the "Radical Reformation" in the *Handbook of European History, 1400-1600: Late Middle Ages, Renaissance and Reformation*, vol. 2 (Leiden: Brill, forthcoming).

[40] See James Stayer, *The German Peasants' War and Anabaptist Community of Goods* (Montreal and Kingston: McGill-Queens University Press, 1991).

[41] See Werner Packull, *Communitarian Experiments during the Reformation. A Narrative History of Hutterite Beginnings: 1525-1545* (forthcoming, Johns Hopkins University Press).

[42] Walter Klaassen, *Living at the End of the Ages* (Lanham, Md.: University Press of America, 1992).

Select Bibliography

(limited, with few exceptions
to writings cited in the text)

Primary Sources

Ausbund, das ist Etliche schöne Christliche Lieder, wie sie in dem Gefängnis zu Passau in dem Schloss von den Schweizer-Brüdern und von andern rechtglaubigen Christen hin und her gedichtet worden. First edition 1564; second expanded edition 1583. Subsequent editions to the present essentially reproduce the 1583 edition, with some minor additions. I have used an edition published at Elkhart, Indiana: Mennonitischen Verlagshandlung, 1880.

Blesdijk, Nikolaas Meyndertsz van. *Christelijcke Verantwoordinghe, Ende billijcke nederlegginge des valschen onghegrondeden Oordeels / Lasterens ende Scheldens: By Menno Symonsz. in eenen Sendtbrief wtgegeuen...* n.p., 1607.

Blesdijk, Nikolaas Meyndertsz van. *Weder-antwoort Nicolaes Meynaertsz van Bleesdijck op zekeren Brief by Gellium onderteeckent / waer in hy sijne meyninge unde oordeel stelt op eenich Tractaet geintituleert Een Christlijcke verantwoordinghe unde billijcke wederlegginghe etc. Geschreven in't Jaer 1545.* n.p., 1607.

Bünderlin, Hans. *Ein gemeyne berechnung uber der heyligen schrifft innhalt...* Strassburg, 1529.

Bünderlin, Hans. *Erklerung durch vergleichung der Biblischen geschrifft, das der wassertauff sampt andern eüsserlichen gebreüchen...* Strasbourg, 1530.

Bullinger, Heinrich. *Heinrich Bullinger Reformationsgeschichte,* 3 vols. Hottinger, J.J. and Vögeli, H.H., eds. Zürich: Nova-Buchhandlung, 1984; reprint of the 1838 edition.

Bullinger, Heinrich. *Der Widertöufferen Ursprung, Fürgang, Secten, Wäsen, fürnemme und gemeine irer leer Artickel, auch ire Gründ, und warumm sy sich absünderind, etc.* Zürich: Froschauer, 1561; photo reprint, Leipzig, 1975.

Concordantz und Zeiger der namhafftigsten Sprüch aller Biblischen Bücher alts und news Testamentss / auffs kürtzest verfasset und zusamen gebracht. n.p., n.d.[ca. 1550].

Denck, Hans. *Hans Denck: Schriften.* Baring, Georg, and Fellmann, Walter, eds. *Quellen zur Geschichte der Täufer,* Vol. 6. Gütersloh: C. Bertelsmann Verlag, 1959-1960.

Egli, Emil, ed. *Aktensammlung zur Geschichte der Zürcher Reformation.* Zürich, 1879; reprint, Nieuwkoop, 1973.

Fast, Heinold. *Der linke Flügel der Reformation.* Bremen: Carl Schünemann Verlag, 1962.

Fast, Heinold, ed. *Quellen zur Geschichte der Täufer in der Schweiz,* 2. Band, Ostschweiz. Zürich: Theologischer Verlag, 1973.

Franck, Sebastian. *Chronica, Zeitbuch unnd Geschichbibell...* Ulm, 1536; photoreprint edition, Darmstadt: Wissenschaftliche Buchgesellschaft, 1969. [First edition Strasbourg, 1531].

Franz, Günther, ed. *Urkundliche Quellen zur hessischen Reformationsgeschichte.* Marburg: N. G. Elwert'sche Velagsbuchhandlung, 1951.

Friedmann, Robert, ed., *Glaubenszeugnisse oberdeutscher Taufgesinnter,* II. Gütersloh: Gerd Mohn, 1967.

Haas, Martin, ed. *Quellen zur Geschichte der Täufer in der Schweiz*, 3. Band (Aarau, Bern, Solothurn). [Unpublished ms. used with permission of Dr. Martin Haas.]

Haas, Martin, ed. *Quellen zur Geschichte der Täufer in der Schweiz*, 4. Band, Drei Täufergespräche in Bern und im Aargau. Zürich: Theologischer Verlag, 1974.

Hoffman, Melchior. *Das XII Capitel des propheten Daniels aussgelegt...* (Stockholm, 1526).

Hoffman, Melchior. *Die eedele hoghe ende troostlike sendebrief / den die heylige Apostel Paulus to den Romeren gescreuen heeft / verclaert ende gans vlitich mit ernste van woort to woorde wtgelecht Tot eener costeliker nutticheyt ende troost allen godtvruchtigen liefhebbers der eewighen onentliken waerheyt.* 1533.

Hoffman, Melchior. *Ein rechte warhafftige hohe und gotliche gruntliche underrichtung von der reiner forchte Gottes ann alle liebhaber der ewiger unentlicher warheit...* (1533).

Hoffman, Melchior. *Warhafftige erklerung aus heyliger Biblischer schrifft / das der Satan / Todt / Hell / Sünd / und dy ewige verdamnuß im ursprung nit auß gott / sundern alleyn auß eygenem will erwachsen sei.* Straßburg: Jakob Cammerlander, 1531.

Hoffman, Melchior. *Weissagung usz heiliger götlicher geschrifft. Von den trubsalen diser letsten zeit. Von der schweren hand und straff gottes über alles gottloß wesen. Von der zukunfft des Türckischen Thirannen / und seines gantzen anhangs. Wie er sein reiß thun / unnd volbringen wirt / uns zu einer straff / unnd rutten. Wie er durch Gottes gwalt sein niderlegung unnd straff entpfahen wirt.* (1529/1530).

Joris, David. *Christlijcke Sendtbrieven...,* 3 volumes. (n.p., n.d.).

[Jost, Ursula] Hoffman, Melchior. *Prophetische Gesicht und Offenbarung der goetlichen würckung zu dieser letsten zeit / die vom XXIIII Jahr biß in dz XXX einer gottes liebhaberin durch den heiligen geist geoffenbart seind / welcher hie in diesem büchlin LXXVII verzeichnet seindt.* (1530).

Krebs, Manfred, ed. *Quellen zur Geschichte der Täufer: Baden und Pfalz.* Gütersloh: Bertelsmann Verlag, 1951.

Krebs, Manfred and Rott, Hans Georg, eds. *Quellen zur Geschichte der Täufer, VII. Band, Elsaß, I. Teil: Stadt Straßburg 1522-1532.* Gütersloh: Gerd Mohn, 1959.

Krebs, Manfred and Rott, Hans Georg, eds. *Quellen zur Geschichte der Täufer, VIII. Band, Elsaß, II. Teil: Stadt Straßburg 1533-1535.* Gütersloh: Gerd Mohn, 1960.

Ein kurtze einfaltige erkanntnuß uff die dryzehen artickell so verlouffens 1572 (sic) Jars zu Franckenthal in der Pfaltz disputiert worden... Manuscript in the Berner Bürgerbibliothek; Microfilm copy in the Mennonite Historical Library, #203; transcribed by the author.

Loserth, Johann. *Quellen und Forschungen zur Geschichte der oberdeutschen Taufgesinnten im 16. Jahrhundert.* Wien: Fromme, 1929.

Mecenseffy, Grete, ed. *Quellen zur Geschichte der Täufer,* vol. 11. *Österreich, I. Teil.* Gütersloh: Gerd Mohn, 1964.

Mecenseffy, Grete, ed. *Quellen zur Geschichte der Täufer,* vol. 13. *Österreich, II. Teil.* Gütersloh: Gerd Mohn, 1972.

Müller, Lydia, ed. *Glaubenszeugnisse oberdeutscher Taufgesinnter,* I. Leipzig: Nachfolger, 1938; New York: Johnson Reprint, 1971.

von Muralt, Leonard and Schmid, Walter, eds. *Quellen zur Geschichte der Täufer in der Schweiz,* 1. Band, Zürich. Zürich: Theologischer Verlag, 1952.

Neumann, Gerhard. "A Newly Discovered Manuscript of Melchior Rinck," MQR 25(July, 1961), pp. 197-

217.

Protocoll, Das ist Alle handlung des gesprechs zu Franckenthal inn der Churfürstlichen Pfaltz / mit denen so man Widertäuffer nennet / Auff den 28. May angefangen / und den 19. Junii dises 1571 jars geendet Heidelberg: Johann Mayer, 1571.

Simons, Menno. *Dat Fundament des Christelycken Leers*. Meihuizen, H.W., ed. The Hague: Nijhoff, 1967.

Schornbaum, Karl. *Markgraftum Brandenburg: Bayern*, Part 1. *Quellen zur Geschichte der Wiedertäufer*, II. Band. Leipzig: Nachfolger, 1934.

Stupperich, Robert, ed. *Die Schriften Bernhard Rothmanns*, I. Münster: Aschendorff, 1970.

Wappler, Paul, ed. *Die Täuferbewegung in Thüringen von 1526-1584*. Jena: Fischer, 1913.

Weisse, Michael. *Gesangbuch der Böhmischen Brüder*. n.p., 1531; facsimile edition: Kassel: Bärenreiter, 1957.

Westin, Gunnar and Bergsten, Torsten, eds. *Balthasar Hubmaier Schriften*. Gütersloh: Gerd Mohn, 1962.

Primary Sources in Translation

Bauman, Clarence, trans. and ed. *The Spiritual Legacy of Hans Denck*. Leiden: E.J. Brill, 1991.

Bender, Harold S. "The Discipline Adopted by the Strasburg Conference of 1568," MQR 1(January, 1927).

van Braght, Thieleman J. *The Bloody Theater or Martyrs Mirror*, trans. by Joseph F. Sohm. Scottdale, Pa.: Herald Press, 1972.

Correll, Ernst and Bender, Harold. "Conrad Grebel's (sic) Petition of Protest and Defense to the Zurich Council in 1523," in *Goshen College Record Review and Supplement*. (Jan., 1926), pp. 23-26.

The Chronicle of the Hutterian Brethren, Vol. I. Rifton, N.Y.: Plough Publishing House, 1987.

Dyck, Cornelius; Keeney, William; and Beachy, Alvin, eds. and trans. *The Writings of Dirk Philips*. Scottdale, Pa.: Herald Press, 1992.

Foster, Claude R., Jr. and Jerosch, Wilhelm, trans. and eds. (Hans Bünderlin) "The Reason Why God Descended...", MQR 42(October, 1968), pp. 260-284.

Furcha, Edward J., ed. and trans. *Selected Writings of Hans Denck*. Pittsburgh: Pickwick Press, 1975.

Furcha, Edward J., ed. and trans. *The Essential Carlstadt*. Scottdale, Pa.: Herald Press, 1995.

Gross, Leonard. "The First Mennonite Merger: The Concept of Cologne," in *Mennonite Yearbook*, 1990-1991, pp. 8-10.

Harder, Leland. *The Sources of Swiss Anabaptism*. Scottdale, Pa.: Herald Press, 1985.

Hostetler, John, Gross, Leonard, and Bender, Elizabeth, eds. and trans. *Selected Hutterian Documents in Translation, 1542-1654*. Philadelphia: Communal Studies Center, Temple University, 1975.

Klaassen, Walter. *Anabaptism in Outline*. Scottdale, Pa.: Herald Press, 1981.

Klassen, William and Klaassen, Walter, trans. and eds. *The Writings of Pilgram Marpeck*. Scottdale, Pa.: Herald Press, 1978.

Matheson, Peter. *The Collected Works of Thomas Müntzer*. Edinburgh: T & T Clark, 1988.

Oyer, John. "The Pfeddersheim Disputation, 1557," MQR 60(July, 1986), pp. 304-351.

Pipkin, H. Wayne and Yoder, John H., trans. and eds. *Balthasar Hubmaier, Theologian of Anabaptism*. Scottdale, Pa.: Herald Press, 1989.

Riedemann, Peter. *Account of Our Religion, Doctrine and Faith*. Rifton, N.Y.: Plough Publishing House, 1974.

Roth, John D., trans. and ed. *Letters of the Amish Division: A Sourcebook*. Goshen, In.: Mennonite Historical Society, 1993.

Scott, Tom and Scribner, Bob, eds. and trans. *The German Peasants' War: A History in Documents*. London: Humanities Press, 1991.

Verduin, Leonard, trans. *The Complete Writings of Menno Simons*. Scottdale, Pa.: Herald Press, 1956.

Waite, Gary, trans. and ed. *The Anabaptist Writings of David Joris, 1535-1543*. Scottdale, Pa.: Herald Press, 1994.

Williams, George H. and Mergal, Angel, eds. *Spiritual and Anabaptist Writers*. Philadelphia: Westminster Press, 1957.

Yoder, John H., trans. and ed. *The Legacy of Michael Sattler*. Scottdale, Pa.: Herald Press, 1973.

Zwingli, Huldrych. *Huldrych Zwingli Writings*, 2 vols. Volume 1, *The Defense of the Reformed Faith*, trans. by Furcha, E.J.; Volume 2, *In Search of True Religion: Reformation, Pastoral and Eucharistic Writings*, trans. by Pipkin, H. Wayne. Allison Park, Pa.: Pickwick Publications, 1984.

Secondary Sources: Books and Articles

Armour, Rollin Stely. *Anabaptist Baptism*. Scottdale, Pa.: Herald Press, 1966.

Bainton, Roland. "The Left Wing of the Reformation," *Journal of Religion*, 21(1941).

Bainton, Roland. *Women of the Reformation in Germany and Italy*. Mineapolis: Augsburg, 1971.

Barrett, Lois. "Women's History/Women's Theology: Theological and Methodological Issues in the Writing of the History of Anabaptist-Mennonite Women," *The Conrad Grebel Review* 10(Winter, 1992), pp. 1-16.

Barrett, Lois. "Wreath of glory: Ursula's prophetic visions in the context of Reformation and revolt in southwestern Germany, 1524-1530." Unpublished Ph.D. dissertation, The Union Institute, 1992.

Bauman, Clarence. *Gewaltlosigkeit im Täufertum*. Leiden: Brill, 1968.

Bender, Harold. "The Anabaptist Vision," MQR 18(April, 1944), pp. 67-88; also in Hershberger, Guy F., ed. *The Recovery of the Anabaptist Vision*. Scottdale, Pa.: Herald Press, 1957.

Bender, Harold. "The Discipline Adopted by the Strasbourg Conference of 1568," MQR 1(January, 1927).

Bender, Harold. "The Historiography of the Anabaptists," MQR 31(April, 1957), pp. 88-104.

Bergmann, Cornelius. *Die Täuferbewegung im Kanton Zürich bis 1660*. Leipzig: H. Nachfolger, 1916.

Bergsten, Torsten. *Balthasar Hubmaier: Anabaptist Theologian and Martyr*, trans. by Estep, Jr., W.R. Valley Forge, Pa.: Judson Press, 1978.

Blanke, Fritz. *Brothers in Christ*, trans. by Nordenhang, J. Scottdale, Pa.: Herald Press, 1961.

Blough, Neal. *Christologie Anabaptiste: Pilgram Marpeck et l'humanité de Christ*. Geneva: Labor et Fides, 1984.

Blough, Neal. "Pilgram Marpeck and Caspar Schwenckfeld: The Strasbourg Years," in Rott, Jean, and

Verheus, S., eds. *Anabaptistes et dissidents au XVIe siecle*. Baden-Baden: Koerner, 1987.

Blough, Neal. "Pilgram Marpeck et les Frères Suisses vers 1540," *in "... Lebenn nach der ler Jhesu ... Das sind aber wir!": Berner Täufer und Prädikanten in Gespräch, 1538-1988*. Bern, 1989, pp. 147-164.

Blough, Neal. "Pilgram Marpeck, Martin Luther and the Humanity of Christ," MQR 61(1987), pp. 203-212.

Bornhäuser, Christoph. *Leben und Lehre Menno Simons'*. Neukirchen-Vluyn: Neukirchener Verlag, 1973.

Boyd, Stephen. "Anabaptism and Social Radicalism in Strasbourg, 1528-1532: Pilgram Marpeck on Christian Social Responsibility," MQR 63(Jan., 1989), pp. 58-76.

Boyd, Stephen B. *Pilgram Marpeck: His Life and Social Theology*. Durham, N.C.: Duke University Press, 1992.

Brady, Thomas A. *Ruling Class, Regime and Reformation at Strasbourg*. Leiden: E. Brill, 1978.

Brecht, Martin. "Die Theologie Bernhard Rothmanns," *Jahrbuch für Westfälische Kirchengeschichte* 78 (1985), pp. 49-82.

Chrisman, Miriam U. *Strasbourg and the Reform*. New Haven, Conn.: Yale University Press, 1967.

Clasen, Claus-Peter. *Anabaptism: A Social History, 1525-1618*. Ithaca: Cornell University Press, 1972.

Coggins, James R. "A Short Confession of Hans de Ries: Union and Separation in Early Seventeenth Century Holland," MQR 60(April, 1986), pp. 128-138.

Cressy, David. *Literacy and the Social Order; Reading and Writing in Tudor and Stuart England*. Cambridge: Cambridge University Press, 1980.

Davis, Kenneth. *Anabaptism and Asceticism*. Scottdale, Pa.: Herald Press, 1974.

De Bakker, Willem J. "Bernhard Rothmann: Civic Reformer in Anabaptist Muenster," in Horst, Irvin B., ed. *The Dutch Dissenters: A Critical Companion to their History and Ideas*. Leiden: E.J. Brill, 1986, pp. 105-16.

De Bakker, Willem J. "Bernhard Rothmann: The Dialectics of Radicalization in Münster," in Goertz, Hans-Jürgen, ed. *Profiles of Radical Reformers*. Scottdale, Pa.: Herald Press, 1982, pp. 191-202.

De Hoop Scheffer, J.G. "Eenige opmerkingen en mededeelingen betreffende Menno Simons," *Doopsgezinde Bijdragen* (1894).

Deppermann, Klaus. *Melchior Hoffman: Soziale Unruhen und apokalyptische Visionen im Zeitalter der Reformation*. Göttingen: Vandenhoeck & Ruprecht, 1979.

Dethlefs, Gerd. "Das Wiedertäuferreich in Münster 1534/35," in Galen, Hans, ed. *Die Wiedertäufer in Münster*. Münster: Aschendorff, 1986.

Dietrich, Christian. *Die Stadt Zürich und ihre Landgemeinden Wahrend der Bauernunruhen von 1489 bis 1525*. Frankfurt; Bern; New York, 1985.

Duerksen, Rosella Reimer. "Anabaptist Hymnody of the Sixteenth Century." Unpublished Doc. Music dissertation, Union Theological Seminary, 1956.

Dyck, Cornelius J., ed. *An Introduction to Mennonite History*, 3rd. edition. Scottdale, Pa.: Herald Press, 1993.

Dyck, Cornelius J. "The First Waterlandian Confession of Faith," MQR 36 (Jan., 1962), pp. 5-13.

Dyck, Cornelius J. "The Middelburg Confession of Hans de Ries, 1578," MQR 36(Apr., 1962), pp. 147-161.

Dyck, Cornelius J. "A Short Confession of Faith by Hans de Ries," MQR 38(Jan., 1964), pp. 5-19.

Eisenstein, Elizabeth L. *The Printing Press as an Agent of Change*, 2 vols. Cambridge, 1979.

Erb, Betti. "Reading the Source: Menno Simons on Women, Marriage, Children, and Family," CGR 8(Fall, 1990), pp. 301-319.

Erb, Peter C. "Anabaptist Spirituality," in Senn, Frank C., ed. *Protestant Spiritual Traditions*. Mahwah, N.J.: Paulist Press, 1986.

Erb, Peter C. *Schwenckfeld and Early Schwenckfelders*. Pennsburg, Pa.: Schwenckfelder Library, 1986.

Erb, Peter C. *Schwenckfeld and Early Schwenkfeldianism: Papers Presented at the Colloquium on Schwenckfeld and the Schwenkfelders*. Pennsburg, Pa.: Schwenkfelder Library, 1986.

Fast, Heinold. "Die Eidesverweigerung bei den Mennoniten," MGB, N.F. 17 (1965), pp. 18-32.

Fast, Heinold. "Hans Krüsis Büchlein über Glauben und Taufe," in Dyck, Cornelius J., ed. *A Legacy of Faith*. Newton, Kan.: Faith and Life Press, 1962, pp. 197-231.

Fast, Heinold. "Michael Sattler's Baptism: Some Comments," MQR 60(July, 1986), pp. 364-373.

Fast, Heinold. "Die Täuferbewegung im Lichte des Frankenthaler Gespräches, 1571," *Mennonitische Geschichtsblätter*, N.F. 23 (1971), pp. 7-23.

Foster, Claude R., Jr. "Hans Denck and Johannes Buenderlin: A Comparative Study," MQR 39(April, 1965), pp. 115-124.

Friedmann, Robert. "Anabaptism and Protestantism," MQR, 24(1950), pp. 12-24.

Friedmann, Robert. "Economic Aspects of Early Hutterite Life," MQR 30(October, 1956), pp. 259-266.

Friedmann, Robert. *The Theology of Anabaptism*. Scottdale: Herald Press, 1973.

Friesen, Abraham. *Thomas Muentzer, a Destroyer of the Godless*. Berkley and Los Angeles: University of California Press, 1990.

Gäbler, Ulrich. *Huldrych Zwingli: His Life and Work*, trans. by Gritsch, Ruth C. L. Philadelphia, 1986.

Geiser, Samuel. *Die Taufgesinnten Gemeinden*, 2. Auflage. Jura, 1971.

Geldbach, Erich. "Toward a more ample biography of the Hessian Anabaptist leader Melchior Rinck," MQR 48(July, 1974), pp. 371-72.

Gerber, Barbara Bettina Gerber. "Sebastian Lotzer: An Educated Layman in the Struggle for Divine Justice," in Goertz, Hans-Jürgen, ed. *Profiles of Radical Reformers*. Scottdale, Pa.: Herald Press, 1982, pp. 72-87.

Gingerich, Barbara N. "Property and the Gospel: Two Reformation Perspectives," MQR 59(July, 1985), pp. 248-67.

Ginzburg, Carlo. *The Cheese and the Worms: The Cosmos of a Sixteenth-Century Miller*, trans. by John and Anne Tedeschi. Baltimore: The Johns Hopkins University Press, 1980.

Goertz, Hans-Jürgen. "Der Fremde Menno Simons; Antiklerikale Argumetation im Werk eines mechioritischen Täufers," in Horst, Irvin B., ed. *The Dutch Dissenters: A Critical Companion to their History and Ideas*. Leiden: E.J. Brill, 1986.

Goertz, Hans-Jürgen, ed. *Profiles of Radical Reformers*. Scottdale, Pa.: Herald Press, 1982.

Goertz, Hans-Jürgen. *Die Täufer: Geschichte und Deutung*. München: Beck, 1980.

Goertz, Hans-Jürgen. *Pfaffenhass und gross Geschrei: Die reformatorischen Bewegungen in Deutschland, 1517-1529*. München: C. H. Beck, 1987.

Goertz, Hans-Jürgen. "Thomas Müntzer: Revolutionary in a Mystical Spirit," in Goertz, Hans-Jürgen.

Profiles of Radical Reformers. Scottdale, Pa.: Herald Press, 1982, pp. 29-44.

Gordon, Bruce. *Clerical Discipline and the Rural Reformation. The Synod in Zürich, 1532-1580*. Bern, Frankfurt, New York: Peter Lang, 1992.

Graff. Harvey J. *The Legacies of Literacy*. Bloomington, Indiana: Indiana University Press, 1987.

Graham, William. *Beyond the Written Word: Oral Aspects of Scripture in the History of Religion*. Cambridge: Cambridge University Press, 1987.

Gross, Leonard. *The Golden Years of the Hutterites*. Scottdale, Pa.: Herald Press, 1980.

Guderian, Hans. *Die Täufer in Augsburg*. Pfaffenhofen: Ludwig Verlag, 1984.

Haas, Martin. *Huldrich Zwingli und seine Zeit*. Zürich, 1982.

Hecht, Linda Huebert. "An Extraordinary Lay Leader: the Life and Work of Helene of Freyberg, Sixteenth Century Noblewoman from the Tirol," MQR 66(July, 1992), pp. 312-341.

Hecht, Linda Huebert. "Faith and Action: The Role of Women in the Anabaptist Movement of the Tirol, 1527-1529." Unpublished cognate essay, Master of Arts, History, University of Waterloo, 1990.

Hecht, Linda Huebert. "Women and religious change: The significance of Anabaptist women in the Tirol, 1527-29," *Studies in Religion* 21(1992), pp. 57-66.

Herschberger, Guy F. *War, Peace, and Nonresistance*. Scottdale, Pa.: Herald Press, 1946.

Hillerbrand, Hans J., ed. *Radical Tendencies in the Reformation: Divergent Perspectives*. Kirksville, Mo.: Sixteenth Century Journal Publishers, 1988.

Horsch, John. *The Hutterian Brethren, 1528-1931*. Cayley, Alberta: Macmillan Colony, 1985.

Horsch, John. *The Principle of Nonresistance as held by the Mennonite Church,*. Scottdale, Pa.: Mennonite Publishing House, 1927.

Horst, Irvin B. "Menno Simons: The Road to a Voluntary Church," in Horst, Irvin B., ed. *The Dutch Dissenters: A Critical Companion to their History and Ideas*. Leiden: E.J. Brill, 1986, pp. 194-203.

Hui, Matthias. "Von Bauernaufstand zur Täuferbewegung," *Mennonitische Geschichtsblätter*, 46(1989), pp. 113-144.

Hulshof, Abraham. *Geschiedenis van de Doopsgezinden te Straatsburg van 1525-1527*. Amsterdam: J. Clausen, 1905.

Irwin, Joyce L. *Womanhood in Radical Protestantism, 1525-1675*. New York: Edwin Mellen, 1979.

Jelsma, A. "De positie van de vrouw in de Radicale Reformatie," *Doopsgezinde Bijdragen*, nieuwe reeks 15(1989), pp. 25-36.

Keeney, William E. *The Development of Dutch Anabaptist Thought and Practice From 1539-1564*. Nieuwkoop: B. De Graaf, 1968.

Kirchhoff, Karl-Heinz. "Gab es eine friedliche Täufergemeinde in Münster 1534?" *Jahrbuch des Vereins für Westfälische Kirchengeschichte* 55/56 (1962/63), pp. 7-21; English translation in MQR 44(October, 1970), pp. 357-70.

Klaassen, Walter. *Anabaptism: Neither Catholic nor Protestant*. Waterloo, Ont.: Conrad Press, 1973.

Klaassen, Walter, "Church Discipline and the Spirit in Pilgram Marpeck," in Horst, I. B., de Jong, A. F., and Visser, D., eds. *De Geest in het geding*. Alphen an den Rijn: Tjeenk Willink, 1978, pp. 169-180.

Klaassen, Walter. "Eschatalogical Themes in Early Dutch Anabaptism," in Horst, I.B., ed. *The Dutch*

Dissenters. Leiden: E.J. Brill, 1986.

Klaassen, Walter. *Living at the End of the Ages*. Lanham, Md.: University Press of America, 1992.

Klaassen, Walter. "Menno Simons Research, 1937-1986," MQR 60(Oct., 1986), pp. 483-496.

Klaassen, Walter. *Michael Gaismair: Revolutionary and Reformer*. Leiden: Brill, 1978.

Klaassen, Walter. "Michael Gaismair," in Goertz, H.-J., ed. *Profiles of Radical Reformers*. Scottdale, Pa.: Herald Press, 1982, pp. 88-96.

Klaassen, Walter. "The Nature of the Anabaptist Protest," MQR 45(October, 1971), pp. 291-311.

Klaassen, Walter. "Spiritualization in the Reformation, MQR 37(1963), pp. 67-77.

Klassen, Peter J. *The Economics of Anabaptism*. The Hague: Mouton, 1964.

Klassen, William. "The Limits of Political Authority as seen by Pilgram Marpeck," MQR 56(October, 1982), pp. 342-364.

Klassen, William. "Pilgram Marpeck: Liberty without Coercion," in Goertz, Hans-Jürgen, ed. *Profiles of Radical Reformers*. Scottdale, Pa.: Herald Press, 1982, pp. 169-170.

Kobelt-Groch, Marion. *Aufsässige Töchter Gottes: Frauen im 'Bauernkrieg' und in den Bewegungen der Täufer*. Frankfurt and New York: Campus Verlag, 1993.

Kobelt-Groch, Marion. "Why did Petronella Leave Her Husband? Reflections on Marital Avoidance Among the Halberstadt Anabaptists," MQR 62(January, 1988), pp. 26-41.

Krahn, Cornelius. *Dutch Anabaptism: Origin, Spread, Life and Thought*. The Hague: Nijhoff, 1968.

Krahn, Cornelius. *Menno Simons*. Karlsruhe: Schneider, 1936.

Krehbiel, Henry P. *War, Peace, and Amity*. Newton, Kan.: Published by the author, 1937.

Kühler, W.J. *Geschiedenis der Nederlandsche Doopsgezinden in de zestiende eeuw*. Haarlem: Tjeenk Willink, 1932.

Laube, Adolf. "Radicalism as a Research Problem in the History of Early Reformation," in Hillerbrand, Hans J., ed. *Radical Tendencies in the Reformation: Divergent Perspectives*. Kirksville, Mo.: Sixteenth Century Journal Publishers, 1988, pp. 9-23.

Liechty, Daniel. *Andreas Fisher and the Sabbatarian Anabaptists*. Scottdale, Pa.: Herald Press, 1988.

Lieseberg, Ursula. *Studien zum Märtyrerlied der Täufer im 16. Jahrhundert*. Frankfurt: Peter Lang, 1991.

Locher, Gottfried. "Felix Manz' Abschiedsworte an seine Mitbrüder vor der Hinrichtung 1527: Spiritualität und Theologie. Die Echtheit des Liedes 'Bey Christo will ich bleiben'," *Zwingliana* XVII (1986), pp. 11-24.

Locher, Gottfried. *Zwingli's Thought: New Perspectives*. Leiden: Brill, 1981.

Loewen, Howard John. *One Lord, One Church, One Hope, and One God: Mennonite Confessions of Faith*. Elkhart, IN: Institute of Mennonite Studies, 1985.

Maier, Paul L. *Caspar Schwenckfeld on the Person and Work of Christ*. Assen: VanGorcum, 1959.

Martens, Helen. "Hutterite Songs: The Origins and Aural Transmission of their Melodies from the Sixteenth Century." Unpublished Ph.D. dissertation, Columbia University, 1969.

Martin, Dennis. "Catholic Spirituality and Anabaptist and Mennonite Discipleship," MQR 62(January, 1988), pp. 5-25.

Martin, Dennis. "Monks, Mendicants, and Anabaptists: Michael Sattler and the Benedictines Reconsidered," MQR 60(April, 1986), pp. 139-164.

McLaughlin, Emmet R. *Caspar Schwenckfeld, Reluctant Radical: His Life to 1540*. New Haven: Yale University Press, 1986.

Mellink, A. F. *De Wederdopers in de Noordelijke Nederlanden, 1531-1544*. Groningen: Wolters, 1954.

Menache, Sophia, *The vox Dei: communication in the Middle Ages*. New York: Oxford U. Press, 1990.

Meyer, Christian. "Zur Geschichte der Wiedertäufer in Oberschwaben" Part I: "Die Anfänge des Wiedertäufertums in Augsburg," *Zeitschrift des historischen Vereins für Schwaben und Neuburg*, I(1874), pp. 227-28.

Müller, Ernst. *Geschichte der Bernischen Täufer*. Nieuwkoop: B. de Graaf, 1972; original edition, Frauenfeld, 1895.

Müsing, Hans-Werner. "Karlstadt und die Entstehung der Strassburger Täufergemeinde," in Lienhard, Marc, ed. *The Origins and Characteristics of Anabaptism*. The Hague, 1977, pp. 169-195.

Müsing, Hans-Werner. "The Anabaptist Movement in Strasbourg from Early 1526 to July 1527," MQR (April, 1977), 91-126.

Mullett, Michael. *The Counter-Reformation*. New York: Methuen, 1984.

Nelson, Benjamin. *The Idea of Usury*, 2nd. ed. Chicago: University of Chicago Press, 1969.

Nelson, Stephen F. and Rott, Jean. "Strasbourg: The Anabaptist City in the Sixteenth Century," MQR (July, 1984), pp. 230-240.

Oosterbaan, J. A. "De broederlijke Vereniging, een voorlopig consolidatiepunt der broederschap." Meihuizen, H. W., Oosterbaan, J. A., and Kossen, H. B. *Broederlijke Vereniging*. Amsterdam: Doopsgezinde Historische Kring, 1974.

Oyer, John S. "Bucer and the Anabaptists," in Krieger, Christian and Lienhard, Marc. *Martin Bucer and Sixteenth Century Europe*. Leiden: Brill, 1993. Vol. 2, pp. 603-613.

Oyer, John S. *Lutheran Reformers Against Anabaptists*. The Hague: Nijhoff, 1964.

Oyer, John S. "The Strasbourg Conferences of the Anabaptists, 1554-1607," MQR (July, 1984), pp. 218-29.

Ozment, Steven E. "Sebastian Franck: Critic of the 'New Scholastics'," in Goertz, Hans-Jürgen, ed. *Profiles of Radical Reformers*. Scottdale, Pa.: Herald Press, 1982, pp. 226-233.

Packull, Werner. *Communitarian Experiments during the Reformation. A Narrative History of Hutterite Beginnings: 1525-1545*. (forthcoming, Johns Hopkins University Press).

Packull, Werner. "Denck's Alleged Baptism by Hubmaier. Its Significance for the Origin of South German-Austrian Anabaptism," MQR 47(October, 1973), pp. 327-38.

Packull, Werner. "Hans Denck: Fugitive from Dogmatism," in Goertz, Hans-Jürgen, ed. *Profiles of Radical Reformers*. Scottdale, Pa.: Herald Press, 1982, pp. 62-71

Packull, Werner. "The Melchiorites and the Ziegenhain Order of Discipline, 1538-39," in Klaassen, Walter, ed. *Anabaptism Revisited*. Scottdale, Pa.: Herald Press, 1992, pp. 11-28.

Packull, Werner. *Mysticism and the Early South German-Austrian Anabaptist Movement, 1525-1531*. Scottdale, Pa.: Herald Press, 1977.

Packull, Werner. "The Origins of Swiss Anabaptism in the Context of the Reformation of the Common Man," *Journal of Mennonite Studies* 3(1985), pp. 36-59.

Pater, Calvin. *Karlstadt as the Father of the Baptist Movements: The Emergence of Lay Protestantism.* Toronto: Univ. of Toronto Press, 1984.

Peachey, Paul. *Die soziale Herkunft der Schweizer Täufer in der Reformationszeit.* Karlsruhe: Schneider, 1954.

Plenert, Wayne. "The Martyrs Mirror and Anabaptist Women," *Mennonite Life* 30(June, 1975), pp. 13-18.

Poettcker, Henry. "Menno Simons' View of the Bible as Authority," in Dyck, C.J., ed. *A Legacy of Faith.* Newton, Kan.: Faith and Life Press, 1962.

Potter, George R. *Zwingli.* Cambridge, 1976.

Pries, Edmund. "Oath Refusal in Zurich from 1525 to 1527: The Erratic Emergence of Anabaptist Practice," in Klaassen, Walter, ed. *Anabaptism Revisited.* Scottdale, Pa.: Herald Press, 1992, pp. 65-84.

Rempel, John. *The Lord's Supper in Anabaptism.* Scottdale, Pa.: Herald Press, 1993.

Robinson-Hammerstein, Helge, ed. *The Transmission of Ideas in the Lutheran Reformation.* Dublin: Irish Academic Press, 1989.

Roper, Lyndal. "Sexual Utopianism in the German Reformation," *Journal of Ecclesiastical History* 42(July, 1991), pp. 394-418.

Rössing-Hager, Monika. "Wie stark findet der nicht-lesekundige Rezipient Berücksichtigung in den Flugschriften?" in Scribner, Robert and Köhler, Hans-Joachim, eds. *Flugschriften als Massenmedium der Reformationszeit.* Stuttgart: Ernst Klett Verlag, 1981, pp. 77-137.

Rupp, Gordon. *Patterns of Reformation.* London: Epworth Press, 1969.

Russell, Paul A. *Lay Theology in the Reformation.* Cambridge, 1986.

Sawatsky, Rodney J., Holland, Scott, eds. *The Limits of Perfection: A Conversation with J. Lawrence Burkholder.* Waterloo, Ont.: Institute of Anabaptist-Mennonite Studies, 1993.

Schaeufele, Wolfgang. "The Missionary Vision and Activity of the Anabaptist Laity," MQR 36(April, 1962).

Scribner, Robert. *The German Reformation.* Atlantic Highlands, N.J.: Humanities Press, 1986.

Scribner, Robert. *For the Sake of the Simple Folk.* Cambridge: Cambridge University Press, 1981.

Scribner, Robert. "Oral Culture and the Diffusion of Reformation Ideas," in Scribner, Robert. *Popular Culture and Popular Movements in Reformation Germany.* London: Hambledon Press, 1987.

Scribner, Robert and Kohler, Hans-Joachim, eds. *Flugschriften als Massenmedium der Reformationszeit.* Stuttgart: Ernst Klett Verlag, 1981.

Schmid, Hans-Dieter. "Das Hutsche Täufertum. Ein Beitrag zur Charakterisierung einer täuferischen Richtung aus der Frühzeit der Täuferbewegung," *Historische Jahrbuch,* XCI(1971), pp. 327-44.

Schultz, Selina G. *Caspar Schwenckfeld von Ossig (1489-1561)....* Norristown, Pa.: The Board of Publication of the Schwenckfelder Church, 1946.

Seebass, Gottfried. "Caspar Schwenckfeld's Understanding of the Old Testament," in Erb, Peter C. *Schwenckfeld and Early Schwenkfeldianism: Papers Presented at the Colloquium on Schwenckfeld and the*

Schwenkfelders. Pennsburg, Pa.: Schwenkfelder Library, 1986.

Seebass, Gottfried. "Hans Hut: The Suffering Avenger" in Goertz, Hans-Jürgen, ed. *Profiles of Radical Reformers*. Scottdale, Pa.: Herald Press, 1982, pp. 54-61.

Seebaß, Gottfried. "Müntzers Erbe: Werk, Leben un Theologie des Hans Hut (1527)." Habilitationsschrift der Theologischen Fakultät der Friedrich-Alexander Universität zu Erlangen-Nürnberg (1972).

Seibt, Ferdinand. "Johannes Hergot: The Reformation of the Poor Man," in Goertz, Hans-Jürgen, ed. *Profiles of Radical Reformers*. Scottdale, Pa.: Herald Press, 1982, pp. 97-106.

Shantz, Douglas H. "The Ecclesiological Focus of Dirk Philips' Hermeneutical Thought in 1559: A Contextual Study," MQR 60(April, 1986), pp. 115-127.

Sider, Ronald J. *Andreas Bodenstein von Karlstadt: The Development of His Thought, 1517-1525*. Leiden: Brill, 1974.

Sider, Ronald J. "Andreas Bodenstein von Karlstadt: Between Liberal and Radical," in Goertz, Hans-Jürgen, ed. *Profiles of Radical Reformers*. Scottdale, Pa.: Herald Press, 1982, pp. 45-53.

Snyder, Arnold. "An Anabaptist Vision for Peace: Spirituality and Peace in Pilgram Marpeck," *The Conrad Grebel Review* (Spring, 1992), pp. 187-203.

Snyder, Arnold. "Beyond Polygenesis: Recovering the Unity and Diversity of Anabaptist Theology," in H. Wayne Pipkin, ed., *Essays in Anabaptist Theology*. Elkhart, Ind.: Institute of Mennonite Studies, 1994, pp. 1-33.

Snyder, Arnold. "Biblical Text and Social Context: Anabaptist Anticlericalism in Reformation Zürich," MQR 65(April, 1991), pp. 169-191.

Snyder, Arnold. "Communication and the People: The Case of Reformation St. Gall," MQR 67(April, 1993), pp. 152-173.

Snyder, Arnold. "The Confession of the Swiss Brethren in Hesse, 1578," in Klaassen, Walter, ed. *Anabaptism Revisited*. Scottdale, Pa.: Herald Press, 1992, pp. 29-49.

Snyder, Arnold. "The Influence of the Schleitheim Articles on the Anabaptist Movement: An Historical Evaluation," *Mennonite Quarterly Review*, 63(October, 1989), pp. 323-344.

Snyder, Arnold. "Konrad Winckler: An Early Swiss Anabaptist Missionary, Pastor and Martyr," MQR 64(Oct., 1990), pp. 352-361.

Snyder, Arnold. *The Life and Thought of Michael Sattler*. Scottdale, Pa.: Herald Press, 1984.

Snyder, Arnold. "Michael Sattler, Benedictine: Dennis Martin's Objections Reconsidered," MQR 61(July, 1987), pp. 262-279.

Snyder, Arnold. "Michael Sattler's Baptism: Some Comments in Reply to Heinold Fast," MQR 62(October, 1988), pp. 496-506.

Snyder, Arnold. "Modern Mennonite Reality and Anabaptist Spirituality: Balthasar Hubmaier's Catechism of 1526," *The Conrad Grebel Review*, 9(Winter, 1991), pp. 37-51.

Snyder, Arnold. "Orality, Literacy and the Study of Anabaptism," MQR (Oct., 1991), pp. 371-392.

Snyder, Arnold and Hecht, Linda H., eds. *Profiles of Anabaptist Women* (forthcoming, WLU Press).

Snyder, Arnold. "Research Note: Sources Documenting Anabaptism in Zürich, 1533-1660," MQR 69(January, 1995), pp. 93-99.

Snyder, Arnold. "Response to J. Denny Weaver," CGR 13(Spring, 1995), pp. 210-15.

Snyder, Arnold. "The Schleitheim Articles in Light of the Revolution of the Common Man: Continuation or Departure?" *The Sixteenth Century Journal*, 16(1985), pp. 419-30.

Snyder, Arnold. "Word and Power in Reformation Zürich," *Archiv für Reformations Geschichte* 81(1990), pp. 263-285.

Snyder, Arnold. "Zollikon Anabaptism and the Sword," MQR 69(April, 1995), pp. 205-225.

Snyder-Penner, Russel. "Hans Nadler's Oral Exposition of the Lord's Prayer," MQR (Oct., 1991), pp. 393-406.

Sommer, Donald. "Peter Rideman and Menno Simons on Economics," MQR 28(July, 1954), pp. 205-223.

Sprunger, Keith L. "God's Powerful Army of the Weak: Anabaptist Women of the Radical Reformation," in Greaves, Richard L., ed. *Triumph over Silence: Women in Protestant History*. Westport, Ct.: Greenwood Press, 1985.

Stayer, James. *Anabaptists and the Sword*. Lawrence, Kan.: Coronado Press, 1976.

Stayer, James. "Die Anfänge des schweizerischen Täufertums im reformierten Kongregationalismus," in Goertz, Hans-Jürgen, ed. *Umstrittenes Täufertum, 1525-1975*. Göttingen, 1977, pp. 19-49.

Stayer, James. "Davidite vs. Mennonite," in Horst, Irvin, ed. *The Dutch Dissenters*. Leiden: Brill, 1986, pp. 143-159; also published in MQR 58(1984), pp. 459-476.

Stayer, James. *The German Peasants' War and Anabaptist Community of Goods*. Montreal and Kingston: McGill-Queens University Press, 1991.

Stayer, James. "The Radical Reformation" in the *Handbook of European History, 1400-1600: Late Middle Ages, Renaissance and Reformation*, vol. 2. Leiden: Brill, forthcoming.

Stayer, James. "Reublin and Brötli: The Revolutionary Beginnings of Swiss Anabaptism," in Lienhard, Marc, ed. *The Origins and Characteristics of Anabaptism*. The Hague: Nijhoff, 1977, pp. 83-102.

Stayer, James. "The Swiss Brethren: An Exercise in Historical Definition," *Church History* 47(1978), pp. 174-195.

Stayer, James. "Thomas Müntzer in 1989: A Review Article," *Sixteenth Century Journal* 21(1990), pp. 655-70.

Stayer, James. "Was Dr. Kuehler's Conception of Early Dutch Anabaptism Historically Sound?," MQR 60(July, 1986), pp. 261-88.

Stayer, James. "Wilhelm Reublin: A Picaresque Journey Through Early Anabaptism," in Goertz, Hans-Jürgen, ed. *Profiles of Radical Reformers*. Scottdale, Pa.: Herald Press, 1982, pp. 107-117.

Stayer, James and Packull, Werner. *The Anabaptists and Thomas Müntzer*. Toronto: Kendall/Hunt, 1980.

Stayer, James, Packull, Werner and Deppermann, Klaus. "From Monogenesis to Polygenesis: The Historical Discussion of Anabaptist Origins," MQR 49(1975), pp. 83-122.

Stock, Brian. *The Implications of Literacy*. Princeton: Princeton University Press, 1983.

Strauss, Gerald. *Luther's House of Learning. Indoctrination of the Young in the German Reformation*. Baltimore: Johns Hopkins University Press, 1978.

Umble, Jenifer Hiett. "Women and Choice: An Examination of the Martyrs' Mirror," MQR 64(April, 1990), pp. 135-145.

Verduin, Leonard. *The Reformers and Their Stepchildren*. Grand Rapids: Eerdmans, 1964.

Verheyden, A.L.E. *Anabaptism in Flanders, 1530-1650*. Scottdale, Pa.: Herald Press, 1961.

Voolstra, Sjouke. "Themes in the Early Theology of Menno Simons," in Brunk, Gerald R., ed. *Menno Simons: A Reappraisal. Essays in Honor of Irvin B. Horst*. Harrisonburg, Va.: Eastern Mennonite College, 1992.

Vos, K. *Menno Simons, 1496-1561*. Leiden: Brill, 1914.

Wackernagel, Philip. *Das deutsche Kirchenlied*, vol. III. Leipzig: Teubner, 1870.

Waite, Gary K. *David Joris and Dutch Anabaptism, 1524-1543*. Waterloo, Ont.: Wilfrid Laurier University Press, 1990.

Weaver, J. Denny. *Becoming Anabaptist*. Scottdale, Pa.: Herald Press, 1987.

Weigelt, Horst. "Caspar von Schwenckfeld: Proclaimer of the Middle Way," in Goertz, Hans-Jürgen, ed. *Profiles of Radical Reformers*. Scottdale, Pa.: Herald Press, 1982, pp. 214-225.

Weiß, Ruth. "Die Herkunft der osthessischen Täufer," *Archiv für Reformations Geschichte* 50(1959).

Williams, George H. *The Radical Reformation*, 3rd. edition. Kirksville, Mo.: Sixteenth Century Journal Publishers, 1992.

Windhorst, Christof. "Balthasar Hubmaier: Professor, Preacher, Politician," in Goertz, Hans-Jürgen, ed. *Profiles of Radical Reformers*. Scottdale, Pa.: Herald Press, 1982, pp. 144-157.

Wolkan, Rudolf. *Die Lieder der Wiedertäufer*. Berlin, 1903; reprint: Nieuwkoop: B. de Graaf, 1965.

Wyntjes, Sherrin Marshall. "Women in the Reformation Era," in *Becoming Visible: Women in European History*. Bridenthal, Renate and Koonz, Claudia, eds. Boston, Houghton Mifflin, 1977, pp. 165-91.

Yoder, Jesse. "The Frankenthal Debate with the Anabaptists in 1571: Procedure, Participants," MQR 36(Jan., 1962), pp. 14-35.

Yoder, Jesse. "The Frankenthal Disputation: Part II. Outcome, Issues, Debating Methods," MQR 36(April, 1962), pp. 116-146.

Yoder, John. H. "The Hermeneutics of the Anabaptists," MQR 41(Oct., 1967), pp. 291-308.

Yoder, John H. *Täufertum und Reformation in der Schweiz, I. Die Gespräche zwischen Täufern und Reformatoren 1523-1538*. Karlsruhe: Mennonitischen Geschichtsverein, 1962.

Yoder, John H. *Täufertum und Reformation im Gespräch*. Zürich: EVZ-Verlag, 1968.

Yoder, Paul, ed. *Four Hundred Years with the Ausbund*. Scottdale, Pa.: Herald Press, 1964.

Zeman, Jarold K. *The Anabaptists and the Czech Brethren in Moravia, 1526-1628*. The Hague: Mouton, 1969.

Zemon Davis, Natalie. "Printing and the People: Early Modern France," in Graff, Harvey J., ed. *Literacy and Social Development in the West: A Reader*. Cambridge: Cambridge University Press, 1981, pp. 69-95.

Zijlstra, Samme. "Nicolaas Meyndertsz van Blesdijk; Een bijdrage tot de geschiedenis van het Davidjorisme." Unpublished Ph.D. dissertation, Rijksuniversiteit Groningen, 1983.

Index

About Pandora Press

Pandora Press is a small, independently owned press dedicated to making available modestly priced books that deal with Anabaptist, Mennonite, and Believers Church topics, both historical and theological. We welcome comments from our readers.

Visit our full-service online Bookstore:
www.pandorapress.com

Lawrence Klippenstein and Jacob Dick, ***Mennonite Alternative Service in Russia***
(Kitchener: Pandora Press, 2002; co-published with Herald Press)
Softcover, lv, 163 pp. ISBN 1-894710-21-5
$17.00 U.S./$20.00 Canadian. Postage: $4.00 U.S./$6.00 Can.
[Diaries and photographs from Russian Mennonite COs]

Nancey Murphey, ***Religion and Science***
(Kitchener: Pandora Press, 2002; co-published with Herald Press)
Softcover, lv, 163 pp. ISBN 1-894710-20-7
$14.00 U.S./$17.00 Canadian. Postage: $4.00 U.S./$6.00 Can.
[Proceedings of the 2001 Goshen Conference on Religion and Science]

Biblical Concordance of the Swiss Brethren, 1540. Trans. by Gilbert Fast and Galen Peters; bib. intro. Joe Springer; ed. C. Arnold Snyder
(Kitchener: Pandora Press, 2001; co-published with Herald Press)
Softcover, lv, 227pp. ISBN 1-894710-16-9
$20.00 U.S./$25.00 Canadian. Postage: $4.00 U.S./$6.00 Can.
[Previously untranslated Anabaptist biblical resource]

Orland Gingerich, ***The Amish of Canada***
(Kitchener: Pandora Press, 2001; co-published with Herald Press.)
Softcover, 244 pp., includes index. ISBN 1-894710-19-3
$18.00 US/$24.00 Canadian. Postage $4.00 US/$6.00 Canadian
[Third printing of this definitive history of Amish of Canada]

M. Darrol Bryant, *Religion in a New Key*
(Kitchener: Pandora Press, 2001)
   Softcover, 136 pp., includes bib. refs. ISBN 1-894710-18-5
   $12.00 US/$17.00 Canadian. Postage $3.00 US/$5.00 Canadian
[Explores dialogue between religious communities world-wide]

Trans. Walter Klaassen, Frank Friesen, Werner O. Packull, ed. C. Arnold
Snyder, *Sources of South German/Austrian Anabaptism*
(Kitchener: Pandora Press, 2001; co-published with Herald Press.)
   Softcover, 430 pp. includes indexes. ISBN 1-894710-15-0
   $40.00 US/$50.00 Canadian. Postage $5.00 US/$7.00 Canadian
[A wide spectrum of newly-translated Anabaptist sources.]

Pedro A. Sandín Fremaint y Pablo A. Jimémez, *Palabras Duras: Homilìas*
(Kitchener: Pandora Press, 2001).
   Softcover, 121 pp., ISBN 1-894710-17-7
   $12.00 US/$16.00 Canadian. Postage $5.00 US/$7.00Canadian
[Spanish. Reflections on the ìhard wordsî of Jesus in the Gospels.]

James C. Juhnke and Carol M. Hunter, *The Missing Peace: The Search
for Nonviolent Alternatives in United States History*
(Kitchener: Pandora Press, 2001; co-published with Herald Press.)
   Softcover, 321 pp., includes index. ISBN 1-894710-13-4
   $26.50 US/$37.50 Canadian. Postage $5.00 US/$7.00
Canadian.
[Focuses on each of the principal periods on United States history.]

Ruth Elizabeth Mooney, *Manual Para Crear Materiales de Educación
Cristiana* (Kitchener: Pandora Press, 2001).
   Softcover, 206 pp., ISBN 1-894710-12-6
   $15.00 US/$20.00 Canadian. Postage $5.00 US/$7.00 Canadian
[Spanish. Manual for creation of Christian education programs.]

Esther and Malcolm Wenger, poetry by Ann Wenger, *Healing the Wounds*
(Kitchener: Pandora Press, 2001; co-published with Herald Press).
   Softcover, 210 pp. ISBN 1-894710-09-6.
   $18.50 US/$21.00 Canadian. Postage $5.00 US/$7.00 Canadian
[Experiences of Mennonite missionaries with the Cheyenne people]

Pedro A. Sandín Fremaint, *Cuentos y Encuentros: Hacia una Educación Transformadora* (Kitchener: Pandora Press, 2001).
Softcover 163 pp ISBN 1-894710-08-8.
$12.00 US/ $16.00 Canadian. Postage $5.00 US/$7.00 Canadian.
[Spanish. Stories and discussion questions for Christian education]
A. James Reimer, *Mennonites and Classical Theology: Dogmatic Foundations for Christian Ethics* (Kitchener: Pandora Press, 2001; co-published with Herald Press)
Softcover, 650pp. ISBN 0-9685543-7-7
$52.00 U.S./$65.00 Canadian. Postage: $5.00 U.S./$7.00 Can.
[A theological interpretation of Mennonite experience in 20th C.]

Walter Klaassen, *Anabaptism: Neither Catholic nor Protestant,* 3rd ed (Kitchener: Pandora Press, 2001; co-pub. Herald Press)
Softcover, 122pp. ISBN 1-894710-01-0
$12.00 U.S./$15.00 Can. Postage: $3.00 U.S./$4.00 Can.
[A classic interpretation and study guide, now available again]

Dale Schrag & James Juhnke, eds., *Anabaptist Visions for the new Millennium: A search for identity* (Kitchener: Pandora Press, 2000; co-published with Herald Press)
Softcover, 242 pp. ISBN 1-894710-00-2
$20.00 U.S./$26.00 Canadian. Postage $4.00 U.S./$5.00 Can.
[Twenty-eight essays presented at Bethel College, June, 2000]

Harry Loewen, ed., *Road to Freedom: Mennonites Escape the Land of Suffering* (Kitchener: Pandora Press, 2000; co-published with Herald Press)
Hardcover, large format, 302pp. ISBN 0-9685543-5-0
$35.00 U.S./$39.50 Canadian. Postage: $7.00 U.S./$8.00 Can.
[Life experiences documented with personal stories and photos]

Alan Kreider and Stuart Murray, eds., *Coming Home: Stories of Anabaptists in Britain and Ireland* (Kitchener: Pandora Press, 2000; co-published with Herald Press)
Softcover, 220pp. ISBN 0-9685543-6-9
$23.00 U.S./$26.00 Canadian. Postage: $4.00 U.S./$5.00 Can.
[Anabaptist encounters in the U.K.; personal stories/articles]

Edna Schroeder Thiessen and Angela Showalter, *A Life Displaced: A Mennonite Womanís Flight from War-Torn Poland*
(Kitchener: Pandora Press, 2000; co-published with Herald Press)
    Softcover, xii, 218pp. ISBN 0-9685543-2-6
    $22.50 U.S./$25.00 Canadian. Postage: $4.00 U.S./$5.00 Can.
[A true story: moving, richly-detailed, told with candor and courage]

Stuart Murray, *Biblical Interpretation in the Anabaptist Tradition*
(Kitchener: Pandora Press, 2000; co-published with Herald Press)
    Softcover, 310pp. ISBN 0-9685543-3-4
    $30.00 U.S./$33.00 Canadian. Postage: $4.00 U.S./$5.00 Can.
[How Anabaptists read the Bible; considerations for todayís church]

Apocalypticism and Millennialism, ed. by Loren L. Johns
(Kitchener: Pandora Press, 2000; co-published with Herald Press)
    Softcover, 419pp; Scripture and name indeces
    ISBN 0-9683462-9-4
    $39.50 U.S./$45.00 Canadian. Postage: $5.00 U.S./$6.00 Can.
[A clear, careful, and balanced collection: pastoral and scholarly]

Later Writings by Pilgram Marpeck and his Circle. Volume 1: The ExposÈ, A Dialogue and Marpeckís Response to Caspar Schwenckfeld
Translated by Walter Klaassen, Werner Packull, and John Rempel
(Kitchener: Pandora Press, 1999; co-published with Herald Press)
    Softcover, 157pp. ISBN 0-9683462-6-X
    $22.00 U.S./$25.00 Canadian. Postage: $4.00 U.S./$5.00 Can.
[Previously untranslated writings by Marpeck and his Circle]

John Driver, *Radical Faith. An Alternative History of the Christian Church*, edited by Carrie Snyder.
(Kitchener: Pandora Press, 1999; co-published with Herald Press)
    Softcover, 334pp. ISBN 0-9683462-8-6
    $33.00 U.S./$36.00 Canadian. Postage: $5.00 U.S./$6.00 Can.
[A history of the church as it is seldom told ñ from the margins]

C. Arnold Snyder, *From Anabaptist Seed. The Historical Core of Anabaptist-Related Identity*
(Kitchener: Pandora Press, 1999; co-published with Herald Press)
    Softcover, 53pp.; discussion questions. ISBN 0-9685543-0-X
    $5.00 U.S./$6.25 Canadian. Postage: $2.00 U.S./$2.50 Can.
[Ideal for group study, commissioned by Mennonite World Conf.]
    Also available in Spanish translation: *De Semilla Anabautista*,
    from Pandora Press only.

John D. Thiesen, *Mennonite and Nazi? Attitudes Among Mennonite Colonists in Latin America, 1933-1945.*
(Kitchener: Pandora Press, 1999; co-published with Herald Press)
    Softcover, 330pp., 2 maps, 24 b/w illustrations, bibliography,
    index. ISBN 0-9683462-5-1
    $27.00 U.S./$30.00 Canadian. Postage: $4.00 U.S./$5.00 Can.
[Careful and objective study of an explosive topic]

Lifting the Veil, a translation of *Aus meinem Leben: Erinnerungen von J.H. Janzen.* Ed. by Leonard Friesen; trans. by Walter Klaassen
(Kitchener: Pandora Press, 1998; co-pub. with Herald Press).
    Softcover, 128pp.; 4pp. of illustrations. ISBN 0-9683462-1-9
    $14.50 U.S./$16.00 Canadian. Postage: $4.00 U.S. and Can.
[Memoir, confession, critical observation of Mennonite life in Russia]

Leonard Gross, *The Golden Years of the Hutterites*, rev. ed.
(Kitchener: Pandora Press, 1998; co-pub. with Herald Press).
    Softcover, 280pp., index. ISBN 0-9683462-3-5
    $24.00 U.S./$27.00 Canadian. Postage: $4.00 U.S./$5.00 Can.
[Classic study of early Hutterite movement, now available again]

The Believers Church: A Voluntary Church, ed. by William H. Brackney
(Kitchener: Pandora Press, 1998; co-published with Herald Press).
    Softcover, viii, 237pp., index. ISBN 0-9683462-0-0
    $27.00 U.S./$29.50 Canadian. Postage: $4.00 U.S./$5.00 Can.
[Papers from the 12th Believers Church Conference, Hamilton, ON]

An Annotated Hutterite Bibliography, compiled by Maria H. Krisztinkovich, ed. by Peter C. Erb (Kitchener, Ont.: Pandora Press, 1998). (Ca. 2,700 entries) 312pp., cerlox bound, electronic, or both.

   ISBN (paper) 0-9698762-8-9/(disk) 0-9698762-9-7
   $18.00 each, U.S. and Canadian. Postage: $6.00 U.S. and Can.

[The most extensive bibliography on Hutterite literature available]

Jacobus ten Doornkaat Koolman, *Dirk Philips. Friend and Colleague of Menno Simons*, trans. W. E. Keeney, ed. C. A. Snyder (Kitchener: Pandora Press, 1998; co-pub. with Herald Press).

   Softcover, xviii, 236pp., index. ISBN: 0-9698762-3-8
   $24.50 U.S./$29.50 Canadian. Postage: $4.00 U.S./$5.00 Can.

[The definitive biography of Dirk Philips, now available in English]

Sarah Dyck, ed./tr., *The Silence Echoes: Memoirs of Trauma & Tears* (Kitchener: Pandora Press, 1997; co-published with Herald Press).

   Softcover, xii, 236pp., 2 maps. ISBN: 0-9698762-7-0
   $19.00 U.S./$21.00 Canadian. Postage: $4.00 U.S./$5.00 Can.

[First person accounts of life in the Soviet Union, trans. from German]

Wes Harrison, *Andreas Ehrenpreis and Hutterite Faith and Practice* (Kitchener: Pandora Press, 1997; co-published with Herald Press).

   Softcover, xxiv, 274pp., 2 maps, index. ISBN 0-9698762-6-2
   $29.00 U.S./$34.00 Canadian. Postage: $4.00 U.S./$5.00 Can.

[First biography of this important seventeenth century Hutterite leader]

C. Arnold Snyder, *Anabaptist History and Theology: Revised Student Edition* (Kitchener: Pandora Press, 1997; co-pub. Herald Press).

   Softcover, xiv, 466pp., 7 maps, 28 illustrations, index,
   bibliography. ISBN 0-9698762-5-4
   $38.50 U.S./$40.00 Canadian. Postage: $5.00 U.S./$6.00 Can.

[Abridged, rewritten edition for undergraduates and the non-specialist]

Nancey Murphy, *Reconciling Theology and Science: A Radical Reformation Perspective* (Kitchener, Ont.: Pandora Press, 1997; co-pub. Herald Press).

　　Softcover, x, 103pp., index. ISBN 0-9698762-4-6
　　$16.00 U.S./$18.50 Canadian. Postage: $3.50 U.S./$4.00 Can.
[**Exploration of the supposed conflict between Christianity and Science**]

C. Arnold Snyder and Linda A. Huebert Hecht, eds, *Profiles of Anabaptist Women: Sixteenth Century Reforming Pioneers* (Waterloo, Ont.: Wilfrid Laurier University Press, 1996).

　　Softcover, xxii, 442pp. ISBN: 0-88920-277-X
　　$28.95 U.S. or Canadian. Postage: $5.00 U.S./$6.00 Can.
[**Biographical sketches of more than 50 Anabaptist women; a first**]

The Limits of Perfection: A Conversation with J. Lawrence Burkholder 2nd ed., with a new epilogue by J. Lawrence Burkholder, Rodney Sawatsky and Scott Holland, eds.
(Kitchener: Pandora Press, 1996).

　　Softcover, x, 154pp. ISBN 0-9698762-2-X
　　$12.50 U.S./$15.50 Canadian. Postage: $2.00 U.S./$3.00 Can.
[**J.L. Burkholder on his life experiences; eight Mennonites respond**]

C. Arnold Snyder, *Anabaptist History and Theology: An Introduction* (Kitchener: Pandora Press, 1995).　ISBN 0-9698762-0-3

　　Softcover, x, 434pp., 6 maps, 29 illustrations, index, bibliography.
　　$38.50 U.S./$40.00 Canadian. Postage: $5.00 U.S./$6.00 Can.
[**Comprehensive survey; unabridged version, fully documented**]

Pandora Press
33 Kent Avenue
Kitchener, Ontario
Canada N2G 3R2
Tel./Fax: (519) 578-2381
E-mail:
info@pandorapress.com
Web site:
www.pandorapress.com

Herald Press
616 Walnut Avenue
Scottdale, PA
U.S.A. 15683
Orders: (800) 245-7894
E-mail:
hp@mph.org
Web site:
www.mph.org